America in Controversy

Contributing Authors

Jerald L. Banninga, *Western Illinois University*

Paul H. Boase, *Ohio University*

Ronald G. Coleman, *Edinboro State*

Donald H. Ecroyd, *Temple University*

Clyde J. Faries, *Western Illinois University*

Robert Friedenberg, *Miami University*

Harry R. Gianneschi, *Western Illinois University*

G. Jack Gravlee, *Colorado State University*

Robert L. Heinemann, *Western State College of Colorado*

D. Ray Heisey, *Kent State University*

DeWitte Holland, *Lamar University*

Dale G. Leathers, *University of Georgia*

R.A. Micken, *Southern Illinois University*

Harold Mixon, *Louisiana State University*

John W. Reed, *Dallas Theological Seminary*

Gladys Ritchie, *Pennsylvania State University*

Allan H. Sager, *Lutheran Theological Seminary*

John H. Sloan, *Memphis State University*

Arthur L. Smith, *New York University*

Charles J. Stewart, *Purdue University*

John L. Sullivan, *University of Virginia*

Thomas L. Tedford, *University of North Carolina*

Ralph Towne, *Temple University*

Jess Yoder, *Cleveland State University*

120120

AMERICA IN CONTROVERSY

History of American Public Address

Editor

DEWITTE HOLLAND
Lamar University

Associate Editors
CHARLES STEWART, *Purdue University*
JESS YODER, *Cleveland State University*

"88"

WM. C. BROWN COMPANY PUBLISHERS
Dubuque, Iowa

Contents

Preface

This book analyzes the rhetoric, primarily oral, of major issues in American history from earliest New England colonization to the present. Personhood of the American Indian in the Massachusetts Colony is the first issue treated and U.S. involvement in the Vietnamese war the last. Planned and researched by twenty-four contributing authors, this work is designed as a comprehensive single volume primary text for courses in the history of American public address and major rhetorical movements in American history. Approaches to some courses will require supplementary speech documents and rhetorical biographies. By the same token, because of the close relationship of the approach of this work to that of the intellectual historian the student of American history may make good use of this book for parallel reading.

America in Controversy is idea and issue centered, placing heavy emphasis on the historical and societal roots of the debates and the impinging events during various periods of controversy, whether the height of the involvement under consideration be three months or thirty years. No attempt is made to report all of the rhetoric on the issues. Excerpts of significant representative oral rhetoric are made and occasionally major contributions of written rhetoric are noted.

Believing that the ideas and supports chosen by the advocates in a given rhetorical situation are the most revealing of the historical residues, these writers present a history of the spectrum of rhetorical stances on major issues controverted in the American experience. As we view the polarity of ideas from typical speeches and other rhetorical forms on the issues selected we can note the evolving American mind and the relationship of rhetoric to its development. Such an approach to the study of American public address ties many loose ends together and provides a framework for analyzing specific speeches, movements, or campaigns from both an internal and external standpoint of criticism. Our volume stands in contrast to works which analyze typical rhetorical choices of an individual speaker, trace rhetorical biography of the "great speakers," or simply present an anthology of speeches for potential criticism.

Each chapter in *America in Controversy* treats a different debate, presenting on each issue at least minimum treatment of a definition, the background/roots, the rhetoric of the polarity of views with major emphasis given to rhetorical stances and supports, developments, and contemporization. Simply, we trace a series of major debates in American history, note their principal arguments and supports, and trace developments. We pay minimal attention to individual speakers or their personalized techniques of speech construction and presentation. Our work does provide the fabric for analysis of speakers and their techniques in persuasion; however, analysis of individuals is left for the student.

The contributors made their plans for this volume through casual interchanges in the Speech Communication Association where they discussed the state of the literature in American public address. Noting the dearth of issue-centered materials and the lack of a single volume text, a committee was formed to seek to answer this need. We recognize in our text the absence of biographical materials and texts of those speeches which often are studied in public address courses. The teacher and student using this volume will find ample supplementary materials readily available to suit their particular inclinations. Use of this text reduces lengthy, tedious library research to set the climate of opinion for speech analysis. Now the student can spend his time examining speakers and their workmanship.

DeWitte Holland
Lamar University

Foreword

I

War, poverty, youth, race, inflation, migrant workers, bussing, and women's liberation, are current subjects of protest in the United States. The American dream is not fulfilled. Protest efforts range from person-to-person buttonhole rhetoric to sit-ins; from parades and rallies to demonstrations and boycotts. Plainly a great number of people are seeking to change our nation. Their sort of rhetoric is not new. It is part of a revolutionary heritage that stretches back to the beginning of organized English communities here. Protest rhetoric is a part of America; when it ceases our dream will be either fulfilled or dead.

The one thing that is unique about America is revealed in its rhetorical history: the enlarging right to protest. This rhetorical history is the story of our efforts at working through people, usually linquistically and discursively, to change the environment. When people, discontent with a situation, lack the political, economic, or social power to change it, they may resort to rhetoric. Such a rhetoric is a substitute for power. When people can't *do* they *talk* or *write* or make other signs of disquiet. This substitution permits the weak, the poor, and the disestablished to seek what they want. While their seeking does not always meet with immediate success, their input into the system through their rhetoric often helps to shape future circumstances.

In the beginning of the American experience most of life was bound rigidly by tradition. However, there were a few areas where discussion, dissent, and persuasion were permitted. As people interacted about the personhood of the Indian, the relationship of church and state, the nature of God and man, they inevitably raised other issues and admitted them to inquiry and advocacy. The admission of rhetoric into a tradition-bound system exerted a determining influence on the future. For rhetoric, once admitted as a legitimate human activity, almost inevitably enlarges its area of concern. The area of concern of rhetoric continues to grow even today, into tomorrow, as shall be emphasized in the chapters that follow. Lately we are more fully realizing that rhetoric is more than public discourse coupled with rhetorical literature. In includes any kind of human behavior short of threat and physical manipulation, designed to modify the environment.

The story of the rhetoric on primary issues in our society outlines the movement of our people into a much wider democratic participation. Undoubtedly, some areas of our corporate life still are bound by tradition, prejudice, and vested interests; but protest continues to chip away in these areas. It is this chipping and its admitted right to existence that permits stability in our institutions while allowing defensible change.

The heritage of a free people, enjoying the enlarged right to persuade others through free speech, press, personal dialogue, and life style, will remain if we use it responsibly and are willing to exercise it and defend it. As much as we dislike protest rhetoric, as much as it disturbs us, it has gotten us to the point where we are on a continuum of freedom. Protest continues; many of the old battles have been won; new issues have arisen with our developing society; there are going to be more new issues to confront. If the scope of our freedom is to grow, protest rhetoric will require full dedication by the participants and a good measure of tolerance from the on-lookers.

II

At this writing there is nothing in print that approaches a complete rhetorical history of the United States. This volume, in presenting representative oral rhetoric on major issues in our history, lays a foundation for such a complete rhetoric.

Since the United States is unique in its rhetorical heritage, what have we done and said about the basic problems that have confronted us? The next few pages trace in chronological sequence major issues in our history and the polarity of rhetorical responses to them. This tracing is an outline preview of the book's twenty-four chapters.

1. One of the first issues confronted by our English forefathers in America was the personhood of the American Indian. This question was probed in halting evangelical efforts during the first decades of the Massachusetts Colony. Even though the royal charter of the Colony instructed the settlers to evangelize the natives, they were slow to integrate the Christianized Indians into the English towns. Colonists even controverted whether the Indian was human enough for evangelization. Minimal evangelistic effort was the inevitable result of this condition.

   Converted Indians were not granted church membership until they were observed for a period of time, sometimes as long as fifteen years. The God of the New England colonists was not large enough to permit the Indian to be both Indian and Christian. The Indian was expected to adopt the Puritan culture. Consequently, Indian evangelism realized a very limited success. The failure of early resolution of the issue of personhood of the American Indian plagues our society to this day.

2. Were civil magistrates to be independent of the church or were they an arm of the church? Should dissenters from the state forfeit their civil rights and be barred from holding government offices? These church-state issues were debated at length by Roger Williams and John Cotton in Massachusetts during the first generation of settlers. Cotton won that battle as the church continued to domi-

nate the state, but Roger Williams won the war—his position was later written into the federal Constitution. The early facing of this issue laid the groundwork for other freedom movements which followed.

3. The second quarter of the eighteenth century was known as the Great Awakening. A shift from a religion that emphasized the absolute sovereignty of God to one that stressed the expression of one's religious experience in the life of the Christian shook the theological foundations and ecclesiastical authority of the established Congregational, Anglican, and Presbyterian traditions. The major issues dealt with the nature of conversion, the place of rationality in religion, the role of personal experience in religion, and the expression of religious beliefs and experience. The debate gave direction and strength to an emerging individualism which wasted little time in finding political expression.

4. With the successful conclusion of the Revolutionary War, grave peace-time problems beset the young republic. The Articles of Confederation, the basic instrument of the national government, provided ample individual and state freedom, but little power for the Federal legislature. The economic crisis threatened the Confederation every bit as much as had the British troops.

   The second Monday of May 1787 and Philadelphia were set down as the time and place for a convention to revise the inadequate Articles. Fifty-five delegates appeared quite agreed on a need for a change. They adopted rules for debate that encouraged unfettered and candid interchange on the basic question of how to establish a stable (meaning powerful) central government and at the same time to preserve liberty. Some forty subsidiary propositions were debated in a three month period leading to the writing of the Constitution of the United States. A flexible equilibrium was set between liberty and authority. The significance of the question which was basically the survival of the new nation, called forth the best efforts in debate to establish a durable free government.

5. Every four years from 1816 to 1832 Congressmen returned to Washington to discuss major revisions of the nation's tariff policy—a portion of the sectional power struggle. Economic arguments were exhausted by 1824 and Congressmen seemed determined to deal with larger political questions in the name of tariff debate. They felt more comfortable in debating constitutional questions like a state's right to nullify laws passed by Congress. The famous Webster-Haynes debate and the confrontation between Andrew Jackson and John C. Calhoun centered on nullification and possible secession of states from the Union. Slavery was part of the hidden agenda in the tariff debates as was the controversy over internal improvements.

6. Congress never debated the constitutionality of federally financed internal improvements, only the nature of financing improvements and what projects

should be constructed—a natural issue in the growing inter-sectional rivalry of the early national period. Jefferson was the first to question national public works by maintaining that a system of federally financed improvements was unconstitutional and therefore illegal. Madison was the first president to veto an improvements bill on constitutional grounds. Monroe took a strong stand against improvements on constitutional grounds, but encouraged maintenance of projects already completed. Adams wanted to establish the right of the federal government to finance improvements and encouraged an all-out program. Jackson opposed Adams' program and declared that no further programs would be approved until the federal debt was paid and until the new program could be initiated. Even then, only "national" projects would receive federal funds. He took an economic, not a legal or moral stand and gradually destroyed the elaborate system of internal improvements fostered during the Adams administration.

7. Though slavery had been with America from the beginning, controversy over it did not achieve prominence until the emergence of the abolition movement in 1830. The conflict was concerned with political, economic, moral, and religious issues. Consequently, the issues were debated in Congress, the lecture circuit, the pulpit, and the press. Opponents of slavery differed in strategies and intensity while the able defenders of slavery were increasingly on the defensive. Unfortunately the conflict was not resolved by reason and debate but on the battlefield.

8. American history through 1900 was one of nearly constant territorial expansion to satisfy the urge to settle and develop land. At first it was a simple matter of taking land from Indians or purchasing lands held by European governments. But Americans then began to confront Mexico and Spain whose governments were not interested in selling or giving away vast territories. Determined to move forward, the United States (motivated by slavery, economic problems, and "humanitarianism") eventually gained Texas, New Mexico, Arizona, California, Hawaii, Cuba, Puerto Rico, the Philippines and many small islands. The rhetoric of American imperialism was one of rationalization, usually justifying actions already taken. Manifest destiny was the ultimate justification: the United States had a responsibility to spread our values, form of government, technology, and civilization to a misguided and underdeveloped world.

9. The black man's place in American society was not settled with the Civil War, but has remained a serious and often violent issue. With the Civil War at an end in 1865, many speakers prophesied the extinction of the black race in America; they could not survive the cold winters of the northern states and the southern states would not tolerate free blacks. The black race survived, however, and other black-related issues like suffrage, economic opportunity, legal justice, and social equality received the nation's attention or inattention. As northern politicians and reformers gradually lost interest in the freed black man, southern

leaders began systematically to eliminate black political power and to place black people into an inferior economic, legal, social, and educational position. Poor whites gained political power in the early 1900s and demanded a harsh rhetorical racism to accompany the strict segregation accomplished in the decades after the Civil War.

10. The rapid industrialization of America following the Civil War—accompanied by periodic economic panics, unemployment, low wages, and terrible working conditions—made confrontations between labor and management inevitable. Labor leaders argued that the issue was a matter of serious infringements upon basic rights and liberties guaranteed by American institutions. They appealed to traditional American values and beliefs in equality, justice, and fair play. Industrial leaders used the widely popular social Darwinism as the basis for their arguments. They contended that the labor issue was a matter of natural selection, whether the inferior—the laborer—was to interfere with the superior—the employer. Men were not guaranteed happiness, only the opportunity to pursue it, they argued. The excesses of industrial leaders, the rise of the progressives and social demands would be heard and labor organizations would be recognized as bargaining agents for workers.

11. During the decades after the Civil War, the American economy, despite periods of serious depression, showed a seemingly endless ability to expand. But the laborer, especially in the agrarian areas of the country, did not share equally in the growing economic wealth. The "little guy" formed a series of organizations—the Grange, the Anti-Monopoly Party, the Greenback Party, the Farmers Alliance, and the Populist Party—to pressure the establishment into changes or to eliminate the establishment altogether. The rhetoric of all these groups was one of total commitment to the cause; there could be no middle ground, no compromise. The leaders of these movements wanted at the very least a fair share of the wealth they produced; at most they demanded all the wealth they produced. Their rhetoric was characterized by careful audience adjustment, extreme motive appeals, and an abundance of facts and evidence.

12. Progressive ministers responded to the abuses of industrialism in post-reconstruction America with the social gospel, a movement designed to bring social and economic justice through appeals to the moral fiber of churchmen. Only one of many protests during that period, the social gospel was primarily an urban movement. Social preachments ranged from pleas to abolish the "existing order" to gentle pleas urging labor and management to cooperate for common social good. On the other side of the issue, positions ranged from moderate concern for personal ethical involvement to total separation of religious and ethical concerns. The progressives were generally lonesome voices crying in the wilderness. How-

ever, in spite of evangelical protestations the social gospel strengthened until by around 1915 the mainstream of protestant Christianity became concerned for the coming of the Kingdom, here as well as in the world beyond.

13. Prior to the Civil War, Americans caught up in the new political freedom overlooked economic inequities in society. But in post-war industrialism rampant social problems did not yield easily to reform efforts within the "free capitalistic" system. Thus out of the events of the era arose the basic issue, "Is economic justice compatible with capitalism?" An array of varied socialists vowed that capitalistic society was based on exploitation of the working class. Economic equity just was not possible within capitalism. Revolution was necessary. The system had to be destroyed or a new one developed that would supercede the old. Socialists dissipated their energies with divisive tactics while successful progressive reforms stole the Socialists' thunder. Repressive patriotism of World War I essentially destroyed the Socialist party for more than a decade.

14. The "Progressive Era" of American history lasted essentially from 1909 to 1919. Its impetus grew out of the populist and labor movements of earlier decades and appeared again during the "New Deal Era." The progressives demanded a wide range of governmental controls—regulations over big business, railroads, food and drugs, natural resources, workmen's compensation, and women and child labor. The cry was for returning government to the hands of the people, a government that would insure a more equal life for all citizens. The muckrakers and their exposés, together with novelists, scholars and speakers enhanced public awareness and concern for problems. Governmental and congressional leaders like Theodore Roosevelt, Albert Beveridge, and Robert LaFollette spent long careers fostering progressive legislation.

15. When war broke out in Europe in 1914, Americans had difficulty comprehending the reasons and scope of the disaster. Our traditional isolationism made it easy to say that we were too proud to fight. But America—partially because of its role as arms supplier to the belligerents—was gradually drawn into the conflict. We searched for a cause to justify entry into the war. The cause became world peace, making the world safe for democracy. When the war came to an end, many American congressional leaders wanted to reestablish isolationism as a foreign policy, but President Wilson proposed a world organization, the League of Nations, to insure peace. The congressional debate over the treaty in general and the League in particular was one of the longest and bitterest in American history. Isolationists attacked the League concept and questioned the assumption that world powers and leaders truly wanted peace. President Wilson and his supporters simply tried to answer the objections as they arose, and lost the debate.

16. From the time Elizabeth Cady Stanton delivered her first public address in behalf of women's suffrage at Seneca Falls, New York, in 1848, until the Nineteenth Amendment became law in 1920, hundreds and thousands of women spoke for the cause of suffrage at every possible occasion. They based their case on the Constitution's Bill of Human Rights, the Bible, and local precedents. A number of states and local governments had given women the right to vote and to hold office but these actions were taken to the Supreme Court and ruled unconstitutional. Undaunted by the high court's decision that neither the Constitution nor its amendments granted women voting rights, the women of the nation organized, lobbied and spoke out to promote their cause. Finally, Congress, the courts, and the nation became convinced and the amendment was passed.

   The women of America were also instrumental in the passage of the Eighteenth Amendment which prohibited the sale and drinking of intoxicating beverages. Frances Willard, Susan B. Anthony, and Carrie Nation were prominent speakers in this movement. Throughout the nation women spoke about the harmful effects of strong drink. They prayed, sang, preached, printed papers, and demonstrated. Some, such as Carrie Nation, gained notoriety by "hatchetations" of saloons. The systematic passing of the amendment, however, did not eliminate the proported evils. Secret drinking, lawbreaking, bootlegging, and related crimes resulted. Consequently the amendment was later repealed.

17. The collapse of idealism during World War I opened the way for empiricism and scientific thinking to catch up with America. Analysis and criticism were turned upon every facet of society and especially those based on tradition. The Christian church, very heavily dependent upon history and tradition was a natural focal point of challenge and question in what is called the Modernist-Fundamentalist controversy. Modernist churchmen, led by Harry Emerson Fosdick, sought more individual freedom for the Christian within an inclusive church fellowship. Fundamentalists, led by Clarence Macartney, J. Gresham Machen, and layman-orator William Jennings Bryan, insisted upon acceptance of the authority of the "Five Points," fundamentals of the faith. The Fundamentalists-Modernists controversy, ostensibly a theological debate, was really one of epistemology. The ultimate concerns then were those of authority. The affirmations of both sides had and still have widespread implications for the very nature of man as a rational being.

18. The national economic catastrophe during the Hoover administration swept a Democrat into the White House. He was Franklin D. Roosevelt, quarterback for the New Deal, a program of quick, strong, affirmative humane federal action. This philosophy of government, fairly consistent during the New Deal, led to a patchwork of good and bad national programs and criticism from several quarters.

Franklin Roosevelt had little trouble defeating Herbert Hoover. Once in office he concentrated on selling his radical program to Congress and to the public, while turning rebuttal of critics over to his chief lieutenants. The success of the Roosevelt administration in selling, primarily through public address, the concept of the welfare state remains one of the major American rhetorical phenomena. Succeeding administrations have been unable to reverse the philosophy reflected in basic tenets of the New Deal.

19. Despite the Fascist build-up in Europe and Japan in the 1930s, isolationists called upon America to remain aloof from foreign involvements. It was not until Franklin Roosevelt's Quarantine Speech of 1937 that the push for internationalism was renewed. As late as 1941 American public opinion was almost evenly divided between those supporting American involvement in World War II and those opposing it. The mood of American changed following the war when America had emerged as a world power in possession of the atomic bomb. The U.S. dollar was the backbone of European economics and we supported the United Nations. The Korean War had some dampening effect on the post-war internationalist spirit. The economic build-up of other industrial nations, loss of international influence, and the failure of the Vietnam venture, along with economic and social problems at home has again shifted the mood of America from internationalism to isolationism.

20. During the decade following World War II, many Americans were concerned about the internal Communist conspiracy which public discourse reported to be penetrating the United States government and institutions. Since America was the only nation in possession of atomic military secrets subversion was a dramatic issue. J. Edgar Hoover warned that subversive infiltration had actually taken place. Loyalty oaths were initiated for government workers; internal security laws were passed by Congress, investigations and hearings stirred up the whole country. Citizens who invoked the Fifth Amendment were treated with suspicion. Guilt by association was common in the charges made. Rarely has America been so directly and immediately affected by public communication.

21. When Rosa Parks refused to follow the orders of the Montgomery bus driver to relinquish her seat to a white man the floodgates of centuries-old frustrations were opened. C. O. R. E., the Urban League, and especially the N. A. A. C. P. had worked quietly toward black dignity for years. The Montgomery story, however, caught the imagination of America, both black and white, and the rhetoric of the current Black Revolution was under way. It was not so much a debate with the opposition as it was an internal struggle over method of achieving the goal of black dignity and freedom. The limited success of Martin Luther King's nonviolence and Malcolm X's separateness gave rise to a New Black Power militancy with primary focus on effect rather than strategy. Tragically, assassins'

bullets took both King and Malcolm X and, following the 1968 elections, the national administration skillfully diverted attention from the plight of blacks. Popular regional black leaders have surfaced since 1968, but none has captured the national black scene.

22. Urged on by a resurgence of idealism in America and public attention via mass media, two groups, students and blacks, led a determined movement to reform some basic societal practices. These rhetorical efforts backed by natural conservative forces have led to much wider freedom of expression. Blacks, stripped of human dignity by an oppressive white society, sought full rights of citizenship at first politically and later economically. During the 1960s students, encouraged by the success of the black revolution and goaded by *in loco parentis* policies at college and societal lip service to basic American values, lashed out at the establishment. These reform efforts, at first dignified and cerebral, were not satisfying to the rhetors and rapidly shifted into confrontational body rhetoric of various kinds. Marches, sit-ins, draft card burning, underground newspapers, etc., appalled the power structure and occasionally violated local laws. Arrests followed and case after case supported a broader right to protest in spite of opposition from the "grassroots."

23. By the mid sixties students essentially abandoned the black revolution in the south and shifted to Students for a Democratic Society leadership on several national issues, especially the war in Vietnam. March after march, and sit-in after sit-in seemed not to affect national policy on the war. With this turn of events youth progressively lost respect for authority and the "system" in general and protest became violent and destructive. The S.D.S. continued a major leadership role as the focal point of the protest shifted first to Berkeley and then to Columbia where tactics became deliberately divisive. The shooting at Jackson State and at Kent State brought a chilling somberness to the national scene and the combatants quietly, if reluctantly, laid down arms. Little change in national policy seemed to have been affected by the youth/student protest of the 1960s but *in loco parentis* has long since died and students now wield considerable power on most campuses. Quiet has returned to the campus—it is an uneasy quiet. Kent State scared everybody.

24. The peace movement came alive anew in the early 1960s and called for a change in East-West relations. With the United States overtly involved in the Vietnam War, the peace movement picked up much momentum. University teach-ins across the nation marked the initial response to the Vietnam War. New organizations joined existing peace organizations and while they were often not in full agreement among themselves they could agree on the theme "end the war and bring the troops home." Strategies of protest differed radically. Spokesmen in the peace movement constantly raised questions that prodded the conscience of

America. A Harris poll of April 16, 1971, indicated that 58 percent of Americans considered the United States' fighting in Vietnam to be morally wrong. At this writing a cease fire has been signed and the task of building a lasting peace has begun.

III

Now that we have traced the role of rhetoric in American history and have sketched the major issues to which rhetoric has been addressed, we are permitted some observations. They may be seen in the approaches to the issues described in some detail in the chapters to follow.

(a) Men seek improvement in their condition, usually rhetorically, when alternatives of hope are presented. However, even an extremely painful condition may not be protested if the abused sees little hope for betterment.

(b) When groups of people and institutions are in a rhetorical campaign it is important that alliances be built as a power base if their rhetoric is to succeed.

(c) The American value system is vital in most persuasive efforts. The role of values is complicated by differing emphases and interpretations of values during different time periods and by differing interpretations of values by opposing persuaders during the same time period.

(d) Much American rhetoric tends to be a justification or rationalization for actions already taken. Our values and national beliefs (e.g., democratic form of government) serve as prime rationalizations.

(e) Successful appeals tend to be moderate in nature and appropriate to a broad base of support among the American populace. Radical ideas or solutions are rarely successful.

(f) Unity and compromise—working through the system—are essential for success in most debates, campaigns, and movements.

(g) "Politics" plays an important role in many decisions on a wide variety of issues. This fact was readily apparent in the tariff issue, World War I and the League of Nations, black man's rights, progressivism, etc. Ostensibly a given debate may appear to controvert a basic premise (e.g., state's rights) when in essence the conflict is a raw power struggle.

(h) For success, goals and strategies should be adapted to fit the requirements of a changing rhetorical situation.

  1. In the event that a given strategy may not succeed the advocate should be prepared to lead a different attack on the problem.

  2. Strategies are less important than progress toward the goal. A rigid leadership committed to "the only way" of goal achievement tends to become doctrinaire even to the extent of means becoming ends.

3.   A given goal may be achieved in whole or in part, leading to a lessening of the need for the rhetorical movement. New realistic and relevant goals must be adopted if the group is to survive.

(i)   When impotent or even irrelevant audiences are addressed, the speaker should make himself aware of the audience potentiality for goal fulfillment.

(j)   Audacious requests may win short term gains in a given rhetorical skirmish due in part to the surprise element.

(k)   Conservatives usually occupying the power establishment position tend to be unexercised by rhetorical threats. This may be due to complacency or general inarticulateness on their part.

(l)   As long as opposing rhetorical movements talk seriously about their controversy, progress may be made toward bringing unity where there is difference.

Readers will discover other patterns or trends as they read about how men and groups have jockeyed rhetorically to lessen their difficulties and enhance their blessings. The ones noted seem readily apparent in several of the issues studied.

1

Puritan Paternalism and Indian Evangelism, 1620-1675

John W. Reed

John Eliot, the Puritan pastor at Roxbury, Massachusetts, was called "the Apostle to the Indians." He labored many years to win converts to Puritanism from among the Indians. Eliot successfully reduced the Indian language to writing, translated the Bible into Algonquin, and taught the Indians to read. He established the converted Indians into what he called "Praying Towns" and carefully catechized them in the elements of Puritan doctrine. After a decade of exhaustive work Eliot invited representatives of the Puritan churches in Massachusetts to come to Roxbury and examine several of the Christian Indians to see if they were worthy of becoming members of the Puritan communion. The examination was to convene on the thirteenth day of the fourth month in 1654.

Ten days before the great event three of Eliot's prospective church members procured several quarts of liquor and got drunk. In the process they also encouraged an eleven year old boy to become drunk. The drunken Indians engaged in rowdy behavior and fighting. Eliot was deeply discouraged but proceeded with the examination of other prospective Indian Puritans.

The interrogations lasted the entire day as the Puritan elders asked many detailed questions relating to Puritan doctrine and church practice. All those present were impressed with the genuineness of the Indians' faith but refused to accept them into the Puritan church. Eliot was told that since the Indians had so recently come out of such "great depth of darkness, and wild course of life"[1] more time was needed to observe their behavior before they could safely be given church status. John Eliot submitted to the decision of the elders and continued his work. The first of his Christian Indians received Puritan church membership in 1660, more than fifteen years after Eliot had made his initial converts.

The long delay in accepting Christian Indians into the church was symptomatic of the standard Puritan method of relating to the Indians of New England and comprised a partial answer to a question that the elders of Massachusetts Bay might have been asked: "Is the Indian a rational human

---

1. John Eliot, "A Late and Further Manifestation of the Progress of the Gospel Amongst the Indians in New England," *Collections of the Massachusetts Historical Society* (Cambridge: Charles Folsom, 1824), 4, 3d series:285.

being fully deserving to be treated as a fellow human and brother?''

Since the Puritans exerted such profound influence upon subsequent American history, their treatment of the Indians in the experience of early colonization was of great importance. If the Puritans could have avoided paternalistic attitudes in their dealings with the Indian, American race relations might have taken a more favorable course. The facts of the colonial experience reveal a prolonged debate over the best methods of treating the Indians that inhabited the American shores. The problem of Indian evangelism was at the center of the controversy.

The Background

When John Winthrop stated the reasons for settling a plantation in New England, he listed as first concern "The ppagocon of the gospell to the Indians." After this purpose, he included such objectives as the acquisition of land and the development of agriculture and commerce.[2] The royal charter of the Massachusetts Bay Colony included a directive that the people were to be governed so as to win the natives to the Christian faith, "which, in our royall intencon and the adventurers free profession, is the principall ende of this plantacon."[3] The seal of the colony of Massachusetts Bay was inscribed symbolically with an Indian holding a bow and arrow in his hands and saying, "Come over and help us." This inscription indicated the centrality of Indian evangelism in the colony's purpose and the ever-present threat of Indian warfare as one of the major deterrents to converting the Indians.

English Superiority — Anthropologists have regarded the New England coastal region as having been the most densely populated area of eastern North America in times prior to colonization by Europeans. Among the major tribes were the Massachusetts, who inhabited the region in the northern section of the colony that took its name as their own. Below them were the Wampanoag and Pequots. What is now Rhode Island was inhabited by the Narragansets and below them were the Mohegans. These people were similar in most ways and all spoke Algonquian dialects.[4]

The site for the location of the Massachusetts Bay Company's settlement was selected on the basis of the fact that the tribes in the area had been decimated by a severe plague several months prior to the colonization attempt. The Puritans spoke consistently of the epidemic being an act of God in clearing the land of Indians in order for the establishment of their colony. The popular view persisted that the Indians' high mortality rate made them fear the English. Johnson reasoned that "by this meanes Christ (whose great and glorious workes the Earth throughout are altogether for the benefit of his Churches and chosen) not onely made roome for his people to plant, but also tamed the hard and cruell hearts of these barbarous Indians."[5] The "Reverend and Learned" Cotton Mather explained that the Puritans had been led by the hand of God to a country prepared by the mor-

2. "Winthrop's Conclusions," *Old South Leaflets* (Boston: Directors of the Old South Work, n.d.) 2, no. 50:1.

3. Nathaniel B. Shurtleff, ed., *Records of Massachusetts Bay* (1853; reprinted New York: AMS Press, 1968), 1:17.

4. William Brandon *The American Heritage Book of Indians* (New York: Dell Publishing Co., 1961) pp. 164-165.

5. J. Franklin Jameson, ed., *Johnson's Wonder-Working Providence 1628-1651* (New York: Barnes & Noble, 1910), pp. 40-41; 79-80.

tality of the Indians. He stated that as high as nineteen out of twenty had died in the pestilence, "so that the woods were almost cleared of these pernicious creatures, to make room for a better growth."[6]

The cause of the plague that destroyed up to a third of the Indian population north of the Narragansett Bay has never been accurately determined but historians generally agree that since the English appeared to be immune, it was probably brought to New England by European explorers and traders. This fatal touch of English influence continued through many years of colonial missionary work. "Ironically, the first victims of disease were usually those the Puritans had most thoroughly converted and civilized."[7] Faithful Puritan leaders saw the hand of God in all the events of life. The death of Indians was an evidence to them that God had given the Puritans the right of superiority in New England. Since the Indians were unchristian and uncivilized, the Puritans felt the responsibility of maintaining law and order. English strategy consistently involved immediate response with force whenever the Indians revealed warlike activity.

In 1637 the Puritans marched in an early morning assault on the Pequot Indians in retaliation for the murder of an English trader. With sword and fire they destroyed some five hundred to seven hundred Indian men, women and children in one bloody night. In addition they sought to destroy every other male member of the Pequot tribe by paying a price for the head of any brave captured. Pequot women and children were sold into slavery in the West Indies. Thomas Lechford wrote of the Indians in 1641: "Since the Pequid war, they are kept in very good subjection, and held to strict points of justice, so that the English may travail safely among them."[8]

The Puritans were careful to keep the balance of power in their favor. European weapons were definitely superior and the advantage gained by the possession of firearms was guarded jealously. Sale of firearms to Indians was forbidden.[9] Winthrop records on September 4, 1632, the case of a man named Hopkins of Watertown. Hopkins sold a rifle and a pistol, with powder and shot, to an Indian. For this act Hopkins was whipped and branded on his cheek.[10]

Some tribes in the Massachusetts Bay area that had been weakened by pestilence submitted to the jurisdiction and government of the English. Their reason for doing so was related primarily to desires for their own survival. The English promised to protect these tribes from the attempts of stronger rival Indians to bring them into subjection. The General Court of Massachusetts often threatened and even executed retaliation against more remote tribes as a result of information provided by these local tribes. This process often resulted in difficulties but the English patiently sought to be consistent in their Indian policies. The Bay Colony attempted to stand behind all treaties that they had made with individual tribes. It can be said to the colonists' credit that any degree of order in the face of constant friction and tension may be considered commendable. Roger Williams, in Rhode Island, often provided information that helped the Bay Colony

6. Cotton Mather, *Magnalia Christi Americana* (New York: Russell and Russell, 1967), 1:51.

7. Alden T. Vaughan, *New England Frontier* (Boston: Little Brown and Company, 1965), p. 306.

8. Thomas Lechford, *Plain Dealing or News from New England* (1767: reprinted New York: Johnson Reprint Corporation, 1969), p. 117.

9. Vaughan, *New England Frontier*, p. 179.

10. James K. Hosmer, ed. *Winthrop's Journal "History of New England" 1630-1649* (New York: Barnes & Noble, 1946), 1:90.

break tribal alliances which threatened English existence and his intelligence helped preserve the English balance of power. In the tragedy of King Philip's War (1675) which finally broke the Indians of New England, it was intelligence provided by evangelized Indians that helped turn the tide to the English.[11]

Theological Barriers to Evangelism— John Cotton, pastor of the church in Boston, was one of the most influential Puritan preachers during the period of 1620-1660. While still a pastor in old England, he had preached the farewell sermon before the departure of a group of Bay Colony settlers on the ship *Arbella*. In this 1630 sermon he stated that the conversion of the Indians was not the main reason for Puritan colonization but was a part of the price the colonists were willing to pay for sharing the land with the Indians.[12] Cotton came to New England in 1633 and it again became evident that Indian evangelism was not of primary importance to him. John Winthrop recorded in his *Journal* in 1641 that Cotton had preached a sermon from Revelation 15:8 and revealed his belief that the present age could expect the conversion of only a few pagans.[13] Cotton also stated this view in *The Way of Congregational Churches Cleared* published in 1648. This treatise was an answer to critics of the Bay Colony form of church government. He said of Indian evangelism, "It is true, there may be doubt that for a time there will be no great hope of any national conversion, till Antichrist be ruined, and the Jews converted."[14] He was referring to a belief that efforts in evangelization among non-Christians would have only minor results until the Roman Catholic church was overthrown and there was an extensive evange-

lization of the Jewish nation.[15] Roger Williams expressed a similar view in *The Hireling Ministry None of Christs.*[16]

It is difficult to determine how much of a deadening influence this view may have had on attempts at Indian evangelism. John Eliot mentioned the idea along with other problems in confessing that the colonists had reason to be humble because they had not worked hard enough to reach the Indians. He recognized that there was "A seale set upon the hearts of the people . . . till the Jewes come in"[17] but this realization did not keep him from prolonged efforts in Indian evangelism. The fact that Eliot continued to work in the face of such obvious discouragement indicates something of the scope of his energy and vision.

Civilization Before Evangelization—The Puritans were extremely careful in their acceptance of new converts from among the Indians. Only a complete change of life and a thorough understanding of Puritan doctrine could constitute evidence of conversion. Thomas Thorowgood had spoken of the Spaniards' mass baptism of professing Indian believers. He had also discussed

11. Vaughan, *New England Frontier*, p. 317.

12. Larzer Ziff, *The Career of John Cotton* (Princeton, New Jersey: Princeton University Press, 1962), p. 62.

13. Hosmer, ed. *Winthrop's Journal* 1:30.

14. Larzer Ziff, ed. *John Cotton on the Churches of New England* (Cambridge, Mass.: Belknap Press, 1968), p. 274.

15. Thomas Thorowgood, *Jewes in Americana* (London: Printed by W. H., 1650), pp. 22-23. Hereafter cited as *Jewes* (1650).

16. Roger Williams, *Complete Writings* (New York: Russell & Russell, 1963), 7:168.

17. John Eliot, "The Day-Breaking of the Gospel with the Indians" *Old South Leaflets* (Boston: Directors of the Old South Work, n.d.), 6, no. 143:14.

Spanish attempts to force Indians into the faith by violent means.[18] The Puritans consistently refused to use such tactics. They demanded that each Indian personally experience conversion in the fullest Puritan sense. This was such a change for the primitive Indian that John Eliot stated:

> But me thinkes now that it is with the Indians as it was with our New-English ground when we first came over, there was scarce any man that could beleeve that English graine would grow, or that the Plow could doe any good in this woody and rocky soile. And thus they continued in this supine unbeliefe for some yeares, till experience taught them otherwise, and now all see it to bee scarce inferiour to Old-English tillage, but beares very good burdens; so wee have thought of our Indian people, and therefore have beene discouraged to put plow to such dry and rocky ground, but God having begun thus with some few it may bee they are better soil for the Gospel then wee can thinke: I confesse I thinke no great good will bee done till they be more civilized, but why may not God begin with some few, to awaken others by degrees?[19]

The idea that civilization was mandatory to the process of Christianizing was quite widespread among the Puritans and Eliot was persistent in his efforts to this end throughout his long career.[20]

Roger Williams did not agree that civilization before evangelism was such a critical matter. In a letter to John Winthrop in 1637, Williams spoke of his ministry to the Narragansetts. The Indians had been receptive to Williams' claims that their religion was inadequate. Williams spoke of Indian willingness to worship the powers and manifestations of nature. The Indians had given Williams the names of thirty-eight of their gods and revealed a desire to add the Puritan God to their list. They were even ready to consent to worship "O God (as they speak)" on the Puritan sabbath.[21] Williams was not interested in such a shallow accep-

tance of Christianity but saw in it a tendency that could result in genuine conversion. In his *Key into the Indian Languages* Williams revealed that he could easily have brought the Indians of the Narragansett Country into "keeping the Englishman's day of worship" but he "was persuaded that God's way is first to turne a soule from it's Idolls, both of heart, worship, and conversation, before it is capable of worship, to the true and living God."[22] It was apparently this reference concerning Indian readiness to add the Puritan God to their list of gods that English critics of Puritanism later confused as Williams' evidence of ability to make thousands of converts.[23] There is little evidence that Roger Williams found many Indians who were willing to make the steps of true conversion. These steps he described as turning to God from idols in the form of "Repentance from dead workes, and Faith towards God, before the Doctrine of Baptisme or washing and the laying on of hands, which containe the Ordinances and Practices of worship."[24] During his long life Williams continued to preach to the Indians. He continually held to a hope that "some of the wildest of them shall be found to share in the blood of the Son of God."[25] William described a group of particularly wild Indians: "The Mauguauogs, or Men Eaters, that live two or three miles West from us make a de-

---

18. Thorowgood, *Jewes* (1650), pp. 26-35.

19. Eliot, "Day-Breaking," 6, no. 143:14-15.

20. Ola Winslow, *John Eliot* (Boston: Houghton Mifflin, 1968), p. 134.

21. Williams, *Writings*, 6:88.

22. Ibid., 1:160.

23. Ziff, *Cotton on Churches*, pp. 275-79.

24. Williams, *Writings*, 1:161.

25. Ibid., 1:85.

licious monstrous dish of the head and brains of their enemies: which is yet no barre (when the time shall approach) against God's call, and their repentance, and (who knowes but) a greater love to the Lord Jesus? Great sinners forgiven love much."[26]

While it appears that Roger Williams did not attempt to civilize the Indians before conversion and there is little evidence that he attempted to Europeanize them after conversion, he did reveal attitudes that primarily favored the English above the Indians. In a letter addressed to the General Court of Massachusetts, October 5, 1654, Williams spoke of his service to the Court in providing intelligence in the Pequot War. He also reminded the Court of his continued attempts to keep peace between the Indians and the English. Williams urged the Puritans to avoid war with the Narragansetts. He reminded the Court that "it be not only possible, but very easy, to live and die in peace with all the natives of this country."[27] Williams continued by urging that the Court avoid overreacting in the face of minor infractions of rules laid on the Indians. He pointed out that the Puritans had gained much support in their cause because of the news of "the glorious conversion of the Indians of New England."[28] Williams then asked what may have been one of the most critical questions of early American history: "I beseech you consider, how the name of the most holy and jealous God may be preserved between the clashings of these two, viz.: the glorious conversion of the Indians in New England, and the unnecessary wars and cruel destruction of the Indians in New England."[29]

This enlightened viewpoint sounds refreshingly modern against its seventeenth century background. Because of such an attitude in Roger Williams, Perry Miller of Harvard indicated that Williams was the only Englishman of his generation who could treat the Indian culture with respect.[30] Yet Williams finished his 1654 letter to the General Court with an admission that if a general war occurred the English would find the Indians seeking to destroy them. Williams found himself bound to English interests whenever a choice had to be made between the Indians and his countrymen:

But I beseech you, say your thoughts and the thoughts of your wives and little ones, and the thoughts of all English, and of God's people in England, and the thoughts of his Highness and Council, (tender of these parts), if, for the sake of a few inconsiderable pagans, and beasts, wallowing in idleness, stealing, lying, whoring, treacherous witchcrafts, blasphemies, and idolatries, all that the gracious hand of the Lord hath so wonderfully planted in the wilderness, should be destroyed.[31]

The Process of Evangelism

John Eliot never seemed to be troubled with the confusion and divided interests that bothered Roger Williams. Eliot had no respect for the Indian culture. He not only sought to civilize the Indians before conversion but also attempted to finish the task after conversion. His method was to establish the converted Indians in what he called praying towns. These towns were Puritan in every respect and were designed to abolish all aspects of Indian culture.

---

26. Ibid., 1:77.
27. Ibid., 4:271.
28. Ibid.
29. Ibid., 4:272.
30. Perry Miller, *Roger Williams, His Contribution to the American Tradition* (New York: Atheneum, 1965), p. 52.
31. Williams, *Writings*, 6:276.

The actual evangelization of the Indians as practiced by Eliot began by the seeking of an initial contact with the Indians to negotiate a preaching opportunity. This resulted in a time of preaching and dialogue and then continued contact until some Indians began to respond. John Eliot described several of his early Indian encounters in *The Day-Breaking, if not the Sun-Rising of the Gospel with the Indians of New England.* The contact on October 28, 1646, was typical of subsequent attempts at evangelization. After a period of prayer Eliot and three other Puritans approached an Indian village near Roxbury, Massachusetts. Following cordial greetings to the tribal leaders, the Puritans bowed in prayer before the Indians. They prayed in English and then one of the Puritans, whose name Eliot did not give, began to preach in Algonquin. Eliot described the experience as follows:

For about an houre and a quarter the Sermon continued, wherein one of our company ran thorough all the principall matter of religion, beginning first with a repetition of the ten Commandments, and a briefe explication of them, then shewing the curse and dreadfull wrath of God against all those who brake them, or any one of them, or the least title of them, and so applyed it unto the condition of the Indians present, with much sweet affection; and then preached Jesus Christ to them the onely meanes of recovery from sinne and wrath and eternall death, and what Christ was, and whither he was now gone, and how hee will one day come againe to judge the world in flaming fire; and of the blessed estate of all those that by faith beleeve in Christ, and know him feelingly: he spake to them also (observing his owne method as he saw most fit to edifie them) about the creation and fall of man, about the greatnesse and infinite being of God, the maker of all things, about the joyes of heaven, and the terrours and horrours of wicked men in hell, perswading them to repentance for severall sins which they live in, and many things of the like nature; not medling

with any matters more difficult, and which to such weake ones might at first seeme ridiculous, untill they had tasted and beleeved more plaine and familiar truths.[32]

After the sermon Eliot asked the Indians if they understood what was said and they responded affirmatively. Eliot then asked if they had questions about the sermon. The village leaders responded with a series of questions primarily related to the cause of thunder, tides of the sea and the wind. The Puritans responded that the answers to their questions were to be found in meditation on the words of the Bible and by praying to the Puritan God:

And wee told them, that although they could not make any long prayers as the English could, yet if they did but sigh and groane, and say thus; Lord make mee know Jesus Christ, for I know him not, and if they did say so againe and againe with their hearts that God would teach them Jesus Christ, because hee is such a God as will bee found of them that seeke him with all their hearts, and hee is a God hearing the prayers of all men both Indian as well an English, and that English men by this meanes have come to the knowledge of Jesus Christ.[33]

The final advice concerned repentance for sins and the confessing of sins to God. Eliot observed that the man who preached said an occasional word or phrase through an Indian interpreter who had accompanied them but the tribesmen listened most attentively when the Englishman was speaking.

An Indian said that he had attempted to pray in his tent as suggested by the English but one of his fellow Indians stopped him by telling him that Jesus Christ only understood English. The Puritans pointed out

---

32. Eliot, "Day-Breaking," 6, no. 143:2.

33. Ibid., 6, no. 143:3.

that since God made all things by Jesus Christ, He also made Indians. Just as Indians understood the things they used in making baskets, so God understood the language of Indians that He had made.

After answering the Indians' questions, the Puritans took opportunity to ask the Indians concerning their views of such things as God being invisible, there being but one God, and how they at that time found peace concerning their sins. When the Indians answered, the English proceeded to explain the Puritan solutions to these problems. Eliot concluded the account:

Thus after three houres time thus spent with them, wee asked them if they were not weary, and they answered, No. But wee resolved to leave them with an appetite; the chiefe of them seeing us conclude with prayer, desired to know when wee would come againe, so wee appointed the time, and having given the children some apples, and the men some tobacco and what else we then had at hand, they desired some more ground to build a Town together, which wee did much like of, promising to speake for them to the generall Court, that they might possesse all the compasse of that hill, upon which their Wigwams then stood, and so wee departed with many welcomes from them.[34]

After many visits to Indian villages and gathering a group of followers, the next step was the establishment of Indian towns. Thomas Shepard, Puritan pastor at Cambridge provided an account of the request of an Indian sachem (chieftain) for such a town near the English at Concord. When the Puritans suggested that it might be wiser to locate the town further from the English, the sachem replied that if the Indians dwelt far from the English, they would not so quickly learn to pray and it would be more difficult for them to hear the Word of God. The English granted the request and the town was organized.[35]

Generally the Puritans continued their attempts to keep the Indian towns as far from their own villages as possible. There appeared to be little real desire to integrate the Christian Indians into the English towns and villages. However, there were several instances of children being given to the English to rear and educate.[36] In 1652 the Bay Colony promised that "if any of the Indians shalbe brought to civilitie, and shall come amongst the English to inhabite in any of theire plantations . . . such Indians shall have allottment amongst the English according to the custome of the English."[37] On the other hand, the English were not allowed to live among the Indians but there were apparently no laws against intermarriage.[38] Vaughan reasoned that the vast cultural differences and a plentiful supply of English women kept the number of racial intermarriages at a minimum.[39]

The number of Indian towns continued to expand. Daniel Gookin recorded descriptions of fourteen praying towns in addition to the Christian Indians of Martha's Vineyard.[40] Gookin also described the severe stricture under which the Puritans placed the Indians before they would recognize any Indians as being worthy of becoming church members. Some Indians were observed for as long as

---

34. Ibid., 6, no. 143:7.

35. Thomas Shepard, "The Clear Sun-shine of the Gospel breaking forth upon the Indians in New-England," *Collections of the Massachusetts Historical Society* (Cambridge: Charles Folsom, 1834), 4, 3d series:38-39.

36. Eliot, "Day-Breaking," 6, no. 143:17.

37. Shurtleff, ed. *Records of Massachusetts*, 3:281.

38. Ibid., 1:140.

39. Vaughan, *New England Frontier*, p. 209.

40. Daniel Gorkin, "Historical Collections of the Indians in New England," *Collections of the Massachusetts Historical Society* (Boston: Muroe & Francis, 1806), 1:180-207.

fifteen years before they were granted membership.

One of the most important elements in Indian evangelism was the translation of the Bible into the Algonquin language by John Eliot. The Roxbury pastor lived a very busy life. In addition to serving the church in Roxbury, he continually visited the Indian towns and labored for years in reducing the language of the Indians into writing, translating the Bible into Algonquin and then teaching the Indians to read it. Eliot's efforts revealed his deep sincerity of purpose and provided one of the brightest pages in this early history of American race relations. His work was carried on without essential training in linguistics and was a remarkable accomplishment for a man of his time.[41]

Much of the financial support for the publishing of the various editions of Eliot's Bible came from a united effort of the colonists and those back in England who were interested in the evangelization of the New England Indians. In 1649 "The Society for Propagation of the Gospel in New England" was organized and continued to provide much of the money for the work of John Eliot. In addition to financial help in the publishing of Eliot's Algonquin Bible, the Society also provided funds for the Indian schools in the praying towns. A special building was built at Harvard College for the training of eligible Indian students. The effort was sincere but the young Indians apparently were not made for scholarship. Few Indians took advantage of the opportunity and of those few who did most died before completion of the program.[42]

Many of the accounts of work among the Indians apparently were written to provide publicity and encourage additional gifts to the Society. Across the years John Eliot was the most consistent fund raiser of those who preached to the Indians. The substantial gifts for the support of the Indian work revealed an awareness on the part of the English of their responsibility to the Indians in the area of the propagation of faith. Evangelism provided the base for almost all English humanitarian enterprises on behalf of the Indians. The Puritan's desire to win the Indians to belief in Christ may have prolonged for many years the conflict that came in 1775 when the two cultures living in New England seemed unable to hold back any longer their ultimate incompatibility.

Can an Indian Be Saved?—From the days of Christopher Columbus, Europe had debated the problem of Indian evangelism. Many held that the native Americans were cannibalistic savages without rational understanding. These people felt that the Indians must be subdued and civilized before there was any possibility of developing religious capabilities. Those who held such views were usually profiting greatly from the Indian slave trade. Bartolomé de las Casas, who as a young man, sailed with Columbus in 1498, emerged as the champion of the Indians. He devoted his life to awaken in Europe the realization that Indians were rational human beings and not mere subjects for manipulation and slavery.[43]

41. John Eliot, "The Indian Grammar begun" *Old South Leaflets* (New York: Burt Franklin, n.d.), 3, no. 51:1-10.

42. Gookin, "Historical Collections," 1:176. Vaughan, *New-England Frontier*, pp. 280-88.

43. The issues of this debate may be studied in Lewis Hanke, *Aristotle and the American Indian* (London: Hollis & Carter, 1959), p. 112; *Hakluytus Posthomus* (Glasgow: James MacLehase & Sons, 1906), 18:176-180; Francis A. MacNutt, *Bartholomew De Las Casas* (New York: G. P. Putman's Sons, 1909), pp. 287-93; Winslow, *John Eliot* pp. 71-85.

Various aspects of this great problem concerning the worth of the Indians and proper methods in evangelizing them constituted one of the earliest controversies in American history.

It is not difficult to assess the attitude of New England settlers toward the Indians and toward the Indian's capacity to receive the message of Puritan religion. The fact that the English were interested in evangelization indicated a Puritan belief that the Indians had a capacity for such an experience. Roger Williams, the founder of Providence, Rhode Island, had learned the Algonquin language before his banishment from the Massachusetts Bay Colony.[44] While ministering in Plymouth in 1631-1632, he established a trading post with the Indians conversing with them in their own language. Williams came to know many Indians and they evidently learned to trust the young Puritan preacher. He spoke concerning an Indian named Oufamaquin who lived near his later home at Providence "that he was pleased that I should here be his neighbor, and that rather because he and I had been great friends at Plymouth."[45] Apparently Roger Williams must have heard complaints from the Indians concerning the colonists' acquisition of lands in New England because he wrote a pamphlet concerning the King's Patent. The *Treatise* is not extant but its basic thrust can be drawn from other sources. John Winthrop referred to the treatise and said that Williams had advised the governor and assistants at Boston "that, claiming by the kings grant, they could have no title, nor otherwise, except they compounded with the natives."[46] Williams was apparently headed toward a viewpoint that might have resulted in a higher regard for Indian rights than America actually came to experience.

The colonial authorities censured Williams for this and other statements in the *Treatise* but were able to work out a reconciliation with him. Roger Williams later clarified his viewpoints in *The Bloody Tenent yet More Bloody*. Williams is the "Discusser" in the following quotation:

I know those thoughts have deeply possessed, not a few, considering also the sinne of the Pattents, wherein Christian Kings (so calld) are invested with Right by virtue of their Christianitie, to take and give away the Lands and Countries of other men. . . .
And I know these thoughts so deeply afflicted the Soule and Conscience of the Discusser in the time of his Walking in the Way of New Englands Worship, that at last he came to a presuasion, that such sinnes could not be Expiated, without returning againe into England: or a publike acknowledgement and Confession of the Evill of so and so departing: To this purpose before his Troubles and Banishment he drew up a letter (not without the Approbation of some of the Chiefs of New England, then tender also upon this point before God) directed unto the King himselfe, humbly acknowledging the Evill of that part of the Pattent which respects the Donation of Land, etc.[47]

This early attempt of Roger Williams to condemn the aggressive land grabbing tendencies of the colonists is counterbalanced by the fact that Williams later sought a Royal charter for his Providence Plantations. He had fairly purchased the land from the Narragansetts and it was true that the charter helped to protect his colony from attack by the Bay Colony. However, Williams' actions indicated that he was a man of his times and his protests against unfair treatment of the Indians concerning

---

44. Williams, *Writings*, 1:84-85; 4:261.
45. Ibid., 6:317.
46. Hosmer, ed. *Winthrop's Journal*, 1:116.
47. Williams, *Writings*, 4:461-462.

the possession of lands did not become a major passion of his life. Later, in the maturity of his years, he spoke of his pessimism concerning English motives in New England, "I fear that the common Trinity of the world (Profit, Preferment, Pleasure) will here be as in all the world beside; that Prelacy and Papacy too will in this wilderness predominate; that God Land will be (as now it is) as great a God with us English as God Gold was with the Spaniards."[48] Those who read the history of the more than three hundred years that have followed this statement by Williams can readily assess its prophetic value.

After more than a decade of trading with the Indians and preaching to them regularly, Roger Williams wrote *A Key Into the Language of America* which he published in London in 1643. His general attitude was one of sympathy and understanding for the Indians. Williams concluded that the Indians were fellow humans descending from Adam and Noah. He found a similarity between the Jewish race and the Indians in some of the words in their vocabulary and in customs such as anointing their heads, giving dowries for wives, and secluding their women during the monthly menstruation period.[49]

Thomas Thorowgood took this idea and expanded it into his work *Jewes in America or Probabilities that the Americans are Jews*. Thorowgood found a large number of similarities between the Indians and the Jewish race in customs, rites, words and manners of speech.[50] Thorowgood argued on the basis of these Indian similarities to the Jews that the Indians must not be neglected in the giving of the Gospel.[51]

The great Indian evangelist, John Eliot of Roxbury, emerged as the most famous of those who seriously sought to preach to the Indians. He wrote a discourse for the second edition of Thorowgood's book in which he generally agreed with Thorowgood's contentions.[52]

The Dregs of Humanity—Thorowgood's writings revealed an important area of thought in relationship to English attitudes toward the Indians of New England. Many pages in his first book were devoted to the subject of Spanish cruelty to the Indians in other parts of North and South America and the West Indies. In contrast to such maltreatment, Thorowgood pleaded for the best peaceable efforts in seeking to win the Indians to Christ.[53] While history suggests that the English of New England treated the Indians of America with less severity than did some other Europeans, it does seem evident that the Puritans and Pilgrims were not without severe problems in their attitudes toward the American aboriginals. Thorowgood stated he was confident that, "the Gospel of Christ shall be revealed in the midst of that yet most Barbarous Nation."[54] He thus classified the New England Indian's society as the lowest form of human life possible. Charles Chauncy, who preached in Plymouth and Scituate and became an early president of Harvard College, gave insight into his own views of the Indians in a sermon in which, among other

---

48. Ibid., 6:319.
49. Ibid., 1:22-23.
50. Thorowgood, *Jewes* (1650), pp. 1-35.
51. Ibid., a.e.
52. Thomas Thorowgood, *Jews in America, or Probabilities that those Indians are Judaical, made more probable by some additionals to the former Conjectures* (London: For Henry Brome, 1660), pp. 1-23.
53. Thorowgood, *Jewes* (1650), pp. 26-35.
54. Ibid., p. 2.

points, he condemned the wearing of long hair by church members. Such hair in Chauncy's view branded a man as having "Correspondency with ruffians and swaggerers and cavaliers yea the vilest persons in the country, yea Indians and Pagans."[55]

This tendency to downgrade the Indians apparently began quite early in the colonial experience. Johnson's *Wonder Working Providence* was an eye witness history of colonization. Johnson remarked in recounting the settlement of the Plymouth Colony that they made tests of "the sordid spirits of the Neighboring Indians"[56] before settling. The phrase "dregs of humanity" appeared in the popular vocabulary of the colonists and was evidence of the general European attitude toward the Indians.[57] Roger Williams agreed that the Indians could be classed with the "dregs of mankind" but were no more bloody than the European whites.[58] John Eliot who emerged as the Puritan most sensitive to Indian needs spoke of them as: "these poore Natives the dregs of mankinde and the saddest spectacle of misery of meere men upon earth."[59] Eliot held that the Indians were immersed in "the deepest degeneracies." He complained:

Wee are oft upbraided by some of our Countrymen that so little good is done by our professing planters upon the hearts of Natives; such men have surely more spleene then judgement, and know not the vast distance of Natives from common civility, and almost humanity it selfe . . . for what Nation or people ever so deeply degenerated since Adams fall as these Indians?[60]

Thomas Lechford gave an insight that might summarize the English attitude toward the Indians. His statement assumed added significance because Lechford, an attorney and solicitor, found himself in opposition to many of the practices of the Massachusetts Bay Colony. He said that the Indians ". . . live much better, and peaceably, for the English, and themselves know it, or at least their Sachems, and Saggamores know so much, for before they did nothing but spoil and destroy one another."[61]

Developments

Eliot and other missionaries to the Indians received discouragement from many sources. Back in England there were those who sought to undermine Puritanism at home and in New England.

Criticism—Robert Baylie, a Presbyterian clergyman, was a major critic of Puritan church practice. He wrote *A Dissuasive from the Errors of the Time* (1645) to which John Cotton gave a detailed answer in *The Way of Congregational Churches Cleared* (1648). Among the arguments Baylie advanced were several that related directly to Puritan policies of Indian evangelism. Baylie used evidence gathered from eye witness reports made by Roger Williams and Thomas Lechford to charge Puritan church practice "exceedingly hindered

55. Charles Chauncy, *God's Mercy, Shewed to His People in Giving them a Faithful Ministry and Schooles of Learning for the Continual Supplyes thereof, Delivered in a Sermon preached at Cambridge, the day after the Commencement.* (Cambridge in New England, 1655), pp. 24-28. Quoted in Babette Levy. *Preaching in the First Half Century of New England History* (Hartford, Conn.: The American Society of Church History, 1945), p. 61.

56. Jameson, ed., *Johnson's Wonder Working* p. 45.

57. Winslow, *Eliot*, p. 72.

58. Williams, *Writings*, 6:307.

59. Eliot, "Day-Breaking" 6, no. 143:13.

60. Ibid., 6, no. 143:14-16.

61. Lechford, *Plain Dealing*, p. 118.

the conversion of the poor pagans."[62] Bay-lie argued that Puritan preachers did not preach for conversion but spent all their efforts on those who were already church members. John Cotton responded that it was the responsibility of Puritan preachers "to attend the work of conversion, both of carnal English, and other nations, whether Christian, or pagan."[63] He asserted that Puritan preaching had resulted in conversions among the children of church members. The reason Baylie had not read evangelistic sermons preached by Puritans was explained by the fact that these sermons had not been put in print. Cotton reminded Baylie that Puritans Thomas Shepard and Thomas Hooker had written extensively on conversion and these treatises had been available in England.

John Cotton continued his rebuttal of Baylie by pointing out the example of the conversion of the Indian Weaquash which Baylie could read about in a twenty-six page tract entitled *New Englands First Fruits.* In addition Cotton reported that colonists from Virginia had requested help from Massachusetts Bay in working with the Indians in their region. In spite of Indian violence in Virginia "God so far forth followed their labors with his blessing in the work of conversion, that sundry of them were effectually wrought upon by the power of the Lord Jesus; whereof some of them came along with our ministers at their return, and are received into our churches."[64] Cotton further indicated that there was a continuing ministry among the Indians of Virginia and that some of the colonists in the West Indies were also seeking help from Massachusetts in Indian evangelism.

John Cotton proceeded to present the work of evangelism as it then existed in

New England. The Indians were slow in learning English, except for trading purposes, and the English had offered to raise Indian children and educate them in English schools. This was a long range program and Cotton emphasized the effective work of John Eliot in Indian evangelism as the best evidence that Baylie's charges were in error.

One of our elders (Mr. Eliot, the teacher of the church of Roxbury) hath (with the consent of the natives) preached to them first by an interpreter, but since having with much industry learned their language, he now preacheth to two congregations of them in their own language weekly. One week on the fourth day to one congregation, who sit down near Dorchester Mill, and another week, on the sixth day, to another congregation of them, who sit down in Cambridge, near Watertown Mill. To ease and encourage him in his work, the ministers of neighbor churches take off by turns his weekly lecture on the third day. The fruit hitherto hath been, the Indians resort more and more to these assemblies, hear with reverence and attention, reform (and make laws amongst themselves, for reformation of) sundry abuses, ask sundry questions for their instruction.[65]

John Cotton turned next to an allegation made by Thomas Lechford in his book *Plain Dealing* that the Puritans had not sent men out to learn the Indian language because they expected the Indians to come in and learn and hear in English. Cotton retorted that Lechford was ignorant both of Puritan practice and of the truth.

I know not whether ever any gave him so weak an account or no: if any so did, it was his rashness, or ignorance both of us, and the truth. But if the author speak it, as a point of our profession or

---

62. Ziff, *Cotton on Churches,* p. 268.

63. Ibid.,

64. Ibid., p. 272.

65. Ibid., p. 273.

practice, that we do neglect the instruction of the Indians, and especially upon such a reasonless reason, I will say no more to it but this, it seemeth there are two sorts of Plain Dealing: plain honest dealing, and plain false dealing, of which latter sort, this speach is.[66]

John Cotton also responded to Robert Baylie's assertion that only Roger Williams, the Puritan outcast who had settled Rhode Island, was effective in Indian evangelism. According to Baylie, Roger Williams had won thousand of converts among the Indians and had made them better Christians than most Puritans. However, Baylie indicated that problems concerning church practice had kept Williams from making full use of his opportunity.

Cotton responded by claiming that Williams's evangelistic efficiency was overstated. In Cotton's view, Williams was so confused over the nature of the church that he had no place to bring his converts for an adequate church relationship. It seemed Roger Williams not only felt that there would be no major conversion of Indians until the Antichrist was overthrown, but he also thought there could be no church at all until this event took place. Cotton maintained that "these and like principles are enough, not only to retard him from the planting of churches amongst Indians, but also to further him in supplanting all the churches of Christ in Christendom."[67] In addition Cotton reasoned that the Indians converted under Williams's preaching were not genuine. The Puritan spokesman used as an explanation of his meaning a Roman Catholic plantation in Maryland where it was reported that forty Indians had submitted to baptism as Catholics after they had been given new shirts by the priests. When the shirts got dirty, the Indians threatened to renounce their baptism if they were not given new shirts. As further indication of Indian fickleness, John Cotton reported the case of a local chieftain, John Sagamore, who confessed faith in Christ after a Puritan clergyman had helped cure him of a sickness. When Sagamore's powwow (medicine man) and other tribesmen threatened him with violence because of his conversion, he relented and went back to his old ways. But John Sagamore soon became ill again, this time with smallpox from which he died. Before his death the repentant chief gave his son to the English to educate, but the boy also died of smallpox. In the view of John Cotton, the converts of Roger Williams were no more stable than was John Sagamore.[68] Cotton's logic may have been weak but his careful rebuttal of opponents provided interesting views of at least part of the controversies that surrounded Puritan attempts at evangelizing the Indians.

Indian Opposition to the Gospel—The primary Indian opposition to the Puritan preachers came from the tribal medicine men. They were called powwows and were next to the chieftains in their power over the people.[69] The powwows feared the loss of influence that came when an Indian was converted to Christianity. Every new convert had to face the immediate opposition of these Indian priests. Many Indians were not able to withstand their strong medicine and fell back into their old ways.[70] The Puritans were convinced that the powwows were agents of Satan and it was expected

---

66. Ibid., p. 275.
67. Ibid., p. 276.
68. Ibid., pp. 277-78.
69. Lechford, *Plain Dealing*, p. 117.
70. Shepard, "Clear Sun-shine," 4, 3d series:51.

that some Indian converts would "totter, back slide, and fall away from what they professed."[71]

Perhaps influenced by the powwows, other members of the tribe sought to discourage those influenced to embrace Christianity. The threat of death was a common practice and some Indians were actually killed. The Puritan preachers considered such attacks on their followers as "temptations of the Devill"[72] and their preaching consistently sought to strengthen the Indian believers to be able to resist.

In the long view it was the Indian chieftains that posed the most powerful threat to the advancement of Puritan evangelism. The converted Indians joined together in Eliot's praying towns and no longer paid tribute to the tribal authorities. This loss of revenue made the sachems wary of the Puritan preachers. Only a few minor sachems became Christians. The greatest inroads of Puritanism came in areas where tribes had been decimated by disease or war. The major tribes retained their integrity and resisted the preaching of the English quite successfully.

On Martha's Vineyard, Thomas Mayhew, Jr. had gained unusual success with the Indians but the tribe with which he worked was small and isolated by being on an island. Mayhew was lost at sea in 1657 and it is not known whether his brand of evangelism might have expanded to other areas.

Missionary efforts in Connecticut were largely ineffective. The problem seemed to center in one of the most powerful New England sachems, Uncas of the Mohegans. Uncas was a master of intrigue. He kept a careful balance in his relationships with the English and with other Indian tribes. In 1642 he participated in the execution of Miantonomo, the powerful young sachem of the Narragansetts.[73] While being careful to keep in political contact with the Puritans, Uncas was equally careful to avoid contact with Puritan missionaries.[74] As late as 1670 Uncas was considered a "great obstruction" to evangelization. The Reverend James Fitch of Norwich found him to be "an old and wicked, wilful man, a drunkard and otherwise very vitious."[75] Fitch summed up the essence of opposition at the level of the tribal leaders:

. . . the sachems did discern, that religion would not consist with a mere receiving of the word; and that practical religion will throw down their heathenish idols, and the sachem's tyrannical monarchy: and then the sachems, discerning this, did not only go away, but drew off their people, some by flatteries, and others by threatenings: and they would not suffer them to give so much as an outward attendance to the ministry of the word of God.[76]

The most conclusive evidence of the Indians' opposition to English civilization and evangelism came in the horrors of King Philip's War. On the eve of this war there may have been as many as 2500 converts to Christianity among the Indians. This number was not more than 20 percent of the New England native population. Most of the converts were in Massachusetts and in the Martha's Vineyard area. Maine, New

---

71. Henry Whitfield, "The Light Apearing more and more towards the perfect Day," *Collections of the Massachusetts Historical Society* (Cambridge: Charles Folsom, 1834), 4, 3d series:48.

72. Eliot, "Day-Breaking," 4, no. 143:17.

73. Thomas Hutchinson, *The History of the Colony and Province of Massachusetts Bay* (1936; reprinted New York: Krause Reprint Co., 1970), p. 118.

74. Vaughan, *New England Frontier*, p. 300.

75. Gookin, "Historical Collections," 1:208.

76. Ibid., 1:209.

Hampshire, Rhode Island and Connecticut Indians were without significant groups of converts.[77] The causes of King Philip's War have been debated for years.[78] Philip was sachem of the Wampanoag tribe. As early as the 1640s his territory within the Plymouth patent was populated with more English than Indians. Philip had seen his power fade as members of his tribe took to English religion and ways. He had traveled to the English courts, had bowed before superior numbers and weapons. Philip apparently moved in a last ditch effort to preserve his power and stop the inroads of English colonization. The incredible story of the war showed that Philip mustered only a part of the Indians to his cause. Some tribes remained semineutral and many refused to participate. The Indians of the praying towns suffered much unfair persecution from the English, but most remained faithful to Puritanism. Many Christian Indians served as scouts in the last stages of the war and helped turn the balance of power to the English.[79] John Eliot bemoaned the fact that after the war the English soldiers became very friendly with the Christian Indian scouts that had aided them and rewarded them with so much strong drink that many became drunken and debauched.[80]

Conclusion

In the end, disease, war and the continual migration of English to America brought the New England Indians into submission. It can be said of the Puritans that they tried harder to maintain peace with the Indians than most other American colonists. However, the motives for such actions can be questioned. As Johnson observed, the colonists had needed the Indians' trade in order

to subsist in their early experiences and had consistently in dealing with the Indians "sought more after their conversion than their destruction."[81] This mixture of English self-interest and concern for the civilization and Christianizing of the Indian revealed the heart of this early American controversy. The worth of the Indian as a human being appears to have been a major problem in the minds of the English. Only a few seemed concerned about Indian evangelism. Those who did engage in such activity were told by Puritan preachers that they had little hope of success. Roger Williams, whose view of the Indian culture may have been the highest of any man of his time, was restricted by his strange views of the church and his constant practice of keeping English interests ahead of his concern for the Indians. John Eliot emerged as the most energetic in seeking to Christianize the Indian. Yet his failure to adjust to the Indian culture and accept the Indian way of life as valid, stood in the way of a true solution to the needs of the New England Indian. If Eliot had respected the Indian culture and had allowed his converts to remain in the tribal structure, the results might have been less threatening to the sachems. The context of subsequent history reveals that the

77. Ibid., 1:207-210.

78. See Douglas E. Leach, *Flintlock and Tomahawk* (New York: Macmillan, 1958) for an updated discussion of the war. Leath provided an extensive bibliography of sources.

79. Gookin, "Historical Collections," 1:228. See also Daniel Gookin, "An Historical Account of the Doings and Sufferings of the Christian Indians in New England, in the Years of 1675, 1676, 1677," in *Transactions and Collections of the American Antiquarian Society [Archaeologia Americana]*, 2 (1836):429-534.

80. Vaughan, *New England Frontier*, p. 321.

81. Jameson, ed., *Johnson's Wonder Working*, p. 43.

key issue of this early controversy was debated on the grounds of actions rather than words. The Puritans may have considered the Indians as worthy candidates for Christianity but their demands that the converts accept Puritan society while being separated from it revealed deeply paternalistic attitudes. It is obvious that the Puritan solution to the Indian problem was inadequate. Ultimately it was the sheer weight of numbers of colonists possessing discipline, organization and firepower that forced the sachems to strike out in desperation. The fragmentation of the Indian tribal system was consistently inadequate in the face of unlimited English migration.

Yet, it must be realized that the Puritans were successful in changing the life patterns of those Indians that were evangelized. When it is remembered that Christian Indians were primarily responsible for turning the tide against the tribal Indians in King Philip's War, the difficulty of making judgments concerning the affairs of those days is severely complicated. The most effective efforts of the English in seeking to help the Indian was in evangelization. This very effort, however, resulted in shifting the balance of power in favor of the colonists. The New England experience became somewhat prophetic in terms of what was to follow in American history. Roger Williams caught the sense of this in a bit of poetry in his *Key to the Language of America* written in 1643:

> Oft have I heard these Indians say,
> These English will deceive us.
> Of all that's ours, our lands and lives.
> In th' end they will bereave us.[82]

In 1698 Cotton Mather preached a sermon in which he discussed the continuing Indian problems that followed King Philip's War. Mather reasoned that the major cause of the colonists' Indian difficulties had been the failure to convert the Indians to the Christian faith.[83]

Efforts at evangelism continued into the eighteenth century but were generally sporadic attempts to reach the severely depleted population of New England Indians. Eleazar Wheelock, founder of Dartmouth College, was an example of a strong advocate of Indian education. He saw the responsibility of evangelization in much the same perspective as had the Puritans of the previous century.[84] Wheelock died in the Revolutionary War and efforts toward evangelism were severely hampered by the fact that many Indians were supporters of the Crown.

The opinions of seventeenth century Indians concerning their experiences with the colonists were not recorded but some contemporary Indians have spoken concerning these past events. Vine Deloria, Jr. stated:

> While the thrust of Christian missions was to save the individual Indian, its result was to shatter Indian societies and destroy the cohesiveness of the Indian communities. Tribes that resisted the overtures of the missionaries seemed to survive. Tribes that converted were never heard of again. Where Christianity failed, and insofar as it failed, Indians were able to withstand the cultural deluge that threatened to engulf them.[85]

Deloria's book impressed Floyd Westerman to write a song entitled "Missionaries" which reflects some of the bitterness felt by modern Indians.

---

82. Williams, *Writings*, 1:185.
83. Mather, *Magnalia*, 2:664-65.
84. Eleasar Wheelock, "Wheelock's Narrative (1762)," *Old South Leaflets* (New York: Burt Franklin, n.d.), 1, no. 22:1-12.
85. Vine Deloria, Jr., *Custer Died for Your Sins* (New York: Avon Books, 1969) p. 106.

. . . Go and tell the savage native
   That he must be Christianized
   Tell him, end his heathen worship
   And you will make him civilized.
   Shove your gospel, force your values
   Down his throat until it's raw
   And after he is crippled
   Turn your back and lock the door.

. . . Missionaries, missionaries, go and leave us all
   alone
   Take your white God to your white man
   We've a God of our own.[86]

It is a strange commentary on America that one of the earliest issues in controversy is still a current and unresolved debate.

BIBLIOGRAPHY

Extensive bibliographical information concerning the Puritans and Indians during the seventeenth century may be found in the following books:

Boorstin, Daniel J. *The Americans: The Colonial Experience.* New York: Random House, 1965.

Leach, Douglas E. *Flintlock and Tomahawk.* New York: Macmillan, 1958.

Vaughan, Alden T. *New England Frontier.* Boston: Little, Brown, and Company, 1965.

The major accounts of Indian evangelism are contained in:

Collections of the Massachusetts Historical Society. Vol. 4, 3d series. Cambridge: Charles Folsom, 1834.

---

86. Copyright © 1970 by Popdraw Music Corp. as contained in "Missionaries" from "Custer Died for Your Sins." Perception Records, a division of Perception Ventures, Inc.; used by permission.

2

Church and State in Massachusetts, 1630-1660

John W. Reed

The settlement of New England was enveloped in continuing controversy, and the relationship of the state to the church was one of the major concerns. Colonists whose views differed from the established standards of the Massachusetts government were promptly punished by the colonial magistrates and continuous offenders were deported to England. Roger Williams emerged in the context of church-state controversies as a man who could not be silenced by banishment. Long after his exile to Rhode Island he continued to speak through his pamphlets. While the transcripts of his sermons and oral debates are not extant, the extensive written dialectic between Williams and John Cotton, the spokesman for the Bay Colony, provided adequate sources for this chapter's consideration of the clash of ideas concerning church and state from 1630-60.

Church-State Backgrounds

Most of the colonists that stepped on American shores accepted the close relationship of church and state as a normal procedure. Europeans for centuries had assumed that whoever ruled the state could exercise the right to determine the religion of the state's subjects. The bloody European wars caused by this assumption gave clear testimony to the depth of the church-state problem.

Many of the people who settled in the new world came as a direct result of church-state conflicts. The Puritans had come under stress of great persecution by the Anglican state church at home. Colonization provided for them an outlet to escape the pressure and to establish in Massachusetts the form of church and state they desired. The development of this colony and the controversy that it stimulated became of great importance to American history.[1]

Church and State in England—By 1600, England had adopted a reformed theology deeply influenced by Luther and later by Zwingli and the Swiss Reformers. However,

---

1. A helpful summary of the nature of the church-state issue in other American colonies may be found in: William Adams Brown, *Church and State in Contemporary America* (New York: Charles Scribner's Sons, 1936), pp. 303-10. See also: Anson P. Stokes, and Leo Pfeffer, *Church and State in the United States* (New York: Harper & Row, 1964), pp. 3-29.

many influences of Catholic theology and practice lingered in the Anglican church. The church elected its own officers, regulated doctrine, administered word and sacrament, ordered public worship and exercised internal discipline. The state provided the support of the clergy, fixed the bounds of parishes, provided buildings for worship, called meetings of the clergy, presided at their meetings and supported church decisions with civil power.[2]

A fiercely militant Protestant nationalism emerged under Queen Elizabeth (1558-1603) and serious attempts were made to stamp out elements of Catholicism completely in the Anglican Church. Seemingly endless arguments emerged over the nature of the church, its leadership and worship. These arguments began to fragment English Protestantism. The Puritans were part of this fragmentation. They pressed for a thoroughly Reformed theology. Elizabeth responded by persecuting them almost as severely as she did the Catholics.

James Stuart (1603-25) followed Elizabeth and urged the Anglican cause even more severely. Nearly three hundred Puritan preachers lost their churches. James created dissension in most areas of English life and his son Charles I (1625-49) was even worse. Charles appointed William Laud as Archbishop of Canterbury (1633-45). Laud was inflexible and the Puritan dissenters had increasing difficulty. Out of these roots of persecution grew not only the New England colony but also the English Civil War under Cromwell.[3]

Massachusetts Oligarchy—The Puritans found in New England the opportunity that they desired to establish their own type of church-state relationship. They were less radical than the Pilgrims at Plymouth in that the Pilgrims were Separatists who desired separation from the Anglican Church. The Puritans were content to reform their own church in New England and not push their relationship with the mother church too far.

A considerable degree of misunderstanding has developed concerning the relationship between the clergy and the civil governors in the Massachusetts Bay Colony. Some historians have inferred that the clergy ruled the colony. Actually the Massachusetts magistrates were all church members but were not ministers. The civil authority was in the hands of qualified laymen and they were zealous in the protection of their supremacy over the affairs of the state.[4]

To understand the position of the Massachusetts Bay Colony in church-state matters it is necessary to study the *Westminster Confession* to which the General Court expressed approval in 1649 and *The Platform of Church Discipline* which was hammered out in a synod of the churches and accepted in 1648.[5] The civil leaders were by these

2. Charles Hodge, *Church Polity* (New York: Charles Scribner's Sons, 1878), pp. 106-7.

3. An excellent study based on extensive reading of the sermons and theological literature of the period may be found in: Charles H. George, and Katherine George, *The Protestant Mind of the English Reformation* (Princeton: Princeton University Press, 1961), pp. 3-72. See also: Wallace Notestein, *The English People on the Eve of Colonization:* 1603-1630 (New York: Harper & Row, 1962).

4. Aaron B. Seidman, "Church and State in the Early Years of the Massachusetts Bay Colony," *The New England Quarterly* 18, 2: (1945), 211-33.

5. Reprints of early position papers including *The Platform of Church Discipline* may be found in Williston Walker, *The Creeds and Platforms of Congregationalism* (New York: Charles Scribner's Sons, 1893).

documents restricted in their involvement with church matters. They could not introduce new articles of faith, rites or modes of worship. They were not allowed to administer sacraments, approve members or prescribe preaching. They could not decide on church matters or controversies without consulting the pastors. These factors contributed a degree of separation between church and state.

On the other hand, the magistrates were responsible for establishing and maintaining the church. They were to keep the church pure by restraining and punishing heretics. They were to provide proper ministers and support them. The magistrates were responsible for seeing that the clergy preached the truth and faithfully fulfilled their duties. Since all magistrates had to be members of the church, and no one could hold office or vote in the colony unless a church member, the civil power was in this sense in the hands of the church. The laws of the church were in large measure the laws of the land.

These views of the colonists were founded on the theoretical basis of Reformed doctrine. An accurate and precise summary of these principles is made by Hodge:

The theory on which this doctrine of the Reformed Church is founded, is, 1. That the State is a divine institution, designed for promoting the general welfare of society, and as religion is necessary to that welfare, religion falls legitimately within the sphere of the state. 2. That the magistrate, as representing the state, is, by divine appointment, the guardian of the law, to take vengeance on those who transgress, and for the praise of those who obey; and as the law consists of two tables, one relating to our duties to God, and the other to our duties to men, the magistrate is, ex officio, the guardian of both tables, and bound to punish the infractions of the one, as well as the other. 3. That the word of God determines the limits of the mag-

istrate's office in reference to both classes of his duties; and as, under the Old Testament, there was a form of religion, with its rites and officers prescribed, which the magistrate could not change, so there is under the New. But under the Old, we find with this Church government the kings were required to do, and in fact did do much, for the support and reformation of religion, and the punishment of idolators; so they are now bound to act on the same principles, making the pious kings of the Old Testament their model.[6]

Sinning Against the Conscience—One of the characteristics of the Puritan mind was inflexibility. Once there was full assurance as to the rightness of the conviction, the mind was set. William Ames, one of the most influential of the Puritan teachers in England expressed this clearly when he concluded the statement of beliefs held by his church: "They hold, that not one of these opinions can be proved contrary to the word of God; and that if they might have leave, that they are able to answer all that hath been written against any one of them.[7]

The Massachusetts Bay Colony found itself repeatedly under attack to move from basic positions. To preserve the purity of the Puritan position procedures were refined to deal with dissenters. John Cotton, who emerged as the leading spokesman for the Bay Colony, gave a clear summary of how dissidents were to be faced (a "blind conscience" would be one that disagreed with Bay Colony conclusions):

First, it is not lawfull to persecute any for conscience sake rightly informed, for in persecuting such, Christ himselfe is persecuted in them. Acts 9.4. Secondly, for an erroneous and blind conscience, (even in fundamentall and weighty points)

---

6. Hodge, *Polity*, p. 116.
7. William Ames, *The Marrow of Sacred Divinity* (London: Edward Griffin, 1642), p. 31.

it is not lawfull to persecute any, untill after admonition once or twice, and so the Apostle directeth, Titus 3.10. and giveth the reason that in fundamentall and principall points of Doctrine, or Worship, the Word of God is so clear, that he cannot but be convinced in conscience of the dangerous error of his way, after once and twice admonition wisely and faithfully dispensed. And then if any one persist it is not out of conscience, but against his conscience, as the Apostle saith Ver 1.1. he is subverted and sinneth, being condemned of himselfe, viz. of his own conscience: So that if such man after such admonition, shall still persist in the errour of his ways and be therefore punished, he is not persecuted for cause of conscience, but for sinning against his own conscience. Thirdly, in things of lesser moments, whether points of Doctrine or Worship, if a man hold them forth in a spirit of Christian meekness and love (though with zeal and constancy) he is not to be persecuted, but tolerated, till God be pleased to manifest his truth to him. Phil. 3.17. Rom. 14.1,2,3,4. Fourthly, but if a man hold forth, or professe any errour, or false way, with a boisterous and arrogant spirit, to the disturbance of civil peace, he may be punished according to the quality and measure of his disturbance caused by him.[8]

In the Bay Colony the civil magistrates were given the responsibility of commanding only those things ". . . which, if men have any tendernesse of submitting to which is truely liberty of conscience, conscience being never in a truer or better estate of liberty here on earth, than when most engaged to walke according to God's Commandments.[9]

Communication and Controversy

The communication procedures employed by the colonists took several forms.[10] At the base was that of individual and group interaction. The lengthy discussions carried on in church synods were apparently crucial in the refinement of doctrine and practice needed to meet assaults on the established ways of the Colony.

The sermon was an important form of communication and involved many hours each week in the life of the average citizen. But sermon content generally reinforced the existing viewpoints of the established doctrinal norms.[11] Sermons were usually not a tool of extended controversy in the early years of the Bay Colony. Those who took to their pulpits to advocate change were quickly brought to trial and if they would not relent, were banished.

Puritan tracts tended to be the most persuasive form of controversial communication. Dissenters silenced by the General Court of Massachusetts could still find an audience if they could get into print. Roger Williams provided the outstanding example of such continued dissent in his impact on the New England way of church and state.

Dissent and Banishment—Cambridge educated, Williams arrived in Boston in February 1631. His reputation as a "Godly minister"[12] had preceded him to New England and, although he was only twenty-eight, the Boston church sought him as teaching pastor. Concerning this significant offer Roger Williams later wrote: "I con-

8. John Cotton, *The Controversie Concerning Liberty of Conscience in Matters of Religion* (London: 1646), pp. 7-8.

9. *The Result of a Synod at Cambridge in New England, Anno. 1646* (London: 1654), p. 8.

10. See George V. Bohman, "The Colonial Period," in *A History and Criticism of American Public Address*, ed. William N. Brigance (New York: Russell & Russell, 1960), 1:3-54.

11. Samuel Eliot Morison, *The Intellectual Life of Colonial New England* (Ithaca, New York: Cornell University Press, 1956), pp. 152-76; Babette M. Levy, *Preaching in the First Half-Century of New England* (Hartford: American Society of Church History, 1945), p. 59.

12. James K. Hosmer, ed., *Winthrop's Journal "History of New England" 1630-1649* (New York: Barnes & Noble, 1946), 1:57.

scientiously refused, and withdrew to Plymouth, because I durst not officiate to an unseparated people, as, upon examination and conference, I found them to be."[13] The Boston church still had ties to the Anglican church back home. In Williams' opinion the church in England was not only impure in doctrine but beyond reformation. He had become a separatist—satisfied only by the severing of all connections with the mother church. To the Boston magistrates, such a view was not only unthinkable but unnecessary. On their side of the ocean, they could do as they wished without undue interference.

John Winthrop noted in his *Journal* (1; 62) that Williams ". . . had declared his opinion, that the magistrates might not punish the breach of the Sabbath, nor any other offence, as it was a breach of the first table." Such an attack on their right to punish those who disobeyed the first four of the Ten Commandments was exceedingly dangerous to the Bay Colony government. The magistrates tagged the young minister as a man to be watched.

Roger Williams went to Salem where the church leaned toward his Separatist views and received him gladly. Shortly after he became the Salem minister, a message arrived from the Boston magistrates. It condemned the congregation for its hasty action. Williams held "dangerous opinions" and in Boston the magistrates "marvelled" that Salem would consider him without first consulting them.[14]

Williams soon moved to the Pilgrim colony at Plymouth where he preached and traded with the Indians. He felt at home with the Pilgrims' strict ways and was beyond the reach of Boston. Apparently Williams soon found that the Plymouth church was not the place for him. He later stated that the Plymouth people professed to be separated but when any of them visited Old England, they frequently attended the Anglican services.[15] Apparently his disaffection was expressed openly. Governor Bradford said of Williams that ". . . he began to fall into some strange opinions, and from opinions to practice, which caused some controversy between the church and him."[16] The differences were strong enough to cause Williams to return to Salem with a group of followers.

At Salem he bought a home, began to farm and to preach. Early in the fall of 1634, John Skelton, the minister of the Salem church, died. Roger Williams was asked to take his place and accepted. Boston was incensed! The magistrates demanded that he be removed. The Salem people were told that until Williams was gone, they could not expect to receive the land on Marblehead Neck that they had requested. Salem protested but the request for the land was pigeonholed by the magistrates.[17]

In his Salem pulpit, Williams attacked the practices of the Massachusetts magistrates. New residents were being required to swear an oath of allegiance to the Bay Colony. Williams contended that many of these people were unbelievers and to make them swear an oath in the name of God was forced worship. His sermons also contained condemnations of the General Court's

---

13. Roger Williams, *Complete Writings* (New York: Russell & Russell, 1963), 6:356. The Writings include seven volumes.

14. Hosmer, ed., *Winthrop's Journal*, 1:62.

15. Williams, *Writings*, 6:356.

16. William Bradford, *Of Plymouth Plantation 1620-1647* (New York: Alfred A. Knopf, 1959), p. 257.

17. Hosmer, ed., *Winthrop's Journal* 1:154-55.

practice of punishing people found guilty of breaking any of the first four of the Ten Commandments.[18]

The Boston government acted. Williams was striking at the very heart of the system. If they gave heed to this babbler (Cotton Mather was later to say that Roger Williams had a windmill in his head),[19] then surely there would be little use for the whipping post, the stocks and the cage. He was summoned to appear before the General Court of July 5, 1635. He was charged with his "errors" and told that he should prepare for the next session where he should give "satisfaction to the court, or else expect sentence."[20] John Cotton, who had taken the Boston pulpit that was rejected by Williams, sought to straighten out the young dissenter.

Back at Salem, the situation was deteriorating. The congregation felt the need for the land on Marblehead Neck and they began to soften. Williams wrote a letter demanding that they separate from the churches of the Bay Colony or else accept his resignation. They were "much grieved"[21] but Roger Williams did not appear again in the Salem pulpit.

He did appear at the Court's session on October 8, 1635, to debate the issues of his dissent. Thomas Hooker was appointed to represent the Court. Roger Williams "broached & dyvulged dyvers newe & dangerous opinions, against the authoritie of magistrates"[22] and Hooker "could not reduce him from any of his errors."[23]

The crucial issues of accusation against Williams were those that involved his Salem preaching and an additional contention that the power of the civil magistrate extends only to the "Bodies and Goods, and outward state of men."[24] It was clear that Williams views were pointing directly to a break between the church and the state. The General Court acted quickly and the next morning the sentence of banishment was read. Williams was given six weeks to get out and was to remain silent until his departure. In a short time, word reached Boston that Williams was preaching regularly in his home. Agents were sent to apprehend him and put him on a ship that was in the Boston harbor ready to depart to England. Before the officers arrived, friends of Williams had warned him of the plot. Although he was very ill, he fled into the snowbound wilderness. His Indian friends cared for him during the winter and in the spring he bought the site of Providence, Rhode Island, from the Narragansett tribe.[25]

A Voice for Freedom—At Providence, Roger Williams established the first truly democratic colony in America. He opened its doors to people of all religions. Even Catholics, Quakers and Jews found themselves welcome at Providence. The Bay Colony looked to their neighbors on the south and declared Williams' unique settlement to be the cesspool of New England.

---

18. *Ibid.*, 1:154.

19. Cotton Mather, *Magnalia Christi, Americana* (1852; reprinted, New York: Russell & Russell, 1967), 2:495.

20. Hosmer, ed., *Winthrop's Journal*, 1:154.

21. *Ibid.*, 1:157.

22. Nathaniel B. Shurtleff, ed., *Records of Massachusetts Bay* (1853; reprinted, New York: AMS Press, 1968), 1:160-61. This record includes the banishment proceedings.

23. Hosmer, ed., *Winthrop's Journal*, 1:162-63.

24. Williams, *Writings*, 1:40-41.

25. A helpful analysis of Williams' clash with the Bay Colony may be found in Leon Ray Camp, "Man and His Government: Roger Williams Vs. the Massachusetts Oligarchy," in *Preaching in American History*, ed. Dewitte Holland (Nashville: Abingdon Press, 1969), pp. 74-97.

The years of establishing the colony were hard. Williams farmed, traded with the Indians, preached, wrote letters to the Boston magistrates and brooded over the implications of his banishment.

While Williams worked and waited in the wilderness, the Civil Wars were beginning in Old England. With these wars came unrest in New England. The people of Providence feared the landgrabbing tendencies of their Massachusetts neighbors. They sent Roger Williams to London to seek a charter for the Providence colony. The long weeks of the ocean voyage gave him the opportunity to begin his writing. First was the *Key into the Language of America.* It was his recollections of the language and customs of the Indians to whom he had preached. The English people were eager for some understanding of the "salvages" and the *Key* helped to provide an audience for Williams' more important pamphlets concerning the relationship of the church to the state. These pamphlets grew out of a letter that Williams had received from John Cotton concerning the banishment. Williams published *Mr. Cotton's Letter Examined and Answered* (London: 1644) and followed it with *The Bloody Tenent of Persecution for Cause of Conscience, Discussed in a Conference between Truth and Peace.*

In the preface to *The Bloody Tenent* Williams explained the core of his contentions:

> . . . what ever Worship, Ministry, Ministration, the best and purest are practised without faith and true persuasion that they are the true institutions of God, they are sin, sinful worships, Ministries, etc. And however in Civill things we may be servants unto men, yet in Divine and Spiritual things the poorest pesant must disdaine the service of the highest Prince: Be ye not the servants of men, I Cor. 14. . . . without search and triall no man attaines this faith and right perswasion, I Thes. 5. Try all things. In vaine have English Parliaments

permitted English Bibles in the poorest English houses, and the simplest man or woman to search the Scriptures, if yet against their soules perswasion from the Scripture, they should be forced (as if they lived in Spain or Rome itselfe without the sight of a Bible) to beleeve as the Church beleeves . . . . having tried, we must hold fast . . . we must not let goe for all the flea bitings of the present afflictions, having bought Truth deare, we must not sell it cheape, not the least grain of it for the whole World, no not for the saving of Soules, though our own most precious.[26]

Roger Williams was able to negotiate a Parliamentary Charter for Providence and returned home triumphantly in 1644.

In Boston, John Cotton puzzled over the *Bloody Tenent.* It had impact on both the old world and the new and was not to be ignored. In 1647, Cotton published his answer: *The Bloody Tenent, Washed, and Made White in the Blood of the Lamb.* He dealt with Williams' ideas and justified the banishment. Cotton declared that Roger Williams had been fully instructed in the Bay Colony's position; therefore, all he had to do was accept their viewpoint. When he did not, he was simply sinning against his own conscience in refusing to be "enlightened." Williams had banished himself! All of this was perfect logic—to a Puritan.[27]

Williams studied Cotton's reply and prepared his rebuttal. The Providence charter was threatened again in 1651 by colonial land sharks and Roger Williams returned to London seeking a Royal Charter. He found the atmosphere charged with revolution. There was growing interest in matters of freedom of conscience. He gained the ear of

---

26. Williams, *Writings*, 3:12-13.

27. John Cotton, *The Bloudy Tenent, washed and made white in the bloud of the Lambe: being discussed and discharged of bloudguiltinesses,* (London, 1647), p. 3. See also Williams, *Writings.* 1:13.

Cromwell and became a friend of John Milton. From his pen came the answer to John Cotton—*The Bloody Tenent Yet More Bloody: By Mr. Cotton's Endeavours to Wash it White in the Blood of the Lamb.* With minute detail, Williams reaffirmed his arguments and added more evidence, mostly from the Bible. Providence ultimately gained its Royal Charter and Williams lived a long life in his free colony.

John Cotton died in 1652—probably before he saw Williams's rebuttal.

Debating the Bloody Tenent—The debate between Roger Williams and John Cotton covered more than one thousand pages and took many years. It was prophetic in a sense of the many prolonged debates that would follow in American history.[28] Almost any attempt to reduce the massive dialectic of the debate to a brief statement must result in oversimplification. Both men wrote for a select audience of their ministerial peers. The rambling argumentation is virtually unintelligible to any mind not drilled in the intricacies of Puritan disputation. Almost all the major issues of the debate centered around the interpretation of biblical texts and concepts. Both men were biblicists who reveled in the minutiae of interpretative detail. The summary that follows is an analysis of the major issues of the debate. The importance of these issues to an understanding of church-state backgrounds in America has been pointed out by LeRoy Moore who asserts that Roger Williams was one of very few to provide a thorough theoretical and theological basis for his views.[29]

The proposition that formed the basis for controversy might be stated as follows: No man should be persecuted by the civil state for worshiping God according to the

dictates of his own conscience. Both Williams and Cotton agreed that those who were guilty of doctrinal error should be dealt with. The clash came over who would punish heretics. Williams contended that only the church should be involved with spiritual matters. Cotton maintained that the civil magistrates were responsible for the punishing of spiritual offenders because theirs was the job of protecting the purity of the church. The end that Williams sought was an individual at peace with his conscience living in a peaceful society. Since persecution for cause of conscience was the major barrier to such peace, he presented the following issues (Volume and page numbers are from *The Complete Writings of Roger Williams*):

1. The Massachusetts Bay Colony practiced the evil of persecution for cause of conscience. Williams offered his banishment as proof. (1:313-47)

2. The doctrine of persecution for cause of conscience was not taught in the Bible by Jesus Christ, Paul or other writers. (1:351-70; 3:52-73,104,167-76; 4:136-62)

3. The implications of typology were opposed to such persecution. (1:347-48, 356-62; 3:178; 4:57-118,164-209) The particular typological interpretation that Williams advocated involved the relationship of the nation of Israel in the Old Testament to later figurative manifestations of Israel on earth. John Cotton felt that the Massachusetts Bay Colony was actually the restructuring of the Old Testament Israel,

---

28. An extended list of these campaigns may be found in: Paul A. Carmack, "Controversial Speaking Campaigns in American History," *The Gavel*, 44 (1962), 20.

29. LeRoy Moore, "Religious Liberty: Roger Williams and the Revolutionary Era," *Church History*, 34 (1965), 57-76.

in Massachusetts, and thus demanded the establishment of a government of religious leaders following the example of the original pattern in the Old Testament. Williams responded by affirming that the Old Testament nation of Israel was only a type or prophecy that found its antitype or fulfillment in the church of the New Testament. If Williams's claims were true, the Bay Colony had no rational claim for their theocratic form of government and no precedent for the rule of the saints.

4. Persecution for cause of conscience was not universally practiced by civil states. Other peoples existed and prospered who did not exercise authority in spiritual matters. (1:336; 3:102,130,240) Some church leaders and civil leaders had opposed persecution for cause of conscience. (3:93-95; 4:120-23)

5. Persecution for cause of conscience destroyed church and civil peace and caused the loss of peace to those individuals who must conform or be persecuted. (1:379; 3:29-39,163-70; 4:15)

6. The civil state should follow these guidelines: Be concerned with civil government and reserve spiritual matters for the care of the church. The state should provide security for assembled worshipers so that they might worship in peace and should only intervene in religious dissent when the dissenters disturbed the civil peace. The state should not hinder those who voluntarily dedicated themselves to religious service from performing this service. (3:61,114-30,214-33; 4:15-45)

7. Full liberty of conscience should be provided for all. There should be no persecution of heretics, sects or unbelievers by the state. The state should not tax the people to finance the church. (3:214; 4:14,210-318)

8. The church should care for those matters that concern herself. The ministry should be financed by the churches. (7:149-87) Religious heretics should be dealt with by the church. The spiritual vitality and growth of the church should keep the sects under control. (1:392-96; 3:38-97; 4:46-57)

The interpretation of the parable of the wheat and the tares (Matthew 13) figured largely in the case that Williams built against Cotton in this area. By the seventeenth century this parable had been discussed intensively by such great theologians as Augustine, Thomas Aquinas, Luther and Calvin. The point of clash concerned the interpretation of the term "field" in the parable. Cotton asserted that the field meant the church and therefore a pure church could never be expected on this earth since the hypocrites and false believers must be allowed in the church until the end of the age. He used this interpretation to justify the entanglement of the Bay Colony churches with the pollutions of the mother church back in England. In opposition to Cotton, Williams insisted that, in the parable, the "field" is the world rather than the church, and the "tares" represent not hypocrites but unregenerate people. The issue then became that the wheat—Christians, and the tares—sects and false religious groups, are to be left alone to live side by side until the harvest time—the end of the age.

John Cotton answered the contentions of Roger Williams by denying any need for the adoption of the proposed resolution. Cotton stated in *The Bloody Tenent Washed*, "I did not think it needful to declare what an Arrogant and Impetuous way was, seeing his request was, not that I should compile a discourse of mine oune:

but that I should return an answer . . . and it is an Answerers part not to Expatiate into declarations, but distinctly and closely to remove Objections." (p. 14)

Cotton proceeded to "remove Objections" found in Williams's contentions. The first argument was met by a flat denial:

1. The Massachusetts Bay Colony did not practice persecution for cause of conscience. Roger Williams "banished himself" because of civil disobedience. [30] Williams had maintained views against the King's authority that could have undermined the security of the Bay Colony in its relation to the Crown. Williams had advocated the view that the "Oath of Fidelitie" could not be sworn by unconverted men since it was an act of worship. By advocating this view Williams "tended to unsettle all the Kingdomes, and Common-wealths in Europe."[31] Persecution for cause of conscience was opposed to all that the Bay Colony believed and practiced. (*Tenent Washed* pp. 3-10).

2. It was agreed that persecution for cause of conscience was not taught in the Bible but punishment for heresy was taught. Most of Williams's interpretations of scripture were irrelevant and immaterial. The typological views of Williams were fanciful and based on erroneous interpretations of Scripture. (*Tenent Washed*, pp. 29-96)

3. It was granted that the civil state should not persecute for cause of conscience but the civil state had a responsibility to keep the church pure by assisting in the punishing of heresy. Williams' evidence concerning other peoples who existed and prospered yet did not exercise authority in spiritual matters related mainly to primitive peoples such as the Indians. As the Indians came to the truth, they would have to accept the responsibility of using civil power to keep the truth pure. Williams's evidence concerning church and civil leaders who opposed civil authority in matters of religion was inadequate. (*Tenent Washed*, pp. 97-182)

4. Persecution for cause of conscience was always wrong but the use of civil power to keep the church pure would preserve peace. Williams' contention that such authority caused the loss of peace was erroneous. The defection of one tribe of Israel caused great trouble to the Old Testament nation. When the church was pure, the nation rejoiced (Psalms 122:6 and Proverbs 28:12). The church was the highest society in the civil state and should receive the best treatment of any segments of the state. God was displeased if the civil state thought the church of little concern to her. If the spiritual peace was disturbed through heresy, civil disturbance followed. Individuals who held dissident views should receive enlightenment and repent. Those who repented would find peace. Punishment given to the unrepentant could cause him to repent later thus restoring peace to him also. (*Tenent Washed*, pp. 11-28, 183-92)

The Means of Peace—Having attempted to place the debate between Roger Williams and John Cotton in its historical and theoretical setting, an attempt will now be made to examine some basic arguments in depth. Most of the assumptions by both men were based primarily on their methods of interpreting the Bible. However, one argument that began in the area of nonbiblical

---

30. *Letter of Cotton to Williams*, 1643, in Williams, *Writings*, 1:13. Many of Cotton's arguments are first stated in this letter.

31. John Cotton's *Answer* to Roger Williams, in Williams, *Writings*, 2:49.

sources was Williams' assertion that persecution for cause of conscience was a destroyer of peace. In Chapter 6 of *The Bloody Tenent*[32] he declared that civil peace involved the peace of the people of the city. He stated that many cities of the world, including the Indian towns of New England, had peace and yet did not possess a "true Church of God." Williams' logic concluded that the presence or absence of a church in a particular community had no relationship to the civil peace of the community. To clarify the point Williams used an analogy:

> O how lost are the sonnes of men in this point? To illustrate this: The Church or company of worshippers (whether true or false) is like unto a Body or Colledge of Physitians in a Citie; like unto a Corporation, Society, or Company of East-Indie or Turkie-Merchants, or any other Societie or Company in London: which Companies may hold their Courts, keep their Records, hold disputations; and in matters concerning their Societie, may dissent, divide, breake into Schismes and Factions, sue and implead each other at the Law, yea wholly breake up and dissolve into pieces and nothing, and yet the peace of the Citie not be in the least measure impaired or disturbed; because the essence or being of the Citie, and so the well-being and peace thereof is essentially distinct from those particular Societies; the Citie-Courts, Citie-Lawes, Citie-punishments distinct from theirs. The Citie was before them, and stands absolute and intire, when such a Corporation or Societie is taken down.[33]

The analogy presented Williams' general principle. Next he gave specific examples of the application of this principle. He stated that in the New Testament city of Ephesus there existed a strong cult for the worship of the goddess Diana. In the same city there was also a Christian Church and a Jewish Synagogue. Williams argued that any one of these three institutions might be altered or completely removed without any effect upon the peace of Ephesus.

In *The Bloody Tenent Washed*[34] John Cotton conceded that the meaning of civil peace was clearly the humane and civil peace of a particular community. However, Cotton stated that since the societies were integral parts of the city, to disturb one society was to disturb the city itself. John Cotton was apparently seeking to turn Williams' argument against himself, for Williams had been first to mention the concept of the church being a society.

Williams responded in *The Bloody Tenent yet More Bloody*[35] that he was not speaking of an enforced destruction on a particular society within a city but rather a voluntary combining or disbanding that could be accomplished without the civil peace being disturbed in any way. He maintained that there could be free controversial discussion and debate within a church—even to the extent that a particular church could dissolve itself—without the civil peace being destroyed. The problem came when the civil magistrates intervened in the free course of persuasive interaction and silenced controversy through persecution.

Williams charged John Cotton with a double fallacy. The first might be called a degree of equivocation—using words or groups of words more than once with different meanings. In Williams's view Cotton used the term "peace" at times to mean spiritual and moral peace and at other times he used the same word to mean material

---

32. Williams, *Writings*, 3:71-74.
33. *Ibid.*, 3:73.
34. pp. 10-11.
35. Williams, *Writings*, 4:68-70.

prosperity. The second fallacy that Williams noted in Cotton's logic was Cotton's contention that every dissident view within the church immediately constituted a breach of the civil peace. This fallacy arose from Cotton's failure to understand the basic difference between the role of the church and that of civil government. Cotton maintained that while the inner peace of the church was spiritually maintained the outward peace of the church must be protected by the civil magistrates. His logic was based on syllogistic reasoning:

> All societies in the civil state must be preserved by the state.
> The church is a society.
> The church must be preserved by the civil state.

In drawing this conclusion John Cotton placed the church as a society in an equal sense with such societies as the fishmongers, haberdashers, and merchants. As a result he found himself in somewhat of a dilemma. Roger Williams could and did argue—if the church was parallel with other societies in the civil state, "is it not partiality in a meer civil State to preserve one onely society, and not the persons of other Religious societies and consciences also?"[36] He then concluded that such obvious partiality and bigotry was based on the selfish motives of people who were afraid to put their church to the test of standing without state support.

> But the Truth is, this mingling of the church and the world together, and their orders and societies together, doth plainly discover, that such churches were never called out from the world, and that this is only a secret policy of flesh and blood, to get protection from the world, and so to keep (with some little stilling of conscience) from the Cross or Gallowes of Jesus Christ.[37]

Cotton had stated that the church was the most important of all the societies in the civil state, and being the highest it deserved the fullest and most instantaneous response from the civil state when problems arose in it. Williams argued that in such a declaration John Cotton destroyed the validity of his syllogism. If the church was above all the other societies, the reasoning was not valid. The societies must be equal in status or the major premise was not universal in its application. In developing this idea Williams went on to say that if Cotton's opinion of the "excellency and preheminence"[38] of the church was carried to its logical conclusion then Cotton had refuted himself. Such an institution as the church could never be properly judged by such an inferior institution as a civil state.

Cotton argued that Williams' proposed separation of church and state would displease God because God would feel that the civil state did not care about the church. Williams answered that the civil state could be concerned about the welfare of the church without judging and ruling it.

Inevitably this argument, as did all of the arguments used by Cotton and Williams, became interwoven into the context of religious ideas. Roger Williams returned often in his argumentation to a belief that was directly related to his entire proposition that the church and the state should be separate. This belief undergirded the attack that Williams made on Cotton's assumption that the peace of the church must be secured by the civil sword. It was based on the concept of typology discussed earlier in this chapter. John Cotton believed that the Massachusetts Bay Colony and the nation of Is-

---

36. *Ibid.*, 4:74.
37. *Ibid.*, 4:74-5.
38. *Ibid.*, 4:76.

rael in the Old Testament were parallel cases. The promises of God that had been placed on the historical Israel were now placed upon the new Canaan in New England. The logic of the parallel case demanded that the "New Israel" be like the old in form of government. Since historical Israel was a Theocracy—ruled by God through religious leaders—so the Israel in New England could justify government by magistrates who were also the ruling elders of the church. Since Israel in the Old Testament allowed only one faith in the land, the Massachusetts Bay Colony was justified in following this example.

Roger Williams consistently answered this argument with the contention that John Cotton was mistaken in his basic assumption. The Bible nowhere taught that the Israel of the Old Testament could be the pattern of a literal physical state under the new "covenant"—the way in which God dealt with man after the death and resurrection of Jesus Christ. The contrary was true: the Israel of the Old Testament was a type—a figure or prophecy—of the New Testament church. The New Israel was the church. The type was physical—the antitype was spiritual. The spiritual domain of the fulfillment of the type was only in the church and did not relate at all to the civil state. To interpret the promise as physical was to do violence to the truth.

The true and living God, is the God of order, spiritual, civil and natural: Natural is the same ever and perpetual: civil alters according to the constitutions of peoples and nations: spiritual he hath changed from the national in one figurative land of Canaan, to particular and congregational churches all the world over; which order spiritual, natural or civil, to confound and abrogate, is to exalt mans folly against the most holy and incomprehensible wisdom of God, etc.[39]

It was on this point that Williams scored one of his most telling blows and indicated why it was necessary for Cotton to continue to refute him. Cotton's entire case was built on the fragile foundation of a curious method of interpreting the scriptures. Since—in Cotton's view—New England was now the favored Canaan of God and he was the chief spokesman of the "divinely appointed" magistrates of the Bay Colony, his word was highly authoritative. If the magistrate was God-ordained, he should have power in God's things.[40] John Cotton fully believed that men—even Roger Williams—were amenable to reason and that the central doctrines of his brand of Christianity were clear and reasonable. When these doctrines were explained by a competent teacher—Cotton being the most competent—no man could remain unconvinced except by suppressing the urging of his own conscience. Behind Cotton's interpretation of the Bible stood the united voice of the Massachusetts Bay Colony. On their own ground, they were invincible.

But Roger Williams no longer stood on their ground or before the judgment bar of their General Court. The Boston magistrates could not silence him in Massachusetts, and it had become increasingly apparent that it was even more difficult to silence him in Rhode Island. His scheme of interpreting the Bible was not institutionally supported as was that of John Cotton. Williams could look back to Old England for partial support from the extreme separatists there but his primary reliance ultimately had to be on his own right to read the Bible and interpret it for himself. While

39. *Ibid.*, 4:80.
40. Cotton, *Tenent Washed*, p. 104.

the modern reader may applaud Williams' independent spirit, the Massachusetts Bay Colony rejected it completely.

The Effects of the Controversy

The task of assessing the effects of the debate between Roger Williams and John Cotton is extremely difficult. It appears that there was virtually no change of opinion experienced by either of the participants. In terms of Massachusetts Bay opinions, Cotton was clearly the victor. Perhaps the most telling effect that Roger Williams had on the Puritan magistrates was that his arguments were strong enough to compel John Cotton to attempt an answer to them. From Williams's point of view, it would seem that debating these issues was part of his character and personality. Late in his life Williams wrote a letter (June 22, 1670) in which he promised: ". . . to discuss by disputation, writing or printing, among other points of differences, these three positions; first, that forced worship stinks in God's nostrils. 2d. that it denies Christ Jesus yet to come, and makes the church yet national, figurative and ceremonial. 3d. that in these flames about religion . . . there is no other prudent, Christian way of preserving peace in the world, but by permission of differing consciences."[41]

The importance of the debate to what eventually became an America that practiced separation of church and state is viewed in many ways. Morgan spoke of Williams' helter-skelter style of putting words on paper and added:

The torrent of words may sometimes have left his readers bewildered, and it surely left them unconvinced, but behind it lay the rare simplicity of an original mind. As Williams uncovered the various consequences of his ideas, he put human society in new perspective; and he demolished, for anyone who accepted his premises, some of the assumptions that encumbered the statesmen of his day and still haunt our own.[42]

Perry Miller said of Roger Williams: "But what he stood for, and still stands for, is the certainty that those who mistake their own assurances for divinely appointed missions, and so far forget the sanctity of others' persuasion as to try reducing them to conformity by physical means, commit in the face of the Divine a sin more outrageous than any of the statutory crimes."[43]

However one may view Williams and the controversy that followed his dissent, it is obvious that the shadow cast by his Rhode Island experiment in separation of church-state relations extends across virtually the entire history of the American experience. His writings were out of print and probably not generally available at the time of the writing of the American Constitution.[44] Yet his influence may have reached the constitution through those he influenced in Old England. The parliament burned *The Bloody Tenent*[45] but could not keep Williams from contact with Oliver Cromwell, John Milton, John Locke and others.

Hudson sees Williams as a direct influence upon John Locke. He points out the close relationship between Williams' written views and those of Locke that appeared shortly thereafter. Through Locke he as-

41. Williams, *Writings*, 4:347.

42. Edmund S. Morgan, *Roger Williams: The Church and the State* (New York: Harcourt, Brace & World, 1967), p. 99.

43. Perry Miller, *Roger Williams, His Contribution to the American Tradition* (New York: Atheneum, 1962), p. 256.

44. LeRoy Moore, Jr., "Religious Liberty: Roger Williams and the Revolutionary Era," *Church History*, 34(1965), 57-76.

45. Miller, *Roger Williams*, p. 238.

sumes that Williams had a profound impact on the American Constitution.[46]

Through his continued controversy Roger Williams apparently made cracks in the foundations of the Puritan Oligarchy. The new independent, revolutionary spirit in Old England and the weight of increasing numbers of more independent people migrating to Massachusetts helped to widen the cracks.

It was such ideas in controversy that opened the way for what emerged as the democracy that became America. The controversy raged in sermons, discussions, debates and when the oral media were stopped by excommunication and banishment, it was the revolutionary tract that kept the issues from dying until finally in 1791 the First Amendment to our Constitution legislated: "Congress shall make no law respecting an establishment of religion, or prohibiting the free exercise thereof." The Puritans themselves had begun the separation of church and state by taking the civil government out of the hands of the clergy. Roger Williams carried it the rest of the way to complete freedom of conscience. He argued for a church that cared for its own affair and a state that cared for civil matters without molesting men in their worship of God. He put his views to work in Rhode Island where America first experienced separation of church and state.

Current Issues

The controversy concerning church-state relations continues in the arena of modern debate. A partial list of these issues includes: the cessation of the celebration of religious holidays; Bible reading and prayer in public schools; reading the Bible and praying over communication media by U.S.

astronauts in space; relaxing of Sunday "blue laws"; removing tax exemptions for religious agencies; removing chaplains from the military forces; state and federal funds for private education.

Advocates for all sides of these and other issues may readily be found across the nation today. The Supreme Court continues to debate these issues and to pass judgments. Voices cry that America was founded on the Bible and the state should continue to be influenced by religion. Other voices cry for a totally "secular state."[47]

This nation in controversy has not and should not lose sight of one of its first and most vital issues—that of the separation of church and state. It should continue to be of concern to all citizens of a great nation who are free to discuss, debate and to decide.

BIBLIOGRAPHY

In addition to sources footnoted in this chapter the following are recommended:

Books helpful in understanding Puritanism:

Haller, William. *The Rise of Puritanism.* New York: Harper and Brothers, 1938.

Miller, Perry. *Errand into the Wilderness.* New York: Harper Torchbooks, 1956.

——. *The New England Mind: The Seventeenth Century.* New York: Macmillan, 1939.

——. *Orthodoxy in Massachusetts 1630-1650.* Boston: Beacon Press, 1959.

46. Winthrop S. Hudson, "John Locke: Heir of Puritan Political Theorists," in *Calvinism and the Political Order*, ed. George L. Hunt (Philadelphia: The Westminster Press, 1965), pp. 108-29.

47. An effective discussion of such issues may be found in: J. Marcellus Kik, *Church & State—The Story of Two Kingdoms* (New York: Thomas Nelson & Sons, 1963), pp. 103-44.

Miller, Perry, and Johnson, Thomas H. *The Puritans—A Sourcebook of Their Writings*. 2 vols. New York: Harper & Row, 1963.

Morison, Samuel Eliot. *Builders of the Bay Colony*. Boston: Houghton Mifflin, 1964.

Waller, George M. *Puritanism in Early America*. Boston: D.C. Heath & Company, 1950.

Wertenbaker, Thomas J. *The Puritan Oligarchy*. New York: Grosset & Dunlap, 1947.

Sources for Roger Williams include:

Garrett, John. *Roger Williams, Witness Beyond Christendom*. New York: Macmillan, 1970.

Miller, Perry. *Roger Williams, His Contribution to the American Tradition*. New York: Atheneum, 1962.

Moore, LeRoy, Jr. "Roger Williams and the Historians," *Church History*, 32 (1963), 432-52.

Winslow, Ola. *Master Roger Williams*. New York: Macmillan, 1957.

Sources for John Cotton include:

Emerson, Everett H. *John Cotton*. New York: Twayne, 1965.

Ziff, Larzer. *The Career of John Cotton*. Princeton: Princeton University Press, 1962.

Representative arguments from the debate between Cotton and Williams may be found in:

Reed, John W. "Man and His Government: Roger Williams vs. The Massachusetts Oligarchy." *Sermons in American History*. Edited by DeWitte Holland. New York: Abingdon Press, 1971.

Of special concern to those interested in rhetoric is:

White, Eugene R. "Puritan Preaching and the Authority of God." *Preaching in American History*. Edited by DeWitte Holland. New York: Abingdon Press, 1969.

An excellent bibliography of colonial materials may be found in:

Boorstin, Daniel J. *The Americans: The Colonial Experience*. New York: Random House, 1965.

3 God, Man, and the Great Awakening

Robert L. Heinemann

The term "Great Awakening" refers to a religious revival which took place throughout the American colonies in the mid-eighteenth century. The term "awakening" itself was no doubt derived in part from the many scriptural references which compare the process of spiritual renewal to an awakening. Such an example is found in Ephesians 5:14, "Awake thou that sleepest, and arise from the dead, and Christ shall give thee light." Conjecture as to exactly who was awakened and to what has received a great deal of attention from historians and critics. One interpretation would say, in effect, that those who were spiritually dead and damned were awakened by God's Spirit to find salvation and eternal life through Christ. Another interpretation might assert that the awakening, taking place in a predominantly Christian culture, was an awakening of believers, a revitalization of faith which had previously existed to some degree. Still another interpretation might be expanded humanistically, and declare, "What was awakened in 1740 was the spirit of American democracy." [1]

The first two interpretations of the "Awakening" are mutually exclusive, while the humanistic interpretation is compatible with either theistic interpretation or possibly an atheistic interpretation. Indeed, a central issue at the time of the Awakening regarded the very source of activity: was it of God or merely a deviate sociological phenomenon? This chapter will, of course, not attempt to settle the issue but rather will seek to describe it, taking into account the times, the men, and the subordinate issues. Finally, a brief appraisal of the overall impact as viewed from the twentieth century will be offered.

Throughout American and world history there have been numerous religious "awakenings." What was particular about this one to merit the stamp "Great"? Time and geography perhaps should be a first consideration. If the Jesus Movement of the 1970s might be considered the latest example of religious revival in America, the Great Awakening might well be considered the first. Although the populating of the new continent came about largely through religious revivals and schisms in Europe, once in America the various sects settled

---

1. Alan Heimert and Perry Miller, eds., *The Great Awakening* (Indianapolis: Bobbs-Merrill, 1967), p. lxi.

down as a complacent establishment. This moderating process continued within the framework of American Calvinism throughout the seventeenth century and into the eighteenth century. Although there were a few brief periods of heightened religious activity, it was not until the period of American history referred to as the "Great Awakening" that religious activity loomed to the forefront and consumed the general interest of a major portion of the colonial population. Although the Awakening was "Great" within the history of our own country, perhaps, within the context of European history, the religious revivals which occurred almost simultaneously in Germany, Holland, Switzerland, France, and England were not quite as "great."

The scope of revival, in terms of time, geography, and percentages of people involved was truly great. It is somewhat difficult to date the Great Awakening since it developed gradually and faded even more gradually. Although, generally, the Awakening occurred simultaneously in all sections of the American colonies, it is possible to identify periods of religious activity with particular geographical areas. The broader scope of the dates might run as follows: New England, 1735-45; Middle Colonies, 1725-58; Southern Colonies, 1739-80. Within this time period, it is also possible to isolate the major thrust of the Awakening, commencing in 1739 and running through 1742.[2]

Although the Awakening seemed to die out most quickly in New England, it should be noted that this is where the conflagration burned with greatest intensity; perhaps greater excesses are harder to maintain over a period of time. Charles Brockwell, an

Anglican missionary in Salem, Massachusetts, at the height of the Awakening wrote home to England concerning the extent of the religious excesses, "It is impossible to relate the convulsions into which the whole Country is thrown by a set of Enthusiasts. . . . Their behaviour is indeed as shocking, as uncomon, their groans, cries, screams, & agonies. . . draw tears even from the most resolute. . . . Such confusion, disorder, & irregularity Eye never beheld."[3] Of course the preceding account was written from the perspective of an anti-revivalist; but the same scope and importance of the event is evident from the pro-revivalist position. Thomas Prince, a highly esteemed Congregational minister and historian wrote to George Whitefield concerning the "Amazing Works," "Our exalted Saviour has been riding forth in his Magnificence and Glory thro' divers Parts of our Land, in so triumphant a Manner as has never been seen or heard among us, or among any other People as we know of, since the Apostles Days."[4]

Some critics have viewed the Great Awakening as primarily an outlet for pent-up social energy. In this context the Great Awakening can be seen as something which filled the lull between the initial settling of the new continent and the Revolutionary War. James Playsted Wood suggests that the energies that are today drained off by

2. Heimert and Miller suggest these narrower dates, p. xiii.

3. Charles Brockwell, "Every Idle Untruth as a Revelation," in *Religious Enthusiasm and the Great Awakening*, ed. David S. Lovejoy (Englewood Cliffs, N.J.: Prentice-Hall, 1969), pp. 65-66.

4. Thomas Prince, "What Shall We Do to Be Saved?" in *Religious Enthusiasm*, ed. Lovejoy, pp. 38-39.

professional sports and recreation found their outlet in an "unparalleled revival."[5] Though such a view seems valid enough, it does not explain the whole story. There were issues involved, issues upon which men were willing to stake their lives and reputations, issues which still haunt the various religious establishments of today.

The Major Issues

The major issues around which the controversy of the Great Awakening revolved can be classified into three general categories: theological, ecclesiastical, and rhetorical. The theological issue centered around the nature and cause of salvation and regeneration, reviving the old Calvinist-Arminian dispute of predestination vs. free will. This theological issue was basic and provided the foundation upon which the other two types of issues were argued. The ecclesiastical issue focused on the legitimacy of itinerant preachers and "exhorters" who invaded the parishes of the established clergy. The itinerants rationalized their action by denouncing as inadequate the "dead" Arminian theology. The established clergy denounced the theology of the itinerants as extreme and unwarranted by scripture. Finally, the rhetorical issue involved the question of how Christian preaching and worship should be conducted; this issue was closely linked with the controversy as to what "faculties" ought to be involved in the Christian "experience." The revivalist, emphasizing the gracious work of the Spirit of God, favored an affective approach, while the anti-revivalists, emphasizing man's ability to make rational moral choices, favored a reserved, rational approach. A favorite invective used by the anti-revivalists against the revivalists was the label "enthusiast." The word at that time meant something quite different from what it means today; it denoted a state of psychological frenzy and unbalance brought about by an individual himself rather than by any true Spirit of God.

It is interesting to note that each side in the dispute gave more or less emphasis to certain types of issues. The revivalists, for the most part, took the offensive on the theological issues. The concept of the "new birth" (John 3:3) was paramount and was interpreted literally as a specific event corresponding to natural birth. Just as birth is beyond the control of the baby, so the "new birth" is beyond the control of the would-be saint. For the most part, this strict Calvinist theology was pressed against the mild Arminianism of the status quo, perhaps most ably represented in the writings of Dr. Charles Chauncy of Boston. The great revivalist preachers of the day, Jonathan Edwards, Gilbert Tennent, and George Whitefield, all emphasized the doctrines of man's total depravity and God's absolute sovereignty.

The anti-revivalists assumed the offensive on the ecclesiastical and rhetorical issues. Throughout the colonies, there was almost universal agreement among the anti-revivalists as to the illegitimacy of itinerant preachers, who were seen as usurping the ministry of the established clergy. In the North, the "Old Light" congregationalists, supported by the seminaries (Harvard and Yale), protested the unorthodox activities and preparation of the "New Light" preachers and "exhorters." In the Middle Colonies, the "Old

5. James Playsted Wood, *Mr. Jonathan Edwards* (New York: Seabury Press, 1968), pp. 86-87.

Side" Presbyterians attacked the Tennents and the "New Side" Presbyterians, which eventually lead to a complete break and the formation of a rival religious body. In the South, Alexander Garden, the Anglican hierarchy, and the civil authorities, all attacked Whitefield and, primarily because of his itinerancy, attempted to discredit him as a proper Anglican minister.

Leading the attack on the rhetorical issue were Chauncy, Garden, and a series of anonymous pamphlets entitled the "Querists." Here, as Edward Collins points out, the charges were primarily generated from the view that the Christian experience and conviction should be primarily of a rational nature rather than affective.[6]

Although the issues stressed depended primarily on the viewpoint of the men presenting them, geography also seemed to play a role. To be sure, all three types of issues were at stake in all three geographical regions, but New England seemed to stress the theological and rhetorical issues, whereas, the Middle Colonies and especially the Anglican South seemed to focus on the ecclesiastical controversy.

To fully understand the issues and their inter-relatedness, one must attempt to examine each type individually, taking into account the various idiosyncrasies of individual speakers and the pecularities of specific rhetorical settings.

The Theological Issues—The main theological issue, which in a logical way was the basis of all other issues, centered on the question of Christian conversion, its nature and its cause. As will be shown, the view taken regarding the cause of conversion, i.e., man's free will or God's sovereignty, strongly influenced the position taken on the nature of conversion.

The Nature of Christian Conversion. One of the first questions to arise concerning the nature of conversion dealt with the time factor: is conversion a gradual or instantaneous happening? A literal interpretation of the concept of "new birth" meant for the revivalist that conversion was a particular event in time. Many of those "awakened" by the revival could readily identify their conversion down to the hour, and could have, so they felt, accurately filled out a spiritual birth certificate. Edwards speaks of the "first sensible act of grace"[7] as being the point at which the believer is first in some way aware of his salvation. Although Edwards, with other revivalists, would strongly assert that "in fact" conversion changes the heart "at once," he does admit that human awareness of the event may differ:

Conversion is a great and glorious work of God's power, at once changing the heart, and infusing life into the dead soul; though the grace, then implanted more gradually displays itself in some than in others. But, as to fixing on the precise time when they put forth the very first act of grace, there is a great deal of difference in different persons; in some, it seems to be very discernable when the time was; but others are more at a loss. . . .

In some, converting light is like a glorious brightness, suddenly shining *upon* a person. . . . In many others it has been like the dawning of the day, when at first but a little light appears, and it may be is presently hid with a cloud; and then it appears again, and shines a little brighter, and gradually increases, with intervening darkness, till at length it breaks forth more clearly from behind the clouds. And many are doubtless ready to date their conversion wrong, throwing by those lesser de-

6. Edward M. Collins, Jr., "The Rhetoric of Sensation Challenges the Rhetoric of the Intellect: An Eighteenth-Century Controversy," in *Preaching in American History*, ed. DeWitte Holland (Nashville: Abingdon Press, 1969), pp. 98-117.
7. Jonathan Edwards, *The Narrative* (Grand Rapids: Kregel Publications, 1957), p. 52.

grees of light that appeared at *first* dawning, and calling some more remarkable experience they had *afterwards*, their conversion.[8]

The point to note about the preceding passage is the assumed existence of some objective moment of conversion. The very idea of dating "their conversion wrong" implies that there indeed is a right date. Although Edwards and most revivalists would admit that the preparation or "awakening" of the heart to its sinful state may be gradual[9] and also that the realization of grace may be gradual, they all would assert that the actual saving work of grace is instantaneous.

In direct contrast to the revivalists, most anti-revivalists held that salvation and conversion was a gradual process beginning with infant baptism and proceeding through the adherence to Christian doctrine and the living of a moral life. The concept of the "new birth" was taken figuratively to simply signify the entry into the Christian way of life. Chief antagonist of the Awakening in the South, Alexander Garden, spoke out against an instantaneous conversion, "the Work of *Regeneration* is not the Work of a Moment, a sudden *instantaneous* Work, but a *gradual* and *co-operative* Work of the *Holy Spirit*, joining in with our *Understandings*, and leading us on by *Reason* and *Persuasion*, from one Degree to another, of Faith, good Dispositions, Acts, and Habits of Piety. . . ."[10] Perhaps the clearest statement of this "gradual process" was offered by Anglican lecturer, Samuel Quincy. Quincy, a good friend of Alexander Garden, after clarifying his own position that the "new birth" signified "no more than that great and mighty Change which visibly appears in Men after they become true Converts to Christianity, and take upon them, not only the Profession, but

the Life and Behaviour of a Christian,"[11] turned to attack the Revivalists' concept of immediate conversion:

Other Misinterpretations of this Doctrine are, that this Work of Conversion or the New Birth, is sudden and instantaneous, and wrought by an irresistable Degree of God's Grace and Power. . . . That Conversion from a wicked Life may not, in some extraordinary Instances, have been very suddenly effected, cannot be doubted; . . . But then that this is the ordinary Method of God's Grace; or that Conversion, in any Instance, is the Effect of irresistable Power, does not at all appear; nay is contrary to the Nature of this great and mighty Change in the Hearts and Lives of Men, which is called Conversion, or the New Birth. For no one is made either very bad, or very good in an instant; Conversion is a progressive Work, and the Principles and Habits of Grace and Goodness, are not infused into us by Miracle, all at once; as the extraordinary Gifts of the Holy Ghost were bestow'd on the first Christians. This some seem to think, who speak of Conversion as an instantaneous Work; but this is not the Case of the ordinary Operations of God's Holy Spirit. He works upon us by way of rational Conviction, and the several Graces of Christianity are acquired by degrees; one Virtue is added to another, and we grow up to the Christian Life by insensible Gradations.[12]

The preceding quotation demonstrates not only the wide gap in the dispute over the time element of the "new birth," but more importantly establishes the basis of this disagreement—the strict Calvinist doctrines of "irresistible grace" and "predestination."

Closely associated with the dispute over the time of conversion was the question of whether a "saved" soul was aware of his

8. *Ibid.*, pp. 59-60.

9. *Ibid.*, p. 34.

10. Alexander Garden, "Two Sermons on Regeneration," in *The Great Awakening*, ed. Heimert and Miller, p. 50.

11. Samuel Quincy, "The Nature and Necessity of Regeneration," *Twenty Sermons Preach'd in the Parish of St. Philip* (Boston, Printed and sold by John Draper, 1750), p. 177.

12. *Ibid.*, pp. 290-91.

preferred spiritual state. Although Edwards, as we have seen, did raise the possibility of not knowing the exact time of conversion, he and other revivalists would seriously question the spiritual state of an individual who had never been aware of God's grace, as it would certainly be made manifest by the work of the Holy Spirit. In fact, the work of the Holy Spirit was one of Edwards' chief concerns. The problem concerning the identification of the work of the Holy Spirit was not so great with the revivalist as with the anti-revivalist, who denied that the entire revival was the work of God. Here then was not only an abstract doctrinal dispute, but a real, live issue, being fleshed out in churches, meeting halls, and fields throughout colonial America: was the Great Awakening truly a mass salvation event? Was this what was happening the nature of Christian conversion?

Enthusiasm or the Work of the Spirit? The anti-revivalist responded with a definite "No." Perhaps the most articulate spokesman for the anti-revivalists was Charles Chauncy. In 1742 he published a sermon entitled *Enthusiasm Described and Caution'd Against.* Although he defined enthusiasm so as to include all those persons who felt "favoured with the extraordinary presence of the *Deity*" and "immediately inspired by the Spirit of God,"[13] Chauncy cautiously attacked directly only the itinerant preachers and exhorters. If the unusual behavior of the revivalists was not to be found in the workings of the Spirit of God, what was the explanation? Chauncy sought to explain the radical activity in terms of a psychological defect caused by "a bad temperament to the blood and spirits." "'Tis properly a disease, a sort of madness," explained Chauncy, resulting when "*melan-*

choly is the prevailing ingredient in their constitution."[14]

And how was one to distinguish between "bad temperament" and the work of the Holy Spirit (a concept which Chauncy refused to deny)? Surprisingly enough Chauncy's first test was the same as that appealed to by Edwards, scripture:

But I come In the second place, to point you to a *rule* by which you may judge of persons, whether they are *enthusiasts*, meer pretenders to the immediate guidance and influence of the SPIRIT. And this is, in general, *a regard to the bible, an acknowledgment that the things therein contained are the commandments of GOD.* This is the rule in the text. And 'tis an infallible rule of tryal in this matter. We need not fear judging amiss, while we keep closely to it.[15]

After delineating his first rule, Chauncy sought to apply it. Quoting indirectly from St. Paul's first letter to the Corinthians and elaborating on the text, Chauncy condemned the revivalists for lacking order and being "busy-bodies."[16]

Following his discussion on the test of scripture, Chauncy introduced a second test: "Next to the Scripture, there is no greater enemy to enthusiasm, than reason."[17] Indeed Chauncy saw reason as not only consistent with the Spirit but as a vehicle of that Spirit as well, "the SPIRIT preserves from delusion. . . .by opening the understanding."[18] If Chauncy disliked the lack of order and the dominance of the emotions over the reason, he was even more

---

13. Charles Chauncy, *Enthusiasm Described and Caution'd Against* (Boston, 1742), p. 3.
14. *Ibid.*
15. *Ibid.*, p. 7.
16. *Ibid.*, p. 12.
17. *Ibid.*, p. 18.
18. *Ibid.*, p. 19.

upset that such emotional behavior should be attributed to the Spirit of God. In a letter to an English friend, George Wishart, Chauncy summed up his feelings:

In performing these Exercises they observed no stated Method, but proceeded as their present Thought or Fancy led them: And by this means the Meetinghouse would be filled with what I could not but judge great Confusion and Disorder; ... These Meetings they would continue till 10, 11, 12 o'Clock at Night; in the midst of them sometimes 10, 20, 30 and sometimes many more would *scream* and *cry out,* or send forth the most *lamentable Groans,* whilst others made great Manifestations of Joy, by *clapping* their Hands, uttering *extatick Expressions, singing Psalms,* and *inviting* and *exhorting* others. Some would *swoon away* under the Influence of distressing Fears, and others *swallowed up with insupportable Joy.* While some were *fainting,* others laboured under *convulsive Twitches of Body,* which they said were involuntary. But in vain shall I pretend to describe all the Proceedings at those Meetings. But what appeared to me most dangerous and hurtful was, that very much Stress was laid on these *Extraordinaries,* as tho' they were *sure Marks,* or, at least *sufficient Evidences* of a just Conviction of Sin on the one Hand; or, on the other, of that Joy which there is in believing, and so of an Interest in the Favour of God.[19]

Chauncy's challenge to the Awakening being attributed to the Spirit of God was taken seriously by all involved in the heat of the event. Especially bothered was Jonathan Edwards, who, as Leslie Stephen points out, was "unconsciously troubled by the strange contrast between the effect and the stupendous cause assigned for it."[20] In answer to Chauncy, Jonathan Edwards published a carefully structured argument, clearly outlining what he considered to be "no signs by which we are to judge a work"[21] and what he saw as "distinguishing Scripture evidences of a work of the Spirit of God."[22] First Edwards stated that any extraordinary behavior such as "tears, trembling, groans, loud outcries, agonies of the body,"[23] etc. are not to be judged one way or the other since scripture is silent on "any such rule."[24] In fact, argued Edwards, it would indeed be strange if there was no or little emotional reaction, considering the great life and death issues involved and considering the many different personalities of the congregation. Further, it is no argument against the work of the Spirit that some people should be moved by the emotional outbursts of others; God always uses "means," and this like the sermon may just be another "means." As in any religious revival, there are always those who "fall away" shortly after the heat of the meetings, and Edwards was quick to assert that the existence of some "counterfeits," was not due reason for discrediting the entire movement. Finally, Edwards defended the revivalist ministers' techniques of preaching on hell, saying that if a hell really exists (a fact generally agreed upon by the majority of opposition), then it is surely something of which all men should be sensible.

In contrast to the various phenomena which were not signs, either of the Spirit or not of the Spirit, Edwards set forth five tests which would establish that the Spirit of God was indeed at work:

---

19. Charles Chauncy, "The Heat and Fervour of Their Passions," in *Religious Enthusiasm and the Great Awakening,* ed. Lovejoy, p. 77.
20. Leslie Stephen, "Jonathan Edwards," *Hours in a Library* (New York: G.P. Putnam's Son, 1904), 2:53.
21. Jonathan Edwards, "Marks of A Work of the True Spirit," in *The Works of President Edwards* (New York: Leavitt & Trow, 1843), 1:525.
22. *Ibid.,* 1:539.
23. *Ibid.,* 1:527.
24. *Ibid.*

1. "When the operation is such as to raise their esteem of Jesus who was born of the Virgin, and was crucified without the gates of Jerusalem. . ."

2. "When the spirit that is at work operates against the interests of Satan's kingdom. . ."

3. When "the spirit that operates in such a manner, as to cause in men a greater regard to the Holy Scriptures. . ."

4. When the spirit "operates as a spirit of truth, leading persons to truth, convincing them of those things that are true. . ."

5. When "the spirit that is at work among a people operates as a spirit of love to God and man. . ."[25]

Edwards concluded his argument by saying, "From what has been said, I will venture to draw this inference, viz., that the extraordinary influence that has lately appeared causing an uncommon concern and engagedness of mind about the things of religion, is undoubtedly, in the general, from the Spirit of God."[26]

Any dispute over the nature of salvation and conversion was inevitably linked to the question of the nature of man. The revivalists saw man as totally depraved and hopelessly lost in sin; consequently his reason was all but useless in finding God, "for the preaching of the cross is to them that perish foolishness" (I Corinthians 1:18). The anti-revivalists, on the other hand, admitted that man's vision had been blurred since the fall, but denied that his reason was totally blind; indeed, this was one of the nobler qualities in man and must be properly used in making the rational choice of the Christian way of life. This brings one to the crux of the entire theological issue: May man choose God, or must God choose man?

The Cause of Christian Conversion. The controversy over man's ability to secure his own salvation through his own belief in Christ has been historically labeled the Calvinist-Arminian issue. Actually, the controversy is wider than this single issue, involving the issues of "irresistible grace" and "eternal security." However, as John Wesley pointed out in his definition of Arminianism, the basic issue is "predestination":

Indeed, the two latter points, irresistible grace and infallible perseverance, are the natural consequence of the former, of the unconditional decree. For, if God has eternally and absolutely decreed to save such and such persons it follows, both that they cannot resist his saving grace (else they might miss of salvation), and that they cannot finally fall from that grace which they cannot resist. So that in effect the three questions come into one, "Is predestination absolute or conditional [upon the will of man]?" The Arminians believe it is conditional; the Calvinists, that it is absolute.[27]

In addition to the Calvinist and Arminian positions, a third hyper-Calvinistic position is possible; this is generally referred to as Antinomianism. This position represents extreme theistic determinism. God does everything both before and after salvation; man is completely passive. The sinner therefore is completely dependent upon God, and his sinfulness then is according to God's will, while the Christian is completely righteous in God's will and hence is not subject to the temporal standards of conduct and morality. In colonial America, Anne Hutchinson was credited with propagating this view, though in reality she was probably quite close to the Calvinism of Edwards. The thin line be-

25. *Ibid.*, 1:539-43.

26. *Ibid.*, 1:546.

27. John Wesley, "What is an Arminian?" in *Great Voices of the Reformation*, ed. H.E. Fosdick (New York: Random House, 1952), p. 516.

tween Calvinism and Antinomianism is the doctrine of "preparation," which the Antinomians deny.[28]

For the most part New England was populated with at least nominal Calvinists. For a colonial preacher at the time of the Awakening to accept the label of "Arminian" as Wesley had would have been the kiss of death. Consequently, most of the vocal opponents of Calvinism were Englishmen, living and deceased. These would include John Tillotson, Samuel Clarke, Thomas Chubb, Daniel Whitby, Isaac Watts, and John Wesley. It was to the arguments of these men, arguments given silent assent by many colonial leaders, that the main defender of the old Calvinism, Jonathan Edwards, addressed himself.

The first direct assault on the Calvinist doctrine of predestination to occur in America came after the height of the Awakening. Yet it must be recognized that there was present during the Awakening an undercurrent of like sympathy. By 1749 American Arminianism was articulated:

Hence it has come to pass that when Men read of God's choosing whole Nations to certain Priveleges (and those in this Life only) they have rashly concluded that *particular Persons are unconditionally* chosen to eternal Life Hereafter. —That when they have laid before them the Character of a very loose and abandoned People, who by their *own* long practised Wickedness, have rendered themselves the Children of Wrath, and fitted themselves for Destruction, they are induced to vilify human Nature itself with the same vicious Character. —That when they hear of our being *saved by Grace,* they conceive of it so as to destroy all moral Agency, and set themselves down with this vain Thought, that nothing of their Part is necessary to Salvation, but if they are designed for it, they shall irresistably be driven into Heaven, whether they will or not. —And if they are not, no Prayers, nor Endeavours will avail. . . .

Thus "stupified and bewildered with Sounds, without attending to the true Sense of Revela-

tion," the pure and perfect Religion of Jesus, (which contains the most refined System of Morality the World was ever blessed with; which every where considers us as moral Agents, and suspends our whole Happiness upon our *personal* good Behaviour, and our patient Continuance in the Ways of Well-do-ing) is in many Places turned into an *idle Speculation,* a *mysterious Faith, a senseless Superstition, and a groundless Recumbency;* and in short, every Thing but what in Fact it is, viz. a Doctrine of Sobriety, Righteousness and Piety.[29]

It was to this new rising spirit of Arminianism that Edwards spoke. His was a valiant, but in many ways vain, effort to reestablish in colonial America the strict dogmatism of Jean Calvin. In his *Institutes of the Christian Religion* (1536) Calvin developed his doctrine of "eternal election, by which God has predestined some to salvation, others to destruction."[30] Since the time of this statement, the doctrine of election and predestination had constituted a major dogma for a large segment of the Protestant church. In fact, the doctrine was staunchly affirmed in the Thirty-nine Articles of the Church of England (Article Seventeen).

Throughout his career, Edwards preached many sermons on the subject of election and predestination. It would at this point be useful to thoroughly examine perhaps one of Edwards' stronger state-

---

28. For a more complete discussion on the differences between Calvinism and Antinomianism see Jonathan Dickinson, "Letter XVIII. Wherein some *Antinomian Abuses* of the Doctrine of Believers Union to CHRIST, or Pleas from it for *Licentiousness* and *Security* in sinning, are considered and obviated," *Familiar Letters* (Boston, Printed and sold by Rogers and Fowle, 1745).

29. Lemuel Briant, "The Absurdity of Depreciating Moral Virtue," in *The Great Awakening,* ed. Heimert and Miller, p. 542.

30. Jean Calvin, *Institutes of the Christian Religion* (Philadelphia: Westminster Press, 1960), 2:920.

ments, *God's Sovereignty*. The text for this sermon is Romans 9:18, "Therefore hath he mercy on whom he will have mercy, and whom he will he hardeneth."

First, Edwards dealt with the nature of God's sovereignty. It appears that Edwards here asserted the freedom of God to will whatever he pleased—"in opposition to any constraint. . . in opposition to its being under the will of another. . . in opposition to any proper obligation."[31] "God's mere will and sovereign pleasure," then, is said to be "without restraint, or constraint, or obligation."[32] However, Edwards was careful to define God's choices and acts as being "without prejudice to the glory of any of his attributes."[33] Thus the "attributes" of God, which to some extent are revealed in the scriptures, set limits on what can and cannot be willed. Actually these might not be so much limits of action as limits of definition. Other limitations to God's sovereignty which arise from his attributes are those specific promises of scripture; God will not break His word.

Edwards next went to the heart of the doctrine of election: God chooses some and damns others arbitrarily that his glory might be manifest. Edwards first dealt with the positive aspect of this doctrine:

God can, without prejudice to the glory of any of his attributes, bestow salvation on any of the children of men, except on those who have committed the sin against the Holy Ghost. . . . Though persons have sinned long, have been obstinate, have committed heinous sins a thousand times even till they have grown old in sin, and have sinned under great aggravations: let the aggravations be what they may; if they have sinned under ever so great light; if they have been backsliders, and have sinned against ever so numerous and solemn warnings and strivings of the Spirit, and mercies of his common providence: though the danger of such is much greater than of other sinners, yet God can save them if he pleases, for the

sake of Christ, without any prejudice to any of his attributes. He may have mercy on whom he will have mercy.[34]

Many a moderate or "Arminian leaning" Calvinist would readily endorse the above view. However, he would begin to balk as the other side of the coin was revealed. Edwards, unflinchingly stated the negative aspects of this doctrine with all of its stark harshness:

There is no person whatever in a natural condition, upon whom God may not refuse to bestow salvation without prejudice to any part of his glory. Let a natural person be wise or unwise, of a good or ill natural temper, of mean or honorable parentage, whether born of wicked or godly parents; let him be a moral or immoral person, whatever good he may have done, however religious he has been, how many prayers soever he has made, and whatever pains he has taken that he may be saved; whatever concern and distress he may have for fear he shall be damned; or whatever circumstances he may be in; God can deny him salvation without the least disparagement to any of his perfections. His glory will not in any instance be the least obscured by it.[35]

After making such a statement, Edwards went to the scriptures to demonstrate that God indeed does arbitrarily choose one individual or nation over others, who would appear to be equally or even more eligible for God's grace. Examples include God's choices of the Israelites over the Egyptians, Greeks, or Romans; Isaac over Ishmael; Jacob over Esau; the Gentiles over the Jews; and Lazarus over the rich man. Moreover, God sometimes chooses children of wicked families such as Abijah, Hezekiah,

---

31. Edwards, "God's Sovereignty," *Works*, 4:549.
32. *Ibid.*, 4:549-50.
33. *Ibid.*, 4:550.
34. *Ibid.*, 4:550-51.
35. *Ibid.*, 4:552.

and Josiah: or he "withholds salvation from those who are the children of very pious parents,"[36] such as Amnon, Absalom, and Manasseh. The New Testament also bears out the fact that "God exercises his sovereignty in calling some to salvation, who have been very heinously wicked, and leaving others, who have been moral and religious persons."[37] God passed over the pious Pharisees and instead chose the publicans, harlots, and dregs of society. All this was done that the glory of God's sovereignty might be known.

Edwards concluded this sermon by putting more of the responsibility for salvation on God than on the individual, "Let you be what sinner you may, God can, if he pleases, greatly glorify himself in your salvation."[38]

Quite similar to this sermon are two others, *God Glorified in Man's Dependence* and *The Justice of God in the Damnation of Sinners.* In contrast to these sermons is one which explicates the doctrine of preparation, *The Manner in Which the Salvation of the Soul is to be Sought.* In this sermon, Edwards stressed how man must work out his own salvation with fear and trembling. Edwards drew a parallel to the physical salvation of Noah. Noah had to embark upon a great undertaking; he could not tire of his task, he could not succumb to the ridicule of his contemporaries, and he had to lay his whole being on the line to accomplish the task. Edwards asserted that he who would seek spiritual salvation is in much the same position as Noah and concluded that "If we undertake this work with the same good will and resolution, we shall undoubtedly be successful."[39] This doctrine then, which stresses the responsibility of the individual in preparing himself by a "great undertaking," constituted the thin line in Colonial thought between orthodox Calvinism and heretical Antinomianism.

A discussion of predestination would not be complete without some mention of Edwards' *opus magnum, A careful and strict Enquiry into The modern Prevailing Notions of that Freedom of Will, which is supposed to be essential to Moral Agency, Virtue and Vice, Reward and Punishment, Praise and Blame.* Published after the Great Awakening in 1754, this work depends on arguments from psychology and physics as well as theology. Edwards' psychological argument is based on the concept of motives: "the will is always determined by the strongest motive, or by that view of the mind which has the greatest degree of previous tendency to excite volition."[40] From the realm of physics, Edwards argued that volition is subject to the law of cause and effect. Though the will is a cause, it is not a first cause and is therefore the effect of something external to itself:

The mind's being a designing Cause, only enables it to produce effects in consequence of its design; it will not enable it to be the designing Cause of all its own designs. The mind's being an elective Cause, will only enable it to produce effects in consequence of its elections, and according to them; but cannot enable it to be the elective Cause of all its own elections; because that supposes an election before the first election.[41]

---

36. *Ibid.,* 4:555.
37. *Ibid.,* 4:556.
38. *Ibid.,* 4:560.
39. Edwards, "The Manner in Which the Salvation of the Soul is to be Sought," in *Works,* 4:376.
40. Edwards, "A Careful and Strict Inquiry into the Prevailing Notions of the Freedom of the Will," in *Works,* 2:7.
41. *Ibid.,* 2:32.

In other words, while admitting that man often has the freedom to act in accordance with his will, Edwards denied the freedom of actually determining one's own will. In terms of the issue of theistic determinism vs. free will, Jonathan Edwards was by far the most eloquent spokesman in the Great Awakening period.

The Ecclesiastical Issues—The major ecclesiastical issue focused on the validity of itinerant preachers and exhorters who traveled from parish to parish, often uninvited. What made the issue even more volatile was the fact that often these itinerants would attack the established clergy as "unregenerate." One of the first ministers in New England to attack the established clergy was the Dutch Reformed minister Theodore Frelinghuysen. Appointed to serve in America by the classis of Amsterdam, he began his ministry in the Raritan Valley, New Jersey, in 1720. Although he was not an itinerant, he did provide a prelude for what was soon to follow by charging "his colleagues in the ministry with being unconverted."[42]

In 1740 Gilbert Tennent dropped a bomb, his "Nottingham Sermon." Using Mark 6:34, "And Jesus, when he came out, saw much People, and was moved with Compassion towards them, because they were as Sheep not having a Shepherd," as a text, Tennent lashed out at unconverted ministers, labeling them "Swarms of Locusts, the Crowds of Pharisees, that have as covetously as cruelly, crept into the Ministry, in this adulterous Generation!"[43] After thoroughly establishing the spiritual lifelessness of the majority of his colleagues, Tennent advised his hearers to "withdraw. . .from the Ministry of a natural Man."[44] Further, he criticized the rule by which parishioners should hear only the ministers of their parish, calling it "a Yoke worse than that of Rome itself."[45]

If Tennent indicted the Colonial ministry generally, the Rev. James Davenport attacked it more specifically, pointing the finger at individual unregenerate ministers. A letter from Chauncy to Davenport reveals that it was the latter's practice upon entering a town to promptly visit the established minister and inquire upon the state of his soul.[46] After hearing the minister out, the Spirit of God would reveal to Davenport, so he claimed, whether the man was living in God's grace or not, and shortly afterward it was Davenport's practice to make such revelation public knowledge. Needless to say, there were many hard feelings generated in those who were publicly declared unconverted and living in sin.

By far the most popular itinerant preacher during and after the Awakening was George Whitefield, an erratic Anglican minister from England. Between the years 1738 and 1770 Whitefield made seven "visits" to America, preaching from one end of the colonies to the other. If he could not find a church, he would rent a hall or preach out in the open field, on the sabbath or on week-days. One of Whitefield's more famous auditors was Benjamin Franklin who described the effect of the great itinerant's oratory:

---

42. John T. McNeill, *The History and Character of Calvinism* (New York: Oxford University Press, 1962), p. 344.

43. Gilbert Tennent, *The Danger of An Unconverted Ministry* (Philadelphia: B. Franklin, 1740), p. 17.

44. *Ibid.*, p. 22.

45. *Ibid.*, p. 21.

46. Charles Chauncy, *A Letter to the Reverend Mr. James Davenport. . . Now in Boston* (Boston: J. Draper, 1742).

I happened soon after to attend one of his Sermons, in the Course of which I perceived he intended to finish with a Collection, and I silently resolved he should get nothing from me. I had in my Pocket a Handful of Copper Money, three or four silver Dollars, and five Pistoles in Gold. As he proceeded I began to soften, and concluded to give the Coppers. Another Stroke of his Oratory made me asham'd of that, and determin'd me to give the Silver; and he finish'd so admirably, that I empty'd my Pocket wholly into the Collector's Dish, Gold and all.[47]

If Franklin willingly gave of his money, Charles Chauncy did not. In fact Chauncy was furious that Whitefield was draining off money which, as he saw it, should rightly go into the church coffers of the local parish:

And some are in the Opinion, it han't been to Mr. WHITEFIELD'S Disadvantage, on *temporal* Accounts, that he has travelled about the World in Quality of an *Itinerant Preacher.* He has certainly made LARGE COLLECTIONS: And if, in the doing of this, he had a *Fellow-Feeling* with the Orphans, 'tis no more than might be expected. No one, I believe, besides himself, can tell the *Amount* of the *Presents,* he received in this Town, as well as in other Places, for his *own proper Use.*[48]

It might be noted in passing that while Chauncy doubted Whitefield's motives and honesty, Franklin had no such reservations, stating that Whitefield "was in all his Conduct, a perfectly *honest Man.*"[49]

It is hard for us today to imagine a situation wherein the itinerant evangelist would be completely ruled out of order by the establishment. Yet this was the case. "The Querists," an anonymous pamphlet published by the New Castle Presbytery indicates the narrow provincialism of the day:

And seeing every ordinary Minister is called to the Oversight of a particular Flock; where is the Order and Decency of leaving a Man's own Flock, and industriously entering other Men's Labours? When

Men strive so hard to dissolve the solemn Tye of the sacred Relation between Ministers and People, under the Notion of Liberty; why may not they plead for the same Liberty in other Relations, if it may be supposed to be for the Benefit of the *Orphan-House* in *Georgia?* [A reference to Whitefield][50]

In most colonies, the sanction against the roving evangelists was only that of the established clergy; in Connecticut, however, itinerants found themselves constrained by civil law. "An Act for Regulating Abuses and Correcting Disorders in Ecclesiastical Affairs" was passed by the Connecticut Assembly in 1742. This act made it illegal for any minister or exhorter to preach in a parish other than his own unless "expressly invited and desired. . . either by the settled minister and the major part of the church of said parish, or, in case there be no settled minister, then by the church or society within such parish."[51] The penalties for breaking the law suited the nature of the lawbreaker: ordained Connecticut ministers would "be denied and secluded the benefit of any law of . . . this Colony made for the support . . . of the gospel ministry";[52] unordained preachers would be subject to "the penal sum of one

47. Benjamin Franklin, *The Autobiography of Benjamin Franklin* (New Haven: Yale University Press, 1964), p. 177.

48. Charles Chauncy, *Seasonable Thoughts on the State of Religion In New England* (Boston, 1743), p. 37.

49. Franklin, *Autobiography,* p. 178.

50. "The Querists: A Short Reply to Mr. Whitefield's Letter," in *The Great Awakening,* ed. Heimert and Miller, p. 141.

51. Connecticut Assembly, "An Act for Regulating Abuses and Correcting Disorders in Ecclesiastical Affairs," in *Religious Enthusiasm and the Great Awakening,* ed. Lovejoy, p. 70.

52. *Ibid.*

hundred pounds lawful money";[53] and "any foreigner, or stranger that is not an inhabitant within this Colony" would "be sent . . . out of the bounds of this Colony."[54]

Although there were those who welcomed the new law, it was criticized by others. Judge Elisha Williams, a friend of the religious revival, pointed out the law was illegal since it violated the *Act of Toleration* by which "all his Majesty's Subjects are so freed from the Force of all *Coercive Laws* in Matters of *Religion*, relating to Worship and Discipline, that they act their own *private Judgment*, without Restraint."[55] Of course the colonial charter specified that Connecticut could not abridge the laws of England, but Williams's appeal was broader than the laws of England; it was the appeal to be made a few years later in the Declaration of Independence and Constitution of the United States, "if there be any Rights, any Priviledges, that we may call natural and unalienable, this is one, viz. the Right of *private Judgment*, and Liberty of worshipping God according to our Consciences, without controul from human Laws."[56]

The Rhetorical Issues—The rhetorical issues can be generally classified into three categories: the setting of preaching, including time and place; the manner of preaching; and the nature of the religious service. All of these issues were dependent on and closely related to the theological and ecclesiastical issues.

The Setting of Preaching. For the itinerant preachers, religion and religious services were not a one-day-a-week thing. Most of the evangelists, patterning their campaigns after those of Whitefield, moved from town

to town preaching every day of the week. Because of this activity the itinerants were accused of taking men away from their "earthly callings." Nathan Cole, a farmer of Middletown, Connecticut, gave the following account of how he and his fellow colonists left their work and hastened to hear the man of God, George Whitefield:

Then on a sudden, in the morning about 8 or 9 of the clock there came a messenger and said Mr. Whitefield preached at Hartford and Wethersfield yesterday and is to preach at Middletown this morning at ten of the clock. I was in my field at work. I dropped my tool that I had in my hand and ran home to my wife, telling her to make ready quickly to go and hear Mr. Whitefield preach at Middletown, then ran to my pasture for my horse with all my might, fearing that I should be too late. . . . The land and banks over the river looked black with people and horses; all along the 12 miles I saw no man at work in his field, but all seemed to be gone.[57]

Perhaps the time of the meetings was more criticized than the place. The main criticism concerning place was that the itinerants often came to towns where they were unwanted—at least by the church or civil authorities. In such cases, the itinerants would have to seek private facilities. Charles Chauncy complained that "they have come into Parishes of their own Accord; and sometimes, by Application made to them from a few disaffected Persons. Sometimes, in order to get the Liberty of the Meeting-House, they have us'd mean

---

53. *Ibid.*, p. 71.
54. *Ibid.*
55. Elisha Williams, "The Essential Rights and Liberties of Protestants," in *The Great Awakening*, ed. Heimert and Miller, p. 338.
56. *Ibid.*, p. 339.
57. Nathan Cole, "Spiritual Travels," in *The Great Awakening*, ed. Heimert and Miller, pp. 184-86.

and indirect Arts; and sometimes . . . gathered Assemblies in the Fields."[58]

The Manner of Preaching. Before considering the manner of preaching, it might be worth noting the "who" of preaching. The anti-revivalists were extremely critical of "who" was preaching. Charles Chauncy reflects an attitude which would surely not be tolerated by today's "liberated" women:

And it deserves particular consideration, whether the suffering, much more the encouraging WOMEN, yea, GIRLS to speak in the assemblies for religious worship, is not a plain breach of that *commandment of the LORD*, wherein it is said, *Let your WOMEN keep silence in the churches; for it is not permitted to them to speak—It is a shame for WOMEN to speak in the church.* After such an express constitution, designedly made to restrain WOMEN from speaking in the church, with what face can such a practice be pleaded for?[59]

The issue over the manner of preaching involved content, style, and delivery. While the content of the anti-revivalists tended to appeal to the intellect, the content of the revivalists sought to work upon the emotions, as the famous sermon by Jonathan Edwards so vividly illustrates:

O sinner! consider the fearful danger you are in. 'Tis a great furnace of wrath, a wide and bottomless pit, full of the fire of wrath, that you are held over in the hand of that God whose wrath is provoked and incensed as much against you as against many of the damned in hell. You hang by a slender thread, with the flames of divine wrath flashing about it, and ready every moment to singe it and burn it asunder; and you have no interest in any Mediator, and nothing to lay hold of to save yourself, nothing to keep off the flames of wrath, nothing of your own, nothing that you ever have done, nothing that you can do, to induce God to spare you one moment.[60]

Likewise, the style and delivery of the revivalist preachers also was geared to arousing the emotions. In sharp contrast to the traditionally well-poised Colonial minister, many revivalist preachers and exhorters "thundered out . . . scolding . . . stamping & beating."[61] One of the most widely criticized aspects of the revivalists' preaching was what might today be considered a strong point, "extemporaneous delivery."[62] David S. Lovejoy indicates the close connection between style and delivery and the emotional-spiritual experience which the revivalists were trying to bring about:

If, as Whitefield suggested, he entered the pulpit full of the "Spirit of God," there was no need, it seemed, for written sermons. "Extempore preaching" became as much a part of the revivalists' style as an appeal to the "affections"; in fact, they were intimately related. A minister read the pulse, or sensed the mood, of his listeners and tailored his message accordingly. The "Spirit of God" moved quickly and a clergyman had to stand ready and move with this spirit, not be tied to a stuffy sermon written in the cool of his study. A sermon had to smell of brimstone, not of the lamp. In the heat of the Awakening a good many ministers forgot their written sermons, even their notes, and preached on the spot as the spirit moved them in an extemporaneous manner. Their method was both exciting and effective, lending to their ser-

58. Chauncy, *Seasonable Thoughts*, p. 40.

59. Chauncy, *Enthusiasm Described and Caution'd Against*, p. 13.

60. Jonathan Edwards, "Sinners in the Hands of an Angry God," *Selected Sermons of Jonathan Edwards*, ed. H.N. Gardiner (New York: Macmillan, 1904), p. 89.

61. Patrick Henry, "The Awakening Reaches Backcountry Virginia," in *Religious Enthusiasm and the Great Awakening*, ed. Lovejoy, p. 58.

62. "The Testimony of the President, Professors, Tutors and Hebrew Instructor of Harvard College in Cambridge Against the Reverend Mr. George Whitefield, And His Conduct," *American Christianity An Historical Interpretation with Representative Documents*, eds. H.S. Smith, R.T. Handy, and L.A. Loetscher (New York: Charles Scribner's Sons, 1960), 1:330,334.

mons and prayers an emotional appeal which was the very essence of revival.[63]

The Nature of the Religious Services. Nor was the preacher the only object of criticism within the revivalist movement; the whole conduct of the religious service was subject to question, the crying out, praying, and other overt activity on the part of the congregation. Charles Chauncy, one of the first to publicly condemn the "disorders," spoke out against the *"EXHORTING*, and *PRAYING*, and *SINGING*, and *LAUGHING*, in the same house of worship, at one and the same time" and compared these excesses to those "the apostle blames in the church of Corinth."[64]

But despite the criticism, censures, and even laws against the radical religious activities, the Great Awakening stands as a landmark of rebellion against the religious and social establishment and the positive assertion of the religious and spiritual rights of the individual.

The Impact of the Great Awakening on American Society

The Great Awakening gave an existential American society a new existential religion. What really "existed" in the life of the individual became more important than an idealized abstract essence. Although Calvinist theology was to see a decline in America, the "existential" aspect of religion flourished, even in such non-Calvinist thinkers as Emerson and Thoreau. Perhaps, because she was faced with a vast wilderness and the job of creating a nation, America naturally was attracted to a religion of hard realities based on gut experience rather than a religion of traditional ideas, formulas, and essences. The "new birth"

became something one could feel, like the heat from the sun or the sweat from a hard day's work. The religious service became either the heat of conception or the birthday celebration of those who were "born again."

The Great Awakening also served to democratize religion in America by fragmenting the religious "monopolies" and legitimatizing free expression of divergent beliefs. The ecclesiastical authority of the Congregationalists, Presbyterians, and Anglicans was shaken, and would never again return to the strict authoritarianism of the past. This was not England, and the radical antics of the Awakening revivalists demonstrated the extent, latitude, and direction of religious tolerance in America. In a true sense, the Awakening laid part of the groundwork for the civil liberties which would be written into the Constitution a few years later; the religious democratization which took place during the 1740s foreshadowed the political democratization which was to occur in the 1770s and thereafter.

To be sure, the exact relationship of the Great Awakening and the American Revolution has been the subject of a great deal of controversy. In sharp contrast to the Heimert position referred to in the beginning of this chapter, Herbert W. Schneider comes to the conclusion that the philosophy which rationalized the break with England "came not from Puritanism, but from contemporary English liberalism and Deism."[65] Although Deism and English

---

63. *Religious Enthusiasm and the Great Awakening*, ed. Lovejoy, pp. 13-14.

64. Chauncy, *Enthusiasm Described and Caution'd Against*, p. 14.

65. *The Puritan Mind* (Ann Arbor: University of Michigan Press, 1958), p. 197.

liberalism no doubt played an important role in the Revolution, they did not play an exclusive role as Schneider seems to suggest. Rather than excluding Puritanism and Calvinism, these new liberal doctrines blended with them. That the Revolution followed a season of Calvinistic individualism was not just chance. The doctrines of election and a personal spiritual relationship with God constitute a most powerful rationale for individualistic and revolutionary behavior. God and the "I," through divine decree and by divine power, can turn the world around. The God of Calvinism asserted the superiority of the elect individual over a corrupt society, asserted the superiority of a righteous minority over a tyrannical majority, and finally asserted the superiority of an oppressed English colony over an unfair and restrictive mother country.

BIBLIOGRAPHY

Two excellent biographies of Awakening revivalists:

Henry, Stuart C. *George Whitefield: Wayfaring Witness.* Nashville: Abingdon Press, 1957.

Miller, Perry. *Jonathan Edwards.* New York: William Sloane, 1949.

For two different interpretations of the theological issues embedded in the colonial social setting, compare:

Heimert, Alan. *Religion and the American Mind.* Cambridge: Harvard University Press, 1966.

Schneider, Herbert Wallace. *The Puritan Mind.* Ann Arbor: University of Michigan Press, 1958.

Two readily available collections of documents and sermons of the Great Awakening:

Heimert, Alan, and Miller, Perry. *The Great Awakening: Documents Illustrating the Crisis and Its Consequences.* New York: Bobbs-Merrill, 1967.

Lovejoy, David S. *Religious Enthusiasm and the Great Awakening.* Englewood Cliffs, N.J.: Prentice-Hall, 1969.

Both books contain excellent introductory essays, and the selection of documents is different in each. Taken together, they cover well the spectrum of material on both sides of all three issues.

Also of interest:

Collins, Edward. "The Rhetoric of Sensation Challenges the Rhetoric of the Intellect: An Eighteenth-Century Controversy." *Preaching in American History.* Edited by DeWitte Holland. Nashville: Abingdon Press, 1969.

A good analysis of the rhetorical issues.

Gaustad, Edward S. *The Great Awakening in New England.* New York: Harper, 1957.

A regional study covering all of the issues in context; written by a church historian.

Morgan, Edmund S. *Visible Saints: The History of a Puritan Idea.* New York: New York University Press, 1963.

A discussion of the ecclesiastical issue, especially from the viewpoint of church membership.

4

The Constitution in Debate

Robert Friedenberg

The Road to Philadelphia

"In all communities there must be one supreme power, and only one," contended Gouverneur Morris mere minutes after debate had opened in the Constitutional Convention. Morris, who was to be the most frequent speaker in the Convention, quickly perceived the essential issue that confronted the delegates. Would they create another government which, seeking to guarantee liberty to individual citizens and states, would weakly rest, as Morris claimed the Articles of Confederation did, "on the good faith of the parties"? Or, would the delegates, seeking to guarantee sufficient authority for a national government, create a supreme power? To the Constitutional Convention of 1787 fell the seemingly impossible task of forming a government which would resolve the conflict between providing for the liberties of individuals and states, and providing sufficient authority to maintain a sound government.

Few events in American history illustrate as clearly as does the Constitutional Convention that the real concerns of men in a free society are reflected in public address. By the summer of 1787 the concern of many Americans was with their govern-ment. Eleven years earlier, scant days after it had appointed a committee headed by Thomas Jefferson to draft a Declaration of Independence, the Continental Congress appointed another committee, headed by John Dickinson, to prepare a form of government for the soon-to-be independent colonies. The Articles of Confederation that Dickinson's committee drafted were shortly adopted by the Continental Congress, and sent to the various states for their approval. Yet, even before the last state had approved the Articles, perceptive Americans recognized their shortcomings.[1]

The Articles of Confederation represented the first attempt at resolving a uniquely American problem in government. In 1776 the Dickinson Committee was charged with preparing a government for a nation of self-reliant individuals who cherished their personal liberties. It was charged with preparing a government for a nation composed of thirteen former col-

---

1. Several states delayed ratification until all states with western land claims relinquished them to the central government. Hence, Maryland never formally approved of the Articles until March 1, 1781, although the exigencies of the period made the Articles operative almost immediately.

onies, each with its own new state government, and each jealous of maintaining its rights. While preserving the independence and liberty of these citizens and states, the Dickinson Committee had to create a government with sufficient authority to bind its citizens and states into a single nation. It was charged, in short, with creating a government which could establish a delicate equilibrium between liberty and authority. The Dickinson Committee failed.

The Dickinson Committee failed because it created Articles of Confederation with, as Alexander Hamilton prophetically warned, a "fundamental defect." That fundamental defect, Hamilton pointed out, "is a want of power in Congress."[2] The Articles had failed to find the delicate point of equilibrium between the liberty desired by individuals and states, and the authority necessary for a stable central government. The Articles were weighted excessively on the side of the individuals and states, to the detriment of the central government.

Though Hamilton was surely a Cassandra, perceiving and proclaiming the shortcomings of the Articles more quickly and more vehemently than his countrymen, his lone voice soon became one in a growing chorus. Essentially, Hamilton was correct when he claimed (in 1780) that "the fundamental defect is a want of power in Congress." Although the Articles provided that "every State shall abide by the determinations of the United States in Congress assembled," there was no means of compelling the states to accept Congressional determinations.

By 1786 the nation faced grave financial problems as a result of Congress's inability to act without state cooperation. Congress's inability to act without state cooperation similarly created serious problems in foreign relations and commerce. Congress's inability to act without state cooperation also created concern that property rights were in jeopardy. These, and other difficulties precipitated by the Articles of Confederation have been thoroughly examined, and consequently need no additional development here.[3]

By 1786 the Virginia Legislature, cajoled into action by Madison, moved to resolve one of the problems created by the Articles. Virginia invited the other states to send delegates to a meeting in Annapolis on the first Monday of September, for the purpose of considering "how far a uniform system in their commercial relations may be necessary to the common interest and their permanent harmony."[4] The report of the Annapolis Convention, shaped largely by Hamilton and Madison, pointed out that commercial problems could hardly be remedied without consideration of the entire fabric of government. To that end the report called on the states to appoint commissioners,

2. Letter, Alexander Hamilton to James Duane, September 3, 1780, *The Papers of Alexander Hamilton*, ed. Harold C. Syrett (New York: Columbia University Press, 1962), 2:401-3.

3. The definitive history of this period is Merrill Jensen's *The New Nation: A History of the United States During the Confederation, 1781-1789* (New York: Alfred Knopf, 1950). Also see Jensen's *The Articles of Confederation* (Madison: University of Wisconsin Press, 1948). An older but highly reliable and recently reprinted study of this period is Andrew C. McLaughlin, *Confederation and the Constitution: 1783-1789.* (New York: Collier Books, 1962). The standard textbook treatment of this period, focusing on the consequence of the shortcomings of the Articles of Confederation can be found in Alfred H. Kelley and Winfred A. Harbison, *The American Constitution: Its Origins and Development* (New York: W. W. Norton and Co., 1963).

4. For a full development of the events preceding the Annapolis Convention, stressing the roles of Madison and Washington, see Chapter 2 of McLaughlin, *Confederation and Constitution.*

To meet at Philadelphia on the second Monday in May next, to take into consideration the situation of the United States, to devise such further provisions as shall appear to them necessary to render the constitution of the Federal Government adequate to the exigencies of the Union.[5]

In February of 1787 the only body legally sanctioned to alter the Articles of Confederation, the Congress, never mentioning the Annapolis Convention, tacitly acknowledged its inability to cope with the nation's growing problems by also calling on the states to send delegates to Philadelphia on the second Monday in May.

Neither the report of the Annapolis Convention, nor the Congressional resolution, specified how the Convention delegates should be selected. Hence the state Legislatures chose the delegates. The result was a Convention dominated by men who recognized the imbalance of the Articles of Confederation, and who sought to redress that imbalance by constructing a stronger central government. As John Roche suggests, "those who get appointed to a special committee are likely to be the men who supported the movement for its creation."[6]

Even when men whose sense of state loyalty transcended their feelings of nationalism or federalism were selected to attend the Convention, they did not go. Patrick Henry was the best known of this group, which also included Richard Henry Lee and George Clinton. Asked why he did not attend, Henry replied, "I smelt a rat."[7] Those who like Henry "smelt a rat," chose to bide their time. The Federalists took the initiative in Philadelphia. The state advocates would be heard at the ratification conventions.

"We hold these truths to be self-evident," wrote Thomas Jefferson in the second sentence of the Declaration of Independence. To the men who came to Philadelphia, there were self-evident truths. Truths which as Hamilton suggested, "are not to be rummaged for among old parchments or musty records." But rather, that can be found "written as with a sunbeam, in the whole volume of human nature."[8] Based on their classical studies, on more contemporary political theorists and history, and on their own experiences, the homogeneous group of nationalists who arrived in Philadelphia reflected the view of their countrymen that there were self-evident truths.[9] "The Founding Fathers believed," writes Martin Diamond, "that true knowledge of the good and bad in human conduct was possible, and that they themselves possessed sufficient knowledge."[10]

What were the self-evident truths that the delegates brought to Philadelphia? Essentially there were four. First, the delegates believed that the function of government is to work for the public good, the

5. Winton U. Solberg, *The Federal Convention and the Formation of the Union of American States* (Indianapolis: Bobbs-Merrill, 1958), pp. 58-59, for the Annapolis Convention Report.

6. John R. Roche, "The Founding Fathers: A Reform Caucus in Action," *American Political Science Review* 55 (December 1961):802. The same point is made by Stanley Elkins and Eric McKitrick, "The Founding Fathers: Young Men of the Revolution," *Political Science Quarterly* 76 (June 1961):212, and by Robert Schuyler, *The Constitution of the United States: An Historical Survey of its Formation* (New York: Macmillan, 1923), pp. 71-72.

7. Quoted in Schuyler, *Constitution of the United States*, p. 75.

8. Hamilton, "The Farmer Refuted," *Papers of Alexander Hamilton*, Syrett; 1:122.

9. For a full development of the concept of self-evident truths see Daniel J. Boorstin, *The Americans: The Colonial Experience* (New York: Vintage Books, 1958), pp. 153-59.

10. Martin Diamond, "Democracy and the Federalist: A Reconsideration of the Framer's Intent," *American Political Science Review* 53 (March 1959):56.

public happiness. Second, they believed that the best government is representative government, and the keystone of a representative government is a frequently elected Legislature. Third, they felt that though the Legislature was the keystone of government, good government also included a distinct Executive and Judiciary, all three of which should check one another. Finally, the delegates felt that good government is government by law, not by men.

That the function of government is to work for the public good, the public happiness, is a constantly repeated theme of the political writing of this period and particularly of the Convention delegates. George Mason gave this idea its classic expression in the Virginia Declaration of Rights when he wrote, "All government is or ought to be instituted for the common benefit, protection and security of the people, nation, or community: of all the various modes and forms of government, that is best which is capable of producing the greatest degree of happiness and safety."[11]

The Continental Congress, in which many Philadelphia delegates had participated, resolved that "a reverence for our great Creator, principles of humanity, and the dictates of common sense, must convince all those who reflect upon the subject, that government was instituted to promote the welfare of mankind, and ought to be administered for the attainment of that end."[12] James Wilson believed that "all government is founded on the consent of those who are subject to it: such consent was given with a view to ensure [sic] and encrease [sic] the happiness of the governed. . . The consequence is, that the happiness of the society is the first law of every government."[13]

It has been suggested that the delegates

to the Constitutional Convention were not concerned with providing for the public good and happiness, but rather for their own good and happiness, through the protection of their economic interests.[14] To suggest that personal gain was the paramount motive in the minds of the delegates to the Constitutional Convention is a totally untenable position.[15] Uppermost in

11. See the "Virginia Declaration of Rights," in *Documents of American History*, ed. Henry Steele Commager (New York: Appleton-Century-Crofts, 1963), 1:103.

12. Worthington C. Ford, ed. *Journal of the Continental Congress*, (Washington: Government Printing Office, 1908), 2:140.

13. Quoted in Clinton Rossiter, *Seedtime of the Republic* (New York: Harcourt, Brace and World, 1953), p. 428.

14. The classic statement of this position is Charles Beard's *An Economic Interpretation of the Constitution of the United States* (New York: Macmillan, 1962). This book was first published in 1913.

15. This suggestion has been made by Beard and his followers. However, such a view does not seem justifiable. Nowhere in the papers of the men who played a major role in calling the Convention is there any evidence to support a claim that they were calling the Convention to advance their own interests. Hence, to accept the Beard position is to suggest that some sort of conspiracy was going on. A conspiracy which was so deep that nowhere in their private letters to one another did the conspirators ever mention it. Moreover, research by men such as Forrest McDonald and Robert Brown makes the Beard position untenable. Recent scholarship has charged, and documented, major shortcomings in Beard's research. Brown, whose study *Charles Beard and the Constitution* (Princeton University Press 1956) is the most thorough indictment of Beard, has clearly illustrated the total lack of correlation between the holdings of the delegates to the Convention, and their behavior toward the Constitution. Additionally, if Beard's charges are correct, and the Constitution was the outgrowth of a conspiracy by the rich who sought to secure and advance their economic position, it is hardly likely that it would have been ratified, as the poorer classes were in control of several states. The ratification debates in Massachusetts, Brown points out, are particularly instructive in this regard.

the minds of the delegates was the desire to form a government which would provide for the public good and happiness.

The second self-evident truth the delegates brought to Philadelphia was a deep belief in representative government. For them, representative government was the government best able to secure the public good. Hobbes, Locke, and Montesquieu who had so impressed Madison, all expressed this idea and were well known by the delegates.

The keystone of such a government, the Convention members believed, was a frequently elected Legislature. The Maryland Declaration of Rights states this view most succinctly. "The right of the people to participate in the Legislature is the best security of liberty, and the foundation of all free government."[16] James Wilson found free elections to be "the point of last consequence to all free governments."[17]

But governments need more than frequently elected Legislatures. Governments also require a separate Executive and Judicial branch, all three able to check one another. This was the third self-evident truth.

George Mason felt that the Legislative, Executive, and Judicial powers should be separate and distinct,[18] and many of the state constitutions which the delegates to Philadelphia had helped to write, deliberately spelled out the separation of the branches of government. Particularly notable in this respect was the state constitution of Massachusetts, written largely by John Adams, and universally acknowledged to be the finest of the state constitutions.[19]

The last of the self-evident truths that the delegates brought to Philadelphia was a belief in the sanctity of written laws: the desire for a government of laws, not men. During the revolutionary period, Thomas Paine had dramatized this belief:

But where, say some, is the king of America? I'll tell you friend, he reigns above, and doth not make havoc of mankind, like the Royal Brute of Great Britain. Yet that we may not appear to be defective even in earthly honors, let a day be solemnly set apart for proclaiming the charter... let a crown be placed thereon, by which the world may know, that so far as we approve of monarchy, that in America *THE LAW IS KING*. For as in absolute governments the king is law, so in free countries the law *ought* to *BE* king, and there ought to be no other.[20]

John Dickinson believed the most important right of any people was to have "a share in their own government, by their representative chosen by themselves, and in consequence of being ruled by *laws* which they themselves approve, not by the edicts of men of whom they have no control."[21]

Their education in the classics, political theory, history, and law, their experiences under Britain during the Revolution, and after, made the group of men who converged on Philadelphia in May of 1787 rather homogeneous in their political

16. Benjamin Poore, ed. *The Federal and State Constitutions, Colonial Charters and other Organic Laws of the United States* (Washington: Government Printing Office, 1878, 1:818.

17. Quoted in Rossiter, *Seedtime of the Republic*, p. 390,

18. See the "Virginia Declaration of Rights," *Documents*, Commager, 1:103-4.

19. During the Convention Adams was serving as the Ambassador to England, while Jefferson was Ambassador to France. However their views, particularly those of Adams who had recently published a study of Constitutions, were well known to the delegates. Indeed, Adams' "Thoughts on Government," originally written as a letter to George Wythe, is perhaps the best short statement of American Political philosophy of this period.

20. Thomas Paine, *The Complete Writings of Thomas Paine*, ed. Philip Foner (New York: Citadel Press, 1945), 1:99.

21. Quoted in Rossiter, *Seedtime of the Republic* p. 398.

thought. They generally agreed on the function of government, on the desirability of a representative Legislature, on the need for three distinct branches of government able to check one another, and on the importance of establishing a government of laws, not men. These were the large ends which they hoped to secure at Philadelphia.

The Methods Used in Philadelphia

The delegates to the Constitutional Convention made a clear and conscientious commitment to decision by debate. That commitment is distinctly reflected in both the rules adopted by the Convention, and those it rejected. In adopting the rules that governed their proceedings, the delegates were giving themselves maximum opportunity to change their opinions, if in the course of the debate they felt that such a change was necessary or desirable.[22]

The best known rule of the Convention, virtually the only one mentioned in most accounts of the Convention, is the secrecy rule, or more precisely, the three rules which provide:

That no copy be taken of any entry on the Journal during the sitting of the House without the leave of the House.

That members only be permitted to inspect the Journal.

That nothing spoken in the House be printed, or otherwise published, or communicated without leave of the House.[23]

The motive for such regulations is clear. The Convention was attempting to provide for a completely free exchange of ideas. George Mason no doubt summarized the delegates' thinking in a letter written two days before the secrecy rules were passed:

It is expected our doors will be shut, and communications upon the business of the Convention be forbidden during its setting. This I think myself a proper precaution to prevent mistakes and misrepresentation until the business shall have been completed, when the whole may have a very different complexion from that in which the several crude and indigested parts might in their first shape appear if submitted to the public eye.[24]

The secrecy rules would protect the delegates from later being held responsible for any remarks they might individually make in the Convention. Their responsibility would be a collective one, for the entire document. Secrecy would insure candor in debate. Subsequent remarks, particularly those of Hamilton, indicate that Mason's thinking was typical of the Convention.[25]

The secrecy rules are by no means the only rules which reflect the Convention's commitment to debate. The delegates decided that "a member shall not speak oftener than twice, without special leave, upon the same question; and not the second time, before every other, who had been silent, shall have been heard, if he choose to speak, upon the subject."[26] This rule provided that everyone would have an opportunity to express his opinion on the topic. No one or two men would be able to dominate the discussion, to the exclusion of

22. The rules of the Convention reflect what one of its students calls the delegates' "Spirit of Rational Inquiry." See Paul Eidelberg, *The Philosophy of the American Constitution* (New York: The Free Press, 1968), pp. 34-35.

23. "Journal of the Federal Convention," in *The Records of the Federal Convention of 1787*, ed. Max Farrand (New Haven: Yale University Press, 1937), 1:5.

24. Letter, George Mason to George Mason Jr., May 27, 1787, in *The Life of George Mason*, ed. Kate Mason Rowland (New York: Russell & Russell 1964), 2:103-04.

25. For Hamilton's comments, see his "Reply to Anonymous Charges," in *Records of the Federal Convention*, Farrand 3:368.

26. "Journal of the Federal Convention," in *Records of the Federal Convention*, Farrand, 1:8.

others. This rule insured that everyone would be heard. Moreover, the Convention decided "that Committees do not sit whilst the House shall be, or ought to be, sitting."[27] Not only would everyone be able to speak, but the work of the Convention would not draw members off the floor. Committee work would never interfere with debate.

Other rules passed by the Convention provided the delegates with the means to reconsider decisions. The Convention bound itself to majority rule. However, in doing so it sought to provide a means of revising its decisions. An initial decision could be wrong. Subsequent events, greater reflection, new or more accurate information, all could alter opinion and fuel new arguments. The Convention did not wish to be bound to its first decision if later debate cast doubt on that decision. This was a commitment to decision by the highest quality of debate, regardless of how long it took to achieve that quality.

One of the rules rejected by the Convention also indicates the Convention's desire to maximize the opportunity for fruitful debate. The Wythe Committee, which drew up the Convention rules, recommended that any member of the Convention should be allowed to call for the yeas and nays and have them entered on the minutes.[28] King and Mason spoke against this motion. King objected because he felt that "changes of opinion would be frequent in the course of business."[29] Consequently, he did not want to bind the members to prior decisions. Similarly, Mason added "that such a record of the opinions of members would be an obstacle to a change of them on conviction, and in case of its being hereafter promulged must furnish handles to the adversaries of the result of the meeting."[30] No

one defended the Committee report, and this proposed rule was rejected.

In some respects the Convention's rejection of this rule is similar to their passage of the secrecy rules. In rejecting this rule, as in approving the secrecy rules, the delegates were providing for candor in debate. No delegate would be held responsible for his individual actions. No obstacle would be put in the path of any who might change his mind as the debates progressed. The effects of debate were being given a maximum opportunity to work. Thus, the rules of the Convention indicate that, though delegates arrived in Philadelphia uncommitted to any specific plan of government, they were firmly committed to the method by which they would build government. Theirs would be decisions through debate.

The Clash in Philadelphia

The conflict between liberty and authority, the liberty desired by states and individuals, and the authority required to run a nation smoothly, is reflected in virtually every one of the almost forty major propositions which were debated in the Constitutional Convention. This point can be well illustrated by focusing on three major debates that developed in the Convention.

The first Convention debate was over the proposition:

Resolved: That the House of Representatives should be chosen by the people of the several states.

---

27. *Ibid.*, 1:16.

28. James Madison, "Notes on the Proceedings of the Federal Convention of 1787," in *Records of the Federal Convention*, Farrand, 1:10. (Hereafter Madison's notes will be cited as Madison, "Notes," with the volume and page numbers referring to the Farrand edition.)

29. *Ibid.*

30. *Ibid.*

This proposal was offered by Randolph in the plan which bears his name, and served as the starting point for debate on May 29. It was first seriously debated two days later. George Mason and James Wilson were the major affirmative speakers. Elbridge Gerry and Roger Sherman were the primary negative speakers, who offered an alternative to popular election of the House of Representatives. They sought to have that body elected by the state Legislatures.

While the full development of this debate has been traced elsewhere,[31] and need not be duplicated here, it is important to recognize why popular election of the House of Representatives prevailed. It prevailed, because along with state legislative selection of the Senate, it represented a reasonable means of attaining an equilibrium between liberty and authority.

This conclusion is reinforced by the arguments used in the Convention. Advocates of popular election of the House felt such an election would lend prestige, stability, and strength to the national government. Wilson suggested that he "was for raising the Federal pyramid to a considerable altitude, and for that reason wished to give it as broad a basis as possible. No government could long subsist without the confidence of the people."[32] Similarly, Madison felt that the government "would be more stable and durable if it should rest on the solid foundation of the people themselves."[33] The Congress established under the Articles of Confederation was selected by and responsible to the states. Hence, the government lacked the authority to control the states. Madison and Wilson were in effect arguing that a federal government selected by the people would be built on a much broader foundation, and deservedly acquire greater authority. As the debate grew heated, Wilson incisively

cut to the heart of the argument. He contended that the new government needed vigorous authority, "and that could only come from the source of authority, the people."[34]

Though negative speakers such as Elbridge Gerry initially suggested that the people could not make wise decisions, they soon dropped this argument. Instead, they submitted that the House of Representatives should be chosen by state Legislatures in order to insure state cooperation with the new government.[35] Gerry, and other negative speakers, seemed fearful that the states would lose their liberty unless they could control the new government. State legislative selection of the House of Representatives offered a means of such control.

The affirmative position prevailed. The imbalance created by the Articles of Confederation which granted excessive liberties to the states was being corrected. The new government would not be dependent on the states. Its authority would be derived from the people and hence be greater than the authority granted Congress under the Articles of Confederation.

Many delegates feared that the pendulum might be tipping too heavily toward an authoritarian central government. They were determined that the second house of the Legislature be selected by the state Legislatures. The first major debate involving the Senate developed over the following proposition:

---

31. Robert Friedenberg, "Toward a More Perfect Union: An Analysis of the Debates in the Constitutional Convention of 1787," (Ph.D. diss., Temple University, 1970).
32. Madison, "Notes," 1:49.
33. *Ibid.*, 1:50.
34. *Ibid.*, 1:132.
35. *Ibid.*, 1:137.

Resolved: That the Senate of the United States should be chosen by the state Legislatures.

Affirmative speakers favoring this procedure for selecting the Senate offered many arguments. But, running through every day's debate on this topic was the argument clearly presented by George Mason almost as soon as the debate opened. The state Legislatures, he claimed, "ought to have some means of defending themselves against the encroachments of the National Government."[36] A Senate elected by the state Legislatures, argued Oliver Ellsworth, would secure state cooperation with the federal government, cooperation he felt the federal government would surely need, while providing as Mason repeatedly argued in these debates, that the states have a means of self defense against the federal government.[37]

Negative speakers, who supported popular election of the Senate, as well as the House, argued that the states had nothing to fear from the federal government. Wilson, the chief negative speaker, felt that the federal government had much to fear from the states. He defended popular election of the Senate to give the federal government strong authority, since its power would be derived from the people.[38] But Wilson's position did not prevail.

While other arguments entered into the debates over the mode of selecting members of the national Legislature, these two crucial provisions of the new Constitution were shaped largely by the delegates' attempts to establish an equilibrium between liberty and authority. Reacting to the excessive liberties granted the states under the Articles of Confederation, the Convention rested one house of the Legislature on the people, thus granting the Congress a source of authority not granted it under the Arti-

cles of Confederation. Yet, fearful that Congressional authority might run rampant, this authority was tempered by allowing the states the opportunity to select the Senate. The new national Legislature found the equilibrium between liberty and authority that was missing under the Articles of Confederation.

The structuring of the office of President also indicates the Convention's attempts to balance liberty and authority. While all the debates involved in structuring that office cannot be discussed here, the most crucial of these debates, and perhaps the most frustrating debate the delegates experienced during the entire summer, illustrates again the Convention's attempt to balance liberty and authority. This debate involved the method of electing the President:

Resolved: That the President shall be elected by special electors selected by the state Legislatures.

No less than seven different methods for selecting the President were advanced in the Convention.[39] Only four, however, received serious attention. The debates over these means of selecting the President reflect the Convention's desire to balance liberty and authority.

The first alternative which received considerable support in the Convention, from men like Randolph and Mason, was Congressional election of the President. How-

---

36. *Ibid.*, 1:155.

37. *Ibid.*, 1:406-07.

38. *Ibid.*, 1:151-54.

39. In addition to use of an electoral college, the Convention heard suggestions that the President might be elected by state Legislatures, by the Congress, by popular vote of the people, by the executives of the states, by a group of Congressmen drawn at lot, and by Congress, voting from a list of candidates, one from each state, elected popularly by each state.

ever, this alternative was ultimately rejected because it robbed the President of any authority. It made him, argued Morris and Madison, a servant of the Legislature.[40] In order to redress the imbalance created by the Articles it was necessary to give the entire new government authority. It was also necessary to give authority to *each* branch of that government. As previously indicated, the delegates believed in the separation of powers. Congressional election of the President would have blended powers, and deprived the President of authority.

The second alternative which received considerable support in the Convention, primarily from Wilson, was the use of popularly elected electors to select the President. Though many arguments were presented against this position, two stand out. Wilson's position was continually attacked on the basis, first, that the people could not make a wise decision, and second, that popularly selected electors would bear the same relation to the people as their popularly elected state Legislatures. This being the case, it was argued that the Legislatures, not a new and confusing body of electors, should elect the President.[41]

Wilson's proposal would have made the President far less dependent on the states than would election by the state Legislatures. It would have granted him greater authority, for like the House of Representatives, he could claim to be the true representative of the people. Aware of the many powers to be vested in the President, including that of Commander-in-Chief, the Convention hesitated to grant him such authority.

The third alternative, hinted at by Gerry and Williamson, was that the President be elected by the state Legislatures.[42] Such a method of election would limit the new

President. He would be dependent on and be constantly courting the state Legislatures. He would, like Congress under the Articles of Confederation, find himself constantly trying to appease the states. Thus this alternative was rejected.

However, if the state legislators were to select an independent group of Presidential electors, the President would not be overly dependent on the Legislatures. His authority would not be undermined. Yet, the states would still have a voice, though perhaps one step removed, in the selection of the President. State liberty would not be in serious jeopardy. The Electoral College represents the Convention's attempt at balancing liberty with authority in the office of the presidency. Moreover, this method also provided, what Morris called "the indispensable necessity of making the Executive independent of the Legislature,"[43] for nowhere in the selection procedure would the national Legislature, the Congress, take part.

Virtually all of the almost forty propositions debated in the Constitutional Convention illustrate that the delegates were trying to balance authority and liberty. This overriding issue appears again and again in the records of these debates. That the Convention found an equilibrium is attested to by the success of the American Constitution.

Characteristics of Convention Debate

Four characteristics of Convention debate warrant our attention. First, debate in the

---

40. Madison, "Notes," 2:52-56.
41. Madison, "Notes," 1:81.
42. *Ibid.*, 1:80.
43. *Ibid.*, 2:500. Ironically, although the Electoral College was designed to provide the State Legislatures a measure of control over the President by allowing them to select his electors, within a few years of 1789 most State Legislatures established popular election of the Electoral College. This in effect implemented Wilson's suggestion.

Constitutional Convention was of the plan-counterplan variety. Second, those positions which prevailed in the Convention were the most ably advocated. Third, by current standards the use of evidence in the Constitutional Convention was poor. Finally, there appears to have been little teamwork among the speakers of the Constitutional Convention.

The debates in the Constitutional Convention were not typical policy debates. They did not involve one side presenting a rationale and program for change, and another side defending the presumption of the *status quo*. At the Constitutional Convention no one had the presumption. None of the advocates wished to support the *status quo* and continue the existing state of affairs. Rather, as indicated previously, for several years before the Convention there was a growing recognition of the need to change the form of government. The Convention was, itself, the culmination of that recognition. Hence, the Constitutional Convention was marked by a clear presumption for a change, but not in favor of any particular change.[44]

In such situations, debates never focus on the need or advantages for change, as both parties already concur in them. Rather, the debate focuses over the means of change. This is what happened at the Convention. Thus, debating in the Constitutional Convention was essentially of the plan-counterplan type.

Secondly, though a detailed analysis of the debates of the Constitutional Convention is not permitted within the limitations of this chapter, such analysis clearly indicates that those positions which prevailed in the Constitutional Convention, and hence manifested themselves in the Constitution of the United States, were more ably advocated than those positions which they defeated.[45] Advocates of the prevailing positions generally built sounder cases for their positions, and were considerably better than their foes in rebuttal and refutation. While each of these statements may not be true of every one of the almost forty debates which developed during the Convention, there does appear to be a clear relationship between the better debating and the positions which prevailed in the Constitutional Convention.

Thirdly, by current standards, the speakers in the Constitutional Convention made poor use of evidence. Their speaking suffered from two deficiencies, when evaluated by current standards. First, they frequently lacked evidence. Second, when they did provide evidence, they frequently failed to cite its source, or otherwise qualify its reliability.

There seem to be several reasons for these shortcomings. First, much of the evidence used may well have been common knowledge in the Convention. Second, the high regard that these men held for each other may have caused them to accept one another's word at face value. The failure of speakers to question one another about evidence lends some support to this explanation. Third, perhaps the use of evidence during this period was simply not as important as it is today, and therefore the strict standards applied in judging evidence today may not be appropriate for evaluating the merits of Convention speakers.

---

44. See Austin Freeley, *Argumentation and Debate* (Belmont, Calif.: Wadsworth Publishers 1966), p. 32, for clarification of the term "presumption for change" as it is used in current debate theory.

45. See the final chapter of Friedenberg, "Toward a More Perfect Union."

John Dickinson well characterized the Convention's use of evidence when, on August 13, he cautioned his fellow delegates that "experience must be our only guide."[46] If the evidence used in the Convention can be considered indicative, the experiences of the delegates in their native areas, both as colonies and confederated states, made experience a major guide of the Convention. Second in importance were the experiences of other governments, primarily, though not exclusively, Britain's and the prior American experience with Articles of Confederation. The evidence used in the Convention confirms Rossiter's claim that "the men of 1787 were, in short, both dutiful wards of the past and creative makers of the future."[47] It also confirms the suggestion of one student of this period who writes that Americans of this era settled their problems "in the arena of experience."[48]

Finally, speaking in the Constitutional Convention was not marked by any appreciable teamwork among the delegates. Three factors emerge in an examination of Convention speaking which illustrate this lack of teamwork.

First, the debates of the Constitutional Convention were marked by a constant repetition of ideas. This repetition of ideas was engaged in by three, four, five, or more speakers all on the same day, frequently in speeches which followed on the heels of one another.[49] Such repetition is not the mark of a preplanned effort, or a coordinated team.

Second, there does not appear to be any division of speaking tasks among the members of the Convention, as might be expected of a coordinated team. Not only would such a division have tended to reduce repetition, but it might also have led to some specialization in speaking. Had there been teamwork, for example, perhaps Madison and Wilson would have been essentially rebuttalists, while, hypothetically, Mason and Franklin might have been exclusively constructive speakers. Certainly, had there been teamwork, we would expect to find certain types of speeches frequently being made by the same man. Yet, this was not the case. Additional evidence that there was no division of speaking tasks is gained by observing that the cooperation that did take place in the Convention seems spontaneous. We find that normally the second speaker simply provided additional evidence for a first speaker's arguments, which seems far more likely to be the result of spontaneous agreement than of preplanned effort.

Finally, no pattern develops among the speakers. We do not see the same group of speakers consistently aiding one another. One would hypothesize that if such assists did take place it would be among members of the same state delegation. The common interests of the state might cause delegates from the same state to work closely together. On some occasions, as during the debates on legislative representation, there was a tendency for this to be true. Yet, far too often for this hypothesis to hold up, delegations were split. Rufus King and

---

46. Madison, "Notes," 2:278.
47. Clinton Rossiter, *1787: The Grand Convention* (New York: Macmillan 1966):19.
48. Boorstin, *The Americans*, p. 154.
49. See, for example, Madison, "Notes," 1:132-37, 359, 468; and Madison, "Notes," 2:43, 53, 56, 235-37, 427-29. Also see *John Lansing, The Delegate from New York: Proceedings of the Federal Convention of 1787 from the Notes of John Lansing*, ed. Joseph Strayer (New York: Kennikot Press 1967), p. 76.

Elbridge Gerry consistently split the Massachusetts delegation. Hamilton rarely agreed with Robert Yates and Robert Lansing in the New York delegation. Luther Martin was frequently in disagreement with the remainder of Maryland's delegation. Franklin was often out of step with his colleagues from Pennsylvania, as on occasion was Wilson. In the Virginia delegation Mason and Randolph frequently disagreed with Madison. The number of divided votes in the Convention gives further evidence that, even among delegates from the same state, there were often sharp differences of opinion which no doubt contributed to the lack of teamwork evidenced in the Convention. Thus, all available evidence points to a lack of speaking teamwork in the Constitutional Convention.

Lessons of the Constitutional Convention

The Constitutional Convention of 1787 must be accorded a position as perhaps the most successful deliberative assembly ever convened. In three short months the fifty-five "demigods" of the Convention, as Jefferson referred to the delegates, created the equilibrium between liberty and authority which had proven so elusive. They created a form of government which provided for individual and state liberties while simultaneously providing the newly created federal government with sufficient authority to govern. The method of their creation was debate.

In the years since 1787 the Constitution has been amended twenty-four times. Each amendment represents an attempt to perfect better the equilibrium between liberty and authority. Each amendment was subject to the rigors of debate in deliberative assembly and the public conscience. In future years as this nation continues to perfect the equilibrium, the Constitution may well be subject to additional amendment. Hopefully, these amendments too will be subject to the rigors of debate.

Though committed to debate as its means of decision making, the Convention could have failed. The success of the Constitutional Convention resulted from many causes. One was surely the use of debate, but there were others.

Invariably one must return to the men. A debate can be only as good as the debaters. Virtually any deliberative body in this nation's history would be enhanced by the presence of members such as Edmund Randolph, George Wythe, Daniel Carroll, Rufus King, Oliver Ellsworth, Roger Sherman, and John Dickinson. Yet these men were only in the second rank of the Convention, which included James Madison, Benjamin Franklin, Gouverneur Morris, James Wilson, and Alexander Hamilton.

Few deliberative assemblies have ever counted so many outstanding men among their membership. Fewer still have ever had such ability distributed throughout the assembly. These men, as well as Charles Pinckney, his cousin Charles Cotesworth Pinckney, John Rutledge, James McHenry, Jared Ingersoll, Robert Morris, Elbridge Gerry, Nathaniel Gorham, George Read, William Paterson, Hugh Williamson, and John Langdon, were not scattered among a Senate of 100 members, or a House of Representatives of 435. They were not scattered among a state Legislature of hundreds, or a massive study commission. All of these men were in a group of only fifty-five delegates to the Convention.

The Convention's smallness and compactness contributed to its success for yet another reason. Because it was small, it made little use of committees. Votes were never made simply on the basis of a committee recommendation. Each issue was thoroughly debated by the entire Constitutional Convention. Sub-committees, which characterize deliberative assemblies today, were rarely used by the delegates at Philadelphia.

A fourth reason for the Convention's success can be found in its nationalistic outlook. This outlook was made possible, in large part, because the delegates did not have to contend with the pressures that today frequently face members of deliberative assemblies. With few exceptions, the delegates were not Virginians, New Hampshiremen, or Pennsylvanians. They were Americans. There was no representative from the Pennsylvania-New York farm belt, the New England shipping industry, or the southern tobacco lands. The delegates did not have to worry about being re-elected from such regions, nor were they bothered by lobbyists. These pressures, which so greatly affect members of deliberative assemblies today, affected the Convention only minimally.

The Convention was, however, subject to one strong pressure. It had to act. Perhaps the fifth cause for the Convention's success was the very real urgency and importance of its activities. These men were not altering a farm subsidy, appropriating money for a highway, or waiving a monopoly law for professional sports. The very existence of their nation demanded that they act. Urgency compelled attendance. Urgency caused members to study issues, rather than rely on a friend's judgment. Urgency prohibited bartering a vote on one issue, to secure a vote on another. Few deliberative assemblies in this nation's history have faced a crisis as grave as that faced by the Constitutional Convention. Perhaps the gravest of issues brings out the best in deliberative assemblies.

As the last delegates signed the Constitution, Benjamin Franklin, observing the sunburst painted on the back of the presiding officer's chair, turned to the delegates standing near him. "Painters had found it difficult," said Franklin, "to distinguish in their art a rising from a setting sun. I have, often and often in the course of the session, and the vicissitudes of my hopes and fears as to its issue, looked at that behind the President without being able to tell whether it was rising or setting: But now at length I have the happiness to know that it is a rising and not a setting sun."[50] If but one lesson is to be learned from the "Miracle at Philadelphia," where, as Franklin might suggest, perhaps the sun first rose on the American Republic, it may well be that public address, the healthy clash among ideas in deliberative assembly and public conscience is the most effective means of perfecting a free society.

BIBLIOGRAPHY

Bowen, Catherine Drinker. *Miracle at Philadelphia.* Boston: Little, Brown and Company, 1966.

  The most popular recent book on the Convention, and superbly written, though lacking in footnotes and other scholarly accessories.

Farrand, Max, ed. *The Records of the Federal Convention of 1787.* 4 vols. New Haven: Yale University Press, 1937.

  The indispensable volumes for any serious student of the Convention. Farrand has assembled not only the notes of Madison and the other delegates who kept accounts of the Convention, but also the official records, per-

50. Madison, "Notes," 2:648.

tinent letters, and many other useful basic materials. The Lansing notes, found after Farrand had published, are the major primary source not in Farrand.

Friedenberg, Robert. "Toward a More Perfect Union: An Analysis of the Debates of the Constitutional Convention of 1787." Ph.D. diss. Temple University, 1970.

Views the Convention as a series of debates and attributes the success of the Convention primarily to the quality of debate. Cf. Perkins below.

Jensen, Merrill. *The New Nation: A History of the United States During the Confederation, 1781-1789.* New York: Alfred A. Knopf, 1950.

Perhaps the most perceptive of recent studies. Jensen finds the Articles to have been a bit more serviceable than does McLaughlin (see below).

McLaughlin, Andrew C. *The Confederation and the Constitution, 1783-1789.* New York: Collier Books, 1962.

Portrays the Convention as the logical outgrowth of the deficient Articles. Cf. Jensen above.

Perkins, Lindsey. "The Convention of 1787: A Study of Successful Discussion," *Western Speech* 18 (October 1954), 213-22.

Attributes the success of the Convention to its utilization of group discussion principles. Cf. Friedenberg above.

Rossiter, Clinton. *1787: The Grand Convention.* New York: Macmillan, 1966.

A sound recent book.

Among other valuable secondary studies are:

Crosskey, William. *Politics and the Constitution in the History of the United States.* 2 vols. Chicago: University of Chicago Press, 1953.

Eidelberg, Paul. *The Philosophy of the American Constitution.* New York: Free Press, 1968.

Farrand, Max. *The Fathers of the Constitution.* New Haven: Yale University Press, 1921.

———. *The Framing of the Constitution of the United States.* New Haven: Yale University Press, 1913.

Warren, Charles. *The Making of the Constitution.* 1928. New York: Barnes and Noble, 1967.

5   The Tariff, Slavery, and Politics, 1828-1833

John L. Sullivan

Every four years from 1816 to 1832 congressmen returned to Washington to discuss major revisions in the nation's tariff policy. When the question arose again in December, 1827, almost all parties gathered at the nation's capitol recognized that a major change was occurring in the nature of the debate over that question. John C. Calhoun's decisive vote against the Woolens Bill at the end of the preceding session had only increased agitation for a protective tariff, central tenet in Henry Clay's American System. The pro-tariff Harrisburg Convention which had met several months earlier upset two important political groups despite its protestation that the meeting was entirely nonpolitical. In the cotton South Thomas Cooper had already questioned the "value of the union" under a protective tariff; the Harrisburg Convention only intensified the feelings he had aroused.[1] Andrew Jackson's leading supporters saw the tariff agitation as a political ploy designed to secure the presidency for John Quincy Adams. These two considerations, heretofore subordinate items at best during the tariff discussions, came to control consideration of the question during the period 1828-33. It is their introduction

and eventual ascendancy which makes the study of the debates particularly interesting to students of rhetoric. Of course neither party politics nor the dual question of states' rights and the South's domestic institution stopped senators and congressmen from discussing economic principles and practices during the Jacksonian period. Their introduction did, however, shift the tone and emphasis of the public disputes over the tariff. In effect the tariff issue became an occasion for their discussion. From a rhetorical standpoint what is significant about the tariff question is the manner in which two heretofore subsidiary concerns came to dominate the strategies of most of those engaged in its discussion. Why did the issue become an occasion for the discussion of concerns which the society considered more basic? How did these questions gain ascendancy? What meaning, if any, does this shift in emphasis, hold for our society today?

1. Thomas Cooper's "Value of the Union" Speech, Columbia, South Carolina, July 2, 1827, in *Niles Weekly Register*, 33 (September 8, 1827): 28-32. A portion of this address is reprinted in William W. Freehling, ed., *The Nullification Era, A Documentary Record* (New York: Harper Torchbooks, 1967), pp. 20-25.

Economics and the Tariff

While focusing on the tariff as an occasion for the discussion of other issues necessarily underplays certain basic economic considerations in the period 1828-33, there is justification for such an approach. Many of those involved in the 1828 discussion believed that political rather than economic concerns controlled the votes of congressmen.[2] Other factors also contributed to turn the debate away from economic principles and toward related issues. One of the major factors was the state of economic thought itself. It was easy enough to argue economic theory in ante-bellum America but next to impossible to accurately test assumptions predicated on those theories. Even "the experts" in the period quickly came to realize the difficulties inherent in discussing such a question. Often they criticized leading economic texts as "too abstruse to be easily comprehended by the unphilosophical mind" and scored the lack of accurate information necessary for economic analysis.[3]

Political rather than economic principles captivated speakers in the 1820's and 1830's. Orators were much more comfortable discussing politics than when called on to evaluate their theories by practical application. Their models, Demosthenes, Cicero, and Quintilian provided few examples of how to deal accurately with the economic complexities of an issue like the tariff. Many of the speakers were neither equipped to handle the intricacies of economic analysis nor were they trained to admire such rhetoric when and if found. As James Buchanan said, "Even if I were able, upon any occasion to be eloquent, Heaven defend me from such objects as hemp and molasses! Of all themes for rhetorical effect, they are the very worst."[4]

Encumbered by complex economic theories, unable to obtain accurate statistics, and unskilled at adapting such material to their audiences, public spokesmen might have been expected to turn to other considerations. Debating the tariff during the period 1828-1833 was made even more difficult by yet another factor. Most, if not all, of the classical economic arguments available had been offered by the debate over the Tariff of 1824 and had failed either to firmly establish or to bring about complete rejection of a protective policy. The protective policy at best had led a precarious existence during the late teens and early twenties. Leading politicians had been on both sides of the issue and often their protective professions were countered by the low duties they established. On occasion the protective tariff suffered as much from the narrow sectional outlook of its supporters as it did from the opposition. Proponents simply had difficulty voting to protect items produced outside their section of the country despite their protestations that they favored a nationalistic policy.

As the ready fund of economic arguments was exhausted without effect, one might expect tensions to grow higher when the topic was again taken under consideration. A brief look at the debates prior to 1828 adds support to the exhausted argument theory. The strong nationalistic

2. Gales and Seaton's *Register of Debates*, vol. 4, pt. 2, Twentieth Congress, First Session, April 23, 1828:2472; *Niles Weekly Register*, 34 (April 26, 1828):137.

3. Joseph Dorfman, *The Economic Mind in American Civilization*, (New York: Augustus M. Kelley, 1966), 2:512-13; *The Banner of the Constitution*, December 5, 1829; *Niles Weekly Register* 33 (October 13, 1827): 100; *Niles Weekly Register* 41 (February 25, 1832): 467.

4. *Register of Debates*, vol. 4, pt. 2, Twentieth Congress, First Session April 2, 1828, 2090.

movement which emerged during and after the War of 1812 numbered John C. Calhoun among its leading exponents. That movement gave the nation its first protective tariff, in part to rescue American industry from its depressed state and also to assure that in the event of another war America would have the materials necessary to conduct it successfully. The British, on the other hand, pursued a policy designed to "glut" the American market "to stifle in the cradle those rising manufactures in the United States which the war had forced into existence contrary to the usual course of things."[5] Before the nation had a chance to evaluate the effects of the Tariff of 1816, organized agitation began for a higher tariff. The depression of 1819 gave added impetus to the tariff forces. In 1820 Henry Baldwin, The Chairman of the House Committee on Manufactures, presented a revised tariff policy designed both to gain revenue for relief of the public debt and for the protection of American industry. Supported by Henry Clay, committee members argued that infant industries required protection. They claimed that an improved manufacturing interest would aid the advancement of both agriculture and commerce. Not only would the tariff create home markets, they asserted, but also it would promote independence by forcing the nation to supply its own food, clothing, and means of defense. The protariff forces also promised lower prices as a long term result of their policy. Additionally, they contended that only by a protective tariff policy could America free itself from British dominance. Finally they pointed out that the tariff would present an additional source of revenue for the nation.

Opposition to the tariff of 1820 came primarily from southern planters and the eastern shipping and mercantile interests. Their representatives attributed both economic and social ills to a protective policy. They denied a causal relationship between a protective tariff and economic improvement. The disadvantages of such a policy far outweighed the advantages. The benefits of a protective tariff, they claimed, were at best temporary; the evils it might inflict were disastrous. Arguing that a nation will always do what it does best, they asserted that the country would best be served by remaining predominantly agricultural. Most importantly the antiprotective tariff forces viewed an increased tariff as a tax on consumers in general to benefit a particular class, the manufacturers, whom they believed were entitled to no special aid.

Congress discussed the merits of the Tariff of 1824 for nearly three months. The debate in the House produced one of the best exchanges on the issue during the period 1816-33 as Henry Clay and Daniel Webster clashed over the nature and value of a protective system.[6] As Clay developed the need argument he described "diminished exports," a "depressed" shipping industry, "diminished" commerce, "successive crops of grain perishing" for want of a market, tight currency, "numerous bankruptcies," low wages and unemployment,

---

5. Speech of Henry Brougham, April 9, 1816, in Edward Stanwood, *American Tariff Controversies in the Nineteenth Century* (Boston: Houghton, Mifflin, 1904) 1:167-68. The speech can be found in *Niles Weekly Register*, (December 28, 1816):283-84. The description of the debates prior to 1828 which follows can be found in greater detail in Stanwood, *American Tariff Controversies*, 1:160-241.

6. Both of these speeches are reprinted in Frank W. Taussig, ed., *State Papers and Speeches on the Tariff* (Cambridge: Harvard University, 1893), pp. 252-385.

the "ravenous pursuit" of public office as a means of income, a growing and "perilous" use of paper money, and above all "the low and depressed" state of all forms of public property. The existing evils, Clay charged, were caused by the absence of legislation to encourage manufactures. As a solution he offered "the American System," a combined program of protective tariffs and internal improvements. Webster, then spokesman for the shipping interests, denied both the cause and effect relationship between the absence of a protective tariff and national distress, and the existence of the distress itself. Both he and Clay traded arguments on the validity of the "home market" thesis, the question of whether the American System was really a national policy or in fact a sectional one, the wage theory of labor, and the concept of balance of trade. In the latter case Webster employed a tactic which would serve him well when he became an advocate of the protective policy. Just as he redefined the terms in treating the balance of trade theory to fit his contentions, so too would he employ this strategy of redefinition when meeting Hayne in their famous debate six years later. Webster's brief treatment of the constitutional aspects of the tariff, while playing a minor part in the exchange with Clay, would plague him when he became an advocate of the system in 1828.

Few of the remarks in the Senate over the Tariff of 1824 matched those in the House, but in the light of future events the speech of Senator Robert Hayne deserves special attention. Not only did Hayne enter a "solemn protest" against the tariff in the "name of Liberty and the Constitution" but also he articulated the growing inflexibility on the question which would mark

Carolina's posture in the years to follow. "I wish it to be distinctly understood," he asserted, "that we will not hold ourselves bound to maintain the system, and if capitalists, will, in the face of our protests, and in defiance of our solemn warnings, invest their fortunes in pursuits, made profitable at our expense, on their own hands be the consequences of their folly."[7] For Hayne and a significant number of Southerners the question of advantage-disadvantage had been resolved.

Although the Tariff of 1824 had been discussed by "some of the ablest men" the country had produced, and "almost all the arguments" pertaining to it had been urged, "preconceived opinions" and sectional interests still dominated.[8] The economic arguments had been offered and still men would not be moved. Since the debaters were unable to test the theories offered, the question remained an academic one. Congressmen began to despair of removing the causes which led their opponents to "shut out the light," to resist the truth, and which "rendered argument useless."[9] Searching for explanations for their failure, both pro-tariff and anti-tariff men examined the motives of their opponents. In the years following 1824, simplistic and potentially dangerous explanations emerged. Reacting to the complexity and ambiguity of the tariff question, speakers began to think in terms of stereotypes, personalization, and oversimplification. The symbols they created as a result further oversimplified and distorted the issue. In their efforts to find a logical rationale for

---

7. *Speech of Mr. Hayne of South Carolina, Against the Tariff Bill. . . April, 1824* (Charleston: A. E. Miller, 1824), pp. 40, 41.

8. *Ibid.*, pp. 3-4.

9. *Ibid.*, p. 4.

their failure and to justify their own position, politicians looked for simple cause and effect relationships to solve the complexities of the tariff question. They were encouraged to ddo so by the very nature of their constituencies. If a question like the tariff confounded the experts, how was the average voter expected to understand it?[10]

Politics and the Tariff

Lack of coordination and narrowness of vision among the pro-tariff forces also contributed to turning the debates of 1828 to political considerations. Other conditions likewise made it possible for politics to dominate those debates. Embroiled in a bitter political campaign, Andrew Jackson had much to lose by debating the tariff question. He numbered among his supporters strong anti-tariff men like George McDuffie and Robert Hayne; in states like Pennsylvania hosts of protectionists flocked to his banner. To neutralize the issue the General's supporters denied its importance. After all the tariff would "undergo full discussion and consideration," a Jacksonite urged, "and be settled by the sober and enlightened sentiments of the country" no matter who won.[11] In short, questions of economic policy had no place in presidential elections. While professing high-mindedness on the tariff, Jacksonites were convinced their opponents hoped to use the question to further their political aims. Robert Hayne warned Jackson that Henry Clay planned to "convert the whole system of internal improvement and the tariff into a political engine" and if possible "ride into power on these *popular Hobbies.*"[12]

Throughout the 1828 electoral campaign the General's supporters confidently came out on both sides of the question. "In a *tariff* state," an Adams man complained, "he is for the tariff and Domestic Manufactures"; in the states opposed to the policy his supporters claim he is against it.[13] Poor communications and the Jacksonite public position that the tariff was beyond party consideration made it difficult for the opposition to turn the question into a national campaign issue in 1828. But if Jacksonites were vague about the tariff as the election approached, Adams and Clay men were by no means united either on the kind or amount of protection they desired. If they officially adopted the report of the Harrisburg Convention as their program then they opened themselves to charges of politicalization; if they did not, then the issue was difficult to develop without a specific proposal. Consequently the section on the tariff in Adams Annual Message to Congress was as vague as Jackson's stand for judicious protection.[14]

When the Twentieth Congress finally gathered in late 1827, the avowed supporters of both Jackson and the administration could no longer hide their views. The audience and the scene were national, not

10. For one answer see Wilcomb Washburn, "The Great Autumnal Madness: Political Symbolism in Mid-Nineteenth Century America," *Quarterly Journal of Speech* 49 (December, 1963), 430.

11. Speech of Worden Pope at Fowler's Garden, Lexington, Kentucky, July 21, 1827, in Richmond *Enquirer*, August 21, 1827.

12. Robert Hayne to Andrew Jackson, Charleston, S.C. June 5, 1827, in John Spenser Bassett, ed., *Correspondence of Andrew Jackson*, 7 vols. (Washington: Carnegie Institution, 1928), 3:359-60. Hereafter referred to as *Jackson Correspondence.*

13. John P. Erwin to Josiah Johnston, Nashville, February 15, 1827, Josiah Johnston Papers, Historical Society of Pennsylvania, Philadelphia.

14. Louisville *Public Advertiser*, December 22, 1827.

regional. The time had arrived to turn abstract support for a "judicious" tariff into a concrete proposal. Northerners and westerners in both camps suspected each others' motives; southerners almost to a man opposed any protective tariff policy. In terms of rhetoric whether or not supporters of the two presidential hopefuls planned to capitalize politically by exploiting the issue is not the point, although some evidence exists that they did. What is central is that in the debate which ensued both camps sought to convince themselves and the general audience that their opponents were politically motivated. The debaters acted upon what they believed to be true—not upon what was true. They widened the gap between their rhetoric and reality by consistently attributing not only political motivation but also better organization and more solidarity of purpose to their opponents than actually existed. The two-valued orientation under which they operated only reinforced already polarized beliefs. The general feeling that the opposition operated upon narrow selfish political premises made discussion about substantive issues virtually impossible. Rather than attempting to change positions, speakers instead sought to reinforce existing attitudes.

One must be careful not to over-emphasize the importance of the belief in the dominance of political motivation. Many of those engaged in the discussions thought that a particular tariff policy did or could cause havoc in their section of the country. They simply could not muster evidence that would convince anyone but their own supporters. For many that was enough; as Philip Barbour explained, "if the Southern people *believed* themselves to be oppressed; it amounted to the same thing as if they *were* oppressed. . . ."[15] This dual sense of political intrigue and fear of economic harm, though supported only by circumstantial evidence at best, forced the debates to turn on questions which, if answered, still could not solve the tariff dilemma.

In control of the Twentieth Congress the first move belonged to the Jacksonites. The feeling that political considerations dominated the tariff question manifested itself almost immediately. The bill reported by the pro-Jacksonite Committee on Manufactures resembled a "pedlar's wagon" because of "the number and mixed character" of the items it covered.[16] From the viewpoint of the pro-tariff forces it looked like the Harrisburg Report as seen in a fun house mirror. Things were all out of shape. The bill catered to sectional interests and satisfied none. Hezekiah Niles called it "*a mockery of the public suffering.*"[17] For items like iron, molasses, hemp, flax, printed cotton and coarse wool, more protection was granted than desired, or in some cases, even asked for. On questions vital to the woolen manufacturers, however, the committee refused to grant the protectionists' requests. A wool grower himself, Congressman Isaac Bates argued that the proposal would "put the knife to the jugular vein of every sheep in the country" and destroy the woolen manufacturers. If the committee had asked for advice on how to frame a bill that could not possibly, pass, or if it could conceivably pass, should not give relief to the manufacturer or sheep raiser, they could not have found one "better suited" for that purpose.

---

15. *Niles Weekly Register* 41 (November 26, 1831):239.
16. *Register of Debates*, vol. 4, pt. 2, Twentieth Congress, First Session, April 14, 1828, p. 2318.
17. *Niles Weekly Register* 34 (March 15, 1828):34.

From the standpoint of the Jacksonites the bill was a master stroke.[18] It took the tactics of the Harrisburg Convention one step further. That meeting hoped to unite diverse industrial and agricultural interests to secure protection; the committee's bill sought to bind regional interests to secure an election.[19] Tariff historian Edward Stanwood called the discussion over the bill and its amendments which followed "wearisome and mutually exasperating," concluding that it was "as impossible as it would be fruitless to summarize the long and technical debates...."[20] Indeed the reading of the more than a thousand columns in the Register of Debates covering the issue represents an exercise in futility. Too many men were unprepared to listen to reason, too few to offer it. The already complex and difficult economic questions when mixed with political motivations all but obscured the great issues of the day. Congressmen preferred to oversimplify the issue, rather than to attempt to understand the complexities of the tariff. It simply was a case in which technological change outstripped decision making. Rather than trying to understand and analyze the changing nature of society which industrialism would bring, the representatives turned the debate into "a mere game of snatch." "Each interest," William Haile of Mississippi noted, struggled to "get the most for itself, by robbing from every other."[21] Some of the bitter exchanges which resulted left orators frustrated and politicians frightened. Trapped by self-interest, lack of knowledge, and their own rhetoric, all parties seemed fearful of reaching a solution and yet anxious to condemn their opponents for preventing one.[22]

The bill which the House and Senate finally approved resembled the committee's recommendations in all but a few details. One opposition member believed it was "incumbered" with most of "the original defects" as well as "other superadded evils, introduced by a majority composed of the friends of the original project and the avowed enemies of the whole system of protection."[23] Just as an observer had predicted party leaders struggled to "get rid of the responsibility" for the bill in anti-tariff areas, while taking credit for it in the pro-tariff districts. At least in the North and West the Jacksonite strategy had defused the tariff issue.[24] Adams men glumly blamed "Jacksonism and southern jealousy" for the bill's odious features and spent their time explaining away their votes for it.[25]

Somehow Jackson had managed to hide behind a "judicious" tariff throughout the debate in Congress. Now the election had to be won; the South needed to know where the General actually stood on the tariff. Along with their pledges of continued support Carolinians sent him pointed suggestions concerning his future

---

18. *Register of Debates*, vol. 4, pt. 2, Twentieth Congress, First Session, March 25, 1828, pp. 1-74.

19. Silas Wright to Azariah Flagg, April 7, 1828, in Robert V. Remini, *The Election of Andrew Jackson* (Lippincott: Philadelphia, 1963), p. 174.

20. Stanwood, *American Tariff Controversies,* 1:272, 73.

21. *Register of Debates*, vol. 4, pt. 2, Twentieth Congress, First Session, April 14, 1828, p. 2329.

22. Charleston *Courier*, April 15, 1828.

23. *Register of Debates*, vol. 4, pt. 2, Twentieth Congress, First Session, April 16, 1828.

24. Letter from Washington, February 20, 1828, *Kennebec Journal*, May 23 and 30, 1828.

25. *National Journal*, April 23, 1828; Charleston *Courier*, April 29, 1828; *Kennebec Journal*, May 30, 1828.

policy.[26] Among them John C. Calhoun expressed best "the better order of things" desired by Carolina: equal distribution of the burdens and benefits of government, payment of the public debt, and "the removal of oppressive duties."[27] Aware of Jackson's political dilemma one southerner warned him to "neither write nor express any positive opinion" on the question because he feared that a statement would produce "a schism" among his friends.[28] Still many found it difficult to maintain "a sullen silence" so essential to preventing such a break.[29] James Hamilton, Jr., George McDuffie, and Robert Barnwell Rhett all spoke angrily about the tariff prior to the election.[30]

Still more moderate voices managed to hold sway in Carolina despite the hard core secessionists already active in the state. Not until after the election did South Carolina and several of her sister states formally protest against the tariff question. In the *South Carolina Exposition* John C. Calhoun outlined the grounds which the South would take on the tariff question. He labeled the tariff both unfair and unconstitutional and affirmed the right of the people of a sovereign state to nullify such laws. When a state took such action, Calhoun explained, the law became null and void there until a remedy was reached. If no solution could be found the state could secede. For the present, he wrote, Carolina would postpone exercising her right so that Congress might right its unconstitutional acts and bring relief to the South.[31] Thus Calhoun removed the issue from the economic realm and placed it on the higher ground upon which American statesmen felt much more comfortable arguing.

However enticing to argue, questions of constitutionality could not deal with eco-

nomic reality. Those who favored direct action against the tariff believed a simple cause and effect relationship existed between it and the South's economic ills. It was and is easier, after all, to look for the causes of one's problems outside one's self. Although some few saw used-up lands, poor agricultural techniques, and inefficient planning and management at the heart of the South's dilemma, most preferred to pin the blame for all problems on the manufacturing interests in the North and their unfair tariff. "Either the tariff or the South must be prostrated," Thomas Cooper argued, "they cannot, will not, exist together."[32] Only a few recognized that southerners dependent "solely on the culture of cotton" would be in "a miserable situation" with or without the tariff if they failed to emulate northern manufacturers. But, as one communicator noted, "South-

26. James Hamilton, Jr. to Andrew Jackson, Washington, May 25, 1828, *Jackson Correspondence*, 3:404; Arthur Hayne to Jackson, Fort Moultrie, Sullivan's Island, S. C., September 20, 1828, *Jackson Correspondence*, 3:436; William W. Freehling, *Prelude to Civil War, The Nullification Controversy in South Carolina, 1816-1836* (New York: Harper and Row, 1968), pp. 141-44.
27. John C. Calhoun to Jackson, Pendleton, S.C., July 10, 1828, *Jackson Correspondence*, 3:414-15.
28. Col. Arthur Haynes to Andrew Jackson, Fort Moultrie, Sullivan's Island, S.C., September 20, 1828, *Jackson Correspondence*, 3:436.
29. James Hamilton, Jr. to Martin Van Buren, Fourt Moultrie, Sullivan's Island, S.C., September 7, 1828, Van Buren Papers, Library of Congress, microfilm ed. ser. 2, reel 7.
30. Freehling, *Nullification Era*, pp. 48-61; Freehling, *Prelude to Civil War*, pp. 147-49.
31. Richard Cralle, ed., *The Works of John C. Calhoun* (Charleston, S.C.: Walker and James, and New York: D. Appleton, 1854), 6:1-59.
32. Thomas Cooper to Martin Van Buren, Columbia, S.C., March 24, 1829, Van Buren Papers, Library of Congress, microfilm ed. ser. 2, reel 7.

ern Pride," "want of capital to [in] vest," and "want of skill" were "difficulties" not easily overcome.[33]

Jackson's election gave the South some reason to hope. Privately he had already told Carolina politico James Hamilton, Jr. that he regretted the discussion of the tariff "under the strong feelings of political excitement that pervaded the whole nation and Congress." In abstract and no doubt calculated terms Jackson expressed the hope that in the future the question could be deliberated "with an eye to the prosperity of the whole Union, and not of any particular part. . . ."[34] This was precisely the point the Carolinians had often made from the platform themselves. The new President was a Carolinian by birth, his Vice President had penned the *South Carolina Exposition*, Calhoun backer Samuel Ingham and southerners John Branch and John Berrien formed part of the cabinet—surely the South had reason to expect some relief.

Jackson's time for acting was limited, however, and the issue was far from being settled in Carolina's interest. One of Jackson's friends warned that the northern and eastern states could not "submit to have the doctrines of Mr. McDuffie imposed upon them." Jackson's own acts and those of his "immediate friends" at the next session of Congress would be important. Those who favored the tariff, he pointed out, would then unite around someone "consistent" with their "true interests."[35] If Jackson opposed it, another supporter argued, "a counter-revolution will be produced & H. Clay will, with his Black legs & all his other crimes be the next president."[36] If, however, the Twenty-First Congress failed to remove the tariff burden from the South, a Carolinian predicted,

"This state will prefer war, disunion, or anything else sooner than submission to a law that we conceive to be so unwise, unjust, unconstitutional and partial in its operations."[37] Caught on the horns of a dilemma Jackson and his advisors carefully sidestepped the issue in the Inaugural Message.

Jackson's message to Congress likewise offered little solace to those who viewed the tariff as an evil which must be immediately eradicated. Indeed one of the weaknesses of the hyperbolic rhetoric which pictured the South in ruins because of the tariff was that it effectively closed the door to all gradual solutions. However many southerners wished to free themselves of the tariff, and not all of them did, even the Carolinians were by no means united on how to accomplish that end. Several options were open to the Carolina members of Congress in 1830. Each of these options called for a different rhetorical strategy.[38]

---

33. Samuel Brown to Josiah S. Johnston, Philadelphia, March 4, 1828, Josiah Johnston Papers, Historical Society of Pennsylvania, Philadelphia. See also "A Cotton Purchaser to Enterprising Gentlemen of South Carolina in the Interior Country," Charleston *Courier*, March 4, 1828.

34. Andrew Jackson to James Hamilton Jr., Hermitage, June 29, 1828, *Jackson Correspondence*, 3:411.

35. Joshua Forman to Martin Van Buren, Albany, February 12, 1829, Van Buren Papers, Library of Congress, microfilm ed. ser. 2, reel 7.

36. Joel Penson to James K. Polk, Nashville, May 13, 1829, in Herbert Weaver, ed., *Correspondence of James K. Polk* (Nashville: Vanderbilt University Press, 1969), 1:262-63.

37. S. R. Townes to Gessner Harrison, Greenville Court House, S.C., October 6, 1828, Harrison Papers, University of Virginia Library, Charlottesville.

38. It is important to recognize that neither Calhoun nor the Carolina delegation as yet controlled affairs even in their own state, let alone in the entire South.

The first strategy rested upon Calhoun's political future. If the Carolinian could secure his right as successor to Andrew Jackson then relief from the tariff would come in some form. A willingness to play the game of politics, however, demanded that rhetoric's Phaedrian horses be held in check. The presidency could hardly be obtained on a platform of disunion. Instead a new majority had be forged. The dispute over the sale of western lands offered that opportunity. A second complementary course remained open. Southerners could attempt to repeal the tariff item by item in the hope of breaking apart the coalition of interests which framed the Tariff of 1828. This course likewise called for a de-emphasis of the question of constitutionality and an end to threat and bluster. Such a moderate and necessarily long run solution was difficult to advocate once the discussion had reached an emotional level. Too many South Carolinians had already committed themselves to a polarized rhetoric in their own state to make this approach viable. A third, more, direct course not only suited the inflamed passions the tariff had aroused but also left Carolinians dependent on their unanimity rather than upon the will of the opposition. This position, which numbered among its earlier advocates James Hamilton, Jr. and George McDuffie, called for the use of a minority veto against majority tyranny. Following its tenets Carolina would rescue the nation from the wayward path it followed. This solution involved more than just the tariff; indeed, it made the tariff merely the occasion for a greater debate. Those who advocated it were less interested in discussion than acceptance. However conservative questions about the meaning of the constitution might be, their stand was a radical one. They possessed the

truth; they alone had seen the evils of the tariff; they alone viewed it as unconstitutional; they alone understood the constitutional remedy. Certainly the alternatives as presented here were never as clear-cut as portrayed from the distance time alone gives. Some Carolinians, for awhile at least, followed all three courses. The debate over the third eventually split South Carolina itself into two parties. Behind all three alternatives lurked an even more important question; the question of the security of a minority life style in a democratic society. The tariff was but one of the symptoms; the disease bore the name, slavery.

Still the symptom, tariff, was the public issue at hand. Nowhere did the dilemma of how to deal with it become clearer than during the first half of 1830. The tariff question had never existed in a vacuum but now its relationship to other issues became painfully evident. More was at stake than just a simple reduction of duties. As the national debt dwindled, the question of surplus revenue the tariff would provide and of its uses raised fundamental questions about the course the nation would follow in the future. Would a surplus be applied to internal improvements, to colonization schemes; would it be simply divided among the states? Was the mere possibility of a surplus a threat to the nation?

Webster and Hayne Clash

Aware of the alternatives open to them, legislators came prepared once more to play the game of politics as the First Session of the Twenty-first Congress met. From December, 1829, through May, 1830, Carolinians probed for legislative means and political alliances to alleviate the conditions under which they suffered.

The exchange which took place between Robert Y. Hayne and Daniel Webster over the Foot Resolution best illustrates the rhetorical dilemma the South faced. If anti-tariff men hoped to forge a new majority by linking the sectional interests of the South and West, such an action called for a rhetoric subjected to participatory democracy, a capturing of the middle ground. This Hayne set out to do in his speech on January 19.[39] Exploring the problems of the South caused by a protective tariff and those of the West created by high priced public lands, Hayne sought to establish a common enemy for both sections. The manufacturers, the supporters of the American System, he argued, had formulated both oppressive policies to serve their own interests. Both policies would lead to the creation of a "great permanent *National Treasury*," which would soon become a "*fund* for corruption." It would enable the federal government to control not only the great interests of the country and its people, but also the states themselves. Thus Hayne pictured a consolidated government controlled by manufacturing interest, the partial remedy he proposed called for an abandonment of the policy of using western land sales as a source of revenue and a rejection of the concept that such sales should be governed by a concern for industry and population size. The other half of the remedy, a second step against the consolidation of government, Hayne left unstated. It was evident enough anyhow; the nation must abandon a protective tariff policy.

Hayne's first speech clearly indicated the basis for a marriage of interests between the South and West. If successful it might not only make western lands cheaper and the tariff lower, but also promote the political ascendency of John C. Calhoun. Hayne's position on western lands was a paradoxical one since cheap western lands would have both drained Carolina of a portion of its population and harmed its economic interests. Carolinians like George McDuffie had recognized the problem five years earlier.[40]

In his first reply to Hayne, Daniel Webster exposed the weakness of his opponent's position both rhetorically and politically. While he devoted much of his speech to the proposition that the East rather than the South was the West's true friend, Webster managed to shift the ground of the debate away from the public land policy. Taking the argument to Hayne, Webster discussed "the Carolina doctrine" and the dreaded issue of slavery. Although he ironically hoped that Hayne was not among those in his state who "habitually" spoke of the Union in "terms of indifference or even disparagement," Webster in effect asked him to defend the beliefs of those who calculated "the value of the Union." Such men, he argued, made the Union "a mere question of present and temporary expediency—nothing more than a mere matter of profit and loss" to be preserved when it suited "local and temporary purpose" and dissolved when it thwarted those purposes. In contrast Webster aligned himself with "the framers of the Constitution"; he, too, believed that the Union was "essential to the prosperity and safety of the

---

39. Unless otherwise noted quotations from the Webster-Hayne debate are from Freehling, *Nullification Era*, pp. 62-95. The entire debate can be found in *United States Telegraph*, February 13, 15, 16, and March 4-8, 1830.

40. "Debate in the Senate of the United States," *North American Review* 31 (October 1830):478. This article, over eighty pages in length, analyzes the Webster-Hayne debate in detail.

States." In doing so he placed the Carolinian at a distinct disadvantage. Hayne could not sit idly by and hear his opposition to consolidation treated as a disunionist doctrine. Talk of union and disunion could not help mold a political alliance between the West and the South. These were not the two alternatives as Hayne saw them in any case. Thomas Cooper, not he, had calculated the value of the Union. Hayne now had to defend one of Carolina's solutions to the tariff. In doing so he would move his state a step closer toward accepting it as the only alternative. To add to Hayne's discomfort and make his rhetorical task even more difficult, Webster had also managed in passing to speak disparagingly of the effects of slavery. Such a charge could not remain unanswered.

Webster's speech had "created sensations" in Hayne's heart.[41] Prompted by Calhoun he now spoke less about the rationale for a South-West coalition; instead he issued a spirited defense of his home state's doctrines and life style. In doing so Hayne relied on two matrices of thought which shaped the pattern of belief for his constituents, the necessity for slavery and an "ardent love for liberty." Few in the South saw any inconsistency in the two clusters of belief. Like most of his southern colleagues Hayne did not like to be drawn out on the slavery question. He accused Webster of enlisting "*the passions of mankind*" and "*the prejudices of the world*" because he even mentioned it. From a rhetorical standpoint its introduction placed Hayne in a dilemma. Undoubtedly he preferred that the subject had never been introduced, but once brought up, it had to be answered. Arguments about the tariff, the constitution, or public lands, however, could hardly be won in its name outside the South.

Liberty bore no national stain. Hayne made it the controlling term for the remainder of his speech. This "most prominent trait in the Southern character" governed his state's course on the tariff question. Like the Virginians who formulated the "good old Republican doctrine of '98," Hayne argued, Carolinians believed that when the federal government exercised "a deliberate, palpable, and dangerous" power not specifically granted to, a state had "the right" and was "duty bound, to interpose, for arresting the progress of the evil. . . ." The protective tariff, of course, was the "gross, palpable, and deliberate violation of the constitution"; the Union could be preserved only by "a firm, manly, and steady resistance" against such "usurpation." So long as the federal government alone judged the extent and limitation of its own power liberty would suffer, Hayne concluded. Carolina would stand for liberty.

Daniel Webster, too, knew something about god terms and much about constitutional law. In his second reply to Hayne he rejected the notion that Carolina was acting in accordance with the Virginia and Kentucky Resolutions. He rejected, too, the "words of delusion and folly—*Liberty first and Union afterwards.*" The national emblem he portrayed for an enraptured audience had "not a single stripe erased or polluted, nor a single star obscured—bearing for its motto, no such miserable interrogatory as—*What is all this worth?*. . . .but everywhere spread all over in characters of living light, blazing on all its ample folds . . . that other sentiment, dear to every true American heart—*LIBERTY* and *UNION*, now and forever, one and inseparable!"

The Webster-Hayne debate represented a turning point in the South Carolina struggle

---

41. *Ibid.*, 476.

against the tariff. Webster had beaten back the attempt to form a South-West alliance.[42] Forced to defend Carolina's proposed remedy for the tariff, Hayne's second speech differed radically in both tone and content from his first. Defense of nullification not only called forth another set of arguments, it also moved the debate over the tariff a step further away from the original grievance. More now was at stake than just the tariff. Hayne's decision to argue on Webster's terms weakened the chances of working within the majority system and gave impetus to the forces calling for immediate action on Carolina's part.

To make matters worse for the anti-tariff forces, Andrew Jackson divorced himself from Carolina's solution at the Jefferson Day Dinner in Washington on April 13, 1830. There he delivered his famous toast to the Union. Calhoun's reply in defense of liberty completed the epigrammatic version of the Webster-Hayne clash. The battle lines were clearly drawn.[43] Hayne and Calhoun had placed liberty before the Union; Jackson and Webster saw the two as synonymous. Carolina might complain as much as she desired; as long as the tariff was the law of the land Andrew Jackson pledged himself to support it.

Slavery and the Tariff

During the next three years the twin matrices of thought which placed liberty over union and demanded defense of the southern life style governed South Carolina's approach to the tariff question. Only George McDuffie's forty bale theory added a new dimension to the economic argument. Although the theory offered a plausible explanation for the complex tariff problem by placing the entire burden of protection on the producer, it was unsound economi-

cally. Economic sophistication, however, was not essential to the propaganda battle McDuffie waged. His argument was well adapted to "the crisis and the community" to which it was directed.[44] However well McDuffie's theory explained the problem, it offered no solution. When Carolinians needed a theoretical explanation of their proposed remedy they turned to John C. Calhoun. For the most part their own explanations of nullification were marked with a calculated ambiguity. Sometimes the doctrine merely meant the application of the Virginia and Kentucky Resolutions, other times, a simple court action, and still other times, the first step toward dissolving the Union. Not until August, 1831, however, did Calhoun find it necessary to publicly proclaim "his real opinions" on the constitutional question in terms that could not be "mistaken or misconstrued."[45] In his Fort Hill Address he outlined the theoretical justification for employing a state veto, claiming its application would save

42. Henry Clay to Josiah Johnston, Ashland, Ky, May 9, 1830, Josiah Johnston Papers, Historical Society of Pennsylvania.

43. Accounts of the dinner can be found in *United States Telegraph*, April 17, 1830, and *National Intelligencer*, April 20, 1830.

44. McDuffie presented his thesis in several forms. William Freehling's excellent description of the theory "as popular propagandists used it" can be found in *Prelude to Civil War*, pp. 193-96; an early version appeared in *National Intelligencer*, May 21 and 25, 1830; James Hamilton, Jr. to James Hammond, Charleston, May 21, 1831, *AHR* 6 (July, 1901):745.

45. New Orleans *Courier* in Baton Rouge *Gazette*, August 6, 1830; Augusta *Courier* in Charleston *Courier*, July 12, 1831; John C. Calhoun to Samuel Ingham, Fort Hill, June 16, 1831, J. Franklin Jameson, ed. "Correspondence of John C. Calhoun," *Annual Report of the American Historical Association for the Year 1899* (Washington, D. C., 1900) 2:294-95; Pendleton, South Carolina *Messenger*, August 3, 1831.

rather than destroy the Union. While states' rights supporters hailed the "profound and masterly" document, Unionists complained that Calhoun had substituted a "multitude of words," "twelve solid columns of ingenious verbiage" for ideas and arguments.[46] While Calhoun would return to the constitutional theme in his famous clash with Webster in 1833, in 1831 he doubted that "any force of argument" could "change public opinion" on the question; only the "coming confusion and danger" would.[47]

Calhoun's assessment that circumstances rather than argument would determine the tariff question rested in part in his belief that the tariff was but "the occasion, rather than the real cause" of Carolina's problems. "The truth can no longer be disguised," he admitted, "the peculiar domestick institutions of the Southern States," and their soil and climate had placed them in a minority position. If the "reserved rights" of the states could not protect Carolina, then southern states must in the end be "forced to rebel" or have "their permanent interests sacrificed, their domestick institutions exhausted by Colonization and other schemes and themselves & children reduced to wretchedness."[48] Indeed so great was the relationship between the tariff, states' rights, and slavery, that James Hamilton, Jr. saw the tariff debates as "a battle at the outposts" which, if won, would not only repulse the enemy but also secure "the citadel."[49]

The fall of 1831 brought the "confusion and danger" which Calhoun had predicted. News of Nat Turner's revolt upset the entire South. Rumors of more plots spread rapidly.[50] State legislatures and local governments quickly passed a series of repressive measures to prevent further outbreaks. Some argued that black men ought not be allowed to preach; others urged suppression of Garrison's *Liberator*. The next step, gibed one newsman, would be to *pass a law to hang* all of the editors north of the Potomac, who do not advocate *Slavery and Free Trade*."[51] Virginians further threw matters into a turmoil by calling for gradual abolition of slavery.[52] Many of the ills they laid to slave labor paralleled the problems Carolinians ascribed to the tariff. As some northerners began to advocate colonization schemes at pro-tariff meetings "the Safety valve of Nullification" took on added importance for the South.[53] If South Carolina could not maintain her constitutional ground on the tariff question, what would happen when northerners began to advocate abolition of slavery?

By the end of 1831 several things became apparent about the nullifiers' rhetori-

46. New Bern, N. C. *Sentinel*, August 24, 1831, in Pendleton *Messenger* September 7, 1831; Mobile, Ala. *Commercial Register*, August 24, 1831; Charleston *Courier*, August 16, 1831.

47. John C. Calhoun to Samuel L. Gouverneur, Fort Hill, August 18, 1831, *Annual Report . . . for 1899*, 2:300.

48. John C. Calhoun to Virgil Maxey, September 11, 1830, in Freehling, *Nullification Era*, pp. 98-99.

49. James Hamilton, Jr. to John Taylor *et al*, September 14, 1830, in Charleston *Mercury*, September 29, 1830; a portion of this letter appears in Freehling, *Nullification Era*, pp. 100-101.

50. Milledgeville, Ga., *Southern Recorder*, October 6, 1831.

51. Providence *American* in *Liberator*, November 5, 1831.

52. See Richmond *Enquirer*, November 4 and 25, 1831, for letters discussing the merits of such a proposal.

53. Letter to Charleston *Mercury* from Philadelphia, September 27, 1831, in Milledgeville *Southern Recorder*, October 13, 1831; Report from Charleston, October 6, 1831, in *Southern Recorder*, October 13, 1831; *Liberator*, November 5, 1831; James Hamilton, Jr. to J. H. Hammond, Rice Hope, Savannah River, January 16, 1832, *AHR* 6 (July, 1901):749.

cal strategy. If Carolinians chose to battle the tariff in constitutional terms, piecemeal reform would not do. A compromise tariff which avoided the question of minority rights would be a hollow victory for those who chose to stand on principle. It was precisely the piecemeal reform which tariffites feared most. Once Carolinians began to treat the tariff as a symptom rather than the disease, they legitimately broadened the list of symptoms to include possible attacks on the institution of slavery and the southern life style.[54] Thus even before the abolitionists were prepared to mount a frontal assault on the southern institution, nullificationists manned the outposts. Giving primacy to the question of minority rights presented special problems. Many of those who agreed that the tariff was unconstitutional remained unconvinced that nullification was the proper remedy. Outside of Carolina the doctrine gained little real support. As it became apparent that South Carolina had to go it alone, the nullificationists sought to unify the state by picturing themselves as the revolutionists of '76 and republicans of '98. They deprecated their opponents as submissionists, cowards, and traitors. Their polarized rhetoric made compromise virtually impossible.

The tariff which Congress passed in 1832 pleased neither the protectionists nor the nullifiers. One observer labeled it an "evasive substitute" which "any clerk in the Treasury could have drawn as well."[55] Only Andrew Jackson seemed satisfied. "The people must now see," he wrote, "that all their grievances are removed and oppression only exists in the distempered brains of disappointed ambitious men."[56] The inability to adjust the tariff on their own terms, however, further convinced the nullifiers that the great struggle at hand was no longer a contest over free trade but rather a battle against the power of consoli-

dated government. For the moment the fate of the southern life style rested on the constitutional argument. As John C. Calhoun pointed out, "If, after ten years of remonstrance and denunciation of the system as unconstitutional, the Southern States should now yield their ground, where can a stand be heretofore made?"[57]

The opposition, too, recognized that "*something* more than the tariff" was now at stake.[58] Indeed Clay backers firmly believed that "nothing would distress" the nullifiers more than "to see the question settled, as they say it ought to be."[59] An increasing number of them began to point out that Carolina's cries against consolidated government and an unjust tariff had slavery as the root cause. One Ohio representative openly charged that "slavery and not the tariff" was "the withering curse" which blighted the South.[60]

---

54. See Freehling, *Prelude to Civil War*, pp. 256-58, for the comments of Hamilton, McDuffie, Calhoun, and Harper on this point.

55. W. H. Overton to Josiah S. Johnston, Crosslands, Louisiana, May 23, 1832, Josiah Johnston Papers, Historical Society of Pennsylvania.

56. Andrew Jackson to John Coffee, Washington, July 17, 1832, *Jackson Correspondence*, 4 (Carnegie Institution, 1929) 462-63.

57. John C. Calhoun to Richard K. Cralle, Washington, May, 1832, *Annual Report . . . for 1899*, 2:321.

58. Richmond *Whig* in Charleston *Courier*, July 3, 1832.

59. Andrew Porter, Jr. to Josiah S. Johnston, Oak Lawn, St. Mary's Louisiana, May 3, 1832, Josiah Johnston Papers, Historical Society of Pennsylvania.

60. Speech of Thomas Ewing, *Register of Debates*, vol. 8, pt. 1, Twenty-second Congress, First Session, February 9-20, 1832, 436; a few northern editors also had begun to develop the point, see Letter to the Portland *Advertiser* from Washington, February 6, 1832, in *Kennebec Journal*, March 1, 1832; Providence *American* in *Liberator*, May 26, 1832; "Spy in Washington" to New York *Courier and Enquirer*, in Columbus, *Ohio State Journal*, December 26, 1832.

Nullification and the Tariff

Frustrated by their failure to achieve a repeal of the tariff in Congress, Carolinians met in convention on November 19, 1832, to turn nullification proposals into state action. Within four days the convention's Select Committee of Twenty-One produced two addresses, a nullification ordinance and its own report. The delegates quickly endorsed all the documents. The pronouncements of the victorious nullifiers were replete with all the standard trappings of an agitative rhetoric, non-negotiable demands, cries of self-righteousness, claims of power, both moral and military, far beyond those actually possessed, and a willingness to sacrifice all for the cause. Orators attached every conceivable popular symbol to their movement. At times patriotic rhetoric almost buried the discussion of the tariff itself. Briefly Carolinians demanded that tariff duties be brought down to a rate of no more than 12 percent and levied on all previously protected and unprotected items. They declared both the Tariffs of 1828 and 1832 null and void on constitutional grounds and set February 1, 1833, as the final date for the payment of duties. Should the federal government then attempt to collect them, Carolina would consider the Union dissolved. Outside of Carolina nullification still gained little support. While the legislatures of some southern states backed a call for a convention none endorsed nullification as a solution to the tariff question.

No matter how much nullificationists believed that they now controlled events, the fate of their movement rested with Andrew Jackson. Should the President act rashly he might do what Carolina had yet been unable to do, unite the South. In time of crisis, George McDuffie had argued five years earlier, the nation demanded a leader with "the judgment to decide with promptitude" what remedy would save the Republic "and the energy to apply that remedy successfully, whatever obstacle may be interposed by foreign force or domestic treason." "Such a man," McDuffie then concluded, "precisely is Andrew Jackson."[61] Now Jackson lived up to McDuffie's prediction. Both in his Annual Message to Congress and in the Nullification Proclamation the President made it clear that he would enforce the law. He too believed the tariff should be adjusted but not at the expense of law.[62]

Jackson's public declaration to support the law won him the plaudits of his pro-tariff opponents. Even Edward Everett admitted that "now that General Jackson is the champion of the Law, for the first time in his life, it seems really hard that he cannot be supported."[63] On January 16, 1833, Jackson sent another message to Congress designed to plug the loop-holes used by Carolina to avoid paying the tariff. The entire package quickly became misnamed the Force Bill. While senators battled over the constitutionality of both the bill and the tariff, a New York editor pointed out that constitutionality no longer mattered. "The southern states" believed themselves "aggrieved," he noted; if they were deluded "no process of reasoning" could convince them of their error. Only

---

61. Speech of George McDuffie before the Mechanics Convention, Hamburg, South Carolina, July 21, 1827, in Richmond *Enquirer*, August 7, 1827.

62. James D. Richardson, ed., *Messages and Papers of the Presidents*. (New York: Bureau of National Literature, 1897), 3:1154-69, 1173-95.

63. Edward Everett to Josiah S. Johnston, Washington, December 23, 1832, Josiah Johnston Papers, Historical Society of Pennsylvania.

action could save the day; the time for discussion had passed.[64]

With the threatened action of Carolina just weeks away Henry Clay acted. On February 12, he offered a compromise tariff. The Kentuckian's proposal offered Carolina much less than she had demanded. Clay denied that he was abandoning the principle of protection and insisted that his program would give the manufacturers "nine-and-a-half years of peace, certainty, and stability." More significant to Carolina than the moratorium on the tariff debate and the gradual reduction of duties which Clay proposed was the opportunity to escape from a potentially disastrous dilemma. Now even Clay was willing to admit that he had misjudged the Carolinians. "Her appeal was not to arms," he told his fellow senators, "but to another power; not to the sword, but to the law." It was "utterly impossible," he claimed, "that South Carolina ever desired, for a moment, to become a separate and independent State." The nullification ordinance may have been a "rash, intemperate" experiment but it did not block tariff revision in Clay's view.[65] All eyes now turned to Calhoun. "He who loves the Union," the Carolinian intoned, "must desire to see this agitating question brought to a termination. . . If the present difficulties were to be adjusted, they must be adjusted on the principles embraced in the bill" offered by Clay. Only "minor points of difference" existed. They could be settled, Calhoun asserted, "when gentlemen met together in the spirit of mutual compromise" and "without at all yielding the constitutional question as to the right of protection. Tumultuous approbation" greeted Calhoun's conclusion.[66] Before the Senate acted on Clay's proposal, a combination of pro-tariff and Jackson men pushed through the Force Bill. Neither Clay nor Calhoun voted. The path was now clear for a tariff adjustment.

With a compromise achieved and the session ended, Calhoun and his followers went home to declare a victory. In March the Nullification Convention rescinded its ordinance.[67] There James Hamilton, Jr. proclaimed that Carolina had triumphed "amidst stupendous difficulties."[68] Others were not so sanguine. What indeed had Carolina and the South won in their acrimonious struggle against the tariff? For those shortsighted enough to see only a simple cause and effect relationship between the tariff and the South's economic ills, victory only proved them wrong. Northerners began to look at those ills and to give the disease another name, slavery.

Conclusion

Perhaps the lessons one can learn from the tariff debates of the 1820s and 1830s are few, but they are sobering ones. The discussions were conducted in an age in which politicians professed to stand for "measures not men," yet even a cursory glance at their treatment of the tariff reveals that few men understood the issue. Fewer still were

64. New York *Evening Post* in Raleigh *Constitutionalist, People's Advocate and State Gazette*, February 5, 1833.

65. Speech of Henry Clay, *Register of Debates*, vol. 9, pt. 1, Twenty-second Congress, Second Session, February 12, 1833, 462-73.

66. Speech of John C. Calhoun, *Register of Debates*, vol. 9, pt. 1, Twenty-second Congress, Second Session, February 12, 1833, 477-78.

67. Raleigh *Constitutionalist, People's Advocate and State Gazette*, May 7, 1833.

68. Speech of James Hamilton, Jr., in Freehling, *Nullification Era*, pp. 183-85; speech of Robert Barnwell Rhett, in Freehling, *Nullification Era*, pp. 186-90.

interested enough to establish a system which would enable them to gain the data necessary to discuss the question intelligently. Far too many distrusted "the metaphysics of that *ignis fatuus* of a science, called political economy."[69] They preferred, instead, to indulge in a kind of political metaphysics of their own. Much of the problem in fact rested with their definition of "measures." Too many disdained "mere questions of policy" like the tariff, preferring instead to debate the great principles of government, "justice," "moderation," and "faithful adherence to the constitution."[70] On those great principles "epic" orations might be delivered. Discoursing about them an orator might command "spirits" which "no other enchanter" could call up. He might mold "the passions at his will" and hold "the rein of every emotion in his hand" but he could not create an intricate economic policy.[71]

The age's love for politics had further confused attempts to shape economic policy and blocked effective debate. One observer noted that he had never seen a tariff passed "where the influence of the proposed measure upon the politics of the country was not obviously a more operative consideration than the effect it was to have upon manufacturing, commercial and agricultural interests."[72] Too often politicians ascribed political motivations where none existed. The resulting ill will did little to promote intelligent discussion. Too often representatives turned the tariff debates into an occasion for electioneering. With a political vision that extended as far as their own districts' boundaries, they preferred "talking to Bunkum" to establishing an economic policy.[73]

Carolina's attitude did little to help solve the economic dilemma engendered by the tariff debate. Seeing the issue as a favorable ground upon which to protect her life style, her inflexible stance and narrow vision greatly endangered the nation. In seeking to defeat the tariff on constitutional grounds she may indeed have been arguing the slavery question at the outposts. In that case her stubborn resistance to exchange of ideas and compromise signaled great danger for the nation in the future. If defense of slavery indeed led her to engage in an agitative rhetoric to assure her aims, it also provoked a like response from a growing number of northern anti-slavery men. Ironically her attempt to prevent discussion of slavery may have indeed hastened its advance as a national issue in the decades to come.

Despite the notable exchanges between Webster and Hayne and Webster and Calhoun on the nature of government which grew out of the tariff question, the debates as a whole hardly did honor to a nation which placed its faith in the ability of her representatives to make correct decisions once given the facts. Too often "statesmen" had simply avoided the complex question at hand and had used the tariff issue as but an occasion for the discussion of other issues.

---

69. Speech of Asher Robbins on the tariff, March 2, 1832, in *United States Telegraph*, May 4, 1832.

70. *United States Telegraph*, in New York *Mercury*, March 16, 1831.

71. "On Schools of Modern Eloquence," *The Knickerbocker* 1 (May, 1833):259.

72. "A Brief View of the Administration of Andrew Jackson," in Raleigh *Constitutionalist, People's Advocate and State Gazette*, June 4, 1833.

73. *Niles Weekly Register* 35 (September 17, 1828):66.

BIBLIOGRAPHY

Christopherson, Merrill. "The Anti-Nullifiers," *Oratory of the Old South, 1828-1860.* Ed. Waldo Braden. Baton Rouge: Louisiana State University, 1970.

Eubanks, Ralph T. "The Rhetoric of the Nullifiers." *Oratory of the Old South, 1828-1860.* Ed. Waldo Braden. Baton Rouge: Louisiana State University, 1970.

These two excellent works should help to explain the rhetorical nature of the nullification struggle in South Carolina.

Freehling, William W. *The Nullification Era, A Documentary Record.* New York: Harper and Row, 1967.

This work is an excellent companion piece to the one listed below. It contains segments of several important speeches on the topic.

———. *Prelude to Civil War, The Nullification Controversy in South Carolina, 1816-1836.* New York: Harper and Row, 1968.

This is an essential work for any student wishing to understand both the tariff struggle and the ensuing nullification crisis.

Remini, Robert, *The Election of Andrew Jackson.* Philadelphia: Lippincott, 1963.

Remini offers the student unfamiliar with Jacksonian politics a readable and interesting account of the 1828 election.

Stanwood, Edward. *American Tariff Controversies in the Nineteenth Century.* 2 vols. Boston: Houghton-Mifflin, 1904.

The standard work on the tariff during the nineteenth century.

State Papers on Nullification. Boston: Dallas and Wentworth, 1834.

These important papers are now available in a DaCapo Press reprint.

Taussig, Frank. *State Papers and Speeches on the Tariff.* Cambridge: Harvard, 1893.

Among the useful items in the volume are the 1824 Webster and Clay speeches on the tariff.

Ward, John William. *Andrew Jackson—Symbol for an Age.* New York: Oxford University Press, 1962.

This paperback version can be extremely useful to the student concerned with Jackson's *ethos* as a factor in the politics of the 1820s and 1830s.

6 Controverting Internal Improvements During the Early National Period

Harry R. Gianneschi and Jerald L. Banninga

The question of how strong the federal government should be received a variety of answers during the early National Period and did much to emphasize the conflict between those who had a conservative view of the Constitution and those who had a liberal view of it. The question, however, might never have been asked had it not been for the controversies over tariff, over slavery, and over internal improvement. The former controversies were congressional affairs; Congress did deliberate over whether there should be a tariff and over whether slavery should be abolished. The internal improvement controversy was a different matter, however. At no time did Congress deliberate over whether there should be internal improvements. Instead, recognizing the need for such programs, when it concerned itself with them it debated the questions of how they should be financed and to what extent specific projects would be of benefit to the entire country. It would be both possible and interesting to study in isolation the various congressional debates concerning internal improvement legislation of the early National Period or the speeches relevant to the subject of such men as Henry Clay and John C. Calhoun.

However, a much broader view of the controversy can be obtained from a study of the State of the Union Messages and the pertinent Veto Messages of Presidents Washington, John Adams, Jefferson, Madison, Monroe, John Quincy Adams, Jackson, Van Buren, Tyler, and Polk. What they wanted in regard to internal improvement had a major impact on the controversy. Although each of these men recognized the need for internal improvement and, without exception, approved appropriations for such purposes, they did not agree on whether it was legal for the federal government to support programs of internal improvement, on whether it was the moral responsibility of the federal government to do so, and on whether it was economically expedient for the federal government to do so. This chapter will therefore focus on the controversy at the presidential level over the legal, moral, and economic justification for internal improvement during the early National Period.

The Legal Basis For Internal Improvement

The Constitution of the United States gives to Congress the "Power To lay and collect Taxes, Duties, Imposts and Excises, to pay the Debts and provide for the common Defence and general Welfare of the United States," and gives it also the power "To establish Post Offices and post Roads."[1] That Hamilton and Madison, in *The Federalist*, offered divergent views on the meaning of the "general welfare" clause of the Constitution, and that the Supreme Court did not affirm the right of Congress to provide internal improvement until 1888 in its decision concerning California *v.* Pacific Railroad Company, made it possible, even expedient, for various interpretations to be advanced during the early National Period.[2]

Both George Washington and John Adams were interested in internal improvement and approved appropriations for lighthouse facilities. But, faced with the more pressing problems of making a new government operational, they did not offer an opinion concerning the legal justification for such improvement. Such was not the case with Thomas Jefferson who quickly established himself as a strict constructionist. In his first State of the Union Message, he warned Congress that "agricultures, manufactures, commerce, and navigation" would be "most thriving when left most free to individual enterprise."[3] Jefferson believed that if such enterprises needed aid it could be provided only "within the limits of our constitutional powers," and that an amendment to the Constitution would first be necessary.[4]

To Jefferson, however, the questions concerning internal improvement and tariff were not entirely separable. In his sixth State of the Union Message, for example,

he argued against dropping the tariff and reasoned that the people's "patriotism would certainly prefer its continuance and application to the great purposes of the public education, roads, rivers, canals, and such other objects of public improvement as it may be thought proper to add to the constitutional enumeration of Federal powers."[5] Much as Jefferson recognized the need for internal improvement, he did not believe such programs were "among those enumerated in the Constitution, and to which it permits the public moneys to be applied."[6] However, he was inconsistent in at least one respect. His rhetoric did not support his actions. During his administration, Congress for the first time appropriated money for the improvement of roads and canals. Jefferson approved the expenditure of $25,000 of federal money for the improvement of a canal at Carondelet, Louisiana; he approved another $18,400 for laying out a road from Georgia to New Orleans; and he approved still another $30,000 for the laying out and making of the first phase of the Cumberland Road.[7] No longer was federal action concerning in-

---

1. *The Constitution of the United States of America: Analysis and Interpretation*, Senate Document No. 39, 88th Congress, 1st Session, p. 40.
2. For a discussion of Supreme Court cases concerned with spending for the general welfare see: *Ibid.*, pp. 144-49.
3. Thomas Jefferson, "First Annual Address," in *The State of the Union Messages of the Presidents: 1790-1966*, ed. Fred L. Israel (New York: Chelsea House Press in association with R.R. Bowker Co., 1967), 1:62. All future references to the State of the Union Messages will also be derived from this source.
4. *Ibid.*, 1:62-63.
5. Thomas Jefferson, "Sixth Annual Address," in *State of the Union Messages*, 1:87.
6. *Ibid.*, 1:88.
7. See *U.S. Statutes at Large* for a listing of federal expenditures for internal improvement.

ternal improvement limited to appropriations for lighthouse facilities. Therefore, if Jefferson's conservative view of the Constitution seemingly delayed the development of internal improvement, his action as President established a precedent for a much broader federal program.

With his inauguration in 1809, James Madison not only inherited a growing internal improvement program, but also the constitutional question surrounding it. In spite of the actual appropriations Jefferson approved during his eight year tenure as President, his rhetoric clearly set a standard for viewing such appropriations as an infringement upon the legal bindings of the Constitution. This attitude, projected by Jefferson in his State of the Union Messages, was, therefore, the position which Madison would seemingly have to accept or reject.

It soon became apparent, however, that Madison was going to take neither position. Instead, he recommended to the attention of Congress "the advantages of superadding to the means of education provided by the several States a seminary of learning," which would be built "by the National Legislature within the limits of their exclusive jurisdiction."[8] Such an improvement, built within the constitutionally sanctioned District of Columbia, Madison believed would be "local in its legal character," but "universal in its beneficial effects."[9] Thus, although strongly supporting the expenditure of federal funds for a university, Madison had managed to bypass the constitutional question.

In his third, fourth, fifth, and sixth State of the Union Messages, Madison ignored completely the question of internal improvement and not until his seventh did he again bring his views to the attention of Congress. Once more, however, it appeared that he was not willing to follow Jefferson's firm stand on the illegality of federal internal improvement programs. Although Madison argued that a system of roads and canals would "richly repay the expense bestowed on them," he refused to assume the responsibility for answering the legal question.[10] Madison both urged the federal government to undertake a system of roads and canals "requiring a national jurisdiction and national means," and reasoned that it was "a happy reflection that any defect of the constitutional authority which may be encountered can be supplied in a mode which the Constitution itself has providently pointed out."[11]

Even in his eighth and final State of the Union Message, Madison refused to take a stand. He again supported internal improvements by arguing for a system of roads and canals which would have "the effect of drawing more closely together every part" of the country, and he again refused to support either the legality or illegality of such legislation.[12] He would go no further than to remind Congress of "the expediency of exercising their existing powers, and, where necessary, of resorting to the prescribed mode of enlarging them."[13]

Madison seemed to know the question but not how to answer it. Indeed, perhaps his hesitant rhetoric concerning the question of the constitutionality of internal improvements explains in part the inconsis-

---

8. James Madison, "Second Annual Address," in *The State of the Union Messages*, 1:108.
9. *Ibid.*
10. James Madison, "Seventh Annual Address," in *The State of the Union Messages*, 1:138.
11. *Ibid.*, 1:138-39.
12. James Madison, "Eighth Annual Address," in *The State of the Union Messages*, 1:142.
13. *Ibid.*

tency of his actions concerning such legislation. Although he approved the expenditure of over $700,000 of federal money for the establishment and repair of roads during his two terms in office, he was the first president to veto an improvement bill on the grounds that it was unconstitutional.[14]

In his Veto Message, Madison explained to Congress that he was "not unaware of the great importance of roads and canals and the improved navigation of water courses," and that he believed "that a power in the National Legislature to provide for them might be exercised with signal advantage to the general prosperity."[15] Nonetheless, he argued, "seeing that such a power is not expressly given by the Constitution, and believing that it can not be deduced from any part of it without an inadmissible latitude of construction and a reliance on insufficient precedents," it would be necessary for him to return the bill in question, unsigned.[16]

Madison's veto of an internal improvement bill on the grounds that it was unconstitutional and the inauguration of James Monroe seemed to bring to an abrupt halt the eight years of presidential indecision over improvement legislation. At his earliest opportunity, Monroe echoed Jefferson's rigid constitutional philosophy concerning such legislation. In his first State of the Union Message, he voiced the opinion that Congress did not possess the power to establish a system of internal improvement. He reasoned that the right was excluded not only from "the specified powers granted to Congress" but also from those powers which are considered "incidental to or a necessary means, viewed on the most liberal scale, for carrying into effect any of the powers which are specifically grant-

ed."[17] With language reminiscent of Jefferson, Monroe suggested "to Congress the propriety of recommending to the States the adoption of an amendment to the Constitution which shall give to Congress the right in question."[18]

It seemed at first that Monroe would take an even stronger stand on the issue than had Jefferson. On May 4, 1822, Monroe returned to Congress unsigned "An act for the preservation and repair of the Cumberland road." He explained in his Veto Message that he objected to its passage "under a conviction that Congress does not possess the power under the Constitution to pass such a law."[19] Monroe explained to Congress that he believed "a power to establish turnpikes with gates and tolls, and to enforce the collection of tolls by penalties, implies a power to adopt and execute a complete system of internal improvement."[20] Such a power, Monroe contended, could "be granted only by an amendment to the Constitution and in the mode prescribed by it."[21]

Contained within the same message, however, was the equally important implication that Congress did have the power

<hr>

14. On March 3, 1817, his last official day as President, Madison vetoed a bill calling for the government to set aside the bonus and the net proceeds of the National Bank for the purpose of establishing a permanent fund for internal improvement.
15. James D. Richardson, ed., *A Compilation of the Messages and Papers of the Presidents* (Washington, D.C.: Government Printing Office, 1896), 1:585.
16. *Ibid.*
17. James Monroe, "First Annual Address," in *The State of the Union Messages*, 1:154.
18. *Ibid.*
19. Richardson, ed., *Compilation*, 2:142.
20. *Ibid.*
21. *Ibid.*, 2:143.

"to make appropriations" for internal improvements.[22] On the same day, out of a desire to clarify his position even further, Monroe sent to Congress a lengthy document entitled "Views of the President of the United States on the Subject of Internal Improvements."[23] Its purpose, he explained was to establish "whether the power to adopt and execute a system of internal improvement by roads and canals has been vested in the United States," and "to ascertain distinctly the nature and extent of the power requisite to make such improvements."[24]

With systematic reasoning, previously not used to answer the legal question surrounding federal improvement, Monroe "examined all the powers of Congress under which the right to adopt and execute a system of internal improvement is claimed and the reasons in support of it in each instance," and concluded "that such a right has not been granted."[25] If, however, Monroe denied to Congress the right to adopt and execute a system of internal improvement, he nonetheless found a basis for internal improvement legislation. He believed that the power of Congress to "provide for the common Defence and general Welfare of the United States," gave to Congress "in the case of internal improvements" the right "to appropriate the money necessary to make them."[26] Monroe clearly differentiated between the right of Congress to appropriate federal money and the right to adopt and execute a system of internal improvement.

The right to appropriate money for internal improvements of national benefit, Monroe argued, did not include the power "to take up the subject on principle."[27] Nor did it include, in his opinion, the powers necessary "to cause our Union to be examined by men of science, with a view to such improvements; to authorize commissioners to lay off the roads and canals in all proper directions; to take the land at a valuation if necessary, and to construct the works; to pass laws with suitable penalties for their protection; and to raise a revenue from them, to keep them in repair, and make further improvement by the establishment of turnpikes and tolls, with gates to be placed at the proper distances."[28]

By thus differentiating between the power to appropriate and the power to adopt and execute internal improvements, Monroe had created a new philosophy regarding the question. Previous to this, in both rhetoric and practice, the power to appropriate funds had been considered one and the same with the power to adopt and execute internal improvement. It was now considered not only a separate power but also legal by the terms of the Constitution itself.

President Monroe, however, was to do even more to encourage the advocates of internal improvement. Having already conceded to Congress the right to appropriate funds for internal improvement, he later found that he was forced to concede other federal powers incidental to that right. In his sixth State of the Union Message, Monroe again asked Congress to recommend an amendment to the Constitution in order to broaden congressional powers concerning improvement legislation. More important,

---

22. *Ibid.*, 2:142.
23. *Ibid.*, 2:144-83.
24. *Ibid.*, 2:155.
25. *Ibid.*, 2:175.
26. *Ibid.*, 2:168.
27. *Ibid.*, 2:175.
28. *Ibid.*

however, he informed Congress, that should it "deem it improper to recommend such an amendment," it would have "the right to keep the road in repair by providing for the superintendence of it and appropriating the money necessary for repairs."[29] He reasoned that if Congress "had the right to appropriate money to make the road they have a right to appropriate it to preserve the road from ruin."[30]

In his seventh State of the Union Message, Monroe broadened still more his interpretation of the constitutional power of Congress over internal improvement. He suggested to Congress "whether it may not be advisable to authorize by an adequate appropriation the employment of a suitable number of the officers of the Corps of Engineers to examine the unexplored ground" to be used for the construction of a canal connecting the waters of the Cheasapeake and Ohio.[31]

Finally, in his eighth and final State of the Union Message, Monroe reasoned that if congressional appropriations were to be used for internal improvement, then Congress had the incidental power to supervise such improvements. He informed Congress that in order to complete "the improvement of the navigation of the Mississippi and the Ohio, of the Harbor of Presqu'isle, on Lake Erie, and the repair of the Plymouth beach" that "the superintendence of them has been assigned to officers of the Corps of Engineers."[32]

Thus, although at first seemingly wanting to keep from Congress the power to adopt and execute internal improvement, Monroe, through his rhetoric, had broadened the powers of Congress over such legislation. Gradually, he had recognized the right of Congress to appropriate funds for the creation, repair, surveying, and super-

vision of internal improvement projects. By the time of John Quincy Adams' inauguration, therefore, the impact of Jefferson's philosophy on the operation of the federal government had been considerably weakened. Madison's refusal to take an executive stand on the question until his last day in office weakened it some and the constantly changing attitude of President Monroe weakened it even more. Because of these two presidents, the legal question surrounding improvement was being asked less and less often and all that seemed to be needed for a federal system of internal improvement was the election of a president willing to finish the task.

The Moral Basis for Internal Improvement

Minutes before being sworn into office, John Quincy Adams, in his first official presidential address to the nation, gave clear evidence that he believed the legal question concerning a federal internal improvement program had been answered to his satisfaction and that he would establish such a program. Adams argued that it would be because of internal improvement that "the unborn millions of our posterity" will be most grateful "to the founders of the Union" and that the "beneficent action of its Government will be most deeply felt and acknowledged."[33] Looking to the day when "all constitutional objections will be

29. James Monroe, "Sixth Annual Address," in *The State of the Union Messages*, 1:198.

30. *Ibid.*, 1:198.

31. James Monroe, "Seventh Annual Address," in *The State of the Union Messages*, 1:211.

32. James Monroe, "Eighth Annual Address," in *The State of the Union Messages*, 1:222.

33. Richardson, ed., *Compilation*, 2:298.

ultimately removed," Adams committed "with humble but fearless confidence" his "own fate and the future destines" of his country on the belief that it was his obligation "to pursue to their consumation those purposes of improvement in our common condition" started or recommended by President Monroe.[34] One salient question remained. How far would Adams go toward diminishing the importance of the constitutional question surrounding such improvement programs?

Adams answered this question less than ten months later in his first State of the Union Message. He did not ignore the constitutional justification for internal improvement legislation but went beyond the Constitution to justify his position. With an arrogance not unusual for him, John Quincy Adams was more than ready to instruct the members of Congress of the basic reason for the creation of government itself and of their responsibility to their constituents. With almost a professorial tone, Adams reasoned that "the great object of the institution of civil government is the improvement of the condition of those who are parties to the social compact, and no government, in whatever form constituted, can accomplish the lawful ends of its institution but in proportion as it improves the condition of those over whom it is established."[35]

"Roads and canals," Adams argued, "are among the most important means of improvement."[36] But, for Adams this was only a part of his system. He argued that "moral, political, intellectual improvement are duties assigned by the Author of Our Existence to social no less than to individual man."[37] In support of this view, Adams asked Congress to provide for a "university," "a public ship for the exploration of

the whole northwest coast of this continent," "the erection of an astronomical observatory, with provision for the support of an astronomer, to be in constant attendance of observation upon the phenomena of the heavens, and for the periodical publication of his observations," and for "the establishment of an uniform standard of weights and measures."[38]

Although the constitutional justification for such improvements was still actively questioned by at least some of his contemporaries, John Quincy Adams would not delay his program.[39] To Adams, the Constitution clearly gave the Congress "the power to exercise exclusive legislation in all cases whatsoever over the District of Columbia," "the power to lay and collect taxes, duties, imposts, and excises, to pay the debts and provide for the common defense and general welfare of the United States," and the power "to fix the standard of weights and measure, to establish post-offices and post-roads."[40] This was the justification Adams gave to Congress as its

---

34. *Ibid.*, 2:298-299.

35. John Quincy Adams, "First Annual Address," in *The State of the Union Messages*, 1:243-44.

36. *Ibid.*, 1:244.

37. *Ibid.*

38. *Ibid.*, 1:244-46.

39. See for example: Thomas Jefferson to William B. Giles, December 26, 1825, in *The Writings of Thomas Jefferson*, ed. Paul L. Ford (New York: G.P. Putnam's Sons, 1899), 10:354-55, in which Jefferson upon learning of Adams' first State of the Union Message explained he viewed "with the deepest affliction, the rapid strides with which the federal branch of our government is advancing towards the usurpation of all the rights reserved to the States, and the consolidation in itself of all powers, foreign and domestic; and that, too, by constructions which, if legitimate, leave no limits to their power."

40. John Quincy Adams, "First Annual Address," in *The State of the Union Messages*, 1:248.

authority for the creation of laws "promoting the improvement of agriculture, commerce, and manufactures, the cultivation and encouragement of the mechanic and of the elegant arts, the advancement of literature, and the progress of the sciences, ornamental and profound."[41]

Adams warned Congress that to refrain from exercising its power "would be to hide in the earth the talent committed to our charge—would be treachery to the most sacred of trusts," and would "cast away the bounties of Providence and doom ourselves to perpetual inferiority."[42] He asked only that Congress "give efficacy to the means committed to" them "for the common good," and "to secure the blessings of peace and promote the highest welfare of our country."[43] If this was meant as a challenge, Congress was willing to accept it.

As a result of the open invitation extended by Adams in his first State of the Union Message, requests for federal funding for internal improvement programs were sent to Washington in ever-increasing numbers. Although the majority of the requests were small and grouped together for legislative efficiency, the total figures reached an all-time high. During the four years of Adams' tenure as President, Congress approved the appropriation of over $1,000,000 for the creation and repair of lighthouses, over $1,000,000 for the creation and repair of a federal system of roads, over $500,000 for the creation and operation of canals, and over $1,500,000 for the improvement of rivers and harbors. John Quincy Adams accepted them all, and more so than any other President of the nineteenth century, established the right of the federal government to operate a massive program of internal improvement.

In 1828, however, John Quincy Adams met defeat at the hands of Andrew Jackson, and Adams viewed the loss not only as a personal defeat but also as the defeat of his goal to establish a national internal improvement program. As Adams reflected in later years: "I fear I have done and can do little good in the world—my life will end in disappointment for the good which I could have done had I been permitted. The great effort of my administration was to mature into a permanent and regular system the application of all the superfluous revenue of the Union to internal improvements."[44] Adams complained that his defeat had kept him from his goal of improving the "physical, moral, and intellectual" capacities of his country, and expressed the fear that the newly elected Jackson would allow what had been established to falter.[45]

The Economic Basis for Internal Improvement

Adams' fear was not without justification. Andrew Jackson, in his first State of the Union Message, laid down two principles which would be used in an attempt to destroy federal internal improvement. Expenditures for internal improvements, Jackson contended, would have to be reduced until the first priority of his administration, the payment of the national debt,

---

41. *Ibid.*
42. *Ibid.*, 1:248-49.
43. *Ibid.*, 1:249.
44. John Quincy Adams to Charles Upham, February 2, 1837, in E.H. Tatum, "Ten Unpublished Letters of John Quincy Adams, 1786-1837," *Huntington Library Quarterly* 4 (April 1941), 382-83.
45. *The Memoirs of John Quincy Adams Comprising Portions of his Diary from 1795 to 1848*, ed. Charles Francis Adams (Philadelphia: J.P. Lippincott & Co., 1874-1877), 8:100.

could be accomplished. More important, however, he believed that, even with the extinguishment of the debt, there were so many difficulties inherent in the system of John Quincy Adams that a new system would have to be developed before internal improvement programs could be reestablished.

President Jackson argued that while internal improvement legislation previously adopted had by some citizens been considered "an infraction of the Constitution" and by others "inexpedient," all believe "it has been employed at the expense of harmony in the legislative councils."[46] Jackson told Congress that in his opinion, difficulties would always "arise whenever power over such subjects" are "exercised by the General Government."[47] He wanted instead a system able to "reconcile the diversified interests of the States and strengthen the bonds which unite them."[48] Such a system, Jackson believed, would be one which would distribute surplus funds "among the several States according to their ratio of representation" so that each State could have its own program of internal improvement.[49]

Although Jackson made it clear that his first priority was the payment of the national debt, his first State of the Union Message gave every indication that he also disagreed with the system of internal improvement established by Adams. In direct opposition, Jackson proposed a system that would take the responsibility for internal improvement away from the federal government and give it to the state governments. Because his system, however, was to be preceded by the payment of the national debt, one question remained. What would Jackson do while waiting for the extinguishment of the debt?

Jackson provided the answer to the question six months later. On May 27, 1830, he vetoed a bill calling for a subscription of stock in the Maysville, Washington, Paris, and Lexington Turnpike Road Company. This he explained to Congress was necessary because, in his opinion, the turnpike would be local and not national in character. Jackson informed Congress that although he did not intend to veto bills "appropriating money for the construction of such works as are authorized by the States and are national in character," he did "not wish to be understood as expressing an opinion that it is expedient at this time for the General Government to embark in a system of this kind."[50]

Jackson seemed to be evaluating internal improvement projects not on a legal or moral basis, but on an economic one. He warned Congress that "appropriations for internal improvement are increasing beyond the available means of the Treasury," and cautioned them concerning such legislation.[51] "Without a well-regulated system of internal improvement," Jackson feared that "the plain consequence must be either a continuance of the national debt or a resort to additional taxes."[52] Jackson would not, of course, allow either of these things to happen.

Yet, while the economic argument seemed to offer a reasonable objection to Adams' system, the remainder of Jackson's message suggested that his negative at-

---

46. Andrew Jackson, "First Annual Address," in *The State of the Union Messages*, 1:303.
47. *Ibid.*
48. *Ibid.*
49. *Ibid.*
50. Richardson, ed., *Compilation*, 2:488.
51. *Ibid.*
52. *Ibid.*, 2:489.

titude was also based upon other convictions. Foremost was his belief that Adams' system lacked focus and was without regulation. Jackson argued that even "assuming the right to appropriate money to aid in the construction of national works to be warranted by the contemporaneous and continued exposition of the Constitution, its insufficiency for the successful prosecution of them must be admitted by all candid minds."[53] He believed that if Congress would "look to usage to define the extent" of its power over internal improvement, it would be "found so varient and embracing so much that has been overruled as to involve the whole subject in great uncertainty and to render the execution of our respective duties in relation to it replete with difficulty and embarrassment."[54]

Even after pointing out the confusion within the system, however, Jackson was not ready to stop his attack upon the internal improvement views of Adams. He went so far as to reason that internal improvement legislation could lead to the eventual destruction of the constitutional system itself. Jackson warned Congress that although all are friends of internal improvement, "none certainly are so degenerate as to desire their success at the cost of that sacred instrument with the preservation of which is indissolubly bound our country's hopes."[55] Jackson argued that the destruction of self-government could even happen if *"expediency"* be made the rule of construction in interpreting the Constitution."[56] This, however, was only his first veto of improvement legislation and other attacks on internal improvement were to follow quickly.

Within days after the Maysville veto, Jackson vetoed another improvement bill. This time it was a bill calling for a subscription of stock in the Washington Turnpike

and Road Company.[57] Considering that only two improvement bills were vetoed by the first five Presidents, Jackson's two vetoes in one week indicated that he would support his rhetorical attack against Adams' system with equally strong action. This, however, was only the beginning.

On December 6, 1830, Jackson used his second State of the Union Message to tell Congress that he was vetoing two more internal improvement bills.[58] Again, Jackson objected to them on the same basic grounds as before. "Mingling the concerns of the Government with those of the States or of individuals," Jackson warned, "is inconsistent with the object of its institution and highly impolitic."[59] He maintained that "the successful operation of the federal system can only be preserved by confining it to the few and simple, but yet important, objects for which it was designed."[60]

During the remainder of his eight years as President, Jackson continued to use his presidential addresses and the power of the veto to support his contention that internal improvements were both economically and politically inexpedient.[61] If anything, his

---

53. *Ibid.*, 2:490-91.
54. *Ibid.*, 2:491.
55. *Ibid.*
56. *Ibid.*
57. See *Ibid.* 2:493, for Jackson's Veto Message.
58. One of the bills called for general appropriations for building lighthouses, light-boats, beacons, and monuments, placing buoys, and for improving harbors and directing surveys. The second bill called for subscription of stock in the Louisville and Portland Canal Company.
59. Andrew Jackson, "Second Annual Address," in *The State of the Union Messages*, 1:323.
60. *Ibid.*, 1:323-24.
61. During his two terms as President, Jackson vetoed an unprecedented seven internal improvement bills. Their dates were: May 27, 1830, May 31, 1830, December 6, 1830 (2), December 6, 1832, December 4, 1833, and December 1, 1834.

attacks in later years were even more profuse and vicious. At a time when most of the country was in agreement, at least in theory, on the question of internal improvement, it is reasonable to suspect that Jackson's effort to stop the system would not have been as successful without his offering at least a hope of another method.[62]

In his final State of the Union Message, however, Jackson, having done all in his power to stop the system both verbally and physically, abruptly dissolved the hope for a new program. Because of the results of the Deposit Act of 1833, Jackson seemingly was persuaded that a distribution of surplus funds was, for any purpose, harmful to the nation.[63] Jackson explained to Congress that "the experience and observation of the last two years" had "operated a partial change in my views."[64] What Jackson called a partial change, however, proved to be far more than that. He argued that with or without a constitutional amendment, recommendations based upon surplus revenue distribution were neither wise nor expedient. To Jackson, surplus funds distribution, at first his answer to federal improvement, caused only "rash speculation, idleness, extravagance, and a deterioration of morals."[65]

The rhetorical impact of Jackson's last message cannot be overestimated. After eight years, the only hope he had offered to the friends of internal improvement was now casually dismissed as being neither wise nor expedient. Jackson left office having done all in his power to demolish Adams' system of internal improvement and having also withdrawn the only alternative which he had at first offered the nation.

Although Jackson had seemingly destroyed the system of John Quincy Adams, the actual federal expenditures for internal improvement during his administration do not reflect this defeat. Because Monroe and Adams had opened the door for massive internal improvement projects, Jackson found himself burdened with the responsibility of seeing those projects continued.[66] Thus, although he had used every means available to halt the federal expenditures for internal improvements, Jackson had the unique distinction of approving more money for such projects than had any of the presidents prior to the twentieth century.

The impact of Andrew Jackson upon the internal improvement issue, however, cannot be measured simply by his accomplishments during his eight years in office. Although he never achieved the complete destruction of the system, he did lay the foundation, through both his actions and his rhetoric, for its eventual downfall. Jackson had stood as a dike against the rushing liberalism of Adams and had not only held back the system but had reversed its course.

This reversal can be seen in the rhetoric and actions of Presidents Van Buren, Tyler,

---

62. At least one historian argues that it was not Jackson but the railroad which put an end to appropriations for roads and canals. See: John W. Burgess, *The Middle Period: 1817-1858* (New York: Charles Scribner's Sons, 1912), pp. 166-89.

63. The Deposit Act of 1833, called for a distribution of the surplus funds to the individual state banks for safe keeping until needed by the federal government. The states, however, interpreted the Act to mean that the federal government was loaning them money to spend as they deemed necessary. Because of this problem, the state banks did not have the money available when they were called upon to return it.

64. Andrew Jackson, "Eighth Annual Address," in *The State of the Union Messages*, 1:454.

65. *Ibid.*, 1:455.

66. Another explanation is that Jackson usually approved general appropriation bills and nearly all appropriations for internal improvement projects were included within such bills.

and Polk. Without exception, they adopted the Jacksonian philosophy toward federally supported internal improvement programs and continued a bitter assault on them. Using rhetoric nearly identical to Jackson's and using the veto, these three presidents saw both the number and the cost of internal improvement legislation go steadily downward with each of their successive terms in office. Finally, by the time of Polk's last year in office, the system nurtured by Adams, had, for all practical purposes, been destroyed. James Polk, in his final State of the Union Message, explained to Congress that he hoped that "the corrupting system of internal improvements... has been effectually checked."[67]

Conclusion

By 1850 the conflict over the issue of a federally supported internal improvement program had ended and the record of the forty-five year controversy over the three major philosophies was left for the historian. The first philosophy, fostered by the legalistic concerns of Thomas Jefferson, centered on the argument that a federal program of internal improvement was unconstitutional and that an amendment would be necessary for such a system to be developed. The second philosophy, fathered by John Quincy Adams, evolved from the contention that federally supported internal improvements should be based on moral grounds and that such improvement was the very foundation for the establishment of government. The last philosophy, developed by Andrew Jackson, centered solely upon the economic inexpediency of such programs related to his desire for the extinguishment of the national debt. In the end, Jackson's economic arguments seemed to have won out.

Yet, if the controversy over the internal improvement issue died temporarily, the question concerning such a system remained. Infrequently discussed during the remainder of the nineteenth century and for the first third of the twentieth century, the issue was brought back to the forefront of national concern in the 1930s. Faced with the problem of widespread unemployment, President Franklin D. Roosevelt assumed responsibility for reestablishing the economy of the nation. One of his solutions was the establishment of a massive federal program of public works designed to improve the transportation, communication, and educational facilities of the nation.

Although initiated because of economic necessity, the federal internal improvement program of the 1930s again raised the question of the responsibility of the federal government to care for its constituents. For the past third of a century, federal internal improvement programs have expanded to such a point that even John Quincy Adams would have had difficulty comprehending them. It seems that the federal government is ever-increasingly accepting the belief that it bears the responsibility of caring for the physical and intellectual needs of its constituents.

BIBLIOGRAPHY

For a descriptive view of early internal improvements see:

Hill, Forest G. *Roads, Rails & Waterways: The Army Engineers and Early Transportation.* Norman: University of Oklahoma Press, 1957.

McGill, Caroline E. *History of Transportation in the United States Before 1860.* Washington: Carnegie Institution of Washington, 1917.

---

67. James Polk, "Fourth Annual Address," in *The State of the Union Messages*, 1:763.

Taylor, George Rogers. *The Transportation Revolution: 1815-1860.* New York: Rinehart & Company, 1951.

The Presidential State of the Union Messages can be found in either collection below; the Veto Messages only in the first:

A Compilation of the Messages and Papers of the Presidents. Edited by James D. Richardson, 10 vols. Washington: Government Printing Office, 1896-1899.

The State of the Union Messages of the Presidents: 1700-1966. Edited by Fred L. Israel. 3 vols. New York: Chelsea House Press, 1967.

See also:

Record of Bills Vetoed and Action Taken Thereon by the Senate and House of Representatives, First Congress Through the Ninetieth Congress, 1789-1968. Washington: Government Printing Office, 1969.

7 Slavery: America's Irrepressible Conflict

D. Ray Heisey

Whether slavery should be extended or be permitted to exist at all was during 1830-1861 the most crucial and far-reaching question that America faced in the nineteenth century. The impact of the controversy touched every fiber in the fabric of American life and the consequences of the ultimate outcome are still with us. In short, the controversy over slavery is one of the most important public debates in American history.

The question had been with America from the beginning, but did not achieve prominence until abolitionism, one of the North's many movements for moral reform, emerged in 1830. Some argued that the question rightfully should be decided by the several states. Others argued that it was not a local problem, but a national one, and should be settled by the federal government in Congress or in the Supreme Court. Still others felt that slavery transcended all levels of government, challenging the very basis of human existence.

As with all social and political issues, slavery was a multi-faceted problem. The sources of that problem were many; the voices that entered the arena were legion. The purpose of this essay is not to duplicate the numerous accounts of the causes of the Civil War or of the basic sources of the antislavery movement.[1] Rather, the objective is to provide for the student of American public address in particular and of American intellectual history in general a rhetorical perspective. Who were the significant voices in the intellectual conflict? What were the chief patterns of thought expressed both in defense of slavery and against it? Finally, what consequences resulted from the rhetorical battle; what legacy did the debate leave us?

Backgrounds

For the purpose of this discussion, five sources of the slavery issue may be identified. The conflict over slavery was political—over the nature of the federal government. Was the federal government, as expressed in the Constitution, a compact

---

1. The reader is referred to such works as the following for general background: Louis Filler, *The Crusade Against Slavery* (New York: Harper & Row, 1960); Gilbert H. Barnes, *The Antislavery Impulse* (New York: Harcourt, Brace & World, 1964); Kenneth M. Stampp, ed., *The Causes of the Civil War* (New York: Prentice-Hall, 1959).

between states which preserved for them the constitutional right to protect their ultimate and separate interests, or, was it a form of government established beyond the possibility of state interposition or nullification, save through revolution?

A second level of the conflict was the clash of industrial northern capitalism and romantic southern imperialism. The North was fast becoming industrialized and developing along strongly capitalistic lines. In contrast to this, the South was an agrarian society, based on a cultural nationalism and a romantic imperialism that sought to bring more territory into its slave empire. It challenged the evils of the class warfare it predicted would follow from free competition.

A third level of this conflict over slavery was the current of humanitarian reform on behalf of the rights of individuals that pervaded early nineteenth-century America. The concept of the rise of the common man was expressing itself through women's activities, in education, in temperance societies, in prison reform and in other causes, but the plight of the slave and the call for his freedom became the central hub of reform.

A fourth impulse behind the antislavery movement was religious. The popular revivals of the 1830s and 1840s and the sweep of the leading evangelists across the country left a residue of spiritual and evangelical benevolence that provided an uncompromising conscience to the crusade.

The fifth, and most concrete, level of the conflict concerned the treatment of the slave and the specific evils arising out of the institution of slavery. The North was repulsed by stories of mistreatment of the slave; the South countered that these were isolated instances and were not grounds for removing a system that generally provided

well for its laboring class. The force and interaction of all of the above dimensions of the problem reveal the seriousness and the complexity of America's nineteenth-century dilemma.

The crusade against slavery, in the sense that we mean it here, began about 1830. It was in 1829 that slavery ended in Mexico, that a debate on the slave trade took place in the District of Columbia which resulted in resolutions condemning the slave trade, that William Lloyd Garrison demanded in the Boston Park Street Church a gradual abolition of slavery, that David Walker, a free slave, published his "Appeal." It was in 1830 that Garrison was sentenced for libel in condemning a slave carrier from Newburyport and went to jail, the first significant court action. It was in 1831 that the famous Nat Turner rebellion occurred, and the subsequent massacre, and the beginning of the important debates on slavery in the Virginia House of Delegates. Perhaps the most striking symbolic salvo of the crusade was the issuing of the first number of the *Liberator* on January 1 of that year. The following year the New England Anti-Slavery Society was formed—the first of its kind in America.

Instead of narrating the slavery debate chronologically, the approach here is to describe representative spokesmen and their patterns of argument as expressed in selected rhetorical documents. First, we shall consider those who were opposed to slavery, and then those who came to slavery's defense.

Slavery Opposed

The most notable abolitionist, of course, was William Lloyd Garrison (1805-65). Garrison, brought up in poverty and a broken home, early learned the printing and publishing trade. Before founding the *Liberator*, he had in 1826 issued for several unsuccessful months *The Free Press*, in 1828 had become editor of the *National Philanthropist*, the first temperance newspaper, and the following year had assisted Benjamin Lundy in issuing the *Genius of Universal Emancipation* Garrison's abolitionist philosophy was succinctly put on the first page of the first issue of the *Liberator*, January 1, 1831:

I will be as harsh as truth, and as uncompromising as justice. On this subject I do not wish to think, or speak, or write, with moderation. No! no! Tell a man whose house is on fire to give a moderate alarm; tell him to moderately rescue his wife from the hands of the ravisher; tell the mother to gradually extricate her babe from the fire into which it has fallen;—but urge me not to use moderation in a cause like present. I am in earnest—I will not equivocate—I will not excuse—I will not retreat a single inch—AND I WILL BE HEARD.

Garrison never wavered throughout his career in his fanatic efforts to abolish slavery. His writing, his speaking, his personal impact on other abolitionists, such as Wendell Phillips and Parker Pillsbury, made Garrison the symbol of northern abolitionism.

His position, as seen in his 1854 address "No Compromise With Slavery" at the Broadway Tabernacle in New York, is stoutly defended as "the highest expediency, the soundest philosophy, the noblest patriotism, the broadest philanthropy, and the best religion extant." That position consists of three assumptions that are developed at some length. An abolitionist, he claims, believes that (1) all men are created equal and that which turns a man into a thing is the worst form of oppression, (2) despite our national heritage of freedom, the wealth, enterprise, literature, politics, and the religion of the land all support the Slave Power, which will bring the

ship of State to destruction, and (3) there can be no compromise of any sort with the evil of slavery, even for the purpose of preserving the Union.[2]

Four years earlier, on July 4, at a meeting in Framingham, Massachusetts, Garrison had performed the ultimate act of defiance against those who wanted to preserve the Union first and abolish slavery second. He had set fire to a copy of the United States Constitution, exclaiming, "So perish all compromises with tyranny!" In 1859, after the death of John Brown, he spoke in Boston, arguing that it was the duty of those who believed in justice and liberty to bring about the dissolution of the Union. Only then could God build a true and enduring Union.

Garrison's primary motive was moral and religious. He invoked the imprimatur of heaven on abolitionism, calling it an essential part of Christianity, not the fruit of fanaticism. Garrison influenced many of the northern clergy with his evangelistic zeal and moral appeal.

If Garrison was the most notable abolitionist, Wendell Phillips (1811-84) was the most impressive. A leading Boston aristocrat and orator, Phillips "was a keener observer and had a more flexible mind than most of his colleagues."[3] When Elijah Lovejoy, an abolitionist editor in Alton, Illinois, was murdered in November of 1837, Phillips became convinced that Garrison's approach was right. Moderation was no longer viable. This murder, along with his marriage to a strong abolitionist in 1836 and seeing

2. The address in edited form may be found in Ernest J. Wrage and Barnet Baskerville, eds., *American Forum* (New York: Harper & Bros., 1960), pp. 169-79.
3. Richard Hofstadter, *The American Political Tradition* (New York: Alfred A. Knopf, 1948), p. 140.

Garrison mobbed in Boston in 1835, prepared Phillips for his historic Faneuil Hall address where he was thrust into the antislavery arena. There he adapted to a difficult rhetorical problem in a singularly successful manner. Following the Attorney General of Massachusetts who had addressed the crowd first and had won applause by comparing the rioters who had killed Lovejoy to the Boston patriots of 1776, Phillips jumped up, was able to turn the tide, indicting the murderers, and ended with the support of the audience and sympathy for the cause of abolition.

Phillips was a radical abolitionist for the remainder of his career, advocating dissolution of the Union, attacking the complacency of the churches, and urging nonparticipation in the political process. Even though his direct influence never moved much beyond the Garrisonian wing of the abolitionists, he was a frequent and popular speaker at antislavery societies and according to Hofstadter was the most valuable acquisition of the New England abolitionists because he "brought to the movement a good name, an ingratiating personality, a great talent for handling mobs and hecklers, and, above all, his voice."[4]

Phillips' forthright and confident approach is well represented in one of his best statements, "The Philosophy of the Abolition Movement," made before one of the antislavery society meetings.[5] His speech opens with the following:

Resolved, That the object of this society is now, as it has always been, to convince our countrymen, by arguments addressed to their hearts and consciences, that slaveholding is a heinous crime, and that the duty, safety, and interest of all concerned demand its immediate abolition, without expatriation.[6]

He then gives a very comprehensive analysis of the abolition movement, documenting the significant events in its history and claiming for it a statesmanship and an effectiveness paralleled nowhere in history. Its success, he continues, is due to the fact that:

It has been marked by sound judgment, unerring foresight, the most sagacious adaptation of means to ends, the strictest self-discipline, the most thorough research, and an amount of patient and manly argument addressed to the conscience and intellect of the nation, such as no other cause of the kind, in England or this country, has ever offered.[7]

The abolitionists have used the proper means to right the public mind on this question, he argues, because they have been able to take "this country by the four corners" and shake it until nothing but slavery can be heard. Wendell Phillips certainly must be credited with holding one of those four corners.

In the political arena John Quincy Adams (1767-1848), after he had been a diplomat, a senator, the Secretary of State and President, served the cause of antislavery as a member of the House of Representatives. His contribution was occasioned by the growing objection in the South to the widespread use of the mail to send abolitionist propaganda. The issue of censorship forced Adams to stand up for the constitutional right of free press and speech. It was in this context that the debate over the right of petition emerged in the late 1830s.

4. *Ibid.*, pp. 141-42.
5. Reprinted in Ernest G. Bormann, ed., *Forerunners of Black Power: The Rhetoric of Abolition* (New York: Prentice-Hall, 1971), pp. 123-44.
6. *Ibid.*, p. 123.
7. *Ibid.*, p. 126.

Abolitionists worked through their representatives to present petitions on the floor of Congress regarding slavery. The right of petition was a constitutional right. When John C. Calhoun offered (in 1836) a motion that would lay on the table all petitions on the subject of slavery, Adams denounced the measure as "a direct violation of the Constitution of the United States, the rules of this House, and the rights of my constituents."[8] The motion passed the House and became known as the famous Pinckney gag. It was repeated each session and in 1840 became a standing rule. The abolitionists were now able to identify a new issue—petitions that were denied a hearing by a standing rule were not petitions. Abolitionism then became associated with the constitutional right of petition.

The abolitionists were successful in convincing the North that their rights were being denied while the South claimed it was a false issue. Adams soon became the leading spokesman in the House for the antislavery cause. In the beginning he carefully objected to the gag rule on constitutional grounds but he finally and openly acknowledged that his war was against slavery, and used every device available to get the subject of slavery on the floor for discussion. His purpose was to stimulate antislavery feeling and provoke southern representatives into a defense of slavery. Adams presented piles and piles of petitions and the flood of them grew. The volume of petitions coming in during the late 1830s sustained the battle for abolitionists' rights and made Adams the greatest spokesman in the House for the antislavery cause.[9] Through him the cause had come to Washington and created an additional national arena for discussion.

Two other agitators who supported the abolitionist cause in Congress and who deserve mention are Joshua R. Giddings (1795-1864), a Whig representative from the Western Reserve of Ohio and Thomas Morris (1776-1844), a Democratic senator also from Ohio. Giddings had been one of Weld's converts and joined the House in 1838 where he "lent his fearless and powerful personality to the petition controversy, disdaining the parliamentary niceties which gave an aura to Adams's campaign."[10] He was censured by his Whig colleagues for presenting resolutions on the case of the *Creole*. After resigning his seat, he went back home where he was reelected by an overwhelming victory. Returning to Washington with an immunity to party discipline, he became a fierce fighter for the right of free discussion.[11] Giddings was relentless and inflexible in his severe attacks on slavery and the slaveholders. He saw abolition as a moral issue that was based on the rights of man.

Senator Morris, first antislavery spokesman in the Senate, was another politician out of Ohio who gave valuable support to the cause.[12] After serving in the Ohio legislature for a number of terms, he was elected to the U.S. Senate in 1833, and served one full term, being expelled from the Democratic Party because of his strong antislavery position. Being a controversial person, he caused much agitation out of the Senate

---

8. Quoted in Barnes, *Antislavery Impulse*
9. *Ibid.*, pp. 129-30.
10. Filler, *Crusade*, p. 103.
11. Barnes, *Antislavery Impulse*, pp. 187 ff.
12. Morris is practically untouched by scholars. For material presented here I am indebted to James R. Crocker, Teaching Fellow at Kent State University, who is engaged in research on the antislavery rhetoric of Morris.

and eventually was nominated as the vice-presidential candidate in the New York Liberty Party.

Morris was a progressive, religious person who supported many liberal causes. His position on slavery was based on the higher law principle. He felt slavery was morally wrong, though the states had the right to resist external interference. Morris opposed the gag rule and restrictions on freedom of the press. He took on such venerable men as John C. Calhoun and Henry Clay. His final and most important speech in the Senate (February, 1839) was in answer to Clay who had charged him with being an abolitionist. The speech was exceptionally long and comprehensive. It included discussion on why the people had the right of petition, why slavery was wrong and why he was opposed to it, why slavery should be feared as dangerous, and what the free states had to do with slavery. This speech was used much by the abolitionists who considered Morris their elder statesman until his death in 1844.[13]

Black speakers remembered for their contribution to the antislavery cause are, among others, Nat Turner, Sojourner Truth, and Frederick Douglass, each for different reasons. Nat Turner (1800-1831), a slave in Southampton County, Virginia, was a religious fanatic who talked of visions and a call from God to lead a battle between black and white. He accordingly made plans to lead a rebellion on July 4, 1831, but it did not materialize until August. Turner and his six conspirators succeeded after midnight on August 21, in killing the family of his owner and gathering guns and additional followers from other plantations. Within two days they had killed 56 whites—men, women, and children—and had gathered approximately 70

slaves to their cause. After a battle with the militia and volunteer soldiers, the rebels were scattered and defeated. Turner escaped until November when he was caught, tried and hanged. The insurrection aroused southern whites, who retaliated by killing 120 Negroes in the aftermath and produced extremely repressive legislation in order to hold down further attempts. It may be argued that Turner's insurrection was a kind of presentational rhetoric that resulted in several significant consequences. It inspired the important debates on slavery in the Virginia House of Delegates in 1831-32; it raised Garrison to sudden fame when people connected the *Liberator* and the Turner rebellion; it helped to bring the plight of the slave and his feeling about it to the attention of the nation; it forced Virginia and the South to defend slavery against antislavery in any form.[14] The immediate consequence certainly was a negative one for the black man, as repressive legislation kept him from staging any significant rebellion after that. "Considered in its necessary relation to slavery," writes John Cromwell, "and as contributory to making it a national issue by the deepening and stirring of the then weak local forces, that finally led to the Emancipation Proclamation and the Thirteenth Amendment, the insurrection was a moral success and Nat Turner deserves to be ranked with the greatest reformers of his day."[15]

A different type of Negro influence was

---

13. Filler, *Crusade*, p. 102.
14. *Ibid.*, pp. 52 ff.
15. John W. Cromwell, "The Aftermath of Nat Turner's Insurrection," *The Journal of Negro History* 5: (April, 1920) 208. I am indebted to John Callahan for his research on Nat Turner in Speech 656 class at Kent State University, 1971.

that provided by the itinerant ex-slave, Sojourner Truth (1797?-1886).[16] Her contribution was not from fomenting a crisis but from exerting continuous influence during a long period of time over a wide geographical area. An illiterate freed slave, an independent voice, Sojourner Truth talked to the common people at the crossroad towns, on the farms, along the roads, at antislavery meetings. As a freed slave with many first-hand experiences to relate, she was able to establish an interest and credibility that brought considerable response and acceptance for the antislavery cause. She won the common people by her rude eloquence and captivating entertainment. She composed songs and sang them; she toured into Canada and the midwest, selling copies of her biography; she met the big names—Garrison, Phillips, Douglass. One of her strengths as a speaker was the successful way in which she adapted to audience situations. When heckled, she remained poised, when ridiculed she responded with dignity. She had a strong, masculine voice, was witty, home-spun, yet profound in her use of language, and was described in 1854 by the *Liberator* as having "genuine soul-eloquence." She brought home to her audiences the evils of slavery and the urgency of removing this blight from the American nation.

Another Negro who achieved even greater prominence in the abolition movement was Frederick Douglass (1817-95). Douglass was born a slave, learned to read, succeeded in escaping, and eventually joined the Garrisonian wing of the movement. He supported immediate abolition, even at the price of violence. Douglass became a well-known lecturer and for seventeen years was editor of the *North Star*, a newspaper for Negroes. In later years he be-

came more moderate and actually separated from Garrison over political involvement, but the impact he made at antislavery society meetings and on lecture tours continued unabated. Though he was very fluent in use of language and possessed a rich, melodious voice, the strength of his power was in his ethos—who he was and what he represented. The power came through well as he adapted to many kinds of audiences and shared with them his experiences as a slave.

As an agitator Douglass was particularly harsh on the churches and clergymen. He believed that "the power that holds the keys of the dungeon in which the bondman is confined, is the pulpit."[17] As a leader, he inspired the abolition movement by his call for moral and physical struggle. In a letter to Gerrit Smith in 1849, he remarked that if there is no struggle, there is no progress.[18] His own life was a testimony to that philosophy.

The antislavery movement was supported by many clergymen who used the influence of their voice and pen. Theodore

16. For bringing together the work that has been done on Sojourner Truth, I wish to acknowledge the efforts of Mrs. Linda L. Moore, a doctoral student at Kent State University, and her unpublished paper, "Sojourner Truth." The chief biographies of Sojourner Truth are Jacqueline Bernard, *Journey Toward Freedom: The Story of Sojourner Truth* (New York: Norton, 1967); Arthur H. Fauset, *Sojourner Truth: God's Faithful Pilgrim* (Chapel Hill: University of North Carolina Press, 1938); and Olive Gilbert, *Narrative of Sojourner Truth* (New York: Arno Press, 1968).
17. See the address by Douglass, "The Right to Criticize American Institutions," in *Forerunners of Black Power: The Rhetoric of Abolition*, ed., Ernest G. Bormann (Englewood Cliffs: Prentice-Hall, 1971).
18. "No Progress Without Struggle, 1849," in *The Black Power Revolt*, ed., Floyd B. Barbour (Boston: T. Porter Sargent, 1968).

Dwight Weld (1803-95) became an ardent antislavery spokesman due to the influence of the British abolitionist Charles Stuart and the New York evangelist Charles G. Finney. Weld's knowledge of antislavery doctrine and his personal zeal combined to make him a powerful leader. He was instrumental in leading the famous Lane Seminary (Ohio) debate on antislavery in 1834. The discussion, which developed into a protracted eighteen night meeting, ended in conversions and devoted efforts to help the free blacks in Cincinnati. The Lane debate and its consequences made an impact throughout other colleges and many feared that similar discussions might occur elsewhere. A conference of college presidents was called and ended in the passage of resolutions demanding that all antislavery agitation be suppressed. The Lane Seminary trustees thereupon acted to abolish the students' antislavery society and to place discussions under censorship.[19] Weld and a large group of the students left and were welcomed warmly at the new college at Oberlin, Ohio.

Weld refused a professorship at Oberlin and continued his antislavery activity as a lecturer and organizer of speakers. He was particularly active in gaining support for new antislavery societies throughout Ohio. An indefatigable researcher, Weld gathered scores of stories on the evils of slavery and other devastating information for himself and to supply his speakers. He wrote many pamphlets and a number of tracts including *Bible Against Slavery*, *Emancipation in the West Indies*, and *Slavery As It Is*. The latter, which had a profound effect on Harriet Beecher Stowe's *Uncle Tom's Cabin*, was widely published by the antislavery societies and served as a handbook for more than a decade.[20] Weld favored immediate aboli-

tion and the establishment of equality for the freed slaves.

Charles G. Finney (1792-1875), who was primarily responsible for Weld's conversion, contributed greatly to the antislavery cause as an evangelist. Finney had had a remarkable conversion himself which redirected his career plans from law to the ministry. Though he never allowed his views on slavery to take priority over his work of evangelism, he sought to arouse public opinion on slavery and often alluded to it in his sermons and prayers.[21] He became a controversial clergyman because of his use of so-called "new measures" in evangelism and because of his reformist doctrines. His Broadway Tabernacle in New York City was burned because of rumors that it was to be a "mixed" church, forcing whites and Negroes to sit together. After he became president at Oberlin College the buildings there were threatened by hostile people who opposed the abolitionist character of the college. Oberlin became a stronghold for antislavery doctrine, while Finney's influence as an evangelist and theologian helped spread the views against slavery. Finney was disturbed, however, when sectionalism and radical abolitionism threatened the division of the churches and the impact of the Great Revival.

Horace Bushnell (1802-76), clergyman, "contributed in no small way to the crystallization of a nation-wide sentiment concerning slavery and its place in American society."[22] Bushnell was foremost a theo-

---

19. Barnes, *Antislavery Impulse*, p. 71.
20. *Ibid.*, p. 139.
21. Charles G. Finney, *Memoirs* (New York: A.S. Barnes & Co., 1876), p. 324.
22. Charles C. Cole, Jr., "Horace Bushnell and the Slavery Question," *The New England Quarterly* 23: (March, 1950) 20.

logian and a pastor, serving as minister of the Congregational North Church in Hartford, Connecticut, from 1833-59.[23] He was one of New England's chief orators, one of America's most creative theologians, and a leading pulpit speaker on social and political affairs. Considering it the duty of clergymen to speak often on public affairs, he himself became known for his views on public education, politics, government, women's suffrage, urban improvements, language, and slavery. In theology he attempted to be a mediator between conflicting points of view and became known for his Christian nurture emphasis as opposed to revivalism. Like Channing, he was a liberal but never went as far as his Unitarian friend. Also like Channing, he opposed the fanaticism of the abolition movement but spoke and wrote much against slavery.

As early as 1835, the year Garrison was mobbed, Bushnell preached a sermon in his church warning of four great dangers facing the country, slavery being one of them. Though he spoke often after that against slavery, his major address on the subject was a Thursday evening discourse on January 10, 1839, in his own church.[24] In it he hoped to present a comprehensive view of slavery as related to the question of abolition. He argued against the obnoxious and evil aspects of slavery, but claimed that the peculiar institution was the South's and should be removed by the South through their legislators. He opposed the agitational nature of abolitionism because of its "sin of ill manners." Where the abolitionists drove hard to put down slavery, they should have sought to conciliate and lead, without earning unnecessary prejudice against themselves. Bushnell felt that the antislavery societies were irresponsible and subject too much to passion instead of to reason. He

called upon his people to refrain from joining these societies, asking them instead to consider other ways of action in the ordinary spheres of life. "The pulpit and the press have their power," he reminded them. "You may raise candidates, question candidates, as you do now, vote, debate, converse, write." He concluded his address with words characteristic of his moderate temperament:

My object is higher and more comprehensive—it is to produce a more united, just and vigorous action on this subject—it is, if possible, to take this movement into the hands of our whole people, give it a new character, and prepare a great stage of progress in it.[25]

Bushnell was severely criticized by abolitionists for his attack upon them and for his comparatively mild opposition to slavery. His discourse was perceived as being designed to bring about "the utter overthrow and annihilation of modern abolitionism."[26]

Throughout his pulpit career, Bushnell continued to speak against slavery, largely focusing on the specific moral evil that it engendered, the violation of the American moral conscience that it produced, the domination of the political government that it caused, and the barbarism that it inflicted on the social progress of the country. He naively believed that history and

---

23. T.T. Munger, *Horace Bushnell* (Boston: Houghton, Mifflin and Co., 1899); Barbara M. Cross, *Horace Bushnell: Minister To a Changing America* (Chicago: University of Chicago Press, 1958).
24. Horace Bushnell, *A Discourse on the Slavery Question* (Hartford: 1839).
25. *Ibid.*, p. 31.
26. Francis Gillette, *A Review of the Rev. Horace Bushnell's Discourse on the Slavery Question* (Hartford: S.S. Cowles, 1839), p. 3.

time would bring an end to slavery, primarily due to the increase in the white population. He saw the Civil War as a divine way of expelling the political heresy of the social compact theory of government and the social falsity of slavery that the founding fathers had permitted to remain.

Bushnell was not an abolitionist. But his importance in he antislavery movement may be that he symbolized the moderate nineteenth-century American who spoke against slavery, helping to mold intangible public opinion without radicalizing it.

Another one of the giants of New England liberals, William Ellery Channing (1780-1842), did much to support the antislavery cause, though he like Bushnell never joined Garrison's abolitionist society. In 1835, the same year that Garrison was mobbed in Boston, Channing published a book called *Slavery*,[27] one of the most influential of published antislavery documents. Channing's reputation as a leading New England divine was without question. He had led the Unitarian battle as early as 1819, achieving an eminence throughout the years that made his published view on slavery a significant contribution to the movement. The book was not well received by Garrison, however, because it was not supportive of the radical abolitionists. Channing argued against slavery because he felt it was morally wrong to deprive man of his human rights, but he was opposed to immediate abolition. "It would be cruelty, not kindness," he said, to give the slave "a freedom which he is unprepared to understand or enjoy." Furthermore, Channing felt that the means of removing slavery was a question for the slaveholder only to answer. The abolitionists' goal of immediatism and their method of public agitation were the two chief objections he had to the

radical movement. Channing was more concerned about what was wise and right than what would be successful.

Though this essay deals with American spokesmen in the slavery issue, there is one other figure who should be considered because of his influence on the American scene, and who as yet has generally been neglected. The Irish patriot, Daniel O'Connell (1775-1847), made a substantial contribution to the American antislavery cause despite the fact that his primary thrust was in helping to shape Irish history.[28]

As early as 1829 O'Connell spoke out against American slavery, and in 1832 proclaimed:

I am an abolitionist. I am for speedy, immediate abolition. I care not what creed, caste, or color, slavery may assume. I am for its total, its instant abolition. Whether it be personal or political, mental or corporeal, intellectual or spiritual, I am for its immediate abolition. *I enter into no compromise with slavery.* I am for justice in the name of humanity, according to the law of the living God.[29]

In 1843, at the peak of his career, O'Connell was criticized severely by the Irish Repeal Association of Cincinnati for his attacks on American slavery. O'Connell responded to this attack with a detailed and lengthy letter which he read in October at a specially convened meeting in Dublin. He

---

27. Published in *The Complete Works of William Ellery Channing* (Christian Life Publishing Co., 1884), pp. 489-528.

28. For research on O'Connell's contribution to antislavery, acknowledgement is made to the work of Carol Wilder, Teaching Fellow at Kent State University, as reported in her unpublished paper, "Ireland Speaks: Daniel O'Connell on American Slavery," 1971.

29. *The Liberator,* September 7, 1849, quoted in Wilder, "Ireland Speaks," p. 4.

developed more than a dozen antislavery arguments, the chief ones being, according to Wilder, (1) "America is criminally inconsistent in preaching liberty and justice while practicing the tyranny and oppression of slavery," (2) "Slavery is inconsistent with all sacred Christian principles," (3) "The negro is not inferior to the white, and his apparent inferiority is the result of a lack of education," and (4) "No Irishman—and no Irish-American—worthy of the name and ancestry could possibly tolerate such a dreadful system of human bondage."

The impact of his letter was widespread. The Dublin group reportedly sent a copy to the American Anti-Slavery Society, along with the signatures of seventy thousand Irishmen who supported O'Connell. The address was read by Garrison at a "Grand Meeting in Faneuil Hall" on November 18, 1843. Great publicity attended the meeting, where Phillips praised O'Connell as "one of the brightest stars in the galaxy" and called him "brother" and "leader." The address by O'Connell was published in the *Liberator* and later as a pamphlet by the New England Anti-Slavery Tract Association.

This significant contribution of the Irish leader was that his method of nonviolent agitation and forceful rhetoric provided needed moral support to the American cause, influenced greatly the thinking of Wendell Phillips, who considered O'Connell's eloquence unequalled in modern times, and forced Irish-Americans to confront the abolitionist argument.[30]

Slavery Defended

In Waldo Braden's volume on spokesmen for the Old South, the public address of the slave defenders is characterized as "a rhetoric of desperation, meaning of course that each group which came forward was ultimately frustrated and in the end smothered by the complexity of the issues, the emotionalism, and the gradual drift toward repression."[31] The speeches of the antebellum South have generally been neglected by rhetorical critics in the wake of the exciting spokesmen for abolition and the compulsiveness of the moral argument that they represented. It has been argued that the northern abolitionist attack forced a southern response that "is intrinsically more interesting than that of the abolitionists because it is more difficult and more complex."[32] The southern response, though it became increasingly uniform and repressive, demonstrated at times telling arguments and a certain intellectual agility.

John C. Calhoun (1782-1850) was probably the South's greatest statesman. His principle of nullification represents one of the earliest arguments that the South entered in the slavery debate. The principle of nullification had been around for some time, being used in various forms and by different states depending on the issue. In 1832 South Carolina called a convention to nullify the Tariff Acts of 1828 and 1832. The economic position of the state had deteriorated and the Tariff Act was interpreted as being discriminatory. Calhoun seized the leadership in this fight and provided the philosophical argument that the Federal

---

30. See Wilder , "Ireland Speaks," p. 23.
31. Waldo W. Braden, ed., *Oratory in the Old South: 1828-1860* (Baton Rouge: Louisiana State University Press, 1970), p. 5.
32. Eric L. McKitrick, ed., *Slavery Defended: The Views of the Old South* (Englewood Cliffs: Prentice-Hall, 1963), p. 2.

Constitution is a compact between states, not an instrument of the people, and that each state may judge whether an act of Congress is applicable to its own situation or in its best interests.

In his now famous speech on the Force Bill given in the Senate in February 1833, Calhoun argued that the developing conflict between the sectional interests of the North and those of the South was a contest, in fact, between power and liberty. He saw the North as the advocate of power and the South as the defender of freedom. Calhoun wanted to see adequate limitations and checks placed on the government of a majority, for the "tendency of all governments, based upon the will of an absolute majority, without constitutional check or limitation of power, is to faction, corruption, anarchy, and despotism."[33] Calhoun's reasoning loomed large in the southern mind. The North was viewed with alarm because its concept of democracy and its moral stand on slavery were threatening the rights of the minority of the South. The principle of a concurrent majority was Calhoun's answer to the dilemma of the tyranny of the majority. He would give the right to the majority in each interest group (North and South) to approve federal legislation before it became law. His answer was also an attempt to prevent what ultimately happened—armed conflict to resolve irreconcilable differences. One side had to beat the other into submission. Calhoun's principle would have protected the minority and prevented the "complete breakdown of the democratic process" which Avery Craven has said is the significant thing about the coming of the Civil War.[34] Of course, it would have frustrated also the success of the antislavery cause.

The slavery issue was crucial for Calhoun and the South because "slavery had become the proving ground of the South's fight to maintain her rights as a minority within the Union."[35] To abolish slavery was to abolish the power to maintain slavery, which in the final analysis was the most important thing. To Calhoun the power struggle between the sections was the heart of the conflict. The coming of the Civil War proved he was right.

Closely related to the argument that States' Rights were more important than nationalism was the South's claim that slavery should not be abolished because it was the bulwark of southern agrarian civilization. Calhoun also supported this part of the South's case for slavery. In his resolutions, introduced in the Senate on December 27, 1837, he argued, "That domestic slavery, as it exists in the Southern and Western States of this Union, composes an important part of their domestic institutions, inherited from their ancestors, and existing at the adoption of the Constitution. . . .."[36]

The South's defense became uncompromising because its very way of life, its traditional inheritances from colonial days, its social values, its culture and sentimental romanticism, its plantation system—all

33. John C. Calhoun, "The Compact Theory of the Constitution," in Wrage and Baskerville, American Forum, p. 112.

34. Stampp, Causes of the Civil War, p. 150.

35. Margaret L. Coit, John C. Calhoun (Boston: Houghton Mifflin, 1950), p. 447.

36. John C. Calhoun, "Speech on the Importance of Domestic Slavery," in McKitrick, ed., Slavery Defended, p. 17.

were at stake.[37] The aristocratic southerner felt that the northern abolitionists were blinded to the reality of slavery as it existed and that their misconceptions should be corrected.

One of these aristocratic southerners was James Henry Hammond, lawyer, editor, governor of South Carolina from 1841-43, and then U.S. Senator. He was a wealthy plantation owner, a frequent speaker and writer in defense of slavery as a basis of the South's agrarian economy. His most noted work, *Cotton Is King*, answers many of the attacks from the North and argues the necessity of slavery to the cotton economy. One of Hammond's chief lines of argument was that the facts and the cricumstances of American slavery spoke for themselves. His vehemence against the abolitionists was not exclusively a result of his arrogance but "was based on what he considered to be a realistic assessment of the situation."[38] In his "Mud-Sill" speech, given in the Senate on March 4, 1858, Hammond argued the Aristotelian notion of superior and inferior social classes, saying that the Negro race is well suited to perform the drudgeries of life. Such a class constitutes "the very mudsill of society and of political government." This relationship, he said, provides a harmonious and stable society and is the greatest strength of the South.[39]

Another southern aristocrat who defended slavery as the basis of the South's civilization was Edmund Ruffin (1794-1865). He was well known for his scientific views of agriculture, his radical views on secession, and his defense of the slavery system. The latter position was well articulated in four pamphlets that he published in the 1850s: *The Political Economy of Slavery*, *The Influence of Slavery*, *African Colonization Unveiled*, and *Slavery and Free Labor Described and Compared.* He argued that slavery is more efficient and more humane than free labor because the laboring class under capitalism suffers from cruel working conditions and extreme competition. Thus slavery promotes an economic system that is more desirable than that of the North. Slavery makes it possible for the southern gentry to pursue a culture and way of life that cultivates mental and social refinement, something the North does not have in its drive for wealth. No people could have been raised from barbarism to an enlightened and refined civilization without the aid of slavery in some form, he said.[40]

Ruffin, along with other "Fire-Eaters" like Robert Barnwell Rhett and William

---

37. For an excellent treatment of these aspects of the Old South see Rollin G. Osterweis, *Romanticism and Nationalism in the Old South* (Baton Rouge: Louisiana State University Press, 1967). Osterweis argues that the South's civilization rested on a tripod: cotton and the plantation system, the institution of Negro slavery, and the cult of chivalry as a manifestation of southern romanticism.

38. Gail C. Ambuske, "A Rhetorical Analysis of the Pro-Slavery Arguments of Governor James Henry Hammond," unpublished paper written for Speech 656, School of Speech, Kent State University, 1971.

39. James Henry Hammond, "Mud-Sill Speech," in McKitrick, *Slavery Defended*, p. 122.

40. Edmund Ruffin, "The Political Economy of Slavery," in McKitrick, *Slavery Defended*, p. 75. I also wish to acknowledge Bruce Landis, "Edmund Ruffin: A Southerner in Defense of His Homeland," unpublished paper written for Speech 656, School of Speech, Kent State University, 1971. Mr. Landis concludes that Ruffin's prejudices and the values of his way of life played a more substantial part in his arguments than so-called facts or objective data.

Towndes Yancey, helped to crystallize southern opinion on the importance of the South's agrarian aristocracy and the impossibility of yielding in any way to northern pressure.[41] These spokesmen were the leading figures in the cause of secession—the ultimate and most radical consequence of viewing the slavery conflict as basically a conflict of northern industrial capitalism and southern agrarian aristocracy. A third base that the southern case touched down on was that slavery had divine sanction. This was a very controversial issue because the abolitionists argued the immorality of slavery and yet the South was able to come back with specific proof texts from the Bible, notably the Old Testament view of slavery, the absence of prohibition of it in the New Testament, and even the admonition of St. Paul for servants to be obedient to masters. McKitrick claims that in their examination of scripture "their Bible argument is really something more than an exercise in equivocation; it is strong historical exegesis, and on this plane the Southern divines had clearly the better of their Northern counterparts."[42]

Representative of the South's appeal to scripture was the work of the Reverend Thornton Stringfellow, a Baptist minister from Virginia. His widely read essay "A Scriptural View" presented three main claims. The first was that the institution of slavery had the sanction of God because Canaan was cursed to be a servant, and after that Abraham, Job, Isaac and Jacob all were great slaveholders who won favor with God for the manner in which they treated their slaves. The second was that slavery "was incorporated in the only national constitution emanating from the Almighty." The Mosaic law, Stringfellow said, included specific authorization for the Hebrews to have slaves as property. The third claim in his argument was that "Jesus Christ recognized this institution as one that was lawful among men, and regulated its relative duties." The primary support here is from the apostolic writers, particularly St. Paul, who advocated proper subordination by servants, whether the masters be good or bad, and never a word was given to the masters.[43]

We have seen that the defense of slavery by the South took three lines of argument: The Constitution was a compact of states that should judge ultimately for themselves what was in their best interest, the agrarian economy and culture were dependent on slavery, and slavery as an institution had the divine sanction of Holy Writ. There was a fourth: slavery was a positive good. Although the South had come to feel this way after the abolition movement had started saying slavery was evil, Calhoun was the first southern statesman of real significance to say so openly in Congress.[44] In his speech on the reception of abolition petitions in February, 1837, Calhoun appealed to facts, boldly stating that the relation between the white and black races in the slaveholding states "is instead of an evil, a good—a positive good."[45]

The crusade against slavery forced the South to come up with its best thinking about the positive aspects of slavery. Gen-

41. For a description and an analysis of these men, see H. Hardy Perritt, "The Fire-Eaters" in Braden, *Oratory*, pp. 234-57.

42. McKitrick, *Slavery Defended*, p. 2.

43. Thornton Stringfellow, "A Scriptural View of Slavery," in McKitrick, *Slavery Defended*, pp. 86-98.

44. Hofstadter, "John C. Calhoun: The Marx of the Master Class," in *American Political Tradition*, p. 79.

45. John C. Calhoun, "Speech on the Reception of Abolition Petitions," in McKitrick, *Slavery Defended*, p. 13.

erally, the argument was that the condition of the slave, in terms of his wants being fulfilled, is one of perfect contentment. George Fitzhugh (1806-81), writer and social philosopher, was the most noted of the proslavery intellectuals.[46] His pamphlet, *Slavery Justified, by a Southerner*, was published in 1850, and later reappeared in his book *Sociology for the South*. In the pamphlet he argues that liberty and equality are destructive in a free society as far as its weaker members are concerned whereas slavery protects the weaker members of its society. The Negroes, comparable to children and women in that they are not capable of taking care of themselves, "are well fed, well clad, have plenty of fuel, and are happy. They have no dread of the future—no fear of want."[47] In contrast to this, he says, the evils of free competition in the capitalist North bring misery, gloomy working conditions, unemployment, squalor, rivalry, and oppression. The system of slavery is given the credit for "peace, quiet, plenty and contentment" in the South.

The positive aspects of slavery were enunciated well by Robert Toombs (1810-85) at Emory College in Oxford, Georgia, in July, 1853. He gave essentially the same speech later in Boston. Toombs, a member of the House of Representatives from 1845-53 and of the Senate from 1853-61, was a leading political figure from the South who at first was a Unionist, but later was forced into a sectionalist position. In his speech he attempts to vindicate his position that a state of slavery is best for the Negro and for society. He confidently asserts:

In glancing over the civilized world, the eye rests upon not a single spot where all classes of society are so well content with their social system, or have greater reason to be so, than in the slaveholding states of the American Union. Stability, progress, order, peace, content and prosperity, reign throughout our borders. . . . These great social and political blessings are not the results of accident, but the results of a wise, just and humane republican system.[48]

Toombs continues by enumerating the "great and valuable rights" enjoyed by the slave. All the privileges of livelihood and comfortable maintenance are secure for him. He enjoys religious privileges and though he is not permitted educational advantages this does not matter because they are unnecessary to his station in society. Instead of wages for his labor, the slave is paid in products themselves. In the long run, this is better than under free labor where wages are dependent upon profit and captial success. The portion due the slave is a charge upon the capital itself. Also, there are laws that restrain abuses and violations of justice and humanity, if the North is concerned about these.

Though proslavery thought in the South demonstrated "intellectual agility," it also demonstrated, as the above arguments show, an inability to criticize itself. Its essential arrogance and rigidity were superior to its responsiveness and self-analysis.[49] The zeal and fervor with which the antislavery forces attacked the proslavery voices virtually precluded the latter from engaging in an honest and thorough self-examination. They were thrown on the defensive early, and from several different fronts, so

---

46. McKitrick, *Slavery Defended*, p. 34.
47. George Fitzhugh, "Sociology for the South," in McKitrick, *Slavery Defended*, p. 45.
48. Robert Toombs, "Slavery in the United States; Its Consistency with Republican Institutions, and Its Effect upon the Slave and Society," in Wrage and Baskerville, *American Forum*, p. 160.
49. For a perceptive presentation of this point, see McKitrick, *Slavery Defended*, pp. 2-5.

that building a respectable defense was the best that they could do.

The Consequences

An examination of the slavery debate reveals the various shades of thought that characterized both sides. It would be an oversimplification to say that this issue caused the Civil War.[50] But it must be said that the debate over slavery facilitated the polarizing influences at work in the minds of northerners and southerners.

The crusade against slavery, begun in rhetoric, escalated into armed conflict that brought emancipation to the slave, the overthrow of a social and economic system, the resolution of a perplexing constitutional question regarding the nature of the federal government, and the almost insurmountable challenge of "reconstruction" for freed blacks, defeated Dixies and victorious Yankees.

The crusade for slavery, begun in defense of a way of life, ended in a failure to examine that way of life in a truly constructive and prophetic manner. The movement toward secession, seen eventually as the only alternative to the North's challenge, brought an abortive and a broken nationalism. With its social, economic, and political strength gone, the South emerged with bitterness, helplessness and only memories of past glory.

The "irrepressible conflict" was seen by some as a deserved penalty for America's national sin and by others as an unnecessary great national trauma that could have been avoided but for the uncontrolled emotionalism and fanaticism of certain irresponsible, self-styled crusaders. In any case, the great questions that had been addressed in the national debate were now answered,

at least for the time being. America has said "no" to the extension and to the existence of slavery. The wisdom of strategical decisions made by both the abolitionists and the proslavery spokesmen as well as the political and military choices that resulted in war is subject to debate. In reality, the latter were rhetorical choices, as well. Those choices will be analyzed by generations yet unborn.

The Legacy of the Slavery Debate

The rhetorical conflict over the slavery issue has produced a classic illustration of what happens when crisis and continuity struggle for priority in the life of a nation. It is a struggle that occurs in every age, though in different forms. The abolitionists had visions of the future and the proslavery voices reveled in echoes of the past. The North saw a new order of human relationships as a national imperative, while the South saw the old order of institutional relationships as an unequalled ideal.

The crusaders who proclaimed a new order for nineteenth-century America had the favorable advantage of a broad range of rhetorical choices in the achievement of their goals. Though the antislavery spokesmen were united in their goal of abolishing slavery, they differed in the best means of accomplishing it. Bormann argues that there were two main rhetorical camps in

---

50. Kenneth Stampp's book *The Causes of the Civil War* attempts to bring together documents organized into seven broad categories of "causes." They are the "Slave Power" conspiracy vs. the Northern "Black Republicans," States Rights vs. Nationalism, Economic Sectionalism, Blundering Politicians, and Irresponsible Agitators, the Right and Wrong of Slavery, Majority Rule and Minority Rights, and the Conflict of Cultures.

the abolition movement—"those who practiced the rhetoric of agitation and those who participated in the rhetoric of conversion." The agitator, symbolized by Garrison, used the strategy of stinging, goading and disturbing the audience, while the evangelist, symbolized by Weld, aimed to convert the listener to the gospel of immediate abolition. The evidence, says Bormann, indicates that the rhetoric of conversion was more successful at mobilizing public support because it placed the movement in the general cultural context and tradition. The agitators were outside this mainstream.[51]

To these two camps should be added a third group who practiced what should be called the rhetoric of reasonableness. Represented by such influential moderates as William Ellery Channing, Horace Bushnell, and John Quincy Adams, these spokesmen rejected the methods of the immediate abolitionists, arguing that the best way to eliminate slavery would be to cooperate with the South in bringing about appropriate legislation. If *by law*, they reasoned, the Negro could be humanized by bringing him into the national church organizations, by honoring the sanctity of the family, by guaranteeing the best southern practice as to the treatment of his person, by providing a program of incentives toward freedom, the system could be removed by a series of short-term reforms rather than a radical tearing up of the roots.[52] Those who called for this more reasonable approach felt the radicals were accomplishing negative results by bringing about alienation rather than cooperation. The moderates wanted to change the system by working from within and not by attacking it from without. Confrontation, they felt, would reduce the options that the South had avail-

able, and that is precisely what happened. The rhetorical escalation of the immediate abolitionists polarized the South against the North so that no cooperation in ridding the nation of slavery could have been conceivable.

Another way of looking at the spectrum of views is described by Elkins[53] as consisting of (1) immediate and unqualified emancipation, the Garrisonian view, (2) gradual immediatism, or immediate emancipation gradually accomplished, the view held by Charles Finney and Theodore Weld, (3) philosophical abolitionism, the view held by Channing and Bushnell, and (4) colonization, the original view that lost out as an option as the abolitionists gained momentum and broadened the base of their support. Whatever terminology one chooses, the important consideration is that the antislavery speakers collectively produced a rhetorical power among a considerable range of viewpoints which raised the crusade "from a reform enterprise to a revolutionary movement which has not yet run its course."[54] They were on the side of history, and from a certain vantage point, of progress. As with any revolution, the potential for violence existed. And war came. The advocates of uncompromising solutions to crisis problems carry this potential, particularly when they clothe their rhetoric in urgent, moralistic and individualistic terms.

---

51. For further elaboration of Bormann's excellent analysis, see his essay "The Rhetoric of Abolition" in his *Forerunners of Black Power*, pp. 1-36.
52. See Stanley M. Elkins, *Slavery*, 2nd ed. (Chicago: University of Chicago Press, 1968), pp. 193-200.
53. *Ibid.*, pp. 178-90.
54. Filler, *Crusade*, p. 280.

On the other hand, the southern spokes-men who defended the old order had the disadvantage of a narrow range of rhetor-ical choices. Defending essentially a closed system, they had little ground on which to maneuver. Those who argue the status quo nearly always have this rhetorical limita-tion. Enjoying argumentative presumption bears little weight in the face of deep moral questions. The proslavery voices, in the final analysis, were narrow and barren. They had the opportunity to reexamine their social order and advocate from it the highest and best of its historical tradition. But they failed. The closed system they were advocating turned in on them at the moment of crisis, rendering them unable to respond in any other way but in a closing mobilization of intense sectionalism. El-kins describes the southern intellect well in the following paragraph:

The minute re-examination of Southern slavery which ought in principle to have occurred-no mat-ter how it should turn out, *pro* or *anti*-did not occur at all. The most outstanding of the proslav-ery statements, even in their flashes of logical genius on such matters as the nature of industrial capitalism, were precisely those which, on slavery itself, were the least equivocal and the most rigid, singleminded, and doctrinaire. The fact that the dialectic was not really an internal one, that the only assaults on slavery to which men in the South paid any attention were coming from the out-side-*this* was the problem, not slavery itself, that both engaged and somehow sapped these men's en-ergies. They were thus unable, in the fullest sense, to think about slavery. At most, they thought in the vicinity of slavery.[55]

The sterility of the southern intellect that Elkins speaks of lends credence to the description that the South's rhetoric was a rhetoric of desperation. Perhaps this de-scription is applicable, in part, to the rhe-torical defense of most "old orders." It

behooves orators of the status quo to dig deep in the inventive process lest they come up with superficial and unenduring an-swers.

If the defenders of slavery practiced a rhetoric of desperation, it is obvious that the antislavery advocates engaged in a rhet-oric of confrontation. In doing so, they contributed to the provocation of a crisis, forcing America to answer Lincoln's di-lemma of a house divided. Out of the crisis developed a continuity in what Hofstadter calls the American cultural and political tradition.[56] This is the challenge that faces rhetors of the contemporary Black Power movement and protesters and revolu-tionaries in the human rights movement. They need to develop a continuity out of it all that perpetuates *the human tradition*, so that America need not face a twentieth-century irrepressible conflict.

BIBLIOGRAPHY

Barnes, Gilbert H. *The Antislavery Impulse, 1830-1844.* New York: Harcourt, Brace, and World, 1964. Emphasizes the religious and midwestern nature of the impulse behind the antislavery movement, in contrast to the economic and New England factors which have dominated the traditional story of anti-slavery beginnings.

Bormann, Ernest G. ed. *Forerunners of Black Power: The Rhetoric of Abolition.* Engle-wood Cliffs: Prentice-Hall, 1971. Anthology consisting of 15 representative speeches and

---

55. Elkins, *Slavery*, p. 207.
56. In the introduction to his book, *The American Political Tradition*, he says, "Above and beyond temporary and local conflicts there has been a common ground, a unity of cultural and political tradition upon which American civilization has stood. That culture has been intensely national-istic and for the most part isolationist; it has been fiercely individualistic and capitalistic." p. x.

writings of leading abolitionists—the evangelicals, the agitators, black speakers, prominent women, and those from the establishment. Excellent introductory essay provides the historical background and describes the leading rhetorical features of the movement. Concluding essay follows through from the post Civil War period to the present, sketching the rhetorical developments relating to civil rights and black power.

Braden, Waldo W., ed. *Oratory in the Old South, 1828-1860*. Baton Rouge: LSU Press, 1970. Prepared under the auspices of the Speech Association of America, this volume consists of ten essays which describe, analyze, and evaluate the peculiar characteristics of selected orators of the Old South and their rhetoric in its behalf. The essays help to destroy the myth of the southern orator as far as his method of speaking is concerned, but do demonstrate the elements of commonality in the message of each.

Elkins, Stanley M. *Slavery: A Problem in American Institutional and Intellectual Life.* 2nd ed. Chicago: University of Chicago Press, 1968. Examines American slavery from several viewpoints that provide a fresh orientation to the problem. Other slave systems in relation to the American system are discussed, as is the impact of slavery on the personality of the Negro. Of particular importance for the student of public address is the chapter on slavery and the intellectual which treats the problem of guilt and reform movements in this country and the relationship between the Transcendentalists and the abolitionists.

Filler, Louis. *The Crusade Against Slavery,*

1830-1860. New York: Harper, 1960. A comprehensive examination of the antislavery movement and its relationship to abolition as well as the other reform movements of the period. It seeks to discriminate among individuals in the movement and their various goals and purposes.

McKitrick, Eric, ed. *Slavery Defended: The Views of the Old South.* Englewood Cliffs: Prentice-Hall, 1963. Presents 15 of the most influential spokesmen for the southern system of slavery and their views (letters, reviews, speeches, treatises) of it as a viable system of labor and a desirable social institution. A brief introductory essay describes the odd combination of intellectual agility and arrogance of the Old South's leading minds. An excellent list of suggested readings for the proslavery side is also included.

Pease, William H. and Pease, Jane H. eds. *The Anti-Slavery Argument.* New York: Bobbs-Merrill, 1965. An excellent anthology of readings consisting of speeches and writings of the leading antislavery spokesmen, representing most of the points of view in the movement.

Stampp, Kenneth M., ed. *The Causes of the Civil War.* Englewood Cliffs: Prentice-Hall, 1959. Stampp attempts to search for the causes of the Civil War by bringing together 91 selected documents by men who lived through the sectional crisis as well as by later historians. They are organized around seven categories: the Slave Power and the Black Republicans, state rights and nationalism, economic sectionalism, blundering politicians and irresponsible agitators, the right and wrong of slavery, majority rule and minority rights, and the conflict of cultures.

8 American Imperialism

John H. Sloan

The time: February 15, 1898. The place: Havana harbor. The event: The explosion of the *Maine*. The result: A similar explosion of an issue which had been smoldering for over half a century in our country, the issue of imperialism. What was that issue? What were the elements of the controversy? What was its resolution? Answers to these questions provide some fascinating, and indeed relevant insights into this important aspect of American foreign policy.

The Issue of Imperialism

The fundamental issue of imperialism is not complex: Should the United States annex extracontinental territories populated by alien peoples? Assuming the answer to this question is "yes," two extremely significant consequent issues emerge: (1) How should such peoples be governed? (2) What are the limits to this type of expansion?

The issue of imperialism is, of course, in reality a specific application of a much larger issue. What should the United States' involvement be in the world community of nations? The range of options has been debated constantly ever since the formal reso-

lution of the issue of imperialism in the early part of the century. Should the United States be an isolationist island unto itself? Can it be? If not, what is our role? Are we the world's policeman? To what extent can we or should we involve ourselves in the internal affairs of other countries? To what extent should we involve ourselves in multilateral or bilateral defense treaties? These are the types of questions which have dominated United States Foreign policy in the twentieth century. Indeed, several of them plague us today. The events of the twentieth century have been directly affected by the issue of imperialism and the rhetoric which attended it.

Background—Obviously, the issue of imperialism did not germinate overnight. The westward movement of the nineteenth century provided a constant invitation and temptation to "wave the flag" beyond the established boundaries. Three specific events were clear illustrations of the manifestation of imperialism before 1898:

(1) The annexation of Texas
(2) The Mexican War
(3) The annexation of Hawaii

In the early part of the nineteenth century, the present states of California, New Mexico, Arizona, and Texas were frontier provinces of Mexico. The Texas territory was particularly appealing to American settlers. As early as 1823, pioneer settlers crossed into Texas.[1] Both President John Quincy Adams and President Jackson attempted to purchase the territory from the Mexican government. "The first offer was received as an insult and the repetition created resentment."[2]

Curiously, the Mexican government encouraged American immigration into the Texas territory. As a result, Stephen F. Austin was able to develop a colony of considerable magnitude and significance. By 1834, the total number of colonists approximated 22,000 (including 2,000 slaves). The colony actually outnumbered native Mexicans in the entire territory by four to one.[3]

Other settlers in Texas were not as calm or as able to integrate as Austin. Sam Houston of Tennessee, David Burnet of Ohio, Branch Archer from Virginia, the Bowie brothers of Louisiana, and the famous Davy Crockett himself were also "settling down" in Texas—and stirring it up as well.

The Battle of the Alamo is well known to every school child. After President Santa Anna's proclamation of 1834 which the settlers of Texas felt was coercive, the Americans set up a provisional government and expelled the Mexican troops from San Antonio. On March 6, 1836, Santa Anna wiped out the entire garrison at the Alamo. Under Sam Houston, General Lamar led a counter-attack of Texans which drove the Mexican troops out of the territory.

Many Americans clamored for the immediate annexation of the newly formed Republic of Texas. An envoy was dispatched from Texas to Washington demanding either recognition or annexation. On his last day in office, President Jackson signed into law the recognition of the Lone Star Republic.

The problem of "imperialism" was clearly at hand. Should Texas be annexed as the twenty-eighth state? President Tyler's answer was "yes," as was the conclusion of Secretary of State John C. Calhoun. Many of the states disagreed on constitutional grounds, and two separate annexation treaties failed, despite strong southern support. The issue was "resolved" when President Tyler, after the election of 1844, pushed through the annexation of Texas via a joint congressional resolution. Thus, Texas was annexed on dubious grounds through extremely dubious means. Expansionists were delighted—as was the South.

The election of James Polk to the presidency guaranteed further expansion. Henry Clay campaigned on an antiexpansion platform, and Polk advocated "reoccupation of Oregon and re-annexation of Texas."[4] He also wanted California. By the time he went into office, Texas was already in the Union. Polk worked on two fronts: to develop a compromise with England on the Oregon territory, and to purchase the California territory from Mexico. On June 15, 1846, the Senate accepted the 49° N. latitude as the northern boundary of the United States. The maneuvers with Mexico were less successful. Irked by the "annexation" of Texas, Mexico had already severed diplomatic relations with the

1. Samuel Eliot Morison, *The Oxford History of The American People* (New York: Oxford University Press, 1965), p. 551.
2. *Ibid.*
3. *Ibid.*
4. *Ibid.*, p. 557.

United States. Despite this, Polk tried to deal with the Mexican government. He appointed Slidell to represent the United States to make this offer: essentially, Slidell was commissioned to assume unpaid American claims against the Mexican government "in exchange" for Mexican recognition of the Rio Grande as the southern boundary of the United States. Slidell was also instructed to make cash offers for New Mexico and California. President Herrera of Mexico refused to see Slidell, but was overthrown by the military on the grounds that he was proposing a treasonous bargain with the United States.

After the Slidell failure Polk ordered General Zachary Taylor to cross the Rio Grande into Mexico (contending erroneously that both banks of the Rio Grande were American soil). General Taylor blockaded Matamoros.

On May 9, 1846, President Polk learned that a band of Mexican soldiers had crossed the Rio Grande and engaged in a brief skirmish with American troops. On May 11, Polk sent his war message to Congress, saying "The cup of forebearance has been exhausted . . . after reiterated menaces, Mexico has passed the boundary of the United States, has invaded our territory and shed American blood upon the American soil." Congress dutifully declared "By act of the Republic of Mexico, a state of war now exists between that Government and the United States."[5]

It was a splendid little war, but there were many who disagreed with the policy. In the *Bigelow Papers*, James Russell Lowell mused:

They just want this Californy.
So's to lug new slave states in

To abuse ye, an' to scorn
    ye,
An' to plunder ye like sin[6]

Henry Thoreau protested the war by refusing to pay his poll tax. His justification for his position, the *Essay on Civil Disobedience*, is one of the more interesting results of the splendid little war.

General Winfield Scott's successful march to Mexico City eventually resulted in the treaty of Guadalupe Hidalgo on February 2, 1848. As a result, Mexico ceded Texas with the Rio Grande boundary, New Mexico (including Arizona) and California to the United States. The United States assumed the unpaid claims and paid $15,000,000 for the new territory.

The Mexican War was dubious but popular. Some American expansionists even wanted to take the entirety of Mexico. Fortunately, Polk decided this was a bit excessive. The "justification" for the war was concocted by an expansionist President, passed by a largely expansionist Congress, and applauded by a significant number of expansionist citizens. The seeds of "manifest destiny" were planted. On the other hand, with the exception of Alaska, our continental boundaries were settled. As a result, the issue of "imperialism" could conceivably have been settled. Obviously, such was not the case.

Prior to the Spanish-American War, the issue of imperialism was revived modestly during the administration of President Harrison. During this time American settlers in the Hawaiian Islands had upset the monarchy and concluded a treaty of annexation with the United States. (This treaty was

---

5. *Ibid.*, p. 561.
6. *Ibid.*, p. 562.

later voided by President Cleveland.) In 1878, President Grant had obtained the naval station at Pago Pago by treaty with native chieftains. Although these were modest incursions into the Pacific, they were in a sense precedent-shattering, for they implied the right of extracontinental annexation. But Americans were not concerned with expansion at this time; domestic problems occuped the bulk of the attention of the public.

The Prelude to War—Richard Hofstadter has asserted that one of the important causes of our involvement in the Spanish-American Was was what he termed "the psychic crisis of the 1890's"[7] Americans were plagued by economic stress. The depression of 1893 affected the entire nation. "Prices and wages struck rock bottom, and there seemed to be no market for anything. It was a period of soup kitchens, ragged armies of the unemployed, fervid soapbox oratory, and desperate strikes."[8]

The farmer was particularly hard hit. Farmers were distressed for a number of reasons during the latter half of the nineteenth century; they were deeply in debt, money was scarce, and the sale of their goods brought them minimum profit. Perhaps the root of their problems was the industrial revolution. Farm mechanization resulted in extraordinary savings in man-hours of labor. The time required to harvest wheat was reduced by 95 percent; corn was machine-harvested in less than half the time required by hand labor. Assuming that more crops would earn more money, farmers invested heavily in farm equipment. With the new equipment, usually purchased on credit, many farmers purchased more land on the same basis. Both farm and urban mechanization encouraged farmers

to specialize, cultivating "cash crops," selling them for a profit, and buying ready-made articles at the store.

Specialization introduced a new problem for the farmer: the middleman, which in the farmer's case was the carrier. He was faced with railroad rates which were high and often discriminatory. "The cost of shipping grain from Chicago to Liverpool was less than from some Dakota farms to Minneapolis."[9] Even with an abundant harvest a wheat farmer was likely to find that the costs of marketing his crops often resulted in losses.

Despite these difficulties, most farmers could exist as long as their products brought them a respectable return and as long as eastern and foreign capital encouraged speculation. In the 1880s farmers suffered reversals on both counts. Farm prices fell even further than prices of other commodities during those trying years. The land boom collapsed at the same time; money became even more scarce, and mortgage after mortgage was foreclosed, 11,000 in Kansas alone from 1889 to 1893. The farmer faced all of these economic problems with debts which were growing at face value; the dollar was three times as valuable as it had been in 1860 due to the limited quantity of money. It is easy to understand why farmers favored any device for expanding the currency, such as free silver.

The defeat of Bryan in 1896 left the common man frustrated. No miraculous reforms were in sight. Business was slow.

---

7. Richard Hofstadter, "Manifest Destiny and the Philippines," in *American Imperialism in 1898*, ed. with intro by Theodore P. Greene (Boston: D. C. Heath & Co., 1955), p. 54.

8. Morison, *Oxford History*, p. 769.

9. Paul Glad, *The Trumpet Soundeth* (Lincoln: University of Nebraska Press, 1960), p. 4.

Trusts were forming. New markets were needed. Frederick Jackson Turner's prophecy in 1893 that the end of the frontier would also end the frontier spirit seemed to have come true.

Inextricably interwoven into the economic gloom pervading the 1890s was a strong humanistic-humanitarian reform movement. The era had not only seen the emergence of populism, but the popularization of utopianism, socialism, and the Christian social gospel movements.

The revolt in Cuba was rhetorically catalytic. It produced the perfect solution to America's problems. American intervention in Cuba could certainly be justified on moral-humanitarian grounds, and extra-continental expansion might provide the economic panacea many Americans were seeking. The embryonic imperialist rhetoric was coming to life, in such addresses as those given by the Reverend J. H. Barrows at Union Theological Seminary entitled "The Christian Conquest of Asia."[10] The Reverend Barrows's thesis was that American commerce and American Christianity would go hand in hand across the Pacific.

Cuba made good copy. Newspaper circulation soared as reports came in of the horrors of the revolt. "Yellow journalism," combined with a renewed outpouring of humanistic protest, helped shape imperialism as an issue. Inevitably, the country was changing course. Attitudes were shifting. "Many businessmen, clergymen, and editors saw the multitudes turning jingo."[11]

On February 15, 1898, the *U.S.S. Maine* was blown up in Havana harbor. The pressure to declare war with Spain proved irresistible to President McKinley. Indeed, according to his own admission a year later, the public had actually *declared* the war.

He said: "But for the inflamed state of public opinion, and the fact that Congress could no longer be kept in check, a peaceful solution might have been had."[12] Clearly, McKinley could have avoided war. The Spanish were trying to negotiate a settlement. The American minister at Madrid had in fact cabled McKinley that he believed the situation could be settled amicably. Even after receiving this message, McKinley concluded his report to Congress on this note: "I have exhausted every effort to relieve the intolerable condition of affairs which is at our doors . . . I await your action."[13]

"The Splendid Little War"—Like Polk before him, McKinley allowed a "'splendid little war" to occur. Unlike Polk, he had no obvious reasons to declare the war. Indeed, the Spanish-American War might be better labeled "the foolish little war" for it had little real economic or moral thrust. The real expansionist-imperialist rhetoric took place during and after the fact, rather than before it.

The war itself was short and simple. The bands played "There'll Be a Hot Time in the Old Town Tonight," and "The Stars and Stripes Forever." Democrats and Republicans alike joined in the contest. Bryan commanded a national guard regiment. "Teddy" Roosevelt ran his rough riders up San Juan Hill. Dewey wiped out the Spanish Fleet at Manila Bay. It was Dewey who emerged as the supreme national hero.

---

10. Julius W. Pratt, *Expansionists of 1898* (New York: Peter Smith, 1951), pp. 234-35.
11. Ernest R. May, *American Imperialism: A Speculative Essay* (New York: Athenum, 1968), p. 95.
12. Morison, *Oxford History*, p. 801.
13. *Ibid.*

Headlines praised his triumph as follows:

Here is How it was Done
    Story of the Greatest Naval Engage-
    ment of Modern Times[14]

Hyperbole abounded in public print. Commodore Winfield Scott Schley was quoted as follows: "Admiral Dewey's victory at Manila must deservedly take its place side by side with the greatest naval victories in the world's history."[15] Even composers were inspired. Margherita Arlina Hamm wrote a "Hymn to Dewey." Victor Herbert composed "The Fight is Made and Won." One of the most popular songs was written by a Kansas lawyer named Eugene Ware. The lyrics are as follows:

    Oh,dewey was the morning
    Upon the first of May
    And Dewey was the Admiral,
    Down in Manila Bay,
    And dewey were the Regent's eyes
    Them orbs of royal blue,
    And dew we feel discouraged?
    I dew not think we dew![16]

Clearly, Dewey was the national hero. And America felt that it had "arrived" as a world power.

Indeed, the war was far less complicated than the peace. Proclamation for the State of War, which began on April 23, had stated that the United States disclaimed "any disposition or intention to exercise sovereignty, jurisdiction, or control over said island [Cuba] except for the pacification thereof, and asserts its determination, when that is accomplished, to leave the government and control of the island to its people."[17] On May 1, Dewey sank the Spanish fleet in Manila Bay. On July 3, the other Spanish fleet was destroyed at Santiago, and shortly thereafter the Spanish

landforces surrendered in Cuba. On August 12, the war ended, having lasted 80 days. We had freed Cuba. But we had also acquired Guam, Puerto Rico, and had claim to the Phillippines. What were we to do with them? The smoldering issue of imperialism suddenly became a reality.

Aftermath: The Issue is Debated

The situation invited rhetoric, and two men were the chief antagonists in the congressional debate on the peace treaty: Albert Beveridge and William Jennings Bryan.

In many respects, Bryan and Beveridge were well-matched. Young, popular, superbly capable orators, they were both magnificent popularizers. Bryan, of course, was better known, having almost attained the Presidency in 1896. And Bryan was in desperate need of a new issue. Although bimetalism was not dead, it had peaked. Bryan's position on imperialism was developed outside the halls of Congress, but it had influence upon the deliberations. He urged that the treaty be adopted, but that as soon after as possible, the "dependencies" should be set free. Essentially, this was the ultimate resolution of the debate. Perhaps of equal significance, it aligned Bryan squarely with the "antiexpansionist" camp.

Albert Beveridge also needed an issue. And he had done his homework. As far back as April 27, 1898, before a shot had even been fired, Beveridge projected him-

14. Mark Sullivan, *Our Times: The United States 1902-1925* (New York: Charles Scribner's Sons, 1926), p. 323.
15. *Ibid.*
16. *Ibid.*, p. 322.
17. Morison, *Oxford History*, p. 801.

self as the spokesman for the imperialists, in his address before the Middlesex Club in Boston at the Grant Anniversary Banquent. Beveridge was a midwest lawyer, had never run for public office, and was thirty-six years old. His speech was a bombshell.

After a few passing allusions to Grant, Beveridge led into his thesis, the justification for empires. He said:

He had the prophet's seer-like sight which beheld, as part of the Almighty's infinite plan, the disappearance of debased civilizations and decaying races before the higher civilization of the nobler and more virile types of men.

He understood that the axioms applicable to thirteen impoverished colonies have been rendered obsolete by history. An echo of the past is not to stay the progress of a mighty people and their free institutions. He had the instinct of empire. He dreamed the same dream that God put in the brain of Jefferson and Hamilton, of John Bright and Emerson, and all the imperial intellects of this race—the drama of American extension till all the seas shall bloom with that flower of liberty, the flag of the great Republic.

He continued:

American factories are making more than American people can use; American soil is producing more than they can consume. Fate has written our policy for us; the trade of the world must and shall be ours. And we will get it as our mother [England] has told us how. We will establish trading-posts throughout the world as distributing-points for American products. We will cover the ocean with our merchant marine. We will build a navy to the measure of our greatness. Great colonies governing themselves, flying our flag and trading with us, will grow about our posts of trade. Our institutions will follow our flag on the wings of our commerce. And American law, American order, American civilization, and the American flag will plant themselves on shores hitherto bloody and benighted, but by those agencies of God henceforth to be made beautiful and bright.

If this means the Stars and Stripes over an Isthmian canal . . . over Hawaii . . . over Cuba and the southern seas . . . then let us meet that meaning with a mighty joy and make that meaning good, no matter what barbarism and all our foes may do or say.

If it means Anglo-Saxon solidarity; if it means an English-American understanding upon the basis of a division of the world's markets so that the results may be just, upon the basis of justice to Ireland so that the understanding may be enduring; if it means such an English-speaking people's league of God for the permanent peace of this war-worn world, the stars in their course will fight for us and countless centuries will applaud.[18]

Later in 1898, Beveridge presented his classic defense of imperialism, "The March of the Flag" in Indianapolis:

The march of the flag. In 1789, the flag of the Republic waved over four million souls in thirteen states and their savage territory which stretched to the Mississippi, to Canada, and to the Floridas. The timid souls of that day said that no new territory was needed, and, for an hour, they were right. But Jefferson, through whose intellect the centuries marched; Jefferson, whose blood was Saxon, but whose schooling was French, and therefore whose deeds negatived his words; Jefferson, who dreamed of Cuba as a State of the Union; Jefferson, the first imperialist of the Republic— Jefferson acquired that imperial territory which swept from the Mississippi to the mountains, from Texas to the British Possessions, and the march of the flag began. The infidels to the gospel of liberty raved, but the flag swept on.

The title to that noble land out of which Oregon, Washington, Idaho, and Montana have been carved was uncertain; Jefferson, strict constructionist of constitutional power though he was, obeyed the Anglo-Saxon impulse within him, whose watchword then, and whose watchword throughout the world today, is "Forward," and another empire was added to the Republic, and the march of the flag went on.

Those who denied the power of free institutions to expand urged every argument and more that we

---

18. Claude G. Bowers, *Beveridge and the Progressive Era* (Cambridge: The Riverside Press, p. 32), p. 68.

hear today; but the peoples' judgment approved the command of their blood, and the march of the flag went on.

The screen of land from New Orleans to Florida shut us from the Gulf, and over this and the Everglades Peninsula waved the saffron flag of Spain; Andrew Jackson seized both, the American people stood at his back, and, under Monroe, Florida came under the dominion of the Republic, and the march of the flag went on. The Cassandras prophesied every phophecy we hear today, but the march of the flag went on. Then Texas responded to the bugle call of liberty, and the march of the flag went on. And at last we waged war with Mexico, and the flag swept over the Southwest, over peerless California, past the Golden Gate to Oregon, and from ocean to ocean its folds of glory blazed.

And now, obeying the same voice that Jefferson heard and obeyed, that Jackson heard and obeyed, that Monroe heard and obeyed, that Seward heard and obeyed, that Ulysses S. Grant heard and obeyed, that Benjamin Harrison heard and obeyed, William McKinley plants the flag over all the islands of the seas, outposts of commerce, citadels of national security, and the march of the flag goes on. Bryan, Bailey, Bland, and Blackburn command it to stand still, but the march of the flag goes on. And the question you will answer at the polls is whether you will stand with this quartet to disbelieve in the American people, or whether you are marching onward with the flag.

But did the opposition say that, unlike the other lands, these lands of Spain are not contiguous?

The ocean does not separate us from the lands of our duty and desire—the ocean joins us, a river never to be dredged, a canal never to be repaired. Steam joins us, electricity joins us—the very elements are in league with our destiny. Cuba not contiguous? Puerto Rico not contiguous? The Philippines not contiguous? Our navy will make them contiguous!

Dewey and Sampson and Schley have made them contiguous, and American speed, American guns, American heart and brains and nerve will keep them contiguous forever.

We are raising more than we can consume. We are making more than we can use. Today our industrial society is congested; there are more workers than there is work; there is more capital than there is investment. We do not need more money—we need more circulation, more employment . . . Think of the thousands of Americans who will pour into Hawaii and Puerto Rico when the republican laws cover these islands with justice and safety! Think of the tens of thousands of Americans who will invade mine and field and forest in the Phillipines when a liberal government, protected and controlled by this Republic, if not the government of the Republic itself, shall establish order and equity there!

It is God's great purpose made manifest in the instincts of our race, whose present phase is our personal profit, but whose far-off end is the redemption of hthe world and the Christianization of mankind.[19]

Beveridge, then, articulated the extreme position of the imperialists:

1. There is economic advantage of a policy of imperialism:
   a. increased productivity
   b. more jobs
   c. increased trade
2. A policy of imperialism is consistent with the westward movement of the nineteenth century.
   a. We have fulfilled our continental boundaries
   b. The next logical step is extracontinental expansion
3. There is a moral reason to "help" peoples of other countries
   a. We can rescue them from tyranny
   b. We can introduce them to democracy
   c. We can make them Christians
4. The governing of new possessions can be settled later as individual circumstances dictate.

Beveridge took his ammunition with him to the Senate in 1898, where he immediately plunged into the debate on the disposition of the Philippines. He had just re-

---

19. *Ibid.*, pp. 74-76.

turned from a trip to the Islands where fighting was still going on between American troops and Filipino revolutionaries. He urged that Americans settle the uprising and govern the Islands. After briefly recounting the now-traditional arguments for imperialism, he concluded:

God has not been preparing the English-speaking and Teutonic peoples for a thousand years for nothing but vain and idle self-contemplation and self-admiration. No! He has made us the master organizers of the world to establish system where chaos reigns . . . He has made us adept in government that we may administer government among savages and senile peoples.

Pray God the time may never come when Mammon and the love of ease shall so debase our blood that we will fear to shed it for the flag and its imperial destiny . . . And that time will never come. We will renew our youth at the fountain of new and gloriuos deeds. We will exalt our reverence for the flag by carrying it to a nobler future, as well as in remembering its ineffable past . . . And so, Senators, with reverent hearts, where dwells the fear of God, the American people move forward to the future of their hope and the doing of His work.

Adopt the resolutions offered that peace may quickly come and that we may begin our savings, regenerating, and uplifting work. Adopt it, and this bloodshed will cease when these deluded children of our islands learn that this is the final word of the representatives of the American people in Congress assembled. Reject it, and the world, history, and the American people will know where to forever fix the awful responsibility for the consequences that will surely follow our failure to do our manifest duty. How dare we delay when our soldiers' blood is flowing?[20]

At this point, the anti-imperialist position was articulated by Senator Hoar of Massachusetts. At the age of seventy-six, Senator Hoar had listened intently to Beveridge's remarks. He had not intended to speak. But Beveridge's rhetoric demanded a rejoinder. The bitter, yet eloquent response is one of the best-known and most biting attacks on imperialism. Hoar said:

I have listened, delighted, as I suppose all the members of the Senate did, to the eloquence of my honorable friend from Indiana. I am glad to welcome to the public service his enthusiasm, his patriotism, his silver speech, and the earnestness and courage with which he has devoted himself to the discharge of his duty to the Republic, as he conceives it.

Yet, Mr. President, as I heard his eloquent description of wealth and glory and commerce and trade, I listened in vain for those words which the American people have been wont to take upon their lips in every solemn crisis of their history. I heard much calculated to excite the imagination of youth seeking wealth, or the youth charmed by the dream of empire. But the words Right, Duty, Freedom, were absent, my friend must permit me to say, from that eloquent speech. I could think of this brave young Republic in our listening to what he had to say [in terms of] but one occurence:

"The devil taketh him up into an exceeding high mountain, and showeth him all the kingdoms of the world, and the glory of them: and saith unto him, All these things will I give thee, if thou wilt fall down and worship me. Then saith Jesus unto him, Get thee behind me, Satan."[21]

As previously indicated, Bryan's compromise eventually passed; the Phillippines were purchased, peace was declared, and a vague promise was made to free the peoples of the Phillippines "as soon as possible." This compromise enraged Hoar, but still placed Bryan in the antiexpansionist camp. And Bryan was destined to get more involved with the issue. While he insisted on retaining a bimetallism plank in the Democratic platform in the 1900 campaign, the key issue was the issue of imperialism.

Bryan was never more cogent or acute than he was in his 1900 acceptance speech. Addressing himself squarely to the moral as well as the practical implications of a policy of imperialism, he argued first that a policy of imperialism is morally indefensible.

20. *Ibid.*, pp. 121-22.
21. *Ibid.*, pp. 122-23.

After quoting at length the words of Henry, Jefferson, Washington, and Lincoln to prove the incompatibility of imperialism and democracy, he asserted that the Philippines had to be granted independence:

There can be no doubt that we accepted and utilized the services of the Filipinos, and that when we did so we had full knowledge that they were fighting for their independence and I submit that history furnishes no example of turpitude baser than ours if we now substitute our yoke for the Spanish yoke.[22]

Developing his second line of argument, Bryan contended that a policy of imperialism would lose us prestige abroad, and might lead to despotism at home, particularly if imperialism would lead to increased militarism. He attempted to distinguish imperialism ("the forcible annexation of territory to be governed by an arbitrary power") from expansionism ("the acquisition of territory to be built up into states").

Bryan's peroration was an eloquent anti-imperialism plea:

I can conceive of a national destiny surpassing the glories of the present and the past—a destiny which meets the responsibilities of today and measures up to the possibilities of the future. Behold a republic, resting securely upon the foundation stones, quarried by revolutionary patriots from the mountain of eternal truth—a republic applying in practice and proclaiming to the world the self-evident proposition that all men are created equal; that they are endowed with inalienable rights; that governments are instituted among men to secure these rights, and that governments derive their just powers from the consent of the governed. Behold a republic in which civil and religious liberty stimulate all to earnest endeavor and in which the law restrains every hand uplifted for a neighbor's injury—a republic in which every citizen is a sovereign, but in which no one cares to wear a crown. Behold a republic standing erect while empires all around are bowed beneath the weight of their own armaments—a republic whose flag is loved while other flags are only feared. Behold a republic increasing in population, in strength and in influence, solving the problems of civilization and hastening the coming of an international brotherhood—a republic which shakes thrones and dissolves aristocracies by its silent example and gives light and inspiration to those who sit in darkness. Behold a republic gradually but surely becoming a supreme moral factor in the world's progress and the accepted arbiter of the world's disputes—a republic whose history, like the path of the just, "is as the shining light that shineth more and more unto the perfect day."[23]

Bryan lost again in 1900, by a significantly greater margin than in 1896. The issue of imperialism did not have the appeal of the issue of free silver. After the Peace of Paris, Americans were more interested in "the full dinner pail" than in the rights of the Filipinos.

The Unresolved Resolution

The issue of imperialism was never specifically resolved. "Teddy" Roosevelt neatly buried it. He evacuated Cuba, initiated self-government in the Philippines, and generally implemented his philosophy of "Speak softly, and carry a big stick." Without overtly carrying out an imperialist policy, he achieved the rights to develop the Panama Canal, and even went so far as to announce the "Roosevelt Corollary" to the Monroe Doctrine: if a country in our hemisphere had internal problems, the United States would exercise "international police power." Although repudiated in 1930 by the State Department, the "Roosevelt Corollary" is an interesting and rather prophetic precedent to policies in the mid-twentieth century.

---

22. *New York Times*, August 9, 1900, p. 1.
23. *Ibid.*

Unquestionably, the United States emerged in the twentieth century as a world power, with an increasingly valid claim to involvement and influences in world affairs, Equally clearly, the United States failed to develop coherent long-term foreign policies to use as guidelines in this broadened arena. The question of isolationism before World War I, Wilson's problems with the League of Nations, the inexorable involvement in World War II, the Marshall Plan to rebuild Europe, the involvement in multilateral defense treaties such as NATO and SEATO, and our involvement in the Indo-China war are all examples of decisions made without an overall international philosophy. In short, we have not as a nation really resolved the questions raised in the beginning of this essay. We are unsure of the extent and degree of our involvement in the world community of nations.

Conclusions

Historically, America has been lured by the siren song of imperialism and expansionism. It enabled us to complete our continental expansion; it helped us justify, in our own minds at least, two "splendid little wars." And, somewhat inevitably, it helped draw us into a position of international leadership during the twentieth century.

The rhetoric of imperialism is typically a rhetoric of rationalization. Historically, arguments for imperialism have been manufactured during or after a decision was made that further expansion was necessary and just. Furthermore, the rhetoric of imperialism seems to be particularly appealing when spirits are at a low ebb; when times are hard (or dull); when the nation needs "a lift" either psychologically or econom-

ically. Unquestionably, the arguments in favor of imperialism have great popular appeal. Combine our "Christian duty" with a demonstration of our power and influence, temper with a strong humanitarian appeal to help those less fortunate than ourselves, and conclude with a strong affirmation that expansionism is economically in our self-interest and one has an appealing, persuasive, popular proposal.

Opponents of imperialism have had limited impact. The wisdom and eloquence of Senator Hoar had minimum effect in 1898. Even Bryan at his best was unable to affect the public mind to any significant extent in the campaign of 1900. One wonders why. A possible reason is the somewhat negative and defensive posture adopted by imperialists. While anti-imperialists were able to react with indignation and logic to the reasoning of the imperialists, they were unable to come up with any concrete positive policies imposing limits on possible expansionist policies. In the twentieth century, the lack of a coherent, long-range policy statement about the extent of our involvement in the world community of nations has left us vulnerable to the continued popular appeal of imperialistic rhetoric. Our policies continue to be somewhat makeshift, inconsistent, and tend to be based upon expediency rather than principle. As a result, the inevitable appeal of imperialist rhetoric poses a constant threat to our policy-making. One wonders if we would now be struggling in the jungles of Southeast Asia if a Bryan or a Hoar had been able to construct policies which would have shaped and perhaps limited our role. One is forced to conclude that until appropriate policies are proposed and implemented, the probability is extremely high that imperialistic policies will recur.

BIBLIOGRAPHY

Beisner, Robert L. *Twelve Against Empire: The Anti-Imperialists 1898-1900.* New York: McGraw-Hill, 1968.

A detailed account of the position of the anti-imperialists during and after the Spanish-American War.

Bowers, Claude. *Beveridge and the Progressive Era.* Boston: Houghton-Mifflin, 1932.

A detailed analysis of Beveridge and his imperialistic views.

Bryan, William Jennings. *The Second Battle: An Account of the Struggle of 1900.* Chicago: W. B. Conkey, 1900.

A personalized and detailed diary of the 1900 presidential campaign. An interesting description of Bryan's unsuccessful attempt to build imperialism into a major issue.

Faulkner, Harold U. *Politics, Reform and Expansion, 1890-1900.* New York: Harper and Brothers, 1959.

A thorough accounting of the climate of the 1890s in this country.

Glad, Paul W. *The Trumpet Soundeth: William Jennings Bryan and His Democracy, 1896-1912.* Lincoln: University of Nebraska Press, 1960.

The definitive account of Bryan's life during his years as leader of the Democratic Party.

Greene, Theodore P., ed. *American Imperialism in 1898.* Boston: D. C. Heath, 1955.

A collection of essays on the issue of imperialism.

May, Ernest R. *American Imperialism: A Speculative Essay.* New York: Atheneum, 1968.

An interpretation of the causes and effects of imperialistic policies.

9 The Black Man's Place: Post Civil War Issues

Clyde J. Faries

Whereas the Civil War solved one problem concerning the black man, it created new ones. No one could tell the freedman just how free he would be. Leaders differed so drastically and so emotionally on what place the black man would hold in postwar America that compromise was unlikely and confusion was certain.[1] Those who feared assimilation of blacks into white society faced those who favored full equality in what portended to be a political and rhetorical death struggle. Those who searched for ways of accommodating all views and those who argued that the problem would solve itself excited little interest.

Even before Lee and Grant met at Appomattox, the lines of battle for Negro rights had been drawn. Issues and proposed solutions were worked out with clarity, but reasons behind these arguments remained vague. Questions of voting rights, labor practices, educational opportunities, justice, and social equality dominated discussion of the black man's fate. Some predicted early extinction of the black race in America; others believed blacks would survive but only as serfs. One group hoped to bring the black man to his freedom slowly and experimentally; another group tried

making them forever wards of the state. Still another segment of the population called for instant freedom and instant citizenship with full protection of all civil rights. The rationale offered for these measures ranged from a belief that blacks are innately inferior to a desire to uphold the American Constitution; but a deeper, unstated problem lay at the root of the conflict.

The Question of Race Extinction

The newly-freed people in the South suffered immeasurable hardships immediately following the war. Unemployed, without property or food, ill-clothed, unsheltered, and generally unprotected, thousands were turned loose upon the land. In search of food, work, or any means of survival, they roamed the roads and trails; travel seemed

---

1. The purpose of the chapter is to investigate the speaking that influenced and revealed decision making concerning the place of the black man in American society from the Civil War to World War I. Minimal space is given to the speaking of black leaders because the writer believes that such speaking played little part in either policy development or community practices.

unsafe and an air of desperation pervaded the countryside. Hunger, exposure, disease, and violence swept through congregated blacks; they died by the hundreds. Some white orators and newspaper editors blandly predicted an end of the race. Said Governor Brownlow, of Tennessee, "Now that the negroes will no longer be cared for and protected by their masters, they will soon die out before civilization and competition, just as the Indians have."[2] This prediction, often voiced and rarely refuted, was not widely accepted.

Such conclusions, however, were not without supporting data. In Charleston, S. C., for example, the mortality rate for blacks was almost three times that for whites[3] and in Mississippi alone, 56,000 black people died during the first year following the war.[4] Men of distinction and honor lent credibility to the extinction thesis. General Robert E. Lee, for example, offered the opinion that Negroes were an "Amiable and social race," looking "more to the present than to their future condition."[5] Such a characteristic indeed would have contributed to their destruction in this country. The fact that 200,000 freedmen flocked to the Union League as a means of survival suggests, though, that Lee's analysis was not accurate. One historian observed "that the race was able to survive the ordeal of freedom was due more to its large numbers and to the blind instinct of self-preservation than to purposeful social habits."[6] Yet, when the Freedmen's Bureau came south with an array of social services and human welfare programs, the tide against the rising mortality rate was turned. The 22 million rations, 148,000 medical treatments, 45 hospitals, transportation for 32,000 persons, and 9,500 teachers contributed by the bureau put an end to the doomsday rhetoric.[7]

The Question of Suffrage

Since extinction was a prediction of fact rather than deliberate policy, the claim generated little opposition. The question of suffrage, on the other hand, developed a heated controversy. White southerners reacted violently to the idea of granting voting privileges to blacks and many pledged their lives toward seeing that such a thing never happened. Antebellum abolitionists looked upon Negro suffrage as the route to racial equality and seemed unwilling to accept less.

President Lincoln undergirded the anti-suffrage campaign. Speaking from the window of the White House in his last public address before his assassination, he explained his controversial policy for the governance of Louisiana. For fear of moving too fast, he said, he had not granted suffrage to black people in that state. He intended to encourage freedmen to ready themselves for the franchise. "The colored man," he explained, "in seeing all united for him, is inspired with vigilance, and energy, and daring to the same end." Lincoln observed that the black man desired the right to vote, but, he queried, "Will he not attain it sooner by saving the already advanced steps toward it than by running backward over them?" Comparing the Negro's position with that of an embryo, he reasoned, "We shall sooner have the fowl

2. "Will the Freed Negro Race at the South Die Out?" *The Nation*, September 14, 1865, pp. 325-27.
3. The *Charleston Courier*, cited in the *Missouri Republican*, September 28, 1869.
4. James Garner, *Reconstruction in Mississippi* (Boston: Macmillan, 1901), p. 124.
5. Francis B. Simkins, *A History of the South* (New York: Alfred A. Knopf, 1959), p. 254.
6. *Ibid.*
7. *Ibid.*, p. 268.

by hatching the egg than by smashing it."[8] Prestige publications likewise supported the movement against suffrage. *Brownson's Quarterly Review*, for example, expressed the hope that blacks would be denied the vote and that no effort would be made to "elevate the negro to the level of the white man."[9] Brownson favored changing the form and condition of servitude from chattel to serf, making blacks lawfully men but not free men.[10] Even the all-black conventions held in Southern states in 1865 and 1866 did not call for the franchise.[11]

President Andrew Johnson continued Lincoln's policy almost without change. Lincoln had wanted to test whether Negro voting would work by granting the franchise to a small number of freedmen in a small section of Louisiana.[12] Johnson suggested permitting educated blacks owning property to vote, but when southern leaders objected, he simply dropped the idea. Both presidents believed philosophically that some day blacks should have suffrage, but neither was willing to set forth a policy showing how and when that goal should be attained. Both sympathized with Lyman Beecher's sermonic theme that suffrage is a natural right that cannot forever be denied a race;[13] yet both denied the practicality of protecting that natural right. Both gave priority to reconciling whites instead of granting suffrage to blacks.

Opponents of the black franchise argued primarily from the standpoint of two positions. They seconded Lincoln's and Johnson's views on practicality, and they maintained that the suffrage amendments were unconstitutional. Wade Hampton, of South Carolina, for instance, urged legislatures to defeat the Fourteenth and Fifteenth amendments on grounds that they were not passed in accordance with American constitutional provision.[14] Beneath his

calm statutory contention, though, lay sharp defiance. White dominance advocates offered the constitutionality objection mainly for consumption outside the South. Therefore, their reply to proposals emanating from northern civil rights groups had a ring of logic. For the South, they had a different strategy. While Equal Rights League conventions resolved that every man should be "equal in the law and equally exercising all rights, political and civil,"[15] southern convention halls rang with "This is a white man's government and intended for white men only,"[16] and southern newspapers echoed the same sentiment. So much hostility developed over the issue that rational discussion became rare. Even in Grant's cabinet meetings the question brought heated debate. John Rawlings, Secretary of War, argued so strenuously against plans to force Negro rights in the South that he fell prostrate upon the floor and had to be carried from the room. "Gentlemen, you cannot do it," he had shouted as he collapsed. Rawlings died a short while after the session.[17]

8. Charles W. Moores, *Lincoln Addresses and Letters* (New York: American Book Company, 1914), p. 222.

9. *Brownson's Quarterly Review* 21 (April, 1864):197.

10. *Ibid.*, 207.

11. August Meier, *Negro Thought in American, 1880-1915* (Ann Arbor: University of Michigan Press, 1963), pp. 5-6.

12. *The Outlook*, 74 (May 30, 1903):264-65.

13. W. S. Scarborough, "The Future of the Negro," *Forum* 7 (March, 1889):86.

14. Wade Hampton, "The Race Problem," *The Arena* 2 (July, 1890):132-38.

15. *Proceedings of the Fourth Annual Meeting of the Pennsylvania State Equal Rights League, 1868* (Philadelphia: 1868), p. 35, cited in Meier, *Negro Thought in America*, p. 4.

16. *Ibid.*

17. *The Missouri Republican*, September 25, 1869.

Forces opposed to President Johnson's Reconstruction policies were equally zealous in fighting for Negro suffrage. Wendell Phillips, a leading abolitionist and minister from Massachusetts, preached in 1864 that the first goal should be emancipation, the second suffrage, and finally complete political and social equality.[18] Congressman Thaddeus Stevens of Pennsylvania joined Phillips on this course, spearheading the congressional campaign. Stevens proposed to withhold Reconstruction from each state until political, economic, and social stability were attained by blacks in that state.[19] He found several war weary representatives amenable on this point, but he could not muster a majority in 1864. Nevertheless, he did achieve momentum for the movement. Through their own Reconstruction vehicle, the Freedmen's Bureau, Congress sent speakers scurrying to different parts of the South, urging blacks to seek the right to vote. Senator Henry Wilson of Massachusetts and Representative "Pig Iron" Kelley of Pennsylvania, among others, won a measure of fame for their southern speaking tours.

To attain Reconstruction under President Johnson, constitutional delegations convening in the fall of 1865 had to accomplish only three things: 1) formal abolition of slavery, 2) repudiation of the Ordinances of Secession, and 3) rejection of Confederate war debts. The softness of this policy fueled the Stevens machine and stronger and bolder congressional opposition countered with the Civil Rights Act of 1866, reducing the representation of states failing to grant Negro suffrage.

Victories in the election of 1866 gave the "radicals" enough strength to take over the Reconstruction process. Consequently, from March 2 to 24 in 1867, they passed into law a series of acts designed to assure the Negro his civil rights. By requiring legislatures to accept the Fourteenth and Fifteenth Amendments to the Constitution before being seated, they assured blacks their citizenship and the right to vote. As a result, Negroes were registered by the thousands. In fact, more black than white people qualified to vote in the South. With approximately 150,000 whites disfranchised by their war activities and a large number refusing in anger to participate, blacks on the rolls outnumbered whites 703,000 to 627,000.[20]

In the new Southern legislatures advocates of Negro suffrage led the deliberations. Alonso Ranzier of South Carolina urged his fellow citizens to accept that the right to vote "belongs alike to the wise and ignorant, to the virtuous and the vicious." He said he hoped that every lawmaker in the state would be inspired to view the voting of blacks as progress and reason. He wanted "every word that puts a limitation upon the manhood of the citizen, so far as regards the right to vote, struck from the record."[21]

Blacks attained a majority only in the South Carolina legislature. Black influence, however, was probably significant in Alabama, Louisiana, Florida, and Mississippi. They won major offices in a few instances— three became lieutenant governors, two U. S. senators, and fifteen U. S. representatives. Although they took over a variety of

18. "Wendell Phillips, Esq., Speech at Annual Meeting of the Anti-Slavery Society, Tremont Temple, Boston, January 28, 1864," *Brownson's Quararterly Review* 21 (April, 1864):195.
19. "Thaddeus Stevens, House of Representatives, January 23, 1864," *Brownson's Quarterly Review* 21 (April, 1864):166-85.
20. Simkins, *History of the South*, p. 271.
21. *Ibid.*, p. 96.

minor offices, these posts were of little influence and often were under white supervision.

Apparent success was deceiving, however, because leaders of the struggling Democratic Party in the South had no intention of accepting the Fourteenth and Fifteenth Amendments. Confederate officers who had returned to their prewar leadership posts under Presidential Reconstruction eased out of public office and began organizing opposition to the new governments. From his base as Dean of the Law School at the University of Mississippi, L. Q. C. Lamar along with James Z. George and others plotted a strategy that was to become a southern prototype. They encouraged Democrats to run for the legislature, helped them win a majority, then advised legislators to turn down the Fourteenth Amendment. When they rejected this amendment, the federal government refused to seat them and a new election was ordered. With their duly-elected representatives denied the right to hold office, Democrats were able to expand their grievances and their support for future revolution. Georgia Democrats won a majority in the legislature, approved the amendments, gained admission to the Union, and then expelled the twenty-eight Negro members from the lawmaking body. Blacks had the right to vote, said the Democrats, but not the right to hold office. The Georgia legislature also was reconstituted. As was the case in Mississippi, the conspirators attracted dissident white people to their cause. With this added strength they could make sure that civil rights laws were never enforced.

Encouraged by the national administration's inability and unwillingness to enforce the law, ex-Confederate leaders pursued plans to "redeem" their states. By coercion, by trickery, by every conceivable devious means they harrassed Negroes, white Republican voters, and election officials until they wore away the nation's will to fight for the Negro's rights. Such tactics were justified, they asserted, because Republican, carpetbagging war scavengers were using blacks to promote their own political fortunes. Henry Grady, noted Atlanta newspaper editor, expressed the popular rationalization of these actions before a New England audience a few years later. "Not in prejudice against the blacks, not in sectional estrangement, not in the hope of political dominion, but in a deep and abiding necessity," said Grady, white people banded together. Northern opportunists, he contended, were tempted by "this vast ignorant and purchasable vote—clannish, credulous, impulsive and passionate." According to Grady, Negroes were easy prey for the demagogue but were insensible to appeals of statesmen.[22]

Under the onslaught of the Redeemers, the enthusiasm of civil rights crusaders faded so fast that their seriousness of intent became doubtful. As soon as resistance appeared strong and enforcement difficult, most abandoned the cause. A reporter for *Nation* speculated that many who acted in behalf of the suffrage measures did so "more from the pressure of a real or supposed political necessity than from the conviction that the newly enfranchised race was really well fitted to make a good use of the right conferred upon them."[23] Even Carl Schurz, strong senatorial advocate of

22. Henry W. Grady, "The Race Problem in the South," in *Masterpieces of Modern Oratory*, ed. Edwin D. Shurter (New York: Ginn and Company, 1906), p. 225.
23. *Nation*, January 4, 1877, p. 53.

black rights, branded Congressional Reconstruction a failure. "That as a class they were ignorant and inexperienced and lacked a just conception of public interest," he said, "was certainly not their fault; for those who have studied the history of the world know but too well that slavery and oppression are very bad political schools." However, he added, "The stubborn fact remains that they were ignorant and inexperienced; that the public business was an unknown world to them; and that in spite of the best intentions they were easily misled."[24]

The issue of black suffrage was not resolved, but opponents of the measure held the upper hand. Southern Bourbons found that they could whip poor southern whites into line by suggesting that if all white voters did not hang together, blacks would take over. Henry Grady termed it racial suicide for whites to divide into factions and bid for the Negro vote. Black people would then rule, he warned, for they would hold the balance of power.[25] Probably a majority of white northerners believed black suffrage was morally right but, under the circumstances, not worth the sacrifice required to achieve it. Schurz, for example, told audiences that is was unwise to put "so large and influential a class of whites in point of political privileges below the colored people." This, he said, "could not fail to inflame those prejudices which stood in the way of a general and honest acceptance of the new order of things."[26] Southern orators, pressing their advantage, appealed for nationwide unity of whites on racial issues.

The extent of the antisuffrage victory became manifest in the election of 1875. When the Governor of Mississippi called upon President Grant for more troops in that election year to keep down intimidation of both Negro and Republican voters,

the President bowed to public pressure against such a move. He replied that "The whole public is tired out with these annual autumnal outbreaks in the South and the great majority are ready now to condemn any interference on the part of the Government."[27] This action left black people without the free ballot and thus left them to the mercy of whites. Some who had fought earnestly for black voting rights recognized defeat whereas others rationalized a kind of victory. A few liberals saw the white dominance arrangement as a solution allowing men with the greatest ability, integrity, and breadth of view to make decisions for each community. Negroes need to be guided, wrote the editor of Nation; people should do everything possible "to induce the negro to vote for the best men. . . and to restrain him from voting for bad ones."[28]

Mississippi Redeemers had gambled that the determination of Negro rights advocates was weak. They had set up committees "to investigate and keep under constant surveillance all county officers"[29] and pledged their lives, fortunes, and honor to win control of the state government by whatever means necessary.[30] They won the election because they were permitted to ignore statutory law and the constitu-

24. Carl Schurz, "A Plea for General Anmesty," in *The World's Famous Orations*, ed., William J. Bryan, (New York: Funk and Wagnall's Company, 1906), vol. 10 (America 3), 33. Hereafter referred to as Bryan, *Orations*.
25. Grady, "Race Problem," in *Masterpieces of Modern Oratory*, Shurter, p. 225.
26. Shurz, "A Plea for General Amnesty," in Bryan, *Orations*.
27. Simkins, *History of the South*, p. 289.
28. *Nation*, January 4, 1877, p. 54.
29. Dunbar Rowland, *Courts, Judges and Lawyers of Mississippi, 1798-1935* (Jackson, Miss.: The Press of Heiderman Bros., 1935), p. 195.
30. *Ibid.*

tion.[31] Systematically, they flogged, murdered, and threatened the opposition to keep them from the polls.[32] President Grant ignored the existence of whole companies of "Home Guard" forces formed unofficially in southern states with well-armed infantry, cavalry, and even artillery, to "see that the election was fair."[33] Under pressure to "let the South settle its own problems," Grant became one of many disgusted but actionless onlookers. The Democrats who took office in 1875 in Mississippi, said the President, were "officials chosen through fraud and violence such as would scarcely be credited to savages, much less to a civilized and Christian people."[34] Fully one-third of those who voted for the winning party, according to the *Jackson Daily Times*, did so entirely because they were coerced.[35] Grant, nevertheless, had acted as the public had desired. Because he never had "a policy to enforce against the will of the poeple," Roscoe Conkling nominated him for a third term.[36] The battle for black suffrage had been lost.

Though successful in redeeming their state and in blocking most blacks from voting, the Southern Democrats' campaign of fear brought a number of negative results. One such outcome was that Southern speakers shaped a rhetoric of desperation and listeners grew calloused to deceptive communication. Candidates overstated the case against Negro suffrage, maintaining that their opponents were seeking Negro rule.[37] The choice, they argued, was between the Democratic candidates and black domination. Those who aspired to office learned to demonstrate a depth of disgust for all who opposed white dominance by a show of colorful epidieictic or gentlemanly disdain. An example of tension-ridden style is seen in an official pronouncement of the Mississippi Democratic White Man's Party along with the Mississippi Democratic Party. The joint statement read:

The nefarious design of the Republican party to place the white man of the Southern states under government control of their late slaves, and degrade the Caucasion race as the inferiors of the African race, is a crime against the civilization of the age which needs only to be mentioned to be scorned by all intelligent minds, and we, therefore, call upon the people of Mississippi to vindicate alike the superiority of their race over the Negro, and their political power to maintain constitutional liberty.[38]

A few leaders such as "Private John" Allen, famous humorist and Congressman from Tupelo, Mississippi, opposed the violent practices of Democrats. Allen tried to reason with black voters and helped stop repressive actions of whites in Lee County.[39] Moderate voices, however, were either drowned out by the clamor for violent action or absorbed by the double-edged oratory that added a rhetorical wink to every conciliatory utterance. Persuasion of black voters usually was done in such a cynical way as to weaken rather than strengthen

31. Albert Kirwan, "A History of Mississippi Politics, 1876-1925," (Ph.D. Diss., Duke University, 1947), p. 3.
32. James Garner, *Reconstruction in Mississippi* (Boston: Macmillan, 1901), p. 209.
33. *Aberdeen* (Miss.) *Examiner*, August 2, 1883.
34. Garner, *Reconstruction*, p. 410.
35. *Jackson* (Miss.) *Daily Times*, Nov. 1, 1876.
36. Roscoe Conkling, "Nominating General Grant for a Third Term," *Orations of American Orators*, ed. Julian Hawthorne (New York: P. F. Collier & Son, 1900), p. 316.
37. C. H. Chamberlain, "Reconstruction of the Negro," *North American Review*, 267, (February, 1879):165.
38. Garner, *Reconstruction*, p. 209.
39. Clyde Faries, "The Rhetoric of 'Private John' Allen," (Diss., University of Missouri, 1964), p. 41.

the credibility of the persuader. After final efforts to gain Negro support, campaigners could be found standing around the polls on election day ready to lead bystanders in a Rebel yell when a "converted" black man voted the "right" ticket.[40]

Another scar left by the antisuffrage campaign is an inaccurate evaluation of what occured. Turn-of-the-century historians, writing state histories of Reconstruction, supported the popular Bourbon idea that Black and Tan governments of the late 1860s and the early 1870s were corrupt, wasteful, and self-centered. Nurtured by popular notions of the need for white dominance, they pictured highly inefficient systems where ignorant blacks held the offices and greedy carpetbaggers made the decisions. Yet, Reconstruction governments offered more in social services than was offered before or after the war, even with uncooperative, subversive Democrats trying to sabotage their every effort. In mockery, property owners charged exhorbitant prices for use of their property, for transportation, and for services on which they had a monopoly; then they attacked the government for wasteful practices. Historians either did not believe or were unwilling to explain that the major obstacle to peace and prosperity for the area was the decision by white leaders that white domination would be the rule. As one contemporary observer explained; under the Reconstruction government, "elections were free, fair, and honest . . . without violence, or disorder, or excessive rancor. The power that they held they put fairly at hazard with each recurring election. They neither cheated nor intimidated nor sought to intimidate their opponents."[41] This was in sharp contrast to the self-perpetuating plans adopted by Southern states after 1875.

Still another result of the suffrage struggle was political confusion and a set of new restrictive state constitutions in the 1890s. In order to keep objectors pacified, campaigners had to speak for equality and to mean white dominance, to call for universal justice and to mean fairness for whites only, and to urge open elections and to mean that Negroes may not vote. Such "understandings" led to ballot box stuffing, fraud, and acceptance of deceit as standard procedure until new constitutions brought a method of legally excluding blacks from the ballot. These new governmental documents contained "grandfather clauses," poll taxes, literacy tests, and a score of other measures designed to bar blacks from the voting booths. These measures disfranchised blacks as they were disigned to do, but, at the same time, they robbed poor whites of the vote and spurred on a redneck revolt that eventually drove the Bourbons from office.

Tired of the Bourbon doublespeak and empowered by new primary election laws to play a deciding role in selecting leaders and influencing legislation, poor white southerners in the early 1900s gave vent to their racial feelings. Now a candidate would be measured by his boldness in stating the class and race prejudices of the majority. As a result, a new breed of racist demagogues (i.e., James Vardaman and Theodore Bilbo of Mississippi, Jeff Davis of Arkansas, Tom Watson of Georgia, and Cole Blease of South Carolina) were inspired to new heights of stump campaigning by taking

---

40. Ruth L. Johnson, "A History of Tupelo," (Master's thesis: Mississippi State College, 1951), p. 23.
41. Chamberlain, "Reconstruction of the Negro," p. 170.

full advantage of the exciting vote-getting power of "lynch-the-nigger" oratory. Stirred by such evocative speaking, whites clamped even tighter restrictions upon black people, showed less charity toward them, and increased brutalities against them.

A fourth, though indirect, consequence of the ruthless campaign against black suffrage was the emergence of black organizations to counter repression. The progressive movement beginning in the 1890s probably staved off organized reaction for a while. However, when the progress proved to be for whites only, a frustrated group of liberal blacks formed the NAACP. The mere existence of such an organization probably raised some hope once again that blacks would gain the vote, but the most immediate value of the NAACP was that it offered a forum for such articulate spokesmen as W. E. B. DuBois, Kelly Miller, and W. Ashbie Hawkins. When both President Theodore Roosevelt and President Taft turned their backs on them, blacks had no reason to believe they would be enfranchised.

By his dismissal of three army companies in Brownsville, Texas, to assuage the feelings of Southern whites and his assertions that lynchings were caused by Negro assaults on white women, Roosevelt disassociated himself with the cause of the blacks. Taft, in his inaugural address, followed suit. "My chief purpose," he told the nation, "is not to effect a change in the electoral vote of the southern states. That is a secondary matter." He would use no force to insure the Negro's right to vote. "What I look forward to," he said, "is an increase in the tolerance of political views of all kinds and their advocacy throughout the southern states." His rationale for such optimism was that the Thirteenth and Fifteenth

amendments were guards against deprivation of the Negro's right to vote and, he said, "The Thirteenth and Fourteenth Amendments have been generally enforced." He admitted that the Fifteenth Amendment had not been generally observed, but, he opined, "It ought to be." He believed he saw a "tendency of southern legislation" toward squaring with the Amendment.[42]

Jubilant Southern leaders counted Taft's address as evidence that the nation now approved rather than merely tolerated their management of racial matters. To some this was progress toward "Southern normalcy." Julian Harris, editor of *Uncle Remus*, saw the Taft administration as a new era opening opportunities for white solidarity. Southern leadership should now split, he suggested, so as to gain a base of influence in the Republican councils, and "the Negro who waits for a federal appointment will turn gray with age."[43]

The Question of Economic Opportunity

At the close of the war, civil rights advocates were optimistic about the Negro's fitting into the free labor economy on an equal basis. General Fisk, for example, reporting in 1866 on freedmen in Tennessee, said, "It is my constant effort to cause them to feel independent and not depend upon the Government, or benevolent association for much aid. My faith in their ability to paddle their own canoes strengthens with daily experience. Let them be accorded even-handed justice," he added,

---

42. *Colorado* (Texas) *Citizen*, March 5, 1909.
43. Julian Harris, "Shall the Solid South Be Shattered," *Uncle Remus* (March, 1909), cited in the *Colorado* (Texas) *Citizen*, March 19, 1909.

"and they will work out their own salvation."[44] Indeed, outside the south, most subscribed to the view expressed by the editor of *Nation*, that "Negroes are always willing to work whey they can get fair treatment and regular pay."[45]

Southern landowners, on the other hand, had their doubts about the value of the black man in a free labor system. Carl Schurz told the President, after an official tour of the South at the end of the war, that he feared blacks would not receive fair treatment. Cotton growers had told him, "You cannot make a negro work without physical compulsion."[46] One Georgia planter had argued that one of his Negroes had shown himself unfit for freedom because he impudently refused to submit to a whipping.[47] Some whites believed that if blacks learned to read and write they would be spoiled for work.[48]

Whereas white southerners held to their demands that they should control working conditions and contracts of blacks, beyond the initial flurry of activity by the Freedmen's Bureau little was done to protect the Negroes' right to fair labor agreements. The black man's future "must be left to those among whom his lot is cast, with whom he is indissolubly connected, and whose prosperity depends upon their possessing his intelligent sympathy and confidence," argued Henry Grady,[49] and a chorus of white leaders echoed the same sentiment. Some blacks also subscribed to this position. A Natchez, Mississippi hack driver, for example, explained to a touring journalist that he liked his freedom, but, if he needed any assistance, he would go back to his old master.[50]

Grady tried to persuade Northern audiences that Negroes were happy and effective under the New South labor system. "We give to the world this year a crop of 7,500,000 bales of cotton, worth $450,000,000 and its cash equivalent in grain," he told one group, adding that "this enormous crop could not have come from the hands of sullen and discontented labor." Such production, he claimed, could come only "from peaceful fields, in which laughter and gossip rise above the hum of industry, and contentment runs with the singing plow."[51] "No section shows a more prosperous laboring population than the negroes of the South," he told another group of listeners; "none [is] in fuller sympathy with the employing and landowning class." In Grady's view, "Self interest as well as honor" forbade anything but the best possible treatment of the Negro laborer.[52]

If some did not accept Grady's point of view, few replied to his claims. President Benjamin Harrison, for example, simply washed his hands of the problem. In his inaugural address in 1889, he berated white southerners for their immorality and failures toward blacks, but he offered no hope for change. Southern leaders could, "by friendly instruction and cooperation," turn the black man into a productive and worthy ally, if they wanted to, he said. They could benefit the country as well as their local communities by creating a better social order and a more progressive econ-

---

44. *DeBow's Review* 30 (March, 1866):325.
45. *The Nation*, 1 (September 14, 1865), p. 325.
46. Carl Schurz, "Can The South Solve the Negro Problem?" *McClure's Magazine* 22 (January, 1904):260.
47. *Ibid.*
48. *Ibid.*, 264.
49. Grady, in Bryan, *Orations*, p. 150.
50. *The Missouri Republican*, September 28, 1869.
51. Grady, "Race Problem," in *Masterpieces of Modern Oratory*, Shurter, p. 221.
52. Grady, in Bryan, *Orations*, p. 148.

omy, he added. However, he pointed out, "A community where law is the rule of conduct and where courts, not mobs, execute the penalties, is the only attractive field for business investments and honest labor."[53] Grady charged that Republican deceit, not Democratic mistreatment, had discouraged the black man. "His first appeal to suffrage was the promise of 'forty acres and a mule.' His second, the threat that Democratic success meant his reenslavement," Grady explained. It should not be surprising, then, that the black man finally decided that his best friends were his white neighbors, Grady surmised.[54]

Orators' efforts to stereotype black laborers reveal the minds of the speakers better than they describe characteristics of Negro field hands. On the one hand they proclaimed that the black man was too lazy to work and on the other that he worked too hard. Some who claimed that Negroes would work only when coerced also maintained that foreign labor may not be the answer because no white person could do the work being done by blacks. The *Charleston Courier* blamed the high mortality rate of freedmen upon self-imposed idleness;[55] yet South Carolina's delegation in Washington expressed grave concern over the number of blacks leaving the state in search of work.[56]

This confusion changed little in the Post-Reconstruction era. According to the *New Orleans Picayune*, the great need for labor in the South and the unreliability of the black man were universally accepted facts. Yet southern employers found no better solution to the labor problem. The editor of the *Picayune*, for example, objected to introducing Chinese workers as an even greater evil. "Grave and widespread social and political evils are anticipated as a consequence of settlement among us of another

inferior, unassimilating and unChristianized race," said the *Picayune*.[57]

The weight of tradition, prejudice, and the entire economic structure stood against a black man's acquiring wealth, property, or position. The few who broke the color barriers during Reconstruction often felt the wrath of their white neighbors. An experience of the Reverend William Baker's personal servant illustrates this. Baker was pleased with his own magnanimity in performing a wedding ceremony with his "boy" and a black girl who had belonged to a Mrs. Madison. The Reverend recalled how gracious Mrs. Madison was to have permitted the ritual to be held in her house and with what loving concern she had told him about the young black girl. "All their money goes, at least that of all the rest of our negroes, [and here the minister added that such was the case with all Negroes,] for bright calicoes, brass jewelry, candy, and all sorts of candied fruit, oysters and the like," said Mrs. Madison. "But poor things! I am so glad you consented to marry them. Try not to laugh; here they come!"[58] As a father would counsel a son, he remembered urging the black man not to marry because there would not be enough money to provide for the two of them. How the minister pitied the poverty of the young couple as they went happily off to begin life together! Yet, how bitterly he spoke of their success when the

53. Benjamin Harrison, "Inaugural Address, 1889," in Bryan, *Orations*, p. 159.
54. Grady, "Race Problem," in *Masterpieces of Modern Oratory*, Shurter, p. 227.
55. *The Charleston Courier*, cited in *The Missouri Republican*, September 28, 1869.
56. *St. Louis Daily News*, January 1, 1882.
57. *The New Orleans Picayune*, cited in *The Missouri Republican*, September 28, 1869.
58. William Baker, *Scribner's Monthly*, 18 (July, 1879), p. 378.

young man went to the legislature and began to make a modest living. He felt sick at the sight of his ex-"personal boy" riding in his own carriage and owning his own small home.[59]

Disgust and anger of whites at the economic prosperity and social ease of a successful black man seem based on a more fundamental concern. Winning in the competition for money, property, and position forbodes possible winning in the competition for a mate. Knowing the depths of this fear, Booker T. Washington and other black leaders following his approach tried to persuade white employers that working Negroes were not a threat to the social system. In an address at the Atlanta Cotton Exposition in 1893, Washington promised property owners that the two races could be as united as the fist in economic matters while remaining as separate as the fingers in all social affairs.[60] At the same time, he called upon blacks to work for self-improvement—cleanliness, education, manners, tradesmanship—before being concerned with politics and social mobility. Whites found such discourse reassuring and encouraged Washington to continue to work for "the improvement of his race."

Washington had concluded that blacks could not gain economic stability through force or through legal processes. They would have to secure the support of white people and this would take time. He assured his brothers that if they were diligent, hard-working, and economical their status would eventually change. "By the way of the shop, the field, the skilled hand, habits of thrift and economy, by way of industrial school and college, we are coming," he said. "We are crawling up, working up, yes, bursting up. Often through oppression, unjust discrimination, and prejudice, but

through them we are coming up," he told them and added that with "proper habits, intelligence, and property, there is no power on earth that can permanently stay our progress." Yet, he warned his fellow black men that they would need "the help, the encouragement, and the guidance that the strong can give the weak."[61] He tried to inspire black men and win the good will of whites.

The Question of Legal Justice

The question of whether blacks would receive justice before the courts in the same measure as whites was not widely debated. The Black Codes had placed "persons of color" in a lower caste and Redemption reaffirmed the spirit of the Code. Under these measures, blacks could marry, make contracts, sue and be sued. Yet interracial marriage, carrying deadly weapons, and testifying in court against whites were forbidden them. Apprenticeship laws permitted Negro orphans to be bound to property owners and vagrancy laws forbade Negroes to "unlawfully assemble themselves together." Congress abolished the Codes when it wrested control of Reconstruction from the President, but the Redeemers reinstituted some of the basic color lines. That blacks should receive separate judicial treatment found little opposition North or South.

---

59. *Ibid.*, 375-81.
60. Booker T. Washington, "Atlanta Exposition Address," in *A Treasury of the World's Great Speeches*, ed. Houston Peterson (New York: Simon and Schuster, 1954), p. 636.
61. Booker T. Washington, "The American Standard," in *The World's Great Speeches*, ed. Lewis Copeland, (New York: The Book League of America, 1942), p. 332.

Southern leaders such as Henry Grady argued that Negroes received greater justice in the South than elsewhere in the nation. Boston merchants heard Grady explain how the South had lifted the slave to heights of which he could never have dreamed in his savagery in Africa and how white Southern gentlemen had been left "a saving and excellent heritage" in their compassionate and masterly relationships with the black man.[62] Northern leaders found it expedient to offer no refutation on legal decisions concerning blacks. In his campaign for the presidency in 1872, Horace Greeley told a Portland, Maine, audience that he heard but one demand coming from the South and that was for justice; he heard only one desire from them, a desire for reconciliation. They wanted to be reunited with the North "on any terms which do not involve the surrender of their manhood."[63] Even liberals such as Carl Schurz, who viewed southern prejudices as one of the nation's major evils, believed it was better to mitigate, to assuage, and to disarm these racial prejudices with "prudent measures" rather than by force or restriction.[64] Appealing for general amnesty in an 1872 Senate speech, he argued that new problems arising from attempts to guarantee rights of blacks were greater than the problem of racial injustice. The main problem was securing "good and honest government to all."[65]

Attitudes toward the justice that should be accorded blacks were reflected in the language and in the presumption that fairness prevailed. Speakers from every section of the country said "The people of the South" when they were referring only to a majority of white southern voters, and called for "universal justice" when they were referring only to justice for whites. A mere pronouncement by a reasonable official that equality before the law reigned throughout the land seemed to gain more adherents than any amount of evidence to the contrary. In his first inaugural address, Grover Cleveland assured the country that "there should be no pretext for anxiety touching the protection of the freedmen in their rights or their security in the enjoyment of their privileges under the constitution and its amendments."[66] Consequently, black men knew they were not being remanded to slavery, white southerners knew they could dominate without federal intervention, and those concerned with equal justice for blacks retained their basis for rationalizing inaction.

Savagery against blacks never ceased, however. Many northern newspapers during Reconstruction and for a few years thereafter published regularly "Southern Outrages," catalouging rapes, murders, beatings, and other cruelties against the freedmen. In Nashville, Tennessee, Elizabeth Childress, a black, was brought to "justice" for "compounding potions" and "speaking words of evil intent to inflict pain and deformity upon" Mrs. Millie Hays, a white.[67] In Wayne County, Mississippi, Nelson Slater, black, and Elizabeth Duke, white, were arrested for cohabitation. When they were found to be legally married (a fact perhaps known to authorities before

---

62. Grady, "Race Problem," in *Masterpieces of Modern Oratory*, Shurter, p. 218.
63. Horace Greeley, "During His Campaign for President," in Bryan, *Orations*, p. 55.
64. Carl Schurz, "An Appeal for General Amnesty," in Bryan, *Orations*, p. 35.
65. Schurz, in Bryan, *Orations*, p. 30.
66. Grover Cleveland, "First Inaugural Address," in *World's Great Speeches*, ed. Copeland, p. 330.
67. *The Missouri Republican*, October 10, 1869.

the arrest), the jury pronounced them innocent, releasing them from legal punishment but opening their status to a public ready to torment them for their code-breaking.[68] The body of a dead Negro with a rope around his neck was found in the water near Des Arc, Arkansas. A jury, hastily summoned, quickly drew the verdict, "death by unknown causes."[69] Two motormen were shot in St. Louis, supposedly by a black man; police rounded up 300 Negroes, each, according to the police, answering the murderer's description.[70] In Marshall, Texas, a Negro being arrested on a minor charge shot the arresting officer. Within minutes, a mob of fifty or so "unidentified" citizens captured and hanged the black man from the water tower as law enforcement officials looked on.[71] Such incidents were widespread and numerous. A black man would be pronounced guilty with minimal evidence if his crime were against a white man. On the other hand, a white man was rarely found guilty of a crime against a Negro. Periodicals reported but usually did not condemn these events.

Correctional practices likewise demonstrated white determination that blacks should not be accorded equal justice before the law. New-South pitchmen maintained that in practice the Negro received perhaps more justice than the white man. "In penal legislation we have steadily reduced felonies to misdemeanors," Grady told audiences in the North. He maintained that this was done to save the black race from its own weaknesses. In the North, he pointed out, one in every 466 black men was in jail, whereas, in the South the number was one in every 1,865. In the North, he added, black prisoners were six times as great in number as white prisoners while in the South the number was only four times as

great.[72] "We treat the negro fairly, measuring to him justice in the fullness the strong should give to the weak, and leading him in the steadfast ways of citizenship that he may no longer be the prey of the unscrupulous and the sport of the thoughtless," Grady said.[73]

Yet the unscrupulous and the thoughtless were not legally restrained. White crimes against blacks generally went unpunished and black crimes against blacks received little attention from law enforcement officials and judges. In Sunflower County, Mississippi, for instance, a black orator aroused a crowd of four to five hundred to walk to Minter's Store on the Tallahatchie River and present grievances. After a brief pacification effort, Colonel Minter called for white people with guns who came in and shot up the crowd.[74] Legal action, if any was taken in such a case, would have been against the agitators. An indignant letter to the editor of the *Colorado Citizen* from William Hart, Rector, Christ Church, Eagle Lake, Texas, illustrates popular white thinking on proper correctional practices. Hart complained that six "well dressed and clean looking young foreigners" were sentenced to serve thirty days on the County Farm at Columbus for vagrancy because they could not pay $15.00 fines. Said Hart, they would be "treated worse than state convicts (for they are not only herded with

---

68. *The Missouri Republican*, September 28, 1869.
69. *The Missouri Republican*, September 30, 1869.
70. *Colorado Citizen*, December 31, 1909.
71. *Ibid*.
72. Grady, "Race Problem," in *Masterpieces of Modern Oratory*, Shurter, p. 223.
73. *Ibid*., p. 229.
74. *The Missouri Republican*, September 26, 1869.

negroes, but with insane creatures)" in this "home of the free."[75]

Almost any crime by a black could be forgiven provided it was committed against a person of the same race and provided white character witnesses could be found. A black citizen of Columbus, Texas, Will Davis, for example, was convicted of murdering his wife with a shotgun. He was spared the death penalty when a few white witnesses testified to his "previous good character and industrious habits."[76] A less heinous crime against a white person brought demands for immediate punishment. In Tiptonville, Tennessee, when three Negro brothers "created a disturbance" near a church, resulting in the death of a deputy sheriff, an angry mob of whites pursued, captured, tried on the spot, and lynched them without fear of any further legal action.[77] Similar scenes were repeated throughout the country without arousing indignation among the majority. Black militants such as W.E.B. DuBois, a few social gospel ministers, and some progressive politicians sought reform, but they were outshouted by vociferous proponents of lynching such as South Carolina's Senator Pitchfork Ben Tillman and an impressive number of less vehement apologists for the practice.

The Question of Social Equality

Racial antagonism following abolition of slavery grew from political fears as well as from the education and economic gaps between the races. The question of social equality, however, was a more fundamental issue than these. At the initiation of their freedom black people did not strive for social equality, yet some whites were concerned that they may have intended even

more than equality. Senator Morgan of Alabama, for example, argued that the main reason Negroes wanted to vote was to gain the same social privileges as white people.[78] "The Negroes have intended," said Morgan, "that the invasion shall not cease until the races have become homogenous through complete admixture."[79] This was the root fear behind almost all racial disharmony. This was at the bottom of the problem of determining the place of black men in American Society. Whites had a pathological dread of miscegenation becoming a two-way practice.

Although rarely mentioned in public discourse, this issue did sometimes appear obliquely when someone discussed amalgamation of the races. The public case against race-mixing was that mongrels inherited only the weakest parental characteristics. Hard evidence did not support the position, but it was merely a facade argument at best and, consequently, was not debated. In an effort to blame Congressional Reconstruction for division of the races, Philip Bruce maintained that sharp separation did not begin until a year or two after the war ended. Attempts at interracial marriage immediately following the war were not uncommon, he argued, because "the kindly feeling which in the age of slavery united the two populations had not yet ceased."[80] Around Bruce's Southside, Virginias plantation social intercourse between black and white may have been a

75. *The Colorado Citizen*, February 19, 1909.
76. *The Colorado Citizen*, October 9, 1908.
77. *The Colorado Citizen*, November 27, 1908.
78. J. C. Price, "Does the Negro Seek Social Equality?" *Forum* 10 (January, 1891):559.
79. *Ibid.*
80. Philip A. Bruce, "The American Negro of Today," *The Contemporary Review* 77 (February, 1900):285-86.

common practice, but across the nation this was not the case. All post-war Southern state constitutions forbade interracial marriage and few people ever condoned it. In fact, when fear of two-way miscegenation reached a peak, white men were even discouraged by the force of social censure from fathering mulato children.[81]

One justification offered for opposing racial equality was a belief that the black race was innately inferior. "The negro . . . has physical, ethical, and psychological peculiarities which differentiate him from all other races of men," said William Holcomb, a southern medical doctor.[82] He offered a vivid description of Negroid characteristics:

The skull is thick, approximating that of a monkey. His bones approach those of an ape. Exceedingly sensitive to cold—must stay in Southern climate. Hair is short and crisp resembling wool. Physically and mentally inferior to caucasians, organically constituted to be [an] agricultural laborer . . . [he is] lazy, feeble willed, only happy under strict discipline, [and] innately servile.[83]

Holcomb concluded his "scientific treatise" by observing that "There will be no negro philosophers, statesmen, warriors, mathematicians, etc . . . . [but] he will outstrip his caucasian brother in achieving those ideal virtues described in the Sermon on the Mount."[84] Advocates of race separation relied upon such "authoritative" data to support claims of white superiority.

With this view of the innate qualities of blacks, some whites adopted race separation as a religion. They tested all public issues for possible racial overtones. Carl Schurz found that southerners "who conversed about every other subject calmly and sensibly would lose their tem-

per as soon as the negro question was touched."[85] One southerner expressed his objections to permitting social interaction by saying, "Elevation of the blacks would be the degradation of the whites."[86]

Fear of elevating the black man and fear of his gaining social equality caused whites to block efforts to create equal educational opportunities. Directors of the Freedmen's Bureau believed that by pumping teachers and money into black schools they could equalize educational attainment of the races within a short time. They failed for two major reasons. First, white southerners threatened, beat, and even murdered Bureau-sponsored teachers until they abandoned their schools. Second, with little academic reinforcement outside the schools, newly-freed students would require a long time to progress very far. Only 5 percent of freedmen could read, and backers of Negro rights had not the patience to stand behind a literacy program long enough to build an atmosphere for learning in black communities.

Booker Washington's technical school at Tuskegee, Alabama, was tolerated, if not supported, because he taught blacks that they should be satisfied with their second-class status. Wherever community leaders tried to upgrade education for blacks either through integration into white schools or through measures to make them truly equal, a storm was raised. Even after the

81. *Ibid.*, 287.
82. William Holcomb, M. D., "Characteristics and Capabilities of the Negro Race," *Southern Literary Messenger* 35 (December, 1861):401.
83. *Ibid.*, 408.
84. *Ibid.*, 410.
85. Schurz, "Can South Solve Negro Problem?", p. 260.
86. *Ibid.*, p. 264.

turn of the century, scattered efforts to integrate schools were still being made and almost always with negative results. In September of 1908, for instance, when the Houston, Texas, school board ruled that the first six grades only should be segregated, white students in the upper grades went on strike. Demanding removal of all blacks from previously all white classrooms, they paraded in front of the school shouting, "No nigger school for us."[87] Such actions prompted Governor Charles Grosvenor, of Ohio, to observe that the only remedy to the problem of social inequality was education of the white people.[88]

Interpretation

Second-class citizenship was the best the dominant race would offer the black man. The fight to attain for him suffrage, economic stability, justice in court, routine civil rights, or social equality in the Reconstruction or Post-Reconstruction era was unsuccessful. So determined and ruthless were those who opposed Negro rights that most advocates of equality withdrew from the contest, rationalizing that their efforts were untimely and their goals overly optimistic. Belief that blacks are innately inferior and fear that miscegenation would flow two ways if black men gained social equality or economic success barred efforts to secure first-class citizenship for freedmen. The position popularized by Henry Grady, that "We are commanded to make good this change of American policy which has not perhaps changed American prejudice—to make certain here what has elsewhere been impossible between whites and blacks"[89] sustained supporters of separa-

tion. Those who wanted integration but failed to work for it found sustenance in the words from Lincoln's Second Inaugural Address: "Neither side," said the President, "anticipated that the cause of the conflict might cease when . . . the conflict itself should cease."

By 1915, progress for the black man had been barred by legislation, by tradition, and by entrenched attitudes of white leaders. The period from the Civil War to World War I saw issues concerning rights of blacks emerge, become the center of heated disputation, and virtually fade from the mainstream of public affairs. The "back to normalcy" philosophy along with the rejuvenated Ku Klux Klan helped maintain this status quo during the 1920s, just as did the great depression of the 1930s. World War II in the 1940s and sit-ins and marches in the 1950s and 1960s wrought some changes. Certain legal obstructions to voting, to the application of justice, and to economic opportunities were removed; yet extra-legal obstacles remained to prevent many blacks from full use of their civil rights, from receiving criminal justice, and from gaining economic stability. If the analyses of black militants of the 1970s are accurate, the barriers to equal opportunity for Negroes are still secured. The basic problem dividing the races remains. The white man's fear of two-way miscegenation has not subsided.

87. *The Houston Chronicle*, cited in *The Colorado Citizen*, October 1, 1908.
88. Charles Grosvenor, "The Negro Problem in the South," *Forum*, 29 (August, 1900):724.
89. Grady, "Race Problem" in *Masterpieces of Modern Oratory*, Shurter, p. 219.

BIBLIOGRAPHY

Anthologies of speeches, such as those given below, provide texts of a number of public addresses relating to issues concerning the black man's rights in the period 1865-1915. Generally, however, the editors have been too selective of both orators and orations to give a broad view of what Americans were thinking:

Shurter, Edwin D., ed. *Masterpieces of Modern Oratory* New York: Ginn and Company, 1906.

Hawthorne, Julian, ed.*Orations of American Orators.* New York: P. F. Collier and Son, 1900.

Peterson, Houston, ed. *A Treasury of the World's Great Speeches.* New York: Simon and Schuster, 1954.

Bryan, William Jennings, ed. *The World's Famous Orations.* New York: Funk and Wagnalls, 1906.

Specialized histories offer much factual data not easily attainable in other sources. Conclusions in these histories do not always flow from the evidence, but the information is carefully documented:

Garner, James. *Reconstruction in Mississippi.* Boston: Macmillan, 1901.

Rowland, Dunbar.*Courts, Judges and Lawyers of Mississippi, 1798-1935.* Jackson, Mississippi: The Press of Heiderman Brothers, 1935.

Simkin, Francis B. *A History of the South.* New York: Alfred A. Knopf, 1959

Wharton, Vernon. *The Negro in Mississippi, 1865-1890.* New York: Harper and Row, 1947.

Woodward, C. Vann. *Origins of the New South.* Baton Rouge: Louisiana State University Press, 1951.

Contemporary magazines contain speeches and commentary on questions of Negro rights. A wider variety of points of view is found in these periodicals than in the histories or the anthologies:

The Arena
Brownson's Quarterly Review
Contemporary Review
Dobson's Review
The Forum
McClure's Magazine
The Nation
North American Review
The Outlook
Scribner's Monthly
The Southern Literary Messenger

Most useful in this investigation were contemporary newspapers. Large-circulation journals carried speeches by American leaders and comments by policy makers. Small town weeklies were equally important in reflecting the attitudes of rural America.

10 Labor Agitation in America: 1865-1915

Charles J. Stewart

Post-Civil War America was a vastly different nation from the one that had flung itself into a fratricidal war in 1861. During the 1850s, small businesses were giving way to corporations, the population was mainly agrarian, railroads and the telegraph were only beginning to link the scattered parts of the nation, and a trade union movement was being heard from for the first time.[1]

The war placed immense demands upon industry to produce munitions, military uniforms and equipment, shipping, and railroads. Billions in government funds, high rates of profit, and low wages produced great personal fortunes. The developing labor movement, on the other hand, was virtually destroyed by the war, low wages, and inflation.

The America that emerged from the war developed rapidly into an urban, industrial nation.[2] Urban centers, swelled by millions of immigrants, grew eight times faster than rural areas. Massive industrialization—spawned by the Civil War, aided by new inventions, and led by the new millionaires—searched unceasingly for new markets and cheap labor. Railroads grew from 35,000 miles of trackage in 1865 to 185,000 miles of trackage in 1895 and crisscrossed the continent, opening nearly every area to the capitalist with money to invest. Unscrupulous "robber barons" and the new moneyed class—Jay Gould, James Fisk, Dan Drew, Cornelius Vanderbilt, John D. Rockefeller, and others—amassed ever greater fortunes, often bleeding companies of capital, overextending stock, and eliminating competition through monopolies, trusts, and other arrangements.[3] "Survival of the fittest" and "rugged individualism" were the slogans of the period; Darwin's *Origin of Species* as interpreted by Herbert Spencer and William Graham Sumner was its bible. Immigrant and prison laborers,

1. For history of the labor movement see John R. Commons, *The History of Labour in the United States*, 3 vols. (New York: Macmillan, 1926); Norman J. Ware, *The Labor Movement in the United States, 1860-1895* (New York: D. Appleton and Co., 1929); and Philip S. Foner, *History of the Labor Movement in the United States*, 4 vols. (New York: International Publishers, 1947).
2. Thomas C. Cochran and William Miller, *The Age of Enterprise* (New York: Macmillan, 1942).
3. Matthew Josephson, *The Robber Barons* (New York: Harcourt, Brace and Co., 1934). For a debate of the contribution of the great capitalists see Allan Nevins and Matthew Josephson, "Should American History Be Rewritten," *Saturday Review*, February 6, 1954, pp. 7-10, 44-49.

women and children, and men who had no other choice provided the cheap labor. At the same time, inventions made production of goods faster and cheaper—eliminating jobs for skilled and unskilled workers.

Economic chaos with periodic "panics" bankrupted thousands of businesses, swelled unemployment ranks, and reduced wages to subsistence or below. Ironically, the depressions worked in favor of the great industrialists, giving them an opportunity to purchase companies (often competitors) at low prices. Standard Oil, Carnegie Steel, and the Pullman Car Company thus grew into giant corporations.

Labor agitation was inevitable, and confrontations with employers frequently ended in bitter strikes and open violence. The names Homestead, Haymarket, and Pullman mark only a few of the major battles between labor and capital.[4] Early leaders of the labor movement's rebirth, such as William H. Sylvis, were veterans from the prewar trade union movement, while others like Eugene V. Debs, Terence V. Powderly, and Samuel Gompers emerged from the ranks during the postwar period. Thousands of workers joined unions, dropped out, and rejoined. The National Labor Union, the Knights of Labor, and the American Railway Union were born, grew to impressive power and size, and dwindled or died before 1900. Only the American Federation of Labor and individual trade unions survived into the twentieth century and enjoyed a fairly steady growth in both size and influence.[5]

This essay focuses on the period 1865-1915, the era of labor's greatest struggles and growth. It seeks answers to these questions: What was the labor issue as voiced by labor leaders? As voiced by industrialists? How did labor propose to solve workers' problems? How did industrialists react to or counter organized labor's solutions? What were probable reasons for labor's successes and failures? Since these questions pertain to a long and complex social movement, they cannot be answered adequately without considering societal values, arguments and ideas, leadership and organizations, and the rhetoric of the period. The objective is a better understanding of the early labor movement, the nature of social movements, and the function of rhetoric in movements.[6]

The Issue From Labor's Point-of-View

Labor spokesmen of the 1860s and 1870s devoted more time to explaining the labor issue than later leaders who were preoccupied with solutions and incessant industrial warfare. These early spokesmen were firm believers in the American system as produced by the founders of the republic, founders who "intended to create a true democracy, where every man should be in the enjoyment of equal rights and priv-

4. The U.S. Bureau of Labor tabulated strike statistics for the 25 year period 1881 to 1905. Strikes and lockouts totalled 38,303 involving 199,954 establishments and 7,444,270 workers.

5. For histories of these unions see Charlotte Todes, *William H. Sylvis and the National Labor Union* (New York: International Publishers, 1942); Terence V. Powderly, *The Path I Trod* (New York: Columbia University Press, 1940); Ray Ginger, *The Bending Cross* (New Brunswick, N.J.: Rutgers University Press, 1949); and Samuel Gompers, *Seventy Years of Life and Labor* (New York: E.P. Dutton and Co., 1925).

6. The analysis of labor agitation is based on 100 speeches by 23 labor spokesmen. Since few industrialists defended their actions and beliefs, the analysis of industrialist reaction is based on 5 speeches, essays by social Darwinists, and studies of labor-industrial conflicts.

ileges."[7] They argued that all men were created equal and endowed with certain human and civil rights given by nature and God and guaranteed by American institutions and charters. Leaders of the 1860s and 1870s had, after all, just come through a bloody civil war fought partially to protect these rights. The opening lines of the 1868 platform of the National Labor Union—the first attempt to unite all unions into a single national body—was the second paragraph of the Declaration of Independence:

We hold these truths to be self-evident: that all people are created equal; that they are endowed by their Creator with certain inalienable rights; that among them are life, liberty, and the pursuit of happiness; that to secure these rights, governments are instituted among men, deriving their just powers from the consent of the governed.[8]

These guaranteed rights and liberties were synonymous with "worker's rights" and "industrial liberty," labor speakers declared, but the "working" or "laboring" class was, in fact, being excluded from both. "Men talk to me of our independence and boast of our constitutional government, and all that it guarantees to us," William H. Sylvis (president of the National Labor Union) said, "but with these spread-eagle gentlemen I do not agree. These things will do very well for Fourth-of-July orations, but not for everyday life."[9]

Labor spokesmen demanded rights and equality in two areas: decision making and a just share of the nation's wealth. The laborer and the employer should be equals and not "master and slave," Sylvis exclaimed. "We profess to recognize manhood in rags or broadcloth, in poverty or riches, and claim for labor the same prerogatives accorded to capital," he concluded.[10] James R. Sovereign (General Master Workman of the Knights of Labor) said "Labor is rated with tools, machinery and material, and it is considered an act of charity to give employment to the working people.."[11] The message was clear. Laborers considered themselves "factory slaves" or "serfs" caught up in "wages slavery"; the labor movement was the road to emancipation. They wanted their manhood recognized and a stance equal to that of the employer; equality meant a voice in determining wages and working conditions. Speaking to the Academy of Social Sciences in 1902, Samuel Gompers (president of the American Federation of Labor) stated:

We find that one of the greatest causes contributing toward the disturbance of industry, the severance of anything like friendly relations between employer and employes is the fact that the employers assume to themselves the absolute right to dictate and direct the terms under which workers shall toil, the wages, hours and other conditions of

7. William H. Sylvis, "Speech Delivered in Birmingham, Pa., September, 1868," in *The Life, Speeches, Labors and Essays of William H. Sylvis,* ed. James C. Sylvis (Philadelphia: Claxton, Remsen and Haffelfinger, 1872), p. 224.
8. William H. Sylvis, "Platform and Principles of the National Labor Union," in *Life, Speeches, Labors and Essays*, p. 284. Stated Sept. 25, 1868.
9. Sylvis, "Speech Delivered in Birmingham," p. 225.
10. William H. Sylvis, "Address Delivered at Chicago, January 9, 1865," in *Life, Speeches, Labors and Essays*, p. 130; and Sylvis, "Address Delivered at Boston, January, 1867," in *Life, Speeches, Labors and Essays*, p. 173.
11. James R. Sovereign, "Annual Address of the General Master Workman," *Proceedings of the General Assembly: Knights of Labor* (1897), p. 13. Delivered Nov. 12, 1897, in Louisville, Kentucky.

employment, without permitting the voice of the workmen to be raised in their own behalf.[12]

"Life, liberty, and the pursuit of happiness" to labor spokesmen meant a greater share in the nation's growing wealth: better education, food, housing, working conditions, hours, wages, opportunity to work, and more leisure time and cultural opportunities. Speakers did not always agree on the proportion of labor's share, however. Terence V. Powderly (General Master Workman of the Knights of Labor) asked for a "full and just share of the values of capital it [labor] helped to create,"[13] while Sylvis stated "that ten per cent of what they [workers] produce is hardly a fair or just proportion to be set aside for their benefit."[14] At times Sylvis, Powderly, and other leaders demanded an "equal" share in the profits of industry. Wendell Phillips remarked: "That's the meaning of the labor movement—an equalization of property."[15] "What is it that we demand? What that we seek?" James Redpath asked and, then, answered his own questions: "Fair play—that is all; equal and exact justice to all men; equality of rights, equality of duties, equality of burdens under the law."[16] Not infrequently labor spokesmen demanded *all* wealth produced by labor. As Sylvis declared in 1868: "We must adopt a system that will divide the *profits* of labor among those who produce them—a system that will drive the vast army of non-producers—paupers upon the producers of wealth—into honorable employment or starvation, for no man has a right to live who does not produce what he consumes."[17] In an earlier speech, Sylvis had asked: "Shall he not dwell in palaces who raises palaces? . . . Shall she not wear who spins; he eat who sows?"[18] Labor was

more valuable than capital, union leaders contended, so labor should receive a fair share, equal share, or all of the profits—the position varying from speaker to speaker and even in the rhetoric of the same individual. Above all, workers should have a voice in determining their share and conditions. From the labor point-of-view, then, the labor issue was a matter of serious infringements upon the basic rights and liberties guaranteed by American institutions. The appeal was to traditional American values and beliefs in equality, justice, and fair play. Abstract concepts like freedom, equality, and pursuit of happiness naturally led to differences of interpretation among labor spokesmen, but as true agitators they offered no definitions. To them the issue was a simple matter of slavery or freedom, equal status or serfdom, and the labor movement was a new emancipation.

12. Samuel Gompers, "Limitations of Conciliation and Arbitration," *The American Federationist* 9 (June, 1902):310. Delivered in Philadelphia, 1902.
13. Terence V. Powderly, "Response to the Address of Welcome by the Virginia Governor," *Proceedings of the General Assembly: Knights of Labor* (1886), p. 11. Delivered Oct. 4, 1886, in Richmond, Virginia.
14. Sylvis, "Address Delivered at Chicago," p. 164.
15. Wendell Phillips, "Wealth and Work," *John Swinton's Paper*, March 23, 1884, p. 1. Address delivered Oct. 31, 1871, place unknown.
16. James Redpath, "The People to the Front," *John Swinton's Paper*, Dec., 14, 1884, p. 1. Date and place of address unknown.
17. William H. Sylvis, "Extracts from Report to the Toronto Session of the I.M.I.U.," in *Life, Speeches, Labors and Essays*, pp. 266-267. Address delivered July 8, 1868, in Toronto, Ontario.
18. Sylvis, "Address Delivered at Chicago," p. 171.

The Issue from the Industrialist Point-of-View

While Charles Darwin's *Origin of Species* was creating a furor in Europe during the 1850s, America was preoccupied with the approaching conflict between North and South. Darwin's work was widely reviewed in the United States in 1860, but the war prevented all but a few intellectuals from giving it serious consideration. The years following the war, however, witnessed an unprecedented philosophical revolution in America.[19]

Darwin's theories, as interpreted by Herbert Spencer and William Graham Sumner, fitted perfectly with a rapidly industrializing nation like the United States that virtually worshipped science and the gospel of progress. Americans had long believed in "individualism"—epitomized by the frontiersman—and saw their republic as the highest form of government, having evolved upward from the monarchy. "Social" Darwinists simply applied the concepts of natural selection and evolution to society.

The new philosophy appealed to the American middle-class with its emphasis on virtues like personal providence, family loyalty and responsibility, hard work, careful management, and self-sufficiency. William Graham Sumner's famous lecture "The Forgotten Man" was devoted to the "clean, virtuous, domestic citizen, who pays his debts and his taxes and is never heard of out of his little circle." "He is the simple, honest laborer, ready to earn his living by productive work," Sumner stated, "We pass him by because he is independent, self-supporting, and asks no favors. He does not appeal to the emotions or excite the sentiments."[20] Darwinists argued that nature, the Declaration of Independence, and the Constitution did not guarantee equality of status or happiness to everyone, but only the opportunity to compete with the rest of society without interference from the government, misguided reformers and philanthropists, or any other unnatural force. If a person was of low status and poverty stricken, he alone was to blame. As Sumner commented, economic life offered rewards to men of good character and ability while it punished the "negligent, shiftless, inefficient, silly, and imprudent."[21] Any effort to change this "natural order" of life inevitably placed an added burden on the "forgotten man"—higher taxes, higher costs, and reduced work opportunities.

Works by social Darwinists (Spencer, Sumner, Youmans, Fisk) sold in the hundreds of thousands. A whole generation of writers, newspaper editors, politicians, teachers, and industrialists was influenced by Darwin's teachings and disciples. Few students, for instance, went through Yale University without coming in contact with Sumner. Even labor leaders were not immune from Darwinism. John Swinton, founder and editor of a labor paper, said laborers were the "natural owners" of all

_____

19. This discussion of Darwinism and social Darwinism in America is based primarily on two sources: Richard Hofstadter, *Social Darwinism in American Thought* (Boston: The Beacon Press, 1960); and Paul F. Boller, Jr., *American Thought in Transition: The Impact of Evolutionary Naturalism, 1865-1900* (Chicago: Rand McNally and Co., 1969).

20. William Graham Sumner, "The Forgotten Man," in *The Forgotten Man and Other Essays*, ed. Albert G. Keller (New Haven: Yale University Press, 1919), pp. 476 and 480.

21. Hofstadter, *Social Darwinism*, p. 10.

things,[22] while Samuel Gompers remarked that workers' recognitions of their wrongs had come "through the gradual process of evolution" and that the trade union was the "natural form of working class organization."[23]

Industrialists saw the suitability of social Darwinism to their needs. Since unrestricted competition was the scientific way of natural selection of the highest quality industrial leaders, they argued against all government interference or regulation. The industrialist was the new "rugged individual;" the corporation was the highest form of industrial organization; and uncontrolled competition was the means of providing for the "survival of the fittest." The laborer was the lowest level of human development, for he had equal opportunity to become a millionaire and had not. He was classed, therefore, with raw materials—something you purchase for production. The industrialist might pity the laborer, but he could not offer such an inferior a voice in wages, hours, or working conditions. Collective bargaining was unthinkable.

Industrialists did not have to defend their position in public. Nearly all newspapers—except the labor press—were owned, controlled by, or in sympathy with the industrialist interpretation of social Darwinism. Leading clergymen like Henry Ward Beecher spoke against the labor movement. Russell H. Conwell, in his famous lecture "Acres of Diamonds"—delivered more than five thousand times, declared that "ninety-eight out of one hundred of the rich men of America are honest. That is why they are rich." On the other hand, he remarked, "I sympathize with the poor, but the number of poor who are to be sympathized with is very small." "Now then, I say again that the opportunity to get rich, to attain unto great wealth, is here in

Philadelphia now, within the reach of almost every man and woman who hears me speak tonight," Conwell declared.[24] Darwinists like Sumner also argued that man should not waste his time on "unscientific" discourse—such as speculating on social issues. Industrialists happily followed this advice and gave virtually no speeches or other discourses on the labor issue.

Ironically, industrialists in practice violated nearly all precepts of social Darwinism. They limited domestic competition through trusts and monopolies, and persuaded Congress to limit foreign competition through tariffs on iron, steel, nickel, copper, marble, wool, wood, and other items. Thus, the uncontrolled competition espoused by corporate leaders did not exist in reality; those controls which did exist favored the industrialist.

From the industrialist point-of-view, then, the labor issue was a matter of natural selection, whether the inferior being—the laborer—was to interfere with the superior being—the employer. The appeal, like labor's, was to traditional American values, but with the interpretation that all men were created with equal "opportunity" to pursue happiness. Forcing employers to share profits or to be governed by workers was a violation of natural and constitu-

---

22. John Swinton, "Organized Labor and Its Accomplishments During the Past Half Century," *American Federationist* 2 (Feb., 1896):217. Address delivered in New York, 1895.
23. Samuel Gompers, "The President's Report," *Report of the Proceedings: American Federation of Labor* (1888), p. 9. Delivered Dec. 11, 1888, in St. Louis. "President's Report," *Report of the Proceedings: American Federation of Labor* (1887), p. 8. Delivered Dec. 13, 1887, in Baltimore.
24. Russell H. Conwell, "Acres of Diamonds," in *American Forum: Speeches on Historic Issues, 1788-1900* ed. Ernest J. Wrage, and Barnet Baskerville (New York: Harper Brothers, 1960), pp. 270-72.

tional rights and dictates—the result would be social degeneration. Labor's interpretation of rights and liberties was upstaged by the new philosophy of social Darwinism—a philosophy believed with religious fervor by American intellectuals, industrialists, editors, and much of the middle class. The industrialist view of the labor issue thus had a wider and more influential following than organized labor's view. The labor movement would continue to flounder until Social Darwinism had run its course and the reform movement, buttressed by progressivism, succeeded in changing American attitudes toward social responsibility.

Solutions Offered by Labor

On occasion each labor leader seemed to have his special notion of the cause of working class woes: Powderly cited the grabbing of land by a wealthy few; Sylvis feared the gold power; Gompers noted unfair competition; Debs indicted the economic system; and virtually all cited unfair legislation. But these were symptoms rather than root causes.

The cause, to which all spokesmen pointed, was centralized, massed wealth in combinations or monopolies. Powderly referred to the "tyranny of aggregated capital,"[25] and James R. Sovereign (General Master Workman of the Knights of Labor) exclaimed that "This government was intended as an asylum for the oppressed and the home of the free, but it is now an oligarchy of wealth and the land of the trusts."[26] Debs and the socialists could see no hope for the capitalistic system, while the majority of labor spokesmen opposed only the abuse of capital. Sylvis said, "Small capitals are productive of happiness and industry; large ones become pernicious. . . ."[27] He did not define large or small. Gompers, a conservative trade unionist, frequently denied any opposition to capitalism. "We only regret that capital is so hedged in with monopolistic privilege, utilized to oppress, that the toiler is forced into economic subjection to its legalized holders," he stated.[28] Speakers rarely attacked a specific industrialist or a specific company with monopolistic powers. Perhaps this was due to the lack of dialogue between labor and capital; labor speakers had no *one* to refute or attack, only conditions and events. Or perhaps generalized attacks on vague, undistinguishable villains is simply a trait of agitation.

All labor leaders agreed that the first step in solving working class problems—in emancipating workers from industrial slavery—was organization. Gompers said the concentration of wealth and power in a few hands made it impossible for the individual to "obtain redress for bad conditions. . . ."[29] Speakers also agreed there should be one labor organization, ultimately becoming international in scope. "The time has now arrived for a more perfect combination of labor," Lyman A Brant told the delegates at the second organization meeting of the A.F.of L., "one that will concentrate our forces so as to

25. Terence V. Powderly, "Annual Address of the General Master Workman," *Proceedings of the General Assembly: Knights of Labor* (1885), p. 6. Delivered in Hamilton, Ontario, Oct. 5, 1885.
26. Sovereign, "Annual Address of the General Master Workman," Nov. 12, 1897, p. 14.
27. Sylvis, "Address Delivered at Chicago," p. 157.
28. Samuel Gompers, "Trade Unions: Their Achievements and Aims," *American Federationist* 6 (March, 1899):6. Address delivered on Sept. 2, 1891, place unknown.
29. Samuel Gompers, "For Industrial Peace," *American Federationist* 9 (Feb., 1902):55. Delivered in New York, 1902.

more successfully cope with concentrated capital."[30]

Unanimity of agreement ended at that point, however, for there was a basic philosophical disagreement about the nature of labor organization. The Knights of Labor was an industrial union—admitting all workers, regardless of trade or training. Uriah S. Stephens, founder and early leader of the K. of L., declared in 1879 that "all the leading minds and close thinkers among the union men in almost all branches are ready for the consummation, and that nothing really beneficial can be accomplished until a complete unification is had . . . ." He concluded, "The time has fully come when *all* trade and labor organizations of every description should be united."[31] The American Federation of Labor was exactly what its name implied—a federation of independent trade unions. Gompers, leader of the A.F. of L. from 1886 to 1924, was the leading advocate of the trade union philosophy. He saw the trade union as "the historic and natural form of working class organization,"[32] and opposed "a great industrial union, taking in any and everyone in a single vast comprehensive organization."[33] Speaking to the Machinists' Convention in 1901, Gompers remarked: "Those of us who have gone through the movement of the Knights of Labor, which is now happily removed from the path of progress; those who have studied the previous effervescent movements of that character, know the danger with which such movements are always confronted."[34] Industrial unionists frequently retaliated in kind. I. D. Chamberlain of the K. of L. said its motto, "an injury to one is the concern of all," was quite distinct from "mere trade unionism."[35] Debs declared, "I aver that the old trade union has not

only fulfilled its mission and outlived its usefulness, but that it is now positively reactionary, and is maintained, not in the interests of the workers who support it, but in the interests of the capitalist class who exploit the workers who support it."[36] This bickering over philosophy resulted in no single union of workers and little cooperation among organizations. For example, when the A.F. of L. helped to organize a strike for the eight hour day in 1886, Powderly withheld the support of the K. of L. even though he believed in shorter hours. In 1894 Debs appealed to Gompers during the Pullman Strike to use his prestige with the General Managers Association to work out a compromise. Gompers refused and watched the destruction of the American Railway Union—an industrial union.

Not only did labor organizations face external obstacles, but most were racked with internal problems. Powderly's annual reports to the K. of L. were a chronicle of organizational nightmares: fights in the

30. Lyman A. Brant, "Opening Address at International Trades Union Congress," *Report of Proceedings: Federation of Trades and Labor Unions* (1881), p. 6. Delivered in Pittsburgh, Nov. 15, 1881.

31. Uriah S. Stephens, "Grand Master Workman's Address," *Proceedings of the General Assembly: Knights of Labor* (1879), p. 102. Delivered in Chicago, Sept. 3, 1879.

32. Gompers, "President's Report," Dec. 13, 1887, p. 8.

33. Samuel Gompers, "Address to the Machinists Convention," *American Federationist* 8 (July, 1901):251. Delivered in Toronto, Ontario, 1901.

34. *Ibid.*

35. I.D. Chamberlain, "Address of the General Master Workman," *Proceedings of the General Assembly: Knights of Labor* (1902), p. 8. Delivered in Niagara Falls, N.Y., Nov. 11, 1902.

36. Eugene V. Debs, "Craft Unionism," *Debs: His Life, Writings and Speeches* (Chicago: Charles H. Kerr and Co., 1908), p. 375. Delivered Nov. 23, 1905, in Chicago.

executive council, power in too many hands, power struggles between leaders and factions, lack of finances, unauthorized commitment of the union to strikes or economic and political schemes, frequent resolutions against the officers at annual meetings, unauthorized newspapers and organizations using the name Knights of Labor, bribery of members to testify publicly against the union, drunkenness, and scores of workers joining only because of an impending strike or a grievance against their employers. The question is not why a union collapsed, but what took it so long to do so? Leadership problems worsened when a union became weak. For instance, Powderly served as General Master Workman of the K.of L. from 1880 to 1893 (the period of its greatest power and size). From 1894 to 1903, when the K.of L. ceased to have annual meetings, there were six different General Master Workmen and constant power struggles and purges. Effective leadership was impossible.

Since the purpose of organization was to bring about change, the obvious question was *how*. One of the earliest schemes was the establishment of cooperatives where every worker was part owner of the company for which he worked. In 1865 Sylvis declared cooperation to be "the true remedy for the evils of society; this is the great idea that is destined to break down the present system of centralization, monopoly and extortion. By cooperation, we will become a nation of employers—the employers of our own labor." Sylvis related his solution to the American tradition of self-help. "But let us not forget that success depends upon our own efforts," he remarked, "It is not what is done for people, but what people do for themselves, that acts upon their character and condi-

tion."[37] A number of cooperatives appeared during the next decade, especially in Sylvis' own machinist trade. After the National Labor Union ceased in 1872 (four years after Sylvis died), the cooperative idea was carried forward by the Knights of Labor. In his first address as Grand Master Workman in 1880, Powderly exclaimed that cooperation "will eventually make every man his own master,—every man his own employer; a system which will give the laborer a fair proportion of the products of his toil. It is cooperation, then, as the lever of labor's emancipation, [to which] . . . the eyes of the workingmen and women of the world are directed . . . ."[38] However, failure of cooperatives in competitive markets, lack of enthusiasm among leaders of the labor movement, and opposition of industrialists led to the collapse of most cooperatives. By 1886 Powderly was decrying the lack of business training among workers. "Of what avail is it to say that we are laboring to establish a system of co-operation, when that which is most essential to the success of co-operation is lacking?" he asked.[39] In 1889 Powderly told of an instance where a cooperative coal mine was established only to discover that the local railroad would not haul the coal.[40]

---

37. Sylvis, "Address Delivered at Chicago," pp. 168,169.

38. Terence V. Powderly, "Address of the Grand Master Workman," *Proceedings of the General Assembly: Knights of Labor* (1880), p. 171. Delivered in Pittsburgh, Sept. 7, 1880.

39. Terence V. Powderly, "Address of the General Master Workman," *Proceedings of the General Assembly: Knights of Labor* (1886), p. 41. Delivered Oct. 8, 1886, in Richmond, Virginia.

40. Terence V. Powderly, "Response to Speeches by Members of the Georgia State Farmers Alliance," *Proceedings of the General Assembly: Knights of Labor* (1889), pp. 95-96. Delivered in Atlanta, Georgia, Nov., 1889.

Socialism was the natural extension of cooperation, but few labor leaders advocated more than government ownership of railroads, telegraph, and some utilities. Only Debs (among leading spokesmen) espoused the total elimination of the capitalistic system and the establishment of a "co-operative commonwealth" in America—our civilization's "crowning glory."[41] Campaigning for the Presidency in 1904, Debs said "the workers have but one issue in this campaign, the overthrow of the capitalist system and the emancipation of the working class from wage-slavery." "Competition is breaking down and co-operation is supplanting it," he declared.[42] Advocates of the "radical" solutions of cooperatives and partial or complete socialism misjudged the American workers and the public. Neither audience was ready to end the system. The worker wanted a bigger share of the wealth, and the labor movement was generally in tune with Gompers's demand for removal of competitive *evils*, not competition itself.

Virtually all labor leaders maintained faith in the democratic process. "The ballot means that labor is no longer dumb, that at last it has a voice, that it may be heard and if united shall be heeded," Debs declared.[43] Speaking to the Labor Reform Party in 1868, Sylvis said workers were "not powerless, for we have one way to escape. The ballot-box is still open."[44] Labor spokesmen pleaded with workers to break old party ties, and to pressure congressmen and legislators "So that a man in taking up the labor question will know he is dealing with a hair-trigger pistol, and will say, 'I am to be true to justice and to man, otherwise I am a dead duck.'"[45] Few speakers favored a separate labor party. Debs's socialist party, for instance, received little support from organized labor. Eltweed Pomeroy

stated the general feeling at the 1895 A.F. of L. convention: "The trades unions as trades unions should not join any party and become partisan organizations. Such is sure death."[46] Perhaps he was thinking of the National Labor Union that joined with the Labor Reform Party in 1869-1870; both were dead by 1872. Spokesmen recognized the frustrations of getting desired legislation through national and state legislatures, but they believed the following laws would be enacted *if* workers would vote wisely: the eight-hour day, land control, limitation of immigration, and elimination of child labor, prison labor, and foreign contract labor. Of the rhetoric of labor studied for this essay, only Justus Schwab, an anarchist, dismissed the democratic process: "We—that is, the Anarchists—do not interest ourselves in politics. We have no faith for the ballot-box, which is superstition of the American people . . . knowing the futility of this struggle of the poor devils against the machinery of the two capitalist parties, we have no faith that they will ever be able to accomplish anything."[47] The faith of labor leaders and their followers in the ability of the democratic process to achieve social change was

41. Eugene V. Debs, "Liberty," *Debs: His Life* p. 333. Delivered in Chicago, Nov. 22, 1895.

42. Eugene V. Debs, "The Socialist Party and the Working Class," *Debs: His Life* pp. 358, 371. Delivered Sept. 1, 1904, in Indianapolis.

43. *Ibid.*, p. 361.

44. Sylvis, "Speech Delivered at Birmingham," p. 225.

45. Wendell Phillips, "The Labor Question," *John Swinton's Paper*, Feb. 10, 1884, p. 1. Delivered in Boston, April, 1872.

46. Eltweed Pomeroy, "Direct Legislation the Workingman's Issue," *Report of the Proceedings: American Federation of Labor* (1895), p. 203. Delivered Dec. 12, 1895, in New York.

47. Justus Schwab, "Interview," *John Swinton's Paper*, Sept. 14, 1884, p. 1. Date and place of interview unknown.

undoubtedly a major reason why the anarchist movement failed. It simply could not achieve a broad base in any segment of the American population.

The strike was the most spectacular and controversial "solution" to labor's problems. It was visible to the public and frequently affected a far greater population than the striking workers and their families, resulting in bitterness toward organized labor. Nearly all leaders of the K. of L. opposed strikes: Stephens wanted to end the strike fund; Hays wanted delegates to outlaw strikes; and Powderly termed strikes "suicidal" and said they gained only temporary relief.[48] Gompers opposed strikes, except as a last resort, but he defended workers' right to strike and preparation for possible strikes. "As a consistent opponent of strikes," he said, "I do find that those organizations of labor which have best provided themselves with the means to strike have continually less occasion to indulge in them."[49] In spite of leaders' opposition to strikes, especially ones unplanned or unnecessary, strikes occurred by the thousands during the period 1865-1915, and labor leaders and organizations bore the blame for most of them. Industrialist opposition to labor's demands too often left the strike as the only alternative. Gompers remarked to the American Academy of Social Sciences, "There are some things which are worse than strikes, and among them I might enumerate a degraded, a debased, or a demoralized manhood."[50]

Violence frequently flared during strikes, especially in the 1880s and 1890s. Labor was blamed even though its leaders opposed all violent acts. For instance, Eugene V. Debs continually exhorted railroaders to avoid violence during the Pullman Strike of 1894, but Debs and the American Railway Union were blamed for the violence that took place and he and the other officers of the ARU served six months in jail after the strike ended. I.D. Chamberlain of the K. of L. said labor ought to attain its rights "with ballots instead of paving stones," and labeled unionists advocating violence as "the most dangerous element of society."[51] The K. of L. was blamed for the infamous Haymarket Riot in 1886, a totally unfounded charge, and suffered a steady decline from that time to its demise. Gompers said "the question of how they [workers] are going to get their rights can only be solved by the organized labor movement—not by revolution, but by evolution."[52] The anarchists arrested after the Haymarket Riot received little sympathy from labor leaders. Gompers presented his views at the A.F. of L. convention in 1887:

I deem it almost unnecessary to say to you that I am no Anarchist nor have any sympathy with or love for anarchy, its methods or its teachings, the calumnious statements of a few journals to the contrary notwithstanding. But I found a strong feeling prevailing among thousands that the con-

48. Stephens, "Grand Master Workman's Address," Sept. 3, 1879, p. 102; John W. Hays, "Report of the General Master Workman," *Proceedings of the General Assembly: Knights of Labor* (1910):14-16, delivered Dec. 6, 1910, in Washington; Powderly, "Address of the Grand Master Workman," Sept. 7, 1880, p. 171; and Powderly, "Address of the Grand Master Workman," *Proceedings of the General Assembly: Knights of Labor* (1882), pp. 278-79, delivered in New York, Sept. 6, 1882.

49. Gompers, "The President's Report," Dec. 11, 1888, p. 11.

50. Gompers, "Limitations of Conciliation and Arbitration," p. 308.

51. Chamberlain, "Address of the General Master Workman," Nov. 11, 1902, pp. 8-9.

52. Samuel Gompers, "A Rough Sketch of a Rugged Individual," *American Federationist* 4 (Jan., 1897), 243. Address delivered Dec. 20, 1896, in Cincinnati.

demned men were about to be executed in defense of the right of free speech and free assemblage and that if they were executed they would die martyrs to the cause of labor. As the representative of a great labor organization I was called upon and entreated to say a word, first, to save them from death, and second, to deprive their movement of the food upon which all spasmodic movements exist,—martyrdom.[53]

Powderly espoused the same hard-line position on anarchists in an address to the K. of L. convention in 1887.[54] In spite of such statements, a large segment of the American populace identified the labor movement with strikes, violence, and anarchism.

Labor leaders preferred arbitration or collective bargaining to either violence or strikes. In 1879 Stephens told the K. of L. "that with this fund [resistance] the day of arbitration has come, and that financial and industrial blunders of the 'strike' have gone, and with them the barbarous persecution, martyrdom, and ostrocism of the worker is over."[55] Stephens' happiness was premature, for decades would pass before anything like true collective bargaining would become common. Samuel Gompers was perhaps the leading advocate of what was generally called arbitration. He recognized the necessity of equal status for its success. "There is no such thing even as voluntary arbitration successfully carried out unless both parties, the contending parties, are equally strong or nearly so," he stated. A man on his back with a boot on his throat, Gompers remarked, could not arbitrate effectively.[56]

Union labels, boycotts of products, and the labor press were additional means used to achieve labor's goals, but speakers devoted little time to them—perhaps because the labor journals and papers devoted so much space to their use and importance.

"Charity" received little and negative attention. Sylvis maintained that a "division of profit will produce harmony in society, elevate morals, increase temperance, and spread true religion more than the combined efforts of all the moral reformers, philanthropists, missionary societies, and pulpits in the country . . . ."[57] "It is worse than pretence," he exclaimed, "to say we cannot consent to receive and pay for your labor on principles of equity, but we will provide you a poorhouse to die in."[58] Addressing himself to "organized charities" in 1899, Gompers proudly stated that during the entire depression of 1893, "charity organizationists were unable to record the fact that one man with a union card in his pocket made application for charity."[59] Charity tended to degrade a man, to get him in a rut, Gompers argued; the real solution was the betterment of wages, hours, and working conditions. Obviously labor leaders, like the remainder of American society, believed in individualism and self-sufficiency.

Thus, labor spokesmen discussed a variety of ways to combat labor's archenemy—

---

53. Gompers, "President's Report," Dec. 13, 1887, p. 12.
54. Terence V. Powderly, "Address of the General Master Workman," *Proceedings of the General Assembly: Knights of Labor* (1887), pp. 1499-1513. Delivered Oct. 4, 1887, in Minneapolis.
55. Uriah S. Stephens, "Annual Report of the Grand Master Workman," *Proceedings of the General Assembly: Knights of Labor* (1879), p. 54. Delivered Jan. 14, 1879, in St. Louis.
56. Gompers, "Limitations of Conciliation and Arbitration," p. 309.
57. Sylvis, "Address Delivered at Boston," p. 199.
58. Sylvis, "Address Delivered at Chicago," p. 154.
59. Samuel Gompers, "On the Attitude of Organized Labor Toward Organized Charity," *American Federationist* 6 (June, 1899):81. Delivered March 20, 1899, in Boston.

centralized, combined wealth. Organization was the first step, they agreed, but the conflicting philosophies of trade vs. industrial unionism prevented any real unity or cooperation among leaders and unions. The trade union organized the "elite" of the working class and—with limited membership and tighter controls—became the dominant form of labor organization until the 1930s and 1940s. "Extreme" solutions like cooperatives, socialism, a labor party, and violence received only limited and short range support in the labor movement. Workers were generally middle-class Americans in values and attitudes, although not in wealth, and supported reform through legislation, peaceful strikes, the ballot box, and arbitration or collective bargaining. The average worker believed in the system and wanted no charity. The A.F. of L. under Gompers appealed best to the middle-class American, and it alone survived and grew in the twentieth century.

Industrialist Reaction to Solutions Offered by Labor

Labor's solutions were anathemas to the majority of industrialists. Workers organized into unions posed an obvious threat to the employer's right and power to determine all aspects of production, including the purchase and use of labor. Industrialists argued that the individual worker should bargain for better conditions and price for his labor; an organization doing it for him was unnatural, if not un-American. They ignored management's organization into giant corporations and trusts.

The industrialists resorted to all kinds of schemes in their opposition to organized labor. Some formed managers' or employers' associations—industry-wide or regional—to confront unions with an organized front. They produced "blacklists" of employees who belonged to unions and circulated these to other industrialists. As a result, workers were expelled from their trades or prevented from getting a job of any kind. Some employers required their workers to sign "iron-clad oaths" or "yellow-dog contracts," swearing they would not join a union. Violation of such oaths meant immediate dismissal from employment. The "lock-out" was employed to break strikes or threats of strikes. For instance, if employees would strike against one foundry in a city, owners of the other foundries would close theirs. Peer group pressure and the adamant stand of the owners were often enough to break the strike and perhaps even a union trying to organize the workers. Employers imported labor—sometimes from foreign countries—to break strikes. When the inevitable confrontation occurred, they hired Pinkerton detectives to protect property and the strike breakers. Pinkertons also acted as undercover agents to undermine unions or to reveal plans and names to employers.

Collective bargaining or arbitration was unthinkable to the majority of employers. How could they bargain with inferiors who had no right to demand anything beyond what the employer was willing to grant? During a particularly bitter coal strike in 1902, President Roosevelt called union and management leaders to the White House to arbitrate their differences. Employers clearly stated their views on arbitration. George F. Baer, president of three coal and iron companies declared: "The duty of the hour is not to waste time negotiating with the fomenters of this anarchy and insolent defiance of law, but to do as was done in the war of the rebellion—restore the majesty of law, the only guardian of a free people, and to restore order and peace at any cost."[60] Concerning miner union offers to negotiate, Baer commented: "Under these circumstances we decline to accept Mr. Mitchell's considerate offer to let our men work on terms he names. He has no right to come from Illinois to dictate terms on the acceptance of which anarchy and crime shall cease in Pennsylvania."[61] The president of the Lackawanna Railroad demanded the destruction of the union, not arbitration: ". . . at once institute proceedings against the illegal organization known as the United Mine Workers' Association, its well-known officers, agents and members, to enjoin and restrain permanently it and them from continuing this organization and requiring them to desist immediately from conspiring, conniving, aiding, or abetting the outlawry and intolerable conditions in the anthracite region for which they and they alone are responsible."[62]

Industrialists could make demands like the above because they controlled the American system, including courts, Congress, state legislatures, and state militias. When confrontations occurred, they could ask courts to issue injunctions forbidding unions to interfere with interstate commerce, the mails, or the nonunion worker's right to work. Courts even tried to deny labor's right to boycott a product or company. The Sherman Anti-Trust Act of 1890—designed to control industrial trusts and monopolies—proved ineffective against companies but very useful in charging unions with "conspiracy." State militias and even federal troops intervened during strikes to prevent violence and often broke strikes as a by-product. The little legislation favoring unions was either amended to be meaningless or was ignored once passed.

The Pullman Strike of 1894 provides a case study of a confrontation between labor and management.[63] The strike began on May 11 when workers at the Pullman Palace Car Company near Chicago (the majority having recently joined the American Railway Union) walked off their jobs, a strike not authorized by the A.R.U. On June 26, after repeated offers to negotiate were refused by the Pullman Company, the delegates at the first national convention of the A.R.U. voted to strike Pullman shops in Kentucky and Missouri and to boycott all Pullman cars, from which Pullman received rent.

The General Managers Association—representing twenty-four railroads terminating in Chicago—opened offices in Pittsburgh, Cleveland, Philadelphia, New York, and Buffalo to recruit strike breakers and established a central publicity office in Chicago to furnish information to newspapers. After minor violence in Chicago, U.S. Attorney General Richard Olney—himself a life-long corporation lawyer, director of several railroads, and on the board of the Burlington Railroad—appointed Edwin Walker, attorney for the Chicago, Milwaukee and St. Paul Railroad since 1870—as special federal attorney to handle the

---

60. George F. Baer, "Statement at President's Conference to End the Coal Strike," *American Federationist* 9 (Nov., 1902):796. Delivered in Washington, 1902.

61. *Ibid.*

62. *Ibid*, 797.

63. For an account of the strike, its causes, and its effects, see Ray Ginger, *The Bending Cross* (New Brunswick: Rutgers University Press, 1949), pp. 108-83.

strike. His first move was to recruit hundreds of special federal deputy marshals—later described by investigators as thugs and hoodlums. Railroads disrupted their schedules to arouse the public against the boycott and attached Pullman cars to trains that did not usually carry them—freights, suburbans, and (most important) mail trains. Two Federal Court judges in Chicago, using the Sherman Anti-Trust Act as the basis, issued an injunction against Debs and other leaders of the A.R.U.—forbidding them to answer questions, to send telegrams, or to urge workers by word of mouth to join the boycott. Debs refused to obey the injunction. On the morning of July 4, President Cleveland—concerned about the mails and urged on by Attorney General Olney—ordered federal troops to Chicago without consulting the governor of Illinois or the mayor of Chicago. His stated purposes were to protect federal property, to prevent obstruction of the mails, to prevent interference with interstate commerce, and to enforce decrees of the federal courts. The General Managers Association announced it would not arbitrate or compromise, while Olney demanded immediate indictment of Debs and his colleagues. Violence and deaths increased greatly after federal and then state troops arrived. Newspapers gave the impression that Debs was masterminding the destruction of Chicago and planning to take over the country. Debs and other A.R.U. leaders were arrested on July 10, released on bail, and then rearrested on July 17. The strike ended a few days later, while the leaderless A.R.U.—its members blacklisted—floundered and died in 1897.

In review of industrialist reactions to solutions proposed by labor, control of the American system and employment of extreme tactics kept the labor movement under control during most of the period 1865-1915. But industrialists who resorted to these tactics, refusing to negotiate any grievances and declining to defend their actions, misjudged the American people as badly as did the anarchists of the labor movement. Public opinion, bolstered by belief in fair play and Christian ethics, would eventually bring about legislation to protect unions, require collective bargaining, and prevent "unfair" employment practices.

Conclusion

The labor movement's floundering for a half century after the Civil War resulted from its inability to establish a broad-based support in the American population—including the "working class." The movement was identified with anarchism, socialism, and the shiftless element of society. In reality the majority of labor leaders opposed violence, strikes, socialism, and charity while advocating capitalism, American traditions and values, and the self-sufficient, hard-working individual.

Labor's identification crisis was partly its own fault. The rhetoric seemed to condemn violence, strikes, and anticapitalistic schemes while its actions seemed to support all three. Speakers demanded a fair share of profits on one occasion, an equal share on another, and all of the profits on yet another. Labor leaders and organizations competed with one another for members, power, jurisdiction, and praise for achievements. Union members were reluctant to give adequate power and finances to union leadership. Industrial unions and trade unions did not cooperate and frequently broke each other's strikes.

The postwar labor movement found itself in a rapidly changing America. Social Darwinism outdated labor's interpretation of American values, and the new industrialist class controlled the American system as no previous class had done. The industrialist could array the newspapers, courts, state legislatures, Congress, police forces, and state militias against the labor movement during any confrontation. Nonunited labor and its presses were no match against the "system."

But the industrial class eventually squandered its broad-based support through its own extremes. The viciousness of uncontrolled competition accompanied by industrialists' double standard—the worker should compete in an open market while trusts, monopolies, and tariffs would reduce competition for the employer—led to demands for government controls. Social reformers, the progressives, and the "muckrakers" in leading newspapers and periodicals presented the ugly side of American life—slums, sweatshops, company towns, financial scandals. The extreme interpretations of social Darwinism were tempered and America developed a new social consciousness.

If there is a point to all of this, it is that an American social movement can succeed only with a broad-based support, and a broad base is possible only when a movement's statements and actions are congruent with the societal values (and special interpretations) of the period. Extreme statements and actions will cost the defendant or agressor in a movement its broad base and, hence, its position or its goals.

The labor movement has achieved nearly all of its original demands since 1915: collective bargaining, powerful organizations, a high degree of cooperation—if not unity—among organizations, child labor laws, elimination of convict labor, safety standards, a minimum wage, stiff laws against or controlling monopolies and trusts, an eight-hour day, and others. The irony is that unions may have become too strong for certain industries and even for society. But the movement is only beginning to organize government employees, teachers, migrant workers, and other groups. Like many social movements, the end may never come, for there will always be new industries, new disputes, new contracts, and men and women working for wages.

BIBLIOGRAPHY

Detailed histories of the labor movement:

Commons, John R. *The History of Labour in the United States.* 3 vols. New York: Macmillan, 1926.

Foner, Philip S. *History of the Labor Movement in the United States.* 4 vols. New York: International Publishers, 1947.

Ware, Norman J. *The Labor Movement in the United States, 1860-1895.* KNew York: D. Appleton and Company, 1929.

Excellent treatments of social Darwinism and its influence on America—especially the impact on industry and the labor movement:

Boller, Paul F., Jr. *American Thought in Transition: The Impact of Evolutionary Naturalism, 1865-1900.* Chicago: Rand McNally and Company, 1969.

Hofstadter, Richard. *Social Darwinism in American Thought.* Boston: Beacon Press, 1960.

Also of interest:

The American Federationist.

Monthly journal of the American Federation of Labor containing many speeches and editorials of labor leaders, both within and outside of the A.F. of L.

Gompers, Samuel. *Seventy Years of Life and Labor.* New York: E.P. Dutton and Company, 1925.

Gomper's autobiography—aimed at reporting his actions and successes as long-time leader of the American Federation of Labor.

John Swinton's Paper, October 14, 1883 to August 21, 1887.

Contains a great amount of editorializing on the labor movement and some speeches of labor leaders.

Powderly, Terence V. *The Path I Trod.* New York: Columbia University Press, 1940

Powderly's autobiography, essentially an apology for the Knights of Labor and his actions as its leader.

Proceedings of the General Assembly: Knights of Labor. (1878-1913)

Records of the annual meetings of the Knights of Labor containing minutes of the sessions and the annual reports of the General Master Workman, the leader of the Knights.

Report of the Proceedings: American Federation of Labor. (1883-1915)

Reports of the annual conventions of the American Federation of Labor containing the minutes of the sessions, the annual report of the President, and speeches of labor leaders and politicians—from both the United States and abroad.

Sylvis, James C., ed. *The Life, Speeches, Labors and Essays of William H. Sylvis,* Philadelphia: Claxton, Remsen, and Haffelfinger, 1872.

This biographical sketch of Sylvis includes the only collection of his writings and speeches.

Todes, Charlotte. *William H. Sylvis and the National Labor Union.* New York: International Publishers, 1942.

This book provides an extensive history of the National Labor Union and a biographical sketch of Sylvis.

11 The Agrarian Protest

Donald H. Ecroyd

From the end of the Civil War to the present day, the American economy has, despite occasional set-backs, shown a seemingly endless ability to expand. We are today producing more goods than ever before; our average income seems to climb higher and higher; as a people we are now better educated, better travelled, better fed, and more likely to own bathtubs than we have ever been.

The presence of surges and resurges of populist dissent throughout this same period, however, points up flaws in the overall fabric. The "better things" have not been uniformly distributed. Not everyone has shared in the growth and the development which the glowing statistics would seem to index. As a result, from time to time special political and social action groups have organized to protect the "little guy" from the "establishment." These groups have taken various forms, including such disparate bodies as the Greenbackers, the Grange, the Populist Party, labor unions, and even today's SANE or the *Common Cause* of John W. Gardner and his associates.

This essay considers the American farmer's special efforts to resolve his problems by persuasion and by politics during the last half of the nineteenth century. Our interest will focus upon three dimensions of what is often called The Agrarian Revolt: (1) the rhetorical problem faced by the depressed farmer as he attempted to shape his own destiny favorably, (2) the rhetorical solutions to that problem which he attempted, and (3) the rhetorical model which seems best to describe what occurred.

The Rhetorical Problem

Between 1860 and the early 1900s the rapid growth of industry left the farmers and miners of the West and South feeling they were in a colonial relationship to the East. As the fortunes of industry climbed, the fortunes of agriculture fell. Since the balance of the population was still rural, the political effect of a depressed agriculture could not be overlooked at the polls. It is, in fact, interesting to consider the relationship of wheat prices to the development and growth of agrarian pressure group organizations and third parties. As Wilfred E. Binkly points out in *American Political*

Parties,[1] every time wheat prices fell, groups of alarmed farmers quickly banded together for purposes of political action. For example, when wheat prices dropped from a Civil War high of $1.05 per bushel to only $.67, the Grange was founded. The price rose again to a dollar, but fell to $.87 in 1874—the year that the Anti-Monopoly and the Greenback Parties were both founded. The price then rose once more, to $1.05 in 1877—and the Grange Movement had run its course. But when prices again fell to $.80 in 1878, the Farmers' Alliance was organized. In 1887 the price was only $.68 a bushel, and three thousand Alliance lodges were organized in that year alone. In 1891 the wheat price dropped to only $.49; and General Weaver, the presidential candidate of the Populist Party, polled over one million votes in the next election. In 1896 the price stood at $.31 and there was a good harvest. In that year William Jennings Bryan, the candidate of the agricultural West, was defeated for the presidency. The appeal of direct actionism obviously increased and decreased with the seriousness of the farm crisis.

Between 1870 and 1890 the Democrats were beginning to carve into the Republican districts of the North. Throughout the country the formerly solid, post-Civil War regional party identities were beginning to crack. In both the normally Democratic South and the normally Republican North, state elections were becoming highly competitive. As more and more states adopted the custom of holding state and national elections on the same day, some of the competitiveness of the state contests became fused with the partisanship of the national campaigns, especially in the North.

By the late 1880s and the early 1890s, then, the established parties were faced for the first time with the need to mount genuine political campaigns. Throughout this entire period the Democrats represented the establishment in the South, the Republicans in the North; but the ability of that establishment to coalesce the broad voter support of an entire state or region was increasingly challenged by the third force pressure of aggressive dissent.

In addition, the period was actually one of see-saw power, with the prevailing Republican supremacy at the national level never being very secure. For example, in 1881 the Republican edge in the Senate was nonexistent: the parties divided evenly, with 37 Republicans and 37 Democrats. In 1883 the division was 38-36, with the Republicans slightly ahead; but Cleveland's plurality in 1884 apparently offset even that narrow margin. In 1888 Harrison was elected by an electoral vote majority, but Cleveland actually had the plurality of votes. In 1892 Cleveland was re-elected, and the Populist Party polled one million votes besides—indicating a clear rejection of the Republican by the voters.

The precariousness of this balance of power, however, made each party carefully responsive to the voiced needs of the region where it was most firmly entrenched. Thus the local and state Republican platforms of the 1890s were clearly designed to appeal to the rising industrialism of the Northeast, while those of the Democrats reflected a largely farm-oriented approach to government. In fact, for over a generation the main effort on the part of each major party had been to find a stand which would reflect and reinforce the biases of its own particular regional base of power. The plat-

---

1. (New York: Alfred A. Knopf, 1962), p. 315.

forms of the nineteens merely extend and reflect this tendency. By 1892, therefore, a fateful cleavage between the industrial Northeast and the rest of the country had developed. Neither major party was willing to address itself to the broad, national problems of the workers, farmers, and miners as a group, because it felt compelled to consolidate its regional strength. As a result, the field was open to the development of some sort of third force which could do battle for the "little guy," whether he lived in the rural South and West or in the urban, industrial Northeast. Hence, during the 1880s and early 1890s the Farmers' Alliance moved almost inevitably to become, first a broad-based pressure group, and finally a true political party, actively campaigning against "the establishment"—whichever of the two older parties that might be. The Populist Party of the early 1890s had a potential power base that was more national than that of either the Republicans or the Democrats; and efforts on the part of Alliancemen to broaden that base by making common cause with labor generally, and with the miners in particular were almost continual. Because its appeal was therefore a broad one, and because it was not held back by the traditional Blue-Gray prejudices that affected the older parties, the Populist Party quickly became a political force that had to be recognized.

Because the farm vote was not so important to the Republican scheme of power as to that of the Democrats, Populism made its greatest impact upon the Republican Party in the agricultural Midwest. Thousands of nominally Republican farmers in this area became militantly Populist. When southern and rural border-state Democrats also drifted over into the Populist ranks by the thousands, the Democratic Party—which recognized the farm vote as its base of power—was precipitated into a support of Bryan a move which clearly marked a wresting of party control from its established leadership. In fact, Bryan's nomination was a triumph of the southern and western wings of the party over the northern and eastern blocks. But the new People's Party had gone too far to withdraw, even in the face of such an apparent victory for its cause. Thus, at the urging of certain Congressional Democrats, the Populists compromised between complete independence and fusion by nominating Bryan also, at the same time naming Tom Watson of Georgia as his running mate. Although this decision was ingenious, it ultimately meant that they had engulfed themselves in the Democratic Party, ending their political effectiveness as a definable third force in American politics.

Bryan was an agrarian, and his platform had no appeal to the urban area. As a result, the Republicans carried every county in the Northeast, and every northern state east of the Mississippi.[2] The Populist Party was dead, and the aggressive, activist phase of the Agrarian Revolt was apparently over.

The Peoples Party, then—the Populists as its members were widely known—represented the culmination of a twenty-five year effort on the part of non-establishment groups to wrest political power from the mainstream parties and their leaders, thus opening the way for bringing about genuine economic and political reform. In order to accomplish this shift of power, only three courses of action were open to the leaders of dissent: to pressure for

---

2. A fascinating analysis of this entire struggle is contained in James MacGregor Burns, the *Deadlock of Democracy* (Englewood Cliffs, N.J.: Prentice-Hall, 1963). See especially pp. 70-80, *passim*.

changes within the existing structures; to create a third party and win elected offices in sufficient number to bring about change; or to create a third party strong enough to force fusion with one of the existing parties. In the end, these three approaches were tried in turn; each with a certain measure of success.

The three approaches share many of the same rhetorical characteristics. For example, all three required that the established parties in their existing form be defined as some sort of enemy, and that the "people" be defined as downtrodden, oppressed, and victimized. Once this polarization was achieved, the way was clear to require the kind of unswerving—perhaps unreasoning—support and commitment suitable for a righteous crusade. All three approaches permitted the semblance of debate to be used as a metaphoric mask to hide rigid, unbending emotional appeals. Regardless of whether the ultimate objective was pressure, independent action, or fusion, the rhetorical problems were identical: the logical problem of establishing a case, and the psychological problem of securing and maintaining committed popular support for it.

In America, entrenched political power is not easy to attack from the bottom up. Many relatively independent voters will hew to a party line even though they object to it. They may switch parties, or split their ticket, but they hesitate to run the status risk of supporting a third party. If the first rhetorical problem of the Populists was to build a case and give it the semblance of logic, the second rhetorical problem ultimately had to be defined as one of *ethos*. Even though a third force group might be logically effective, it still had to face the problem of overcoming a negative image as

a bunch of "crackpots," "kooks," or even "anarchists." As O. Gene Clanton observes in *Kansas Populism: Ideas and Men*, "The path of reform could be made much smoother almost overnight if these same principles were embraced by urban, middle-class spokesmen and championed in the name of the middle class."[3]

The odds against success for a splinter group are stacked by the American heritage of a strong two-party system. In the post-Civil War period, however, it is a matter of historical fact that with few exceptions, all reform proposals in American politics were introduced by third parties rather than by the two major parties. Difficult as it was to gain a hearing, there was, in other words, some tradition of grudging success for the third force approach. It was therefore almost inevitably a last step that the Agrarian Revolt culminated in a political party, and it was also in keeping with the pattern of history in the last half of the nineteenth century that the goals of that party were finally achieved through fusion rather than by breaking the two-party tradition.

The populism of the late 1800s gained its ends from the established parties by clearly demonstrating the seriousness of its purpose; by polarizing the society of which it was a part; and by raucously confronting the staid power of the stable leadership of the nation. The way the Agrarian Revolt met its task of getting recognition is a fascinating case study, and one that is not to be written off lightly by rhetorical theorists of our day as being relevant only to the dead history of a century ago. The spirit of populism—the revolt of the "little guy" against the "establishment"—is not dead. A third

---

3. (Lawrence: University Press of Kansas, 1969), p. 243.

force in politics may again challenge the established, mainstream political parties and their leadership. In our time it is the poor, the black, and the young who feel in a colonial relationship to the government; but the metaphors of polarization, frustration, and attack are not dissimilar from those of the farmer, the miner, and the laborer who rose up in righteous wrath in the 1870s, 1880s, and 1890s. If the parallel continues, the power struggle of our day has only begun, and "the people" will yet be heard.

The pattern of the populist endeavor of a century ago can be described in three steps, each one roughly approximating one of the possible alternative avenues to the development of a power base for reform which have previously been described.

Step 1. Relatively isolated small groups began to look beyond their purely local dilemmas to establish broadly-based groups such as the Grange in order to gain leverage by which to bring about reform within the established parties. Similarly, other small groups organized as splinter parties on a national basis, hopeful of finding some way of affecting national party politics by direct challenge. Neither of these efforts was especially successful, however, for neither the Grange nor the active third party groups of the period ever defined true long-range goals. Once the short-run objectives of the Granger Laws were achieved, for example, the political clout of the Grange was ended. Also, even the most successful third party groups—as, for example, the Greenbackers or the Anti-Monopoly Party—never achieved widespread membership, for the focus of their appeal was too narrow. Discontented farmers, representing the stable, conservative element in the rural society of

the South and West, did not readily identify with "radicals"; nor did they consider the breaking up of monopolies or the issuing of greenbacks to be true panaceas for all the ills they faced.

Step 2. As the success of the Grange in affecting legislation became an admitted fact, however, and as the agricultural recession continued, farmers determinedly bent their efforts toward the establishment of a truly effective pressure group. Since the Grange was by now a conservative organization with little interest in political action, it was necessary to turn to a new group—the Farmers' Alliance. The Farmers' Alliance was from the beginning a politically oriented organization. It first acted as a pressure group, but quickly entered into active participation in local politics, and finally developed a national political program and mounted a national political campaign.

Step 3. The heady success of having Populism become a national force, however, led to an effort to conserve gains on the part of the party leadership. After all, power which has been gained can be lost again! Congressmen, senators, and governors had been elected. Over a million presidential votes had been cast for a Populist candidate. The established parties were running scared, and the Democrats seemingly offered a *bona fide* opportunity for successful fusion. Thus the 1896 election came about with Bryan as the only presidential candidate in history who has been run simultaneously by two parties, each with its own candidate for Vice-President. Bryan, of course, lost; but the effect upon the Republicans was nevertheless profound. McKinley was forced to look beyond the satisfaction of eastern business interests to develop his legislative program. The Progressivism of the early 1900s—even the ebullient politics of Teddy Roosevelt—are identifiable extensions of the populist spirit, and the legislation of this period had clear roots in the programs of the People's Party. New laws protected labor, controlled interest rates, regulated the railroads, led to the direct election of senators, enfranchised women, and ultimately even established prohibition. The Agrarian Revolt, although seemingly ending with the defeat of Bryan, actually continued until the years of World War I. The zealotry of the little man paid off. His commitment to his cause forced the major parties to toe the line which he drew. The forces of good and evil were known in the land, and the metaphors of the common man's enmity for the forces of Big Business and Big Government have not yet died in our ears.

The Rhetorical Solutions Attempted

Let us reiterate that the Agrarian Revolt faced two essential rhetorical problems. The first was to define its case, and to secure agreement to the stock issue of its debate with the established parties. The second was somehow to generate a positive *ethos* that would permit the spokemen of the reform case to gain a hearing with voters who were not readily willing to identify with any radical cause.

During Step 1 of the Revolt, as previously outlined, the efforts which were made were sufficiently impromptu and sufficiently scattered that it is probably not appropriate to consider the identification of any theory of rhetorical choices in other than individual instances. During the later part of Step 2, however, a "rhetoric of calamity howling"—to use William Allen White's phrase—begins to emerge.

Kansas was the hotbed of Populism as a political movement. Her People's Party leaders were the men and women who first led the way to the creation of a new national third party that was broader than just the Farmers' Alliance. The Kansas People's Party Manifesto later became the basis of the national platform that was adopted at Omaha in 1892. The Weaver campaign for the presidency was frequently referred to as "Kansas-izing" the nation. Kansas was the source of the movement's greatest strength, and the scene of its greatest triumphs.

With the possible exceptions of Tom Watson of Georgia and Ignatius P. Donnelly of Minnesota, Mary Elizabeth Lease of Kansas was Populism's most potent speaker. The Populist vote in 1892 sent five out of the seven congressmen elected, as well as one senator, to Washington; elected a Populist governor; wrested the state legislature out of the hands of the Republicans for the first time in many years; and mandated that all ten of Kansas' electoral votes were to be cast for Weaver.

Because of these reasons, then, we will look at the "rhetoric of calamity howling" through the focus of the Populist movement in Kansas.

Dr. Maurice Natanson, a philosopher and former American Council of Learned Societies Scholar, says in the April, 1955, issue of the *Quarterly Journal of Speech*, that the "proper province of rhetoric" has not even yet been clearly agreed upon. After some review of various efforts at definition, Dr. Natanson concludes that the fundamental difficulty has been that no one has drawn a sharp enough distinction between the theory of rhetoric and its practice.[4] Although he himself then goes on to discuss a "philosophy of rhetoric," rather than to explore the exact nature of the difference he has suggested, the duality is an interesting one to consider.

It is, of course, a truism that the body of rules, methods, and practices which makes up rhetoric is the result of observing speakers in action and analyzing what it was that they did in the light of their acceptance by their auditors. From Corax to Korzybski the theories of rhetoric, and—if you will—the philosophy of rhetoric, have grown as a result of both empirical and scientific observations. Once the inductions leading to the rules become established as having merit, the conscious application of these rules begins, leading in some cases to the establishment of what might definitely be called "oratorical eras." Some such periods have been given names by scholars to indicate the homogeneity of the speaking which took place within a certain time. The so-called "Age of Classical Oratory" offers an example. In this age the speakers were clearly Attic or Asianist in their fundamental rhetoric, and the speeches of Demosthenes, Pericles, Gorgias, and Isocrates have identifiably similar characteristics.

Other eras, though unnamed, are equally identifiable. In American public address, for example, such speakers as Patrick Henry, John C. Calhoun, William Jennings Bryan, and Franklin Delano Roosevelt are each one somehow peculiarly characteristic of his own age. The clarion qualities of a Bryan-esque passage are instantly recognized as being of the late 1800s, and when a contemporary speaker continues these older speechways in our own day, we invariably refer to him as being an "old-style orator." Such examples suggest to us that the identifiably homogeneous speech characteristics of a group or of an age are probably the result of a conscious application of some rhetorical rules and principles.

From this perspective, then, it must be remembered that Populism as a political movement grew out of the Farmers' Alliance, and that a regular part of the Alliance program was its educational activities. Alliance men and women all over the nation, like high school and college debaters of today, were at the *same* time reading the *same* books and pamphlets on economic, social, and political questions; considering them under the guidance of the *same* discussion guides, and learning from them a common method of evaluating evidence and framing arguments. Through training, Alliance people grew accustomed to discussing, debating, and lecturing as parts of their own lives, for every local group held panels, debates, and other "speakings" regularly. "The brethren," in other words, trained themselves conscientiously in public speaking and in parliamentary practice.

Examples of the nature of this training are many. For instance, a Richard Cordley wrote an article in the April, 1892, *Agora*[5] discussing rhetorical criticism in terms of "the man, the subject, and the occasion," as advanced by Webster, and adds "the audience" as well. The Topeka *Advocate*, for May 2, 1894, carried a lengthy letter urging on Populist speakers, simplicity of style and clarity of organization. It was signed "A Linn County Farmer." The Wichita *Morning Eagle* reprinted some advice to stump speakers from *Lippincott's Maga-*

---

4. pp. 133-139.
5. *Agora* was a little magazine published briefly during the 1890s at Burlington, Kansas. Cordley's article is entitled "Snags in the Current," and appears in vol. 1, pp. 195-200.

zine regarding audibility and saving the voice from unnecessary strain.[6] The *Kansas Commoner*, August 28, 1890, urged Alliance lecturers to stick to their points without deviation from truth or conviction, and without being overzealous or abusive. Such items were common. People evidently read them, as well as complete texts or lengthy precis of speeches, editorials commenting upon speeches, refutations of speeches, and the like, with interest. The typical newspaper of the period is witness to the interest of Kansans in oratory.

A close study of the speakers of the Populist Movement in Kansas leads readily to the conclusion that all this advice was sought and applied; that there *was* a real "rhetoric of calamity howling"—an actual body of rules, methods, and accepted practices which influenced the speechmaking of the "Pops," and which helped give to the movement itself its homogeneity. Three of these identifiable rhetorical principles will be named, and an effort will be made to show how the acceptance of these principles by Populist speakers affected the speechmaking of the movement.

Most easily pointed out was the basic principle of Populist rhetorical invention— that facts and evidence are important sources of proof. This rhetorical conviction resulted in so many speeches being given in which so many statistics were cited and so many authorities quoted, that this aspect of Populist speaking, unfortunately, became a byword. It must be admitted that there was a certain difficulty, however, in that the local Populist speakers had almost no materials available to them for use other than those drawn from their own experiences or from the books, pamphlets, and newspapers published by the Alliance itself. Thus many factual items were in a sense the common property of both speaker and listener before the speech itself ever began. Also, the more popular of the Populist orators spoke so often that they had little if any chance even to write, much less re-write, their speeches. Thus even illustrative materials, jokes, and anecdotes sometimes became common property also. In an effort to offset this danger, newspapers frequently presented lists of "quotable quotes," sometimes even editorializing on them. The party itself put out "sourcebooks" of quotations from Republican speeches (or Democratic speeches in the South) which could be used as grist for rebuttal and for "turning the tables" or *reductio ad absurdum*. But even these efforts were not enough, and Alliance-men in Kansas laughed at the story which made the rounds about one of Jerry Simpson's particularly eloquent illustrations. It seems that many who heard it remembered that they had heard it used before by another speaker, almost word for word! Some of them asked him about it. His reply was reported to have been, "I put the quotation marks in, but you couldn't hear them."

The Populist speaker, then, viewed the considerable use of evidence as a desirable rhetorical technique, and sprinkled his speeches liberally with statistics, quotations, and examples.

Populist speechmaking was, however, primarily an emotional activity. Although facts, figures, quotations from authority, and other sorts of evidence were used, they were always used within a two-fold context. First: the facts were known already to most of the members of the audience, as we have already seen. There was no real

---

6. An undated clipping, collected by the Kansas State Historical Society, Topeka.

need to establish them further. What *was* needed was to secure a positive, overt reaction to those facts. Second: the speechmaking that was done was mostly a mixture of pure attack with what might be described as agressive refutation. This focus reflected the argumentative job that the speakers were about—a "sales promotion job" rather than one of teaching. It is, therefore, futile to try to discuss these speeches in terms of the usual Aristotelian categories. The logical and the emotional appeals are far too closely interwoven to make very meaningful the usual distinctions between them.

It is true, however, that practically any speaker in the movement could give figures showing the course of debt and poverty, the strength and wealth of Wall Street, or the exorbitancies of railroad and line elevator charges. Not only were these facts known, they were unmistakably understood. Each statistic, after all, represented the mortgaged home of a neighbor; each dollar charted as debt represented wheat to be raised and sold from which no personal comfort could be derived; each percent of inflation tabulated meant extra hours of personal labor.

With these hard realities in mind, a second identifiable rhetorical principle comes as no surprise: that persuasion stems not only from facts and from one's ability to use these facts motivationally, but also that there is great persuasive force in the bold use of the more obvious motivating appeals. Characteristic, for example, were appeals to the creative urge, to the fighting urge, to independence, loyalty, pride, and sympathy. After all, a new group was organizing to do battle with the older and more established order; and to wrest from the monied and corrupt bankers, in-

dustrialists, and politicians that independence of the people which had been taken away! Such appeals to the sympathies led the attacked to call the Populists "calamity howlers." Appeals to the independent spirit of man caused them to be "anarchists." Their insistence upon loyalty to the new third party. and their pride in their accomplishments led to the epithet, "cranks." But such appeals led also to a large and devoted following who remained loyal to party leaders for many stormy years.

A third identifiable rhetorical principle, clearly related to the two already listed, was that of audience adjustment. The calamity howler was an expert at the art of audience adaptation, and he knew how to appeal to his hearers specifically, as well as in general. Anyone who wanted to could speak at an Alliance meeting. Hamlin Garland, in his novel, *A Spoil of Office*, comments upon the "oration" of a farmer at just such a meeting. Although his picture may be somewhat overdramatized and heightened for narrative purposes, it is probably suggestive of what was fairly typical. "His clothes were faded to a russet brown, and his collarless neck was like wrinkled leather, and his fingers were covered with cots; but he was a most impressive orator. His words were well chosen, and his gestures almost majestic. He spoke in a conversational way, but with great purpose and sincerity." As a heroine of the story remarks, "There are hundreds of farmers who can talk like that."[7]

Special audience techniques were many, but one of the commonest was to cast the speech into the real, or sometimes hypo-

---

7. Serialized in the *Arena*. For this quotation, see the episode in vol. 6 (June, 1892):111.

thetical, aspect of a debate. Thus ability at refutation and attack, ready wit, and sarcasm became established as oratorical prerequisites. Other special techniques included the use of music and of group singing to set a sense of "belonging." Songs were made up to be sung to familiar evangelistic tunes, and the speeches were often alternated with musical selections by such groups as the Pratt Mandolin Band and the Haviland Glee Club. The meetings were carefully staged to "build" to the address of the day. Committees worked hard to make each local affair a success. The parades were designed to include most of the later audience, as did the picnics. The group singing further unified the listeners and made them even more responsive. The suspense of a good conflict, the holiday gaiety of a large audience, the dedicated, fanatical zeal of the partisan—all combined to make the occasion for Populist speechmaking emotionally electric.

Three rhetorical principles, then, have been suggested as underlying Populist speechmaking: one concerning the use of facts and evidence; one concerning the use of standard motivation techniques; and one concerning audience analysis and adaptation. The educational program of the Alliance taught hundreds of farmers and their wives the country over how to stand up and be heard.

Rhetoric, says Aristotle, "finds its end in judgement." The rhetoric of calamity howling was clearly persuasive rhetoric. Its tenets were aimed at the searching out of all the available means of proof, but with a special emphasis upon those means which could move or excite. The principles followed were principles applicable to agitation—to attack, and to special pleading. The Populist speaker knew his audience. He

knew his topics. He knew how to adapt his ideas to the needs and tastes of his listeners. His rhetoric was limited in its philosophic dimensions, but it was precise and pragmatic. Its purpose was to polarize: to define adherents and the "enemy." Once the enemy is known, he can be controlled; once adherents are sufficiently committed, they represent a powerbase which will equalize the arguments and bring about the desired change.

In Kansas the principal Populist leaders were Senator William A. Peffer, Governor Lorenzo D. Lewelling, Congressman Jerry Simpson, Mrs. Annie L. Diggs, and Mrs. Mary Elizabeth Lease. These five Populist leaders, as well as many others, spoke in churches, in country school houses, at picnics and barbecues. In many cases so large was the number of people who came, that two, three, and even four speakers were called into action simultaneously in order to address them all at once. Once, as the editor of the Hutchinson *News* put it in his effort to describe one of the most successful of the mass meetings, "You had but to sit down almost anyplace and wait, and a speaker would come around and go to making a speech directly."[8] People took their politics seriously in the 1890s. Political meetings had an importance that was social as well as political. There were few competing events, thus the meetings were usually well attended and the speech made a vital impression upon the listeners.

Genuine debate was common. Mrs. Lease, for example, almost always asked for questions or debate at the end of one of her speeches. Once at Waushara a minister arose and spoke against Willits, the Populist

_____

8. Sept. 26, 1890.

candidate for governor. Mrs. Lease promptly cross-examined him, wrung from him
that he was a Republican, and that this was
the sole basis of his hatred for Willits. She
then, "with withering sarcasm," made him
out to be a fool "amid the wildest cheers
from the audience."[9]

When considering the effectiveness of
such techniques, we must remember that
the frontier was still very close to people.
Direct actionism was still an important part
of the political philosophy of the day;
while democracy and individualism, to paraphrase Carl Becker, were not a philosophy
but a way of life. Religion was firmly interwoven into all thought, and the crusading
spirit was a typical reaction to any prolonged or general evil. Notice the lack of
subtlety with which Mrs. Lease approaches
her argument in this very representative
passage:

The moral conscience has been quickened, the
heart of the nation aroused, and we are asking, in
all earnestness, "with malice toward none and
charity for all," which of the political parties can
best solve the problems of the day? And we answer
unhesitatingly, that party which is most in accord
with the teachings of Christ and in harmony with
the safe-guard of human liberty, the constitution
of the United States. . . .[10]

As a fascinating contrast of mood, observe the excessive emotionalism of the
same orator when she trumpeted to the
multitudes in one of her mighty perora-
tions:

We will stand by our homes and stay by our
firesides by force, if necessary, and we will not pay
our debts to the shark loan companies until the
government pays its debts to us. The people are at
bay; let the blood hounds of money who have dog-
ged them so far beware.[11]

With her famed battle phrases, "Down

with the Red Dragon of Wall Street!" and
"Raise less corn and more hell!" Mrs. Lease
was the most vivid of the rough-and-tumble
Populist orators. But even staid Senator
Peffer, with his chestnut-brown beard wav-
ing down his chest to a length below his
belt-buckle, was capable of a stirring passage. Notice the way he moves from logical
material to that which is purely emotional
in this typical excerpt from one of his
speeches:

If you will take the prices of cattle in Chicago
in the year 1883, about the beginning of the recent
decline, you will find that the average value of cattle in that market was $38.00 a head, while in 1890
the average value of the same class of property was
only $18.00 a head, less than one half. . . .It is an-
swered in reply to this particular statement that a
dollar buys more today than it bought in 1867.
That is what we are complaining about. It buys
more labor, it buys more wheat, it buys more of
any kind of property that the producer has to
sell. . . .We are asking why it is, why it is that the
wages of labor are so low compared to what they
were a few years ago; we ask why it is that the value
of property is so low compared with a few years
ago; we ask why it is that women are compelled to
work in the factories today, many of them making
shirts for example, at from 30 to 50 cents a dozen,
and little boys pants at six cents a pair or at $1.08 a
week? Poor little creatures beginning their hard
task as the first gray streaks appear upon the hori-
zon, doing the weary-some work during the long
hours of the day until the hours of night settle in
the streets of the city. We ask why these things are
occurring.[12]

Consider the task of one who would attempt to oppose such fervid spell-binding.
Even if he were to discredit the logic, the

---

9. *The Advocate* (Topeka), August 27, 1890.
10. "The Great Quadrangular Debate," (Mrs.
Lease's speech, Dec. 18, 1893, Salina, Kansas),
published by *The Open Church*, Salina, 1894.
11. *Star*, Kansas City, April 1, 1891.
12. *Daily Capital*, Topeka, Oct. 2, 1891.

emotional effect of the attack would remain. To paraphrase a cliché, the only way to meet such fire would be with fire! The ideas and the use of *ad hominem* appeals are so interwoven that they cannot be readily separated. The end result is a verbal message which is inflammatory to the point that a middle position cannot be assumed as a response with any hope of success. The polarization is complete: those who would oppose the speaker are unthinking, vicious, or worse; those who would support him are wise, virtuous, and just.

Annie L. Diggs, herself a famed Populist lecturer and writer, says in the April, 1892 *Arena:* "Nothing can stand before it [the farmers' movement] because the time is come. The purpose for which was all this preparation must be attained. The quickened race conscience will no longer be at ease while hunger and cold torment the millions."[13] In a party pamphlet on money that was circulated in the campaign of 1894, M. W. Cobun, its author, says:

> I do not believe the time has yet come when people will submit to the rule of tyrants. I believe the patriotic spirit of '76 is again being re-kindled in the hearts of the people. I believe universal liberty will again sweep over this entire country with plutocratic despotism chained to her chariot wheels.
>
> But one thing we should not forget is that God reigns. We should take God into our politics. Take our religion into our politics, not partisan politics, for I fear that is of evil origin. But the true politics, the science of government that makes it possible for us to serve God under our own vine and fig tree, according to the dictations of our own conscience, none daring to molest or make us afraid.[14]

As Raymond C. Miller observes in his unpublished doctoral dissertation, "In objective and in method, they were not a political party; they were a crusade."[15]

The Rhetorical Model

The populist movement of the late 1800s culminated in the activity of the Populist Party. In this later stage the movement became a political and economic crusade that had its own powerful theology. The rhetoric appropriate to such a fixed set of opinions is not a rhetoric of alternatives, but is instead a rhetoric designed to cut off the possibility of negotiation or compromise. If such a rhetoric is successful, it will not be possible to disagree on any point of the basic dogma without running the risk of seeming to be evil to those who have accepted the dogma. The single criterion for rhetorical effectiveness is whether or not the listener becomes a convert.

The first point of Populist theology is necessarily an article of faith. It might be stated this way: the people, if properly and correctly informed, will do the right thing. This premise was in turn based upon complete assurance that the truth was known, and that only the known version of truth could possibly be *truly* "American," or *truly* acceptible to God. The ancient concept which the Romans voiced, *"vox populi, vox dei,"* will always find undoubting adherents among any supporters of a populist cause. The Populists of the 1890s were no exception. To them, virtue was inherent in the common man; big business and big government were inherently evil.

---

13. "The Farmer's Alliance and Some of its Leaders," *Arena* 5 (April, 1892) :591.

14. *A Treatise on U.S. Money,* n.p., 1892, p. 19 (included in *People's Party Pamphlets,* vol. 1, collected by the Kansas State Historical Society, Topeka.).

15. "The Populist Party in Kansas", University of Chicago, 1928, p. 184.

A second premise assumed that work is a virtue, and that virtue is always rewarded. If man does not work, he sins; if he does work, he should receive the fruit of his toil. Thus no economic system can have a morality, and man must constantly be on guard against such corrupting systems. "The Red Dragon of Wall Street," to use Mrs. Lease's phrase, is preying on the people. If such is not the case, why does not a man receive a suitable reward for his labor? And how can the ever-growing profits of eastern bankers and moneylenders be accounted for? Obviously such men must be evil, for they prosper without labor. Down with Big Business! Let outrage be heard! "Raise more hell and less corn!"

The third premise is that man not only can be better than he is, but he is better than he was. Evils in the system must be corrected by law in order that men may continue their God-given progress. As the motto of the state of Kansas proclaims, "ad astra per aspera"—to the stars through difficulty! This moment is the preordained moment for God's cause to be forwarded. Those who would deny His will are of evil origin.

The nature of this theology determines the unyielding cast of the entire Populist debate. When an advocate assumes that he is unquestionably correct, he can only assume with equal fervor that one who differs is unquestionably wrong. Unwavering faith in one's cause can only lead to unswerving rigidity.

The nature of this theology also provided a conceptual "set" for the Populists—and, to a certain extent, for their opponents. This "set" affected the reality of the linguistic messages which were encoded, permitting symbolic sweeps of metaphor across mundane denotation and into moral judgment. Polarization became a rhetorical end, and the speakers ultimately ceased to address themselves to issues alone, but turned instead to a galaxy of values which rotated around their issues. Thus Mrs. Lease deals with the hapless Waushara minister, and readily confounds argument with exhortation in speech after speech. Such rhetoric is used to define selfhood—to create identity; not to enter into a logical consideration of the possible outcomes of some course of action.

Such a *rhetoric of being*, based upon a theology which brooks no compromise, deals with the rhetorical problems of logic and ethos in a way undescribed by the Greeks or the Romans. The first step is the creation of an audience, which must then be sustained by rhetoric.

The speakers of the agrarian revolt found a ready-made self-developing audience in the carefully controlled Alliance meetings. The customary publications and public lectures of this organization are a clear example of the cyclic form called for by a rhetorical model based upon rigid, righteous appeals. The Alliance defined for its membership the economic and political truths which were the basis of its case. The elements of this case were then programmed for instruction, and the conditioning of the audience began. The People's Party simply took over the already operating system. The real purpose of the rhetoric was never to affect those who could bring about change directly. The model was not the legislative chamber or the court. Instead, the purpose of the rhetoric was almost exclusively to create an audience of converts, and motivate them to a confrontation of power with the "enemy," thus bringing about change through sheer fright. The model was more like Skinner's training of pigeons to dance by the use of electric shock than it was like the development of a forensic argument. When the "little guy" faces "the establishment," the power is too unequal for a *rhetoric of becoming* which can tolerate alternatives or encourage compromise. Only when the two adversaries have equal power can such reasonable processes of argument begin.

Thus, in Step 1—that first stage of the agrarian revolt described early in this essay—no rhetorical system could truly be identified. In Step 2, however, a rhetoric of self-persuasion begins to be discernable. It might be summarized by a position which would declare: We have been systematically deprived. The suppression of our selfhood has been deliberate. The enemy has done this to us. The enemy must be eradicated.

Such a rhetoric has no real interest in program development. The ploy is to define and control the enemy. Persuasion is considered to be synonymous with coercion. By creating polarization and thus fear, the argument is won. The absence of logic cannot even be assumed to be bad, for a discourse which succeeds may or may not have been any better had it been more reasonable. For what could be more successful than success?

This sort of rhetorical model has frightening currency in our present world, for populism is not dead. The Populist Party of the 1890s was only incidentally a product of its own time and place and circumstances. Populism is a manifestation of a trend or tradition that has long inhered to American culture. The spirit of populism, in one sense, develops in history as a case study in democracy. But in another in-

stance, it can become a case study in the repressive tactics of the mob attempting to force a respectable, well-ordered society into submission. The difference would seem to lie in the rhetoric used.

In the Agrarian revolt of the nineteenth century, the rhetoric moves from self-persuasion to confrontation to coercion, and its tactics are metaphoric and metaphysical.

BIBLIOGRAPHY

Buck, Solon J. *The Agrarian Crusade.* New Haven: Yale University Press, 1920.

Clanton, O. Gene *Kansas Populism: Ideas and Men.* Lawrence: University Press of Kansas, 1969.

Durden, Robert Franklin *The Climax of Populism.* Lexington: University of Kentucky Press, 1965.

Hicks, John D. *The Populist Revolt.* Minneapolis: University of Minnesota Press, 1931.

Hofstadter, Richard *The Age of Reform: From Bryan to F.D.R.* New York: Alfred A. Knopf, 1955.

Nugent, Walter T.K. *The Tolerant Populists: Kansas Populism and Nativism.* Chicago: University of Chicago Press, 1963.

The first of the above books which should be read is still unquestionably the indispensable analysis by John D. Hicks. Later controversy over the essential character of Populism as a movement is summarized in the first thirty-two pages of the study by Nugent. Below are listed an interesting collection of various Populist documents and commentaries, including only two speeches by Populist leaders, however; and my own unpublished doctoral dissertation, in the appendix of which is the only collection of speeches that I am aware of.

Ecroyd, Donald H. "An Analysis and Evaluation of Populist Political Campaign Speech Making in Kansas 1890-1894." Ph.D. dissertation, University of Iowa, 1949.

Tindall, George B., ed. *A Populist Reader.* New York: Harper & Row, 1966. (A Torchbook paperback).

12 The Social Gospel

Paul H. Boase

The existing order has already served over-time. It is now senseless and growing worse. To spend and be spent mending it is to waste one's life. . . .The present order cannot be mended; it can only give birth to the new order, the regenerate civilization.[1]

By substituting "establishment" for "existing order" a new leftist student agitator on a riot-torn college campus in the spring of 1970 could have found these sentiments rhetorically palatable. Actually, the words, delivered in a "solemn, slow, impressive manner,"[2] fell from the lips of an ordained clergyman and reached the ears of an upper middle-class audience in conservative Boston during the "Gay Nineties." On that occasion Professor George D. Herron, the Congregational "Jeremiah" from Grinnell, Iowa, outlined the radical position of a passionate reform movement that gathered momentum following Reconstruction and finally, interlaced with "Progressivism," reached maturity as the social gospel, a popular theological position with many clergymen on the eve of World War I.[3]

The radical rhetoric that tortured the conscience of the church and terrified the "establishment" during the last quarter of the nineteenth century bears striking resemblances to the agitation of the 1970s.

The issues, while shifting slightly, show few signs of disappearing completely. When George D. Herron, the dynamic apostle of Christian socialism, his "tongue touched with fire,"[4] warned Bostonians that "Revolution of some sort is not far off,"[5] he was addressing an economically comfortable, affluent religious folk who had witnessed dramatic industrial growth and expansion, to them fully as amazing as space probes and moon landings. But just as the concerned of the 1970s find poverty and pollution in the midst of plenty, so, too, the

---

1. George D. Herron, "The Opportunity of the Church," *Arena* 15 (December, 1895):42. The edited address is in Paul H. Boase, ed., *The Rhetoric of Christian Socialism* (New York: Random House, 1969), pp. 94-104.
2. Robert T. Handy, "George D. Herron and the Kingdom Movement," *Church History* 19 (1950):105.
3. See Richard Hofstadter, *The Progressive Movement: 1900-1915* (Englewood Cliffs, N.J.: Prentice-Hall, 1963), and for an account of social gospel activism and theological modification by neo-orthodoxy see Donald B. Meyer, *The Protestant Search for Political Realism, 1919-1941* (Berkeley: University of California Press, 1960).
4. Excellent description of Herron's platform techniques in Charles Beardsley, "Professor Herron," *Arena* 15 (April, 1896):784-796.
5. Boase, *Rhetoric of Christian Socialism*, p. 95.

nineteenth-century reformer saw his nation bursting with economic potential, yet still unable to provide the good life for the farmer and the oppressed laborer. His cities, replete with mansions, also housed the poor in slums not unlike the modern ghetto. Even worse, the wealthy and politically powerful, many pious, regular attendants at divine worship, could still "grind the faces of the poor," engage in deadly combat with their brother merchants, and rape the nation's natural resources.[6]

An increasingly concerned group of articulate ministers and laymen sensed the glaring contradiction between the environment and the human behavior they observed on the one hand and the Christian ethic they professed and preached on the other. Clearly, the dilemma called for a new rhetorical stance, a painstaking search for causes and a careful evaluation of solutions. If ecclesiastical action were deemed necessary, what procedures were meet, right, and their bounded duty? The sermons and lectures of clerics and laymen alike reveal the nature of the issues, their analyses of the problems, and the differing remedies they prescribed. Few clerics were bothered by any so-called distinction between words and action. Rhetoric to the minister was action supreme, ordained by the Lord, blessed by St. Paul as the "foolishness of preaching" and powerful enough to change men's lives and alter the direction of economic and political trends. To examine the development of social Christianity, describe the various rhetorical positions of the social gospelers and their antagonists, and to evaluate their contributions to the church and to society constitutes the primary focus of this chapter.

The Origins of Social Christianity

Religion has often occupied stage center in the drama of reform. The concepts of the so-called social gospel antedate Christianity, defying location in place and time or in sect and denomination. A growing awareness of sharp contradictions in economic or social conditions in which the strong oppressed the weak moved prophets from Moses to Isaiah and from Amos to Micah to cry out against the inequities and to exhort men to restore a just balance and live together as brothers. Jesus set forth the ideal in his vision of a heaven on earth and his followers in all ages have striven sporadically with limited degrees of success to establish that kingdom.[7]

In America the Puritan fathers dreamt of "a new Heaven and a new Earth" and later generations, inspired by democratic impulses and equalitarian drives provided a fertile soil for the social gospel. Indeed, nearly all of the social reform movements during the early nineteenth century received their dynamic impetus from men inspired by the Christian ethic and even the most conservative churches contributed substantially to social reform.[8] When George D. Herron addressed the Bostonians in 1895, he eulogized the scriptural and modern prophets who risked death to carry

---

6. Matthew Josephson, *The Robber Barons: The Great American Capitalists*, 1861-1901 (New York: Harcourt, Brace & World, 1962), pp. 317-25.

7. See Handy, "George D. Herron," 97-115.

8. Timothy L. Smith, *Revivalism and Social Reform in Mid-Nineteenth-Century America* (New York: Abingdon Press, 1957), gives a well-documented account of the evangelical impact on reform.

the message of social salvation, praising in particular William Lloyd Garrison. Many in Herron's audience had fought in the Civil War, helped to free the blacks, and received their inspiration from antislavery sermons of churchmen like Henry Ward Beecher, Theodore Weld, and Gilbert Haven.[9]

Few of Herron's listeners, however, realized that industrialism, spawned in part by the need for northern weapons, would hatch an economic monster capable of dooming another portion of the human race to servitude and slum compounds as miserable as the cotton field and the slave quarters. Following the Civil War only a mere handful of religious leaders looked with sympathetic eyes or raised their voices to defend the wage slave locked in mortal combat with his capitalistic overlord. As the industrial machine manufactured millionaires, it also produced the unsavory by-products of recurring depressions to the accompaniment of strikes, lockouts, bombings, and violence. The pulpit leaders following Reconstruction generally sided with the wealthy, advocating repressive measures for labor as brutal as the slave whip. Indeed, if the gentle persuasion of a policeman's club failed to produce law and order, then use "bullets and bayonets," advised Henry Ward Beecher's *Independent*, "canister and grape—with no sham or pretense."[10]

The hostile, unsympathetic attitude of the church and its leaders both lay and clerical weighed heavily on the conscience of Benjamin Orange Flower, the editor who published Herron's address and who might well have been a member of his audience. One of the earliest of the muckraking journalists, B.O. Flower consistently prodded

the church and her spokesmen to focus their attention on the plight of the poor rather than on their "palatial, stone, heaven-piercing, turreted temples." The Christian clergy, he wrote, were crass "materialists" who paid less attention to the teachings of their Master than the "Sadducees of old." Accusing ministers of hiding their talent, "trucking to wealth and cringing before a cynical and supercilious element," the editor pointed his pen at eminent divines who presided over wealthy parishes of Boston "within cannon shot" of squalid poverty, reminding them that *"their responsibility is as great as their apathy is marked."* Ever the optimist, Flower attributed ministerial complacency to timidity or ignorance, both inexcusable and capable of correction. For the timid he urged a more careful study and application of Christ's teachings and example and for the ignorant, a visit one day each week with the "miserables of society."[11]

Ministers who breathed the factory fumes or who, like Walter Rauschenbusch, found themselves near "Hell's Kitchen" planted in industrial soil amid urban squalor developed true rapport with the "miserables" and became the eloquent spokesmen for the social gospel. Farm pastors in rural

9. See Gilbert Haven, *Sermons, Speeches and Letters on Slavery and Its War* (Boston: Lee and Shepard, 1869), and Robert T. Oliver, *History of Public Speaking in America* (Boston: Allyn & Bacon, 1965), pp. 226-245; 373-382.
10. Henry F. May, *Protestant Church and Industrial America* (New York: Harper & Row, 1949), pp. 92-93.
11. "The Power and Responsibility of the Christian Ministry," *Arena* 4 (November, 1891):767-768.

villages found it difficult to achieve brotherly kinship with the immigrant laborer, often feared as a socialist or anarchist and prone to violence and revolution. Furthermore, the religion of the sweating masses, if they had any, was probably "the dwarfing and deadening power of a Roman Catholic ritualism," cited even by the liberal Lyman Abbott as a contributing cause of lethargy and lack of ambition in the poor.[12] Many of the farmers were far from rich and they and their clerical leaders had heard Populist orators like the "Sage of Nininger," Ignatius Donnelly, the "Sockless Socrates," Jerry Simpson, and the "Kansas Pythoness," Mary Lease, castigate the railroads and the eastern establishment.[13] But a genuine alliance of rural and urban forces never occurred; thus, the social gospel sprang primarily from the city and as a reaction to industrial abuse.

The apathy of the clergy and the reluctance of the church to do battle in behalf of either the farmer or the laboring masses during the post-Civil War era is clearly understandable. Following a massive reform movement, including a fratricidal conflict, the inevitable impulse is to retreat to normalcy, lick one's wounds, and get back to a less controversial gospel. Ministers and laymen, tired of struggling with a monstrous social and economic evil, returned to more traditional behavior, namely, the castigation of personal sin and the preparation of souls for heaven. What occurred in the market place and the halls of Congress seemed far less important than the local church program or the political maneuvers in a Methodist Conference.

Immediately following the Civil War, a layman tried to convince the "Father of the Social Gospel," Washington Gladden, "that with the destruction of slavery moral issues were likely to disappear from our politics. . . .and that religion and politics were no longer likely to be brought into such close relations." Neither Gladden nor his friend and frequent correspondent, Henry Demarest Lloyd, accepted the layman's appraisal and Gladden himself saw no rest for reformers until the millenium.[14] Lloyd, the fiery antimonopoly crusader and author of the classic volume, *Wealth Against Commonwealth*,[15] had long demonstrated his zeal for social issues, entering the arena with his commencement oration at Columbia College in 1867, on the exploitation of Africa and the alliance of missions with economic interests.[16] Then on Sunday, November 13, 1887, two days after the execution of the Haymarket bombers, he faced the Ethical Culture Society of Chicago to deliver a stirring social gospel message while the nation, still trembling from massive labor riots, caught a frightful glimpse of imminent revolution in successive upheavals. Lloyd's address, "The New Conscience," a caustic attack on complacent Christianity and a ringing appeal for the church to man the battlements of

12. Lyman Abbott, "Christianity Versus Socialism," *North American Review* 148 (April, 1889):452. See Boase, *Rhetoric of Christian Socialism*, pp. 67-77 for complete edited text.

13. John D. Hicks, *The Populist Revolt* (Lincoln: The University of Nebraska Press, 1961), pp. 159-70. See also Samuel Eliot Morison, *The Oxford History of the American People* (New York: Oxford University Press, 1965), p. 790.

14. "The Duties of Citizens," November 3, 1874 (unpublished sermon), Washington Gladden Papers, Ohio Historical Society Library, Columbus, Ohio.

15. Henry Demarest Lloyd, *Wealth Against Commonwealth*, ed. Thomas C. Cochran (Englewood Cliffs, N.J.: Prentice-Hall, 1963).

16. James Dombrowski, *The Early Days of Christian Socialism in America* (New York: Columbia University Press, 1936), p. 121.

reform once again, stated clearly that freedom for blacks was only the beginning. "Ceaseless growth means ceaseless emancipation," he declared and "One by one the cries of the imprisoned and imprisoner blend into the strains of a widening freedom."[17] Turning to one of the great reform preachers, Henry Ward Beecher, whose liberal theology helped to pave the way for the social gospel,[18] Lloyd singled out one of Beecher's recent pronouncements as damning evidence of the conservative, complacent, laissez-faire attitude of the church and its ministers. "We have struck the shackles from the slave, and made him free and a citizen," Beecher declared amid enthusiastic applause. "Now he must take care of himself, and work out his own social and industrial salvation," to which Lloyd asked pointedly, "When you work with him, and divide proceeds into profits and wages, will the God of Plymouth Church considerately turn his back, so as not to see whether you love your neighbor as yourself?" Using the Negro as his foil, Lloyd then expanded his analogy, concluding bitterly that Beecher's remark characterized the typical middle-class attitude toward the laboring masses.[19]

While Lloyd's characterization of a Church, its ministry at ease in Zion, complacent, wealthy, and self-satisfied aptly described the majority, a few potential prophets donned the camel's hair and cried in the wilderness. One of their number, Walter Rauschenbusch, remembered the "Gay Nineties" as lonesome days and William Dwight Porter Bliss, the St. Paul of Christian socialism, could only dredge up sixty-two socially concerned preachers in response to a challenge by Terrence V. Powderly, head of the Knights of Labor, to produce even ten.[20] The remainder in the church, exhausted from a confrontation with slavery, dazzled by the wealthy entrepreneurs in the pews, overwhelmed by evolution, under attack by such eloquent agnostics as Robert Ingersoll or blissfully unaware of city problems moved decisively toward a defensive rhetorical posture. Nearly all clerics reexamined their basic tenets, searching for the root causes of distress, and advocated plans they considered Christian solutions to the industrial problem and the distressing conditions of poverty and suffering that marred our otherwise prosperous nation.

Understandably, the churches and their spokesmen, while reading the same Bible and often subscribing to the same creed were as sect-ridden as Christendom itself on the causes and even more divided in finding appropriate solutions. The seekers cut across all denominations and faiths, including such figures as Rabbi Gustave Gottheil, Father Edward McGlynn, and representatives from all the major Protestant denominations. In the early years following the Civil War, the principal Protestant reformers sprang from Congregational, Unitarian, and Episcopal backgrounds, joined later by the Northern Baptists, Presbyterians, Lutherans, and Methodists. All of

---

17. Henry D. Lloyd, "The New Conscience," North American Review 147 (September, 1888):325.

18. While Horace Bushnell and Theodore Munger deserve greatest credit for breaking down the harsh Calvinistic doctrines to a more humanitarian position, Beecher also popularized the "new theology" and was credited with freeing Lloyd from the shackles of the "ancient faith." See May, Protestant Church and Industrial America, p. 159.

19. Lloyd, "New Conscience" p. 330.

20. Walter Rauschenbusch, Christianizing the Social Order (New York: Macmillan, 1912), p. 9.

the leaders with few exceptions were basically propagandists, speakers, teachers, and agitators although a few turned politically activist and many participated in the charitable and educational ventures of the so-called "institutional church."[21]

The Means of Communication

The promoters of the social gospel employed a wide variety of means to persuade laymen, scholars, farmers, businessmen, laborers, and ministers to modify their religious attitudes and embrace a new social creed. Their primary focal point was toward the educated middle and upper classes rather than toward the poor laborers, and their failure to reach the toiling masses produced intense emotional stress in the socially conscious layman and minister. Gladden frequently received frantic notes from ministerial colleagues seeking advice and assistance on ways and means of reaching the laborer.[22] Even his Sunday School Superintendent, C.S. Carr, wrote bitterly about their church's inability to reach "the common people, the unfortunate . . . ones Jesus came to live with and died for, the ones who are not successful, who are ignorant, and vulgar, and foolish. . . ." Then pointing to Gladden's communication failures Carr wrote: "I hear you preach. I entirely agree with what you say, since I know how you define certain words. The only trouble with the matter is, it does not lead to any practical result. The people do not need so much, today, to be told what to do, as they need to be shown how to do it."[23]

In 1898, H. Francis Perry, the pastor of Chicago's Englewood Baptist Church, attempted to discover the causes and find the cures for the communication breakdowns

he observed between the clergy and the working class. Sending a questionnaire to several working men and their leaders, including such notables as Samuel Gompers, Perry reached the depressing conclusion that the average minister's ethos with labor was nonexistent or near zero. He found several reasons for the credibility gap, including the laborer's belief that the church was allied to the "rich man, who oppresses him," the failure of the preacher to "treat living issues," clerical prejudice against trade unions, the charging of rent for pews, and most distressing of all—"stale and uninteresting sermons overly freighted with theology and too skimpy on practical preaching."[24]

The remedies the workmen and their leaders proposed would not have shocked preachers actively proclaiming the social gospel. In fact they were exhorting their brethren with strikingly similar rhetoric, although most, with the possible exception of George D. Herron, would not have gone as far as the Reverend Herbert N. Casson, a one-time Methodist preacher who had formed a labor church in Lynn, Massachusetts, and pessimistically appraised the

21. Provided athletic clubs, libraries, medical care, day nurseries, discussion groups, etc. Russell Conwell's Baptist Temple in Philadelphia had one of the most extensive. See W.D.P. Bliss, ed., *The New Encyclopedia of Social Reform* (New York: Funk & Wagnals, 1908), pp. 629-630, and A.I. Abell, *The Urban Impact on American Protestantism, 1865-1900* (Cambridge: Harvard University Press, 1943), pp. 137-65.
22. C.M. Roberts to Gladden, February 22, 1900. Washington Gladden Papers.
23. C.S. Carr to Gladden, January 4, 1900. Washington Gladden Papers.
24. H. Francis Perry, "The Workingman's Alienation from the Church," *American Journal of Sociology* 4 (March, 1899):621-29.

"Church" as "a spiritual opium joint."[25] In his bitter answer to Perry, Casson found "no hope of social reform through the church as it exists today." Particularly heartwarming to the socially conscious was a plea to all ministers to educate themselves in sociology and economics, "Apply the Sermon on the Mount. . . .Preach of a heaven on earth. . . .Visit the laboring man. . . .study his needs" and "Be our champion." Perry was unwilling to accept all the charges and warned that the laboring man's alienation often stemmed from faults within himself rather than in the church and further contended that the Jesus lauded by the average workingman was "not the Christ of the Gospels." Intensely annoying to the Chicago preacher was the "thoroughly false" charge about "stale" sermons, but he did admit the need for more intensive study of urban problems and conceded the potential power of the rich to seal a preacher's lips. But, said he, "It is culpable beyond ordinary cowardice for a preacher of righteousness to sell his conviction for gold, and such a man would be frowned out of the fellowship. . . ."[26]

Whether stale or fresh, the sermon, the lecture, the spoken word from the pulpit, in the classroom, and at the summer institute and discussion seminar comprised the initial, major thrust of the social movement in the church. In the discussion groups and institutes the informal conversation probably did its work of persuasion quietly and was recorded largely on the mind and heart of the participant, but the organizers also employed a variety of techniques, including book reviews, prepared papers, "quiz clubs," and even physical culture programs and dinner meetings. One such group, formed by George D. Herron and announced as "The First Institute of Christian Sociology" included at one of its dinner meetings in Burlington, Iowa, men and women from all walks of life. "Capitalists, clerks, mechanics, lawyers, and laborers sat side by side, and young scions of aristocracy passed buns and cold ham and coffee to men with fingers knotted with toil."[27]

The message originally designed for the ear rather than the eye soon invaded the print media. As the movement gained momentum toward the end of the century, a flood of articles, pamphlets, editorials, books, essays, and even best-selling novels reached the clergy and the general reading public. Virtually all of the major spokesmen for the social gospel, both clerical and lay put their sermons and lectures into print. Washington Gladden confessed that all but six of his thirty-one volumes were "printed as they were preached with almost no revision."[28] The same format of speech to print held true for Richard T. Ely, professor of economics at the University of Wisconsin, probably the most influential of many laymen associated with the social gospel whose widely publicized *Social Aspects of Christianity* was first presented as a lay sermon.[29] The radical George D.

25. May, *Protestant Church*, p. 248.

26. Perry, "Workingman's Alienation," 622-29.

27. *The American Institute of Christian Sociology*, Labadie Collection, University of Michigan, Ann Arbor (1893), p. 14. See C.H. Hopkins, *The Rise of the Social Gospel in American Protestantism: 1865-1915* (New Haven: Yale University Press), p. 187, who points out that union labor favored, while business interests criticized, Herron's efforts to bring these classes together.

28. Washington Gladden, *Recollections* (Boston: Houghton-Mifflin, 1909), p. 411.

29. Robert T. Handy, ed., *The Social Gospel in America, 1870-1920: Gladden, Ely, Rauschenbusch* (New York: Oxford University Press, 1966), pp. 180-84.

Herron's several volumes during the 1890s were nearly all sermons or lectures,[30] and at the opposite extreme, a spokesman for the conservative wing of the social gospel, the dramatically eloquent Joseph Cook, published his popular Boston Monday Lectures in British and American newspapers and later in eleven volumes.[31] Yet, with both the spoken and written word, the leaders were more successful in influencing their brethren in other pulpits than they were in reaching the average man in the pew and, as noted earlier, their stirring words in behalf of the oppressed fell on only a fraction of the downtrodden.

Still, the editor of the *Nation* feared that the rabble might possibly hear or read the radical pronouncements and shuddered at the possible consequences. A conservative publication and stout defender of the status quo, the *Nation* cautioned George D. Herron and other clergymen "preaching and writing about socialism" to "address themselves to the audience whose ear they have, and not to an audience whose ear they have not." Pointing out that the normal attendant at church, mostly from the upper classes, hearing Herron rave about the pending revolution would simply dismiss his sermon with a remark about "How earnest Mr. Herron is!" or "He gave us a very eloquent discourse" and then "go about their business as before." But, warned the editor, when Herron's inflammatory remarks reach the ears of the poor, they will conclude that even wealthy church members accept and condone the arguments thrust upon them by "reckless socialist agitators" and will conclude, therefore, that the rich were in fact robbers and would demand forthwith an immediate redistribution of the wealth.[32]

Analysis of the Causes

Although many socially concerned Christians were genuinely disturbed about the unequal distribution of wealth, or at least a shortage of greenbacks, and realized that this absence of legal tender contributed substantially to the discomfort of farmers and laborers, they were not sure whether the lack of money constituted a cause or an effect. In the minds of most pious churchgoers the basic cause of human suffering could be traced directly to the sin of an individual, usually the one in pain. When man succumbed to any of a multitude of sins the flesh was heir to, the inevitable effect was to bring distress to himself and others. Laziness, drinking, gambling, and other deadly sins led straight to the gutter, poorhouse, and drunkard's grave. Russell Conwell, eloquent exponent of the gospel of wealth, clarified the axiom to the vast audiences who listened again and again as he retold the story of Ali Hafed who sold his farm filled with "Acres of Diamonds" to travel the world over in a vain search for the precious stones. Piety and poverty, Conwell assured his listeners, could not dwell in the same person. Since the two conditions were patently contradictory an infinitesimal number of the poor merited our sympathy because, said he, "There is not a poor person in the United States who was not made poor by his own shortcomings or the shortcomings of someone else." And, since Conwell detected sin in only about 2 percent of the wealthy, the basic cause of poverty

30. Hopkins, *Rise of Social Gospel*, pp. 186-87.
31. *Dictionary of American Biography*, 4, 371-72.
32. *Nation*, May 3, 1894, pp. 323-24.

must lie at the doorstep of the poor.[33] Washington Gladden, on the other hand, finding sin in rich and poor alike, rebuked labor for its personal sins and capital for its greed, selfishness and failure to give the worker his fair share.[34] In a sermon entitled "The Parasite's Creed" he lashed out at a society where those who worked hardest and longest were nearest the poor house and those who toiled not were furthest from want, reminding his Columbus congregation that "great multitudes of human beings . . . draw their living directly from the lives of their fellow men; whose constant effort it is to live in idleness upon the fruits of other men's labor; to give nothing or as little as possible in return for what they receive."[35]

To other social gospel leaders on the radical left the parasite, the "Robber Baron," and the starving laborer were alike, all sufferers in a pagan, ruthless, unchristian system and victims, therefore, of social sins within the establishment. The poor man, contrary to Conwell's thesis, remained powerless to extricate himself from his chafing shackles and his capitalist overlord was likewise impotent to break the links and ease the burdens of his employees lest he forfeit his fortune to his nearest competitor. Indeed, the economic and political system drove man into sin, even tempting Cain to murder his brother. Built on rugged individualism, unholy competition, and the overpowering need for cheap labor, capitalism seemed to encourage the clever and unscrupulous, often pious churchmen as well, to claw their way to the top over the bodies of industrial foes and exploited workers.

A third answer came curiously enough from the world of natural science. Taking his lead from Darwin's *Origin of the Spe-*cies, Herbert Spencer adapted the concepts of evolution to the social sciences, deciding that just as the processes of natural selection and survival of the fittest applied to the animal kingdom, they likewise explained the evolution of man in the realm of economic, social, and political affairs. William Graham Sumner, to be treated in more detail later, led the way as the evangelist for Social Darwinism and was joined in turn by a substantial number of influential preachers who felt they had happily discovered the cause of poverty and temporary suffering rooted in the fibre, structure, and divine nature of creation.

A majority of the clergy continued, even as some do now, to rail against Darwin for attacking the Bible and bastardizing mankind by suggesting that Adam and Eve were not our first parents. But a few, like John Fiske, saw the benevolent hand of God in the evolutionary process and ultimately the versatile theory managed, quaintly enough, to serve both the champions of the status quo and the crusaders of the social gospel. The former used it to justify private enterprise and rugged individualism and the latter linked evolutionary processes to the optimistic progressivism that swept the country at the start of the twentieth century.

---

33. Russell H. Conwell, "Acres of Diamonds," in *American Forum: Speeches on Historic Issues, 1788-1900*, ed. Ernest J. Wrage and Barnet Baskerville (New York: Harper&Brothers, 1960), pp. 263-75.
34. Washington Gladden, "A Plain Talk with Workingmen," *Christian Union*, July 30, 1885, p. 8; idem, "A Plain Talk with Employers," *Christian Union*, July 23, 1885, pp. 8-9.
35. Unpublished sermon, January 17, 1891, Washington Gladden Papers.

Those hardy entrepreneurs who had risen to the top found Social Darwinism a reassuring and comfortable rationalization. Even reformer types, like Henry Ward Beecher, eagerly embraced Spencer's doctrine in part to reconcile science with theology and justify his own preferential position. During the catastrophic railroad strike of 1877 the eloquent preacher assured both rich and poor alike that "God has intended the great to be great and the little to be little."[36] Most of the prosperous at least saw no reason to question God's good judgment and if the system were divinely authorized it could hardly be blamed for being itself or doing its thing.

The Remedies

The solution for the Social Darwinists was frighteningly simple but neither the capitalists nor the reformers were willing to bide their time and wait on evolution. The social gospelers in particular believed that God wanted all men, great and small, to be brothers rather than jungle fighters grasping for survival. They could not reconcile slum ghettos, the fierce battles raging between capital and labor and between warring entrepreneurs with their conception of the brotherhood of man under the fatherhood of God. Even the industrial captains failed to follow Spencerian principles. Some had probably never heard of evolution, and their philanthropies, often criticized by the reformers, did not promote the elimination of the unfit.[37] Due to the intricate complexity of the issue and the divergent analyses of the problem causes, the men in the pulpit, even those most concerned socially, were uncertain about their roles and the limitations of their jurisdiction to speak and act, if indeed there were rhetorical limits.

Lord Bryce in his perceptive two-volume classic, *The American Commonwealth*, wrote understandingly of the ministerial dilemma, pointing out that as church and state separated, the minister whose authority at the beginning of the nineteenth century was akin to the bishops in Western Europe had by the last quarter of the century lost his ethical appeal in the realm of politics. Citing Henry Ward Beecher as an exceptional case when he joined the mugwumps in the presidential canvas of 1884, Bryce concluded that "It is only on platforms or in conventions where some moral cause is to be advocated, such as Abolitionism was thirty years ago or temperance is now, that clergymen can with impunity appear."[38] Activist clerical participation in so-called political affairs still produces explosive confrontations between ministers and laymen on the proper role of the church in secular affairs.[39]

However, the fact that ministers could bridge the gap between the personal and the political on the temperance issue helped keep social impulses alive in the churches during the intensely complacent period following the Civil War. Further, it was no accident that Frances Willard, eloquent leader of the WCTU, also joined the

36. Dombrowski, *Early Days of Christian Socialism*, p. 5.
37. Gladden raised a mighty furor with his protest (1905) of John D. Rockefeller's missionary gift of $100,000, which he labeled "tainted money." See Jacob H. Dorn, *Washington Gladden: Prophet of the Social Gospel* (Columbus: Ohio State University Press, 1966), pp. 240-67. Also Joseph F. Wall, *Andrew Carnegie* (New York: Oxford University Press, 1970), pp. 376-97 on Social Darwinism.
38. James Bryce, *The American Commonwealth* Vol. 2, (Chicago: Charles H. Sergel & Co., 1891), p. 582.
39. D.J. Hamblin, "Crunch in the Churches," *Life*, October 4, 1968, pp. 79-82.

Christian socialists, helped to edit their official organ, *The Dawn*, and gave unqualified support to the Knights of Labor in their demands for a living wage and the eight-hour day. Her enthusiasm for reform took her to the platform as the champion for laborers, farmers, Christian socialists, suffragettes, peace advocates, and prison reformers, all topics that ultimately came under the social gospel umbrella.[40]

In their obsession with things personal in religion, clergymen have seldom encountered opposition to their preaching against so-called vices of individuals, such as gambling, sabbath breaking, profanity, dancing and drinking. But in the shadowy no-man's-land where sinner's vices slopped over into public affairs or business concerns, the preacher spoke in uncertain tones and his congregation often listened with only half an ear. Early in the nineteenth century, the venerable Buckeye circuit rider, James B. Finley, encountered this classic opposition to ministerial involvement in social and economic matters when he attempted to enforce the Methodist rules on drinking. A licensed exhorter in his own denomination advised him to "preach the Gospel and let people's private business alone," or quit the ministry.[41] Undaunted, Finley continued his crusade and at mid-century led his Cincinnati Conference a step closer to the social gospel position, urging them "to speak less, and act more. . . .We hold the Maine Liquor Law to be as agreeable to pure republicanism, as it is to the spirit of the Gospel. . . .We are tired of sculling; let us have two oars to the boat—moral suasion and legal backing.[42]

The preachers of the Gilded Age broke sharply on the "need issue," trying to decide whether to apply religious ethics primarily to the individual or to the system. Would social and economic problems melt away if the saving grace of Jesus were adequately applied to the hearts of all men from the richest capitalist to the poorest wage earner? C.M. Morse shocked many readers of *The Methodist Review* in 1891 with a resounding, No! "I state it as a fact," Morse declared adamantly, "that if every individual in the United States should be 'regenerated' in an hour this wholesale conversion of the community—under present methods—would not result in a single reform in the industrial and social world." The major thrust of his argument was that regeneration must incorporate three steps, namely, "faith in the founder of the Christian religion," meaning the "personal, inward experience. . . a changed attitude toward God." The second element required the "saved" to investigate carefully all the problems related to human welfare and finally, to obey and imitate the founders of the Christian Church. The present evangelical tradition, he maintained, has totally ignored the last two essential demands. Consequently, he found in modern industrial society about the same number of "wicked men" and "regenerated men" both engaged with equal ferocity in the unholy race for riches. "They monopolize the land, they own the money, they operate the railroads, they engage in speculation, they profit by corporate power, trusts, and monopoly of every kind, they absorb the results of toil. . . and riot in luxury, while labor 'strikes' and starves!"

40. Boase, *Rhetoric of Christian Socialism*, pp. 78-87. See Mary Earhart, *Frances Willard: From Prayers to Politics* (Chicago: University of Chicago Press, 1944), pp. 210-59.
41. James B. Finley, *Autobiography* (Cincinnati: Methodist Book Concern, 1853), p. 250.
42. *Minutes Cincinnati Methodist Conference for the Year 1852* (Cincinnati: Methodist Book Concern, 1852), pp. 34-35.

Employing a somewhat earthy metaphor, Morse noted the "All classes of men now sit under the droppings of the sanctuary," but "the teachings from the pulpit have no appreciable influence upon the social movements of the day."[43] Washington Gladden tended to agree. Early in his pulpit career he rejected the premise that a "saved" man would automatically turn his attention to social injustice or that a group of "saved" men would seek to establish Christian relationships in industry. Rather than Christ's law of love ruling their lives, they were more likely in Gladden's view to honor the law of supply and demand.[44]

William Dwight Porter Bliss, the indefatigable missionary for the Christian socialists and editor of *The Dawn*, answered the exponents of personal salvation in the first issue on May 15, 1889. Rejecting the proposition that "What we need is a change of heart, not a change of system," Bliss argued analogically, asking what action a family would take if they found their home filled with sewer gas. Would they, he inquired, declare that their sole need was for a change of heart rather than a change of drainage?[45]

Persuasive support for the efficacy of individual salvation came curiously enough from a moderate leader of the social gospel. Lyman Abbott, a successor to Henry Ward Beecher at Plymouth Church and editor of *The Christian Union*, was the first to open the pages of a religious paper to a discussion of industrial and social problems. He was not unwilling to tackle social and economic ills, yet in an article for *The North American Review* in 1889, he contrasted the methods of Christianity with socialism in combatting social evil and quite understandably gave the nod to Christ.

The primary business of the church, Abbott insisted, was "to make men and trust that out of right manhood will grow right systems." Using Jesus as his primary authority he pointed to Christ's refusal to attack the existing order. He made no attempt to change the social order, offered no new system of taxation, proposed no labor legislation. Although Phariseeism was a dominant hierarchial system, Christ leveled his shafts at "the Pharisee" rather than "at the *ism.*" To abolish evil in the state, Abbott concluded, you must eliminate evil from individuals and "if we leave the sin in the individual, all social reform will result only as a change in the form of social evil."[46]

A strange, yet thoroughly understandable, remedy for nineteenth-century misery came from the Social Darwinians who assured the planners and tamperers with both systems and individuals that they were wasting their time. Nature and natural forces in society would, if not disturbed, work through evolutionary processes to select those individuals adapted to survive. The best course of action was in fact no action, a comforting thought for those who were enjoying the good life under the status quo. Pursuing this doctrine with relentless logical consistency, William Graham Sum-

43. C.M. Morse, "Regeneration as a Force in Reform Movements," *Methodist Review* 5th ser., no. 74, 7 (November, 1891): 929; Reply by R.F. Bishop in no. 74, 8 (March, 1892): 303-04; a second article by Morse no. 74, 8 (November, 1892): pp. 876-83.

44. Gladden, *Recollections,* p. 251.

45. *The Dawn*, May 15, 1889, pp. 2-3. For edited version see Boase, *Rhetoric of Christian Socialism*, pp. 59-66.

46. Abbott, "Christianity Versus Socialism," 449-451. See Boase, *Rhetoric of Christian Socialism*, pp. 67-77 for edited text.

ner furnished strong rhetorical proofs to sanctify *laissez-faire* and slow down if not annihilate the forces of social reform.

Sumner's pessimistic gospel of progress linked to survival of the fittest represented an almost direct antithesis to the optimistic, millenarian message of reform proclaimed by the social gospelers. Hofstadter picturesquely characterized Sumner as a "latter-day Calvin," preaching "the predestination of the social order and the salvation of the economically elect through the survival of the fittest."[47] By extending the analogy, the social gospel preachers could proclaim instead an Arminian concept of economic salvation open to all through God-given cooperation and Christian brotherhood.

Although Sumner defended the accumulation of riches for the best of the "select," he was no happier with the conniving, ruthless plutocrat who wormed his way to power and manipulated the government to his advantage than he was with the reformer who dreamed of establishing socialistic planning. Both were equally guilty of destroying the natural competition of the free market place. A one-time preacher who forsook the pulpit for a teacher's desk at Yale, he carried his strong moral conviction, his admiration for inductive proofs, his hatred of shams, and his love for the "forgotten man" to the public platform and the journals of the day.[48] The vigor of his style and the incisiveness of his logic on the platform and in the printed page made him no easy antagonist.

The establishment of the American Economic Association helped inspire one of Sumner's representative rhetorical blasts. Initiated largely by Richard T. Ely, the charter members of the association em-braced a large number of social gospel preachers, including Lyman Abbott, Leighton Williams, and R. Heber Newton. Washington Gladden helped Ely and the committee write their "statement of principles," advocating economic reformation through scientific study, legislative action, and the ministrations of the church. A number of conservative economists joined, but not Sumner whose essay, "The Absurd Effort to Make the World Over," aptly expressed his contempt for the association and its objectives.[49]

Ironically, Sumner's piece first appeared in *Forum*, neatly sandwiched between two articles on reform.[50] It followed a discussion of proposed new temperance legislation and immediately preceded "The Programme of the Nationalists" by Edward Bellamy, author of the intensely popular

47. Richard Hofstadter, *Social Darwinism in American Thought* (Boston: Beacon Press, 1955), p. 66.
48. The hope of the nation for Sumner rested with the "Forgotten Man," eulogized again by President Nixon in the campaign of 1968: Also a near relative of "silent majority." Nixon used nearly verbatim Sumner's words: "The Forgotten Man is delving away in patient industry, supporting his family, paying his taxes, casting his vote, supporting the church and the school, reading his newspaper, and cheering for the politician of his admiration, but he is the only one for whom there is no provision in the great scramble and the big divide." *Social Darwinism: Selected Essays of William Graham Sumner*, introduction by S. Person (Englewood Cliffs, N.J.: Prentice-Hall, 1963), p. 132; and P.H. Boase, "Campaign 1968: Rhetoric According to Peanuts," *Ohio Speech Journal* 7 (1969):5.
49. Ralph H. Gabriel, *The Course of American Democratic Thought*, 2nd ed. (New York: Ronald Press, 1956), p. 248. See Handy, *Social Gospel in America*, p. 179, and Hopkins, *Rise of Social Gospel*, pp. 116-17.
50. William G. Sumner, "The Absurd Effort to Make the World Over," *Forum* 17 (March, 1894):92-102.

socialistic, utopian novel, *Looking Backward*. The novel inspired a spate of Nationalist Clubs, enrolling a sizable number of ministers, particularly Christian socialists. Many other novels, written by preachers, carried the social gospel message, the most popular being Charles M. Sheldon's *In His Steps*, which sold 23,000,000 copies and was made into a movie.[51]

In his essay, Sumner singled out Bellamy for special treatment, ridiculing his oversimplified concept of economics and his tendency to trace the suffering of society to a single cause, a fault not peculiar to social gospel reformers alone nor confined to Bellamy, although he was surely guilty. Men of all classes were basically good, thought Bellamy, but were innocent victims of the competitive struggle for survival. Dr. Jekyll, however, would soon replace Mr. Hyde when industrial democracy, brotherhood, and state regulation of the economy supplants the brutalizing, "hideous, ghastly mistake" of competition.[52] Sumner scoffed at Bellamy's assumptions, particularly his claim of the all-sufficient healing power of democracy to solve our problems. "We may find that instead of democratizing capitalism we have capitalized democracy—that is, have brought in plutocracy," to Sumner a far more grievous condition.[53]

Sumner did not escape sharp challenges from the best minds in the scientific and Christian world. His chief antagonist among the scientists was Lester Ward who twitted Sumner for his relentless crusade against the reformers who must also be products of evolution and therefore should be allowed to survive or perish as dictated by the immutable laws of nature.[54] Among the social gospel preachers, the moderate Washington Gladden, while rejecting social-

ism, felt that if the church had done her duty "No such social cleavage as that which has parted industrial society into warring classes would ever have occurred. . . .We must lay the entire blame on the church for it belongs to her."[55]

To the radical George D. Herron, the doctrines of Social Darwinism were darkest heresy. In the sermon that launched him on his spectacular career as the foremost propagandist of Christian socialism, he branded Sumner's philosophy as "the principle upon which Cain slew his brother." Invited to Plymouth Church in Minneapolis on September 22, 1890, he delivered "The Message of Jesus to Men of Wealth," and lifted himself to national prominence, dramatizing the theme he spread across the land during the next decade. His message, free from theological dogma but filled with emotional fire, resembled closely the evangelical sermons his audience had heard at camp meetings. His intensely personal appeal directed to professing Christians urged total sacrifice, appealing to his listeners to dedicate themselves wholly to the Kingdom of Heaven in business, industry, and the state.

In his stirring peroration at Minneapolis, delivered, no doubt, with the impressive solemnity that characterized his speaking, he personalized the issue by asking: "Is the

---

51. See Hopkins, *Rise of Social Gospel*, p. 143.
52. See Gabriel, *American Democratic Thought*, p. 222.
53. *Social Darwinism: Essays of William Graham Sumner*, p. 177.
54. Thomas F. Gossett, *Race: The History of an Idea in America* (Dallas: Southern Methodist University Press, 1963), pp. 160-68.
55. "The New Evangel," November 30, 1908 (Mss. sermon), Washington Gladden Papers. See Boase, *Rhetoric of Christian Socialism*, pp. 115-32 for edited version.

Gospel of Jesus livable?" Obviously it was, and fortifying his remedy with divine authority, he issued a new kind of altar call. "God is calling today for able men who are willing to be financially crucified in order to establish the world's market on the Golden Rule basis." Avoiding the evangelist's standard appeal to eschew the personal sins of the flesh, he urged his hearers instead to grasp life's richest reward, and join God's annointed in making "the market place as sacred as the church. You can make the whirl of industrial wheels like the joyous music of worship. . . .And where you go," he promised the faithful, "flowers of hope will spring in your footprints. You can bear the weak in your arms, and set the captives of poverty free."[56]

Herron also found some thorns along his path. The vibrant new approach to conversion and his specific application of the Sermon on the Mount to industry and state produced startling effects, both positive and negative throughout the nation. Some were inspired to carry forth his plan of social redemption to its ultimate logical conclusion and others like President David Starr Jordan of Stanford to concede that he "is a rank humbug."[57] When Herron was in California on an extensive speaking tour, the nineteenth-century Ezekiel, as one Golden Stater labeled him, ran into violent criticism from C.O. Brown, pastor of the First Congregational Church in San Francisco. Confronting Herron during the discussion period following his first address, Brown denounced his Congregational colleague "as an anarchist, whose teachings meant destruction to all established institutions."[58] Joseph Cook, popular Boston lecturer and conservative whose support of mild reform was inspired in large measure

by his fear of socialism and revolution, spoke in Brown's church during the controversy. Understandably, he ridiculed Herron, assuring the congregation that "the best thought of this country from Plymouth Rock to Golden Gate, commends the position of your pastor. . . ."[59]

Herron's defenders, including many of the leading ministers on the West Coast were equally vehement, accusing Brown of "Calumny, misrepresentation, injustice, unfairness," and quoting Herron out of context. Identifying the Grinnell professor with Jesus, his supporters concluded that Christ himself would have received the same treatment and encountered the same criticisms.[60]

Anarchistic or not, Herron's appeal produced concrete activist responses, inspiring not only Sheldon's best seller, *In His Steps*, but also the establishment of a Christian Commonwealth Colony twelve miles east of Columbus, Georgia. An Oberlin theological student, Ralph Albertson, who had studied the works of Henry George and Edward Bellamy and talked at length with Washington Gladden, invited Herron to speak at his Springfield, Ohio, Congregational Church during the panic of 1893. Deeply impressed with Herron's words, he traveled to Chicago the following year and witnessed at first hand the Pullman strike, thereby reaching the conclusion that labor

56. George D. Herron, *The Christian Society* (New York: Fleming H. Revell, 1894), pp. 119-20. See *American Forum*, Wrage and Baskerville, pp. 276-82.

57. *The Oberlin News*, June 13, 1895, p. 4.

58. Adeline Knapp, *et. al.*, "Prof. George D. Herron: The Man and His Work in California," *Arena* 4 (September, 1895):111.

59. *The Oberlin News*, June 20, 1895, p. 4.

60. Knapp, *et. al.*, "Prof. George D. Herron," 110-28.

war conducted by workers was as unchristian as the competitive struggle that produced the conflict. Following a season of intensive soul-searching and extensive communion with several like-minded Christians, he and they decided to replace the materialistic, competitive struggle with a new communal society totally committed to Christian brotherhood. The colony opened its doors in November, 1895 to all, irrespective of economic status. Operating in a purely democratic framework, it adopted a totally communistic arrangement for conducting its business.

The experiment attracted the attention and admiration of many prominent figures, including Count Tolstoy who maintained correspondence with the members. Although the settlers worked at agriculture and simple manufacturing, they secured their greatest income and contributed most significantly to the rhetoric of reform by printing an excellent journal called *The Social Gospel*. It carried news of social Christianity, editorials, book reviews, and feature articles, reaching a circulation of about two thousand in America and Europe. Many leading scholars and churchmen dedicated to Christian socialism helped edit or contributed articles and the highly respected journal was given credit for popularizing if not originating the name later applied to social Christianity.[61]

By the time the colony folded in the spring of 1900, it had reached some three to four hundred persons during the previous four years. Causes of the failure included weather, disease, and a vicious plot by a small band of traitors who proved too materialistic and selfish to be reached by the law of love, obliging the founders to resort to the legal force they were determined to avoid.[62] Interestingly, in 1942, two

young preachers established a nearly identical community only a few miles from the original site. Clarence Jordan, author of the "Cotton Patch" versions of the New Testament, and one of his Baptist colleagues, Martin England, set up Koinonia Farm unaware of the earlier venture but, according to Jordan, following the same "broad, general principles" except for a greater stress on racial brotherhood.[63]

Rhetorical Evaluation of the Social Gospel

A few nineteenth-century pulpit leaders in league with a small but brilliant coterie of religiously motivated laymen relied mainly on spoken and written discourse for awakening a sleeping church to the rediscovery of its social mission and the modification of its unbending individualistic approach to theology and economics. Indeed, they may have placed too much faith in the power of words to move men to action. Or perhaps they overestimated the potency of their pulpit oratory. Only partially successful in arousing a deep and active social concern in the average churchgoer, this colorful band of reformers nevertheless left their indelible impression on Christendom as they marched into the present century alongside the Progressives, supremely confident of total, imminent victory. But once again the

---

61. Hopkins, *Rise of Social Gospel*, pp. 196-97.
62. See Dombrowski, *Early Days of Christian Socialism*, pp. 132-70, for a full account.
63. Correspondence with Dr. Jordan, August 9, 1967. Jordan's untimely death at age 57 in 1969 prompted Hal Gulliver in the *Atlanta Constitution*, November 3, 1969, to refer to him as a "gentle man" who "had guts when it took guts to have guts." Jordan's account of the founding of Koinonia Farm is in Boase, *Rhetoric of Christian Socialism*, pp. 146-61.

millennial vision faded, submerged in waves of pessimistic cynicism, brought on by hot and cold wars, a noble but disappointing experiment in national prohibition, another depression, labor riots, and the apparent failure of the democratic ideal to cope with racism, war, poverty, pollution, and the ghettoes.[64]

The preachers of the "Gilded Age" for a variety of reasons faced nearly insuperable odds in their struggle to adapt a new social gospel to an economically respectable, middle-class congregation. Most of their listeners and many of their own conservative colleagues showed unmistakable symptoms of suffering from the Horatio Alger syndrome. Divinely sanctioned inequities in wealth appeared nearly everywhere throughout the country, but the pious and ambitious were bound to win. The system might contain a flaw or two, but the door of success was open wide to all but the impious and slothful. Moreover, the new evolutionary doctrines of Social Darwinism offered scientific proof of the efficacy of *laissez-faire.* An occupant of the pew found it easy to believe that working men generally enjoyed an adequate income, even when forced to support a family of five or six on a dollar a day, unless, as Henry Ward Beecher warned, he smokes or drinks beer.[65]

Conservative leaders like G. Frederick Wright of Oberlin helped fix attitudes inimical to social gospel philosophy by reminding his readers that even Jesus was resigned to the continuing and inevitable presence of the poor and assuring all that the "cares and responsibilities and rewards of riches can belong only to a few." Most, however, were convinced that the few increased only as the many developed habits of thrift, temperance, hard work, and piety. And in a

nation rich in resources and land, one or two Carnegies furnished sufficient proof to establish the gospel of wealth as axiomatic. Further, any attempt to distribute the wealth more equitably raised the frightful spectre of socialism and communism, neither condemned by the liberal wing of the social gospel. The conservatives offered statistical evidence that such plans would raise each worker's pay infinitesimally and deny the responsible entrepreneur the necessary capital for growth.[66]

These attitudes frequently hostile to the social message rendered audience adaptation, never an easy task, a constant plague to the reformers. Messages that might have moved the absent poor often fell on the deaf ears of the attending rich. The acid-tongued socialist agitator, Daniel DeLeon, smiled wryly as he watched William Dwight Porter Bliss attempt to sell socialism and trade unionism to a well-heeled Episcopal audience in Boston. "It seemed like pouring water on a duck's back to ask them to give up their wealth. . . .Asking God and landlords and speculators to change their tactics is more absurd than trying to make a hungry lion lay down in peace besides a lamb!"[67]

64. See Gabriel, *American Democratic Thought,* p. 280, who wrote: "When Rauschenbusch contemplated in his imagination that Kingdom of God destined, one day, to become an earthly reality, he saw that it was nothing else than the democratic dream come true."

65. *The Christian Union,* August 1, 1877, cited in William Bos and Clyde Faries, "The Social Gospel: Preaching Reform, 1875-1915," in *Preaching in American History: Selected Issues in the American Pulpit,* ed., DeWitte Holland (Nashville: Abingdon Press, 1969), p. 227. Also D.P., "What Does Henry George Mean? What is Said on Both Sides," *Methodist Review* 5th Ser., no. 69, 3, (September, 1887): 763-69.

66. G. Frederick Wright, "Ministers and Mobs," *Bibliotheca Sacra,* 49 (October, 1892): 676-81.

To offer a ravenous industrialist or an ambitious would-be capitalist a viable solution proved nearly impossible and the message, therefore, often suffered from an overdeveloped "need step" and an underdeveloped "plan," a not infrequent weakness in the affirmative debate case. Stimulators rather than activists, their diagnoses were more perceptive than their prescriptions which often sounded sentimental and utopian.[68] The intricate economic and political problems they portrayed so vividly would vanish if men simply followed the Golden Rule. And a few idealists like "Golden Rule" Jones, mayor of Toledo, and "Golden Rule" Nash of Cincinnati, came very near to proving it. With Gladden the crusaders could point to the sky and watch the stars in their courses lead mankind toward a brighter tomorrow, but they were not always able to find an earthly solution for today. The *Nation*, for example, criticized Gladden for the vagueness of his program outlined in *Tools and the Man*, charging him and the Christian socialists with fuzzy thinking in treating abstract, complex organizations like the state, society, and the government as though they were subject to the same kinds of persuasion as the individual. "No careful thinker will permit himself to reason in this way any more than deliberately to attribute sex to a war-vessel."[69]

George D. Herron consistently used this general appeal with his audiences, exhorting civilization, church, and state to seek rebirth lest they miss the "divine social kingdom."[70] Like many of his brethren, Herron was at his best with emotional proof and at his worst with facts, statistics, dialectic, and logical proof. Indeed, he seemed to glory in avoiding scientific analysis, insisting that "Great spiritual facts and principles are not apprehended but distorted by the intellect." Further, his growing hostility toward the "establishment" raised the ogre of anarchy. His dim view of the institution of marriage itself, followed by his divorce and remarriage, ultimately shattered his ethos with the church.[71]

Many social gospel preachers suffered myopic vision in other spheres as well, particularly in the realm of race, a fault more apparent today than during the nineteenth century since most of their audiences then held similar views of Anglo-Saxon superiority. They not only neglected the black following the Civil War but found it difficult to develop sympathetic rapport for the immigrant worker who failed to share their own ethnic background.[72]

Still, the fundamental premises of Christian brotherhood and the individual's responsibility for social service has continued to inspire succeeding generations to apply the Christian ethic to all facets of life. Man turned his eyes from sky to earth and recognized the immanent as well as the transcendant nature of God. Eulogizing the impact on his own mission of Walter Rauschenbusch, the greatest of the social gospel leaders, Martin Luther King, Jr. credited him with giving "American Protes-

---

67. *People*, May 2, 1899, cited in Howard H. Quint, *The Forging of American Socialism* (Indianapolis: Bobbs-Merrill, 1963), p. 126.

68. See *Time*, June 14, 1971, p. 56, for a discussion of the failure of the social gospel to meet the issue of "individual sin."

69. "Christian Socialism," *Nation*, May 25, 1893, 381-82.

70. George D. Herron, *The Christian State* (New York: Thomas Y. Crowell), pp. 61-62. See also, "The New Social Apostolate," *Arena* 25 (May, 1901):486-91.

71. May, *Protestant Church*, pp. 250-56.

72. Gossett, *Race*, pp. 176-97.

tantism a sense of social responsibility it should never lose."[73] Not many modern theologians, laymen, or protestors talk about the "social gospel," but they still use the rhetoric and employ many of the same premises as their nineteenth-century counterparts. As long as poverty, materialism, and war infect this planet a small group of concerned preachers and laymen will proclaim and debate the timeless issues of the social gospel.

BIBLIOGRAPHY

Excellent sources for both the negative and positive ferment appear in the denominational journals and newspapers:

The Andover Review. A religious magazine attuned to social concerns.

Arena. A secular magazine, an enthusiastic supporter of the struggle.

Bibliotheca Sacra. A religious magazine with social concerns.

The Christian Union (*Outlook* after 1893). Founded by Henry Ward Beecher and later edited by Lyman Abbott. Carried excellent articles and essays.

Methodist Review A religious magazine with social concerns.

Nation. Secular magazine; usually a skeptical detractor from the struggle.

Watchman (Baptist). Took the conservative position.

Zion's Herald (Methodist). Took the liberal position.

Abell, A. I. *Catholicism and Social Action. A Search for Social Justics, 1865-1950.* Notre Dame, Ind.: University of Notre Dame Press, 1960.
The Catholic contribution to the struggle about the social gospel.

American Forum: Speeches on Historic Issues, 1788-1900. Edited by Ernest J. Wrage and Barnet Baskerville. New York: Harper & Brothers, 1960.
Includes an analytical essay and speeches by Herron, Sumner, Carnegie, Henry George, and Russell Conwell.

Boase, Paul H., ed. *The Rhetoric of Christian Socialism.* New York: Random House, 1969.
Collection of essays and speeches.

Carter, Paul. *The Decline and Revival of the Social Gospel.* 1956 Reprint. Hamden, Connecticut: Shoe String Press, 1971.
Brings the social gospel into the twentieth century.

Dorn, Jacob H. *Washington Gladden: Prophet of the Social Gospel.* Columbus: Ohio State University Press, 1966.
A definitive biography which covers a wide variety of issues and speakers.

Faulkner, Harold U. *Politics, Reform, and Expansion, 1890-1900* New York: Harper & Brothers, 1959.
Helps to place the movement in perspective.

Handy, Robert T., ed. *The Social Gospel in America 1870-1920: Gladden, Ely, Rauschenbusch.* New York: Oxford University Press, 1966.
Collection of essays and speeches.

Hofstadter, Richard. *The Age of Reform.* New York: Alfred A. Knopf, 1955.
Helps to place the movement in perspective.

Meyer, Donald B. *The Protestant Search for Political Realism, 1919-1941.* Berkeley: University of California Press, 1960.
Brings the social gospel into the twentieth century.

Wrage, Ernest J., and Baskerville, Barnet, eds. *American Forum: Speeches on Historic Issues, 1788-1900.* New York: Harper & Row, 1960.
Includes an analytical essay and speeches by Herron, Sumner, Carnegie, Henry George, and Russell Conwell.

---

73. Martin Luther King, Jr., *Strength to Love* (New York: Harper & Row, 1963), pp. 165-68.

13 Socialism: Path to Economic Justice, 1890-1912

DeWitte Holland

During the 1870s and 1880s, in the United States, few people disagreed that there was maldistribution of the basic goods of society. This problem was viewed as economic injustice by most but the emerging plutocracy and their social Darwinist mentors. Reform efforts arose from every quarter; the churchmen, the farmers, the middle class citizens, the workers, the intellectuals, and even from a few millionaires. The land was potentially ripe for the automatic collapse of capitalism and the rise of the socialist state.

Both Karl Marx and Friedrich Engels felt boundless optimism for socialism in America. In 1879 Marx wrote, "The United States have at present overtaken England in the rapidity of economic progress. . .the masses are quicker, and have greater political means in their hands to resent the form of a progress accomplished at their expense."[1] Following the spectacular rise of the Knights of Labor and the 1886 New York City mayoralty campaign of Henry George, Engels predicted that since no medieval ruins barred the way to classless socialist society, "Once the Americans get started it will be with an energy and violence compared with which we in Europe shall be mere children."[2] But in spite of the prime conditions and the rosy predictions of the great collectivists, socialism did not become, and has not become a significant political or economic factor in the United States. In the face of such conditions this chapter will examine some of the rhetoric of the period of the rise of socialism in America, 1890-1912, to ferret out some of the reasons why socialism failed. Specifically we will look at the major rhetorical strategies addressed to the issue of economic equity through public control of the means of production and distribution.

The Issue

Achievement of economic equity or justice was the issue debated in the battle between capitalism and socialism. The aims of socialists were stated tersely by Eugene Debs in 1904:

---

1. Quoted in Hayim Greenberg, "Socialism Reexamined," *International Socialist Forum* (London), June, 1942. p. 2120.
2. Letter to Schluter, No. 222, in *Karl Marx and Friedrich Engels: Selected Correspondence, 1846-1895* (New York: International Publishers, 1934), p. 497.

The socialist party is not and does not pretend to be a capitalist party. . .The socialist party is. . .a revolutionary working class party whose historic mission is to conquer capitalism on the political battlefield, take control of government and through the public powers take possession of the means of wealth and production, abolish wage slavery and emancipate all workers and all humanity.[3]

Socialists disagreed on the means of attaining the goals suggested by Debs, but they were in total agreement that capitalism was the root cause of all social and economic ills. It was quite clear to socialists that society was built on capitalistic exploitation of the working class. The workman produced the wealth and the capitalist extracted all of it save a subsistence pittance for the workers.

The Republican and Democratic parties were viewed alike as being capitalistic parties, differing only in being committed to different sets of capitalist interests. Debs suggested specifically that:

The capitalist class is represented by the Republican Democratic, Populist and Prohibition parties, all of which stand for private ownership of the means of production and the triumph of any one of which will mean continued wage slavery to the working class. . .The Republican and Democratic parties or to be more exact the *Republican Democratic party* represents the capitalist class in the class struggle. . .with either of these parties in power, one thing is always certain and that is that the capitalist class is in the saddle and the working class under the saddle.[4]

The scientific and political socialists agreed with the utopian communitarian socialists of earlier days on the general goal of social and economic justice. The utopians, however, withdrew from society and sought rationally, collectively and peacefully, without resort to class warfare, to establish a community of brotherhood. The scientific socialists did not quarrel greatly with the utopians; they went their separate ways in seeking to establish social and economic justice. The political or scientific socialists had quite enough difficulty dealing with dissidents in their own ranks. Indeed, most of their rhetoric and unhappily most of their energies were dissipated through in-fighting on the subsidiary issue of the best means to bring about socialism in the body politic.

The Background

Apathy to twenty years of persistent efforts of socialist immigrant proselytizers following the Civil War gave way under the shocking news that "red" agitators were to blame for the bloody Chicago Haymarket riots. This news, though not fully correct, was bolstered when the people correctly discovered that the socialists were playing a major supporting role in the notable 1886 third party New York City mayoralty campaign of Henry George, famous for his single tax proposals. Even so, few Americans outside the confines of major U.S. cities had ever heard of socialism and few of these held any great fear of socialist ideas. They were rather confident of the strength of American political democracy. Andrew Carnegie capsulated the popular mind of the day regarding socialists when he held them to be "a parcel of foreign cranks whose communistic ideas were the natural growth of unjust laws in their native land."[5] Patently to him American political

3. Eugene V. Debs, *Debs: His Life Writings and Speeches* (Chicago: Charles H. Kerr and Co., 1908), p. 358.
4. *Ibid.*, p. 352.
5. Andrew Carnegie, *Triumphant Democracy: or Fifty Years' March of the Republic* (New York: Charles Scribner's Sons, 1886), p. 348.

democracy was the solution to their problem.

The Haymarket affair produced the first "red" scare in American history and gave rise to a "red" baiting campaign of great magnitude. Socialists, lumped with anarchists despite their mutual hatred for one another, became targets for yellow journalism, politicians seeking an issue, and professional patriots. At least the patriots had a real issue, for the socialists generally were not patriotic.

By the mid-1880s the rapid growth of industry, virtually unchecked by ethics, unbridled by government, and spurred onward by the motivations of social Darwinism, was leading to cut-throat competition and to corporate combinations. Henry Demarest Lloyd called attention to the "Trustification of American Industry."[6] The growth of American business following the Civil War was helpful to too few of our citizens. The small businessman with a vision of unlimited expansion in a slaveless America found himself slipping backward in an uphill fight or squeezed out entirely by pressure from capital combinations. The farmer's hope for prosperity urged on by free land and adequate transportation vanished in a flood of mortgages, exorbitant freight rates, falling prices, and closed frontiers. The worker's quest for a better standard of living, job security and economic stability, or the dream of moving into his own business or farm was shattered by nightmare depression, decreased wages, unemployment, and a labor market deliberately loaded by management with hordes of foreign bodies. The few "captains of industry" and a slowly rising middle class did profit from the system and naturally fought to preserve it.

The rapid and dramatic growth of the American economy toward industrial capitalism gave rise to social problems that were underscored by the violent railroad strike of 1877, the Eight-Hour Day strike, the Haymarket Square incident of 1886, and by swelling labor unrest in the early 1890s. Sprawling urban slums spawned by the new industrialism became ugly and continuingly troublesome sore spots on the American scene.[7]

The unfettered expansion of Chicago following the great fire of 1871 is unique but in many ways typical of events throughout urban America of that period. The poor lived in wretched, disease-ridden slums while the well-to-do lived in mansions. Anything from which someone could make a profit was permissible, and for thirty years the city reveled in an orgy of money-making. Nature was destroyed as the air hung heavy with the stench from the packing houses and inadequate sewers. Lives, too, were polluted as Marshal Field could spend $75,000 on a birthday party for his son while thousands of clerks in his stores earned three to six dollars a week.

If the demand for meat lessened, thousands of Armour meat packinghouse workers could be laid off without notice to starve without managerial pang of conscience. Nor was it any real concern to Mr. Swift if a worker in his packing house broke a leg on the job. The unfortunate one was simply turned into the street and another hired to replace him. Such were inexorable manifestations of social Darwinism reflected in the laws of business. Men who

---

6. Cited in Howard H. Quint, *The Forging of American Socialism* (Columbia, South Carolina: University of South Carolina Press, 1953), p. 28.
7. Ira Kipnis, *The American Socialist Movement 1897-1912* (New York: Greenwood Press, 1968), p. 3.

could not rise to the top were ground under.[8]

The growth of business and industry was not accompanied by a comparable rise in the wages for the workman, nor was the conspicuous luxury living of the giants of industry coupled with even decent housing for most urban laborers. Farmers, laborers and little merchants watched profits and prestige of "trustified" business and industry soar as their own standard of living and social status decayed.

Farm income dropped steadily in the time between 1870 and 1900. Grain prices were just about halved during that period and Kansas farmers turned to burning corn instead of fuel, since it was cheaper. Their condition was further threatened by company-set freight rates on farm produce and on farm machinery shipped to the farmer. Moreover, the farmers required increasing amounts of sophisticated machinery, produced and distributed by unregulated manufacturers.

Many farmers, compelled to seek work in the urban areas, helped to overpopulate further a labor market that was already flooded with hundreds of thousands of foreign laborers recently flushed into it. Such conditions along with increased competition between companies led to concerted efforts by employers to cut wages. In at least one known incident a Pennsylvania management organization offered a $10,000 bonus to any mine operator who could successfully lower wages.[9] As capital became centralized and competition lessened, large companies divided the market for a given product or service and drove lesser competitors out of the field. Thus more men at the bottom were pressured into seeking ways to beat the system.

It is only natural that the farmer and the laborer, the primary victims of the economics of the system, were among the first to seek relief. The farmers organized as the Populists and the laborers as union men. Others joined; churchmen as social gospelers (though not all of them were anticapitalist); the intelligentsia as Nationalists or socialists of one stripe or another; few protesters, if any, were Republicans. But there were anticapitalists and there were anticapitalists. Some wanted utterly to destroy the system, slowly or immediately, while others merely wanted to rearrange it so that they would have what they viewed as a more equitable share of it.

Socialists

The socialist variety of anticapitalism was imported from Europe. It rose above nationalism, being neither patriotic nor American. However, if one uses the term broadly, the United States has a rich socialist tradition. It dates back as early as the seventeenth century, well before the transplanting of German class-conscious socialism in the mid-nineteenth century. Several religious, secular, and perfectionist communitarian settlements had been attempted in America, usually in response to the charisma and vision of a leader or in application of social theories such as those of Welshman Robert Owen or French utopian Charles Fourier.

During the 1840s in Germany and especially following the unsuccessful uprising

8. Ray Ginger, *Altgeld's America 1890-1905* (Chicago: Quadrangle, 1965), p. 8.(Paperback edition)

9. DeWitte Holland and Robert Oliver, eds., *A History of Public Speaking in Pennsylvania* (State College, Pa.: Pennsylvania Speech Assoc., 1971), p. 336.

of 1848, German radicals added their influence to the American socialist tradition. These socialist colonists tore American socialism away from its utopian pattern and attempted to weave it into a revolutionary pattern. They could not agree on a common strategy for attacking capitalism and though actively organized they remained relatively unnoticed by the general public. Sensational publicity growing out of the Haymarket riots and some successful literary rhetoric changed all that.

Nationalists—Lawrence Gronlund's, *Cooperative Commonwealth* of 1885 was no ordinary book. It was the first effort by an American socialist to analyze the American economy in Marxist terms. The work, thoroughly Marxist except in omission of the class struggle thesis, which Gronlund could not lower himself to include, rejected remedies and improvements in the capitalistic system. Socialism was the only solution to check the decreasing real wages of the worker.

Gronlund's book, hardly a record-breaking best seller, was not read widely outside of socialist circles. However, it made a profound impression on one Edward Bellamy who in 1887 published his famous utopian novel, *Looking Backward* which incorporated much of the socialist message of *Cooperative Commonwealth*. Bellamy, an unknown literary figure, brought his readers squarely face-to-face with the unpleasant realities of industrialism in America and dramatically extolled the abolition of the competitive principle in social and economic relationships. His work, instantly a best seller, sold upwards of 500,000 copies and is widely credited by friend and foe alike with having made socialism respectable in America.

Bellamy's rhetorical novel, written for the "cultured and conservative class,"[10] while thoroughly Marxist in indictment of industrial capitalism, also rejected the class struggle thesis. He could see no good in the competitive principle in any phase of human activity but denied the use of violence or coercion to usher in the impending social change to the cooperative system. A strong appeal of the work was that while it severely indicted industrial capitalism, it demonstrated that the middle class could be protected in the change process.

Visions of the "nationalist" society, portrayed in *Looking Backward*, so impressed two young Boston journalists that they formed a Nationalist Club in their city to work for the realization of Bellamy's dream. After three months of ground work, the club was formed with quite an impressive membership of intellectuals and reformers. Their publication, *The Nationalist Magazine*, was launched in May of 1889, and served as house organ in the establishment of other clubs in a holy war of battling for the social and economic salvation of the downtrodden.[11]

Following the principles of the Boston club a chain of clubs emerged from coast to coast and beyond to England, Canada, and New Zealand. Most U.S. cities of consequence housed at least one club, and within two years after the founding of the Boston club 165 groups had been chartered.[12]

The middle class character of the Nationalist Club movement attracted a prominent and distinguished membership. People from the working class rarely joined and thus the clubs were not populated by a

---

10. Quint, *Forging*, p. 80.
11. *The Nationalist Magazine*, 3 (1890):110.
12. Quint, *Forging*, p. 82 ff.

membership whose grievances they were seeking to correct. Ministers, rabbis, labor leaders, a few millionaires, veterans, and a variegated bevy of reformers flocked to the meetings. Numbered among them were Clarence Darrow, Samuel Gompers, W. D. P. Bliss, and a Daniel DeLeon who was soon to dominate a phase of the socialist movement for the rest of his life.

The rapid growth of the movement in the middle class lent credence to the cries of oppression of the working class. Here was a large group of respectable people outside of the oppressed group that agreed with the workers and sought to go beyond reform to revolution, albeit it gradually and in a dignified manner. The fledgling Socialist Labor Party took careful and hungry note of the growth of Bellamism, for they desperately needed a respectable, native-born, middle-class American base within their membership.

The Nationalists, the most moderate of pure socialists in America, were basically middle class and did not hold to the class struggle, a doctrine which was never widely popular among Anglo-Saxons. They, like the English Fabians, insisted that the transition to socialism would be made gradually and peacefully as a natural terminal stage in capitalistic development. The increasing tendency toward industrial concentration meant the ultimate and final destruction of the existing capitalist order.

Bellamy, the originator of Nationalist thought, argued that the cooperative commonwealth would be brought in through increased government control of all industries. He was quite willing to work toward that end through government takeover of local utilities and transportation facilities. This mundane, utilitarian approach was anathema to the true Marxist spirit. Further, the Nationalists were patriotic and rejected the Marxist contention that a closer bond existed among the wage-earners of the world than among the workers and capitalists of a given country. Generally, the Nationalists were firm believers in the freedom mission of America. They maintained that Anglo-Saxon countries lived under governments conducive to peaceful change and thus would be the way-showers to a higher and better and more humane type of government.[13]

With keen insight Bellamy pointed out that political democracy is worthless without corresponding economic democracy. In one, the people collectively control their government; in the other, people collectively control the means of production and distribution. Economic democracy constituted the chief objective of the Nationalists. According to Bellamy:

Nationalism. . .is the doctrine of those who hold that the principle of popular government by the equal voice of all for the equal benefit of all. . . should be extended to the economic organization as well; and that the entire capital and labor of the nations should be nationalized and administered by their people through their chosen agents for the equal benefit of all under an equal law of industrial service.[14]

With only political democracy great capitalists still may exercise overwhelming economic forces in behalf of their own private interests. "The industrial system of a nation like its political system," Bellamy asserted, "should be a government of the people, by the people and for the people. Until economic equality shall give a basis to

13. Quint, *Forging*, p. 88 ff.
14. *Ibid.*, p. 92.

political equality the latter is but a sham."[15]

The cooperative commonwealth would come slowly, methodically and in accord with the inevitable economic evolution of capitalism. Bellamy pointed out that:

They (the Nationalists) propose no revolutionary methods, no hasty or ill-considered measures provocative of reaction, no letting go of the old before securing a hold on the new; but an orderly progress of which each step shall logically follow the last, and shall be justified to the most short sighted by its immediate motives and results without invoking any considerations of ultimate ends. Those who wish to go only a step at a time, we welcome as allies, and we pledge them the cooperation which is not the less cordial and considerate because of the fact that results which they regard as ends seem to us as means to ends.[16]

The Nationalist program first was to embrace certain semi-public businesses and then extend to others; the controlling idea being always to avoid the disruption of business and undue hardship to individuals. Bellamy urged full compensation to owners of plants taken over by a city, state, or nation.

The rank-and-file worker was not satisfied by the very pleasant and apparently sound theoretical generalities of the Nationalists leaders. The workers wanted immediate relief from their plight. A program of practical implementation was called for not only by the workers but the great group of middle class people in the movement. Bellamy then spelled out a five point program of specific goals, all of which required some political action and widespread organizational activity. However, in actual practice Bellamy opposed political action to carry out the aims, fearing that it would corrupt and weaken the movement. Even idealistic Nationalists were potential victims of the lure of public office.

The Nationalists wavered on some specific demands of the workers, notably the eight hour day, and did not channel their energies into a specific organization. Rather, they sought to work through any existing reform organization or political party to realize their general goals. But Nationalism and especially *Looking Backward* did serve to enlarge collectivist understanding and broaden the base of socialism from a small group of immigrant working class radicals to include a middle class of native-born Americans. They "brought socialism up from the work shops and beer gardens into the libraries and drawing rooms."[17] Nationalists did figure strongly in the reform movement in the early 1890s and laid the foundation for a stronger reform tide with the coming of the muckrakers and progressives a decade later.

Christian Socialists—*The Dawn*, principal propaganda weapon of the Christian Socialists, edited by W. D. P. Bliss, made its first issue only eight days after its parent organization of Christian Socialists was formed in May, 1889. The motto of the organization was "He works for God who works for man." Bliss had been a charter member of the Boston Nationalist Club but was generally suspicious of its leadership which was controlled by impractical theosophists and Civil War veterans. Prior to the time of Bliss only a very few radical Christian Socialists had dared to utter their thoughts. True, there had been many social gospelers but most of them stopped short

15. *Ibid.*
16. Edward Bellamy, "First Steps Toward Nationalism," *Forum* 10 (1890):183.
17. Harry Thurston Peck, *Twenty Years of the Republic, 1885-1905* (New York: Dodd, 1906), p. 735.

of declaring that there were fundamental inherent evils within the capitalistic system.

The emergence of Christian Socialism was a logical development of the leftward drift in several Protestant denominations after the Civil War. The early social gospelers were far from progressive in their ethical concerns. Christian ethics for the temporal world was to uphold the established order. One of the ways of doing this was to convince the poor that they too had a vested interest in the established order and should submit to its dictates. But as more progressive Christian thinkers such as John R. Commons, Richard T. Eli and Washington Gladden began to analyze their contemporary society, the society undergirded by the Christian church, they increasingly discovered a dearth of social justice.

Rhetorically the left wing for Christian Socialists was best represented by George D. Herron and William Dwight Porter Bliss. With moderate success during the 1890s they both worked at promoting several socialistic organizations and journals. Both Bliss and Herron were men of the cloth and each engaged in a prodigious amount of activism for socialism. Bliss attracted only a small amount of public attention compared to that accorded the clerical radical, George Herron.

Bliss's approach to socialism followed gradualism, but on occasion he was swept away by his enthusiasm for a Christian cooperative commonwealth and made extreme statements, "We say let there be a revolution. . . Let us to arms. Let us sing the 'Marseillaise! Only let it be a revolution that shall get to the bottom of the question. . . Let it be an uprising not of the third or the fourth or the fifth estate but of all estates of all God's children against the

slavery to mammon."[18] Bliss accused the Nationalists of not going far enough along the road to socialism. In fact, he chided them for refusing to acknowledge themselves as socialists. He heartily supported labor and upheld the striking switchmen of the New York Central Railroad in 1890. He defended their resort to adequate protective measures when attacked. "If corporations have the right to arm private detectives and fire upon almost any pretext, why has not organized labor an equal right to form, arm and drill a similar body to defend themselves."[19]

Following the unsuccessful Homestead strike in 1892 Bliss suggested that some good would come from the strike in that it would turn working men to socialism. Trade unions, as the strike demonstrated and as Daniel DeLeon suggested, simply did not have the ability to control massive corporate combinations. Only the state could do that.

Bliss was subject to criticism from both the left and the right. Visiting a fashionable Philadelphia Episcopal church he was described in *People*, the paper of the Socialist Labor Party, as follows:

Rev. W.D.P. Bliss of Boston spent a week in this city lately preaching socialism and trades unionism in one of the Episcopal churches. It was amusing to see him dressed in a long white gown and to hear his denunciation of plutocrats and his pitiful appeals for the poor, while his slim audience of well dressed people in their costly church made it seem like he was accusing a lot of masters in the absence of their servants. It seemed like pouring water on a duck's back to ask them to give up their wealth for charity or for municipal control, instead of going to the poor and telling them to help themselves by

18. *The Dawn* 3 (April, 1892):4.
19. *The Dawn* 1 (Sept., 1890):197.

combining like the rich do. Asking God and land-lords and speculators to change their tactics is more absurd than trying to make a hungry lion lay down in peace beside a lamb.[20]

From the time of the organization of Christian Socialists in 1889 until 1896 Bliss was the primary spokesman for most of the radical Protestant clergymen. He was quite like Bellamy in his approach to socialism. Both were gradualists and followed the brotherhood of humanity concept of Christianity. Both denied the class struggle thesis and both looked on humanity as an organic whole. Bliss engaged in several organizational efforts, none of which achieved the success of the Nationalist movement. But his work was important in helping to keep alive the Nationalist tradition after it had given way to Populism and other reform efforts.

George D. Herron, Congregational minister, rose rapidly from obscurity in the last decade of the nineteenth century. His motivations were somewhat different from those of most other Christian Socialists. He believed socialized social order to be the coming of the Kingdom of God on earth, a way for the true expression and the full fruition of religion. Herron focused his criticisms, not so much on the abstract ethical system of the capitalists, as on the capitalist himself. He spoke of the world of business as "unspeakably corrupt," "the chief danger to the nation," and "greatest enemy of human life." According to him Christians should recognize:

That what we call civilization is but the organized and legalized robbery of the common laborer, [and] until we have a revolutionized comprehension of the fact that our churches and government, our arts and literature, our education and philosophies, our morals and manners, are all more or less the expression and deformities of this universal robbery, drawing their life and motives out of the vitals of the man who is down and underprivileged, out of his unpaid labor and exhausted life—until then, I say, our dreams and schemes of a common bond or better society are but Phillistine utopias; our social and industrial reforms but self conceit.[21]

Herron came to the public's attention in 1890 when he delivered a sermon, "The Message of Jesus to Men of Wealth." It was essentially a plea for the rich to show mercy to the poor. That was one thing, but his vitriolic indictment of the foundation of society was quite another. This kind of talk closed many of the doors to Herron and set him on a path that led to his being defrocked.

Herron continued to play an active role first in the Socialist Labor Party and later in the Socialist Party, but his effectiveness was minimized after his departure from the institutional church. He was gifted, talented, eloquent, but powerless without his institutional platform. He was of some general service to the Socialist Party later on but he was not one to give himself modestly and unselfishly to a cause.

The Socialist Party—By 1896 the Nationalists and the Christian Socialists had spent their course and the short-lived Populists committed "hara-kiri" in throwing their support to the Democrats and William Jennings Bryan. Things looked dark indeed for socialism until the spring of 1897 when the American Railway Union met in Chicago under the direction of Eugene Victor Debs. The convention, however, was not concerned with union affairs. Debs's pur-

20. *People,* May 2, 1899.
21. Cited in Albert Fried, ed., *Socialism in America* (New York: Doubleday, 1970), p. 344.

pose was to establish a new socialist organization, an organization that would be broad enough to include the entire leftist movement in America.

The conservative Republican victory over William Jennings Bryan in 1896 drove Debs into socialism. In a special message to the American Railway Union in 1897 he avowed, " I am for socialism because I am for humanity. We have been cursed with the bane of gold long enough. Money constitutes no proper basis of civilization. The time has come to regenerate society—we are on the eve of the universal change."[22]

The ARU had only a vague idea of establishing some kind of socialist organization. Factions could not agree on structure and goal for the planned organization but when the colonizing group of the movement split in 1898 to go off to the state of Washington, the Social Democratic Party emerged. Debs, the main spokesman and party symbol, ran in the 1900 presidential election as quite a contrast to the stereotype of socialist. He was not a foreigner, not an intellectual, and not a fanatic. He was a mild, pleasant, humble, mid-western American who had come up from the ranks of the working man and spoke, with heart, the simple, plain, yet eloquent language of his countrymen.

Debs was able to win the confidence of the old line (mainly immigrant) socialists who were unhappy with the established but very sectarian Socialist Labor Party and in the summer of 1901, at Indianapolis, Social Democrats and a large group of dissident Socialist Labor Party members united to establish the Socialist Party of America.

The moderates within the socialist party were pragmatic and wished to make socialism relevant to the workaday world and problems of the people. For them the issue

was whether to become a movement or remain a sect. The revolutionaries on the other hand were less optimistic that capitalism would evolve into socialism of its own accord. They were concerned for accelerating the class conflict and bringing about a single apocalyptic leap into socialism. The party developed some semblance of unity by permitting itself to enroll simultaneously both the moderate and the revolutionary.

The Socialist Party opposed the immediacy of the American Federation of Labor. The party, however, had substantial support from the workers, particularly from skilled workers, many of whom were members of the conservative A.F. of L. But the party refused to make the mistake of waging war on the A.F. of L. for the sake of industrial unionism. Its policy was to work from within the prevailing union structure to seek to convince the majority of the members to come over to the socialist side.

The Socialist Labor Party—The smashing Republican victory of 1896 was a melancholy happening among the reforming radicals. Only the Socialist Labor Party without any immediate goals seemed unaffected by the turn of events.

The membership of the Socialist Labor Party was originally composed predominantly of German immigrants and most often meetings on both national and local levels were conducted in German. This practice did not attract many native English-speaking Americans to the movement.

In New York Daniel DeLeon had been a lecturer at Columbia University and a leading light and spokesman for the first Na-

_____

22. *Ibid.*, p. 379.

tionalist club there when in the fall of 1890 he joined the Socialist Labor Party. Within six months he was the party's national lecturer and only a few weeks later he assumed the editorship of *People*, the official English language weekly of the party. The failure of the Nationalists to adopt a definitive program and his own reading of Marxist literature brought him to his decision to join the SLP. That choice was a pivotal moment for American socialism. By this time the Knights of Labor was essentially dead and the American Federation of Labor was emerging as the primary national labor organization. Through a series of maneuvers DeLeon sought but failed to win over the A.F. of L. Thus the die was cast for the organization of the Socialist Trade and Labor Alliance, a competing labor organization. These events of the 1890s marked the boundaries of the debate for the next generation both within the socialist organization and in its ideological controversy with capitalism. The controversy raged heatedly until about 1912, the time of the apex of socialist power.

Daniel DeLeon joined the Socialist Labor Party when the battle was raging between the trade union and the political action elements. He felt that such a debate over tactics was unrealistic since it divided the energies of the group so that neither would be able to mount sufficient offensive to make a comprehensive plan of attack on capitalism. DeLeon maintained that if socialists were to make any headway in the United States they would have to battle their opponents on all sides at all times. "A victory in politics without a corresponding triumph in the trade union room would simply lead to social catastrophe, since the capitalist would still hold the key to power through his continued and unchallenged

ownership of the means of production and distribution.[23]

DeLeon and his new friends in the SLP dedicated themselves to making a radical revolutionary party resting firmly on a class struggle basis and rejecting all compromises with capitalism whether on the industrial or the political front. "If you have the economic organization alone," said DeLeon, "you have a duck flying with one wing; you must have a political organization or you are nowhere. . .make no mistake: the organization of the working class must be both economic and political. The Capitalist is organized on both lines. You must attack him on both."[24]

DeLeon's group chided the American labor movement for its lack of class consciousness. This lack necessarily resulted, he maintained, in the permanency of capitalism in its present industrial form. The labor movement tended to accept the middle class attitude that workmen and the bosses or capitalists were united by ties of human brotherhood. Consequently it was immoral to fight the bosses since they were brothers. Purely and simply, trade union leaders, according to DeLeon, merely acquiesced to exploitation of the workers. "Instead of being a militant class conscious organization, ever watchful of the interest of the worker and ever ready to do battle," against conditions that continued to degrade them, the trade union movement had "reduced itself to a mere benevolent organization, doling out charities for the sick and death-benefits, thus taking upon itself the functions of an ambulance service on the industrial battlefield, taking care of the

---

23. Quint, *Forging*, p. 146.
24. *Ibid.*, p. 147.

wounded, burying the dead, and stripping itself of all other functions."[25]

DeLeon felt that such a timid position could only fail as capitalistic industrial ownership became more and more concentrated. Strikes and boycotts would then be felt with less and less impact. In industries where complete monopolies existed strikes and boycotts would be absolutely worthless. This then called for industrial unionism and that was precisely what DeLeon and the SLP sought to establish—revolutionary industrial unionism, and that closely linked with the Socialist Labor Party. Thus, at a special meeting at Cooper Union to honor the "progressive" delegates attending the national convention of the A.F. of L. DeLeon made a brief, warmly received address. The response heightened when he declared, "Just as you snatch a pistol from the hand of a highwayman, so you have the right to snatch excessive property from those who hold it. . .one class does all the work, and the other does nothing, save marry its daughters to rotten European princes." Finishing his address he offered a resolution which was enthusiastically adopted:

Whereas   issue between the capitalist class and the laboring class is essentially a political issue involving such modifications of our institutions as may be required for the abolition of all classes by transferring to the whole people as a corporate body the land and machinery of production.
Resolved, that we socialists of New York, in mass meeting assembled, urge upon all our fellow workingmen throughout the United States the necessity of joining the Socialist Trade and Labor Alliance now being organized for the purpose of placing the labor movement in its only true and national lines—the lines of international socialism.[26]

The newly formed S. T. & L. A. and the SLP together as the economic and political arms of socialism were to usher in the classless cooperative state.

DeLeon's purpose in organizing the competing labor organization was not "dual unionism" as charged by Samuel Gompers of the A.F. of L. His purpose was clear and ominous for trade unionism, nevertheless. The A.F. of L. and the Knights of Labor could not be ignored nor had they been successfully "bored from within." It was the aim of the new alliance to organize the unorganized men and with their aid to try to reform craft unions (The A.F. of L. was a federation of craft unions). Following this policy, war could not be avoided. However, the Alliance, after an early burst of success when some two hundred organizations were chartered, rapidly fragmented primarily due to central authoritarian leadership. The small remnant remaining merged with the International Workers of the World in 1905.

Radicals—When the I. W. W. was organized in 1905 in Chicago almost every major radical voice in America was represented—Eugene Debs, Daniel DeLeon, Lucy Parsons (widow of the famed anarchist Haymarket martyr) and syndicalist Bill Haywood, leader of the Western Federation of Miners. Only at the outset was it big enough to hold Debs, DeLeon and Haywood. Debs withdrew in 1906 and DeLeon was ousted in 1908 in a coup planned by an I. W. W. group more enamored of anarchy than of socialism. In the same year the I. W. W. constitution was amended to exclude any mention of political action. The I. W. W. dialogued over direct action, sabotage,

25. *Ibid..*, p. 151.
26. *New York World*, Dec. 14, 1895.

and the general strike and developed an American version of Anarcho-Syndicalism.[27]

DeLeon had wanted to fight capitalism on the civilized plan of political action. He labeled the opposition in the I. W. W. (primarily unskilled and migratory workers) "slum proletarians," and charged them with "veiled dynamitism." This "overall" brigade simply ousted DeLeon from the organization, whereupon he acted typically and formed his own group of I. W. W. (the Detroit faction) in opposition to the "beggars" (the Chicago faction).[28] DeLeon's group struggled along politically with other group fragments that he had generated in a few short years.

The Chicago faction, known as Wobblies, lead by Bill Haywood pushed direct action and sabotage. This ultimately lead to a complete break with the regular socialists who disavowed violence in favor of political action. The issue of violence surfaced sharply prior to the 1912 Socialist Party convention in a journalistic debate between Debs and Haywood. The latter wrote, "No Socialist can be a law-abiding citizen. When we come together. . .the purpose of our minds is to overthrow the capitalist system, we have become conspirators then against the United States government. . .I again want to justify direct action and sabotage. . .the trade unionist who becomes a party to a contract. . .removes himself from the class struggle." Debs countered Haywood. "If I had the force . . .I would use it. . .but I haven't got it, and so I am law abiding under protest—not from scruple." On the other hand, sensing the political futility of such a program for law-abiding American workers Debs added, "Direct action will not appeal to. . .them while they

have the ballot and the right of industrial and political organization. .I am opposed to sabotage and direct action. I have not a bit of use for the propaganda of the deed. These are the tactics of anarchist individualists and not of Socialists collectivists."[29]

The 1912 Socialist platform triggered the debate on sabotage versus political action when the conservatives made it clear that they intended to drive the reckless Wobblies (nickname for certain I. W. W. members) out of the party. Prominent Milwaukee socialist, Victor Berger, reported, "In the past we often had to fight against Utopianism and fanaticism, now it is anarchism again that is eating away at the vitals of our party."[30] As the lines became clearly drawn the antisabotage plank was adopted by a 2-1 margin.

But the I. W. W. and Haywood were at the zenith of their popularity in 1912, having staged twenty-eight strikes in which fifteen hundred people were arrested. By then they had perfected their mass-action "free speech" technique which flooded a town— and jails—with Wobblies, sailors, lumberjacks, and migratory workers if one of their speakers was muzzled. "Wobblies" became a household word as had socialist and anarchist, and was no better understood than they were.

---

27. Theodore Draper. *The Roots of American Communism* (New York: Viking Press, 1957), p. 16-17.

28. Daniel Bell, *Marxian Socialism in the U.S.* (Princeton, N.J.: Princeton University Press, 1967), p. 68.

29. *Ibid.*, p. 76.

30. *Ibid.*, p. 75.

Opposition to Socialist Rhetoric

Just as there was common ground for anti-capitalism, there was commonality of opposition to all forms of socialism. All those opposed to socialism agreed to or shared in private property accumulation for capital use. We shall look briefly at the resistance to socialist rhetoric from three groups: the Populists, organized labor, and more direct spokesmen for the capitalist system. Most resistance to socialism was indirect in the guise of reform activities critical of but operating within the capitalist system.

Populists—"Wealth belongs to him who creates it and every dollar taken from industry without an equivalent is robbery. . . The interests of rural and civic laborers are the same; their enemies are identical."[31] So read not a socialist document but the 1892 Omaha platform of the People's Party (Populist). Certainly, socialism and populism did have similarities as radical movements since both represented strong protests against the concentration of economic power in the hands of a few. They agreed that the special privileges of the wealthy came through monopolistic control over the means of production and distribution. Both would resort to the state to redress grievances. But the comparison ends there for their spirit and purpose was quite dissimilar. The Populists, founded in Kansas and drawing largely from agrarian interests of the Midwest and South, wanted to reform capitalism, not destroy it. They simply wanted to cut out monopolistic practices at points adversely affecting them. Beyond that they wanted to safeguard their own farming interests within competitive capitalism that encouraged small independent self-reliant producers.

"Socialism would only replace one master for another; the monopolist by the community, substitute one slavery for another." This was the stock argument of Populists concerning socialism. "All of the systems of anarchy and socialism are based upon a supposed quality [goodness] innate in man which history from the earliest moment of his existence has disproved."[32] The tense marriage of socialism and populism reflected agreement on some of the ills of society but the two were far apart on the solutions to national economic problems.

Labor—Clearly if socialism is to progress far in a capitalistic society it must have the support of labor—the segment most vulnerable to exploitation from concentrated capital. Quite early in the game, however, the Socialist Labor Party gave up on the American Federation of Labor, the largest and most potent trade union organization in America. But other collectivist elements worked carefully and quietly within the A.F. of L. to capture it for socialism. During the 1893 A.F. of L. convention, Thomas J. Morgan offered a resolution condemning, "as inhuman and destructive of the liberties of the human race," a societal system which denied labor to a man willing and eager to work and then treated him as an outcast and arrested him as vagrant for not working. Further he stated "that the right to work is the right to life, that to deny the one is to destroy the other. That when the private employer cannot or will not give work the municipality, state or na-

---

31. Morris Hillquit, *History of Socialism in the United States* (New York: Russell & Russell, 1965), p. 291.
32. Quint, *Forging*, p. 211.

tion must."[33] The resolution went further to commit the Federation to a political program of action for the worker.

During the year that followed, the Morgan political program was generally widely accepted in the union locals and city federations and in some cases political efforts were made. The continuing industrial crisis, rising working class unrest, "industrial army" marches on Washington, and the injunction that crushed the Pullman strike and the American Railway Union augered a complete socialist take over of the A.F. of L. at the 1894 Denver convention. But Samuel Gompers, skilful and determined against socialism, had planned well for that meeting. Through cunning parliamentary maneuvers, a group of Gompers' supporters cut the heart out of the collectivist program of the convention. Then spurred on by Charles Southern, stalwart standby of the labor movement who felt that the "Populists could solve satisfactorily the labor question without aid of the socialist falsifiers and boodlers, who have been too long leading our German-American wage earners through a slough of despond,"[34] Gompers carefully and systematically, over a period of years, excluded socialists from power in the A.F. of L.

The pivotal 1894 division of the A. F. of L. marked a course that has denied socialist forces a large part of their most needed support, organized labor.

Voices of the Status Quo—The socialist movement faced an uphill climb in addressing a society shot through with social Darwinism, competitiveness, and individualism. Because the power was firmly held by the establishment little real organized opposition to socialism was necessary. Sporadic verbal pot shots were taken at Debs

and his philosophy during presidential campaigns but the day-to-day anti-socialistic rhetoric was left largely to the newspapers, the articulate social Darwinists, and the conservative clergy.

Because major daily presses were owned by establishment interests antisocialist charges were front page headlines while socialist answers often were suppressed or buried in inside pages. As the newspapers controlled public opinion, socialists were able to do little to compete with their opponents in this medium. For the most part Socialists had to rely on their own small presses and stump speeches to counteract a vested newsprint rhetoric.

In the 1908 presidential campaign, Debs toured the country in a small train dubbed the "Red Special." Prior to its arrival in major cities, newspapers often put down a barrage of anti-Debs print. Opponents accused him of belittling the flag and finally his honesty was attacked in the *Free Press* headline of Detroit:

> Debs, in Luxury
> > Ignores Crowd
> Sleeps in Magnificent Palace Car
> > While Followers Wait
> > In Vain
> Flunkies Guard Leader
> From the Common Herd[35]

Socialist and trade-union papers refuted the stories but their readership was already pro-socialist. The opposition carried the power, the channel to the public mind, and would not open that channel to socialism. This type of experience continues now as

---

33. *Ibid.*, p. 66.
34. *Ibid.*, p. 68.
35. Ray Ginger, *The Bending Cross* (New Brunswick: Rutgers University Press, 1949), p. 279.

leaders in the current black revolution report difficulty in getting full and fair coverage via the media for their unpopular
minority views.

The oracle of social Darwinism following
the Civil War was William Graham Sumner,
ex-clergyman turned college professor and
social analyst. His basic assumptions on
limited natural goods and his thinking on
competition and survival generally reflected and permeated the "laissez faire"
public mind of post-Reconstruction America. Fixed natural social laws, if permitted
to operate unfettered in a free enterprise
society, were to produce a better society.
These laws would reward the frugal and diligent and penalize the violator of immutable social laws. The gutter drunk was
there rightfully and should not be helped;
nature was eliminating the weak; the rich
man deserved to be so, for he was strong,
diligent, and honest.

During the last third of the nineteenth
century Sumner and his disciples thundered against forces of reform, protection-
ism, socialism, and governmental intervention in economics. Sumner cannot be
faulted for inconsistency. The protective
tariff was just as evil as welfare programs.
"It would be hard to find," he said, "a
single instance of direct assault upon
poverty, vice, and misery, which has not
either failed or ... entailed other evils
greater than the one which it removed."[36]
This sort of half truth had and still holds a
strange national appeal and was broadly accepted by the populace.

The conservative protestant clergy, with
some exceptions, served the middle and
upper class culture and through their
preachments aided in sustaining a mentality in strong opposition to socialism. Men
of the "captains of industry" genre, John

D. Rockefeller and Daniel Drew for instance, were spirited laymen giving strong
financial support to their churches. It was
only natural then, even if wrong, for the
minister to sanctify the status quo. Suggestive, if not typical of their number, was
Russell H. Conwell of Baptist Temple,
Philadelphia, preacher par excellence of
the gospel of wealth. Enthralled crowds
flocked Sunday morning and evening to
hear him sanctify wealth and belittle the
poor. "There is not a poor person in the
United States who was not made poor by
his own short comings or the short comings of someone else ... get rich ... to
make money honestly is to preach the
gospel. ... Ninety-eight out of one hundred rich men in America are honest. That
is why they are rich."[37] Conwell delivered his "Acres of Diamonds" sermon, a
theological pep talk to the rugged individ-
ualist more than five thousand times over
a period of some forty years. Its thoughts,
so enthusiastically received, were in dia-
metrical opposition to the spirit of
brotherhood implicit in socialism.

Progress of the Socialist Party

In 1900 Debs received 95,000 votes in his
bid for the presidency. This increased to
nearly 900,000 in the 1908 election. Party
membership increased from less than
10,000 to more than 1,000,000. In 1900
Socialists held but few offices. In early

36. *Social Darwinism: Selected Essays of William
Graham Sumner*, (Englewood Cliffs, N.J.: Prentice-Hall, 1963), p. 24.
37. Russell H. Conwell, "Acres of Diamonds," in
*American Forum: Speeches on Historic Issues
1780-1900*, ed. Ernest J. Wrage and Barnet Baskerville, (New York: Harper and Brothers, 1960),
pp. 263-75.

1912 they held over a thousand in various parts of the country. In 1900 hardly more than 30 socialist newspapers and magazines were printed, but by 1912 the number had soared to 323, some having very large printings, including the *Appeal to Reason*, with a circulation at times of more than three-quarters of a million. In 1910 the first socialist congressman, Victor Burger of Wisconsin was sent to Washington and some 1,000 socialists held elective offices, including 56 mayors. This was the age of the "muckrakers" and the whole country seemed to be going progressive. The socialists benefited from the general trend and at the same time probably profited from a less dogmatic tone in their own appeal as reflected in the words of Morris Hillquit in 1910:

Our principal efforts must be directed towards the propaganda of Socialism among the workers, but they should by no means be limited to that class alone . . . the ultimate aims of the movement far transcend the interests of any one class in society . . . farming interests . . . small traders and manufacturers . . . professionals . . . intellectuals . . . "Jimmie Higginses" (all) recognize the hopelessness of their struggle against large capital concentrated in the hands of modern industrial monopolies and trusts. . .[38]

The Socialist Party began to slip in most vital indexes of growth after 1912. The decline was not at the time regarded as ominous and there was optimism that the party's fortunes would rise again to higher levels of achievement. The leaders did not foresee World War I, America's entry into the war, and the revolution in Russia.

But World War I would not go away from America. Socialists had to take a stand, an official stand that was almost unanimous against the war. That position alienated the native born membership and aroused the indignation of the Wilson administration. Debs along with other socialist leaders was sent to prison for antiwar activities. A general deflation of idealism and rising economic conditions in the 1920s further decimated the diminished socialist ranks as did the importation of Russian communist thinking, heady with success from the Bolshevik revolution. The apparent popular support for socialism shown in the presidential votes may well be interpreted as a result of Deb's personal ability and magnetism rather than commitment to socialist doctrine.

Between 1890 and 1912 Socialists failed to focus their efforts. Their moderates were pessimistically unrealistic in supposing that the "system" could not reform itself through the regular legislative process or through economic measures short of common ownership of the means of production and distribution. The Marxists were optimistically unrealistic in assuming that Americans would join the class struggle and overthrow the capitalists. Socialism had many enemies, but they did not seem to take socialism seriously nor was that really necessary, because the establishment controlled the sources of real power and the media avenues to the public mind. Moreover the socialists dissipated much of their limited energies through internal sectarian bickering.

In asking for the impossible, one asks for failure. This is essentially what socialism did during its period of ascendency, 1890-1910. Thus as the collectivists haggled among themselves they made few new friends and added no new alliances to their persuasion. Others distressed about the

---

38. Bell, *Marxian Socialism*, p. 22.

abuses of the system—organized labor—some within the church—agrarians—and ultimately the progressives, found ways to make life just a little bit easier for the downtrodden of the system. Opportunity passed for the socialists and history moved on to the concerns of patriotism, World War I, then to the Roaring Twenties and the focus on two chickens in every pot.

Contemporizing

Socialism more than the Populism or the Greenback movement is now remembered. Eugene Debs rather than James B. Weaver, the 1892 Populist presidential candidate who polled over a million votes, is now remembered. Reform movements sought change within the system but socialism challenged the very nature of capitalistic power itself. But remembered or not it is not a viable autonomous political or economic force today. In spite of ample opportunities to enter more fully into the political life of America it did not and has not done so—it was a captive of its own ideological dogmatism on the nature of American capitalism: and this in spite of usually being labeled reformist or right-wing by international socialists. If all the predictions concerning the decay and doom of American capitalism had come to pass, the socialist movement would have Americanized itself more fully. It gained a shaky foothold in American life for a time because it partially fulfilled a need. That need was a diagnosis and solution of the ills of the American economy. This diagnosis was incisive and insightful but the socialist predictions and solutions just were not within the bounds of realization. The Progressives stole their thunder and made at least some reforms within the system.

Now a "New Left" emerges, growing out of the civil rights movement, protests against the Indo-China war, and the youth rebellion. It is loose and amorphous in organization but dogmatic in tone and seems quite unwilling to coordinate its efforts with potential friends. Like the Socialists of 1890-1912, it too is keen on diagnosis but short on realizable programs. History seems likely to repeat itself.

BIBLIOGRAPHY

Bell, Daniel. *Marxian Socialism in the United States.* Princeton: Princeton University Press, 1967.

A highly documented, well written monograph of 212 pages, including careful indexing. Draws heavily from the rhetoric of the period, written and oral, and from intellectual history. Readable and sophisticated.

Debs: His Life, Writings and Speeches. 3d ed. Chicago: Charles H. Kerr & Company, 1908.

A biographical sketch, speeches, and writings. Poorly written and edited, but does have authorized documents. Bears copyright of *The Appeal to Reason,* socialist newspaper.

Dombrowski, James. *The Early Days of Christian Socialism in America.* New York: Columbia University Press, 1936.

Covers topically the period 1870-1900, major figures, organizations, rhetoric both oral and written. Well written and documented.

Fried, Albert, ed. *Socialism in America.* New York: Doubleday, 1970.

A documentary history from early American religious utopian communities to the Third International, 1919. A clear introduction to the movement, written understandably and simply.

Quint, Howard H. *The Forging of American Socialism.* Columbia: University of South Carolina Press, 1953.

A monograph covering the period 1886-1901, intensively, preceded by an introductory sketch of the period. Carefully documented, indexed, and with a bibliographic essay.

14 Progressivism

Harold Mixon

The years 1900-1913 are frequently called "the Progressive era." The title suggests the character of the time: it was a period of reform, a part of what Harold Faulkner has designated "the quest for social justice." Progressivism was not an isolated phenomenon, but a part of a reform spirit which spanned four decades and included other movements such as the agrarian protest of Populism and the labor movement. Progressivism is somewhat difficult to define, but it may be viewed as an attempt to return to emphasizing the right of the individual—every individual—to equal opportunity, an opportunity which had been seriously eroded by the transition of America from a rural, agricultural society to an urban, industrial society whose most obvious characteristic was the rise of the large corporations.

In a sense the goals of Progressivism were conservative, almost reactionary, though the means by which those goals were sought were liberal by any standards. The Progressives sought protection of public rights by the regulation of big business through such specific measures as control of railroad rates, protection of the worker through mandatory workingmen's compensation laws and regulations regarding the employment of women and children, protection of the consumer through pure food and drug laws, and protection of the

nation's natural resources through a vigorous program of conservation. The Progressives were also interested in having the government returned to the hands of the people by reforms such as direct election of senators and the enactment of a system of referendum and recall. This chapter will summarize the historical context of Progressivism and examine ways by which the Progressives used rhetoric to further their cause.

The Historical Context of Progressivism

The last four decades of the nineteenth century witnessed the development of America from a small-town, agrarian society to an impersonal machine age society.[1] Such a

---

1. For the historical context survey that follows, we are indebted to many sources, notably: George E. Mowry, *The Era of Theodore Roosevelt,* The New American Nation Series, ed. Henry Steele Commager and Richard B. Morris (New York: Harper & Brothers, 1958), pp. 1-15; Ida M. Tarbell, *The Nationalizing of Business, A History of American Life,* ed. Arthur M. Schlesinger and Dixon Ryan Fox, Vol. 9 (New York: Macmillan, 1936); Harold Underwood Faulkner, *The Quest for Social Justice, A History of American Life,* ed. Arthur M. Schlesinger and Dixon Ryan Fox, Vol. 11 (New York: Macmillan, 1931), 27-51; Avery Craven and Walter Johnson, *The United States: Experiment in Democracy* (Boston: Ginn and Company, 1957), pp. 441-562; Richard Hofstadter, *The Age of Reform* (New York: Vintage Books, 1955).

development was predictable, even inevitable. America possessed the prerequisites for an industrial society: rich natural resources and a rapidly expanding railroad system.

The development of large corporations, many of which deserved the title of "monopolies," came with the transition from an agrarian to an industrial nation. The monopolies assumed a variety of forms. The "trust," which originated with the Standard Oil Company, was an arrangement under which stockholders in various companies turned their shares over to a central board of trustees from which the stockholders received certificates in return. In 1892 trusts were declared illegal, and the device known as a "holding company" replaced the trust. Legalized in New Jersey in 1888, the holding company permitted a corporation to purchase stock in competing companies with the result that the corporation could control the policies of those companies. The holding company afforded a workable means for avoiding prosecution under the Sherman Anti-Trust Act. Under various guises the monopolies flourished in oil, steel, railroads, and other essential businesses.

Large corporations were able to control key industries, and to engage in practices unfair to competitors, to the public at large, and to the workers within the industries. The corporations fixed prices within their fields, and thus eliminated small competitors. There were no effective controls over the quality of goods produced, nor any guarantee to the consumer that he was actually receiving the goods he thought he purchased. Wages were easily controlled, and were frequently so low that workers lived in abject poverty, managing only a marginal existence and most often receiving no protection in the form of mini-

mum wages, safety and health standards, compensation for injury or loss of time from work due to illness, survivor benefits, or retirement income.

At the local, state and federal levels, monopolies used political influence to prevent the passage of unfavorable legislation or the vigorous enforcement of existing laws. When enlightened states such as Massachusetts, New York, Kansas, and Oregon attempted reforms, such as laws to protect workers, companies appealed the laws in court suits. Initially the Supreme Court upheld the states in such regulation, as in the famous Slaughterhouse Case of 1873 and in contests over state control of railroad freight and passenger rates. Beginning in the 1880s, however, the states increasingly lost the support of the Supreme Court, which ruled in 1886 that a corporation was a person and was therefore entitled to all the protection afforded an individual under the "due process" clause of the fourteenth amendment to the United States Constitution. In 1890 the Supreme Court prohibited state regulation of railroad rates, and gradually adopted a laissez-faire attitude toward big business.

Labor organized to protect its rights. However, the impact of the unions was lessened substantially by a variety of measures employed by the corporations, including the use of spies to infiltrate the unions, legal action against the unions, the use of strike-breakers, lockouts, and the formation of the organization known as the National Association of Manufacturers. The problems of domestic labor were intensified by the influx of large numbers of immigrant, unskilled workers. The defenders of these management-slanted conditions were known collectively as "the conservatives." The title was a broad one, and not all conservatives approved of all aspects of the status quo. As will be seen later, some conservatives recognized that substantial inequities existed in American society, but unlike the Progressives, they urged that the problems could be solved without recourse to radical reform legislation.

The basic problem of conservatives was to justify the concentration of wealth in the hands of a few while so many were very poor. If such a rationale could be given, it would presumably cover the social evils generated by the means used to acquire the wealth. The conservatives based their justification upon the concept of economic individualism; an idea inherent in the founding of the United States, they argued. The conservatives held that in a free, laissez-faire economy it was inevitable that some men, by virtue of ability, hard work and persistence, would accumulate greater material wealth than other men. This belief not only sanctioned the acquisition of large fortunes, but actually conferred praise and honor on the Morgans, Rockefellers, Carnegies and others whose very wealth demonstrated them to be men of exceptional ability. Thus, the president of the Board of Trustees of Columbia University accepted a painting of John D. Rockefeller with the comment that Rockefeller's great fortune was "both a badge and a reward of intelligence and energy."[2]

From the premise that every individual has the right to acquire as much wealth as his ability and initiative permit, the conservatives concluded that attempts to interfere in the process, whether from the government regulation or union pressure, were to be resisted. Conservatives had at least two formidable weapons: they controlled the legislative process and they found the judiciary increasingly sympathetic to their position. These weapons, coupled with the advantages conferred by wealth and their position as "the Establishment," allowed Conservatives to mount substantial resistance to the reform movement.

The reform movement brewing in America since the 1870s came to a focus in progressivism. The movement was more than an attempt to right the injustices which had grown out of industrialization. It shared with Populism the keen sense of such injustices as discriminatory rate schedules employed by the railroads which made life difficult for the farmer. Progressivism shared with the labor movement concern over low wages, hazardous and unhealthy working conditions, inadequate compensation for disabling injuries, and lack of provision for retirement income. Like earlier movements, progressivism saw the answer in government intervention, but it differed in at least two significant respects. Unlike Populists and the labor forces, the Progressives were not highly organized; though sharing mutual objectives and at times cooperating to achieve those goals, the Progressives were largely individuals lacking the cohesiveness of earlier movements. Furthermore, the Progressives were not radicals; they favored the elimination of the abuses of big business by government regulation rather than government ownership of services and industries.

The attempts at Progressive reform originated at the local level.[3] There the Progressives found economic corruption lay behind much of the political corruption, and

2. Russel Nye, *Midwestern Progressive Politics* (East Lansing: Michigan State University Press, 1959), p. 129.
3. For a description of the conditions in the cities, see Lincoln Steffens, *The Shame of the Cities* (New York: McClure, Phillips & Co., 1904).

concluded that the best way to eliminate political corruption was to eliminate the privilege that led to corruption.

In spite of limited success, Progressives at the city level repeatedly encountered restrictive control of state legislatures over municipal government. Thus, some Progressives focused their efforts on reforming state governments.[4] In Kansas, W. R. Stubbs, William Allen White, and Victor Murdoch fought within the Republican Party to elect Progressives and to enact Progressive legislation. From 1910-12 Governor Woodrow Wilson made New Jersey notable among Progressive states, and Hiram Johnson, after his election in 1910, secured in California an impressive record of Progressive reforms, including the removal of railroad interests as the controlling force in politics, the establishment of a commission to regulate railroad rates, the adoption of initiative, referendum and recall, and the passage of a workmen's compensation law.

In Wisconsin, Robert La Follette established and achieved an ambitious set of goals: a commission to determine railroad rates on the basis of the value of railroad investments; railroad taxes based on actual property value of the railroads; an income tax; prohibition of railroad passes to politicians; antilobby laws; limitation of campaign spending; initiative, referendum and recall; conservation of natural resources; and the cooperation of the University of Wisconsin in improving the state.[5]

But just as the city Progressives had found limits set on what they could accomplish, so also the state Progressives encountered limitations. The most significant was highly organized industry and finance that transcended state lines. This forced Progressives to turn their attention to reform through the federal government.

The most significant period for national progressivism began with the administration of President Theodore Roosevelt. When he assumed office following the death of McKinley, Roosevelt believed that the future of American democracy was endangered by the concentration of power in the hands of a few financial groups. However, he differentiated between good and bad trusts, and insisted that he was not opposed to trusts as such, but only to the abuse of their power. His first step was to establish the Department of Commerce and Labor and a Bureau of Corporations with power to investigate activities of interstate corporations. He also secured the enactment of legislation to speed the processing of trust cases in the courts and to provide money for the prosecution of those cases.

In his second administration, Roosevelt continued his "trust-busting" activities, but, a very pragmatic consideration brought a change in his strategy. He recognized that "trust-busting" was not solving the problem because the elements of the dissolved trusts were simply reintegrating in new forms and continuing the same activities as in the past. Therefore, Roosevelt decided to move only against the "bad" trusts, those which failed to pass on benefits of increased productivity to the consumer.

Roosevelt's administration extended governmental regulation into other areas. Roosevelt was intensely interested in the

4. For a description of conditions at the state level and of attempts to do something about them, see C. C. Regier, *The Era of the Muckrakers* (Chapel Hill: University of North Carolina Press, 1932), pp. 83-107.

5. For an account of the La Follette era in Wisconsin, see Robert S. Maxwell, *La Follette and the Rise of the Progressives in Wisconsin* (Madison: State Historical Society of Wisconsin, 1956).

plight of the workingman, and he attacked their problems on three fronts. First, he secured passage of a workman's compensation act for all government employees. Second, he obtained factory-inspection and child labor laws for the District of Columbia. And third, he set a significant precedent when he moved by "executive action" to settle the anthracite coal strike of 1902.

In 1906, Roosevelt took a large step toward a cherished goal of the Populists. The Hepburn Act, passed in that year, gave the Interstate Commerce Commission specific authority to regulate railroad rates. Although the legislation was disappointing to some Progressives because it failed to base rates on the value of railroad property and cost of services, it was, nevertheless, a step toward providing relief and equity for small shippers.

Another area in which Roosevelt secured significant Progressive legislation was consumer protection. Food processing was often carried out under notoriously unsanitary conditions, and both food and drugs—particularly patent medicines—frequently were not what they were claimed to be. To correct these and other abuses involved in the processing of food and drugs, Roosevelt secured the passage in 1906 of a federal meat-inspection law and the Pure Food and Drug Act.

Finally, Roosevelt worked for another major goal of the Progressives: the conservation of natural resources which were being exploited by big business for its own profit. In the face of substantial opposition, Roosevelt moved to protect the forests by placing much forest land under the Department of Agriculture. In 1907 he appointed the Inland Waterways Commission, whose recommendations led to the calling of a national conservation confer-

ence. In addition, Roosevelt secured the passage of the Reclamation Act which led to irrigation projects.

When he was elected to his second term, Roosevelt vowed not to seek re-election; however, he obviously hoped to see the continuation of his Progressive program in the administration of his hand-picked successor, William Howard Taft. Taft apparently wanted to carry on Roosevelt's reforms, but his concept of the presidency differed radically from that of Roosevelt. Roosevelt had operated on the premise that the President has all powers not specifically denied to him by the Constitution, and he frequently took the initiative in attempting to secure reforms. Taft's philosophy that the President had only those powers specifically enumerated in the Constitution permitted the initiative to shift from him to a Congress which was under conservative control. Furthermore, Taft antagonized the Progressives by supporting the Payne-Aldrich Tariff in 1908, by his failure to support them in their attack on the powers of House Speaker "Uncle Joe" Cannon, and in the Ballinger-Pinchot controversy. As a result, in spite of a respectable slate of Progressive legislation passed during Taft's administration, he alienated the Progressives and his old friend Theodore Roosevelt, who considered Taft an opponent of reform.

The Progressives' disappointment with Taft had interesting repercussions for the nation's voters, for it led to Roosevelt's decision to seek another term as President of the United States. In a bitter primary campaign and a stormy Republican nominating convention, Taft's conservative supporters were able to secure his renomination for a second term, and Roosevelt led many of his fellow-Progressives into the formation of the Progressive Party, with Roosevelt nominated as the presidential candidate. When the Democrats nominated Woodrow Wilson as their candidate, Americans were faced with choosing a President from among three candidates, one of whom was a conservative, with the other two advocating programs which, for all the candidates' disclaimers to the contrary, were similar.

The nation chose Wilson, and when his vote was combined with the votes polled by Roosevelt and the Socialist candidate Eugene Debs, the reform movement had a clear mandate from the public. Though he is considered a transition figure in many respects, Wilson was able for a time to continue the reform movement. Supported by a Democratic Congress, Wilson complied an impressive record of genuinely Progressive legislation: the Underwood Tariff Act, the Federal Reserve Act, the Federal Farm Loan Act, the Warehouse Act, the Federal Trade Commission, the Clayton Antitrust Act, the Seaman's Act, the Merchant Marine Act, the Adamson Act, the Smith-Lever Act, and the Smith-Hughes Act.

Wilson's reform program was brought to a halt by World War I, and after that conflict the control of the country passed to conservative Republicans until 1932. In spite of the pessimism of some reformers, the first two decades of the twentieth century had achieved a remarkable record of social reforms; another Roosevelt and his "New Deal" were to mark a resurgence of the Progressive spirit.

The Rhetoric of Progressivism

Reduced to its simplest terms, the rhetorical challenge facing the Progressives was twofold. Their ultimate objective was to secure the passage of legislation to achieve their reforms. To do this, however, they had to contend with a Congress whose lower house was ruled by Speaker "Uncle Joe" Cannon, and whose both houses were heavily populated with or influenced by the interests which the Progressives sought to control.[6] In addition to skill in maneuvering the legislation through Congress, the Progressives needed the support of an aroused public. Progressive rhetoric therefore had to serve two functions: to publicize the need for reform thereby enlisting support for Progressives measures, and to move Progressive measures through the legislative process.

The initial impetus toward reform came in the written rhetoric of Progressive literature which provided both an indication of the need for reform and an ideological basis. The most popular of such literature was the work of the "muckrakers."[7] From 1903-12 these authors produced a succession of exposes which explored the corruption and inequities of politics and big business. The movement began in October, 1902, with the publication of an article about political corruption in St. Louis.[8] Public response was so enthusiastic that by 1904 most major magazines were carrying essays of this type. The articles attacked political corruption at all levels: city, state, and federal.[9] The practices of big

6. For a description of conditions which faced the Progressives in the Senate, see David Graham Phillips, "The Treason of the Senate," *Cosmopolitan*, March 1906, pp. 487-502, 628-38.

7. For an excellent overview, see Regier, *Era of the Muckrakers*.

8. Claude H. Wetmore and Lincoln Steffens, "Tweed Days in St. Louis," *McClure's Magazine*, October, 1902, pp. 577-86.

9. As examples, see Lincoln Steffens, "The Shame of Minneapolis," *McClure's Magazine*, January 1903, pp. 227-39; C.P. Connolly, "The Story of Montana," *McClure's Magazine*, 1906, pp. 341-61; 451-65; 629-39; Phillips, "Treason of the Senate," pp. 487 ff.

business were subjected to detailed examination;[10] even the press was not immune to scrutiny, for the muckrakers charged that the press was frequently indebted to special interest groups and accused at least one of the national wire services of being a monopoly.

In addition to the muckrakers there was a group of capable novelists who exposed corruption and unfair practices in government and business. These writers included Upton Sinclair, Jack London, Winston Churchill, Booth Tarkington, David Graham Phillips, and William Allen White.

The literature of progressivism also included the work of scholarly writers who supplied the philosophical basis for the reform movement. Frederick Jackson Turner gave a historical perspective with his essay on "The Significance of the Frontier in American History," and Throstein Veblen sought to make the public aware of the vast power of interest groups in such works as *The Theory of the Leisure Class* and *The Theory of Business Enterprise.* Herbert Croly in *The Promise of American Life,* organized Roosevelt's thinking and supplied him with a basis for his program of regulating rather than destroying trusts.[11]

The major contribution of Progressive literature to the reform movement was its stimulation of public awareness of the conditions that needed correction. By fact and fiction these writers made vivid the corruption and dishonesty in politics and business in a way that bare recital of the facts could not have done. Most of these writers were committed to capitalism as a viable economic system. They did not crusade for the abolition of capitalism, but for the reform of its abuses.

Also among the Progressive ranks were some of the most capable speakers of the time. Theodore Roosevelt, Albert Beveridge, and Robert La Follette acquired national prominence as spokesmen for the Progressive cause. Their speaking on behalf of progressivism will be considered here as examples of the kind of speaking by which the reformers sought to publicize and enlist public support for their program.

Like many of his fellow Progressives, Roosevelt was not initially a reformer. In fact, while in the New York legislature he voted against a minimum wage law and a twelve-hour work day on the grounds that both measures were "purely socialistic."[12] His conversion to progressivism was gradual, with his term on the Civil Service Commission and the Police Commission being key stages in the process. In both positions he had opportunity to observe firsthand the inequities and corruption which resulted from political influence, and he began to move to correct them.

As President and later as private citizen Roosevelt received and accepted numerous invitations to speak. In a variety of settings which ranged from ceremonial events to campaign speeches, he publicized his program of reforms. He delivered the opening addresses at both the Deep Waterways Convention[13] and the Conference on the Conservation of Natural Resources.[14] On both occasions he developed at length the need

---

10. As examples, see Ida M. Tarbell, "The Rise of the Standard Oil Company," *McClure's Magazine* 20 (1902-3), pp. 115-28; 248-60; 390-403; 493-508; 606-21; Ray Stannard Baker, "The Right to Work," *McClure's Magazine* 1903, pp. 323-36.
11. Mowry, *Era of Theodore Roosevelt,* p. 222.
12. Robert T. Oliver, *History of Public Speaking in America* (Boston: Allyn and Bacon, Inc., 1965), p. 499.
13. *The Works of Theodore Roosevelt,* ed. Hermann Hagedorn (New York: Charles Scribner's Sons, 1926), 16:109-18. Hereafter referred to as *Works.*
14. *Works,* 16:119-26.

to protect America's forest, water and mineral resources against exploitation by private business. Even when the occasion did not immediately suggest a Progressive theme Roosevelt might use the opportunity to publicize a reform which happened to capture his enthusiasm at the moment. For instance, in a dedication ceremony for the new state capitol building at Harrisburg, Pennsylvania,[15] he defended his campaign for federal government regulation of large corporations and one of the most comprehensive statements of his reform program, the "New Nationalism" speech at Osawatomie, Kansas, was delivered to a meeting of the G. A. R.[16]

Roosevelt began his speeches from a set of basic premises whose truth he seemed to think self-evident. He assumed the principle that every individual is entitled to certain basic rights, including the opportunity of self-development to the highest degree of his capability. Whenever these rights are threatened, the government has the responsibility to protect them. He assumed the principle of a strong national government, to which belonged all powers not expressly denied by the Constitution; a corollary of this assumption was the principle that whenever local or state governments cannot protect the rights of citizens, it is the prerogative and responsibility of the federal government to take action. Finally, he assumed that sovereignty rests with the people, and should not ever be construed as irrevocably delegated by the people to their elected representatives.

The reform program which Roosevelt advocated in his speeches was a practical expression of these premises. His speeches repeated a number of basic ideas. He urged the regulation of big business in the interests of fairness to all, and he insisted that

the only agency capable of effective regulation was the federal government. For example, federal control of the railroad rates and revision of the tariff must reflect the interests of the people as well as the interest of business. Roosevelt advocated a graduated income tax and an inheritance tax; a program to protect America's forests, water, gas and oil resources, election reforms through the use of the short ballot, the direct primary, and direct election of senators. His major original contribution to the reform program seems to have been his campaign for judicial recall which would give the people the power to overturn court decisions in suits contesting the constitutionality of legislation.

In the development of these themes Roosevelt on occasion cited statistics, as in a conservation speech where he wanted to establish the seriousness of the soil erosion problem, "Still the loss from soil wash is enormous. It is computed that one-fifth of a cubic mile in volume, or one billion tons in weight of the richest soil matter of the United States, is annually gathered in storm rivulets, washed into the rivers, and borne into the sea. The loss to the farmers is in effect a tax greater than all other land taxes combined, and one yielding absolutely no return."[17] He sometimes used specific examples. "The best way to test the merits of my proposal," he observed in a speech advocating the use of judicial recall,

is to consider a few specimen cases to which it would apply. Within the last thirty years the Court of Appeals of New York has been one of the most formidable obstacles to social reform, one of the most formidable obstacles in the way of getting in-

---

15. *Works*, 16:69-75.
16. *Works*, 17:5-22.
17. *Works*, 16:116.

dustrial justice, which men who strive for justice have had to encounter. Among very many other laws which this court has made abortive, or decided not be laws on the ground that they conflicted with the Constitution, are the following. . . .

Roosevelt then enumerated four laws for reforms which the court had negated.[18]

His most common method of development was simply to state and explain his position. For example, in a speech on the regulation of corporations, Roosevelt asserted the need for a broad versus a narrow interpretation of the Constitution, "If we interpret the Constitution in narrow instead of broad fashion, if we forsake the principles of Washington, Marshall, Wilson, and Hamilton, we as a people will render ourselves impotent to deal with any abuses which may be committed by the men who have accumulated the enormous fortunes of to-day, and who use these fortunes in still vaster corporate form in business."[19] Aside from invoking the four revered names, there is no real proof for his assertions.

Roosevelt's speeches frequently sounded like a series of confident assertions rather than logically-supported arguments. The result might have seemed arrogant in other men, but Roosevelt made it work. One explanation for this practice was undoubtedly his immense personal popularity and the respect which audiences held for him since the beginning of his term as Vice-President of the United States. For the American public he was the hero of San Juan and by the time his Progressive ideas began to emerge he had the prestige of the President of the United States. When he spoke, he placed his own popularity and prestige behind the reform movement, and what he *was* transmuted rather ordinary

speeches into an effective means of securing popular support for the program.

Albert J. Beveridge served in the United States Senate from 1899-1905. When Roosevelt bolted the Republican Party to form the Progressive Party, Beveridge joined him, serving as temporary chairman and keynote speaker for the first Progressive Party Convention in 1912. He worked for the Progressive Party until 1916 when he returned to the Republican Party.

Beveridge received numerous invitations to speak on a variety of occasions ranging from ceremonial events to campaign speeches. In his speeches on progressivism, he based his ideas on certain fundamental premises. The most important of these had to do with the nature of government. Like Roosevelt, Beveridge believed in a strong federal government. For Beveridge, the issue of states' rights had been settled conclusively by the Civil War, and he believed the United States Constitution gave to the federal government all powers necessary to promote the common welfare. The "common welfare" became a touchstone by which social conditions were to be measured, and any condition which threatened the public good was to be corrected by the government. When states failed to correct abuses, or were unable to do so because of the nature of the problem, the federal government must assume the responsibility.

From these premises Beveridge developed a number of themes in his speeches for social reform. The most recurrent and fully-developed theme was the need for regulation of large corporations. His view of big business was perhaps one of the most

18. *Works*, 16:197-99.
19. *Works*, 16:71.

charitable among the Progressives, for Beveridge did more than view the corporations as necessary evils. He openly expressed admiration for their accomplishments, but like his fellow-reformers, he carefully distinguished between "good" and "bad" trusts.[20] "A trust is a good trust," he noted, "when it performs the work for which it has been organized, and produces better goods at cheaper prices and delivers them to the consumer more conveniently than a dozen different concerns could do so. The consumer is the sovereign factor. The well-being of the masses is the result of e   y   development that endures."[21] On the other hand, "A trust is a bad trust when it raises prices dishonestly and without other reason than to satisfy the greed of its managers."[22] Therefore, trusts should not be destroyed but regulated to prevent malpractices. Other themes used by Beveridge included the need for federal controls to guarantee pure food and drugs to the public, the need for tariff revision, direct primaries, and the need for legislation to prevent child labor and to guarantee the rights of the working-man.

In the development of these themes Beveridge sometimes relied on explanation and general assertions which appealed to the common sense and common knowledge of his audiences. However, Beveridge provided more evidence to support his positions than Roosevelt. He demonstrated an ability to use statistics effectively by converting them into terms meaningful to his audience. In arguing against the position that all corporations ought to be dissolved, Beverdige cited statistics to prove that big business was aiding rather than harming the farmer, the businessman, and the laborer:

"Organizations of industry are ruining you," cried the Opposition to the American farmer four

months ago. "That is so," answered the farmer. "For last week I paid off the mortgage on my farm executed during the last Opposition administration." (In the last six years the American farmers paid off $300,000,000 of mortgages on their farms.)

"Organizations of industry are ruining you," the Opposition declared to the American working-man. "That is so," answered the American working-man, "for I am steadily employed at higher wages than ever were heard of in this or any other country in any period of human history; my home is full of comforts; my children are at school." (In the last five years the average wage of the American working-man has increased nearly fifteen per cent; and the number of men employed has increased by the million.)

"Yes, I am being ruined by organizations of industry," admits the American working-man, "because five years ago I was forced to take my savings out of the savings-banks of the country in order to live; today I am putting my savings into the savings banks of the country against the day of possible Democratic disaster in the future." (In five years American working-men have increased their deposits in savings-banks over a thousand million dollars.)

"You are slaves of organized industry; go back to the early days when American labor was free and unoppressed," the Opposition cried to the American working-man four months ago. "I agree with you," answered the American working-man, "and I find as evidence of my slavery and of the industrial liberty of American toilers in the old days, that in 1850, with a population of 23,000,000 the working-men of the Republic had on deposit in savings institutions $44,000,000; whereas to-day, with a population of nearly 80,000,000 the working-men of the Republic have on deposit in savings-banks over $2,500,000,000—I find that with only three times the population the Nation had in 1850, American working-men have on deposit in savings-banks alone *sixty times as much* ready cash as their free and prosperous brothers had fifty years ago." Thus the savings-banks confound the Opposition's oratory. Figures are fatal to falsehoods.

---

20. *The Meaning of the Times*, (Indianapolis: Bobbs-Merrill, 1908), pp. 444-51; 160-61; 205-8.
21. *Ibid.*, p. 144.
22. *Ibid.*

"Organizations of industry are destroying you," cried the Opposition to the American manufacturer only four months ago. "That is clear," answered the American manufacturer, "because during the last six years I have added only 200,000 new factories to the old ones and increased the capacity of the old ones nearly one hundred per cent. It is true because I am running my works by night as well as by day; whereas, five years ago I ran them only a few hours in day time and sometimes not at all. It is true because five years ago banks would not loan me money on any security, and now they send solicitors to get my custom."[23]

Beveridge also used specific examples in supporting his theses. In arguing for the right of the federal government to exercise powers not specifically granted by the Constitution, he noted President Washington's use of federal troops to suppress lawlessness in Pittsburgh and President Cleveland's use of the army in the Pullman labor controversy.[24]

Beveridge was not as widely reported as was Roosevelt, but he did speak often on the subject of Progressive reforms. If his basic ideas frequently sound like echoes of Roosevelt, the speeches were nonetheless clear and compelling even though they develop the themes with less appeal to speaker ethos. Like Roosevelt, Beveridge was a significant publicist for the reform cause among the public at large.

A third orator active in seeking public support for the Progressive cause was Robert La Follette. He served in the United States House of Representatives from 1885 to 1901; was Governor of Wisconsin from 1901 to 1905; and served in the U.S. senate from 1905 to 1925. From 1905 to 1912 he worked for reform while remaining within the structure of the Republican Party. In 1912, he attempted to secure the presidential nomination of his party, but was thwarted when Roosevelt regained command of the Republican insurgents. La Fol-

lette regained control of the Republican Progressives in 1920, and was responsible for initiating the Teapot Dome investigation.

In describing La Follette, Carrol P. Lahman noted that "for the rank-and-file 'Half-breeds,' as the conservatives or 'Stalwarts' called the Progressives, La Follette and the reforms he espoused were indistinguishable. For them La Follette *was* reform."[25] This characterization could be generalized further: for the public at large La Follette was reform.

Early in his political career, La Follette formed the habit of taking his program directly to the people through pamphlets and public speaking. Over and above the campaign oratory, La Follette used public speaking to educate the people in the need for reform and to bring public pressure to bear on recalcitrant state legislatures which blocked his reform program. Beginning in 1897, he adopted the practice of touring county fairs, where he would spend up to eight hours a day lecturing the people on the necessity for reform. He continued this practice with notable success, especially during his governorship.[26]

La Follette also employed the Chautauqua circuit and the lyceum. On these platforms he used essentially one speech which he called "Representative Government." He kept the speech fresh and current by the use of new material from the changing political scene. La Follette himself observed,

23. *Ibid.*, pp. 205-6.
24. *Ibid..*, p. 11.
25. Carroll P. Lahman, "Robert M. La Follette," in *A History and Criticism of American Public Address*, ed. William Norwood Brigance (New York: Russell & Russell, 1960), 2:947.
26. Belle Case La Follette and Fola La Follette, *Robert M. La Follette* (New York: Macmillan, 1953), 2:121-28.

concerning the effectiveness of these lectures, "In this way I have made a thousand or more chautauqua and lyceum addresses, and have pretty well covered all the states of the union except New England and the Old South. I believe these addresses were the most practically effective work I have done, in a national way, for the Progressive movement. . . ."[27]

Considered a radical by many of his contemporaries, La Follette based his ideas on premises which were no more radical than those of Roosevelt or Beveridge. He was committed to the basic soundness of the capitalistic system, and he never sought to have that system overthrown. In this respect, La Follette was true to his agrarian background, for the midwestern farmer needed the capitalistic system to survive as much as did the eastern corporation.[28] La Follette viewed the evils stemming from the large corporations to be transient, not inherent, features in the free enterprise system, and felt it was a responsibility of government to restore equality of opportunity to the individual. To achieve this goal, the government must be responsive to the will of the people; this premise formed the basis for La Follette's demands for changes in the election machinery.

Based on these premises La Follette urged acceptance of a program of specific reforms which he developed in speech after speech. He argued for government control over the size of corporations when they grew large enough to threaten the equal opportunities of other businesses. He wanted a fair system of taxation of railroads, a system which would be based on an evaluation of the actual worth of the railroads, and he sought rate schedules which were reasonable and determined by scientific means. His bitter experiences with machine politics led him to seek election reforms, es-

pecially the direct primary, which would permit the people more voice in the choice of their representatives. He favored tariff revisions which would provide protection for American products without affording special advantages to the large corporations. Using these and other themes, La Follette proposed reforms which aimed at essentially the same results as the other Progressives, though his proposals differed in some details.

The most distinctive characteristic about La Follette's speeches was not the themes but the manner in which they were developed. To a greater degree than Beveridge and Roosevelt, La Follette presented the people with highly detailed, factual evidence in support of his claims. In a speech to a county fair audience, he developed the need for railroad rate regulation by citing long tables of freight rates which showed that the people of the particular community he was addressing were paying more to ship their wheat than were the people of Iowa and Illinois who were the same distance from the markets. He also showed his audience that these freight charges actually constituted a tax on production, and he pointed out that the people of Wisconsin were paying annually a total of $10,000,000 in city, county, and state taxes while paying over $47,000,000 for transportation in the same period of time.[29] This example illustrates the kind of statistics and specific instances with which La Follette flooded his audiences.

---

27. *La Follette's Autobiography* (Madison: University of Wisconsin Press, 1960), p. 131.
28. Gordon F. Hostettler, "The Political Speaking of Robert La Follette," *American Public Address*, ed. Loren Reid (Columbia: University of Missouri Press, 1961), p. 119.
29. Belle La Follette, *Robert M. La Follette*, pp. 168-69.

Sometimes he presented his evidence in a strikingly novel form known as the "roll-call." La Follette would enumerate a list of legislation and explain the significance of the bills for his audience. He would then go through a roll-call of the legislators, indicating how each legislator had voted on the specific items of legislation, concluding with the suggestion that the audience consider carefully which legislators had acted in the interests of the people. He put this method to good use in dealing with recalcitrant state legislatures and he continued to use it when he became a member of the United States Congress.

The use of factual evidence implied a high degree of trust in the intelligence of his audiences, and the response of the people indicated that the confidence was not misplaced. Although La Follette's speeches tended to be quite lengthy, his audiences apparently listened willingly. Evidence of this is provided by the reaction of county fair audiences during his tour of 1903: when La Follette would suggest that he had to shorten his speech so the races could begin, his listeners would respond with cries of "Never mind the races; let them go over until tomorrow." With shouts of "Go on" and applause, the crowd would insist that he continue, and the audience would increase rather than decrease in size.[30]

As a national leader of progressivism, La Follette's effectiveness was probably limited by two factors. In the first place, he was closely linked with the Midwest in his thinking and his appeal, and this association narrowed his appeal to the national audience. The second factor, which developed only after the period covered in this chapter, was his isolationism, a view reflected in his votes against the entry into World War I. Though the position may have reflected that of his constituents, his opposition to the war resulted in a vicious campaign of unfavorable publicity that severely damaged his image with the nation at large.[31] His role as spokesman for the reform movement at the national level undoubtedly suffered as a consequence.

The Congressional debates on reform presented a different set of rhetorical problems from those encountered when the Progressives spoke before civic clubs, on ceremonial occasions, to Chautauqua or lyceum audiences, or to the farmers assembled at the county fair. The Progressives were a minority in Congress, especially in the Senate. In the House of Representatives, they had to contend with the powers of an unfriendly Speaker of the House, and in both houses there was the powerful factor of precedent. It was a major accomplishment to get a bill on the floor for debate. This setting contrasted sharply with the audiences faced outside the halls of Congress. Furthermore, the congressional debates demanded a set of skills different from those required for the speeches before the public at large, for not only did congressional speaking demand the ability to develop constructive speeches, but it also called for skill in refutation and rebuttal, the ability to think and respond rapidly, and a thorough command of the facts.

Beveridge was classed by a senatorial opponent as one of the three great debaters of the Senate, and Beveridge's debates with Senators Quay and Foraker over the question of statehood for Oklahoma, Indian Territory, Arizona and New Mexico, along with his attack on the Payne-Aldrich Tariff Act have been designated as the three most

---

30. *Ibid.*, p. 169.
31. Hostettler, "Political Speaking of Robert M. La Follette," p. 121.

notable debates of his senatorial career.[32] However, his marathon speech in support of his proposed amendment to the bill to prohibit child labor in the District of Columbia was also an excellent demonstrations of his debate ability. This speech deserves closer examination both as a specimen of Beveridge's debating and as an example of the general ability of the Progressives.

In January, 1907, the United States Senate had before it a bill to prohibit child labor in the District of Columbia. In an effort to extend the prohibition to the entire United States, Beveridge proposed an amendment which would ban the interstate transportation of goods produced by child labor. Beginning on January 23, Beveridge spoke for three days in defense of his amendment. "The course of this argument," he noted early in the speech, "will be this. First, to state the facts; then to show the legality of the remedy I propose. For if the facts convince the Senate that this is a national evil of such a crying nature that it ought to be cured; and if I can show that the method I propose is within the power of Congress, of course the conclusion is that the law must be enacted."[33] To develop the need for his proposal, Beveridge began by asserting that a large proportion of the nation's labor force consisted of children. He cited documented statistics which showed that, as high as they were, the child employment figures of the census were unrealistically low estimates of the number of children actually employed.[34] He then spent two days introducing notarized affidavits which testified to the cruel conditions under which children worked.[35] Using cause-effect relationships, he established the disastrous consequences of child labor under those conditions: first, it would impair the health of the children or

even cause their death,[36] and second, it would result in "the deterioration of the race, the production of a degenerate class in this Republic."[37]

To establish that it was within the power of the federal government to take action in the matter, Beveridge organized his attack in the form of refutation of the two major arguments which had been used against federal action. He refuted the argument that the states ought to handle the problem, by replying that the states could not, even if they had the will, cope with the situation. In support of this position Beveridge reviewed the existing laws against child labor on a state by state basis, and concluded that the states had never had uniform laws, without which state action would never be successful.[38] He then asserted that states do not pass or enforce good child labor laws because of pressure from interest groups; he produced affidavits testifying to the resistance to such laws and to the lack of enforcement of existing ones.[39] To refute the argument that federal action would be unconstitutional, Beveridge replied that the authority to regulate interstate commerce was explicitly conferred on the federal government by the Constitution, and he cited court decisions and the opinions of

32. Herold Truslow Ross, "Albert J. Beveridge," in *A History and Criticism of American Public Address*, ed. William Norwood Brigance (New York: Russell & Russell, 1960), 2:937.
33. *Congressional Record*, 1907, 41, pt. 2:1553.
34. *Congressional Record*, 1907, 41, pt. 2:1552-53.
35. *Congressional Record*, 1907, 41, pt. 2:1553-57, 1792-1801.
36. *Congressional Record*, 1907, 41, pt. 2:1802-5.
37. *Congressional Record*, 1907, 41, pt. 2:1805-7.
38. *Congressional Record*, 1907, 41, pt. 2:1808-11.
39. *Congressional Record*, 1907, 41, pt. 2:1817-22.

legal experts to support his interpretation.[40] The speech ended with an appeal for favorable action on the amendment.

During the presentation of the speech, Beveridge demonstrated his ability to respond effectively to the questions of his colleagues. He was interrupted frequently by questions from the floor. Two exchanges will illustrate his manner of handling such questions. Senator Spooner asked, "Does the Senator think he is any more earnest in the discussion of child labor than the remainder of his colleagues?" "Yes; I think a good deal more earnest than some," replied Beveridge. "I doubt the Senator's accuracy," responded Spooner. Beveridge concluded the exchange with, "I think I am more earnest—a good deal more. I have been earnest enough to spend nights and days and weeks and months in accumulating testimony. I have been earnest enough to appeal to the American people all over the country during the last campaign from as far west as Nebraska to as far east as Maine. Has the Senator done as much?"[41] Later in the speech, Beveridge defended the amendment against charges by Senator Spooner and Senator Perkins that the proposal would lead to abuse of power. In reply, Beveridge quoted legal opinion that abuse of power was no argument against the existence of that power, and he showed by specific examples that the same potential for abuse of power existed in other legislation, but it had proven to be no problem.[42]

La Follette was also recognized as an able Congressional debater, defending the Progressive cause in many key debates. One of his best performances was his reply to Aldrich during the debate on the Payne-Aldrich Tariff Act. The force of La Follette's speech is attested to by Beveridge's evaluation, "It was murder and sudden death today. La Follette tore the cotton schedule to pieces. I told Dillingham that even if La Follette were the devil himself, his statements were unanswerable."[43]

If congressional speaking of Progressives is viewed as a whole, one of the strongest impressions which emerges is the technical soundness of the oratory. As was illustrated in Beveridge's speech on child labor, the Progressives demonstrated an ability to construct coherent, logical arguments, supported by substantial amounts of factual evidence. The speakers also held their own in floor debate. There can be little doubt that the Progressives' speaking contributed substantially to the success of their legislative program.

The Opposition

The conservatives were not silent during the Progressive onslaught. Under the mounting pressure for reform, capable, articulate, and sometimes eloquent spokesmen fashioned a written and spoken apologia for the conservative cause. Probably the most famous and scholarly literary defense of conservatism came from Yale's William Graham Sumner. In books and monographs, Sumner attempted to apply Darwin's biological concept of the fittest to the social world. Accepting the accumulation of wealth as a measure of social fitness, Sumner concluded that it was only natural that some individuals—the fittest—would acquire great wealth. Thus, some men ac-

---

40. *Congressional Record*, 1907, 41, pt. 2:1822-26, 1867 ff.

41. *Congressional Record*, 1907, 41, pt. 2:1802.

42. *Congressional Record*, 1907, 41, pt. 2:1875, 1882-83.

43. Claude G. Bowers, *Beveridge and the Progressive Era* (New York: Houghton Mifflin, 1932), p. 345.

cumulated great fortunes because of natural law.[44]

Speakers of the period including George Harvey attempted to popularize individualism. In a speech dedicating a statue of John W. MacKay, Harvey observed that:

... the success of America is a triumph of individualism.... Possession of exceptional intelligence and manifestation of extraordinary energy count for naught if the incentive of personal award be withheld. However pleasing may seem the notion of all members of the human race participating share and share alike in the total product, obviously it is the theory of mediocrity which instinctively hates ability and invariably seeks undue advantage.... History proves conclusively that the only hope of the mass is the development of able individuals.[45]

Conservatism commanded the services of some of the ablest orators of the day, among them Joseph Choate and Chauncy DePew. However, the two men best known today as defenders of conservatism were Elihu Root and Henry Cabot Lodge. There is perhaps some irony in Root's identification with conservatism, since he was a long-time friend of Theodore Roosevelt and served as Roosevelt's Secretary of State, 1905-09. However, as senator from New York during the years 1909-15, Root became closely associated with the Conservative cause.

Root left no systematic presentation of his conservative philosophy, but an examination of his speaking on social and political issues suggests some basic premises from which he began. His reaction to the Progressive reforms was an outgrowth of his attitude toward the role and function of government, an attitude clearly outlined in a series of lectures given at Princeton University. According to Root, the essential characteristics of government as set forth by the Constitution of the United States were essentially five in number. First, it must be representative, and by "representative" Root meant that government was to be by legislators who acted in behalf of the people. Secondly, constitutional government must recognize the primacy of the individual, and must protect his liberty by specific limitations on the power of government. Thirdly, constitutional government distributes its powers among the legislature, executive, and judiciary, and sets specific limits on the powers of each department. Fourth, the Constitution clearly distinguishes between the powers of the national government and the powers of the state governments, and sets clear limits upon the powers of each. Finally, it vests the interpretation of the validity of laws in the courts, which must pass on each case as it arises.[46]

In frequent speeches in the United States Senate and to audiences composed of educators, lawyers, businessmen and politicians, Root applied these principles to specific reforms advocated by the Progressives. With respect to the regulation of big business and the reform of abuses growing out of the trusts, he was willing to admit, like the Progressives, that big business had brought problems. However, he differed from the Progressives in the solution which he urged, for Root felt that the solution should first come from the business community itself, which ought to recognize

---

44. Twelve of Sumner's more significant monographs have been collected in *Social Darwinism* (Englewood Cliffs, N.J.: Prentice-Hall, Inc., 1963).

45. George Harvey, *The Power of Tolerance* (New York: Harper & Brothers, 1911), pp. 243-44.

46. Elihu Root, *Addresses on Government and Citizenship*, ed. Robert Bacon and James Brown Scott (Cambridge: Harvard University Press, 1916), p. 91.

that the solution of these problems was in the best interests of the business world. If big business failed to correct the abuses, the states must assume the responsibility themselves. If the states failed to act, they would be inviting the national government to intervene, a highly undesirable result which would set the precedent for further federal assumption of prerogatives which rightly belonged to state governments.[47]

The aspect of the Progressive reforms which alarmed Root most was the proposal to democratize government by the introduction of such measures as the direct election of senators, initiative, referendum and recall, and judicial recall. He strongly opposed the direct election of senators as a major blow to his cherished principle of representative government,[48] and he opposed initiative and referendum because they encroached on the powers specifically given to the legislature under the Constitution and because he did not believe the people to be capable of passing judgment on legislation.[49] He objected to the idea of subjecting judges to the possibility of recall by popular vote because this violated his concept of an independent judiciary and because, once again, he doubted the competency of the people to decide such matters.[50]

A second spokesman for conservatism was Henry Cabot Lodge, Root's colleague in the United States Senate. A member of a wealthy and socially prominent New England family, Lodge had served as instructor at Harvard University and as a member of both the Massachusetts House of Representatives and the United States House of Representatives before becoming United States Senator in 1893. Like Root, Lodge was a friend and sometime supporter of Theodore Roosevelt.

Lodge's conservatism as expressed in numerous speeches in and outside of the Senate, exhibited interesting contrasts with Root. Lodge's wealth was inherited, and he was repulsed by the newly-developed industrial millionaires whom he considered vulgar, immoral, and lawless. He accepted the development of large corporations as inevitable, and he concluded that attempts to stop such consolidation would be both fruitless and disastrous. However, unlike Root, Lodge favored moderate regulation of big business by the federal government, if for no other reason than that failure to exercise moderate restraint might lead to socialism, which he considered highly undesirable. He opposed some of Roosevelt's proposals, such as one to fix railroad rates, as being too strong, but he did not reject the federal government's right to exercise some regulation.[51]

Like Root, Lodge resisted the attempts of the Progressives to democratize government by making it more responsive to the will of the people. Specifically, he opposed the popular election of United States Senators, the use of initiative and referendum, and the proposal for recall of judges.[52]

Though it is as dangerous to speak of "the" Conservative response as it is to speak of "the" Progressive challenge, the speeches of Harvey, Root, Lodge and others suggest the outline of a Conservative position in the debate. The Conservatives

---

47. *Ibid.*, pp. 363 ff.
48. *Ibid.*, pp. 257 ff.
49. *Ibid.*, pp. 269-70.
50. *Ibid.*, pp. 387 ff.
51. Henry Cabot Lodge, *Speeches and Addresses.* (New York: Houghton Mifflin, 1909), pp. 410-414.
52. Henry Cabot Lodge, *The Democracy of the Constitution.* (New York: Charles Scribner's Sons, 1915), pp. 88 ff.

had what almost amounted to a reverence for the institutions and traditions of the status quo. They were particularly devoted to the idea of individualism, which they felt authorized the acquisition of large fortunes. The evils which had developed in association with big business were transient, not inherent in the system, and while abuses ought to be cured, the responsibility for corrective action lay primarily with the business community itself and secondarily with the state governments. If the federal government had any authority in the matter (and by no means were all of the Conservatives willing to grant the federal government that much) the extent of legitimate action by the national government was moderate regulation. Proposals to make the government more responsive to the people met with almost universal opposition from the Conservatives, who seemed to have an instinctive distrust of the masses.

Interpretation

The best of the speeches on behalf of conservatism were *creditable* performances from the standpoint of basic rhetorical criteria. Well-organized and sometimes well-supported by exposition and argumentation, they might have won adherents in more dispassionate times. However, the first two decades of the twentieth century were anything but dispassionate; fed by the work of the muckrakers and the publicity provided by Progressive speakers, public discontent demanded reform, and the conservatives found themselves defending an unpopular position which was perhaps beyond real defense.

On the other hand, the Progressives made rhetoric an effective tool in achieving reform. Through literature and through speeches on a variety of occasions, the Progressives made the American public aware of the need for reform. Through legislative speaking they were able to assist reform laws through Congress. It was observed earlier that there were ideological ties on the one hand between progressivism and populism and on the other hand between progressivism and the "New Deal" of the 1930s; it might be added that there were methodological similarities, too, for progressivism shared with these two companion movements an extensive use of public speaking.

BIBLIOGRAPHY

The following readings were selected from the standpoint of their general accessibility and on the basis of the quality of their treatment of the subject. Many of the readings contain excellent bibliographies.

General Background:

Faulkner, Harold Underwood. *The Quest for Social Justice. A History of American Life.* Edited by Arthur M. Schlesinger and Dixon Ryan Fox. New York: Macmillan, 1931.
Schlesinger, Arthur Meier. *The Rise of the City. A History of American Life.* Edited by Arthur M. Schlesinger and Dixon Ryan Fox. New York: Macmillan, 1933.
Tarbell, Ida. *The Nationalizing of Business. A History of American Life.* Edited by Arthur M. Schlesinger and Dixon Ryan Fox. New York: Macmillan, 1936.

The Progressive Movement:

Hofstadter, Richard. *The Age of Reform.* New York: Vintage Books, 1955.
Mowry, George E. *The Era of Theodore Roosevelt. The New American Nation Series.* Edited by Henry Steele Commager and Richard B. Morris. New York: Harper and Brothers, 1958.
Regier, C. C. *The Era of Muckrakers.* Chapel Hill: University of North Carolina Press, 1932.

Progressive Speaking:

Lahman, Carroll P. "Robert M. La Follette." *A History and Criticism of American Public Address.* Edited by William Norwood Brigance. New York: Russell & Russell, 1960.

The Meaning of the Times. A collection of Beveridge's speeches. Indianapolis: Bobbs-Merrill, 1908.

Murphy, Richard. "Theodore Roosevelt." *A History and Criticism of American Public Address.* Edited by Marie Kathryn Hochmuth. New York: Longmans, Green and Company, 1955.

Ross, Herold Truslow. "Albert J. Beverdige." *A History and Criticism of American Public Address.* Edited by William Norwood Brigance. New York: Russell & Russell, 1960.

The Works of Theodore Roosevelt. Edited by Hermann Hagedorn. 20 vols. New York: Charles Scribner's Sons, 1926.

Conservatism:

Garraty, John A. *Henry Cabot Lodge.* New York: Alfred A. Knopf, 1953.

Leopold, Richard W. *Elihu Root and the Conservative Tradition.* Boston: Little, Brown and Company, 1954.

Lodge, Henry Cabot. *The Democracy of the Constitution.* New York: Charles Scribner's Sons, 1915.

Lodge, Henry Cabot. *Speeches and Addresses.* New York: Houghton Mifflin, 1909.

Root, Elihu. *Addresses on Government and Citizenship.* Edited by Robert Bacon and James Brown Scott. Cambridge: Harvard University Press, 1916.

Root, Elihu. *Men and Policies.* Edited by Robert Bacon and James Brown Scott. Cambridge: Harvard University Press, 1917.

Schriftgiesser, Karl. *The Gentleman from Massachusetts: Henry Cabot Lodge.* Boston: Little, Brown and Company, 1945.

15 World War I and the League of Nations

R.A. Micken

The beginning of World War I in 1914 was, at first, utterly incomprehensible to people in the United States, and it was to pose problems peculiar to the "New World." Over 13.5 million foreign-born persons lived here; 5.5 million of them were still aliens. Dozens of foreign language newspapers were published for immigrants, providing all the printed communication for many. In some parts of the country German was the language of the school, the church, and the home.

At the beginning of the war, however, most Americans followed President Wilson's advice to remain neutral in thought and action. "The great majority of Americans regarded the European war as a dramatic spectacle in which their own country was not concerned."[1] To leaders impatient to get about the business of finishing this new land of promise, the war was an irritating interruption. They were more than just too proud to fight, as Wilson stated; they were simply too busy to fight.

President Wilson remained insistently impartial during the first two years of the war. He proclaimed our neutrality on ten different occasions in the first four months. Members of Wilson's administration were inclined to be pacifists, the Secretary of State being no less a speaker for peace than William Jennings Bryan.

As the war dragged on, however, several factors began to crystallize public opinion in favor of Great Britain and her allies. The language and basic culture of the United States were Anglo-Saxon. Britain liquidated heavy investment in America and purchased vast amounts of American goods. Clearly, interests engender sympathies and customers are backed against noncustomers. At the same time, Germany lacked communication facilities, controlled no Atlantic cables, and had no political possessions in North America to use as information-distributing centers. Submarine warfare, the arrogant behavior of the German government, and the ineptitude of German diplomacy (as exemplified by the infamous Zimmerman message to Mexico) brought the United States ever closer to joining the allies.

President Wilson began to take a firmer attitude against the Kaiser's government

---

1. Herbert Adams Gibbons, *An Introduction to World Politics* (New York: Century Company, 1923), p. 25.

and set about finding ways of making a holy war out of the inevitable struggle. If Americans were to shed blood, it must be a crusade, a "people's war" as Wilson called it. He appropriated the idea of a great league for peace among all nations and, under the leadership of William Howard Taft, a movement called the League to Enforce Peace gained a large following among diverse elements of the American populace. Much to his later embarrassment at the time of the Senate debates on the League of Nations, even Henry Cabot Lodge favored this league proposal. Wilson sent his close advisor, Colonel House, to Europe to carry on feverish efforts to end the war. If the United States were forced to fight, it could now enter the war on the side of the angels.

World War I

On the evening of April 2, 1917, President Woodrow Wilson appeared before a joint session of the House and Senate and delivered his war message, placing the United States with the allies and against Germany. He reviewed the preceding two years and described events which had led to our entry into the war. German submarine warfare was, he said, warfare against all mankind. The United States was interested only in the vindication of right. He realized the solemn and tragic nature of the step he was taking, but recognized his constitutional duty to take it. He told Americans what this declaration of war would involve and announced that the struggle would be financed as far as possible by taxation. He repeated our motives and declared that "a steadfast concert for peace can never be maintained except by a partnership of democratic nations. The world must be made safe for democracy." Almost parentheti-

cally he congratulated the Bolsheviks who had just overthrown the Czar in Russia. We were the "sincere friends of the German people," he remarked. Our intent was to confront their autocratic government. Wilson concluded his war message with these lines:

It is a fearful thing to lead this great people into war, into the most terrible and disastrous of all wars . . . but the right is more precious than peace and we shall fight for the things which we have always carried nearest our hearts—for democracy, for the right of those who submit to authority to have a voice in their own government, for the rights and liberties of small nations, for a universal dominion of right by such a concert of free peoples as will bring peace and safety to all nations and make the world itself at last free . . . The day has come when America is privileged to spend her blood and her might for the principles that gave her birth and happiness and the peace which she has treasured.[2]

This speech was a magnificent American call to arms. It was designed to remove all the dissonance created by American aversion to war. We were forced into war by a great potential destroyer of democracy; it was our moral obligation to fight. Thus, Americans could go to war as crusaders and with clear consciences.

Support in the Senate was nearly unanimous, with the exception of Senators Norris and LaFollette. Senator Lodge, Wilson's great antagonist, was moved to say "Mr. President, you have expressed in the loftiest manner the sentiments of the American people." Four days later the Senate declared war by a vote of 82-6 and the House endorsed the resolution 373-50.

But Wilson's message was not universally

---

2. A. Craig Baird, *American Public Address, 1740-1952.* (New York: McGraw-Hill, 1956), pp. 224-32.

applauded. Cynics were not impressed with making the world safe for democracy. Pacifists were convinced that Wilson had been forced into endorsing a rich man's war and they demonstrated throughout the country. Troops were called out to protect the Capitol.

With the United States now at war with the Central Powers, it seemed necessary for a people previously committed to studied neutrality to become adequately belligerent. Within a week or two after the declaration of war, the President set up the Committee on Public Information with George Creel in charge. Creel's organization was to whip up love of country along with hatred toward the enemy, and to direct these sentiments into a wide variety of channels—fund raising, greatly accelerated war industry, and fighting and dying in the armed services.

A remarkable propaganda campaign was instituted, accompanied by restrictions on the printing of hostile material and the throttling, or at least the minimizing, of all pro-German or pacifist utterances. Also, Hollywood produced such features as "The Wolves of Kultur" and "The Beast of Berlin," calculated to stir up hatred of the enemy. Poster art reached some kind of height with a creation showing Uncle Sam pointing a finger at the young men of the nation and bearing the caption "I want *YOU* for the United States Army."

An interesting phenomenon was the organization of the Four-Minute Men. Local volunteers gave four-minute talks in theaters and halls throughout the country. Each state had its Chairman, and there were over seventy-five thousand speakers before the war ended, including such well known personalities as Douglas Fairbanks, Mary Pickford, and Teddy Roosevelt.

The rules for the capsulated public address, as given in May, 1917, went as follows:

The speech must not be longer than four minutes, which means there is no time for a single wasted word.

Speakers should go over their speech time and time again until the ideas are firmly fixed in their mind and cannot be forgotten. This does not mean that the speech needs to be written out and committed, although most speakers, especially when limited in time, do best to commit.

Divide your speech carefully into certain divisions, say 15 seconds for final appeal; 45 seconds to describe the bond; 15 seconds for opening words, etc., etc. Any plan is better than none, and it can be amended every day in the light of experience.

There never was a speech yet that couldn't be improved. Never be satisfied with success. Aim to be more successful, and still more successful. So keep your eyes open. Read all the papers every day, to find a new slogan, or a new phraseology, or a new idea to replace something you have in your speech.[3]

Delivery was not neglected. Speakers were urged to have their friends criticize them pitilessly so that they might eliminate weaknesses in presentation. Cliches, such as "doing your bit," "your country needs you," and the like were to be shunned because they lacked force.

Bulletins were distributed containing lists of subjects: the draft, Liberty loans, the nation in arms, why we are fighting, food conservation, the income tax, the meaning of America, the Red Cross, and a great many others. Undoubtedly the speakers should receive credit for influencing high enlistment for factory and battlefield, and the heavy oversubscription of Liberty

---

3. Cedric Larson and James R. Mock, "The Four-Minute Men," *Quarterly Journal of Speech* 25 (February, 1939):99.

and Victory bond issues. But, according to Larson and Mock, "Recognition of the important part played by the Four-Minute Men, the official World War organization of speakers in a special division of the Committee on Public Information, 'in holding fast the inner lines' to use President Wilson's phrase, has been somewhat overlooked by historians of the Wilsonian Era."[4]

The war effort also depended in large measure upon the statements of the chief executive. Regardless of his reputation for being cold and academic in his speaking, Wilson proved to be a great phrase-maker. Some of his lines were on every tongue before the war ended: "peace without victory," "the world must be made safe for democracy," "this is a people's war," and "open covenants openly arrived at."[5]

The campaign of the Committee of Public Information had its tragic aspects. With such a desperate and explosive assignment, the war makers were soon threatening constitutional rights. Those responsible for getting maximum effort for victory found it difficult in the emotionalism of the times to be entirely fair, and advocates of uncomfortable points of view were soon facing what appeared to be undue persecution. The active pacifists came from widely separated areas of society. Senator Norris of Nebraska, from the Progressive group, took the floor on April 4, 1917, to explain his negative vote against the declaration of war. After conceding that some people might have honest, patriotic motives for engaging in the war, he said that many were moved by selfish motives and hopes of gain. He felt that his countrymen were taken in by the great combination of wealth that had a direct financial interest in American participation. To whom he asked, does the war bring prosperity? He answered his own question:

> Not to the soldier, who for the munificent compensation of $16 per month, shoulders his musket and goes into the trench, there to shed his blood and die if necessary; not to the broken-hearted widow, who waits for the return of the mangled body of her husband; not to the mother who weeps at the death of her brave boy . . . War brings no prosperity for the great mass of common and patriotic citizens.[6]

Senator Norris, resuming his lifelong attack on the malefactors of great wealth, told how war brought prosperity to Wall Street and the munitions makers. He summarized bluntly, "Their object in having war and in preparing for war is to make money. Human suffering and sacrifice of human life are necessary, but Wall Street considers only the dollars and the cents."[7]

Robert LaFollette from Wisconsin skirted the edge of serious trouble when he inveighed against profiteers and decried the loss of freedom of speech.

While these powerful and prestigious legislators fought for peace, labor and the common man found an advocate in Eugene V. Debs, leader of the Socialist Party of America. Just a month before the war was declared Debs had written an editorial for *New York Call* magazine which stated the Socialist position on the war:

4. *Ibid.* Shortly before the Armistice, the College Four-Minute Men were organized, and public speaking instructors were sought as chairmen.

5. R. T. Oliver, "Wilson's Rapport with his Audience," *Quarterly Journal of Speech* 27 (February, 1941):79.

6. Richard Hofstadter, ed., *Great Issues in American History* New York: Vintage Books, 1959), p. 221.

7. *Ibid.*

Wall Street and the ruling class in general are seeking to have it appear that we must go to war with Germany . . . The people of the United States and the people of Germany have not the slightest grievance against one another. Left to themselves, they would be on terms of perfect amity and peace . . . It is not the people but the ruling class of the United States and Germany that want the war and they want it for purposes entirely their own. The people of both countries have everything to lose, including their lives, and absolutely nothing to gain by such a war.[8]

Debs blasted away at the evils of preparedness until 1918 when he delivered his Canton, Ohio, speech. Because of this rather rambling effort, which contained only six references to the war, he was sent to prison for violation of the Espionage Act. Although Debs insisted upon his patriotism, President Wilson refused to release him.

Two Roosevelts appeared on the other side in the preparedness confrontation. Theodore castigated President Wilson for his early hesitation and helped to develop an Army even before conscription; Franklin Delano, as Assistant Secretary of the Navy, was instrumental in clearing channels for cooperation between the American and British Fleets.

The League of Nations

The Wilson government had decided well before the war that the great unifying purpose would be a world organization for peace, and once the war was under way the President continued to stress this goal. On January 8, 1918, he delivered his Fourteen Points speech. The idea of the Fourteen Points did not originate with Wilson, any more than the League concept. As General S. L. A. Marshall reported in a rather unkind way:

Just as the historic paper jelled, Lloyd George talked to the British Trades Unions Congress where he said, "the settlement of the New Europe must be based on such grounds of reason and justice as will give some promise of stability, therefore, we feel that government with the consent of the governed must be the basis of any territorial settlement in this war." Wilson felt dished, such were his chagrin and disappointment that he proposed canceling his own speech. His advisers convinced him that Lloyd George had but scratched the surface and that he must carry on for the sake of humanity. He was not only willing; re-reading his own scholarly prose, he warmed to enthusiasm.[9]

The Fourteen Points as they appeared in Wilson's speech were as follows:

1. Open covenants openly arrived at.
2. Freedom of the seas.
3. Removal of economic barriers.
4. Reduction of armaments.
5. Adjustment of colonial claims in the interests of subject peoples.
6. Evacuation of Russian territory and free determination of Russian national policy.
7. Evacuation and restoration of Belgium.
8. Evacuation of French territory; Alsace and Lorraine to be returned to France.
9. Readjustment of Italian frontiers on lines of nationality.
10. People of Austria, Hungary, to be accorded opportunity for autonomous development.
11. Rumania, Serbia, and Montenegro to be evacuated, and Serbia given access to the sea.
12. Non-Turkish nationalities in the Ottoman Empire to be assured autonomous development; the Dardanelles to be opened to ships of all nations.
13. Poland to be made independent, with access to the sea.

---

8. *New York Call*, March, 1917.
9. S. L. A. Marshall, *The American Heritage History of World War I* (New York: American Heritage Pub. Co., 1964), p. 265.

14. Formation of a general association of nations with the mission of preserving world peace.[10]

Although this speech was delivered to a small gathering in Congress, it achieved a gratifying response from the international audience to whom it was addressed. German and Austrian officials expressed approval of the sentiment; Lenin was delighted; and Clemenceau gave grudging endorsement. However, Ludendorff, effectively in command of Germany at the time, dismissed it as a figment of the imagination.

When the Armistice came on November 11, 1918, President Wilson was ready to assure the adoption of a League of Nations that would make the world safe for democracy. He departed for Versailles to get at the job. Conservative leaders in both parties viewed with alarm the idea that our president should leave the country; no President had ever left our shores while still in office.

The League of Nations controversy probably started on January 22, 1917. On that date the President first told Congress specifically of his intentions regarding a league, and at that point Senator Henry Cabot Lodge "parted company with the idea of a league of nations."[11]

On January 8, 1918, Wilson presented his Fourteen Points to a joint session of Congress, the fourteenth point being virtually a debate proposition: "A general association of nations must be formed under specific covenants for the purpose of affording mutual guarantee of political independence and territorial integrity to great and small states alike."[12]

On November 15, after the Armistice, Senator Poindexter and others engaged in heated debate over the league, and the question seemed continually on the floor of the Senate. More discussion occurred over Knox's Resolution 361, which asked that any league plan be postponed until a later date so peace could be arrived at without delay. The controversy continued throughout January of 1919 and not until February 13, 1919, was the constitution for the League of Nations officially accepted and incorporated into the Treaty of Versailles—the first twenty-six articles.

While earlier arguments for and against a league were of necessity diffuse and hypothetical, after February 15, 1919, advocates and opponents had a specific and detailed document to which they could point. Arguments tended to center on "the League," rather than on "a league" as formerly. Senators had the Paris version of the revised League Covenant read into the *Congressional Record* early in June, almost as soon as the Peace Conference had accepted changes and before Wilson was ready to submit it. This unprecedented action provided the defenders and attackers of the League with a definite basis for debate.

Many speeches that did not occur in the Senate must be taken into account. The Lowell-Lodge debate, held at Harvard on March 19, 1919, demanded notice in subsequent speeches in the Senate, and William Howard Taft was refuted almost daily on some point on the Senate floor even though he himself was not present in the chamber. Several of President Wilson's addresses must also be considered as part of the debate.

---

10. *Ibid.*
11. Denna F. Fleming, *The United States and The League of Nations* (New York: G. P. Putnam's Sons, 1932).
12. Henry Cabot Lodge, *The Senate and the League of Nations* (New York: Charles Scribner's Sons, 1925).

The Speakers—There have been efforts to divide the senators into several camps on the question of the League of Nations: the Mild Reservationists, the Strong Reservationists, the Irreconcilables and the Non-Reservationists. It is not useful to sustain the subtle distinctions between Irreconcilable and Reservationist or between Mild or Strong Reservationists. President Wilson suggested that all opponents of the Covenant, as presented to the Senate in July of 1919, were grouped together whether they spoke of reservations or amendments.

Several leading figures in the debate deserve special attention. Henry Cabot Lodge, Chairman of the Foreign Relations Committee, was recognized leader of Republican activities in the Senate and a center of power and influence difficult to overestimate in the League of Nations battle. He was the master of senatorial maneuver, the finished product of years on the Senate floor, a combination of natural talent and practice. His speeches were well-organized and effectively worded; almost startling in contrast to the effusions of Williams, Lewis, and Borah. Speaking of Lodge's opening address against the Covenant on February 18, 1919, Denna Fleming wrote:

As a first speech for the negative it would have been a classic in any debate. The address was moderate in tone. There were strong shades of sarcasm in places, but no trace of the violence evident in other recent speeches . . . It was so wholly reasonable and cold blooded that it would be difficult for the defenders of the League to take hold of it.[13]

William E. Borah merits a place next to Lodge among those who defeated the Treaty of Versailles and the League of Nations. Critics either called him "provincial, blind, and unethical,"[14] or hailed him as one "who believed with a deep and personal honesty that internationalism in any form would lead only to world domination."[15] In 1919 when the President brought back from Paris the first draft of the League Covenant, Borah was ready to meet and defeat this new threat to our national isolation. He had a reputation as a man of the people with an unreasoning devotion to the founding fathers, factors that made him one of the most effective men who "murdered peace," and at the same time removed him from the Lodge group which generally bears the onus of the deed.

Borah is chiefly remembered for his speeches of February 21 and November 19. In the first he called forth all the forces of nationalism and isolationism, winding up with a mixture of native American hero worship and the saws of Polonius. In the second he sounded the death knell of the Covenant. As Albert Beveridge said, "This is one of the best things you ever did—one of the best anybody ever did. It is clear, simple, convincing, exalted . . . Nobody can answer it—nobody will try to answer it."[16]

James Reed from Missouri, called Lodge's Democratic ace-in-the-hole, was characterized by one contemporary as "A redoubtable debater, quick thinking, pungent in speech," a man "with plenty of brains and a criminal lawyer's ability to fit his talents to any cause which paid a good retainer."[17] He was a chronically adverse critic. As early as 1917 and already at odds

13. Fleming, *United States and the League* p. 136.
14. *New York Times*, November 1, 1919, p. 2.
15. Karl Schriftgiesser, *The Gentleman From Massachusetts* (New York: Little, Brown, 1926), p. 308.
16. Claudius O. Johnson, *Borah of Idaho* (New York: Longmans, Green and Co., 1936), p. 245.
17. A. D. Howden Smith, *Mr. House of Texas* New York: Funk and Wagnalls, 1940), p. 332.

with the administration, he warned readers of *The Forum* that Congress was indulging in a kind of legislative follow-the-leader.[18]

Philander C. Knox from Pennsylvania opposed the League of Nations because the League Covenant had been created before the Peace Treaty proper had been disposed of. He spoke in favor of his resolution calling for separate consideration of League and Treaty, and criticized the text of the Covenant as hastily drawn and hence carelessly worded. The *Boston Transcript* said Knox's speech of March 1, 1919 on the League would "change votes in the Senate, change outside opinion, and change the course of the world."[19]

Gilbert Hitchcock, nominal leader of the pro-League forces in the Senate, was so completely overshadowed by the President that he cannot be blamed or praised for any of the legislative results attributable to the Senate. He consistently disclaimed any skill in rhetoric and was "no match for the wily Lodge" in debate.[20] In a Senate speech on October 25, 1919, Hitchcock declared:

> Mr. President, one of the peculiar characteristics of orators, both real and presumptive, is the tendency to totally disregard facts. Depending more upon their ability to convince by well-constructed and well-delivered sentences, they pay less attention to close analysis than do those who are not so gifted. If a fact stands in the way of their forensic eloquence so much the worse for the fact.[21]

Friends of the League could not help wishing that he might have had less contempt for and more facility with effective rhetoric.

John Sharp Williams participated frequently and at great length in the League debates. He talked too much, and, even though he was able to "achieve amazing lucidity whatever the circumstances," he did

more than his share in turning the treaty debate into what he called "the most incoherent gabfest in human history."[22]

Thomas J. Walsh's comments on the Covenant were printed at length in a Sunday edition of the *New York Times* in 1919. The *Times* said of him, "Senator Thomas J. Walsh of Montana is one of the men in Washington who see the President frequently, and was one of the last to be with him before his departure for Europe."[23] Several magazines and newspapers strongly urged that Walsh be a member of Wilson's Peace Commission, but Walsh stayed at home in the Senate and at widely spaced intervals contributed some of the strongest speaking for the League cause. On July 21, 1919, for instance, he answered Senators who viewed Article Ten with alarm. Reed, Borah, and Lodge who took delight in baiting Hitchcock and others, paid Senator Walsh the compliment of either no comment or mere token objection.

Porter J. McCumber of North Dakota was an ultra-conservative Republican who usually stuck to the party line. On the League of Nations question, however, party affiliation meant nothing to McCumber. He fought constantly for U. S. entry into the League and aligned himself firmly and at times bitterly against Republican

---

18. *The Forum* 58 (October, 1917), p. 403.
19. "Summary of Newspaper Opinion on League Debate," *Literary Digest*, March 15, 1919, p. 12.
20. Schriftgiesser, *Gentleman*, p. 334.
21. U. S. Congress, Senate, *Congressional Record*, Sixty-sixth Congress, First Session, 1919, 58, pt. 8:7493.
22. George C. Osborn, *John Sharp Williams, Planter-Statesman of the Deep South* (Baton Rouge: Louisiana State University Press, 1943), p. 449.
23. *New York Times*, February 23, 1919.

colleagues of long standing. When he offered reservations he did so, not to make the League too unpalatable for ratification, but to secure acceptance of the League even at some sacrifice to the original document. He was the only Republican to vote for unconditional acceptance of the League on November 19. Perhaps Senator McCumber states his view best in a speech of March 3, 1919, "I cannot stand back and say, 'Oh let the world be damned; we can take care of ourselves.' There is some obligation resting on the American people to help maintain the peace of the world."

Among the pro-League speakers was Claude Swanson of Virginia, to whom fell the empty honor of making the opening speech for the League after July 10,[24]

J. Hamilton Lewis of Illinois was perhaps the most adequate defender of the League on the floor of the Senate throughout February, 1919. Key Pittman of Nevada was author of a proposal for interpretative reservations, reservations which simply stated the Senate's view without demanding complete reconsideration and adoption.

It is difficult to arrive at a judgment of the senate of 1919. Creel was probably too critical when he wrote of the Senate debate on the League, "Where once a Webster, a Clay, and a Calhoun debated great issues of conscience and high ability there was the squabble of hucksters."[25] Howden Smith called it a "very good run-of-the-mill Senate,"[26] and that is perhaps a more accurate characterization.

The Alignments—The alignments during the debate were easily discernible:

1. Administration vs. Senate
2. Democrat vs. Republican

3. Internationalist vs. Isolationist-nationalist
4. Wilson vs. Lodge.

The first of these divisions was as old as the Constitution. From the very founding of our nation, the power of the President and the Senate in treaty making has been a point of contention. Washington was the first president to feel the chafing effects of the treaty provision embodied in the Constitution. "He [the President] shall have power, by and with the advice and consent of the Senate, to make treaties, provided two-thirds of the Senators present concur . . ."[27]

The difficulty has remained, just as certain framers of the Constitution had feared it might, and as John Hay, Secretary of State under Theodore Roosevelt, declared "there will always be thirty-four per cent of the Senate on the blackguard side of every question." The inability or unwillingness of the president and the Senate to get together on treaties in critical situations has been the subject of study and comment throughout our history.

Politics was a second divisive agent in the League debate. Too frequently the question of For or Against became a question of Democrat or Republican. In the uproar following the submission of the treaty in 1919, the advocates of ratification spoke often of the political motives of their opponents, and those who wished to veto the treaty seemed anxious that the opposite political party bear the blame.

---

24. Thomas R. Marshall, *Recollections: A Hoosier Salad* (Indianapolis: Bobbs, Merrill, 1925), p. 331.
25. George Creel, *The War, the World, and Wilson* (New York: Harper and Bros., 1920), p. 362.
26. Howden Smith, *Mr. House*, p. 333.
27. *U. S. Constitution*, Art. 2, sec. 2.

When the discussion of a League of Nations began early in the war, Wilson had majority support in the Senate, but never two-thirds. After the elections of 1918, however, the Republicans attained a party majority of two. At midnight on March 3, 1919, just before the close of the session, Senator Lodge submitted his famous Round Robin resolution, declaring that the thirty-nine signatories (only five of them newly-elected) were opposed to the "constitution of the league of nations in the form now proposed to the peace conference . . . " All of these signatories were Republican, and Lodge seemed concerned about accusations of political motives. He remarked, "We did not think it desirable to ask any Democrat to sign. We knew there were Democratic Senators opposed to the League, but we did not wish to involve or embarrass them . . . "[28] Regardless of Lodge's solicitude, the Round Robin was a party alignment on the League question and it was so interpreted. Excerpts from the *Congressional Record* reveal this:

Mr. Robinson: . . . I will ask the Senator from Colorado another question: Did he see press reports published widely throughout the United States during the last 10 days that the Senator from Mass., as leader of the majority, and the Senator from Kansas (Mr. Curtis) as whip of the majority, had sent a telegram to every Member of the present majority, urging them to refrain from discussing the proposed league of nations treaty until a partisan conference, a Republican conference, could be held, and the Republicans in the Senate should thereby be afforded an opportunity to reach a conclusion whether or not they would stand for a league of nations in the treaty or oppose it; . . . ?

(Mr. Thomas of Colorado took the floor but did not answer the above question of his colleague. Rather he congratulated himself on his absence from the Senate during the "reign of Theodore Roosevelt" and was indulging himself in a review of a former speech in which he apparently took

some pride, when Lodge interrupted in order to answer Mr. Robinson's question for Mr. Thomas.)

Mr. Lodge: The Senator from Colorado certainly did not read any statement of mine which in the least resembled that which the Senator from Arkansas has stated. The request made by the Senator from Kansas and myself was that they would refrain from interviews or making statements until they had an opportunity to consult with their colleagues. There was no suggestion of any partisanship in it. We are as nonpartisan as anyone could be.

Mr. Thomas: Of course the Senator meant his Republican colleagues.

Mr. Lodge: I did not say that.

Mr. Thomas: I know the Senator did not say it, but no other Senators were honored by the request.

(Here the Senators digressed to discuss the specific rights and duties of the Senate in regard to treaty making, and Mr. Lodge was reminded by Mr. Thomas that he himself [Lodge] had once insisted on the President's right to negotiate treaties without Senate intervention.)

Mr. Robinson: The Senator from Mass. has stated the action of himself and his colleague, the Senator from Kansas, in telegraphing their associates the request already referred to—that they not discuss the league of nations treaty until a conference could be held—was nonpartisan. I should like to be informed whether the Senator from Massachusetts was speaking humorously or in all seriousness?

Mr. Lodge: I was speaking in all seriousness. We have not said a word about it. Not one word has been said in any conference held by the Republicans.

Mr. Robinson: I will ask the Senator from Massachusetts another question. Is it a fact that no one but Members on that side of the chamber were requested to refrain from discussing the treaty until the conference could be held?

Mr. Lodge: Certainly. Our request was addressed only to Senators to whom we had a right to address such a request.

Mr. Robinson: The Senator saw, of course, the statement in the press of a number of Senators on

---

28. Lodge, *Senate and League*, pp. 119-20.

that side of the Chamber to the effect that they refused to be a party to making the league of nations treaty a partisan issue and that they regarded his action in submitting that request as a partisan act. He saw that statement of course?

Mr. Lodge: No; I did not see it.[29]

Party alignment is clearly evident in three separate votes taken on the ratification, November 19, 1919. The first two ballotings were taken on the ratification of the covenant with the fourteen reservations affixed.

First Vote

For		Against	
Republicans	35	Republicans	14
Democrats	4	Democrats	41

Second Vote

For		Against	
Republicans	34	Republicans	13
Democrats	7	Democrats	38

The third and final vote was on unconditional ratification.

For		Against	
Republicans	1	Republicans	46
Democrats	37	Democrats	7

Senator McCumber of North Dakota was the only Republican to vote for unconditional ratification of the League of Nations.[30]

A third alignment on the League question was Internationalist vs. Isolationist. Much of the rhetoric of the Senators with strong political motives and of those involved in the battle of executive vs. legislative was intertwined with Internationalist-Isolationist arguments.

A fourth division on the question was the personal animosity between Lodge and Wilson. The personal factor did not appear prominently in the debates or the votes, however, but it "removed any basis for cooperation which may have existed between them."[31] Wilson refused to speak on the same platform with Lodge as a result of this bitterness, and Lodge continued to vent his spleen upon the President five years after the League's defeat.

The Argument—An analysis of the case for the League is difficult because it was inseparable from the text of the Treaty of Versailles. There had been a concerted move on the floor of the Senate in December, 1918, to have the whole question of a league postponed until the treaty had been disposed of. Senator Knox suggested this in Senate Resolution 361, but President Wilson ignored the desires of Knox and other influential Senators. He virtually dared them to do their worst with the Treaty and the League in the same document. In a speech delivered immediately after Lodge's Round Robin resolution, Wilson told the opposition that he would bring a treaty

---

29. U. S. Congress, Senate, *Congressional Record*, Sixty-sixth Congress, First Session, 1919, 58, pt. 1:162-63.

30. Figures given are based on the following: Royden Daingerfield, *In Defense of the Senate* (Norman: University of Oklahoma Press, 1933), pp. 251-52; Lodge, *Senate and League*, pp. 191-92.

31. Fleming, *United States and The League*, p. 9.

back from Paris with the Covenant "not only in it, but so many threads of the treaty tied to the Covenant that you cannot dissect the Covenant from the treaty without destroying the whole vital structure.[32] The President had strong support for his insistence that the treaty and the league should be inseparable because the Central Powers had offered to surrender only with the understanding that the treaty would follow Wilson's Fourteen Points.[33] Peace could not have been achieved on any other basis at the time of the Armistice. The League's being a part of the Treaty of Versailles produced a great deal of argument on the question and strongly affected opposition strategy.

The proposition for the League debate was whether the Senate of the United States should ratify the Covenant of the League of Nations as constituted in the first twenty-six articles of the Treaty of Versailles. There were only three issues in the debate, and they can be observed clearly from the argument on the Senate floor:

1. Does the world need and desire peace?
2. Is international organization the best way to secure peace?
3. Does the League of Nations provide the proper plan for international organization?

On the first issue, pro-League speakers repeatedly identified the evident *need* for world peace with a universal *desire* for world peace, while several anti-League speakers declared that they failed to see any conclusive evidence of a universal desire for peace. No speaker on either side denied the *need* for peace, and had the issue been advanced by the pro-Leaguers as one of need alone, this would doubtless have been admitted at once.

Isolationists denied specifically the assumption in the second issue that an international organization was needed to secure peace. Borah, Johnson, and Reed stated that international organization was not the only way to secure peace and indeed that it was no way to get permanent peace.

The third issue, the League of Nations, was the most consistently contested. Mild reservationists, men who never denied either the need and desire for peace or the propriety of some form of international organization, often found fault with the details of the Covenant. There is no doubt that certain opponents of the proposed League took a negative stand solely from their conviction that it was not the proper plan for achieving a noble aim.

Irreconcilables like Borah and Johnson omitted nothing from their condemnation of the League. They doubted that everybody in the world wanted peace and opposed *any* world organization.

The argument on the Senate floor seems to have been spontaneous, with speakers rising at random to express their thoughts on the issues. The debate became a process of attack by League opponents followed by refutations from its defenders. As a result the issues appear as negative issues with the affirmative case emanating from President Wilson outside the Senate chamber. The specific arguments, negatively stated, were: We must not ratify the League of Nations Covenant because:

---

32. *New York Times*, March 4, 1918.
33. *Washington Post*, October 13, 1918. The German Government requested an Armistice, declaring that it "accepted the terms laid down by President Wilson in his address of January 8 and in his subsequent addresses as to the foundation of a permanent peace."

1. It will force us to abandon the "no entangling alliance" policy of Washington.
2. It will nullify the Monroe Doctrine.
3. It will force us to surrender our sovereignty.
4. It will assure war, not peace.
5. It will force us to fight all over the world in defense of Article 10.
6. It sanctions, by denying the right of revolution, the oppression of weaker peoples such as the Irish and the Shantung Chinese.
7. It provides a threat of outside meddling in our domestic affairs, such as Oriental immigration.
8. It subordinates us to Great Britain by giving her a six-to-one vote superiority.
9. It assures the perpetuation of the bad features of the treaty of Versailles.
10. It is unconstitutional.

The bulk of the debate between February 15 and November 19, 1919, centered on these arguments, several ultimately taking the form of reservations around which the public mind and the will of the Senate crystallized.

When President Wilson carried his cause to the people in September, 1919, he too had assumed the burden of refuting these negative charges. For instance, in Helena, Montana, on September 11, he answered five objections—the withdrawal clause, Article 10, the Monroe Doctrine nullification, interference with domestic affairs, and the Shantung settlement. At a luncheon in San Francisco one week later he met the same objections and commented on the British vote discrepancy. At Pueblo, Colorado, on September 25, his last speech, Wilson was still concerned with answering negative arguments.

Some anti-League speakers did not confine themselves to the list of standard arguments, but dealt with Anglophobia, fear of papal dominance, hatred of kings, fear of Negro supremacy, and dread of Communism. As the debate wore on speakers occasionally lost their poise and exchanged bitter personal remarks. Brandegee questioned Hitchcock's sanity and Williams called Borah a "Prussian."

The use of statistical evidence was particularly interesting. The pro-League speakers reported that the results of newspaper polls favored a league, and brandished favoring petitions with thousands of signatures. On one occasion Hitchcock and Borah engaged in a long discussion of the significance of such statistics. Since nearly all polls favored the pro-Leaguers, Borah charged that they asked about *a* league, not necessarily *the* League which the Senate was debating, and that they revealed nothing about the popular attitude toward minor or major changes in the text of the Treaty. Even if it could be proved the public was heavily in favor of the League, Borah declared, he would still fight against it because he knew the Covenant was wrong.

Speeches rang with adoration for great Americans: Washington, Hamilton, Adams, Jefferson, Monroe, and Lincoln. Lodge, Knox and other more restrained League opponents used these appeals occasionally, but the more violently disposed opponents depended heavily upon them. Borah's famous speech of November 19, 1919, for example, was built entirely around the infallibility of Washington's statesmanship.

The **Strategies**—The forces in favor of

the League strove to convince the people that the return of official peace depended upon the signing of the Treaty of which the League was a part. They attempted to identify their cause with the cause of world peace, and at the same time to link any opposition to the Covenant with antipeace forces. By urging immediate ratification, pro-League speakers tried to make it seem that those objecting to the first twenty-six articles of the Versailles Treaty, either in detail or as a whole, were not only responsible for the inconveniences and frustrations of a continuing state of war after the armistice of November, 1919, but were also the enemies of permanent peace. This inevitable strategy was apparent in all pro-League maneuvers both in and out of the Senate.

A strategy of the anti-League group consisted of delay in consideration of the Treaty while it dissuaded the public from blind acceptance of the League as a source of all good. The anti-League group recognized the prevailing sentiment for early and permanent peace which the pro-League group had identified with the League of Nations Covenant. Senator Lodge later discussed the inception of this strategy in his book on the League of Nations debate.[34] Borah, the first Senator with whom he had talked about the situation, visited him in Washington toward the end of April to "talk over the course to be pursued in regard to the League of Nations and the Versailles Treaty generally."

I then said to him that . . . the following conditions, as I saw them, existed. The great mass of the people, the man in the street, to use a common expression, the farmers, the shopkeepers, the men in small business, clerks and the like, in short the people generally, did not understand the treaty at all, had had no opportunity even to read the provisions of the League, except in the draft which Mr. Wilson had brought back when he returned in Feb-

ruary, and that, knowing nothing about any of the details of the treaty, their natural feeling was "now the war is over and let us have peace as quickly as possible."
The second condition was that, what I may call the vocal classes of the community, most of the clergymen, the preachers of sermons, a large element of the teaching force of the universities, a large proportion of the newspaper editors, and finally the men and women who were in the habit of writing and speaking for publication, although by no means thoroughly informed, were friendly to the League as it stood and were advocating it.[35]

Lodge and Borah agreed that defeating the League by a direct vote was impossible at that time. Lodge believed the public needed educating on the subject, and he deliberately planned to use the debate in the Senate for that purpose. As he later wrote:

The value of the great and I think I may say historic debate in the Senate was that every day the American people learned more clearly what the Covenant of the League of Nations which Mr. Wilson presented to them really meant, what dangers it threatened and what perilous purposes it might conceal. It was a very remarkable debate. It rendered an immense service in the *instruction of the people.*[36]

The strategy employed by advocates of the League in debate on the Senate floor seems to have been one of defense. The pro-League Senators seemed to feel that a *prima facie* case having been made for their proposition by the President and Taft, their task was simply rebuttal. They entered into the argument only to reinforce the case after it was attacked. Perhaps those charged with putting the League through the Senate were over-confident, although Hitchcock's repeated announcements of confidence

---

34. Lodge, *Senate and League*, pp. 146-211.
35. *Ibid.*
36. *Ibid.*

late in the debate may also have been akin to whistling in the graveyard. They may have leaned too heavily on President Wilson, for:

A considerable majority of the Senators to whom Mr. Wilson presented the Treaty of Versailles on July 10, 1919, were either dourly hostile or lethargic in their reception of him, and this applied to many members of his own party, who felt that he had slighted them in the past, or else resented his misstep of last October, which had cost them the control of Congress and the flow of patronage and appropriations to which they had been accustomed.[37]

Perhaps some Democrats felt little genuine conviction on the question, or entertained little hope of success from the start.[38] In June, 1940, Senator Key Pittman, Chairman of the Senate Foreign Relations Committee, said in an interview, "I guess that even then we knew the country wasn't ready to give up that much sovereignty."[39] The anti-League strategy of appending reservations, nullifying Article 10 for the United States made our withdrawal from the League almost a matter of whim. The Lodge group could maneuver the League advocates into a position where they were forced to vote against the League as presented for ratification. As the controversy progressed, anti-League speakers repeatedly forced the defenders to make uncomfortable choices:

1. Is the League an innocuous "debating society"? (In which case it isn't worth bothering with.)
2. Is it a super-state, blotting out nations and running everybody's affairs? (In which case we must have none of it, since as Americans we have nothing to gain and everything to lose from such an organization.)
3. Will the League prevent all war? (In which case it must be circumvented lest it destroy the right of freedom-loving peoples to revolt.)
4. Will it guarantee war through Article 10? (If so, of course, it runs counter to the avowed purpose of its most enthusiastic advocates and would be worse than the status quo.)
5. Is our obligation under the League moral? (If so, how will it be enforced when put to the test in situations unfavorable to our interests?)
6. Is it legal? (In which case it flatly assures us of sending our boys all over the world to fight for the things of no real concern to them.)

By posing these dilemmas Reed, Johnson, Borah and other anti-League Senators kept Hitchcock and other pro-League Senators busy fighting off the appearance of inconsistency. Senator Walsh of Montana was harder to handle than most League advocates. On the matter of dilemma 5, for example, he simply said it made no difference whether one called an obligation legal or moral, as long as he met it.

Affirmative forces stressed the opposition's failure to suggest alternatives. Despite the implications in Wilson's challenge during his western trip that enemies "put up or shut up," the anti-League forces did propose alternatives during the debate.

---

37. Howden Smith, *Mr. House*, p. 330.
38. Letter from John Sharp Williams to Wilson, quoted in Joseph R. Tumulty, *Woodrow Wilson as I know Him* (New York: Doubleday, Page and Co., 1921), p. 502.
39. Interview with R. A. Micken, on the occasion of the Senator's speech to the graduating class of 1940 of Montana School of Mines, Butte, Montana.

Senator Knox discussed one on March 1; LaFollette proposed one on November 18; Thomas offered one on July 29; and Senator Reed talked of codifying international law as a preventative measure against disturbances of world peace. In fact, isolationism was, by implication, an alternative plan. Borah thought the United States could best serve the people of the world by remaining aloof from all association with other nations that might involve the loss of sovereignty. Thus, she could throw her weight on the side of justice once wars started or were threatened.

It was not easy for Senators to gauge or analyze their audiences. The immediate audience in the capitol might vary from a handful of colleagues on the floor and a scattering of the curious in the galleries, to full attendance of the members, packed galleries, and thousands standing outside trying to get in. Occasions such as Borah's speeches of February 21 and November 19, the Reed speech of February 22, and the Lodge speeches of February 28 and August 12, drew packed chambers. The galleries were often both large and troublesome; Chairman Marshall waged a ceaseless and futile battle to keep the galleryites from cheering what they liked and hissing and booing what they did not like. Senator Williams of Mississippi fought with the crowds, charging they were composed of anti-League partisans and packed with Irish league haters. He was booed violently after Lodge's speech of August 12, when he accused Lodge of making a show of himself for the benefit of the galleries.

Senators came and went throughout the speeches, often coming in only to respond to roll call. Senator Hitchcock spoke of opposition orators talking to empty benches on many occasions in their effort to monopolize debate, and frequent absence of a quorum.

Some Senators carried their arguments to the voters, but Lodge preferred to remain in Washington and use the Senate as a sounding board.[40] The effectiveness of the debating of League opponents was acceded by friends of the League. As Irving Fisher, an avowed pro-Leaguer, wrote in 1923, "The great progress made by the little band of irreconcilable Senators in affecting public opinion is thus a testimony to the power of persistent advertising."[41]

William Allen White observed, "Between December, 1918, and June, 1919, the Hero of the Armistice became, in the hearts of millions of Americans, the betrayer of the American birthright. They felt that in making them part of the United States of the World, he was making them less important as citizens of the United States of America."[42] Another newspaperman said, "If to the people, a large majority of them, the was was merely distasteful, the peace, the League of Nations, was odious, a menace."[43]

The elections of 1918 and 1920, designated as they were by League advocates as tests of League support,[44] strongly indicated opposition to the Covenant, or at the very least indifference to its fate. The election was no "solemn referendum" on League acceptance, as Wilson had wished it to be, but the voters could scarcely have been deceived as to the true Republican at-

---

40. *New York Times*, August 29, 1919.
41. Irving Fisher, *League or War?* (New York: Harper and Bros., 1923), p. 109.
42. William Allen White, *Masks in a Pageant* (New York: Macmillan, 1928), p. 386.
43. Mark Sullivan, *Our Times* (New York: Charles Scribner's Sons, 1935) 6:117.
44. Tumulty, *Woodrow Wilson*, pp. 500-502.

titude on the League in 1920, even though there were protestations of Harding's interest in a league of some sort. Some of the credit for the indifference among the people must belong to the opponents of the document and to their debating in the Senate.

Conclusion

This study of the rhetoric of World War I and the League of Nations debate reveals a great deal about American values and the issue of war and peace. Traditional American pragmatism and morality lead us to oppose the material waste and the animalistic barbarism of war. When war breaks out and the United States inevitably is drawn into it—not infrequently by our own actions like selling war materials to the belligerents (pragmatism)—we search diligently for a cause—make the world safe for democracy (Morality). Thus, we are reacting to evil forces; we are defending ourselves and the good of mankind; we have no choice but to fight. The requirements of pragmatism and morality have been met; dissonance has been effectively (and often happily) reduced. Although we assume the role of a long-suffering people opposed to the evils of war and propaganda, we tend to be proficient in both. The rhetoric of President Wilson and his fellow Americans before and during World War I appealed to these traditional American values; it prepared us for our role as "savior" of the democracies.

The League of Nations seemed to fit perfectly into the American value system. It was democratic in nature, was opposed to war, and was "invented" by American ingenuity. How could it fail to gain support in the United States? That is was ahead of its time—too early for Americans to accept—is only part of the answer. But a more complete answer must include the American value system and form of government. Proponents of the League failed to take into account feelings of national pride, self-sufficiency, independence, and freedom of action ingrained in most Americans. These feelings tended to outweigh opposition to war—a war that ended—and League opponents argued that the debate over the League was actually delaying permanent peace. Traditional American isolationism returned with the Armistice in 1918, and so did political partisanship.

Wilson failed to appreciate the need to involve congressional leaders (of both political parties) in his plans for the League of Nations and, more importantly, for American entry into the League. He discovered painfully, like presidents before and since, that no president can " go it alone." Congress must ultimately approve or disapprove treaties and major international agreements. Wilson foolishly allowed old animosities between himself and congressional leaders to remain and even angered some potential supporters. The strong opposition to the League wisely grasped the offensive in the League debate, appealing to traditional values dear to the American voter. Proponents of the League spent their time defending and explaining the League, a concept that seemed foreign and even threatening to American values. The League was doomed from the start.

Thus, the importance of values in our persuasive efforts cannot be overemphasized. At the same time, unity and compromise between the branches of our government and the major political parties is absolutely necessary for successful persuasive efforts. It was tragic that the right combination of value appeals and cooperation was found to get America into war, but the combination was lost that could get America into the League of Nations and could thus, perhaps, have averted World War II.

BIBLIOGRAPHY

Bailey, Thomas A. *Woodrow Wilson and the Lost Peace.* New York: Macmillan, 1944.

Baker, Ray S., and Dodd, William E. *The Public Papers of Woodrow Wilson.* Authorized. New York: Harper and Brothers, 1925-27.

Braden, Waldo W. "A Rhetorical Criticism of the Invention of William E. Borah's Senate Speeches on the League of Nations, 1918-1920." Ph.D. Diss., State University of Iowa, 1942.

Daingerfield, Royden. *In Defense of the Senate.* Norman: University of Oklahoma Press, 1933.

Fleming, Denna F. *The Treaty Veto and the American Senate.* New York: G. P. Putnam's Sons, 1930.

———. *The United States and the League of Nations, 1918-1920.* New York: G. P. Putnam's Sons, 1932.

A well-balanced presentation of the League of Nations controversy; in many ways the most authoritative treatment available.

Henderlider, Clair. "An Evaluation of the Persuasive Techniques of Woodrow Wilson in His League Of Nations' Speeches, September 4-25, 1919." Ph.D. Diss., State University of Iowa, 1945.

Howden Smith, A. D. *Mr. House of Texas.* New York: Funk and Wagnalls, 1940.

Interesting treatment of President Wilson's friend and aid. Colonel House may well have been the man most instrumental in framing the President's international thinking.

Larson, Cedric, and Mock, James R. "The Four-Minute Men," *The Quarterly Journal of Speech* 25 (1939):97-112.

Link, Arthur S. *Woodrow Wilson and the Progressive Era.* New York: Harper, 1954.

Lodge, Henry C. *The Senate and the League of Nations.* New York: Charles Scribner's Sons, 1925.

A revealing treatment of the Wilson-Lodge controversy by one of the principals.

Marshall, Thomas R. *Recollections: A Hoosier Salad.* Indianapolis: Bobbs, Merrill, 1925.

How the debate looked to the presiding officer.

Taft, William H. *Taft Papers on the League of Nations.* New York: Macmillan, 1920.

Papers on the subject of international organization by the man who led the advocates of a league before the government took over.

Wish, Harvey. *Contemporary America.* New York: Harper and Brothers, 1945.

This is a discussion of the Wilson Era which presents a fair and understanding point of view about men and issues during World War I.

16 Suffrage and Prohibition: Integrated Issues

Ronald G. Coleman

The issues of suffrage and prohibition from the colonial period through the time of the enactments of the Eighteenth and Nineteenth Amendments were perhaps more interwoven than any other issues of that period. Volsteadism was one of the major concerns which prompted the woman speaker to rise to the platform, and as she denounced the demons of drink she was speaking out for herself and thereby aiding the cause of her suffrage. Her advocacy inevitably linked the causes of prohibition and woman suffrage. The analysis here will thus cover the two issues.

Suffrage Issue: Background

Even though some few colonial women were active in public affairs, they were generally hard to attract to activism in the budding woman's movement prior to the Civil War. "Marriage was the ultimate goal of every girl's life, it was the only success she could achieve. Failure to marry was synonymous with failure in life for the women of that period."[1] And it was almost certain that a woman seen speaking on a public platform was not the marriageable kind.

Nevertheless, a restricted movement did

begin. The early years have been called the "Age of Experimentation," and are noted for the public speaking efforts of such women as Maria Chapman, Elizabeth Philbrook, Lydia Child, Lucretia Mott, and Abbey Kelly.[2] Then came the Civil War years which saw women speakers primarily concerned with furthering the effectiveness of the Union forces.

The end of the war brought to a close the preliminary chapter of women's oratory. The excitement of Civil War issues was gone, and women saw fit to begin in earnest the struggle for their own emancipation and enfranchisement.[3]

The Suffrage Movement: 1865-1920— With the emancipation of the slaves and the right of the black man to vote theoretically insured, the exponents of suffrage saw an opportunity to strike out for secur-

---

1. Lillian O'Connor, *Pioneer Women Orators* (New York: Columbia University Press, 1954), p. 8.
2. Doris Yoakum, "Women's Introduction to the American Platform," in *History and Criticism of American Public Address*, ed., William N. Brigance (New York: Longman's, Green and Company, 1955), 1:153.
3. *Ibid.*, 1:187.

ing the vote of women. Speakers for women's rights felt that the opportunity was ripe for a total movement:

To withhold suffrage from women is a degradation of the female sex, giving the right to vote to women would highly improve and refine our elections, and lastly, if she cannot vote, she is not represented. . . . Those in favor of woman suffrage . . . [have] a rational argument in them, while those on the other side . . . [make] illogical appeals to the prejudices and theories which the received state of things naturally produces and maintains.[4]

The reaction against these advocates became immediately apparent. "Although the present status of women is in many respects one of wrongful abridgment, and although they ought to have facilities for education and occupation opened to them in many hitherto untried ways, society should nevertheless make a resolute stand against admitting them to share in any sort of government."[5]

During the decade following the Civil War there was a surge of public interest in woman's suffrage. Individuals, pro and con, made their views known through speeches and articles. Many of these reactions were brought about by specific situations or series of events. One such incident involved the suffragette, Mrs. Sarah Huntingdon, who had applied for the right to vote in the Grant election, and was permitted to register by the Board of Selectmen of Norwalk, Connecticut.   She   was,   nevertheless, brought to trial, where the prosecutor claimed   that   "according   to   the   Constitution of Connecticut, women are precluded from the rights of elective franchise, and; therefore, the action of the selectmen, in admitting Mrs. Huntingdon, was void."[6] The counsel for the defense argued that the decision was to be made by the Board of Selectmen. The court's decision favored

the   prosecutor's   argument   and   Mrs. Huntingdon was not permitted to register.

Magazine editors were assailed with opinions on the subject. "If the vote is given to women, free government, and with it liberty and opinion, would fall."[7] Women should "set a Christian example, cultivate moral principles in the home, and forward moral education and Christian civilization."[8] A woman writing to the editor of *Harper's* suggested that women were certainly inferior to men in strength and intellect, that the greater achievements of the race had been made by men, and that Christianity confirmed the subordinate position of women by allotting to men the "hardship in plain language and positive precept."[9]

The response on the positive side was just as active. Some men felt that active political life on the part of women would stimulate the welfare of the nation. "The family would acquire a new element of interest that would do everyone concerned a tremendous good."[10] A letter appeared in *Harper's* asserting that suffrage was an unalienable right of which women were being unduly deprived. The influence of women in politics would purify public affairs and

4. Jennifer Foster, "A Woman in Reply to Dr. Lieber," *The Nation*, July 11, 1867, p. 35.
5. John Bushnells, *North American Review* 109 (November, 1878):556.
6. "The Would-be Woman Voter in Connecticut: A Temporary Disappointment," *New York Times*, November 6, 1872, p. 7.
7. Goldwin Smith, "Female Suffrage," *Popular Science Monthly* 5 (November, 1874):427.
8. "Female Suffrage," *Harper's* 41 (November, 1874):494.
9. "A Letter to the Christian Women of America" *Harper's* 41 (November, 1874):438-46.
10. J.E. Cairnes, "Woman Suffrage as Affecting the Family," *Popular Science Monthly*, 6 (April, 1875):16.

"alleviate the entire tone of political life."[11]

There were a few successes achieved by the women during this period. The first legislative assembly of Wyoming in 1869 gave the right to vote to women who were also allowed to hold offices on the same terms as men. In 1870 the Territory of Utah extended to its women citizens electoral franchise but in 1887 they were disenfranchised by the Edmunds Bill. The actions of these territories was possible because territories, unlike states, had no constitution, but derived their frame of government and power to make laws from the Organic Act of Congress. The Organic Act specified male citizens as enfranchised only for the initial election; after that, subsequent elections and voter qualifications were prescribed by the legislative assembly of each territory.[12] In each instance the only restriction concerning possible women's right to vote was that the suffrage right and holding office were limited to citizens of twenty-one years of age, or persons above that age who had declared their intention to become citizens.

The Governor of Wyoming, commenting on six years of suffrage in his Territory, said, "It is simple justice to say that women, entering for the first time in the history of the country upon these new and untried duties, have conducted themselves in every respect with as much tact, sound judgment and good sense as men."[13]

During the next five years, 1876-1880, the direction of the women's efforts shifted slightly from a direct concern with the voting franchise to what seemed to be more immediately perceived concerns. The comparison between male and female status in relation to employment was a complex one. Where women had been able to secure positions similar to those of men, discrimi-

nation was obvious in the form of unequal renumeration. In 1878 a woman doing mill work was paid about one-half of what men made.[14]

But in addition to discriminatory practices regarding salaries, women found it difficult to penetrate into professional fields. For example, an interesting incident occurred when a Wisconsin woman applied for admission to the legal bar of that state. In response to the application, Chief Justice Ryan said that "a woman lawyer would obliterate almost all distinction of sex in one statutory corpus Juris . . ." causing women to claim the privilege of all offices under statutes "municipal and state, executive, legislative, and judicial." According to Judge Ryan, such a privilege would infringe upon the constitutional rights of male suffrage and qualification.[15]

It is obvious from even a hasty glance at the speeches and articles of the time that many of the opponents of woman's suffrage saw voting as an added burden beyond woman's capacity. But despite the multitude of criticism, the slow movement toward recognition was beginning to show results. By 1880 the struggle for the voting privilege brought about an experimental election in Boston. Women were given the opportunity not only to vote but to run for office as well. No women were actually elected, but the occasion pointed up the facts that there were women who displayed

---

11. "Letter to the Editor," *Harper's,* 42 (March, 1875):443.
12. Mary A. Greene, "Results of the Woman-Suffrage Movement," *Forum,* 17 (March 1899), 31.
13. E.L. Godkin, "Female Suffrage," *The Nation* 36 (March 8, 1883):204.
14. Charles Elliott, "Woman's Work and Woman's Wages," *North American Review* 135, No. 309 (August 1882): 140-42.
15. *New York Times,* February 27, 1876, p. 17.

the determination necessary for political life, that there were political parties in the city willing to nominate women for office, and that there were women who were worthy of the responsibility of nomination.[16]

However, the 1880s brought about a stunning defeat for the cause of the suffragists. Despite their tedious efforts to further the cause, the Women's Suffrage Act was found unconstitutional. William Baker had pushed the bill until it had passed; then, overnight, a few congressional members came to the conclusion that to allow women voting privileges would be unconstitutional and that nothing short of an amendment to the Constitution would remove the disability. D.W. Travis declared, "The constitution states that every male citizen has the right to vote and says nothing about females, and it would be necessary for an amendment to the constitution to allow women to vote."[17]

At the times of the adoption of the Fourteenth and Fifteenth Amendments (1868 and 1870) women had hoped that their way to the polls would be opened. Consequently, in various sections of the country attempts were made by the ladies to compel the registrars of elections to register them as legal voters. Women in Pennsylvania, California, Missouri, and the District of Columbia sued the election officials for refusal to accept their votes. The uniform decision in each case had been that the two amendments were applicable only to the freedman of color and to existing rights and privileges.

There were several instances of statutes, ordinances, and municipal charters which allowed some form of suffrage to women within a limited territory, and/or for a special occasion. These included the statute extending school suffrage to the women of the city of Wilmington, Delaware; that which allowed the women taxpayers of Cooperstown, New York, to vote on local improvements; the occasional special laws submitting a vote on local improvements; and a provision in Arkansas and Missouri which allowed women to sign petitions for or against liquor licenses.

T.W. Higginson wrote one of the most informed articles to appear during the 1880s on the subject of suffrage. He summarized the potential of suffrage's impact:

It is a curious feature of the Women Suffrage movement that, after half a century of discussion, neither friends nor foes seem to get to appreciate the vastness of the political change proposed. . . .

Not often in the history of the world has a body of voters deliberately opened its ranks to admit a reenforcement larger than itself. Yet, in almost every one of the older States of the Union this will literally happen on the day when women are enfranchised. In sixteen of the states, women outnumber the men by the census of 1880.[18]

By 1890 the issue rested with the Supreme Court for it was alleged that the Fourteenth Amendment covered suffrage for women. But the court never interpreted the technicalities that would have transferred half the nation's sovereign power to women. The arguments which raged during the early 1890s were arguments of early republicanism. Such approaches were confronted with likewise timeworn rebuttals, including the suggestions that enfranchisement of women would result in the degradation of women and the unsexing of

---

16. *New York Times*, January 6, 1880, p. 9.
17. "Considering New Laws," *New York Times*, February 10, 1880, p. 4.
18. T. W. Wigginson, "Unsolved Problems in Women Suffrage," *Forum* 2439 (1886):2.

men.[19] When the right of Colorado women to vote on the federal level was proposed the Supreme Court answered "No." The experience of Colorado was cited:

Over two years elapsed between the original act of legislation conferring suffrage on women and the final decision that the act was void. During this time women had voted, held office, and served on juries. The experiment had thus received a considerable trial. After the territory was organized as a state, the question was submitted to the voters of the state. They had whatever light was afforded by the previous experiment; the provision proposed, extending suffrage to women, was defeated by ten thousand majority.[20]

More disappointments came. In Illinois the law of 1891 conferring school suffrage upon women was declared partly unconstitutional by the Supreme Court; the New York law of 1892 allowing women to vote for school commissioners was declared unconstitutional by the Court of Appeals; and in California in 1893, the governor vetoed the school suffrage bill on the ground of its unconstitutionality.

By the beginning of the twentieth century American women were living under rather different circumstances from those of their nineteenth century sisters. Even though the legal changes in their position had been uneven among the states, enough successes had been secured to encourage the organization of a league that corresponded to a "Militant Movement." This united effort incorporated a program of propaganda which eventually secured women's right to vote. The first point of this feminine propaganda was a constitution which was formulated on action which was clear, logical and aggressive. Briefly stated it consisted of:

1. The union of women of all shades of political thought and of all ranks of society on the single issue of their political enfranchisement.
2. Action independent of all the political parties of men.
3. The undivided attack on the government of the day, which, having the power to enfranchise women, omits to do it.[21]

Critically analyzing contemporary social issues, the militant women identified those they felt to be most menacing as:

1. Debasement of moral standards in politics and business.
2. Absorption by a few, at unwarrranted cost to many, of the common wealth.
3. Unreasonable and violent expression of resentment by the multitude.[22]

The propaganda policy they devised indicated that "the first duty is to educate the public and to popularize the issue. The second is to pressure the government into giving the woman the right to vote."[23] A further stage of the propaganda policy was the effort to make some promise for the future by showing the wrongs that had been committed by the male leaders in the past:

Power is the one thing men cannot continue to exercise morally. This is the reason why the kings and their favorites of olden times were so corrupt. They had the monopoly of power. It is the explanation now of the greed and graft and

19. Helen H. Gardener, "Shall Women Vote?" *Arena* 15 (April, 1893):67.
20. "Woman Suffrage in the West," *Outlook*, June 23, 1900, pp. 430-31.
21. Mrs. B. Borman Wells, "The Militant Movement for Women Suffrage," *The Independent*, April 23, 1908, pp. 901-3.
22. "The Necessity of Woman Suffrage," *North American Review* 183 (October 5, 1906):69.
23. Wells, "Militant Movement," p. 901.

corruption in political and commercial circles. And it indicates the reason also why the wickedness of men is worse than the badness of women. We do not have policemen to look after the mothers of families, nor the young ladies, nor the old maids, but we need them more particularly to take care of the men who have an instinct to get drunk and vote.[24]

The religious aspect of woman's suffrage bears note. Efforts were made to gain assistance for the cause by securing support from church leaders. The Rev. Madison Peters probably spoke for many clergymen when he said, "All the men and women shall be equal in freedom, and common fellowship is the message of the twentieth century."[25]

And so, by the end of the first decade of the twentieth century, although nineteen states had no form of suffrage, the women were able to point to some successes:

    4 states had equal suffrage
    2 states had municipal suffrage
  22 states had school suffrage
    2 states had tax paying suffrage
    3 states had school and tax paying suffrage.[26]

The final phase of the women's program was about to begin.

On May 4, 1912, ten thousand woman suffragists marched on parade in New York City. Despite the *New York Times'* dire prediction that "should women get the right to vote, they will play havoc with it for society and for themselves . . . if men are not firm enough to prevent them,"[27] the parade was instrumental in the creation of a national recognition of the suffrage movement's power.

By election day, November 3, 1912, further victories had been achieved. The women had engaged in active campaigns to publicize the relative values of women's votes. They brought to attention the states and countries where women were enfranchised and pointed out that men in those places generally considered the movement successful. With the help of such campaigners as Jane Adams, one of the most effective speakers for the suffrage cause, May Wright Seawell, honorary President of the International Council of Women, and Ada James, daughter of the senator who sponsored the initial suffrage bill, one and a half million women voters were added to an equal number of women who had already been entitled to cast their ballots that day. There were now ten states where women had the right to vote: Washington, Oregon, Idaho, Wyoming, Utah, Colorado, Kansas, Arizona, California, and Michigan.[28]

When the nation's women's clubs held a convention in Chicago in 1913 the principles of equality were endorsed by the group and the action was termed "the most important endorsement of women's suffrage in the history of the movement."[29] The events in Chicago began a series of legislative successes. Progress was made early in 1915 when the women of Chicago were allowed to vote in the city elections.[30] The movement continued to advance when seven more states adopted a resolution for a constitutional amendment granting woman

---

24. Mrs. L.H. Harris, "Woman and the Future," *The Independent* May 14, 1908, pp. 1090-91.
25. Madison Peters, "American Impressions," *The Independent*, April 23, 1908, p. 394.
26. Elsie Moore, "The Suffrage Question in the Far West," *Arena* 41 (July, 1909):414-19.
27. "10,000 Women March for Votes," *Literary Digest*, May 18, 1912, p. 41.
28. Ida Husted Harper, "Votes for Three Million Women," *Review of Reviews* 46 (December, 1912):739.
29. "Clubwomen for Suffrage," *Literary Digest*, July 4, 1913, p. 4.
30. "The Chicago Ladies Campaign," *Literary Digest*, May 1, 1915, p. 1038.

suffrage. In the fall of 1915, the resolution was submitted for approval to the people of four of the states—Massachusetts, New Jersey, New York, and Pennsylvania.[31]

One of the interesting developments of the period was the utilization of public opinion polls to determine the merits of the suffrage movement. Such a poll was taken by the *New York World* which surveyed the prominent business and professional men of the city. The results of this particular poll showed a strong majority against the issue; only clergymen and architects were in favor of enfranchisement. New York suffragists were not alarmed by the verdict, pointing out that it did not register the opinions of the workingmen; only those of the professional class. Said Mrs. Carrie Chapman Catt:

> Men are not enfranchised because they would make a better government, but because in common fairness each class must have a ballot [sic] share in determining the nature of the government for which and to which they were responsible. Some people have difficulty in seeing that there is a special woman's point of view that no man can represent. We shall never have a government that will represent all people equally until women have the vote.[32]

Another poll reflected the position of women in the state of New York toward suffrage. This tally showed that 75 percent of the women favored the vote for women, thus refuting a popular men's claim that women did not really want to vote. A church poll in Manhattan showed that 80 percent of its women members favored suffrage.[33]

The following year, 1916, was a relatively calm one in regard to the suffrage movement. However, in this year all of the major political parties in the country endorsed the suffrage movement, and in the 1916 elections the suffragists supported candidates who favored enfranchisement.[34] Toward the end of the year the Women's Suffrage Party began making plans for a hard fight in 1917. Included in their plans were further unification of the organization, conformity throughout the nation, careful appointment of efficient workers, and more campaigns out-of-doors.[35]

As the year 1917 advanced, so did the battle for enfranchisement. There were now fifteen states allowing women to vote. Then in April, the Rhode Island Senate gave its women the right to vote in presidential elections.[36] Within a month of this action, estimates showed that more than eight million women were qualified to vote in the next presidential election.[37] Late in the year some fifty workers and officers of the New York State Women's Suffrage Party went to the White House to urge President Wilson to try to persuade the general population to vote for women's suffrage, a request that he honored.[38] In fact, the president was greatly in favor of the enfranchisement. When a delegation headed by Mrs. Carrie Chapman Catt, President of the National Woman Suffrage Association, and

31. "New Women's Laws in Many States," *New York Times*, June 18, 1915, p. 5.
32. "Suffrage Leaders Unafraid of Poll," *New York Times*, April 27, 1915, p. 9.
33. "Woman Suffrage and the Church," *Literary Digest*, May 15, 1915, p. 1156.
34. "Suffrage Planks Not Enough," *Literary Digest*, July 1, 1916, p. 6.
35. "Suffragists Plan 1917 Fight," *New York Times*, November 22, 1916, p. 9.
36. "Favor Votes for Women," *New York Times*, April 12, 1917, p. 13.
37. "Woman Suffrage Marching On," *Literary Digest*, May 5, 1917, p. 1320.
38. "President Puts Suffrage to Fore," *New York Times*, October 26, 1917, p. 1.

Dr. Anna Howard Shaw, Honorary President, called at the White House, Wilson stated:

> . . . I welcome the opportunity to say that I agree without reservation that the full and sincere democratic reconstruction of the world for which we are striving, and which we are determined to bring about at any cost, will not have been completely or adequately attained until women are admitted to the suffrage, and that only by that action can the nations of the world release for the benefit of future generations the full ideal force of opinion or the full humane force of action.
>
> The service of women during this supreme crisis [World War I] of the world's history have been of the most signal usefulness and distinction. The war could not have been fought without them, or its sacrifice endured. It is high time that some part of our debt of gratitude to them should be acknowledged and paid, and the only acknowledgement they ask is their admission to the suffrage. Can we justly refuse it?
>
> As for America, it is my earnest hope that the Senate of the United States will give an unmistakable answer to this question by passing the suffrage amendment to our Federal Constitution before the end of the session.[39]

Later the President went before the Senate and urged the adoption of the Woman's Suffrage resolution as a war measure. After five days of debate the measure was defeated. Although the vote distribution showed that suffrage was not a party issue, the President had been unable to swing any votes. Upon hearing the outcome, Wilson expressed his concern by stating that the passage of this bill was vital to the winning of the war.[40] Debate on the issue was reopened but nothing was really accomplished. The suffragists did not expect the amendment to go before the Senate for another vote until after the November elections. They hoped that during those elections some candidates who favored suffrage would displace those senators who had voted against it. They expected a re-

versal of the decision with the new Congress.[41] Their expectations were soon realized. The Federal Amendment to the Constitution was passed by Congress on May 21, 1919.

The last phase of the struggle now shifted to state ratification. By the end of 1919, twenty-two states had ratified, but fourteen more had to give their approval before the three-fourths majority could be attained. The suffragists hoped to see ratification completed by February 1, 1920.

The National American Women's Suffrage Association met for the last time in December, 1919. The convention agenda included suggestions for providing the quick passage of state ratification. With victory in sight the women returned to those states which had not called special legislative sessions to consider the resolution.

On August 16, 1920, the Tennessee state legislature passed the amendment. Tennessee was the thirty-sixth state to voice approval; the amendment was now law. More then nine million women joined the 17.5 million women who had already been granted the right to vote through state enactments. The struggle for women's right to participate fully in Democracy's responsibilities was finally completed.

Suffrage: The Rhetorical Approach— Whatever the direct causes for the movement's success, it is doubtful whether such would have been accomplished without the tremendous efforts of the women orators. From the time Elizabeth Cady Stanton de-

---

39. "Wilson Spurs Fight for Woman's Vote," *New York Times*, June 14, 1918, p. 10.
40. "Wilson Makes Suffrage Appeal, but Senate Waits," *New York Times*, October 1, 1918, p. 1.
41. "The Suffragists Carry Fight to the Polls," *New York Times*, October 3, 1918, p. 12.

livered her first public address at Seneca Falls, New York, until the Amendment was passed, hundreds of women spoke incessantly for the cause at every possible location and in every situation. In their arguments, the majority of the speakers presented a myriad of facts, statistics, and methods of reasoning. They employed the use of direct reference, particularly quoting from the authorities of the times—Bible, Constitution, etc.

Perhaps the greatest barrier which the speakers had to overcome was the containing element of their so-called "appropriate sphere." Almost all of the material utilized in their speaking had to be that which was acceptable within this "sphere." The use of the rhetorical proofs, "ethos," "pathos," and "logos" was thus fashioned through an added condition. Because of this added element, the speakers were concerned with their own character, intelligence, and good will, always in relation to the public's granting recognition to woman's "sphere." They, likewise, employed pathetic and logical proofs based on the assumptions of what was considered moral and humane—thus, within their designated "sphere." But, as the years progressed the "appropriate sphere" of woman's position in society crumbled under the increased activity of suffrage speakers. With this change in attitude, the speakers sought to find sources for their arguments other than the home and church.

The new sources were, to be sure, of a varied nature. Nevertheless, no matter what sources were found, the logical arrangement of the material showed marked resemblances to the lines of argument as described by Aristotle in his *Rhetoric.* The most commonly used were those of definition, deduction, and induction, including cause and effect, generalization, analogy, authority, and reductio ad absurdum. The speakers utilized almost every phase of the Aristotelian standards; yet, it is doubtful as to whether or not this implementation was purposeful. What concerns the rhetorical critic is that the techniques "were" employed and that their use can be defined in the extant speeches.

The measuring of the oratorical effectiveness of these speeches, either separately or as a movement, is difficult to establish. To determine individual effectiveness of each is almost certainly not possible. The success of the speeches collectively can be equated with the success of the movement—women were eventually enfranchised. The speakers were the suffrage movement and its success was theirs. The hypothesis can be, then, that the rhetorical devices used by the suffragists in their speaking were effectively employed since the desired "response" was ultimately achieved. That they did use rhetorical devices is likewise obvious since Aristotle's principles are more than evidenced in the texts.

Some capsule statements can be made of the speakers of the movement of 1869-1919:

1. The dispositions of the various audiences changed as the movement progressed; greater respect was given to the women speakers as they proved their abilities to speak as well as demonstrated their responsible nature.

2. Two general approaches were taken by the suffragists (as represented by the two initially separate woman's suffrage organizations); the establishment of enfranchisement through recognition on a state basis, and through an amendment to the Federal Constitution (more of a national basis.

3. The speakers were not geared to achieve their goals by force, but were able to dem-

onstrate (in terms of numbers) the ready support that was slowly coming to their side.

4. The movement was, for the women speakers, a representative effort conducted along the principles upon which the government had been founded; they saw in their efforts a culmination of the declarations of democracy.

5. The movement for woman suffrage was concurrently performed with other reform movements and many of the speakers were involved in handling dual roles: (a) accomplishing suffrage, and (b) achieving certain humanitarian and reform responsibilities not inconsistent with the need for woman's enfranchisement.

6. The sources of ideas which were incorporated in the speeches were as unlimited as the ingenuities of the women who voiced them.

7. There was effective utilization of ethics, emotion and logic in the rhetorical methods of the speakers.

8. The nature of ethical proof was such that the speakers were ever aware of the social conditions which had preceded the movement and/or which were constantly shifting as the movement continued.

9. The nature of the emotional proofs was such that no criticism suggesting that the speakers were hypersensitive, high strung, or unable to control themselves upon a rational basis could be substantiated.

10. The methods by which the speakers reasoned (logical proof) were conducive to the rules of logic, rarely representing idle thoughts poorly expressed or substantiated; close out statements were not the general pattern, but were instead ideas supported completely with examples, illustrations, comparisons, etc.

11. Little pattern development for the speakers' ideas can be determined other than that they were quick to posit the initial purpose of their task: suffrage and their individual interpretation of its meaning.

12. The "invention" of the women speakers was a responsible approach to rhetoric and their speaking represented an able contribution to oratory.

The general campaign for the woman suffrage in America has long been ended. The rhetorical invention which represented the agitation, organizing, education, pleading, and persuading has been the subject for this study. No more will the arguments voiced by these women be heard. They had succeeded in securing that which they believed to be their inalienable right: political enfranchisement.

In the struggle to achieve that right, women had some unusual experiences. They learned what may be termed strange things, particularly about the American political system. The authoritative history of woman suffrage fills six volumes; hundreds of individual stories make up pages upon pages in history texts, biographies, and relative works; and endless articles appear in a wide range of periodicals.

Prohibition

Abuses of overindulgence in alcoholic beverages have a long history in the English heritage of America. The close association of "strong drink" with serious personal and social problem situations has generally been an admitted issue. Most often women and children took the brunt of the impact of the husband's heavy drinking. It was thus natural that the American woman and wife would spearhead the drive for control of strong drink. This movement lead not to control but to the legal prohibition of the sale of liquor in the adoption of the Eighteenth Amendment.

Temperance: Background—As with the issue of woman suffrage, the motives which drove speakers to speak out so violently against strong drink also had their roots in colonial times. The earliest legislation passed by the colonials was against the "fire water" of the Indians. Laws were invoked to prevent sale of intoxicants to Indians and to prevent a public display of drunkenness on the part of the white man. However, these laws were often the subject of much controversy. In 1644 the County of Pennsylvania ordered that since "it is not fit to deprive the Indians of any lawful comforts which God alloweth to all men by the use of wine" those who were licensed to retail wines were permitted to sell it to the red men. Massachusetts in the same year followed the example of Pennsylvania. In 1649 Rhode Island granted a license to Roger Williams permitting him to sell wine or "strong water" to the Indians.[42]

The economic argument against the use of intoxicants caused the Massachusetts colony to forbid the sale of such beverages to servants and apprentices. But most of the early colonial legislation was directed to regulation of the consumer rather than the seller. Among such provisions were the prohibition of sale to persons under stated ages, the limitation of the amounts which could be sold to one person, and the closing of inns and public houses at fixed times. As early as 1650 the liquor traffic was taxed for revenue purposes. In that year, the Connecticut colony levied an excise tax on liquors manufactured in the colony and a duty on imported liquors.[43]

The most significant legislation directed against the beverage liquor traffic during the colonial period was that in Georgia, where Governor Oglethorpe on his arrival in 1763 decreed that the importation of ardent spirits was illegal. The following year he secured from the Counsellors of Georgia

prohibition for the importation of rum. Oglethorpe also persuaded the English Parliament in 1775 to prohibit the importation of spirits by the colony, but this was revoked in the following year. A few years later Georgia enacted a law providing that no liquor license should be granted to followers of certain named trades "who should be capable of getting a livelihood by honest labor and industry."[44]

The licensing system came into use early. In 1663 the Massachusetts Bay Colony provided that liquor could not be sold without the Governor's official permit. This policy was later changed to provide for the issuance of licenses by the court. The sale of liquor in New York was limited to company stores, and in Connecticut the sale was limited to certain persons. The first saloon in America was opened in Boston in 1625, and the first brewery built in Massachusetts by a Captain Sedgwick in 1637.

The first definite action against the use of distilled spirits in the newly formed United States occurred in 1777 when the war board of the Continental Congress circulated among the troops a pamphlet setting forth scientific reasons why not to use liquor. General George Washington had previously, on March 25, 1776, in orders issued at Cambridge, Massachusetts, urged the officers of the Continental Army to prevent the soldiers from the frequent danger of tipping-houses. Various colonies had provided for the issue of rum in the rations for the troops, but after this order from Washington, the states generally substi-

---

42. Frances Willard, *Glimpses of Fifty Years. The Autobiography of An American Woman* (Chicago: Women's Temperance Publ. Assn., 1889), p. 57.
43. Foster R. Dulles, "Temperance in the United States," *Arena* 3 (January, 1899):321.
44. Willard, *Glimpses*, p. 324.

tuted beer for distilled liquors in the daily ration. On September 20, 1776, the Continental Congress forbade the sale of liquor of any kind to soldiers. Largely as a war measure, Congress appealed to the various colonial legislatures to prohibit the distilling of grain.[45]

During the years that followed the individual appeals toward temperance became identified with a determined, almost fanatical movement. The strength of the movement was largely derived from the rural areas of the country where a puritanical attitude still prevailed. It was these forces, allied through careful organization, which the women brought to bear against the problems created by the city saloon.

The Anti-Saloon League, the Women's Christian Temperance Union, and the Temperance Society of the Methodist Church remained in the forefront of this campaign. Under zealous and untiring leadership, dedicated members of these groups worked unceasingly to arouse public opinion to the necessity of outlawing the liquor trade. Drinking was held to be responsible for the degradation of municipal politics, the vicious life of the slums, and the country's high rate of industrial accidents. The saloon itself was luridly depicted as the source of all evil in what was becoming a degenerate urban society.[46]

The movement, gathering as it did, so much support from the rural church-going element of the population, did not entirely fit into the pattern of the more general reforms associated with the "progressive efforts" of the late nineteenth century. According to Richard Hofstadter:

It was linked not merely to an aversion to drunkenness and to the evils that accompanied it, but to the immigrant drinking masses, to the pressures and amenities of city life, and to the well-to-do classes and cultivated men. It was carried about America by the rural-evangelical virus: ,the country Protestant frequently brought it with him to the city when the contraction of agriculture sent him there to seek his livelihood.[47]

But this is only part of the story. In the South large landholders favored prohibition to keep liquor from their Negro farm hands; in the North manufacturers similarly sought to protect themselves from employee drinking problems. There was also a conservative urban element which did not necessarily feel very strongly about drinking itself, but was ready to support any movement which would do away with the recognized evils of the old-time saloons which were so often directly owned or controlled by the brewery interests.

The advocates of prohibition often had a dogmatic, intolerant attitude toward moderate drinkers that had not characterized the proponents of temperance. They gave a highly moralistic tone to their campaign, but were never greatly concerned over the means they employed to stamp out the liquor traffic. The Anti-Saloon League in particular was guilty of using its position to intimidate candidates for public office.

Working tirelessly, the prohibitionists succeeded in having their way in state after state. By the turn of the twentieth century, some twenty-six states had anti-saloon laws in one form or another, and thirteen were absolutely dry. A federal law, the Webb-Kenyon Act, was passed in 1913 forbidding the transportation of liquor into states where its sale was illegal.

45. Foster R. Dulles, *The United States Since 1812* (Ann Arbor, Mich.: University of Michigan Press 1924), p. 78.
46. Willard, *Glimpses*, p. 375.
47. Richard Hofstadter, *The Age of Reform* (New York: Alfred Knopf, 1955), p. 143.

However, it was only after World War I that final victory for prohibition was won. At that time the charge went up that prohibition was something that had been "put over" on the country while the nation was absorbed by larger issues, and while the men were overseas. Little acknowledgement was given to the tremendous momentum gained for the movement during the long struggle of the previous century, much of which had been accomplished through the women's platform.

Temperance: The Rhetorical Approach— Three women orators were outstanding among the many speakers and lecturers, men and women, who took to the platform on the issue of prohibition: Frances Willard, Susan B. Anthony, and Carrie Nation.

Frances E. Willard was born September 28, 1839, in Churchville, New York. Churchville was a fine example of the puritanical little settlements which abhorred such worldly amusements as card playing, dancing, and the theater. The town fathers proudly boasted that there was never a profane word heard in their sinless little community.[48] Frances's home in Churchville, and later in Oberlin, Ohio, and Janesville, Wisconsin, was strongly religious. "The opportunities that came to the children . . . were opportunities to be useful: to read, to study, to work with their hands, to love each other, and to be most reverent to nature and nature's God."[49] It is of interest to note that while they were living in Ohio, Frances' mother enrolled in Oberlin College where she was active in a Rhetorical Society organized for "mutual protection."[50]

Very early in life the Willard children were made to sign an abstinence pledge cut from a popular magazine and pasted in the family Bible. Each child's signature was preceded by the signature of the parents. Frances seemingly lived this childhood pledge for her entire life:

A pledge we make, no wine to take,
Nor brandy red that turns the head,
Nor fiery rum that ruins the home,
Nor whiskey hot that makes the sot,
Nor brewer's beer, for that we fear,
And cider, too, will never do;
To quench our thirst we'll look to bring
Cold water from the well or spring.
So here we pledge perpetual hate
To all that can intoxicate.[51]

Miss Willard had a highly successful career as an educator before she entered the field of temperance work. She graduated from Northwestern Female College, Evanston, Illinois, and taught at that school. She accepted the presidency of the Evanston College for Ladies in 1871, and when it merged with Northwestern University in 1873 she was named Dean of Women there.

In 1874 Miss Willard resigned her post as Dean and became corresponding secretary of the National Women's Christian Temperance Union. In 1879 she was elected president and held the office until her death.

The first public mention of her aspiration toward a worldwide organization of Christian women was made in 1875, in a paper called *Our Union*, the official organ of the National Women's Christian Temperance Union. The next autumn in a convention address, Miss Willard placed her idea

---

48. Mary Earhart, *Frances Willard: From Prayers to Politics* (Chicago: University of Chicago Press, 1944), p. 24.
49. *Ibid.*, p. 103.
50. Willard, *Glimpses*, p. 34.
51. Anna A. Gordon, *Frances E. Willard* (Chicago: W.C.T.U., 1898), p. 32.

before her fellow members. Mrs. Mary Clement Leavitt, of Boston, Massachusetts, was given an opportunity to make a reconnaissance tour around the world, gathering support from women of all nations. The results of this tour were drawn up in the now famous Polygot Petition for Home Protection.

The document was written in Miss Willard's workshop in Evanston, Illinois, in 1884, and first presented in Washington, D.C., February 15, 1895. At this time Miss Willard spoke for several hours as seven thousand people listened intently at Convention Hall. Her speech provided a complete history of the petition and its seven million signatures.[52] The talk was directed to "the government of the world, collectively and severally." It was recorded and translated into many languages and circulated throughout the world. The entire list of signatures was presented to each government. By virtue of the petition the W.C.T.U. intended to bring to the entire world the American woman's concern for the alcohol and opium traffic.

Miss Willard's work in reform quite naturally led her into politics and she joined the national Prohibition Party and exerted great influence in its executive council. It is impossible to separate her work for prohibition from her interest in woman's suffrage. It was a time in history when the two areas were concurrent, and accordingly judged together. Women leaders saw that by securing political rights they would gain the power to attack many of the evils besetting their homes.

Miss Willard was aware of ethical proofs since such concepts were directly part of her character and background. Perhaps two aspects predominate: her religious beliefs and her concern for humanity.

Susan Brownell Anthony's personal background did much to affect her actions and ideas concerning temperance just as did Miss Willard's. Susan was born into a Quaker family on February 15, 1820, near Adams, Massachusetts, and her Quaker environment provided guidelines when she ventured into the "outside world."

While teaching at Canajoharie, N.Y., she became involved with a "Daughters of Temperance" society and gave her first public speech at a meeting of one of these unions.[53] Her moderate success here coupled with an interest in becoming involved in the suffrage movement, prompted Miss Anthony to speak at a New York State Teachers' Convention. "We are told that a bombshell would not have created greater commotion. For the first time a woman's voice was heard in a teacher's convention. Every neck was craned, and a profound hush fell upon the assembly."[54]

Immediate reactions to her demands for equal pay and freedom of speech for all women belonging to the organization were mixed. In fact, the boldness of her move alienated many women from her cause; many were suspicious of her early efforts, regarding them as too avant-garde.

Throughout the course of her career, Miss Anthony spoke in almost every state and territory of the Union. She spoke without manuscript or notes and often the only inspiration she needed was a makeshift audience. Even in the most hectic situations her strong contralto voice could be heard

---

52. *Ibid.*, p. 147.
53. Alma Lutz, *Susan B. Anthony: Rebel, Crusader, Humanitarian* (Boston: Beacon Press, 1959), p. 5.
54. "The Strenuous Life of a Woman Reformer," *Current Literature* 40 (May, 1906):492.

clearly by audiences of several thousand. She used a strongly argumentative style and carried conviction by the lucid and intense reasoning which she combined with an acute sense of earnestness. She disliked the limitation of writing, but realized its power and gave considerable time and labor to printed rhetoric.[55]

Most notable (probably notorious) among temperance speakers was Carrie Nation. She launched here career by becoming a very active participant in the local W.C.T.U. in Medicine Lodge, Kansas. There were seven "joints," as she called them, operating in the town and this gave her great concern. "She became determined to rid not only Kansas, but the world of the places, which she regarded as dens of vice and breeders of sin and misery."[56]

After being elected president of the New Barara County chapter of the W.C.T.U., Carrie began to crusade on her own against the evil of alcohol. She dug up an old organ and serenaded the various saloons, choosing the W.C.T.U. battle songs which were not calculated to fill her listeners with cheer. Yet, by and large, she was then considered "just a character." Thus, she decided on a stronger course of action. She entered the first saloon! The proprietor, Mart Strong, seized her by the shoulders and cried, "Get out of here you crazy woman!" But Carrie brushed him aside and raised her voice in lusty song:

Who hath sorrow? Who hath all woe?
They who dare not answer no,
They whose feet to sin incline
While they tarry at the wine.
They who tarry at the wine cups,
They have sorrow; they have sorrow.
They who tarry at the wine cups,
They have woe.[57]

Emboldened, Carrie invaded other joints, and other women, inflamed by her wailings and infected with her savage zeal, followed her. The populace of Medicine Lodge began to grow uneasy. In Henry Durst's place she threw herself on her knees and prayed long and hysterically, and informed him that he was going to hell. Her "hatcheting" attacks on the saloons followed in the inevitable encouragement that success brought. Her saloon smashings were spectacular events and drew large crowds of viewers to experience the glamour and excitement. Whether these people endorsed her actions or not, she drew them to the scene. She thus succeeded in keeping the temperance cause before the public, a tactic of which was extremely important to the cause's ultimate success.

Most of her early speeches were given on the steps of a saloon, and she became very effective as a mob speaker. She developed a question and answer technique which would bring the crowd to quick acceptance of her forthcoming actions, smashing the saloon:

Look children! What is that place?
A hell hole! (sometimes the crowd
                would respond)
What else?
What do they sell there?
Hell-broth and devil soup!
What do they do?
They murder souls!
What must we do to such a place?
Smash it![58]

_____
55. Ida H. Harper, *Life and Work of Susan B. Anthony* (New York: Bowen-Merrill, 1898), Appendix.
56. Stewart H. Holbrook, "The Times of Miss Willard and Mrs. Nation," *Dreamers of the American Dream* (New York: Doubleday, 1957), p. 95.
57. J.L. Dwyer, "Lady with the Hatchet," *American Mercury*, March, 1929, p. 31.
58. Herbert Asbury, *The Great Illusion* (Westport, Connecticut: Greenwood, 1968), p. 230.

Such a catechism illustrated her most effective technique. The use of repetitious questions in which the mob could take part was rooted in her childhood experiences with the Negro revivals and proved extremely useful in approaching her audiences.

On February 21, 1901, Carrie began publication of her own temperance paper. Her aim was to keep the public informed of temperance achievements and to enlist followers. The *Smashers Mail* contained many editorials written by Carrie. They were long rambling dissertations on the liquor traffic with an occasional shrewd comment on government or politics buried in a mass of violent objurgations. The bulk of the paper's content was composed of letters and poems which were sent in by the desperate women of the United States. The paper eventually achieved a rather wide circulation and succeeded in adding new fuel to keep the temperance fires burning.

This was the period of the great social reformers. The speakers found, however, that their greatest problem lay in reaching the public. They could gain support in small areas through their speeches, but without any modern devices for mass communication, it was necessary for them to speak at every possible opportunity in order to establish any depth of support. Thus when Carrie was approached by James E. Furlough, who proposed a tour of the Chautauqua circuits and a series of speeches in New York and other eastern cities she accepted. She was warned, however, not to bring her hatchet because liquor was legal in many of the states in which she would be speaking.

Mrs. Nation started her lecture tour in Chicago where she received a very cold reception; even the mayor refused to see her. In New York she appeared at Carnegie Hall where she gave a speech attacking women's fashions, including the wearing of corsets. In Washington, she tried to gain an interview with the President, but Roosevelt refused to see her. Carrie promptly raised a commotion by publicly denouncing the President and calling him a bloodthirsty, cigarette-smoking rummy.

In the following months of that summer after the episode in Washington, Sister Carrie lectured, argued, fought and was arrested. In November she reached Cleveland. Here she held a public exhibition of smashing a keg of beer and issued her "Four Rules for Longevity":

1. If you would live long, walk past twenty saloons a day.
2. If you must pour liquor, pour it down the sewer.
3. Don't chew tobacco unless you prefer to take your food predigested at forty.
4. Drink all the water you want, whenever you want.[59]

Carrie reached and enlisted her supporters through speeches and news publicity. Her calls were basically appeals to the women of the nation whose lives had been made miserable by the evils of drink. These appeals, oftentimes violent in tone, were geared to the emotions.

Often she sought the aid of the children:

My precious little children: I send you greeting and ask you to help me destroy that which is on the streets and protected by the police and the city officials to destroy you my darlings. I want every one of you little ones to grab up a rock and smash the glass doors and windows of these hell holes. You will do your duty and enroll your name on the pages of undying fame, and place yourself on the side of God and humanity.[60]

---

59. Dwyer, "Lady," p. 327.
60. Asbury, *Great Illusion*, p. 162.

Carrie Nation was more or less a self-styled speaker. The reforms for which she campaigned were the results of her personal experiences and for this reason she saw all from a personal point of view and with scarcely anything but emotion. As a speaker she tended to be ranting, chaotic, abusive, and at times quite ridiculous. Her effectiveness usually lay in the fact that her points of view concerning her subject were shared by the crowd to which she was speaking—most of which shared them on a personal basis. Even so, Carrie Nation had a way of talking which aroused people to follow her, often those who had previously been opposed to her position. Wherever she spoke large crowds gathered to listen. She had her own idiom of well-worn catch words and remarks which underscored the vigor of life.

Her speeches were vituperative, egocentric, prohibitive, mystical and violent. Carrie Nation's rhetoric was reflective of her childhood. . . . Her poor schooling and deeply religious background were the most exemplified.[61]

Public recognition did not come immediately for Carrie Nation, neither did the recognition from the temperance groups. It was not until the Topeka W.C.T.U. presented her with a gold medal that public approval came. This gained her more support and some of the other temperance unions began to employ her "smashing" tactics as their own.

"Publicity was Carrie Nation's most important contribution to the cause of prohibition. It inspired similarly obsessed women, it compelled almost immediately a noticeable tightening of law enforcement and it was responsible for the passage of many new regulatory statutes."[62]

"Prohibition owes as much to Carrie Na-tion as to any other agent of God, male or female, clerical or lay."[63] She was the chief architect of that ill-considered phase of American life that brought this country to so much misery, crime, and gangsterism. "Carrie's extraordinary methods did more to effect the enforcement of prohibition laws than had been accomplished in twenty years by the ineffectual campaign of churches and temperance organization."[64] Her sensational saloon hatchetation lured large crowds of the curious to witness her antics. Some stayed to help or to cheer, but whether the crowds agreed with her or not is not of great moment. She did keep the temperance movement in the news, a very necessary ingredient to the final victory of her cause.

The adoption and repeal of Prohibition in the United States are best understood in the larger movement of temperance and as part of American social reform. Prohibition and temperance developed, remained and declined in relation to the general framework of public opinion and social conflict concerning drinking in American culture. While the word "temperance" suggests moderate usage, it became identified with abstinence during the second quarter of the nineteenth century. In the early development of the antialcohol movement in the United States, the objective was temperate use and not abstinence. While the objective of abstinence became dominant the name temperance remained with organizations and came to be a general label for the anti-alcohol movement. But it was one thing to

61. S. Young, "American Don Quixote," *New Republic*, November 23, 1932, p. 7.
62. Asbury, *Great Illusion*, p. 213.
63. Dwyer, "Lady," p. 31.
64. Asbury, *Great Illusion*, p. 94.

have passed the Eighteenth Amendment and quite another to gain compliance with it. Laws which operate against segments of the population with strong counter-sentiments can seldom expect complete compliance. The extent of the enforcement of Prohibition is a matter of considerable debate. What can be said with some certainty is that, especially in urban areas, it was far from obeyed nor was it enforced.

How much alcoholic consumption occurred during the years of the Eighteenth Amendment is open to question. There is more agreement that illegal manufacture and sales of liquor went on in the United States on a large scale, especially after 1923. In general, Prohibition was enforced wherever the population was sympathetic to it. In the larger cities where sentiment was strongly opposed to Prohibition enforcement was much weaker than in rural areas and small towns.

In the configuration of values characteristic of American middle classes, self-mastery, industry, thrift, and moral conduct have been signs of the attainments of prized character traits. Self-denial has been viewed as a necessary step to the achievement of social and economic success. Drunkenness and indulgence are signs of unethical conduct because they are signs of a lack of personal control. The rural native American of the nineteenth century respected temperance ideals. Sobriety was virtuous and in a community dominated by the middle class, it was necessary to social acceptance and self-esteem. As American life began to change with the advent of urbanization and the influx of immigrants these values were challenged. Prohibition demonstrated for a while at least the dominance which was reflected in abstinence. As contemporary America became far more oriented toward different values of leisure and self-indulgence, the old standards were quickly eliminated and/or modified. The issue of temperance lasted only so long as the moral fiber of society considered it worthy of discussion. The present day finds it discussed only as an analogy to what society now considers greater ills.

Conclusion

It was to take nearly a generation before the country discovered that Prohibition had created more evils and dangers than it had prevented. Carrie Nation's offspring was not merely nonuse of alcohol; it was a host of other monsters: the speakeasy, the hip flask, secret drinking and immoralities of all kinds, lawbreaking, bootlegging, and the rise of organized crime and gangsterism on a level never before considered imaginable.

Prohibition rhetoric was temporarily victorious, but its success brought unforseen evils, clearly indicating that a law violating basic values of a democratic people cannot long endure. Prohibition rhetoric had cleverly identified its plan with God, home, motherhood, and patriotism but had failed to examine carefully the cause-effect relationships in its indictments. After a year or two of prohibition with prohibition rhetoric silent, the general public began to realize that they had been sold a faulty solution to an admitted problem. Repeal brought a halt to prohibition and called forth a new effort to control the abuses of alcohol through sales licensing procedures.

The concept behind women's suffrage, on the other hand, continues to find fulfillment in our society. The passage of the Nineteenth Amendment brought the enfranchisement of some 26 million women of voting age.[65] What effect all of this had upon the nation as a whole is hard to determine. Certainly, few, if any, of the promised or threatened events actually did materialize. The fears of the "antis" were never quite substantiated. Women divided along party lines, voted, not in blocks, but rather according to the issues.

For several years the issue of equality was satisfied with enfranchisement. Today the interpretation of that issue has given rise to the woman's liberation movement which refocuses the issue for yet additional changes. The old arguments continue! However, the success is defined as "total equality" with men, a condition much more difficult to identify than political responsibility. Through this movement American society continues to move to free its citizenry from restraints, legal, traditional, or societal that restrict fulfillment of each individual. No doubt the struggle for recognition of full personhood and citizenship for American women will continue until unbelievers, both male and female, are converted.

BIBLIOGRAPHY

Asbury, Herbert. *The Great Illusion.* 1950. Reprint. Westport, Connecticut: Greenwood, 1968.

An "informal" yet complete history of prohibition.

Davis, Paulina Wright. *A History of the National Woman's Rights Movement.* 1871. Reprint. New York: Collectors Editions, Ltd., 1970.

Reports of meetings and speeches of the early movement leaders.

Krout, John A. *The Origins of Prohibition.* 1925. Reprint. New York: Russell and Russell, 1967.

An excellent summary of the early days of the movement.

Lee, Henry. *How Dry We Were: Prohibition Revisited.* Englewood Cliffs, N.J.: Prentice-Hall, 1963.

A complete review of the "dry" era in American history.

Stanton, Elizabeth Cady; Anthony, Susan B.; Gage, Matilda J.; and Harper, Ida H. *History of Woman's Suffrage.* 6 vols. 1881. Reprint. New York: Collectors Editions, Ltd., 1971.

A collection of personal reflections, articles, news clippings, speeches, and letters.

Willard, Frances. *Glimpses of Fifth Years. The Autobiography of an American Woman.* 1889. Reprint. New York: Collectors Editions, Ltd., 1970.

The autobiography which describes the total development of the W.C.T.U.

---

65. Eleanor Flexner, *Century of Struggle* (Cambridge: Harvard University Press, 1959), p. 324.

17 Modernists and Fundamentalists Debate Restraints on Freedom, 1910-1930

Allan H. Sager

Religionist Sherwood Eddy wrote out of the mid-twenties, "Today literally everything is challenged and questioned—God, man, the soul, the mind, personality, religion, morality, marriage, the church, the state, the social order. Whatever else it is, ours is not an 'age of faith.' Doubts are raised in every branch of study and every area of life."[1]

"Every branch of study and every area of life" is hardly manageable as a research topic to be encompassed within a single chapter. Then what arena might one cast prime focus on in order to epitomize the conflicting currents of thought and the basic issues in debate during the times? J. Gresham Machen, a leading proponent of Presbyterian conservatism, provides directive counsel when he says that if the presumption of the age is that every inheritance from the past must be subject to searching criticism, "then no institution is faced by a stronger hostile presumption than the institution of the Christian religion, for no institution has based itself more squarely upon the authority of a by-gone age."[2]

Accordingly, this study focuses primarily upon that clash in the religious arena which has come to be called "the funda-mentalist-modernist controversy" as an illustration of the conflict over traditional restraints on individual freedom which so rocked the first third of the twentieth century.

The fundamentalist-modernist controversy, which has been christened the nation's most spectacular quarrel on religious doctrine, involved an aggressive conservative movement within almost every major Protestant denomination in the United States against liberal elements within the churches and against certain scientific or secular interests—notably evolution—in American civilization. In the former sphere, fundamentalists attempted by credal definition and imposition to exclude from the churches, and particularly from the control of their educational and missionary institutions, those whose pilgrimage of faith was leading them away from the traditional expression of entire bodies of teachings and practices which had long

---

1. Sherwood Eddy, *New Challenges to Faith* (New York: George H. Doran Company, 1926), p. 212.
2. J. Gresham Machen, *Christianity and Liberalism* (New York: Macmillan, 1923), p. 4.

been regarded as sacrosanct and unchanging. Liberals fought for an inclusive fellowship while seeking to refashion Christianity in the interests of freedom, vitality, and relevancy. Evolution with its philosophical premise of inevitable progress represented a threat of paramount proportions to the fundamentalists. For most of them the logic of the evolutionary hypothesis seemed to demand recognition that man's dignity lay in his rise from brute ancestry, an admission damning to their understanding of the biblical account of creation and thus calling into question the factual reliability of the Bible, their authoritative handbook on all subjects.[3]

Points at issue were ostensibly theological. The "Five Points" regarded as the *sine qua non* of fundamentalism were the infallibility of the Bible, Jesus' Virgin Birth, his Substitutionary Atonement, his Resurrection, and his Second Coming. But at a deeper level, the base of the conflict was more epistemological than theological. The fundamentalist-modernist controversy was a debate over the question of what constitutes authority in the Christian religion.

A reporter of the *American Review*, John M. Mecklin, illustrated the primacy of the question of authority by depicting the manner in which the fundamentalists approached it:

It is in its idea of authority . . . that Fundamentalism finds itself most at variance with our modern culture. The seat of authority for the Fundamentalist lies outside the individual and is independent of the social order in which he lives. It is supernatural, bookish and other-worldly. Its sanction is found in the miracles of an infallibly inspired Bible. Mingled with this supernatural authoritarianism is undoubtedly the feeling that authority in some form is necessary to the survival and effective operation of institutional Christianity. Without authoritative creeds and forms—no effective leadership, no successful training and discipline in

Christian character, no certainty of belief, no spirit of reverence, no salvation from sin.[4]

Joseph Leighton, professor of philosophy at Ohio State University, similarly reflected, "Fundamentalism . . . is a movement to preserve the absolute authority of the traditional cosmology and historiography, because this authority is believed to be indispensable to the preservation of the authority or supremacy of the Christian scheme of conduct and religion."[5]

Rejecting the principle of external authority, modernists such as Harry Emerson Fosdick and William Pierson Merrill declared their willingness to "trust wholeheartedly in spirit."[6]

Thus, a grave cleavage threatened Protestantism in America. Albert C. Dieffenbach, prominent Unitarian champion of religious liberty, described the fray as "two spiritual worlds, irreconcilable, met in inevitable collision. Nothing like it [has] been seen in

---

3. This study is based upon research completed for the writer's doctoral dissertation, "The Fundamentalist-Modernist Controversy, 1918-1930, in the History of American Public Address," (Northwestern University, 1963). Some of the research findings were highlighted in the thirteenth chapter of *Preaching in American History*, ed. DeWitte Holland (Nashville: Abingdon Press, 1969).

4. John M. Mecklin, "The Challenge of Fundamentalism," *American Review* 2, no. 5 (September-October, 1924); 482.

5. Joseph Alexander Leighton, *Religion and the Mind of To-Day* (New York: D. Appleton, 1924), pp. 21-23.

6. See the editorial, "What Is a Modernist?" *The Presbyterian* 94, no. 6 (February, 1924). Fosdick, credited with being "Modernism's Moses," is quoted as having said, "An external and inerrant authority in matters of religion is one of the historic curses of religion." To Merrill is ascribed these words, "Protestantism must frankly and fully abandon the whole notion of external authority. . . ."

Christendom in four hundred years."[7] Machen epitomized the momentousness of the basic issues in conflict when he declared:

The differences between fundamentalism and modernism are not mere surface differences which can be amiably waved aside or disregarded, but they are foundation differences, structural differences, amounting in their radical dissimilarity almost to the differences between two distinct religions. . . . Two world-views, two moral ideals, two sets of personal attitudes have clashed, and it is a case of ostrichlike intelligence blindly to deny and evade the searching and serious character of the issue. Christianity, according to fundamentalism, is one religion. Christianity, according to modernism, is another religion. . . . Christianity is hardly likely to last much longer half-fundamentalist and half-modernist. It is not merely the aggressiveness of fundamentalism that is forcing a choice, it is the inherent nature of the issue itself.[8]

Suddenly religion became newsworthy. News of the controversy was regularly bannered in the great metropolitan dailies and received repeated commentary in popular periodicals of the day such as *The Century Magazine*, *The World's Work*, *The Literary Digest*, *The American Mercury*, *The New Republic*, *North American Review*, and *The Forum*. O.E. Brown, claiming to make a "calm survey of modernism," suggested how widespread was concern over the controversy when he stated that "as never before, we may safely say, the religious questions are being discussed in all places where men get together, and being discussed as well by men of all types. There is virtually no agency that is meant to contribute to the molding of our more serious public mind that is not devoting time and space to the problem of Modernism."[9]

Illustrative of the widespread interest in the issue being controverted was the public reaction to the Straton-Potter debates of 1923-24. *The Christian Century* sketched it best: "The debate between Dr. John Roach Straton and Dr. Charles Francis Potter, Baptist and Unitarian clergymen, respectively, has gathered a ringside equalled only by national pugilistic contests. The next debate is to be held next week, and for this occasion reporters have engaged 100 seats. The debate is considered of such national importance that it will be broadcast by WJZ, the station of the Radio Corporation of America."[10] The first debate of the series, on the proposition that the Bible is infallible, was held in December of 1923 in the Fifth Avenue Baptist Church, New York City. The large auditorium was filled to overflowing and there were hundreds unable to gain admission. The second debate on evolution was set for Carnegie Hall. The Associated Press sent out a 2,500 word story on the first debate to more than two thousand newspapers throughout the United States, and an examination of the files of these papers indicates that in a very large number of instances they used the material sent. The Hearst syndicate played up the debates to 15 million readers. Thousands of listeners east of the Mississippi heard the debates by radio. The reporter for *The Christian Century* concluded: "These various publicity enterprises are carrying the issues of the two ministers to

7. Albert C. Dieffenbach, *Religious Liberty, the Great American Illusion* (New York: William Morrow and Company, 1927), pp. 63-64. Dieffenbach, often somewhat an alarmist, was hardly exaggerating when he declared, "Today is the most militant time in religion since Luther's day."

8. Ned B. Stonehouse, *J. Gresham Machen, A Biographical Memoir* (Grand Rapids: Eerdmans, 1955), p. 366. This section is a reprint from an article written by Machen for the January 3, 1924, issue of *Christian Century.*

9. O.E. Brown, "Modernism: A Calm Survey," *The Methodist Quarterly Review* 74, no. 3 (July, 1925):388.

10. "The Straton-Potter Debates," *Christian Century* January, 1924, p. 120.

the remote corners of the country and setting tongues to wagging in the most distant
Main street of the nation."[11]

The Controversy in Historical Perspective

William Warren Sweet's insistence that theology and theological unrest are directly
conditioned by the times affords a rationale for this section. In 1930 he wrote:

At no period in the history of American Christianity has there been more rapid change in the theological scene than has been witnessed within the past
generation. The principal reason for this fact is the
radical revolutionary changes which have been taking place in the whole political, economic, social
and religious climate of the world. For after all,
theology is not final truth handed down from
above, but grows out of man's condition; it comes
out of a human background.[12]

Sweet's thesis calls for a brief review of
that "human background" and the "radical
revolutionary changes" which took place in
"the whole political, economic, social and
religious climate" of the post World War I
American scene.

In his informal historical excursion
through the twenties, Paul Sann, a sensitive
chronicler, used the fittingly descriptive title, *The Lawless Decade.*[13] And lawless it
was, as social, civil, criminal, political, and
moral laws stood largely ineffectual before
a new preoccupation with self-expression.
Liquor—good, fair, bad, or deadly—flowed
freely between Armistice and Repeal, carrying with it a tide of iconoclasm. Barriers
of tradition and custom fell. People were
no longer willing to allow their operation of
business, government, or church to be inhibited by the restraining hand of the past.
Thousands of returning doughboys flecked
off the confetti of victory parades and
marched to new conquests which earlier

Victorian morals had forbidden. They were
able to pack away their heroes' khakies, but
were neither able nor willing to box away
the new cosmopolitan spirit born on a
myriad of fronts around the world. Tightly
reasoned provincial notions had become taboo to them. Having risked their lives to
make the world safe for democracy, they
were now ready to "find" life by risking the
safety of past customs and conventions.

The adage, "A penny saved is a penny
earned," may have paid safe and sure divi-
dends at the interest window before the
war, but it was neither big nor daring
enough for the twenties. The bull market
on Wall Street, inflated credit, and boundless commercial romanticism afforded a
treasure hunt open to all. Speculation in
land was hardly less resistible, especially
when the voice of William Jennings Bryan
joined those luring moneys from stocks to
Florida sands.

Socially and economically "lawless,"
Americans forsook political traditions as
well. Wilsonian idealism was bent on a new
crusade for international harmony through
the League of Nations. Obsessed by belief
in his mission, Wilson refused to admit that
the day for crusading under the banner of a
puritan conscience was over, and so his optimism gave way to sentimentalism as both
his health and his influence were dissipated.
Americans not only rejected foreign entan-
glements, but even carried their isolationist
zeal into movements intent upon closing
the gates to immigration. "Pure" Protestant American stock was to be kept unsul-

---

11. *Ibid.*
12. William Warren Sweet, *The Story of Religion
in America* (New York: Harper and Brothers,
1930), p. 584.
13. Paul Sann, *The Lawless Decade* (New York:
Crown Publishers, 1957).

lied, and the Ku Klux Klan arose as its self-appointed guardian, militantly rallying membership and strength against Negroes, Jews, Catholics, and Orientals.[14]

Meanwhile, Republican politicians searched for the most nearly perfect political expression of this age of reaction, and chose Warren G. Harding. Amiable, handsome, and proficient in the vernacular, Harding rode to easy victory on the wave of a "retreat to normalcy." Political corruption during his presidential term exhibited but another of the machinations of "the lawless decade."

While "lawless" adequately epitomized the age for many, F. Scott Fitzgerald, the official troubadour of the flapper, using bathtub gin for the ceremony, christened it the "Jazz Age."[15] And without question it was an age which even in its fun and frolic departed from the conventional score. The flapper and hip flask were fitting symbols, jazz and syncopation its music, and Helen Morgan its typical songstress. Brookhouser described Miss Morgan and the age she symbolized, " 'Why Was I Born?' she asked in a tear-choked little voice, and the people in the speakeasies sobbed in their drinks because they really didn't know. . . . And didn't care much, then. It was enough to be alive . . . and having fun and frolic."[16] And frolic they did as Lloyd Morris strikingly portrayed in his popular review of the twenties:

Over the land, youth was convinced that life was lousy, but that sex might be swell. The word "neck" ceased to be a noun; abruptly became a verb; immediately lost all anatomical precision. . . . In Muncie, Indiana, a judge of the juvenile court told the investigating Lynds that the family bus had become a house of prostitution on wheels. The new use was expedient, and prevalent . . . Sheiks and their shebas flocked to the movies to see "Women Who Give," and "The Queen of Sin." They sang and danced to "Hot Lips" and "Baby, I Need Lovin.'" Two and one half million literates emptied the newsstands of Bernarr McFadden's *True Stories*. In New York City's austere temple of classical music, Paul Whiteman offered the first performance of George Gershwin's "A Rhapsody in Blue."[17]

---

14. John Moffat Mecklin, professor of sociology at Dartmouth, made the point that Fundamentalism and the Ku Klux Klan "have much in common." "Both profited immensely from the post-war fears which stampeded so many men and women back to ancient loyalties. The one hundred per cent Americanism of the Klan finds its parallel in one hundred per cent orthodoxy. Both movements, while apparently assuming a national significance since the war, have their roots in the past." Mecklin then specified some of the parallel features he observed: "The Klan is prevailingly a small-town movement and fails signally to gain any foothold within the larger cities and the industrial centers. The stronghold of Fundamentalism is found likewise in the small towns and countryside where the intellectual and religious life has been least affected by modern culture. Fundamentalism is strongest in rural communities. Tennessee, with its famous Fundamentalist anti-evolution law, is seventy-five per cent rural. In all that vast region stretching from Virginia to Texas and Oklahoma, together with a large section of the Middle and Far West, the rural population far outnumbers the urban. Urban leaders in politics, education or religion are at the mercy of the rural mind. . . .The Klan and Fundamentalism are alike, finally, in their tendency to appeal to 'direct action.' The Klan seeks through its mask and clandestine political combinations to coerce men and women into one hundred per cent Americanism. The Fundamentalists, on a somewhat higher level, are seeking through legislation to combat science and to compel the people of a free country to retain the orthodox faith. It was hardly an accident that on his death Mr. Bryan was proclaimed as the greatest of all the Klansmen." See John Moffatt Mecklin, *The Survival Value of Christianity* (New York: Harcourt, Brace and Company, 1926), pp. 6-8.

15. F. Scott Fitzgerald, "Echoes of the Jazz Age," in *These Were Our Years*, ed. Frank Brookhouser (Garden City, N.Y.: Doubleday, 1959).

16. *Ibid.*, p. 170.

17. Lloyd Morris, *Postscript to Yesterday* (New York: Random House, 1947), p. 69.

"Normalcy" was being ushered in by the ubiquitous wail of the saxophone. It was the Era of Wonderful Nonsense. Witness a procession of weeping women eleven blocks long filing past the mortal remains of Rudolph Valentino. For some it was the Get-Rich-Quick era. To the sports journalists it was the Golden Age. To the bluenoses, it was the Dry Decade. But it was left for Frederick Lewis Allen, one of the period's most popular commentators, to put it most simply and adequately when he spoke of the "New Freedom" in a "New Era."[18] The times left very little unturned. Most of the old playing rules for the game of life were being rewritten. America was throwing off the shackles. Prohibition invaded the American's right to pamper—or ruin—his own insides, so he flouted it. The Semi-Victorian morals of the horse-and-buggy days inhibited his right (and hers) to enjoy a long night out, so the old codes were discarded. The age of ballyhoo invented a new retort to all old-fashioned moralists, "Aw, you're nuts!"

Adventurously, it was time to tilt lances at a myriad of targets—not only to puncture hypocrisy, but to initiate a whole revolution in manners, morals, interests, and outlooks. And nowhere was that more evident than in the new literature of the twenties produced by such pioneers in realism and honesty as Sinclair Lewis, Sherwood Anderson, Edgar Lee Masters, Floyd Dell, F. Scott Fitzgerald, Henry L. Mencken, and other such adventurous spirits.

For instance, in 1931, F. Scott Fitzgerald looked back upon the decade just completed and catalogued how the growing freedom regarding eroticism could be illustrated in the literature of the twenties:

We begin with the suggestion that Don Juan leads an interesting life (*Jurgen*, 1919); then we learn that there's a lot of sex around if we only knew it (*Winesburg, Ohio*, 1920), that adolescents lead very amorous lives (*This Side of Paradise*, 1920), that there are a lot of neglected Anglo-Saxon words (*Ulysses*, 1921), that older people don't always resist sudden temptations (*Cytherea*, 1922), that girls are sometimes seduced without being ruined (*Flaming Youth*, 1922), that even rape often turns out well (*The Sheik*, 1922), that glamorous English ladies are often promiscuous (*The Green Hat*, 1924), that in fact they devote most of their time to it (*The Vortex*, 1926), that it's a damn good thing too (*Lady Chatterley's Lover*, 1928), and finally that there are abnormal variations (*The Well of Loneliness*, 1928, and *Sodom and Gomorrah*, 1929).[19]

The tabloids, both instigating and recording periodic waves of contagious excitement over fads, fashions, or dramatic events, specialized particularly in sports, crime, and sex. Crossword puzzles, question-answer books, and Mah Jong covered the country like widespread neuroses. Confession and sex magazines found a ready market once their publishers mastered the art of arousing the reader without rousing the censor. Parades were frequent, their relative success measured in tons of ticker tape. County fairs were hardly less frequent, their relative success measured by the number of acres of Fords parked at the rear of the grandstand. Superstitions made a remarkable recrudescence, as Edwin E. Slosson related in his *Sermons of a Chemist:*

Amulets and charms are again in fashion. The ouija [sic] board rivals the typewriter in the production of literature. Palmistry is a popular pursuit. A mint of money has been made out of those who were willing to believe that the disease, sex, religion and

---

18. Frederick Lewis Allen, *Yesterday* (New York: Harper & Brothers, 1931).
19. Fitzgerald, "Echoes," in *These Were Our Years*, Brookhouser, p. 178.

race of a distant patient could be determined by electronic oscillations of a drop of blood or ink. Rainmaking, one of the earliest of the magic arts, is today a profitable profession. . . . The thirteenth seat in the parlor car is hard to sell, and the thirteenth floor is eliminated from some of our newest hotels.[20]

No attempt is here made to claim that parties to the fundamentalist-modernist quarrel were personally swept up in these primitivisms. It cannot be denied, though, that these sudden and radical changes did much to dissolve traditions and old restraints, and thereby did much to exaggerate tensions in the challenge to the old-time religion.

Technological Changes—The impact of technological changes ought also to be sketched. First, there was the development of the "production line" and the consequent rapid increase of such a product as the automobile. In 1915 there were fewer than 2.5 million cars registered in the United States. By 1920 there were over 9 million; by 1925, nearly 20 million; by 1930, over 26.5 million.[21] Concrete roads with banked curves, automatic traffic lights, roadside diners, tourist homes and tourist cabins, filling station after filling station, and the inevitable used-car lots accompanied and abetted such growth. But the changes went well beyond merely modifying the American landscape. As urbanites moved to the suburbs and as farmers and businesses moved ever further from the railroad station and railroad town, the far-reaching social effects of America-on-wheels became evident. The broadening of geographical horizons came both as goal and as consequence. Rural isolation was no longer tolerated. Describing a wave of prosperity among the farmers of the Midwest,

Ray Stannard Baker had said in 1900 that when a farmer did well, the first thing he did was to paint the barn; the second was to add a porch to his house; the third was to buy a piano; and the fourth was to send his children to college. "By the mid-twenties," reported Frederick Lewis Allen, "the purchase of a car was likely to come even before the painting of the barn—and a new piano was a rarity."[22]

But the automobile was a not wholly unmixed blessing, for with it came an ever increasing number of deaths on the highways. As Allen also reported, in 1922 some less than 15,000 had been killed by automobiles in the United States. By 1930 the toll had more than doubled to over 32,000—a sad and symbolic commentary on what happened when the "new freedom" was coupled with a new concentration of power. In a sentence, Allen epitomized the social impact of the automobile:

If the car was . . . a frequent source of family friction ("No, Junior, you are *not* taking it tonight"), as well as a destroyer of pedestrianism, a weakener of the churchgoing habit, a promoter of envy, a lethal weapon when driven by heedless, drunken, or irresponsible people, and a formidable convenience for criminals seeking a safe getaway, it was nonetheless indispensable.[23]

An adjunct to the automobile in diminishing social isolation was the radio. Eighteen months after station KDKA opened in East Pittsburgh on November 2, 1920, to

---

20. Edwin E. Slosson, *Sermons of a Chemist* (New York: Harcourt, Brace and Co., 1925), pp. 125-26.
21. Frederick Lewis Allen, "The Changes It Wrought," in *These Were Our Years*, ed. Frank Brookhouser, (Garden City, New York: Doubleday, 1959), p. 143.
22. *Ibid.*, p. 148.
23. *Ibid.*, pp. 142-43.

carry the Harding-Cox election returns, there were 220 stations on the air. Three million homes had sets by 1922, and after the booming voice of William Jennings Bryan at the Democratic National Convention of 1924 called radio "a gift of Providence," the line for receiving sets grew ever longer so that by 1925, the listening audience was put at 50 million.[24] In its first decade, radio reached into every third home.

Even as the automobile weakened the churchgoing habit but at the same time made it possible for larger groups of people to travel longer distances to church, so the radio also afforded a potential for mixed responses. It gave the pulpit and lecture platform an expansion never before dreamed of, but it also tempted many to stay home and listen rather than to go and hear. The typical attitude of the religionist toward the radio was positive, as Ozora S. Davis, historian of American preaching, noted:

Those who foresee the speedy coming of the time when worship will be comfortably enjoyed at home by listeners-in, who will remorselessly tune out the dull preachers and the imperfect music and tune in on the interesting preachers and the fine choirs, do not reckon with the power of the visible speaker, the worshiping congregation, and the demand for fellowship in worship. Probably the gains have been more than the losses up to the present time in respect to the visible congregation. . . . It is undoubtedly safe to say that the radio will not dethrone preaching but will, in the end, give the true preacher still greater power over a wider audience.[25]

That such optimism carried over into action is indicated by the report that during 1929, 70 stations associated with the National Broadcasting Company were utilized in the presentation of 531 religious programs under representative Protestant sponsorship in which 268 preachers had part, representing 20 denominations, 49 cities, and 15 states.[26]

Ethos of the Age—Far less subtle than the wavelengths of radio were the waves of cynicism and disillusionment which bombarded the era. Cynicism during the twenties gave birth to a new word, "debunk." Inelegant but expressive, the term capsuled much of the mood and mind of the time, especially among the intellectuals of the age. Endlessly questing, yet lacking a sense of direction; pregnant with power, yet lacking motivation; boisterous and gay, yet victimized by poor morale—so were the twenties—an age which appeared fabulously capable of creation, but determined to waste that potential. With his usual incisiveness, Walter Lippmann charged, "What most distinguishes the generation who have approached maturity since the debacle of idealism at the end of the War is not their rebellion against the religion and the moral code of their parents, but their disillusionment with their own rebellion."[27] Regarding the dissolution of the ancestral order for the modern man, Lippmann reported, "There is no moral authority to which he must turn now, but there is coercion in opinions, fashions and fads."[28] The manifest inadequacy of such new "authorities" heightened the disillusionment.

The greatest literary prophet of the disillusionment was Joseph Wood Krutch, of whom Reinhold Niebuhr said, "Here is a man who has lost all faith but is not happy

---

24. Sann, *Lawless Decade*, p. 39.
25. Ozora S. Davis, "American Preaching," in *Religious Thought in the Last Quarter-Century*, ed. Gerald Birney Smith (Chicago: University of Chicago Press, 1927), pp. 205-6.
26. "Religion on the Radio," *Christian Century* March 26, 1930, p. 405.
27. Walter Lippmann, *A Preface to Morals* (New York: Macmillan, 1929), p. 17.
28. *Ibid.*, p. 9.

about it."[29] Krutch established that the disillusionment among intellectuals went much deeper than dissatisfaction with the fads and fancies of the day. Writing toward the end of the twenties, he explained, "We are disillusioned with the laboratory, not because we have lost faith in the truth of its findings, but because we have lost faith in the power of those findings to help us as generally as we had once hoped they might help."[30] Krutch was unique only in his ability to articulate the *Zeitgeist*. What to many seemed an enigma became for Krutch a clearly seen dilemma: knowledge makes all faith in life's highest values impossible; yet knowledge is the only value worth seeking; so, we seek most avidly that which is most certain to destroy life!

Intellectual Climate of the Times—If such was the mood of the age, what were the substantive intellectual currents which swept it along? What ideas and forces were prominent in that intellectual milieu in which the fundamentalists and modernists contested? Gaius Glenn Atkins, speaking specifically of the intellectual backdrop for the fundamentalist-modernist controversy, reported: "Behind these contestants were the vaster deployments of philosophy, psychology and science, changed social attitudes, economic pressures, class and culture antagonisms."[31] Of these forces, science, psychology, and philosophy require at least brief additional commentary.

The impact of science and the scientific spirit on the age is illustrated by excerpts from sermons of the period. Albert W. Beaven opened a sermon entitled, "The Scientific Spirit in the Spiritual Realm," with, "This is unquestionably the age of science."[32] He then elaborated, "Science has moved into realm after realm, conquering new eras, discovering causes, collating facts and offering to mankind ever newer weapons with which to fight its battles and added resources with which to enjoy life. This result has been largely attained by an attitude on the part of men. We may describe it as the 'scientific spirit.' "[33] Finally, Beaven attempted to describe this "scientific spirit" with some precision:

First, it proceeded on the assumption that there is a body of facts worth knowing.
Second, that there is a fundamental unity which binds these various phenomena into the relationship of cause and effect and that the laws of cause and effect can be discovered and relied upon to be the same in each part of the universe.
Third, that man's mind is capable of finding these facts and seeking these causes.
Fourth, to find them requires an open minded seeking of truth, willingness to follow where it leads, sacrificial patience and unlimited experimentation to ascertain and establish the facts.
Fifth, that the resources uncovered by these discoveries could, and should, be applied to the various needs of humanity.[34]

Another minister, Minot Simons, noted for urging theism as a realistic option in the face of mechanism and humanism, similarly credited the impact of science:

Multitudes of men and women today have come under the influence of the scientific habit of mind. They are no longer willing merely to accept. They desire to know why and what and how. They are

---

29. Reinhold Niebuhr, "Book Review," *Christian Century*, May 1, 1929, p. 586.
30. Joseph Wood Krutch, *The Modern Temper: A Study and a Confession* (New York: Harcourt, Brace and Company, 1929), p. 76.
31. Gaius Glenn Atkins, *Preaching and the Mind of Today* (New York: Round Table Press, 1934), p. 233.
32. Albert W. Bleaven, "The Scientific Spirit in the Spiritual Realm," *Christian Century Pulpit* 1, no. 2 (November, 1929):12.
33. *Ibid.*
34. *Ibid.*, 12-13.

subjecting all doctrines and all traditional authorities to a frank scrutiny. Authorities must make good or they are discarded. There is a growing passion for reality in the modern world. It is bringing to pass a new outlook upon the world and a profound desire to discover the truth about it. Ideas are no longer sacred because they are old, but only because they are true.[35]

Science and religion, or more properly, the scientific spirit and theological dogmatism, were not new antagonists. Sherwood Eddy, speaking in the twenties about the conflict over evolution, said that "the present conflict between science and theology is only the last of at least five great issues that have arisen between them."[36] Without attempting to detail the recurring arguments in the continuing conflict, it should be noted that a sizeable and influential group never took up arms, contending that it was not possible for true science and genuine religion ever to clash. A spokesman for this viewpoint was J. Arthur Thomson:

Science and Religion are incommensurables, and there is no true antithesis between them—they belong to different universes of discourse. Science is descriptive and offers no ultimate explanation; Religion is transcendental and interpretative, implying a realization of a higher order of things than those of sense-experience. . . . The so-called "conflict between science and religion" depends in part on a clashing of particular expressions of religious belief with facts of science, or on a clashing of particular supposedly scientific philosophies with religious feeling, or on attempts to combine in one statement scientific and religious formulations. . . . But the bulk of the conflict is due to a misunderstanding, to a false antithesis between incommensurables.[37]

While some allowed science and religion to reign as co-sovereigns in mutually exclusive fields, others saw the issue not in terms of a possible both/and, but in the clear cut terms of an either/or. The spirit of the latter was well described by William Louis Po-

teat in his 1925 McNair Lectures given at the University of North Carolina:

Only yesterday a few gentlemen, sincere, devout, and capable . . . waked up to find, as they thought, the scientists secretly digging out the foundations of Christianity. Their excitement and alarm spread rapidly and widely. Trained for the most part in prelaboratory days, they could not be expected to have the scientific habit or attitude. Invoking a man-made theory of inspiration most unfair to the precious documents of our faith, and committed to a bald literalism of interpretation, they take the role of defenders of the faith and in its name propose, by ecclesiastical and legislative enactment, by executive order, by organized propaganda, by inquisition and the refinements of modern torture, to crowd the eagle back into the shell and then, in Voltaire's famous phrase, crush the infamous thing. . . . Once more the old slogan comes out of retirement—"religion or science," "Moses or Darwin."[38]

If science—specifically, the sciences of biology and geology—rippled the intellectual currents of the day, psychology ruffled them. Indeed, Walter Marshall Horton claimed that psychological theories posed the greatest threat to the religionist:

35. Minot Simons, *A Modern Theism* (Boston: The Beacon Press, 1931), p. 4.
36. Eddy, *New Challenges*, p. 30. The first of the issues was between the conceptions of a flat or a spherical earth. The second was over whether the sun or the earth was the center of our solar system. The third came with the discovery of the law of gravitation and subsequent insistence upon the supremacy of "natural law." The fourth was between the exponents of the discoveries of geology and the supporters of the conventional orthodox chronology established in 1650 by Archbishop Usher. The fifth issue was the question of evolution.
37. Cited by H.H. Lane in *Evolution and Christian Faith* (Princeton: Princeton University Press, 1923), pp. 184-85.
38. William Louis Poteat, *Can A Man Be A Christian To-Day?* (Chapel Hill: University of North Carolina Press, 1926), pp. 34-35.

Psychology is that science which most nearly affects our deepest religious interests. A man may remain relatively indifferent when science remolds his picture of the inanimate world, or even his picture of the place of mankind among the animal species; but when science thrusts her dissecting-knife in among his vitals, and proposes to deal with all his inmost motives, hopes, and aspirations as coolly as she deals with frogs and worms in the zoological laboratory, then it takes a tough mind to remain impartial. Already there are signs of panic in the theological camp.[39]

At least three different schools of psychology are relevant to the context of the controversy: behaviorism, psychoanalysis, and Gestalt psychology.

The psychology of behaviorism, introduced by Professor John B. Watson in 1915, insisted that our only certain knowledge of human beings was confined to our study of their overt actions. Men's behavior rather than mental states or streams of consciousness was therefore the important field for study. The impact upon religion of this new school of thought is obvious in light of such a question as the following: Is religion to be judged in terms of behavioral tests (as many modernists urged) or may it be conceived and practiced primarily as a matter of precise doctrine or correct opinion—in assent to formulas and shibboleths (as fundamentalists typically argued)?

Psychoanalysis broadened the scope of psychology. Reclaiming the forgotten and unrecognized elements of the past, it opened the whole realm of the subconscious. At its best, it suggested a healthy self-criticism and candor, revealed assorted hidden dangers and ills, and supplied a therapy. At its worst, it supplied the rationale for libidinal self-expression which confused freedom with license, and came to typify the age.

At the same time that behaviorists were giving almost exclusive attention to man's outward behavior and psychoanalysts were probing the subconscious, the Gestaltists were emphasizing the insight that man is not all mind, or body, or sex, but that man is *man*, a unit, a whole. The leaders of this school showed dissatisfaction with the old atomistic psychology with its hair-splitting distinctions, with its artificial "faculties" of the mind, and with its minute analysis which dissected details only to miss the significance of the whole. Behavior, they insisted, must rather be conceived as a constant series of *Gestalten*, or configurations. This school of thought definitely influenced the modernists as they showed increasing awareness of larger contextual relationships and of the interdependencies of different religious and social systems.

Next we turn to the philosophies of the day, for if, as John Herman Randall, Jr., suggested, "the Fundamentalists do not, and the Modernists do, accept present-day philosophies,"[40] some attention must be given the philosophical milieu as basic to an understanding of the cleavage.

A dominant philosophy of the nineteenth century much affecting the subsequent development of Christian thought was romanticism. At least three elements in the superstructure of Christian thought during the early twentieth century were attributable to the quarry of romanticism, according to Henry Sloane Coffin.[41] First

---

39. Walter Marshall Horton, *Theology in Transition* (New York: Harper & Brothers, 1939), pp. 14-15. The quotation comes from a section first published in 1931.
40. John Herman Randall, Jr., *The Making of the Modern Mind*, rev. ed. (Cambridge: Riverside Press, 1940), p. 542.
41. Henry Sloane Coffin, *Some Christian Convictions* (New Haven: Yale University Press, 1915), pp. 3-5.

there was the belief that religion is something more and deeper than belief and conduct—that it is an experience of man's whole nature, and that it consists largely in feelings and intuitions which we can but imperfectly rationalize and express. Closely associated was a second emphasis that the Divine is represented to man by symbols that speak to more parts of his nature than to his intellect. Coffin, speaking as a modernist, called attention to the practical impact of this second emphasis:

One of our chief complaints with the historic creeds and confessions is that they have turned the poetry (in which religious experience most naturally expressed itself) into prose, rhetoric into logic, and have lost much of its content in the process. Jesus is to the mind with a sense of the Divine the great symbol or sacrament of the Invisible God; but to treat His divinity as a formula of logic, and attempt to demonstrate it, as one might a proposition in geometry, is to lose that which divinity is to those who have experienced contact with the living God through Jesus.[42]

A third evidence of the impact of romanticism on theology was the teaching that God is immanent in his world—that He works as truly "from within" as "from above." Deity and humanity were no longer regarded as two distinct and different phenomena. To the romanticist, no man was without "the inspiration of the Almighty." Applied to the God-man, Jesus Christ, the new emphasis insisted that Jesus was not so much God *and* man, as God *in* man.

The romanticists' view of God as good-as-the-best-of-men streamed off into humanitarianism, dominant enough in the twenties to merit separate treatment as a philosophical current. Under its aegis, theology spoke more often of the character of Jesus of Nazareth than of God's sovereign decrees and ordinances. The emphasis fell upon the humanity of Jesus and upon our

ability and duty to become like Him. It was natural that a passion for social righteousness, much emphasized by the modernists, should result from this concern.

It must not be supposed that the impact of these several intellectual currents—science, psychology, and philosophy—was as diverse and separatistic as this treatment might suggest. The effect was cumulative and holistic, and so in summary the composite effect of the intellectual milieu upon man's purposes, ideals, hopes, and beliefs during the twenties may be sketched:

1. A method of inquiry and of judgment arose that discredited reliance upon authority and tradition.

2. Particular beliefs vanished before advancing knowledge of nature, of history, and of mind.

3. Men acquired increasing voluntary control over conditions and areas that religion traditionally assigned to superhuman powers. At the same time, there arose a sharper awareness that certain phases of life (e.g., "id") were beyond man's conscious control or the seeming guidance of a god.

4. The whole mental atmosphere changed as ancient fears, attitudes of submission, and reliance upon the dim or the imagined were supplanted by a self-confident realism.

5. If men were not quite able to muster a welcoming attitude toward change, at least expectation of changes became habitual and normal as the most alive citizens of the twenties sensed their own capacity to produce such changes.

---

42. *Ibid.*, pp. 4-5.

Ecclesiastical Milieu

"The non-church-going male who, in 1920, took off his hat when he passed a church, by 1930 kept his hat on, and more than likely considered the local parson as a figure of fun."[43] To understand such commentary, one must note not only the general secular tenor of the times, but review also what was happening within the ecclesiastical setting.

It has already been noted that the age challenged and questioned literally everything. In this spirit, sermon and lecture titles were frequently cast in the form of queries: "Shall the Fundamentalists Win?," "Shall Unbelief Win?," "What is Religion For?," "Can I Believe in God?," "Brute or Brother?"

In a questioning age, topics framed as questions draw attention. But to hold attention, the spirit of inquiry and quest must pervade the content as well. Especially the modernist preachers felt that the very life of the church depended upon asking relevant questions and searching for reliable answers. Earlier, a steadfast social order, patterned morality, the unchallenged priority of evangelical Protestantism, Sundays kept reasonably free from commercialism, and the relative simplicities of life and interest had all combined to sustain the churches. The dissolution of these forces had by the twenties affected every phase of church life and presented a special challenge to the pulpit either to build new or to brace up the tottering old foundations of theology and ethics.

Theological training had also undergone changes. There was a definite trend away from furnishing clergy with a carefully articulated doctrinal system, a select library of theological authorities, and a fair storehouse of texts and standard homiletical materials. Atkins said of the changed conditions, "Theological educators generally are trying to bring their work into the full current of the life and mind of their time. A seminary like Union in New York is really a kind of theological university."[44] As the seminaries built sizeable endowments, some were able to free themselves completely from denominational dependency, and presented a program of free scholastic inquiry for students drawn from all denominations.

What were the dominant and recurring themes in the sermonic efforts of these clergy? Perhaps there is no better single exhibit than that popularly styled report on a survey of sermons recorded in the *Ladies Home Journal.*[45] A loosely controlled subject analysis of 800 sermons of the time revealed that "spiritual self-culture" was the dominant motif in 213 of them. Most of the remainder dealt with such subjects as literature, plays, science, history, current events, efficiency, and success. Only 38 were biblical-expository or textual, while 13 were evangelistic. Allowing for a sample bias which favored liberal sources, it must yet be conceded that the pulpit, with some sensitivity, was reflecting the changing concerns of the day.

Outline of the Fray—But the pulpit was far more than a mirror of the changing times. It was also the dominant battleground for theological strife. Broadly, the stirrings traced this pattern: In the late

---

43. Archie Robertson, *That Old-Time Religion* (Boston: Houghton-Mifflin, 1950), p. 81.
44. Gavis Glenn Atkins, *Religion in Our Times* (New York: Round Table Press, 1932), pp. 78-79.
45. Alvin E. Magary, "Pulpit 'Pep': Is This What the Church Most Needs?," *Ladies Home Journal*, 33 (May, 1916):19, 92.

nineteenth century there were a few heresy trials, with a temporary return to peace about 1900. Then a movement of protest hardened from the time of the publication of *The Fundamentals*[46] between 1909 and 1912, reaching its full maturity in the early twenties. The orthodox defenders in each denomination organized and bid for control, using all the weapons which a burgeoning technology and an elocutionary rhetoric made available. By the middle of 1925, fundamentalist strength began appreciably to wane so that by 1930 fundamentalism was no longer viable as a force, having succumbed less to the modernists than to the changed tenor of the times.

Parties to the Conflict—The name of the controversy itself—fundamentalist-modernist—specified the two major contending parties. But labels become libels when we rigidly insist upon dividing the American Protestants of the twenties into fundamentalists or modernists, for in so doing, the rich variety and colorful individuality of historical persons are lost in the hypothetical polar types. Furthermore, between the liberals and conservatives stood a sizeable group of moderates who rejected the tendencies of both extremes.[47] The Rt. Reverend James E. Freeman, Bishop of Washington, in a sermon entitled, "The Greatest Story Ever Told," articulated the position of the noncombatants:

Today in the midst of a disordered and distracted world there is no reasonable ground for theological controversy. Now as never before the insistent demand is for a Church that can present with unfailing fidelity the supreme Saviour of men, without obscuring or rendering uncertain or ambiguous His mighty teachings. . . . In the midst of a condition that literally imperils our Christian civilization there is no room for the controversialist, no time for the discussion of those questions that tend to

strife and division. To increase bitterness or party rivalry at such a critical time as the present when unity of action is indispensable to the securing of the most sacred interests of life, is folly, and can issue in nothing but disorder and confusion worse confounded. The great body of the laity, of every class, are calling for a faith expressed in simple terms that will serve to stabilize, refresh and inspire them in the midst of the world's confusions and distractions.[48]

While some pleas to put down the fight were reasoned, albeit passionately, appeals of a more superficial nature were made by others to stem the controversy. An editorial in the *Chicago American*, for instance, under the caption, "Too Bad They Differ," lamented, "It seems a pity that clergymen should be impelled by their conscience to quarrel. It is as though children, discussing Santa Claus, should quarrel, one saying 'Santa has a long white beard and reindeer,' and another 'Santa has a clean shaven face and an airplane.' Why not say, 'We all love

---

46. *The Fundamentals: A Testimony to the Truth.* 12 vols. (Chicago: Testimony Publishing Company, 1909-12).

47. Following World War I, the newer "fundamentalist" and "modernist" labels largely supplanted the older "liberal" and "conservative" dichotomy. Some commentators on religion insisted that "the older and the newer contrasted pairs of terms are not quite coextensive in meaning," for the conservative-liberal terms are "predominantly intellectualistic and refer mainly to attitudes towards doctrines and policies," while the fundamentalist-modernist labels are "broader in scope and take in all experience." See James H. Snowden, *Old Faith and New Knowledge* (New York: Harper and Brothers, 1928), p. 17. For purposes of this study, the sets of terms are used interchangeably.

48. James E. Freeman, "The Greatest Story Ever Told," in *If I Had Only One Sermon to Preach*, ed. Charles Stelzle (New York: Harper and Brothers, 1927), p. 195.

Santa Claus,' and not quarrel about definitions?"[49]

The moderates were unwittingly supplied with an aphoristic defense of their position when Francis L. Patton, a stalwart conservative Presbyterian who disliked labels, declared, "Speaking for myself I confess that I do not wear either of these labels, for I am enough of a modernist to feel that I have a right to live in the twentieth century and too much of a fundamentalist to renounce my heritage of faith for the sake of being in fashionable company."[50]

The historical contours of the controversy have been traced out in detail elsewhere.[51] Our purpose at this point is to focus more specifically upon the contrasting mind sets of the contesting parties.

Fundamentalism as a Mentality

Fundamentalism as a mentality is not a perspective imposed upon this study, for it was a frame of reference often used during the controversy. A.W. Nagler in giving the Charles Wesley Bennett Lectures during May, 1923, defined the essence of fundamentalism as a mentality:

Fundamentalism is an attitude of mind, and an attitude is hard to define. Speaking in general terms we are led to say that a Fundamentalist is one who is so anxious about the value of the past that he fails to see values created or revealed today. He clings tenaciously to traditions because they have been cherished by "our fathers," because they have been handed down as a sacred deposit which is to be accepted without question. He stresses the faith that is believed instead of the faith that believes; doctrinal soundness above practical utility. He loses sight of doctrinal effectiveness in his emphasis upon doctrinal fastidiousness. Having a static instead of a dynamic *Weltanschauung* he is philosophically adverse to change, because change threatens to bring upheaval in its wake.[52]

No more inclusive single characteristic of fundamentalism as a mentality could be given than Nagler's charge that it was "philosophically adverse to change." So defined, fundamentalism becomes a near synonym for "traditionalism," as Leighton explained:

What is Traditionalism? Briefly, it is the assumption that in the traditional dogmas and ecclesiastical forms of so-called Catholic Christianity are to be found whatsoever is necessary to the salvation of the individual and society. In complete and obedient acceptance of all that has been handed down *from of old* alone is salvation. Traditionalism is the attitude which holds that all saving truth was given *once and for all time to the Fathers.* Our business is to preserve it intact and to abide by it. Its favorite formulas are: "The Holy Catholic Church teaches thus and so"; or, "The Fathers of the first six Christian centuries teach thus and so"; or, "The ecumenical councils decreed thus and so"; or, "The Bible teaches thus and so." Woe betide him who thinks otherwise. No modern doctrines or principles, however well-grounded on facts, or however illuminating as guides to action, can be true or right if they are not in complete harmony with the ancient traditions. If modern science—physics, astronomy, biology or psychology—is not in harmony with the traditions, so much the worse for modern science. It is Devil's lore.[53]

Though primarily emphasizing religion, Leighton included in his exposition "all our traditionary moral, social, legal, political and economic institutions and customs"

49. "Too Bad They Differ," *Chicago American*, April 13, 1925; reprinted in *The Open Court* 39, no. 11 (November, 1925):682.

50. Francis L. Patton, *Fundamental Christianity* (New York: Macmillan, 1926), p. 2.

51. See especially Norman F. Furniss, *The Fundamentalist Controversy, 1918-1931* Yale University Press, 1954).

52. A. W. Nagler, "The Witness of the Early Church to Fundamentalism," (Charles Wesley Bennett Lectures, May 24, 1923), p. 4.

53. Leighton, *Religion and the Mind*, pp. 24-25.

which represent "the bondage of the living to the dead," and summarized his thesis by affirming that "the central myth of the traditionalist is that the holy tradition is fixed, complete and self-consistent."[54]

The fundamentalists' mind-set at times provoked modernists to forsake measured terms in referring to them. The roll call of epithets by which fundamentalists claimed to be maligned included: *dogmatists, separatists, cranks, medievalists, ignoramuses, ku-kluxes, landmarkers, obscurantists, reactionaries, nonprogressives, narrow-minded, unscientific, uneducated, uncultured, back numbers, moss-backs, bigots, crass literalists, traditionalists, hopelessly benighted,* and *funny-mentalists.*[55]

Other commentators reported that fundamentalists' tendency to rest supinely in the past was due to such psychological factors as temperamental inertia, a vaguely defined fear of new truth, a bitterness of spirit, a distrust of reason linked with an emphasis upon emotion, doubt in human ability to solve ultimate problems coupled with reliance on divine agency, a longing for certainty, and a nostalgia which spilled over into sentimentality.

Help in uncovering the causative elements in the mental makeup of the fundamentalists comes first from Reinhold Niebuhr, already in the twenties an astute critic of the American religious scene. Crediting the fundamentalist mentality with being an inevitable product of the uncertainties of the time, Niebuhr said, "Frantic orthodoxy is never rooted in faith but in doubt. It is when we are not sure that we are doubly sure. Fundamentalism is therefore inevitable in an age which has destroyed so many certainties by which faith once expressed itself and upon which it relied."[56] As portrayed before, the psycho-

logical climate of the twenties was one in which men were made to feel that the foundations beneath them were tottering, if indeed not crumbling. Fundamentalists sensed that the supreme task before them was the buttressing of the old foundations and that certainly the future of Christianity—if not of humanity—depended upon the spirit and thoroughness with which they accomplished that task.

54. *Ibid.*, p. 25. Granting Leighton's definition of the fundamentalist mentality, one commentator charged that "the worst fundamentalism" is found in American political thought. "Religion is not the only field in which fundamentalism challenges science. It is not the most important field. There is more fundamentalism in the political than in the religious thought of the American people today, and it works greater injury both to the cause of national progress and to the interests of the social order.

"Even the most casual observer of our political psychology must have noticed that there are literally millions of Americans who decline to accept things on faith in the realm of religion, but who do not have the slightest compunction about swallowing the catch-words, phrases, formulas, and slogans that go to make up a creed in politics. They scoff at the miracles of Holy Writ, but are continually looking for the miraculous in government. . . .

"The modernist in religion wonders how anybody, in spite of astronomers and geologists can believe that this world was created in six days of twenty-four hours each; but he himself finds no difficulty in believing that the Constitution of the United States was struck off as a finished job in four months. We do not call that belief fundamentalism; we call it patriotism." William B. Munro, "The Worst Fundamentalism," *Atlantic Monthly* 138, no. 4 (October, 1926):451, 459.

55. Cf. Curtis Lee Laws, "Fundamentalism from the Baptist Viewpoint," *Moody Bible Institute Monthly* 23, no. 1 (September, 1922): 15; and G. W. McPherson, "The Modern Movement in Religion," *King's Business* 15, no. 12 (December, 1924):812.

56. Reinhold Niebuhr, "Shall We Proclaim the Truth or Search for It?," *Christian Century*, March 12, 1925, p. 345.

Modernism as a Mentality

In a sermon strikingly entitled, "If Jesus Were a Modernist," Harry Emerson Fosdick gave this summary estimate of what it meant to be a modernist:

Modernism is the intellectual endeavor to harmonize our religious thinking with the new world-view that science has brought. . . . It springs from the mental discomfort of having religion in one compartment of the mind and scientific information in another. . . . The Modernist cannot endure that bifurcation of the mind. He wants to get himself together. He cannot live with his intellect in the twentieth century and his theology in the first, and so he is trying to untwine the vines of his religious life from the trellis of the old world-view and make it twine around the trellis of the new world-view.[57]

Modernist spokesmen were divided in specifying the goals they championed. Some advocated simply a *restatement* of Christian truths in a more contemporary idiom; others promoted the *rediscovery* of the religion of Jesus out of the centuries-old deposit of truths about Him; and finally, there were those who advanced a radical *reconstruction* of Christian theology along more naturalistic lines.

Shailer Mathews, in contrasting his views of modernism and fundamentalism, became a leading spokesman for modernism understood primarily as a mentality intent upon uncovering the abiding elements in religion:

The issue between modernism and fundamentalism is not one of mere theology. It is rather a struggle between two types of mind, two attitudes toward culture, and in consequence, two conceptions of Christianity. . . .
Modernism is not a theology or a philosophy; it is the historical method of thinking about the Bible and Christian doctrine. Fundamentalism is a theology and centers around theology. The Modernist is attempting to utilize the methods of the histori-

cal and allied sciences to discover the permanent values in his religious inheritance. The Fundamentalist starts with authority and demands the acceptance of the formulas in which their values have been affirmed by the church of the past. To him such authority sets limits not only to thought but to the method of thought. He and the Modernist are evidently not debating on the same plane.[58]

A year later Mathews elaborated that thesis by clarifying, "The Modernist is a critic and an historian before he is a theologian. His interest in method precedes his interest in results. . . . In brief, then, *the use of scientific, historical, social method in understanding and applying evangelical Christianity to the needs of living persons is Modernism.*[59]

Mathews declared that modernism was concerned with addressing "the needs of living persons." Such concern involved the intent to restate Christian historic experience in terms that would catch the attention and command the respect of thoughtful moderns. To emphasize the fact that creeds of another day sounded archaic and unreal to modern men, modernists employed any number of analogies. Some saw traditional religion as a crustacean—building a permanent shell over itself which, though at first a serviceable instrument,

---

57. Harry Emerson Fosdick, "If Jesus Were a Modernist," *Christian Century Pulpit* 1, no. 1 (October, 1929):13.

58. Mathews suggested the plane on which modernists moved as he said in summary, "Modernism is an expression in the field of Christian faith of the new social mind which is the result of the development of experiemental science, the rise of democracy and new understanding of social and economic facts." Shailer Mathews, "Fundamentalism and Modernism," *American Review* 2, no. 1 (January-February, 1924):1.

59. Shailer Mathews, *The Faith of Modernism* (New York: Macmillan, 1924), pp. 31, 35.

soon became a damaging limitation to growth. Such modernists were insistent that the shell be sloughed off periodically, and that a new one be built to accommodate and preserve the ever-changing forms of life. Then there was the "kernel and husk theory" which other modernists used to explain that what fundamentalists saw as dangerous iconoclasm and willful disregard of "fundamentals" was simply a shucking of the husks so that the essential kernel of truth might be more accessible. The third and least radical of the analogies was the "acorn and oak theory." This theory emphasized that there was a legitimate—indeed, necessary—development of ideas and doctrines. Germinal life, present from the beginning, realized a continuity through changing growth forms. Common to all three of the analogies was the modernists' striving to preserve a real connection with the past while recognizing the need for doctrinal revision. That is to say, modernists held that all doctrinal formulas were relative to the historical situation and the *Zeitgeist* of the age in which they were created.

A modernist was one who believed in the possibility of a synthesis between the essential truth of his religion and the essential truth of modernity.

Orientation which had no welcoming attitude toward change was condemned by the modernists as ruling out the possibility for progress. The Cole Lectures given by Fosdick at Vanderbilt University in 1922 under the title, "Christianity and Progress," gave persuasive formulation to the compatibility—indeed, the inevitability—of Christianity and progress. In a series of questions (less queries than arguments for his thesis), Fosdick had declared:

No one can long ponder the significance of our generation's progressive ways of thinking without running straight upon this question: is not Christianity itself progressive? In the midst of a changing world does not it also change, so that, reacting upon the new ideas of progress, it not only assimilates and uses them, but is itself an illustration of them? Where everything else in man's life in its origin and growth is conceived, not in terms of static and final creation or revelation, but in terms of development, can religion be left out? Instead of being a pond around which once for all a man can walk and take its measure, a final and completed whole, is not Christianity a river which, maintaining still reliance upon the historic springs from which it flows, gathers in new tributaries on its course and is itself a changing, growing and progressive movement?[60]

Four years later the form of Fosdick's argument became much more directive as assertion replaced query:

The one utter heresy in Christianity is thus to believe that we have reached finality and can settle down with a completed system. That is the essential denial of the living God, who cannot have said his last word on any subject or have landed his last hammer-blow on any task. It is strange that in religion we so desperately cling to static, settled, authoritative finality as though that were our safety and our strength. In no other realm should we dream of such an attitude. Says Froude, the historian, "If medicine had been regulated three hundred years ago by Act of Parliament; if there had been Thirty-nine Articles of Physic, and every licensed practitioner had been compelled, under pains and penalties, to compound his drugs by the prescriptions of Henry the Eighth's physician, Doctor Butts, it is easy to conjecture in what state of health the people of this country would at present be found."[61]

The "love of truth," the appeal to experience, the readiness to accept new know-

---

60. Harry Emerson Fosdick, *Christianity and Progress* (New York: Fleming H. Revell 1922), pp. 127-128.
61. Harry Emerson Fosdick, *Adventurous Religion* (New York: Harper and Brothers, 1926), p. 6.

ledge from any well-attested sources—these were emphases of enduring strength in modernism during that age when the category of *becoming* was substituted for *being*, when the conception of relativity replaced that of the absolute, and when progress was heralded over immobility.

An excellent epitome of modernism as a mentality was supplied by William Merrill in 1925:

Such a movement, spiritual, elastic, growing, cannot be shut in a definition or set in a formula. But its main outlines have been sketched. In the practical workings of his religious experience, the liberal Christian puts his trust in the free human intellect; welcomes truth from whatever source; rejoices in the scientific method; adopts its clear results; and is ever ready to reopen questions and to reexamine evidence. He wants the Church kept a large, inclusive, comprehensive body. Internally he finds all his faith and hope realized in personality, preeminently in the supreme personality, Jesus Christ. And he cares supremely for present, vital spiritual experience.[62]

The Duel Over Evolution

In the Spring of 1925 while Fosdick was readying his farewell sermon to the First Presbyterian Church of New York (resignation from which had been precipitated by Presbyterian governing powers as led by Clarence Edward Noble Macartney, a stalwart Presbyterian clergyman of Philadelphia) which was to close "the Fosdick case," legislators in Tennessee were preparing a bill forbidding the teaching of evolution in the schools of that state, an action which was to culminate in the Scopes trial (storm center for evolution).[63] The Dayton "Monkey Trial" brought the issues separating the two parties to the public's attention in an unprecedented quantity and manner. It was on the issue of evolution

particularly that fundamentalists showed their full strength.

Actually, fundamentalists hit upon evolution by chance, for their attack upon evolution was not part of their original five-point program. The thrusting of evolution into the spotlight must be attributed largely to William Jennings Bryan. According to Bryan, Fosdick and Darwin were the church's main enemies, and he fought both of them relentlessly. As it became clear that the Presbyterian ecclesiastical system was adequate to deal with Fosdick, Bryan narrowed his attention to evolution. In a speech at Mountain View, California, given in October, 1924, Bryan said, "All the ills

_____

62. William Pierson Merrill, *Liberal Christianity* (New York: Macmillan, 1925), p. 63.
63. Evolutionists were battled by the fundamentalists even as were the modernists. Often, indeed, the action was coextensive, for most modernists were also evolutionists, though many evolutionists (notably scientists and educators) were not so much concerned with doctrinal disputation as with academic freedom. Maynard Shipley, President of the Science League of America, epitomized concern for freedom in the classroom when he said, "Since all modern scientists are in agreement as to the overwhelming preponderance of evidence in favor of the theory—or fact—of organic evolution, the determination of twenty-five million or more thoroughly organized Fundamentalists to debar by law the teaching of evolution *even as a theory of biology* presents a very serious problem. But even more grave is the menace to freedom of teaching in general. . . .What the friends of science are really supporting, or trying to protect, is not so much a unanimous conclusion of the scientists, as the validity of the method of science, and the moral right and duty of the scientists to make known to the students in our tax-supported schools the results of their researches. . . .No lover of liberty would seek to deprive even the most rabid Fundamentalist of his right to freedom of speech. But when he seeks to apply a religious test to any law-abiding, properly educated citizen applying for a position as a teacher in our public schools, it is high time to object!" *The War on Modern Science* (New York: Alfred A. Knopf, 1927), pp. xii, 8, 30.

from which America suffers can be traced back to the teaching of evolution."[64]

Shortly after Bryan began his formal crusade against evolution in 1921, he was joined by other fundamentalist spokesmen in proclaiming that "evolution is the root of discord."[65] John Roach Straton, Baptist preacher of New York City who was variously described as the Archbishop of Fundamentalism or Fundamentalism's Pope, said in an address at the Moody Bible Institute in 1923:

The wave of immorality which is menacing the integrity, even of our boys and girls in their tender years, has had an origin that is easily traced. It dates from that time when the dark and sinister shadow of Darwinism first fell across the fair fields of human life. If man is a descendant of the beast instead of a child of God, then we need not be surprised if we find him inclined to live like a beast. Monkey men make monkey morals, and a false and godless materialistic philosophy that glorifies the flesh at the expense of the Spirit is the one colossal menace of today.[66]

William Bell Riley, fundamentalist leader in the upper Midwest, was no less vocal about the demoralizing consequences of evolution than Straton, and a great deal more active in propagandizing the thesis. His opening remarks in a debate with Maynard Shipley, President of the Science League of America, in the Los Angeles Bible Institute auditorium, June 19, 1925, before nearly five thousand people manifested his anti-evolutionism:

We are to consider the most burning question of the present day,—a subject which in its natural ramification involves every form and interest of life on this globe, namely, the hypothesis of evolution. My part in this debate will be to prove to your satisfaction that the hypothesis is unscientific, unscriptural, and anti-Christian, and to deduce from that demonstrated fact the conclusion that its teaching in tax-supported schools should be no longer tolerated, and that its defense and propaga-

tion in denominational schools is at once the defense and propagation of a falsehood that can have but one fruit: the undoing and practical destruction of such institutions; while its final and more far-reaching effect will be the overthrow of the State, or our highest and best form of civilization.[67]

Riley and Bryan led the movement to preserve fundamentalism's stand on evolution in the schools. First, *church* schools had to be freed and kept safe from "evolutionist error." "One test of sanity," Bryan remarked, "is to put the suspected person in a tank into which a full stream of water is running and tell him to dip out the water. If he has not sense enough to turn off the inflowing stream of water before he begins to dip, he is declared insane. Can the churches escape a similar judgment if they permit church schools to discredit, during the week, the Bible used in Sunday-school and church?"[68] As to the *public* schools, Bryan

---

64. *Ibid.*, pp. 254-55.

65. The Fundamentalists' doctrine of the Bible was in Bryan's estimation basic to maintenance of the Five Points, and the basic threat to the Bible Bryan saw as evolution. "What is it that. . . .progressively whittles away the Word of God and destroys its vitality? I venture to assert that the unproven hypothesis of evolution is the root cause of nearly all the dissension in the church over the five points under discussion." Bryan, "The Fundamentals," *Forum* 70, no. 1 (July, 1923):1675.

66. John Roach Straton, "How Rationalism in the Pulpit Makes Worldliness in the Pew," (Chicago, 1923), p. 5.

67. W. B. Riley, "Evolution: Unscientific, Unscriptural, Anti-Christian!," *King's Business* 17, no. 7 (July, 1926):385. The intensity of Riley's hatred of evolution was signaled also in his summary estimate of the controversy, "Never in history has Christianity itself been so menaced as by Modernism, which is only another name for Darwinism." Riley, *Inspiration or Evolution* (Cleveland: Union Gospel Press, 1926), p. 138.

68. William Jennings Bryan, *Seven Questions in Dispute* (New York: Fleming H. Revell Company, 1924), p. 154.

insisted that "teachers in public schools must teach what the tax-payers desire taught—the hand that writes the pay check rules the school."[69]

The arguments advanced in behalf of antievolution legislation were typified by W.B. Riley in an address in advocacy of an antievolution bill delivered before a joint open session of the Minnesota State Senate and House, March 9, 1927. Riley supplied five arguments:

1. It is conceded to be constitutional. . . .
2. It is admittedly a popular demand. . . . [Riley here claimed that "this is no Riley movement" but "a popular demand of the people," and "ours is a government by the people."]
3. It is most manifestly fair. . . . [Paraphrased, the argument ran: if you're going to put out of the schools "the creative theory," be fair now and force out also "the evolutionary hypothesis."]
4. It restricts no scientific research. . . . What we are demanding is that the philosophy wait until the bones are discovered and the facts are forthcoming, before it boasts itself a science or braggartly demands adoption. . . .
5. State legislation is the one and only way of redress. . . . The State has a right to legislate for itself, and is not yet under the feet of a self-appointed oligarchy of Darwinites.[70]

Verbal denunciation of the evolutionists was much too mild for the rabid actionists among the fundamentalists. A correspondent of the *Greensboro Daily News*, for example, suggested that only inquisitorial devices would adequately rid the country of evolutionists:

This evolution idea has and is poisoning the minds of more people who are fool enough to listen to it. Truth Seeker has given his remedy for war, I will give mine: Take the evolutionists, infidels and these no-hell teachers out somewhere and crucify them head downward and we will have a better country and world to live in and instead of these evolution theories and easy-way ideas, teach the

people the Word of God to go by, to live by and to die by and all will be well.[71]

Evolutionists, confident of the mounting evidence for evolution's reliability, were little affected by such vindictive threats. Slosson reflected their calm confidence:

If the Fundamentalists were to burn up all the books on evolution, as the papers report they are being burned in certain communities of our country, if they should prohibit the teaching of evolution all over the world, that would not suffice. They would have to go further and chisel out all the fossils throughout the earth, for if they remain in the rocks somebody is sure to find them in time and draw the same inferences from them as to their age and origin. Suppose even this could be accomplished and all the paleontological evidences of

---

69. *Ibid.* Specific application of the argument was made in a letter to the editor of *The Forum* in the issue of August, 1925, (p. 28) after Mr. Scopes had challenged a Tennessee law making the teaching of evolution punishable by fine or imprisonment: "The right of free speech cannot be stretched as far as Mr. Scopes is trying to stretch it. A man cannot demand a salary for saying that which his employers do not want said, and he cannot require his employers to furnish him an audience to talk to, especially an audience of children or young people, when he wants to say what the parents do not wish said."

70. W. B. Riley, "Five Reasons for the Adoption of this Anti-Evolution Bill," *Christian Fundamentals in School and Church* 9, no. 2 (April-June, 1927):33-39. When the Texas legislature was considering an antievolution bill, J. Frank Norris, colorful fundamentalist from Fort Worth, appeared before the House legislature in 1925 where he called evolution "the most damnable doctrine that has come out of the bottomless pit." He continued, "So far as I am concerned, so help me God, I will not be a party to wink at, support, or even remain silent when any group, clique, crowd or machine undertakes to ram down the throats of Southern Baptists that hell-born, Bible-destroying, deity-of-Christ-denying, German rationalism known as evolution." See Shipley, *War on Modern Science*, pp. 171-72.

71. Cited by *Christian Century*, November 22, 1923, p. 1526.

evolution eliminated from the earth, evolution would still remain as active an agent as ever in the molding of living beings. Shutting our eyes does not affect the external world. It only makes us stumble about in it. [72]

Most modernists, convinced of "the paleontological evidences of evolution," became theistic evolutionists. They professed that evolution was the systematic, law-abiding means by which God had established and through which he governed the universe. Fosdick, for instance, said, "The great poem on creation with which the Bible opens is a magnificent expression of faith in one supreme God and in this universe as his handiwork, but it is not modern science." [73] Fosdick was saying in essence that the Bible tells us *who* was responsible for creation; science alone authoritatively tells us *how* it was accomplished.

While theistic evolutionists [74] professed to see the hand of God behind natural law and behind cause and effect relationships, many evolutionists banished God. Applying Occam's principle of parsimony, they insisted that in a world of matter and life marked by an orderly and continuous chain development from lower to higher forms of life there was no need for the old antinomies of a natural sphere and a supernatural sphere, or for the idea of an irruption of one sphere into the other. [75]

Other evolutionists were unwilling to have religion and science pitted as antagonists. Accordingly, at the instigation of Professor R.A. Millikan, winner of a Nobel prize, the following statement was prepared and signed by fifteen foremost scientists, sixteen religious leaders, and fourteen men of affairs:

We, the undersigned, deeply regret that in recent controversies there has been a tendency to present science and religion as irreconcilable and antagon-

istic domains of thought, for in fact they meet distinct human needs, and in the rounding out of human life they supplement rather than displace or oppose each other.

The purpose of science is to develop, without prejudice or preconception of any kind, a knowledge of the facts, the laws, and the processes of nature. The even more important task of religion, on the other hand, is to develop the consciences, the ideals, and the aspirations of mankind. Each of these two activities represents a deep and vital function of the soul of man, and both are necessary for the life, the progress, and the happiness of the human race. [76]

But despite claims to legitimate spheres for both science and religion, fundamentalist and evangelical modernist spokesmen alike decried the fact that the age-old issue between science *and* religion became in the twenties more one of science *as* religion.

Argumentation over evolution climaxed in the Scopes trial [77] where the jury's duty to affix guilt or innocence was not limited

---

72. Slosson, *Sermons of a Chemist*, p. 231.

73. Fosdick, *Adventurous Religion*, p. 121.

74. Bryan strikingly assessed theistic evolution in these terms, "Theistic evolution may be defined as an anesthetic which deadens the patient's pain while atheism removes his religion." See Gail Kennedy, ed., *Evolution and Religion* (Boston: D. C. Heath and Company, 1957), p. xiv.

75. Anti-theistic notions were seldom propagated by true scientists, but rather by the devotees of scientism. Darwin, for example, modestly disclaimed any right to pass judgment outside his scientific speciality. It was most often the "popularizers" of the "assured findings of science" who confidently announced that "science had undermined religion," or that "science finds no evidence of God in the world"—implying thereby, more often than not, that that was because God wasn't there to be found. See William Pierson Merrill, "Science Has Its Heretics," *Christian Century*, November 13, 1929, pp. 1406-7.

76. "Theology, Religion and Science," *American Review of Reviews* 68 (July, 1923):89.

77. The most complete account of the Scopes trial is *Bryan and Darrow at Dayton* (New York: A. Lee, 1925), compiled by Leslie H. Allen from the court record and various statements issued at the time.

to Scopes, but was, in the minds of many, generalized into a verdict between Christianity and evolution—not to say, science.

The defense initially made token effort to have the case dismissed on legal technicalities. Failing in this, they decided upon two broad strategies: (1) to shake the beliefs of fundamentalists through expert testimony,[78] and (2) to arouse the world to an awareness of the fundamentalists' threat to freedom through a dramatization of select fundamentalist teachings and practices.[79]

E.T. Stewart, Attorney General, had a simple strategy for the prosecution: this is the law; this is what Scopes did; therefore, he should be found guilty under the law and sentenced. But Bryan was not nearly so ready to settle for a cheap victory. "These gentlemen . . . did not come here to try this case," he asserted; "they came here to try revealed religion. I am here to defend it. . . ." Bryan, of course, carried a gallery of supporters into the defense action. Some three years before the trial, Bryan's supporters already credited him with having put Darwin on the run, and they were intent upon celebrating a significant duplication of the action. Bryan, viewing the event as but the climax of his antievolution crusade, saw no need for new arguments or new strategies. His general strategy remained essentially threefold in steps: (1) Insist that the laws of a sovereign people are to be obeyed and not flaunted.[80] (2) Claim that the theory of evolution is nothing more than an hypothesis,[81] and is palid and feeble before the verity of God's revelation. (3) Declare that evolution means "evil-ution" when it gets into places where it can pollute the minds of youth by calling attention to their brute ancestry rather than their divine birthright.

What were the consequences of the trial

78. The judge, having first sent the jurors out, listened to defense references to such terms as the Paleozoic Era and the Heidelberg Man before deciding that such testimony of the imported scientists was irrelevant—not to say irreverent—to the issues at hand and would not be allowed as an official part of the record.

79. With the testimony of his scientific experts disallowed, Darrow called for Bryan to take the stand as an expert on the Bible. Darrow disclosed his intent of revealing the lack of sound evidence behind Bryan's "expertness" when he said, "We have the purpose of preventing bigots and ignoramuses from controlling the education of the United States. . . ."

80. An antievolution law had been duly passed by the sovereign people of Tennessee. While Bryan's opponents saw him as restricting the educational enterprise, he saw himself as defending the democratic process. In a letter to the editor of *The Forum*, Bryan clarified this point, "As an individual, Mr. Scopes is perfectly free to think and speak as he likes, and the Christians of Tennessee will protect him in the enjoyment of these inalienable rights. But he was not arrested for doing anything as an individual. He was arrested for violating a law as a *representative* of the *State* and as an employee in a school. As a representative, he has no right to misrepresent; as an employee, he is compelled to act under the direction of his employers and has no right to defy instructions and still to claim his salary." 74, no. 2 (August, 1925):28.

Bryan had long insisted that while the constitutional separation between church and state excused the state schools from the positive teaching of the Bible—that "constitutional separation" prohibited alike the union of church and state and the union of state and atheism or infidelity. To denials that evolution destroys faith, leading men to agnosticism, Bryan retorted, "It is not sufficient to say that *some* believers in Darwinism retain their belief in Christianity; some survive smallpox. As we avoid smallpox because *many* die of it, so we should avoid Darwinism because it leads many astray." Cited by Rollin L. Hartt, "Down with Evolution," *World's Work* 46 (October, 1923): 610.

81. Bryan apparently never understood that a scientific "hypothesis" is a carefully formulated provisional statement to be used in furthering more exact research—that it is modifiable—and that it is called an hypothesis expressly to avoid dogmatically closing any investigation before all the facts have been carefully considered. Instead, Bryan cleverly identified a scientific hypothesis with a "guess," and by doing so found it possible to ridicule the proposal that teachers be permitted to teach "irresponsible guesses" when they contro-

in the light of the declared issues at stake? Neither the merits nor the demerits of the theory of evolution were convincingly established by the trial. Those who expected clarification confused the courtroom or public platform with the study, the classroom, and the laboratory. Neither questions of biblical scholarship nor science are amenable to the eloquence of orators or the devices of attorneys. Why then should the fundamentalist spokesmen—and particularly Bryan—have chosen to battle so strenuously over the issue of evolution in this setting? Was not the choice rhetorically motivated? Bryan knew his powers with an audience, provided the issue for which he was contending was sufficiently vital and concrete—qualifications that evolution handily met. In short, fundamentalists, backed by extraordinary advocates, pinned their hopes on the public forum—only to be ridiculed at the bar of public opinion by the Dayton fiasco.

There is no evidence that the Scopes trial changed many minds. It is safe to conjecture, however, that some measure of enlightenment must have resulted from perusal of the large number of volumes, magazine articles, and columns of newsprint which the Scopes trial called forth on the fundamentalist-modernist controversy in general, and the issue of evolution in particular.

John Scopes himself championed the significance of the case not as settling the legal issue in which the case was grounded nor as providing a spotlighted platform for a forensic contest between two well-known verbal pugilists, but as abetting "better understanding between the various factions involved" and hopefully as stirring "a new spiritual awakening."[82]

Scopes' hope for the revival of true religion as a result of the trial was largely unrealized. If anything, religion was hurt. Darrow's ridicule of Bryan was generalized to a ridicule of fundamentalism—if not of Christianity in general, and this is an age when there were already more laughing at the church from the outside than working in the inside. On the other hand, millions of persons all over the world who had laid their religion aside for the more absorbing pursuits of the twenties awoke to a new discussion of what it was all about. The world stirred, however temporarily, from its preoccupation with radio, automobiles, movies, and parades to wonder about the origin and destiny of man.

As it was for so many of the activities of the twenties, public reaction to the Scopes trial was out of all proportion to that which objective analysis of the event should have called forth. This fact would suggest that people were reacting more to that which the trial symbolized than to that which it concretely expressed. Certainly the trial symbolized for many modernist and evolutionist sympathizers the perils of "religious obscurantism," while to conservatives it symbolized the perils of the secularization of our culture as old authoritarian restraints were challenged in open battle. As an event in the controversy, it symbolized the last major fundamentalist offensive and their subsequent decline in prominence.

---

verted the clear teachings of the Bible. Bryan, in seeking to strengthen this point, called attention to the fact that some modern scientists had "abandoned Darwinism." Confusing modification with abandonment, Bryan was not able to refute the fact that while the theory was continually modified in its particulars, there seemed to be increasing unanimity as to the general usefulness of the conception of evolution.

82. See "Letters to the Editor," *Forum* 74, no. 2 (August, 1925):26.

The Issues Reconsidered
in Summary and Conclusion

The questions dividing the fundamentalists and modernists were ostensibly theological. Speeches, sermons, news headlines, literary essays, and full-length volumes all announced that the controversy hinged on such things as the doctrines regarding the Bible, the Second Coming of Christ, the Virgin Birth (Jesus' origin), and evolution (man's origin). Yet, unravelling of the theological involvements of the doctrinal particulars still leaves one with the feeling that the base issue has not been touched. What question lay behind all the theological skirmishing? Was not the single most fundamental question this: where is the seat of authority in religion? Does it reside in some book, in some creed, in some institution, in some person; or is it rather to be found within man himself? The question at root was thus less one of theology than of epistemology—what is the ground of religious knowledge?

In answer to what constitutes authority in the Christian religion, two views were contending for mastery among American Protestants during the twenties. The fundamentalist contended that the Bible was his sole basis of authority, claiming it to be a special, unique revelation of Divine truth and therefore the court of final appeal. The modernist asserted that the individual's autonomous reason was the only authority. This dichotomy is oversimplified, of course, for in practice, the epistemological issue was not so clear cut.

To make controversy profitable, there must be an accepted basis of knowledge by which to test the arguments advanced. But just such an accepted basis consistently held by all was lacking. Fundamentalists,

for example, repeatedly attempted to show the reasonableness of one or other of their contentions. But when that reason to which they appealed in some instances was turned against others of their contentions, they were quick to claim the "higher authority" of a revelation accepted by faith. For a controversialist to enter the arena and support his case by arguments which appeal to reason, and then to shift his ground and demand a judgment in his favor on another basis, annuls opportunity for sound argumentation performed in the interest of discovering reliable knowledge. Nor do the modernists escape critical judgment, for while fundamentalists practiced some inconsistency in their shiftings to various courts of appeal, modernists set up a pseudo-court where, in effect, they themselves interchanged roles as client, judge, and jury. Modernists, as a rule, appealed to reason, but they failed, of course, to establish by reason the contention that reason alone authoritatively establishes reliable knowledge. That is to say, one can neither impeach nor vindicate Reason when it is at the bar of Reason that the case against her has to be tried.

To pledge acceptance of reason as a test for discovering reliable religious knowledge, and then in the end to decline its jurisdiction by ducking out into the safe and convenient asylum of "faith" hardly satisfies the requirements for profitable controversy. On the other hand, to validate one's methodology by the use of that methodology is to be caught in the circular snare of making assumptions (presuppositions) prove their own validity. The judgment seems harsh, but inescapable: the theological issues of the fundamentalist-modernist controversy could not proceed to a profitable resolution because the controversialists were mired in unresolved epistemological issues. Because of this, in short, the encounter was less truly a controversy to ascertain "truth" than it was a campaign to secure votes. As such, it constitutes a fascinating study in the history of American public address.

Epilogue

Ecclesiastical power shifted from the fundamentalists to the modernists in the late twenties and early thirties. Liberalism was, however, not long to enjoy its newly won supremacy. Immediately it faced harsh criticism. When "optimistic liberalism" collapsed in the thirties, fundamentalists took too much credit for themselves, believing that the lances of earlier days had finally done their mischief. Actually it was a self-critical dialectic that led prominent modernist leaders into what has been called "reconstructed liberalism,"—not capitulation to fundamentalists. The movement "beyond modernism" was not a retreat by battered forces so much as it was the admission by certain modernists that their theological premises no longer passed the pragmatic test of realistic relevancy. Several exhibits illustrate the point but it was left for Harry Emerson Fosdick to shatter the easy optimism of modernism. Characteristically, Fosdick chose the medium of public address by which to drop what William Hordern, analyst of contemporary theology, has called "an unexpected depth charge into the sea of theology."[83] In a widely publicized confessional sermon, "Beyond "Modernism," delivered at his Riverside Church and published in *The Christian Century*, December 4, 1935, Fosdick acknowledged that the modernist theology he had so long championed no longer was adequate. The press immediately grasped the headline value of

the event and boldly announced that the leader of the modernist forces had found his liberal religion inadequate and was returning to the God—if not the theology—of the fundamentalists.[84] Fundamentalists were gleeful and liberals cringed at what appeared to be gross betrayal. Few bothered to note what Fosdick had actually said.

Fosdick's charge, in the main, was this: modernism in its vitally necessary function of speaking relevantly to the times had overextended itself to the point where it became so identified with the prevailing culture that it could no longer significantly "stand out from it and challenge it." Modernism had been dangerously sentimental, said Fosdick, in harboring the delusion of inevitable progress, had been so absorbed with a man-centered culture that it had played down the reality of God, and had too often lost its "ethical standing-ground and its power of moral attack" through its harmonizations and accommodations with existing mores.

While old-line liberals were going "beyond modernism" in the direction of the European neo-orthodoxy, a new generation of fundamentalists sought to keep alive the chief theological emphases of their tradition. L.C. Rudolph, for example, reported in 1958:

An interdenominational atmosphere of fundamentalism, usually without the historic issue of evolu-

---

83. William Hordern, *A Layman's Guide to Protestant Theology* (New York: Macmillan, 1955), p. 108.

84. Fosdick's 1935 sermon, not unlike his 1922 sermon, "Shall the Fundamentalists Win?" was significant primarily for its symbolic character. An articulate leader of the American theological scene had issued a cogent statement of sincerely felt convictions around which others could rally or with which they could take clear exception. Both sermons are bold exhibits of the history-shaping potential of public address.

tion, is still offered for all who seek it. Education may range from a respectable Bible college or seminary, with professors carefully trained but not "corrupted" by leading universities, to the barest memory chain of proof texts passed along firsthand or in pulp literature. Economic status may vary from the solidity of the Christian Businessmen's Association to the poverty of some pentecostals. Publications may vary from the carefully edited *Christianity Today* to the anti-Semitic rantings of Gerald L.K. Smith in *The Cross and the Flag*. The variety is impressive and disconcerting. . . .[85]

The terms "fundamentalist" and "modernist," fixed as apparently permanent labels in the twenties, find occasional prominent display in the news media of today. When Billy Graham conducted his "Greater Chicago Crusade" in the summer of 1962, for example, the *Chicago Daily News* bannered the following eight column, forty point headline: "Sin—Fundamentalist vs. Modernist View."[86] Even our astronauts are not immune from being characterized in terms of these labels. Following the space flight of Lieutenant Colonel John H. Glenn, Jr., the Reverend Frank A. Erwin, pastor of the Little Falls United Presbyterian Church to which the Glenn family belongs, reported that Glenn was "neither a fundamentalist nor a liberal."[87] And in his 1963 article "How to Tell a Baptist from a Methodist in the South," George Harmon, religion editor of the *Jacksonville Journal*, reported that "Southern Baptists are Jacksonville's primary depository of Protestant conservatism, or fundamentalism. Methodists have been shifting theologically leftward for many years, and have become the South's color guard of liberal Protestantism, also called modernism."[88]

Though such references continue, they remain, by and large, on the periphery of Protestant church life in America today. Generally, the label of "heresy" is now re-

served for other forces active on the contemporary scene.[89] Yet, the existence and persistence of such skirmishings into the present calls for some explanation. Is it not true that those issues so openly agitated during the twenties embody age-old philosophical, psychological, and theological problems: authority versus rebellion, dogma versus reason, revelation versus experience, affirmation versus negation, ancient creeds versus new formulations, orthodoxy versus heterodoxy, tolerance versus intolerance, evolution versus revolution, old faith versus new knowledge, urbanism versus ruralism, established institutions versus schismatic sects, narrow ecclesiasticism versus a widely inclusive fellowship, "correct" theology versus concern for relevant ethics, tyranny versus liberty, and a haven of spiritual inertia versus the continually tensioned struggle for new spiritual insight? These and like queries agitate minds during every age and require but cogent expression from articulate spokesmen

---

85. L. C. Rudolph, "Fundamentalism," in *The Church Faces the Isms*, ed. Arnold Black Rhodes (New York: Abingdon, 1958), pp. 60-61. Rudolph attempts to systematize the "impressive" and "disconcerting" variety of fundamentalists today by speaking of pietistic fundamentalism, rationalistic fundamentalism, and militant fundamentalism.

86. *Chicago Daily News*, June 2, 1962, p. 7.

87. See *Christianity Today*, March 16, 1962, p. 31.

88. George Harmon, *Harper's Magazine* 226 (February, 1963):59. Harmon's contrasting of Southern Baptists with Methodists supplies a contemporary commentary on the beliefs of fundamentalists and modernists.

89. See, for example, John M. Krumm's book, *Modern Heresies*, in which he speaks of naturalistic humanism, the "positive thinking" heresy, the heresy of secularism, the antisecularist heresy, deism, universalism, the "divine spark" heresy, the heresy of denominationalism, the heresy of papal infallibility, the heresy of individualism, the heresy of spiritualism, and the like. (Greenwich, Conn.: Seabury Press, 1961).

to thrust them, however temporarily, into
the forefront of public consciousness.

BIBLIOGRAPHY

Sources helpful for understanding the theological climate of the twenties:

Atkins, Gaius Glenn. *Preaching and the Mind of
    Today.* New York: Round Table Press, 1934.
——. *Religion in Our Times.* New York: Round
    Table Press, 1932.
Aubrey, Edwin Ewart. *Present Theological Ten-
    dencies.* New York: Harper and Brothers,
    1935.
Henry, Carl F.H. *Fifty Years of Protestant Theo-
    logy.* Boston: W.A. Wilde Company, 1950.
Horton, Walter Marshall. *Theology in Transition.*
    New York: Harper and Brothers, 1939.
Sweet, William Warren. *The Story of Religion in
    America.* New York: Harper and Brothers,
    1930.

For some of the most carefully reasoned
rhetoric in the dispute:

Machen, John Gresham. *The Origin of Paul's Reli-
    gion.* New York: Macmillan, 1921.
——. *The Separateness of the Church.* Sermon
    preached at the Presbyterian Theological
    Seminary, Princeton, N.J., March 8, 1925.
    Calcutta, India: The Evangelical Literature
    Trust, 1925.

A sample of William Jennings Bryan's rhetoric on evolution is found in:

Bryan, William Jennings. *Bryan's Last Word on
    Evolution.* Chicago: The Bible Institute Col-
    portage Association, 1925.
——. *In His Image.* New York: Fleming H. Revell,
    1922.

For perspective on the thinking of Harry
Emerson Fosdick and Clarence E. Macartney, leading rhetoricians on the issue, see:

Fosdick, Harry Emerson, *Christianity and Pro-
    gress.* New York: Fleming H. Revell, 1922.
——. *The Living of These Days: An Autobiogra-
    phy.* New York: Harper and Brothers, 1956.

——. *The Modern Use of the Bible.* New York:
    Macmillan, 1924.
Macartney, Clarence Edward. *Christianity and
    Common Sense.* Chicago: John C. Winston
    Company, 1927.
——. *The Making of a Minister: Autobiography of
    Clarence Edward Macartney.* Great Neck:
    Channel Press, 1961.
——. "Shall Unbelief Win?", a response to Fos-
    dick's "Shall the Fundamentalists Win?"
    Both sermons appear in *Sermons in American
    History.* Edited by DeWitte Holland. Nash-
    ville: Abingdon Press, 1971.

Also of interest:

Furniss, Norman F. *The Fundamentalist Contro-
    versy, 1918-1931.* New Haven: Yale Univer-
    sity Press, 1954.
    A definitive history of the controversy. Ori-
    ginally presented as a Ph.D. dissertation un-
    der the same title, Yale University, 1950.

Gray, L. Jack. "A Study of Protestant Preaching in
    the United States, 1920-1929." Ph.D. disser-
    tation, Southern Baptist Theological Semin-
    ary, 1948.
    A study dealing generally with Protestant
    preaching in the United States during the
    1920s.

Gustafson, Cloyd V. "The Sociology of Funda-
    mentalism: A Typological Analysis Based on
    Selected Groups in Portland, Oregon and Vi-
    cinity." Ph.D. dissertation, University of Chi-
    cago, 1956.
    A sociological treatment of fundamentalism.

Meyer, Donald Burton. "The Protestant Social
    Liberals in America, 1919-1941." Ph.D. dis-
    sertation, 2 vols., Harvard University, 1953.
    Concerned with those Protestant clerics who
    by the end of World War I self-consciously
    conceived their task to be agitating and work-
    ing for basic changes in the economic and so-
    cial arrangements of society.

Miller, Robert Moats. *American Protestantism and
    Social Issues, 1919-1939.* Chapel Hill: Uni-
    versity of North Carolina Press, 1958.
    Originally presented as a Ph.D. dissertation,
    Northwestern University, 1955, under title,
    "An Inquiry into the Social Attitudes of
    American Protestantism, 1919-1939."

18   The New Deal

G. Jack Gravlee

"I pledge you, I pledge myself, to a new deal for the American people." These memorable words, uttered in a precedent-breaking convention address in Chicago, July 2, 1932, by the new Democratic presidential nominee, were followed with a call for "a new order of competence and courage. This is more than a political campaign; it is a call to arms."[1] As the strains of "Happy Days are Here Again" faded, the American people were about to become involved in not just another campaign, another election, another transfer of power. Franklin Delano Roosevelt's "New Deal," later simultaneously praised and cursed, was destined to become the label for a new era; an era that marked the shifting of political gears. Offered originally as a means to pull the nation from the depths of depression, it ultimately altered social, political, and economic cornerstones unlike any changes accomplished by any other American administration in so short a time.

Meaning and Duration

What was the New Deal? Simply stated, it posited that a strong federal government must administer and control solutions to national problems, particularly during times of crisis, in order to insure maximum happiness. Of course a strong central government necessarily would determine when a problem was national in scope and would prescribe its proper solution.

Roosevelt described the "compass of my policy as a 'concert of interests'—North and South, East and West, agriculture, industry, mining, commerce and finance."[2] This "concert of interests" was combined with "interdependence"[3] of the people within the republic which meant the necessity "of distributing wealth and products more equitably, of adapting existing economic organizations to the service of the peo-

---

1. Franklin D. Roosevelt, *The Public Papers and Addresses of Franklin D. Roosevelt*, ed. Samuel I. Rosenman (New York: Random House, 1938), 1:659 (hereafter cited as Roosevelt, *Public Papers*).
2. Lowery LeRoy Cowperthwaite, "A Criticism of the Speaking of Franklin D. Roosevelt in the Presidential Campaign of 1932" (Diss. University of Iowa, 1950), p. 309.
3. See Roosevelt's "Address on Railroads," Salt Lake City, Utah, September 17, 1932, in Roosevelt, *Public Papers*, 1:712. Also, in Cowperthwaite, "Criticism," pp. 310-17.

ple.''[4] "Translated into practical application, it becomes the duty of the state in
times of great national economic disorder
to provide for those who, through no fault
of their own, are without means of livelihood. In short, when private economic
systems break down, the state becomes the
provider for its unfortunate wards.''[5]

The New Deal did not alter the basic tenets of the American Constitution but only
the interpretation of that Constitution.
That is to say, it did not burn the bridges
and make it impossible ever again to return
to a less expansive interpretation of federal
power.

What was the duration of the New Deal?
Historians often speak of the "First New
Deal" encompassing the years 1933-34,
and the "Second New Deal" taking place
1935-37. By the year 1938, the New Deal
had spun its course and attention of necessity shifted to foreign policy.[6] This chapter
will not attempt to follow exactly the historians' divisions. Rather, it will be concerned with three definite divisions of rhetoric within the New Deal period: the 1932
campaign, 1933-34 explication of programs, and the 1935-36 defense of those
programs.

Selling the New Deal: The 1932 Campaign

While Roosevelt "was by no means a political unknown by the summer of 1932," the
voter "who read his daily newspaper and
popular magazines" would have had a
three-faceted "mental picture": "(1) the
'magic' of his name, (2) his reputation as
the popular and progressive Governor of
the Empire State, and (3) the legend of his
heroic struggle against the ravages of a crip-
pling disease.''[7] Even so, this gubernatorial
reputation likely was based more on the

725,000 reelection plurality he acquired in
1930 than on any specific reform measures.
The New Deal was accepted probably because the people were sick to death of Hoover and found Roosevelt refreshingly vigorous and articulate by comparison. The
Republican President considered relief to
be an individual, community, and state responsibility. He would "support adequate
measures for relief of distress and unemployment" only after the national budget
was balanced. Such recalcitrance and insen-
sitivity served as catalysts for the challenging Democratic program.

The first presidential campaign afforded
the populace a chance to hear and accept
FDR's depression remedies. Between September 12 and November, 7, 1932 he campaigned in 37 states, covered over 25,000
miles by train, delivered 16 major addresses, 67 less important addresses and hundreds of brief rear-platform appearances,
for a total in excess of 1,000 speeches.[8] His
speeches offered the expected indictment
of the incumbent administration and went
into greater detail than usual in spelling out
specific remedies. Probably more than any
other single factor, they reflected the candidate's empathy for the downtrodden
which contrasted sharply with Hoover's apparent sullen aloofness. Even before the
nomination, in a radio address, FDR had
spoken of implementing "plans that . . .

---

4. This passage is from Roosevelt's famous "Address on Progressive Government at the Commonwealth Club," San Francisco, Cal.. Sept. 23, 1932,
in Roosevelt, *Public Papers*, 1:752.
5. Cowperthwaite, "Criticism," p. 323.
6. For a concise historical overview of these years,
see Dexter Perkins, *The New Age of Franklin
Roosevelt, 1932-45*, (Chicago: University of Chicago Press, 1967), pp. 4-80.
7. Cowperthwaite, "Criticism," pp. 153,155.
8. *Ibid.*, pp. 33-34, 102-03, 39-40, 78-79.

put their faith once more in the forgotten man at the bottom of the economic pyramid."[9] Using this theme repeatedly, the candidate tailored his speeches carefully to fit his audience. Of course he continued to be Governor of New York and had to return to Albany on occasion to mind the store. But in his speeches he was weaving a bond of trust that four successive challengers could not effectively penetrate.

Typical of his candid problem-solution approach to issues, Roosevelt asserted that agricultural difficulties were aggravated by federal neglect. His address at Topeka, Kansas, "A Restored and Rehabilitated Agriculture," September 14, became the cornerstone of subsequent legislation. Not the savior with all the answers, he emphasized, "I have come here not alone to talk to you about farms and farming. I have come just as much and even more to listen and to learn. . . . I want to avoid on the one hand political skywriting, and on the other hand political wisecracking." After pointing to success in dealing with "the farmers of New York" by applying "practical and definite action" rather than "appointing commissions and calling conferences," he described "our economic life today" as "a seamless web" and modified a Lincoln expression, "This Nation cannot endure if it is half 'boom' and half 'broke.' "[10] He was aware of the problems facing that audience:

Farming has not had an even break in our economic system. The things that our farmers buy today cost 9 percent more than they did before the World War—in 1914. The things they sell bring them 43 percent less than then. These figures, as of August first, authenticated by the Department of Agriculture, mean that the farm dollar is worth less than half of what it represented before the war.[11]

He offered some general solutions:

We must have, I assert with all possible emphasis, national planning in agriculture. We must not have, as now, the scattering of our efforts through the heterogeneous and disassociated activities of our governmental agencies dealing with the problem. On the other hand, we must avoid the present tendency to jump from one temporary expedient to another. We need unity of planning, coherence of our Administration and emphasis upon cures rather than upon drugs.[12]

He followed with more specific remedies:

First, I would reorganize the United States Department of Agriculture. . . .
Second, I favor a definite policy looking to the planned use of land. . . .
. . . third . . . national leadership in the reduction and more equitable distribution of taxes. . . .
. . . refinancing of farm mortgages. . . .
. . . a substantial reduction in the difference between the prices of things the farmer sells and the things he buys . . . by restoring international trade through tariff readjustments.[13]

Then, he explained in detail the six "essential specifications of a workable plan" upon "which most of the reasonable leaders of agriculture have agreed."[14]

And so it went throughout the campaign as he spoke about railroads, tariff negotiations, electrical power, social justice, business interests, unemployment, social welfare, the federal budget, farm mortgages, governmental and private credit, and his overall philosophy of government.

Roosevelt made the general role of the proposed New Deal quite clear throughout the campaign, typified by these statements

9. Roosevelt, *Public Papers*, 1:625.
10. Above excerpts from Roosevelt's text as authenticated in Cowperthwaite, "Criticism," pp. 496-97, 499-500.
11. *Ibid.*, p. 500.
12. *Ibid.*, p. 501.
13. *Ibid.*, pp. 502-04.
14. *Ibid.*, pp. 506-07.

in Boston, October 31: "whenever the States themselves are unable [to provide relief] . . . the Federal Government owes the positive duty of stepping into the breach . . . in addition to providing emergency relief, the Federal Government should and must provide temporary work wherever that is possible . . . the Federal Government should expedite the actual construction of public works already authorized."[15] He pledged an overall plan of "Federal action" that obviously did not repel the voters who delivered almost 60 percent of the total to Roosevelt.[16]

The First New Deal: Rhetoric of Affirmative Action (1933-34)

First Inaugural—"This nation asks for action, and action now." These were the words of the First Inaugural that captured the attention of the immediate audience,[17] although the address is better known for the more catchy "the only thing we have to fear is fear itself."[18] It was a tense situation that bleak March 4 in Washington, and the tenseness of the moment permeated every phrase the new President uttered. Gone was the levity, the blare of campaigning, the clever dart at the opponent. After moving past 500,000 cheering spectators lining the streets, FDR was administered the oath at 1:08 P.M. on the main steps of the Capitol by Chief Justice Charles Evans Hughes. No one knew what to expect, but the world would be tuned in to whatever transpired. From 9:30 A.M. until 4:00 P.M., 178 American radio stations were linked for the inaugural program. Short wave took the ceremonies to England, Germany, Switzerland, Holland, South Africa, New Zealand, and Australia. Nearly 75 microphones were operative "at the White House, the Capitol,

the Senate chamber, various hotels, along Pennsylvania Avenue, attached to portable transmitters strapped on the backs of special announcers in crowds, in automobiles . . . in airplanes and blimps flying over Washington."[19] Security was particularly tight as the possibility of assassination and radical overthrow of governmental processes was not remote.[20] These were desperate times that excited desperate people.

Mixed with this air of desperation was a spirit of excitement. A change was on the way. Arthur Krock noted that "the mood of Washington" was to "welcome the 'new deal,' even though it is not sure what the new deal is going to be. It is ready to be enthusiastic over any display of leadership, any outline of a reconstruction program."[21] The Inaugural Address offered (1) candor, "the time to speak the truth, the whole truth, frankly and boldly";

15. *Ibid.*, p. 622, and Roosevelt, *Public Papers*, 1:851-52.
16. David C. Whitney, *The American Presidents* (Garden City: Doubleday & Co., Inc., 1969), p. 372.
17. *New York Times*, March 5, 1933, p. 1.
18. Roosevelt, *Public Papers*, 2:11-16; Franklin D. Roosevelt, *F.D.R. Speaks*, Phonodisc, Washington Records, 1960, side 1.
19. *New York Times*, March 4, 1933, p. 4.
20. As if national crises were not enough, personal misfortune stalked the new Democratic leader. On a platform in Miami, Flordia, February 15, an assassination attempt on FDR by Joseph Zangara resulted in the shooting of the Mayor of Chicago, Anton J. Cermak. Mr. Cermak seemingly was on the road to recovery, his situation then became critical and he died two days after the Inaugural. Also, two days before inauguration, Thomas J. Walsh, 73 year old Senator from Montana and Attorney General designate in the new Cabinet, died of a heart attack on a train enroute to Washington from Havana with his bride of one week. *New York Times*, March 7, 1933, p. 1, and March 3, 1933, p. 1.
21. "Roosevelt Arrival Heartens Capital," *New York Times*, March 3, 1933, p. 2.

(2) encouragement, "our common difficulties . . . concern, thank God, only material things"; (3) identification of failure, "Practices of the unscrupulous money changers stand indicted in the court of public opinion"; (4) identification of solutions, "Our greatest primary task is to put people to work . . . endeavor to provide a better use of the land . . . strict supervision of all banking and credits . . . an adequate but sound currency." But, alarmingly, the line most robustly cheered threatened that if "Congress shall fail . . . I shall ask the Congress for . . . broad Executive power to wage a war against the emergency, as great as the power that would be given to me if we were in fact invaded by a foreign foe."[22]

Early Action—His first full day in office, the President signed the Proclamation for an Extraordinary Session of Congress, ordered a bank holiday, called for a Governors' Conference at the White House, and issued a radio invitation for cooperation from all veterans, while Herbert Hoover slept twelve hours.[23] It was apparent from the outset that the immediacy of verbal communication would be crucial to the new administration:

Monday, March 6: FDR addressed the Governors' Conference. Discussions conducted at Conference on financial plans. Treasury Secretary William H. Woodin arranged for two press conferences daily to "keep the public advised."

Tuesday, March 7: Scores of individual meetings and small conferences held on national matters, primarily economic in nature.

Wednesday, March 8: FDR outlined bank plans in a White House conference with a group of Congressmen led by Senator Joseph P. Robinson of Arkansas. FDR's first press conference with spontaneous questions and answers. He agreed to hold press conferences twice a week—Wednesday at 10:00 A.M. for afternoon reporters and Friday at 4:00 P.M. for morning reporters.

Friday, March 10: Second press conference.

Saturday, March 11: FDR issued statements from the White House concerning the Los Angeles earthquake and the method for reopening banks. FDR announced his first radio report to the people for the next day.

Sunday, March 12: First "Fireside Chat," 10:00-10:15 P.M. from the White House study, explaining the banking situation over national radio networks.[24]

The first eight full days in office, the President delivered two radio addresses, conducted two press conferences, presided over a two-day Governors' Conference, held scores of meetings and discussions that involved a multitude of subjects. Arthur Krock said moving from "the dying, functionless Hoover government" to the New

---

22. Roosevelt, *Public Papers*, 2:11-15.
23. *New York Times*, March 6, 1933, pp. 1,6. See also, Roosevelt, *Public Papers*, 2:16-18. This plea was made to veterans because (1) payment to ex-servicemen was the largest single item in the budget, (2) he was about to request a decrease in pensions and other benefits, (3) veterans were well organized with a strong lobby, (4) their opposition to smaller payments could be anticipated. *New York Times*, March 5, 1933, section 8, p. 1, and March 11, 1933, p. 2.
24. *New York Times*, March 6, 1933, p. 1; March 7, 1933, p. 2; March 8, 1933, pp. 1, 12; March 9, 1933, pp. 1, 3; March 11, 1933, pp. 2, 3, 7; March 12, 1933, pp. 1, 2; March 13, 1933, pp. 1, 3. See also Roosevelt, *Public Papers*, 2:17-66.

Deal was like changing "from an ox-cart to Frank Hawk's airplane."[25]

The presidential voice was not the only one advocating action and a shift in governmental involvement. Many addresses of explanation, attack, and defense were delivered over one or more of the major radio networks on a coast-to-coast hook-up. There was a series of speeches by ranking administrators informing the public about their specific departments:

April 24, 1933, Homer S. Cummings, Attorney General, radio address;

April 28, 1933, Jesse H. Jones, Director, Reconstruction Finance Corporation, before American Society of Newspaper Editors, Washington, D.C.;

May 1, 1933, Henry A. Wallace, Secretary of Agriculture, radio address;

May 8, 1933, Harold L. Ickes, Secretary of Interior, radio address;

June 14, 1933, Henry Morgenthau, Jr., Governor of the Farm Credit Administration, radio address.[26]

These speeches gave some history of the departments involved, suggested their basic purposes and procedures, then went on to develop some future goals of accomplishment.

The Cabinet and staffers carried the message concerning New Deal programs of increased federal power and probably spoke for the majority of the electorate. Even opportunistic Senator Huey Long, who had pushed his "Share Our Wealth" ideas since 1932, found it necessary to praise "our great President . . . who is so ably serving us at the present time . . . our President has not only kept faith both before his nomination but he kept faith after nomination."[27] On the other extreme, traditional conservatives also supported the innovations, as indicated by resolutions adopted by the Co-lumbus, Ohio, Chamber of Commerce, May 12, 1933, expressing "complete confidence in President Roosevelt . . . we stand ready and willing to assist the President in every possible way in his program to restore industry and relieve unemployment."[28] So the people just wanted to get out from under the depression and did not seem overly concerned with any shifts in basic political structure or philosophy.

Reaction—Major detractors evolved in two categories:

1. Right wing opponents shocked at the "unconstitutional" excesses of the New Deal; and

2. Left wing opponents irritated at the timidity of New Deal programs. Obviously, the ultimate in political acumen and nimbleness probably would fail to please these two divergent elements.

While surfacing somewhat slowly after the one-sided election of 1932, right wingers decried New Deal "unconstitutionality" and hailed puritanical "rugged individualism." These speakers resisted change, avoided specifics, yearned for those mythical "good old days" that would somehow return if we trusted the teachings of "our forefathers"—those same forefathers who, for some unexplained reason, did not them-

25. "Roosevelt in Swift Pace Revitalizes Government," *New York Times*, March 12, 1933, section 4, p. 1.
26. Address by Homer S. Cummings, May 12, 1933, U.S., Congress, House, *Congressional Record*, 73rd Congress, 1st Session, 1933, 3347-48; *ibid.*, Senate, Address by Jesse H. Jones, May 10, 1933, pp. 3110-11; *ibid.*, House, Address by Henry A. Wallace, May 4, 1933, pp. 2884-86; *ibid.*, House, Address by Harold L. Ickes, May 9, 1933, pp. 3096-98; *ibid.*, House, Address by Henry Morgenthau, Jr., June 15, 1933, pp. 6187-88.
27. *Ibid.*, Senate, March 23, 1933, p. 788.
28. *Ibid.*, House, May 15, 1933, p. 3429.

selves patiently await the mysterious blessings of political inertia. Thus, speakers like Rep. John B. Hollister of Ohio cranked out discourses of suspicion:

Hamilton and Marshall would have been aghast at some of the governmental manifestations which we today accept as normal, and I am afraid that poor Thomas Jefferson has grown calluses from turning rapidly in his grave at the mere thought of how far we have departed from his principles.

The Constitution was conceived on the theory of rugged individualism. . . .[29]

Mr. Hollister censured "the Frankenstein of 'government in business,' " but somehow did not find tariffs in conflict with this concept. Also, he did not find "solutions" to be "the province of my talk tonight." Nevertheless, others agreed. Sterling E. Edmunds, an author who was characterized as "a friend to the Constitution," labeled the "Government at Washington as the Federal octopus . . .

with its now numberless tentacles reaching out into every city and every county, into every hamlet and every home in the land, crushing out civil liberty and self-government, debauching the manliness and self-reliance of our people by pandering to the venality of large groups and classes; and through the taxing suckers of its ugly prototype, draining the lifeblood from all property, from all trade, and from all industry.[30]

The most poignant threat to the First New Deal came from another category, a left wing that rankled for more expansive social programs. The leading agitator until his death in 1935 was Huey Pierce Long, the demagogic Governor turned Senator who knew how to read the pulse of the downtrodden and to prescribe his magic elixir for all social ills. Somehow simplistic "pie in the sky" remedies have a charm and a magnetism all their own for those with de-

pressed hope who in normal times would know better. In a radio address, March 17, 1933, over NBC, Mr. Long quoted a few lines from Oliver Goldsmith:

"Ill fares the land, to hastening ills a prey,
Where wealth accumulates and men decay:
Princes and lords may flourish, or may fade;
A breath can make them, as a breath has made;
But a bold peasantry, the country's pride,
When once destroyed, can never be supplied."[31]

He intended to invest his political future in this "bold peasantry" by lashing out at those with means. Even as he praised Franklin Roosevelt, he continued to press for his Share Our Wealth program. During these desperate times, Long's proposals had appeal:

With more than we can eat and more than we can wear and more houses than we can live in, there is greater distress among the people of America today to get something to eat and something to wear and a place to live than there was in times of famine. Simply because a few have desired to accumulate all the wealth, even though they impoverished all the balance of the people.[32]

A month later, Long repeated his "fight for the decentralization of wealth" in another nationwide radio address and announced with considerable sarcasm and gross misstatement "that the President of the United States and the other great statesmen of finance have swallowed our demand, hook, line, and sinker." Such desperate folly as "I have undertaken to bring about a reopening of all banks"[33] would have been ludicrous had Long been a less effective politician.

---

29. *Ibid.*, May 9, 1933, pp. 3094, 3096.
30. *Ibid.*, May 29, 1933, p. 4514.
31. *Ibid.*, Senate, March 23, 1933, p. 786.
32. *Ibid.*, p. 787.
33. *Ibid.*, pp. 2211-12.

By June, Long probably became *persona non grata* to anyone hopeful of regular party support. By then he was particularly abrasive concerning executive power, bureaucracy, regulatory codes, states' rights, monetary conditions, and somehow worked them all into a single performance in the United States Senate on June 7:

The only way we can do anything in this Congress is to authorize the President of the United States to suspend the Constitution of the United States and the antitrust laws and everything else that the people are living under. . . .
. . . the Secretary to the President . . . the secretary to the Secretary . . . the supervisors . . . the assistant supervisors . . . the secretary to the supervisors . . . the supervisors of the secretaries. . . .
The President of the United States not only can, but the chances are 999 to 1 that he will, have hundreds of thousands of agents . . . combing literally the face of the earth. . . . Some little old country woman grinding up hogs in the fall of the year who dares to use the ordinary process of making link sausage, and put a single pound of it on the market, or swap it with a neighbor for a sack of potatoes, would be violating the provisions of this law, and be liable to arrest and imprisonment in the penitentiary. . . .
We have lost State rights. We not only have surrendered what the Union won in 1865, but we have, by such pernicious and abortive legislation as this, surrendered the freedom not only of the black but of the white people of the United States. . . .
. . . the money of the United States . . . is liable to be wood; it is liable to be zinc; it is liable to be wild honey. . . . If we had adopted the Wheeler bill, we would have known that gold and silver were going to be the only commodities called money in the United States.[34]

But Burton K. Wheeler was of another political genre. His main theme was the remonetization of silver, as reflected in a typical radio address, April 22, 1933, "For several years I have been trying to tell the American people that our primary money was not sufficient." Supposedly he did not want any "listener to . . . misinterpret my

attitude toward the national administration" which was "profound admiration" for the "President and his coworkers."[35] But admiration is hardly believable when, in the same address, these condemnations rang forth:

When we delegate to the Secretary of Agriculture the power to tax the people almost at will; when we give the President the power to dictate wage reductions, reductions in the pensions paid; when we give him full authority over the railroads and then give him the right to fix the gold content of the dollar . . . we are . . . coming mighty close to setting up a dictatorship in the White House. . . .
[My proposals] would have done more for the farmers of this country than all the farm legislation . . . advanced by professors, economists, or farm leaders.[36]

While not quite as abrasive as Huey Long, Wheeler's speech was antiintellectual, antiexecutive power, and probimetallism with an implication that other national problems could be solved if his recommendations were adopted.

Other radicals were equally egoistic. The various shades of farm, labor, and socialistic spokesmen seemingly battled each other for the limelight. For instance, John A. Simpson, president of the National Farmers Union, enjoyed considerable radio air time in a series of verbose addresses that supported the Wheeler bill "for the remonetization of silver at the ratio of 16 to 1," condemned bankers, attacked the "farm-relief measure" as "the biggest economic legislative folly ever presented to the National Congress," resoundingly declared "that everything that has been done up to this date is . . . foolish and useless," and appealed for a letter writing-membership

34. *Ibid.*, June 7, 1933, pp. 5174-77.
35. *Ibid.*, April 22, 1933, p. 2148.
36. *Ibid.*, pp. 2149-50.

campaign because his organization was the only one sincerely dedicated to the best interests of all farmers.[37]

Response—Faced with these divergent groups, what was Roosevelt's speaking strategy? In his first two "Fireside Chats," he chose to continue the analytical report approach. March 12, 1933, he spoke "about banking . . . what has been done in the last few days, why it was done, and what the next steps are going to be." In fifteen minutes he moved from fundamental economics to future projection:

First of all, let me state the simple fact that when you deposit money in a bank the bank does not put the money into a safe deposit vault. It invests your money in many different forms of credit—bonds, commercial paper, mortgages and many other kinds of loans. In other words, the bank puts your money to work to keep the wheels of industry and of agriculture turning around. . . .
One more point before I close. There will be, of course, some banks unable to reopen without being reorganized. . . .
I do not promise you that every bank will be reopened or that individual losses will not be suffered, but there will be no losses that possibly could be avoided. . . .[38]

"Tonight, eight weeks later," May 7, the President spoke to the American people "for the second time to give you my report; in the same spirit and by the same means to tell you about what we have been doing and what we are planning to do." He spoke about congressional cooperation, employment, Tennessee Valley, public works, farm relief, hours for labor, transportation, and international conferences.[39] His third address, a July 24 reflection of "the hundred days which had been devoted to the starting of the wheels of the New Deal," developed into a persuasive appeal for accelerated cooperation with the Recovery Act.

He seemed somewhat discouraged by the slowness with which "small employers" agreed to codes and concluded with a bandwagon appeal for the NRA Blue Eagle:

In war, in the gloom of night attack, soldiers wear a bright badge on their shoulders to be sure that comrades do not fire on comrades. On that principle, those who cooperate in this program must know each other at a glance. That is why we have provided a badge of honor for this purpose, a simple design with a legend, "We do our part," and I ask that all those who join with me shall display that badge prominently. . . .[40]

The fourth "Fireside Chat," October 22, 1933, was a mixture of defense for current programs and stinging rebuke for the critics. He reviewed the accomplishments of specific programs, declared "we are on our way" even though "I am not satisfied" with all factors. But he seemed most upset over unfair criticism:

Ninety percent of complaints come from misconception. For example, it has been said that N.R.A. has failed to raise the price of wheat and corn and hogs; that N.R.A. has not loaned enough money for local public works. Of course, N.R.A. has nothing whatsoever to do with the price of farm products, or with public works. . . .
Some people are putting the cart before the horse. They want a permanent revaluation of the dollar first. . . .
Doubtless prophets of evil still exist in our midst.[41]

---

37. *Ibid.*, March 25, 1933, pp. 908-13; April 22, 1933, pp. 2145-47; May 27, 1933, pp. 4461-63. Simpson wanted rustic authenticity in these letters to Congressmen: "Use lead pencil if you do not have ink. Do not ask the children how to spell the words. Let it be your own production from beginning to end. That is the kind of letter that makes an impression here."
38. Roosevelt, *Public Papers*, 2:61-65.
39. *Ibid.*, pp. 160-68.
40. *Ibid.*, pp. 295-303.
41. *Ibid.*, pp. 420-27.

By late 1933, Roosevelt's communication success was attributed to effective use of the radio, popularity with White House correspondents, a working-writing wife interested in social welfare, and a staff of writing professors. Some of these endeavors shocked crusty political professionals.[42] Throughout the First New Deal, presidential associates were constantly in the news. More often than not their communicative adroitness, "plain folks" attributes, and basic common sense were highlighted. The American people, through the media, probably became acquainted with more official and unofficial White House advisors than ever before in American history.

In 1934, Roosevelt delivered only two national "Fireside Chats," but he conducted numerous press conferences and embarked on extensive tours that were highlighted by formal and informal public utterances. The June 28 "Chat" pinpointed possible issue areas for 1934:

Are you better off than you were last year? Are your debts less burdensome? Is your bank account more secure? Are your working conditions better? Is your faith in your own individual future more firmly grounded?
. . . Have you as an individual paid too high a price for these gains? Plausible self-seekers and theoretical die-hards will tell you of the loss of individual liberty. . . . Have you lost any of your rights or liberty or constitutional freedom of action and choice?[43]

Through rhetorical questions, he placed two issues squarely before the people—financial and constitutional—and seemed content to trust their judgment before visiting and speaking in Haiti, Puerto Rico, Virgin Islands, Colombia, Panama, and Hawaii. On the return western swing, he delivered a mixture of ceremonial and political addresses in Oregon, Washington, Montana, North Dakota, Minnesota, and Wisconsin during August.[44] The second "Fireside Chat" of 1934 followed on September 30. He reviewed the New Deal record again, paying particular attention to the National Industrial Recovery Act and the National Recovery Administration.[45]

The elections of 1934 are something of a phenomenon: "Rarely in American history does the party in power increase its congressional representation in a nonpresidential election year. But in 1934 the Democrats won 332 seats in the House, as against 313 in 1932, and in the Senate increased their numbers from 50 to 69."[46]

From all indications, affirmative action, some meagre gains, and believable public discourses enhanced administration credibility. On the other hand, New Deal critics were swinging wildly: "Let us compare some of the recent acts of the Federal Government with the decrees of dictators, and measure them by the yardstick of the Constitution."[47] "I believe in rugged individualism. . . . We've taken better care of the idiot than we have the genius. . . . recent social legislation is the most dysgenic move of which modern man can conceive. . . . Will it be rugged individualism or ragged collectivism?"[48] The "British Government is . . . not seeking popular acclaim in secular in-

42. Paul Mallon, "Roosevelt Gets His Story Over," *New York Times Magazine*, November 19, 1933, pp. 1-2.
43. Roosevelt, *Public Papers*, 3:314-15.
44. *Ibid.*, pp. 343-75.
45. *Ibid.*, pp. 413-22; *Vital Speeches* 1(Oct. 8, 1934):3-6.
46. Perkins, *New Age*, p. 25.
47. Ex-Senator James A. Reed, "The Constitution of the United States," delivered Sept. 17, 1934, *Vital Speeches* 1(Oct. 8, 1934):6-11.
48. George B. Cutten, President, Colgate University, "Rugged Individualism," delivered Sept. 20, 1934, *Vital Speeches* 1(Nov. 5, 1934):70-72.

dustries by the distribution of subsidies, but by treading the wise path and setting the country on a sure foundation that is having lasting results." [49] While his opponents sounded like desperate men seeking issues, the President could attribute success to pursuing a course "a little left of centre," [50] and articulating policies that apparently made good sense to the American voter.

The Second New Deal: Rhetoric of Defense (1935-1936)

The First New Deal demonstrated that reforms could be initiated and protesters from the far right neutralized successfully. This is not to say that conservative spokesmen would not be heard from again. But, more and more, speeches concentrated on money problems, unemployment insurance, child labor laws—[51] some of those same subjects vocalized and popularized by Senator Huey Long, Father Charles E. Coughlin, and Dr. Francis E. Townsend. Franklin Roosevelt usually avoided challenging an opponent directly inasmuch as such practice risked marginal gains at the expense of considerable loss in prestige for himself, and granted free publicity to an adversary. So, he used "hatchet men" for these chores, men such as Hugh Johnson, James Farley, Joseph Robinson, and Harold Ickes, [52] who on occasion would use scathing language in stripping an issue to its barest essentials. In addition, they served as lightning rods for rebuttal. Roosevelt's apparent immunity to much of the adverse criticism that befell such oratory remained one of the amazing rhetorical phenomena of the New Deal.

Voices from the Left—Buffeted by the 1934 elections, the administration apparently decided—not entirely of its own choosing—to have a showdown with the increasingly popular far left. Long and Coughlin were obvious targets. So, in March, an unemployed ex-Director of the National Recovery Administration, Hugh Johnson, uncorked the opening blast at both the right and the left that would get a response from Long over NBC radio in three days and from Coughlin over the same network in seven days. A verbal war was on that would be decided partially with Long's assassination toward the end of the year and finally with FDR's overwhelming reelection in 1936. Undoubtedly the threat from the left was considerably more intense than cursory hindsight indicates today.

On Monday, March 4, 1935, at a testimonial dinner in the Waldorf-Astoria Hotel, New York, General Johnson reviewed the achievements of the New Deal before observing:

49. Ex-Senator Walter E. Edge, "The British Deal and the New Deal," delivered Sept. 24, 1934, *Vital Speeches* 1(Oct. 8, 1934):16-17.
50. Ann O'Hare McCormick, "Still 'A Little Left of Centre,'" *New York Times Magazine*, Nov. 25, 1934, pp. 3, 17.
51. For a few selected examples, see E. W. Kemmerer, "The Public Debt and Inflation," delivered Dec. 19, 1934, *Vital Speeches* 1 (Jan. 28, 1935):286-88; Joseph W. Byrns, "Plans for the New Congress," delivered Jan. 7, 1935, *Vital Speeches* 1(January 28, 1935):264-66; E. P. Hohman, "The Four-Way Plan of Unemployment Insurance," delivered January 7, 1935, *Vital Speeches* 1(January 28, 1935):270; William D. Guthrie, "The Federal Child Labor Amendment," delivered Jan. 7, 1935, *Vital Speeches* 1(January 28, 1935):271-72; Benjamin M. Anderson, "The Farm Problem, the Export Trade and Our General Industrial Equilibrium," delivered Jan. 10, 1935, *Vital Speeches* (January 28, 1935):279-84.
52. See William Scott Nobles, "A Rhetorical Study of the Public Speaking of Harold L. Ickes in the 1936 Presidential Campaign," Diss. Louisiana State University, 1956.

It has been said that these extraordinary measures were not authorized by the people in the 1932 elections. What utter rot! Why, after they were all clearly shown, the people, at the 1934 elections, gave the President and what he had done one of the most overwhelming approvals they have ever uttered. Men of both parties who otherwise had not a Chinaman's chance went into this Congress because they pledged to support those plans.

As he got warmed up, he zeroed in on those who now seemed no longer to need the New Deal:

Something has happened since the last election. Some of our economic kibitzers and political pansies, who have been sniping at the President's plans since the beginning, say that things have been getting so much better, that our free people do not feel the need of any more spontaneous cooperation and yearn for their rugged individualism back again. That is a bunch of bunk!

Then he explored the two fringes that were causing all the trouble:

We used to talk about two parties and a lunatic fringe. Just now I think there are three groups—rather than parties—and that now two of them are lunatic fringes.

The first fringe is the Old Guard itself and its hereditary following. They are what they are because yesterday they were—and their fathers before them—and for no better reason. They learn nothing and they forget nothing. They believe that property and profits come first and that, if you take care of them the humanities will take care of themselves. . . .

The second fringe is the residue. They have emotions rather than beliefs. They are like a harp-of-the-winds upon which any breeze can play a tune and they do not care a hoot about the essence or form of any government that blocks their desires or restricts their impulses. . . .

He reserved the bulk of his bitterness for the two major exponents of the left:

Huey Long and Father Coughlin are rapidly appearing as leaders of the second—the emotional—fringe. . . .

Two Pied Pipers have come to Hamelin Town—and you will recall what the Pied Piper was—a magician who, by tooting on a penny whistle, could step into the leadership of rats—or charm innocent children from the safety of their homes. But our two Pipers are not concerned about rats. They are piping out of the City gates with more and more abused babies at their heels. You can laugh at Father Coughlin—you can snort at Huey Long—but this country was never under a greater menace. . . .

It is not what these men say that is dangerous. It is the devilish ingenuity of their way of saying it. Put down on paper it doesn't make sense. "Every man a king" and "$5,000 a year for everybody" would draw the proper "oh yeah" from nine people out of ten, but it is no less ridiculous than "two cars in every garage" or "two chickens in every pot [promises of President Hoover]," which turned out to be two chickens in every garage. . . .

"Ahm not against de Constitution. Ahm fo' de Constitution. Ahm not against p'ivate p'op'ety. Ahm fo' p'ivate p'op'ety. All mah plan says is tax 'em down—till nobody has mo' dan six million dollahs capital and one million dollahs income. Six million dollahs capital an' one million dollahs income is enough fo' any man!"

Can you beat it? There's language anybody can understand and the tortured talk and four-dollar words with which economists answer that baby is too much for about 99 per cent of people including myself. Who is going to dispute with Huey that six millions of capital and one million income is enough for any man? But try and get it! . . .

This brings me to a part of this speech that I do not relish making. I like Huey Long. He is one of the most plausible Punchinellos in this or any other country. He is an able little devil and I can't help but gleefully admire his cast-iron cheek and his rough and tumble readiness to take on all comers including the august Senate of the United States in session assembled.

For Father Coughlin, I have even a closer sentiment. I agree with much that he says. I think he has done more to interest the average man in politics than anybody. At a very poignant moment in my life—my farewell to NRA—[53] just before it went under the ether and had its intestines removed and wrapped up in a warm wet towel, he sent me a message that touched my heart. . . .

_____
53. Delivered October 1, 1934. For text, see *Vital Speeches* 1(Oct. 8, 1934):12-14.

I have my full share of the common failing and that warm message makes it very hard for me to say what I know must be said. . . .

The most dangerous revolutionary in the world is the sincere one—the more sincere the more dangerous. Also, in this country, at least, it is the opinion and not the garb or station of the man who holds it that counts. . . . But I think there is an exception to the rule when it applies to revolutionary propaganda in the mouth of a priest of the Roman Catholic Church. . . .

Of recent months there has been an open alliance between the great Louisiana demagogue and this political padre. . . . On a recent Sunday, Father Coughlin announced at the conclusion of a sermon on money and politics, which contained a direct attack on the President of the United States, that his topic would be taken up later in the evening by a distinguished Senator. And sure enough across the evening air, replacing the good father's melodious burring, came the cane-brake drawl of Huey Long expounding that priestly and saintly discourse. And the first voice that Huey heard when he gave up the microphone was that of Father Coughlin congratulating him. . . .

We expect politics to make strange bedfellows but if Father Coughlin wants to engage in political bundling with Huey Long, or any other demagogue, it is only a fair first move to take off that Roman Catholic cassock. . . .

What are we going to do about it? There is just one thing to do and that is to finish what we started and give democratic leadership adjusted to crisis something of a chance.

That goes for everybody. It goes for industry. . . . It goes for labor. . . . It goes for agriculture. . . .

It goes for finance. . . . It goes for the unemployed . . . who ought to carry on patiently for just a little longer and tell the Father Longs and Huey Coughlins—or whatever it is—that they are taking their religion from their church and their political leadership from their statesmen and that they are not in the market for any shoes made by a milliner or hats by a cobbler or magic financial hair tonic put up by partnership of a priest and Punchinello guaranteed to grow economic whiskers on a billiard ball overnight.[54]

This speech was an interesting combination

of gentleness, bombast, humor, pleading. It attracted immediate attention.

The following Thursday, March 7, 1935, over NBC radio, "Punchinello" answered "The lately lamented, pampered ex-Crown Prince, General Hugh S. Johnson," who "is a great soldier though he never smelt powder or heard a cap snap, and a great lawyer though he never tried a lawsuit." After he related a couple of homespun yarns about a "colored lady in Mississippi" and "old David Crockett" out possum hunting, he proceeded to mix self-accolades with New Deal condemnations as if no changes had been forthcoming since Hoover's defeat:

The trouble with the Roosevelt administration is that when their schemes and isms have failed, these things I told them not to do, and voted not to do, that they think it will help them to light out on those of us who warned them in the beginning that the tangled messes and experiments would not work. . . .

There was one difference between Roosevelt and Hoover. Hoover could not get the Congress to carry out the schemes he wanted to try, because we managed to lick him on a roll call in the United States Senate. . . .

The kitchen Cabinet that sat in to advise Hoover was not different from the kitchen Cabinet which advises Roosevelt. Many of the persons are the same. . . .

I was one of the first men to say publicly. Mr. Roosevelt followed in my track a few months later, and said the same thing—we said that all of our trouble and woe was due to the fact that too few of our people owned too much of our wealth. . . .

So there you have it, ladies and gentlemen; both Hoover and Roosevelt swallowed the Huey Long doctrine.

Although they supposedly "swallowed" his "doctrine," Long noted, with accompanying asides on his legal prowess, that New

---

54. Hugh S. Johnson, "Pied Pipers," delivered March 4, 1935, *Vital Speeches* 1(March 11, 1935):354-60.

Deal execution was not only hopeless, but un-American:

> Now since they have sallied forth with General Johnson to start this holy war on me, let us take a look at this NRA they opened up around here about two years ago. They had parades and Fascist signs, just like Hitler and Mussolini. . . .
> It would take forty lawyers to tell a shoe shiner merchant how to operate and be sure he didn't go to jail. Some people come to me for advice as a lawyer on trying to run their business. I took several days and couldn't understand it myself. The only thing I could tell them was it couldn't be much worse in jail than it was out of jail with that kind of a thing going on in the country, and so to go on and do the best they could. . . .
> Now it is with the PWA, WRA, GINS and every other flimsy combination that the country finds its affairs in business where no one can recognize it. More men are now out of work than ever. The debt of the United States has gone up ten billion more dollars. There is starvation; there is homelessness; there is misery on every hand and corner. But, mind you, in the meantime, Mr. Roosevelt has had his way. He is one man that can't blame any of his troubles on Huey Long. He has had his way.
> Down in my part of the country, if any man has the measles he blames that on me; but there is one man that can't blame anything on anybody but himself and that is Mr. Franklin De-La-No Roosevelt. . . .

Of course the Kingfish could not allow his time to expire before appealing to this national audience once more with

> that plan taken from these leaders of all times and from the Bible, for the sponsoring of which I have been labeled by American men as a madman and pied piper and demagogue . . . that plan of our Share Our Wealth Society. . . .
> You will find it in the Book of Deuteronomy, from the twenty-fifth to the twenty-seventh chapters. You will find it in the writings of King Solomon. You will find it in the teachings of Christ. You will find it in the words of our great teachers and statesmen of all countries and of all times. . . .
> Write me, wire to me; get into this work with us if you believe we are right.[55]

Appealing for the sympathy often bestowed on the underdog kicked around by higher authority, Long characterized himself as the sane voice against a madcap bureaucracy with only God and "these leaders of all times" on his side. It was the kind of appeal that General Johnson had called "language anybody can understand" with a potpourri of pie-in-the-sky promises and blistering sarcastic bombast. Long must have figured that if it worked on the Louisiana hustings its success would be assured over NBC. But he was cut down by an assassin's bullet in the fall and never was able to test his program in the next national election. His self-appointed successor, the Reverend Gerald L.K. Smith, never captured the following or attention enjoyed by Long.

The air waves were still reverberating when Father Charles E. Coughlin addressed an NBC radio audience on Monday, March 11, a week after Johnson's salvo. He chose to direct his response more to the General while professing unconvincing support of the President. As leader of the Radio League of the Little Flower and the National Union for Social Justice, he intermingled appeals for organizational support. Coughlin's constituency probably was identified less clearly than Long's at this time, so any lambasting had to be handled with care. While vigorous in language, the priest tried a more analytical, self-sacrificial, pseudo issue-oriented approach; passing Johnson off as an inconsequential has-been, a discredited spokesman for Wall Street. When considered in the perspective of subsequent events, it is difficult to be-

55. "Our Blundering Government and Its Spokesman—Hugh Johnson," *Vital Speeches* 1(March 25, 1935):391-97.

lieve that the egoistic Coughlin delivered all of these comments candidly:

My Dear General Johnson, I am not important nor are you. But the doctrines which I preach are important. While you were content to vomit your venom upon my person and against my character, the American public is fully cognizant that not once did you dare attack the truths which I teach. . . .

These people, so you have intimated, are rats being led by the Pied Piper. Must that be the metaphor which you employ to describe the wreckage which your kind has created?

My friends, I appeal to your charity, to your good judgment, to your sense of social justice to bear no ill will against General Johnson. Your intelligence informs you that he is but a faithful obedient servant willing to express in his own grotesque manner the thoughts which are harbored in the mind of his master [later identified as Bernard Baruch].

Coughlin tried to document that he had supported FDR long before Johnson's arrival:

Where were you in 1930 and 1931 while we were advocating New Deal on Sundays and feeding thousands in the bread line on Mondays? . . .

Where were you in 1932 when our same group was advocating the election of Franklin D. Roosevelt? . . .

Where were you in 1933 and 1934 when our beloved leader, consecrated to drive the money changers out of the temple, was hampered and impeded by your master, Bernard Manasses Baruch? . . . you strutted upon the stage of this depression like a comic opera general. . . .

Who originated the slogan of "Roosevelt or ruin?" . . .

The real enemies who are boring from within have been you and your group of Wall Streeters, of international bankers. . . .

My friends in this audience, I still proclaim to you that it is either Roosevelt or ruin. . . .

The fantastic fusillade of false charges which the genial ghost, the kind chocolate soldier and the sweet prince of bombast so engagingly publicized, certainly were not potent enough to arouse my wrath.[56]

The next year Father Coughlin's tune changed dramatically. In a radio address, June 19, 1936, he stepped forth to explain "why I do not find it morally possible to support either the Republicans and their platform or the Democrats and their promises." His 1936 analysis casts grave doubts on his 1935 veracity:

My friends, what have we witnessed as the finger of time turned the pages of the calendar? Nineteen hundred and thirty-three and the National Recovery Act which multiplied profits for the monopolists; 1934 and the AAA which raised the price of foodstuffs by throwing back God's best gifts into His face; 1935 and the Banking Act which rewarded the exploiters of the poor, the Federal Reserve bankers and their associates, by handing over to them the temple from which they were to have been cast!

In 1936, when our disillusionment is complete, we pause to take inventory of our predicament. . . .

It is not pleasant for me who coined the phrase "Roosevelt or ruin"—a phrase fashioned upon promises—to voice such passionate words. But I am constrained to admit that "Roosevelt and ruin" is the order of the day because the money changers have not been driven from the temple.

And what was the solution offered for delivering the country from "the banker's party"? He announced that the National Union for Social Justice would endorse Congressman William Lemke of North Dakota, with the prediction:

Behind it will rally agriculture, labor, the disappointed Republicans and the outraged Democrats, the independent merchant and industrialist and every lover of liberty who desires to eradicate the cancerous growths from decadent capitalism and avoid the treacherous pitfalls of red communism.[57]

---

56. "A Reply to Gen. Johnson," *Vital Speeches* 1(March 25, 1935):386-91.

57. "A Third Party," *Vital Speeches* 2(July 1, 1936):613-16.

Since when banker control simultaneously represented the dual threat of decadent capitalism and red communism was never made clear. But it hardly mattered. By 1936, the New Deal was addressing itself to the conservatives of the right, properly realizing that the radical left had been suppressed sufficiently.

Finally, from the left, came the Townsend Plan, a program to provide $200 a month for everyone over sixty provided he spent the sum before the next pay period. It was to be financed from a 2 percent sales tax which seemingly was a major weakness. Townsend Clubs evolved, as did opposition. When competing with a Huey Long Share Our Wealth program, any plan that must be "explained" by a statistician is in trouble—particularly when the statistician is clever, amusing, and unconvinced:

> Dr. Townsend's demand for a revision of the science of arithmetic by law gives especial timeliness to this discussion. Behind him is a long line of illustrious precedents. There have always been men who demanded that human will be elevated above fact, above reality or above natural law. Sometimes the effort has succeeded. We are told that the seas parted for the children of Israel at the command of Moses. More often the attempt has failed. King Canute, possibly through lack of votes or the right statistical control, did not persuade the tides to obey his command. More recently there have been proposals to abolish history, but history has not yet disappeared. I anticipate the same with respect to the multiplication table, which the Townsend Plan, with the most commendable of motives, would supplant.[58]

In the 1936 national campaign, the Plan was ignored by the major parties and opposed by Coughlin, Lemke, and the Socialist candidate, Norman Thomas.[59]

What were President Roosevelt's verbal contributions to the Johnson- Long-Coughlin fracas? On the surface—none. Delivering his only "Fireside Chat" of 1935 a

month following this exchange, he remained aloof from the controversy and chose instead to emphasize positive accomplishments, pointing optimistically toward future goals, concluding:

> Never since my Inauguration in March, 1933, have I felt so unmistakably the atmosphere of recovery. . . . We have survived all of the arduous burdens and the threatening dangers of a great economic calamity. . . . Fear is vanishing and confidence is growing on every side, faith is being renewed in the vast possibilities of human beings to improve their material and spiritual status through the instrumentality of the democratic form of government.[60]

Voices from the Right—In late summer, 1935, even before the death of Huey Long, verbal emphasis shifted from left to right. Certainly in mainly ignoring the radicals, Presidential addresses contributed to this shift. But, from a more practical standpoint, Roosevelt's attention had to remain fixed on major party opponents, all of whom adhered to more conservative philosophies.

Unfortunately for their cause, GOP top level leadership offered vague, inarticulate denunciations throughout 1935 and 1936. Herbert Hoover spotted the evils of "regimentation and bureaucratic domination . . . centralized under an enormous bureaucracy in Washington." For solutions he advocated, in typical Hooverese, "fundamental American principles," "constitutionally conducted government," a "rebirth of the Republican party," "effective

---

58. Stuart A. Rice, "Is the Townsend Plan Practical?" delivered Dec. 28, 1935, *Vital Speeches* 2(Jan. 27, 1936):263.

59. Norman Thomas, "The Townsend Plan and Cough Drops," delivered July 18, 1936, *Vital Speeches* 2(Sept. 1, 1936):755-58.

60. Roosevelt, *Public Papers*, 4:140.

participation of the States and local governments in relief," and forthrightly declared his support "for productive genius, for expansion of enterprise, for economic recovery, for restoration of normal jobs, for increased standards of living, for reform of abuse of governmental or economic powers, and for advance from outworn modes of thought."[61] In short, he was for just about all those things that everyone else was for.

Wendell Willkie, then President of Commonwealth and Southern Corporation, before his friends of the United States Chamber of Commerce, declared that the inhibiting force was "fear"—"the fear of American industry today is the fear of the hostile attitude of Government itself." Of course he paid the expected disrespect to "a Federal Bureaucracy at Washington" before arriving at the astounding, albeit highly prejudiced, conclusion that "the electric utility business will do more to lift this country out of the depression, take more men out of the bread lines and off relief rolls than any other industry and . . . do more than the Government itself can do with all its expenditures."[62] Why this "electric utility business" had failed to work its magic during the depression years, 1929-33, under a friendly administration was never clarified.

Republican newspapermen were similarly vocal and vague. Colonel Robert R. McCormick, editor and publisher of the *Chicago Tribune*, concluded that contemporary Washington was populated by "extremists," guided a "dictatorship," "inflamed with the policies of Moscow," and determined to reduce state governments "to the status of provinces."[63] Frank Knox, publisher of the *Chicago Daily News* and GOP Vice Presidential candidate in 1936, predicted certain disaster to follow

"the present wildly profligate spending policy of this administration."[64]

Senator L.J. Dickinson of Iowa summarized the overall GOP opposition to the New Deal as succinctly as any speaker:

Through a series of laws, enacted by a subservient Congress under what has been called the "new deal," there is projected and under way the gradual alteration of fundamental relationships between the Federal Government and the 48 States. The Constitution itself is being subtly undermined, with transfer of control over the Nation's economic life to the central authority set up as a new and revolutionary political objective. A vast bureaucracy is being erected which seeks to supervise, in an unprecedented economic and socialistic experiment, all public and private enterprise. Without mandate from the people, we are being regimented under a new social philosophy into a totalitarian State. Our traditional individualism is to be sacrifi[c]ed for dependence upon Government crutches and Government doles for everybody and for every purpose.[65]

Most of the issues, real and counterfeit, that evolved in the 1936 campaign had already been explored by the end of 1935. Left wing spokesmen, serving a concoction of guaranteed income, share the wealth, social justice, and old age pensions, scattered their shots with reckless abandon at any suspected target. In the process they often were caught in overstatement, inconsistency, unredeemable promise, and basic incompetency. The Longs, the Coughlins, and the Townsends were not short on

61. "A Call to Republicans," delivered March 23, 1935, *Vital Speeches* 1(April 8, 1935):441-43.
62. "The New Fear," delivered May 1, 1935, *Vital Speeches* 1(May 20, 1935):538-41.
63. "The Torch of Liberty," delivered May 4, 1935, *Vital Speeches* 1(May 20, 1935):524-26.
64. "A Policy of Abundance," delivered June 7, 1935, *Vital Speeches* 1(July 1, 1935):639.
65. "Broken Party Pledges," n.d., *Vital Speeches* 1(Sept. 9, 1935):801-07.

plans—but, their plans came off as undesirable, impractical, and unworkable schemes for acquiring political office. On the other hand, right wing spokesmen, led by GOP orators, had no solutions at all. They were not sure whether any difficulties existed, but if they did the Roosevelt remedies were at least unconstitutional. They demonstrated a lack of both imagination and compassion in condemning New Deal programs without posing reasonable alternatives. This gross shortcoming persisted throughout the decade. Hoover's call for a "rebirth of the Republican party" implied the weakness, the questionable existence, of an organization charged with suggesting alternative programs. Small wonder the voters flocked to the Democratic column in such numbers. Their speakers were the only members of organized parties that simultaneously tried to identify problems and to recommend rational solutions.[66]

For sheer number of political speeches, January, 1936, made it obvious that this was the dawn of an election year. The President delivered his annual Message to Congress on January 4, repeating some of his Inaugural points: "We have earned the hatred of entrenched greed . . . unscrupulous moneychangers. . . who failed through their own stubbornness and their own incompetence. . . . They seek the restoration of their selfish power. They offer to lead us back round the same old corner into the same old dreary street."[67] It sounded like campaign season again. The Republican response, complete with charges of "showmanship," "klieg lights," "packed galleries," and "a professional claque," was forthcoming on January 6, 1936, from Senator Dickinson,[68] and on January 10 from New York Congressman James Wadsworth over NBC radio.[69] Roosevelt's Jackson

Day Address was delivered on January 8,[70] followed by GOP retorts from Merle Thorpe, Editor of *Nation's Business* and economist James Warburg on January 15, and Herbert Hoover on January 16.[71] FDR spoke at Newark on January 18, with subsequent addresses at the end of the month from Alfred E. Smith, January 25; Bainbridge Colby, January 27; Joseph T. Robinson, January 28; William E. Borah and Alfred M. Landon, January 29.[72] Obviously the opposition was rolling out the heavy cannon. Three presidential addresses had gained response from nine nationally publicized speakers. But, even so, the constant theme of the responses carped on New Deal usurpation of the Constitution without offering tangible plans for employment, housing, labor, industry, and tax problems.

Prior to the national conventions in June, the oratorical pace continued with three groups gaining attention: Democrats, Republicans, and anti-New Deal Demo-

---

66. As Dexter Perkins, *New Age*, points out (p. 40), "The Congress of 1935 turned out a grist of legislation that compares with, and perhaps exceeds in significance, that of the 'Hundred Days.'" Less ballyhoo evolved over many of these items apparently because Republican efforts to marshall public opposition to increasing federal power were failing miserably. These failures should have suggested to the GOP a need to alter its basic philosophy before embarking on another national campaign.

67. Roosevelt, *Public Papers* 5:13-14. Also in *Vital Speeches* 2(Jan. 13, 1936):220.

68. "The State of the Union," *Vital Speeches* 2(Jan. 13, 1936):222-24.

69. "The Session Opens," *Vital Speeches* 2(Jan. 27, 1936):265-67.

70. *Vital Speeches* 2(January 27, 1936):277-79. Also in Roosevelt, *Public Papers*, 5:38-44.

71. *Vital Speeches* 2(Jan. 27, 1936):257-61, 267-75.

72. As reported in *Vital Speeches* 2(January 27, and February 10 and February 24, 1936): 279-80, 282-90, 296-302, 304-07, 314-18.

crats. Democratic speakers usually explained in some detail a specific New Deal subject familiar to them, and probably assigned by higher party authority: Senator Louis Murphy of Iowa, "The New Farm Relief Plan," February 10; John G. Winant, Chairman of the Social Security Board, "The Social Security Act," March 30; Arthur B. Ballentine, former Under Secretary of the Treasury, "Promoting Social Security," April 25; Daniel C. Roper, Secretary of Commerce, "Increasing Employment," April 28; Henry A. Wallace, Secretary of Agriculture, "Making the Most of the Home Market," May 4.[73] Broad, general subjects, such as those developed by Secretary of State Cordell Hull, "Fighting the Depression," March 5, and President Roosevelt's Jefferson Day Address, "My Economic and Social Philosophy," April 25, were exceptions.[74] But even in the more philosophical statement, the President took seemingly diverse economic problems and applied them to simple, common, national circumstances:

Nebraska's corn and Eighth Avenue's clothing are not different problems; they are the same problem. Before the war, a Nebraska farmer could take a two-hundred pound hog to market and buy a suit of clothes made in New York. But in 1932, to get that same suit of clothes he had to take two and a half hogs to market. Back in the Twenties a cotton farmer had to raise seven pounds of cotton to buy one pair of overalls. By 1932, however, he had to raise fourteen pounds of cotton to get those New York overalls.

Thus, he had citizens in three different sections of the country able personally to identify with the vivid analysis.

During the same period, Republican speakers usually were broad and general in upholding Constitution, Supreme Court, freedom, liberty, morality, confidence, courage, "economy of plenty," "abolition of child labor," "old age pensions," "better housing," thrift, honor, hard work, and the "people's sovereignty." They condemned centralization, regimentation, Mr. Wallace, Professor Tugwell, dictatorship, "Brain Trusters," "basic principles of Bolshevistic Russia," "political bureaucracy," debt, inflation, fear, monopolies, taxes, "planned scarcity," and secret Democratic funds.[75] But poor Herbert Hoover was preoccupied in most of his speeches explaining why his administration could not be blamed for depression and Roosevelt's administration could not be praised for recovery:

Mr. Roosevelt is anxious that the American people shall believe that the nation was "in ruins" when he took office. . . .

I hardly need restate the fact, now well-established by disinterested economists the world over, that America was shaking itself clear of the depression, under its Republican administration, in June-July, 1932. . . .

Prosperity had actually swung around the corner. . . . After Mr. Roosevelt's election in 1932 we alone of all great nations were set back.[76]

Mr. Hoover's idea of "a program" for the

---

73. As reported in *Vital Speeches* 2(February 24, May 4, and May 18, 1936): 341-44, 477-81, 488-91, 511-18, 526-29.
74. Hull Address reported in *Vital Speeches* 2(March 23, 1936):378-81; FDR in *Vital Speeches* 2(May 4, 1936):487-88. FDR address also in *Public Papers*, 5:177-82.
75. For examples, see Wheeler McMillen, "A National Agricultural Program," delivered February 24, 1936, *Vital Speeches* 2 (March 9, 1936):352-55; William E. Borah, "Issues Before the People," delivered March 22, 1936, *Vital Speeches* 2(April 6, 1936):412-15; William O. Donovan, "The Case Against the New Deal," delivered May 17, 1936, *Vital Speeches* 2(June 1, 1936):553-55; Daniel O. Hastings, "Reply to President Roosevelt," delivered May 17, 1936, *Vital Speeches* 2 (1 June 1936): 564-68.
76. "Effects of the New Deal," delivered April 4, 1936, *Vital Speeches* 2(April 6, 1936):445.

GOP to steer the nation back on the proper course included: "A restoration of morals in government. A revival of confidence and courage in the destiny of America. Real policies of economic and social regeneration in place of the New Deal extravaganzas. Realistic, drastic and immediate reforms."[77] Republicans let the Democrats talk about "Nebraska's corn and Eighth Avenue's clothing," "a two-hundred pound hog," "a cotton farmer," "seven pounds of cotton," and "New York overalls." These were the "gut" issues, the things that mattered, to the American voter.

Democratic defectors numbered among their ranks two former presidential candidates, a United States Senator, a former Secretary of State, a former Assistant Secretary of War among the more elite group. Alfred E. Smith, the most vocal of the group delivered his famous New Deal denunciation before the wealthy American Liberty Leaguers, January 25. He called for a return to the Democratic platform of 1932 and tossed in several questionable, confusing, and unsupported assertions:

> at the end of three years we are just where we started. . . .
> And we have been such brilliant speculators that we are paying thirteen cents a pound for it . . . and it can be bought in any one of ten cotton markets of the South today for $11.50 [per cwt.] . . .
> The young brain trusters caught the Socialists in swimming and they ran away with their clothes . . . they want to disguise themselves as Karl Marx or Lenin.[78]

The administration responded to Smith through a brilliant broadcast rebuttal delivered January 28 by Senator Joseph T. Robinson of Arkansas. The Senator not only was a Roosevelt floor leader but ran with Smith as the Vice Presidential candidate in 1928. He characterized the "Happy Warrior" as a former battler for the common man who for greed and "thirty pieces of silver" had defected to the other side. He used Smith's style, "Let's look at the record," addressed his comments directly to Smith with biblical undertones, and made the New Yorker seem to elevate money over humanity. His sarcasm was most incisive:

> Your charge that the Roosevelt administration is fostering socialism and communism is so ridiculous it's actually funny. Honestly, Governor, I think you've been seeing things under the bed, you know, those Communist spies that our good friend Ham Fish is always talking about. Where have I heard that charge of socialism and communism before? Oh, now I recall, that's the identical charge that Herbert Hoover made against you in 1928.[79]

Jim Farley slammed at "the du Pont Liberty League, that collection of multimillionaires, and their satellite lawyers and paid propagandists."[80] Even an anti-New Dealer classified the League as a "most politically stupid and inept organization . . . candidates would climb trees or jump down manholes to avoid being indorsed by it."[81] But Smith continued to rattle on about "States' rights," "the people's Constitution," communists in the Democratic Party, and how Ickes, Wallace, Hopkins, and Tugwell did not deserve elevation because they were not "Democratic leaders."[82]

---

77. "Constructive American Alternatives," delivered May 14, 1936, *Vital Speeches* 2(June 1, 1936):556.
78. "Peripatetics," *Vital Speeches* 2(February 10, 1936):282-86.
79. "Jacob's Voice," *Vital Speeches* 2(February 10, 1936):287-90.
80. "The New Deal and Its Critics," delivered May 20, 1936, *Vital Speeches* 2(June 1, 1936):551.
81. Frank R. Kent, "An Anti-New Deal Democrat Speaks," delivered Sept. 9, 1936, *Vital Speeches* 2(Oct. 1, 1936):812.
82. "I Am an American Before I Am a Democrat,' delivered Oct. 1, 1936, *Vital Speeches* 3(Oct. 15, 1936):16-19.

Following the vigorous 1936 campaign, the Democrats took 46 out of 48 states and 62.5 percent of the popular vote. What were the reasons for Roosevelt's smashing success? Laura I. Crowell suggests that:

he was walking in the direction in which history was moving the nation; the incidence of recovery put strong weapons in his hands; he was able, in one of the greatest stump-speaking campaigns of all time, to deepen and to rebuild, where necessary, the faith of the majority in his leadership toward the goals which he envisioned for the country.[83]

What did the Republicans do wrong? As challengers, they:

should have taken the offensive, driving Roosevelt to a defense of the policies of his administration. In this campaign . . . the incumbents became the challengers, constantly enforcing the comparison . . . between the New Deal years and the preceding Republican administrations. . . .[84]

So the Second New Deal ended. From a beginning of defense, the Democrats, by the end of 1936, were definitely on the attack—a tribute to the persuasive ability of spokesmen for the incumbent party. In 1937 came the abortive Supreme Court fight.[85] But the principles of the New Deal were established. Succeeding administrations have been unable to reverse significantly these concepts as reflected especially in contemporary treatment of social and economic crises.

Conclusions

Roosevelt brought to the presidency three basic philosophies of government that surface in his speeches: the federal government should be strong; the federal government should be action-oriented, responding immediately to all demonstrated needs; the federal government should meet problems based on humane demands rather than on narrow legalistic interpretation.

In order to apply these broad philosophies to specific cases, New Deal spokesmen, led by President Roosevelt, used several devices. *First*, they utilized primarily the direct communicative channel afforded by oral discourse. By comparison, their opponents often were overwhelmed, frustrated, and defeated by their own verbal ineptness.

Second, specific subjects were developed with specific evidence, primarily in the form of applied examples, with great effect. This tactic undoubtedly contributed toward listener understanding and gave reason for the people to support the New Deal in such numbers. The broad, sweeping generalizations, so woefully applied by GOP speakers in 1936, registered no telling effect.

Third, there was admirable adaptation to available verbal channels. With the radio the primary medium, FDR immediately comprehended its one-to-one relationship between *the* speaker and *a* listener, as opposed to the one-to-mass relationship of the speaker to a live audience. The "Fireside Chats" reflect this comprehension. Roosevelt's "Forgotten Man" was first and foremost *a* man, a nonmass figure, and the verbal channel made that man feel even more certain that the New Deal was his own personal government.

Fourth, "hatchet men" were used to strike out verbally against people or poli-

83. "An Analysis of Audience Persuasion in the Major Campaign Addresses of FDR in the Presidential Campaign of 1936," Diss. University of Iowa, 1948, pp. 475-76.
84. *Ibid.*, pp. 476-77.
85. For an excellent study, see Bernard F. Phelps, "A Rhetorical Analysis of the 1937 Addresses of F. D. Roosevelt in Support of Court Reform," Diss. Ohio State University, 1957.

cies that the President could not afford to attack. Both the fire and the quality of these attackers often was impressive.

Fifth, effective verbal communication, coupled with appropriate action, encouraged the citizens to turn to a federal government for solutions, often by-passing completely local and state levels from which no "Fireside Chats" evolved, no regular press conferences were held, and no organized speaking tours emanated.

BIBLIOGRAPHY

Brandenburg, Earnest, and Braden, Waldo, "Franklin Delano Roosevelt." *A History and Criticism of American Public Address*, Vol. 3, 1954 Reprint. Edited by Marie K. Hochmuth. New York: Russell and Russell, 1965. An excellent chapter giving an overview of Franklin Roosevelt's speaking from the approach of rhetorical canons.

Perkins, Dexter. *The New Age of Franklin Roosevelt, 1932-45.* Chicago: University of Chicago Press, 1967. A short paperback; recommended as an aid to the reader in following the major events that correspond with the speaking described in this chapter.

Roosevelt, Franklin D. *F.D.R. Speaks.* Phonodisc. W-FDR 7-8. 4 sides 2 volumes. Washington Records, 1960. The best available collection of F.D.R. voice recordings. A collection that contains more complete speeches is needed, however. Authorized edition; abridged. "Speeches se-lected, edited, and annotated by Henry Steele Commager." The last speech is read by F.D.R. Jr. Introduction by Mrs. Eleanor Roosevelt.

Roosevelt, Franklin D. *Public Papers and Addresses of Franklin D. Roosevelt.* 1938-1950 Reprint. Edited by Samuel I. Rosenman. 13 vols. New York: Russell and Russell, 1969. For the most part these texts are taken from speech manuscripts which do not always correspond exactly with the words ultimately delivered.

Rosenman, Samuel I. *Working with Roosevelt.* New York: Harper, 1952. Extremely well-written. A unique text that gives firsthand accounts of intricate speech preparation procedures and the inner-workings of Roosevelt's staff, from the first gubernatorial campaign through the presidency. By a member of the New Deal staff.

Three studies are cited as being exceptional because they provide carefully authenticated speech texts far more accurate in reflecting what the speaker actually said than those usually found in anthologies:

Cowperthwaite, Lowery LeRoy. "A Criticism of the Speaking of Franklin D. Roosevelt in the Presidential Campaign of 1932." Ph.D. dissertation, University of Iowa, 1950.

Crowell, Laura. "An Analysis of Audience Persuasion in the Major Campaign Addresses of FDR in the Presidential Campaign of 1936." Ph.D. dissertation, University of Iowa, 1948.

Phelps, Bernard F. "A Rhetorical Analysis of the 1937 Addresses of F.D. Roosevelt in Support of Court Reform." Ph.D. dissertation, Ohio State University, 1957.

19   Isolationism vs. Internationalism, 1937-1970

Ralph Towne

I suppose, for example, we will have to assume that the isolationist argument will have at least nine lives, for the reason that it pleases the average man because it spares him any immediate inconvenience or sacrifice, and it flatters his sense of power to feel that America can live alone and like it.

—Adlai Stevenson, January, 1951.[1]

There is a solidarity and interdependence about the modern world, both technically and morally, which makes it impossible for any nation completely to isolate itself from economic and political upheavals in the rest of the world, especially when such upheavals appear to be spreading and not declining.

—Franklin Roosevelt, October, 1937.[2]

The argument between isolationism and internationalism has been bitter and persistent for the last forty to fifty years in the United States. Almost all shades of opinion have been expressed from the right extremists, the America Firsters and the McCarthyites, on the one hand, through to the "one worlders," the United World Federalists, on the other. This cat and dog fight, particularly since 1937, has been at the heart of the foreign policy considerations of our country, and plays a significant role in the relationships the country has established with its neighbors in the contemporary, shrunken and violent world. It is the purpose of this chapter to trace the clash which has been raised on the public platform, not so much by the extremists but by the most responsible elements in our government, since 1937. The aim is to make apparent some of the major speakers, to discover the fundamental issues they argued, and to understand the rhetorical strategies they have used and may be using today.

In the study we should not be surprised to find the people of the United States torn by a schizophrenic frame of mind when they turn to a consideration of what foreign policy is best for the country. Charles Lerche, in addressing himself to the weaknesses of American public opinion, concludes that:

Finally, we must mention the American preference for dichotomies. Americans generally have an all-or-nothing attitude in international affairs; the dominant national assumption is that the only alternative outcomes of a situation are extreme ones. Public attitudes think only of total peace or total war, total love or total hatred, Russian friend-

---

1. Adlai Stevenson, "There Are No Gibraltars," *Vital Speeches*, 17 (February 15, 1951):287.
2. Franklin Roosevelt, "Quarantining War," *Vital Speeches*, 4 (October 15, 1937):3.

ship or Russian enmity. This simple black-or-white formulation of problems grows out of the first three points we have made above [lack of information, impatience, emotionalism] and, in turn, influences each of them.[3]

Thus, America defends a policy of isolationism, at one time, which draws the country within its borders and lets the rest of the world fend for itself; and, at the next period of time, it stresses an internationalist policy which accepts the responsibility of saving the world from its self-destructive penchant.

The Apex of Isolationism

So deeply rooted in the American mind, from the cautions of George Washington and Thomas Jefferson against "permanent" and "entangling" alliances to the massive sentiment expressed against our participation in World War II in the late 1930s, is the isolationist design that it is truly a wonder that the pattern has ever been broken. As Paul Seabury noted in his Bancroft Prize winning investigation of foreign policy:

What isolationism did mean as an historic policy was an explicit American commitment—one so consistently followed as to be almost a constitutional understanding—not to employ its diplomacy and force persistently and purposefully in explicit concert with other nations, either to maintain international peace, to extend its sphere of influence outside the Western Hemisphere, or to guarantee the integrity, territorial or otherwise, of any European nation or alliance. In this sense, until the mid-twentieth century, the old role of America in world politics, while at times a very substantial one, was to rely chiefly upon its own strength and resources, to act or not to act "at times and places of its own choosing," and to interpret its own national purposes and destiny as distinct and separate from that of any other nation or group of nations.[4]

Until only the last two or three decades,

then, isolationist philosophy has been the fundamental position controlling the foreign relations of this country. The isolationist foundations, in fact, have been so strong that the decided change of recent years has been made more interesting; but the very strength of those foundations also serves as a warning to the country that the shift of attitude, while apparently real, may have some days of struggle ahead.

Isolationism reached its peak of action in the country probably with the defeat of participation by the United States in the League of Nations whereas isolationism's loudest voice received expression during the later half of the 1930s. The public attitude against extensive American participation in concert with other nations also was at an all time high in the period 1937 through 1939 and was still active in 1940 and 1941. In a public opinion survey in 1937 the public reacted as follows:

If another war like the World War [WWI] develops in Europe, should America take part again?

Yes, 5%   No, 95%

AIPO, February 14, 1937.[5]

The attitude pretty clearly shows a definite desire of the American public in 1937 to avoid participation in a European war. Further indication of this reticent attitude is revealed in a series of polls regarding the use of American ships to transport war goods to England and France as well as modifica-

---

3. Charles Lerche, *Foreign Policy of the American People* (Englewood Cliffs, N. J.: Prentice Hall, 1967), p. 121.
4. Paul Seabury, *Power, Freedom and Diplomacy* (New York: Vintage Books, 1963), pp. 38-39.
5. Hadley Cantril, ed., *Public Opinion, 1935-1946* (Princeton: Princeton University Press, 1953), p. 966.

tion of the Neutrality Acts to help the allies. As late as August 20, and September 11, 1939, the following results were obtained:

> Should our government allow American ships to carry goods anywhere or should our ships be kept out of war zones?
>
> > Carry anywhere, 16%
> > Keep out of war zones, 84%
> >
> > AIPO, August 29, 1939.[6]

> Should England and France be required to carry the goods away in their own ships?
>
> > Yes, 90.2% No, 5.8%
> > No Opinion, 4%
> >
> > AIPO, September 11, 1939.[7]

From September 21, 1939, through May 26, 1940, four polls were taken on the question below and the combined result of these polls are indicated.

> The Neutrality Law prevents American ships from traveling in the war zones in Europe. Should this law be changed so that American ships can carry supplies to England and France?
>
> > Yes, 18% No, 74%
> > Undecided, 8%
> >
> > AIPO, May 29, 1940.[8]

It was not until as late as April 25, 1941 that more of the American public polled agreed to American help being offered for the protection of shipping to Britain; even then the percentage of favorable responses was below 50 percent.

> Should the U.S. Navy be used to guard ships half way across the Atlantic Ocean, when the ships are carrying war materials to Britain?
>
> > Yes, 49% No, 43%
> > No Opinion, 8%
> >
> > AIPO, April 25, 1941.[9]

Thus, even as late as April, 1941, large numbers of the American public were holding for an isolated American position. The qualified exception to this position is revealed only with a poll which posed the hypothetical defeat of the Allies. When asked to consider their attitude, given a possible defeat of Britain, the public did then accept the idea that America should participate; but apparently, this hypothetical evil had to be expressed by the pollsters. The public would not recognize the possibility on their own.

> If it appears certain that Britain will be defeated unless we use part of our navy to protect ships going to Britain, would you favor or oppose convoys?
>
> > Favor, 71% Oppose, 21%
> > No Opinion, 8%
> >
> > AIPO, April 8, 1941.[10]

To defend the position of isolationism there was no want of spokesmen from 1937 to 1941. Many an extremist spoke loudly and frequently. Their case was often, if not always, an oversimplified view of the world as being composed of two kinds of nations, the good and the evil. America represented the good and the evil ones were exemplified

---

6. *Ibid.*, p. 1127.
7. *Ibid.*
8. *Ibid.*
9. *Ibid.*, p. 1128.
10. *Ibid.*

by almost everyone outside the borders of the United States. After this dichotomy was "established," many spokesmen argued that United States participation in the wars carried on by the "bad guys" could only lead to the extinguishing of democracy and freedom in our country. Martin Dies, chairman of the Committee on Un-American Activities, the infamous Dies Committee, delivered an address on NBC radio from Washington, D.C., September 17, 1939. In this speech he developed the standard pattern suggesting first that the times were critical, that democracy was everywhere challenged by dictatorships, that Communism, Nazism, and Facism were " . . . modern cults of the ancient pagan religion of Statolatry or the worship of the state."[11] He next used testimony presented before the Dies Committee to show there were terrible external threats from "out there" and concluded. "There is no doubt in my mind that the greatest contribution we can make to the cause of freedom and democracy at home and abroad is to stay out of Europe's war which can only result, so far as we are concerned, in bankruptcy, prolonged depression and ultimate dictatorship. With God's help we must, we will remain free."[12]

But there were the famous as well as the infamous upholding the isolationist point of view. Reasonable men evaluated the struggle abroad, compared what they saw with the strength of America and its principles as they understood them, and concluded that the United States should remain aloof. In this camp were men like Arthur Vandenberg, Herbert Hoover, William Borah, Robert Taft. And, while on occasion they got involved in some of the cases of the more extreme exponents, their cases were also much less black and white, much better thought out including argu-

ments based more frequently on principle than on name-calling and moral tirades against other people and situations.

In a Senate speech against increased defense expenditures, February 27, 1939, Vandenberg developed his point of view. He showed, first, that he was all for ". . . . thoroughly adequate defense; I believe in rational preparedness,"[13] and added that he had voted for every regular army and navy appropriations bill throughout his eleven years in the Senate. He continued, however, by asking:

But, Mr. President, adequate for what? This is the controlling question.
Adequate for what? Adequate to implement national defense in the traditional American sense of minding our own business? To that I can uncompromisingly answer, "Yes."
Adequate for what? Adequate to sustain the realities of the Monroe Doctrine in the sense that we cannot allow alien ideologies to close in upon us through Western Hemisphere approaches? Again, "Yes."
Adequate for what? To implement the President's Chicago speech [the Quarantine Speech] which talked of quarantines and suggested the use of American sanctions against so-called "aggressor nations" on the continent? This time, "No," unless the sanctions are the deliberate and conscious order of Congress, reflecting the conviction of the whole American people.
Adequate for what? That I repeat is the key question.[14]

This "key question" was argued in terms of possible answers. He believed, first, that if just "national defense in the traditional American sense of minding our own business" was being sought, there was no need for new appropriations. If, however, there

11. Martin Dies, "The Challenge to Democracy," *Vital Speeches*, 5 (October 1, 1939):762.
12. *Ibid.*, 765.
13. Arthur Vandenberg, "Peace or War for America," *Vital Speeches* 5 (April 1, 1939):354.
14. *Ibid.*, 354-55.

was need for expansion of the military to begin some more positive action in the name of defense, a problem arose built on the dangerous misconception that we could "thrust ourselves into foreign quarrels and mold alien destiny by methods 'short of war.' "[15] He went on to suggest that when the country did enter the conflict it might well put destiny beyond its control. In such a circumstance the nation would no longer be in control of the "tragic traffic lights." The point that was offered was that America should never take the first step without being ready and willing to take the final step. "Otherwise we invite not only humiliation but also the complete disintegration of our international influence."[16] He, at this point, developed his case by arguing the relevance of George Washington's warning concerning the engagement by the United States in European struggles to the situation in 1939, and concluded that, "We all have our own sympathies and our natural emotions in behalf of the victims of national or international outrage all around the globe; but we are not, we cannot be, the world's protector or the world's policeman. The price of the association would be the jeopardy of our own democracy."[17]

Robert Taft's case, made on radio before the American Forum of the Air, January 22, 1939, was similar in significant ways to Vandenberg's, but it also developed several other lines of argument. After noting Franklin Roosevelt's annual message to Congress on January 4, which pictured the world in flames and wherein there were calls for higher defense spending which Taft did not find excessive, he noted the changing definition of "national defense" that we have already observed as a line of argument in the Vandenberg speech of a month later. Taft found Roosevelt suggesting that the United States should be respon-

sible for the protection of morality and democracy all over the world and Taft then commented that this was a new thought to America. "No one has ever suggested before that a single nation should range over the world, like a knight-errant, protecting democracy and ideals of good faith, and tilting, like Don Quixote, against the windmills of Fascism. The unsoundness and danger of such a course was eloquently set forth by Senator Borah over a national radio forum on March 28, 1938 [treated below]."[18] He developed, next, that the neutrality legislation could keep us out of war, and that the country could stay out if determined to do so. He, then, suggested that the nation should be determined because of war's destructiveness to that which it seeks to save. With World War I, "We learned that modern war defeats its own purposes. A war to preserve democracy resulted in the destruction of more democracies than it preserved."[19] Further, war would go far to destroy democracy in the United States as well. "We have moved far towards totalitarian government already. The additional powers sought by the President in case of war, the nationalization of all industry and all capital and all labor already proposed in the bill before Congress, would create a socialistic dictatorship which it would be impossible to dissolve when the war ended."[20]

He suggested that the country should feel compassion for the English condition and should let them know that we cared

---

15. *Ibid.*, 355.
16. *Ibid.*
17. *Ibid.*, 357.
18. Robert Taft, "Let Us Stay Out of War," *Vital Speeches* 5 (February 1, 1939):255.
19. *Ibid.*
20. *Ibid.*

greatly, but that we must remain neutral. He concluded that, "many justifiable criticisms can be made of the neutrality act, and of any special type of neutrality. But the horrors of modern war are so great, its futility so evident, its effect on democracy itself so destructive, that almost any alternative is more to be desired."[21]

The speech by William Borah, previously referred to by Taft, was an address given during the National Radio Forum arranged by the *Washington Star* and broadcast over NBC, Monday, March 28, 1938. In this speech Senator Borah included most of the arguments we have observed, developed by Vandenberg and Taft. He set out his case, from the beginning, in the spirit of Washington and Jefferson, and first concluded that it is the duty of the United States to be friends with all nations without making judgments as to the right and wrong of any country's particular system. His evidence for this position was the example of the United States' recognition of the French during its revolution showing that while America did continue recognition, no one did this with an approval of the horrors accompanying the revolution.[22] He proceeded from this example to a criticism of the Versailles treaty. He reasoned that Austria, by the terms of the treaty, was left open to an invasion from Hitler and with whatever treatment Austria had received from Hitler, it could be no worse than that from its friends at Versailles. Conclusion: Our recognition of a fact does not necessarily imply our agreement with that fact. This point of view, by the way, is not unfamiliar to our ears today. We have often heard it advanced by those recommending the recognition of Communist China, for instance.

With the foregoing conclusion in mind, he moved to a refutation of the argument that it is proper for us to support democracies in their struggle against dictatorships—the "save the world for democracy" argument. His premise here was that nations do and must act out of motivations of self-interest; he combined this thought with his prior conclusion: "A nation does not, and can not, choose its friends because of approval, or disapproval, of theories or practices, political or otherwise. . . . We went into the World War [WWI] to make the world safe for democracy and we made it a breeding camp for dictators."[23] Here was another expression of the argument developed by Senator Taft ten months later. Borah concluded this point by quoting George Washington, "There can be no greater error than to expect, or calculate upon, real favors from nation to nation. It is an illusion which experience must cure, which a just pride ought to discard."[24]

Next he moved to an argument which should be particularly familiar to us today and which will be encountered again in the analysis, later in the chapter, of the contemporary state of isolationism. Borah suggested that the problem with democracies at that time, including the United States, was that they were "bleeding inwardly."[25] Given this assumption, he observed that the country must prepare a national defense, then work for internal repair. There was a vast army of unemployed, poverty stricken people, poorly clad and poorly fed. The danger to the nation from abroad "is remote, highly problematical."[26] The danger was within our own borders:

---

21. *Ibid.*, 256.
22. William Borah, "Our Imperative Task," *Vital Speeches*, 4 (April 15, 1938):386.
23. *Ibid.*, 387.
24. *Ibid.*, 388.
25. *Ibid.*
26. *Ibid.*

I do not minimize what all this [the enemies of liberty, the enemies of religion, the Communist and Fascist doctrines] means to the people of this country and all that they cherish. But I do contend most earnestly that the first line of defense against such enemies is the clear mind, the sturdy character, and the loyal heart of the citizen. Against these systems there is, in the last analysis, no security, no protection, except the security and protection found in the contentment, and happiness, the prosperity and the devotion of the people.

I know of no course we as a people could pursue more definitely calculated to establish a totalitarian government in this country than by permitting ourselves to be involved in foreign wars.[27]

Pressing on to a strong conclusion the senator noted that, "war is always the eternal enemy of democracy, the friend of Communism, and the father of fascism."[28] The climax of the address had been reached. Senator Borah closed with one more argument that is anticlimatic and that appears to be almost an afterthought. He asked his audience to consider just whom they should support. England? But then whose position? Eden's, no negotiation; or Chamberlain's, negotiation? France? But they were closely allied with Russia. So whom? The problem is that in Europe the situation was fundamentally unsound. To the question, "Who then makes war?", Borah responded by quoting from an editorial from the *London Times*:

The answer is to be found in the Chancellories of Europe among the men who have too long played with human lives as pawns in a game of chess, who have become enmeshed in formulas and the jargon of diplomacy that they have ceased to be conscious of the poignant realities with which they trifle and thus will war continue to be made until the great masses who are the sport of professional schemers and dreamers say the word which shall bring, not eternal peace, for that is impossible, but a determination that wars shall be fought only in a just and righteous and vital cause.[29]

The case of the isolationists was made.

The extremists tended to stand on an oversimplified "There is evil out there" position. The more moderates included arguments which analyzed the destructive nature of war, the purpose of a nation's foreign policy in terms of self-interest, and the need for solving one's own internal problems. The cases were built with two fundamental lines of support. First, an appeal to the "principles" of Washington and Jefferson; second, to an analysis of the unsatisfactory conclusion of World War I. The solution posed by all of the isolationists of the thirties: stay out of the problems of Europe and the Far East.

The Beginnings of Internationalism

When we consider internationalism we must clearly establish what we mean. It does *not* mean simply a policy wherein the United States will act outside its borders. The United States had, in fact, done this on numbers of occasions prior to the mid-twentieth century. In the country's excursions into the Far East defended by Beveridge in his historical address "The March of the Flag," and in the expansionist activities of Theodore Roosevelt, America went out well beyond its borders. World War I was a clear example of participation of the United States, apparently with other nations to "make the world safe for democracy." But none of these activities were done in a true spirit of partnership with other nations. The nation tended to ride in on a white charger to "save" the world, an entity totally apart from the United States.

In this sense, until the mid-twentieth century, the old role of America in world politics, while at

---

27. *Ibid.*
28. *Ibid.*
29. *Ibid.*, 389.

times a very substantial one, was to rely chiefly upon its own strengths and resources, to act or not to act "at times and places of its own choosing," and to interpret its own national purposes and destiny as distinct and separate from that of any other nation or group of nations.[30]

For a brief moment in 1919 and 1920, a few people under the leadership of Woodrow Wilson advocated a different policy, a policy of internationalism. Wilson's dream was truly the participation of America in a covenant of nations, the League of Nations, to eliminate war from the globe. The conception was broad and deeply bound to a common effort of nations working in concert. But first the Senate and then the nation in the elections of 1920 sent the ideal to defeat.

This true internationalism hardly appeared again in the country until the speech made by Franklin Roosevelt in Chicago for the dedication of the Outer Drive on October 5, 1937: the Quarantine Speech. The thoughts expressed there were present in the many speeches Roosevelt made on international affairs from then until December 7, 1941, when the country entered the war.

The Quarantine Speech apparently grew directly from Roosevelt's extreme concern over the direction of affairs of the world from 1931 to 1937. The times were increasingly grave. Roosevelt expressed concern in a letter in 1936 to James M. Cox "Nevertheless, I am still most pessimistic about Europe and there seems to be no step that we can take to improve that situation."[31] Again, on May 17, 1937, FDR wrote to the United States ambassador in Rome that "Anything, of course, that postpones war is that much to the good. The progress of the disease [notice the disease illusion that was to become the basis for the Quarantine Speech four months later] is slowed up but

the disease remains—and will probably prove fatal in the next few years."[32]

From 1931 to October 1937, much had happened abroad which might well have caused some pessimism. In September, 1931, the Sino-Japanese war had begun with the so-called explosion of the South Manchurian Railway outside Mukden and the Japanese invasion of Manchuria. In 1933, Hitler was elected Chancellor of Germany. He began active purges in June, 1934. July, 1934, brought the murder of Dollfuss, the Austrian Chancellor, in the Vienna *putsch*. Mussolini led his first attacks in Ethiopia in December, 1934, and continued until the conquest of that country was completed in May, 1936. Hitler gave up all pretense of following the troops and arms restrictions of the Versailles treaty in March, 1935, when he established a new German program of compulsory, universal military training. Within the three days following March 7, 1936, Hitler's troops marched on and occupied the demilitarized Rhineland.

At this point, events began to move more rapidly. The Spanish Civil War, with the rebels supported by Hitler and Mussolini, started in July, 1936. October, 1936, saw the formal establishment of the Rome-Berlin axis. Japan and Germany entered into a pact in November which was joined by Italy in 1937, completing the unification of the Axis powers. Now, the armaments race was on in earnest.

---

30. Seabury, *Power*, pp. 38-39.
31. Letter from FDR to James Cox written aboard the USS Indianapolis, December 9, 1936, Franklin Delano Roosevelt Library (FDRL), President's Personal File (PPF), 53.
32. Letter from FDR to Wm. Phillips, May 17, 1937, FDRL, Presdient's Secretary File (PSF), 1. Diplomatic Correspondence; Italy, 1933-41, 1945; Box 10, Folder: Wm. Phillips, 1937-38.

This brief sketch recalls a few of the more obvious directions the world was taking at the time FDR gave the Chicago speech. The situation was dark and getting darker. The major threats were obvious. And Roosevelt rose in Chicago to try to get an isolationist nation to think of joining with other nations to stop the growing dangers.

Roosevelt accepted two major tasks in his Quarantine Speech. First, he made clear how serious the state of the world was to him. Second, he developed arguments against the isolationist beliefs so prevalent in 1937.

First, then, he sought to have the people understand the seriousness of the situation as he understood it. He defined the threat of the Axis powers as being an attack against all that was decent, and further, an attack against civilization itself.

To paraphrase a recent author "perhaps we foresee a time when men, exultant in the technique of homicide, will rage so hotly over the world that every precious thing will be in danger, every book (and) every picture, (and) every harmony, every treasure garnered through two milleniums, the small, the delicate, the defenseless—all will be lost or wrecked or utterly destroyed."

If these things come to pass in other parts of the world, let no one imagine that America will escape, that America may expect mercy, that this Western Hemisphere will not be attacked and that it will continue tranquilly and peacefully to carry on the ethics and the arts of civilization.

No, if those days come "there will be no safety by arms, no help from authority, no answer in science. The storm will rage till every flower of culture is trampled and all human beings are leveled in vast chaos."[33]

To discredit the isolationists, he used the metaphor of a contagious disease that needs to be quarantined:

It seems to be unfortunately true that the epidemic of world lawlessness is spreading.

And mark this well! When an epidemic of physical disease starts to spread, the community approves and joins in a quarantine of its patients in order to protect the health of the community against the spread of the disease.[34]

Thus, from issue one, we are seriously threatened, and from issue two, the threat is spreading like a contagious disease. Therefore, we must join with others in a quarantine. Isolationism will not serve us. "America hates war. America—*America* hopes for peace. Therefore America *actively engages* [italics my own for emphasis] in the search for peace."[35]

The battle lines were drawn by Roosevelt that day in Chicago. He was to carry the fight to the country again and again between 1937 and our entry into World War II. And the battle was waged mostly by Roosevelt or other members of his administration. The case was made most often in terms of alternatives, *i.e.*, if the country did not actively attempt to seek proper solutions, all that America stood for was lost. The conditions were serious and immediate. Cordell Hull spoke out on the issue prior to the Quarantine Speech.[36] And Henry Stimson developed the point before the Foreign Relations Committee of the Senate on April 5, 1939, by first recognizing that a traditional policy of the United

33. Quarantine Speech, (FDRL) Speech files; Speech of October 5, 1937, p. 3. With his speech manuscripts, it was Roosevelt's habit to ad lib during their delivery. The manuscript used here shows this improvisation as taken down by a stenographer. Parentheses indicate material deleted from the speech at the time of delivery. Underlining indicates materials added during delivery. The manuscript of the Quarantine Speech used was that at the FDRL as corrected in this system.

34. *Ibid.*, p. 6.

35. *Ibid.*, p. 8.

36. For example, see Cordell Hull, "The Position of our Secretary of State," *Vital Speeches*, 3 (September 1, 1937):702-03.

States was one of mutual respect for other nations' sovereignty as "prevails among gentlemen in ordinary life."[37] He, then, discovered that the situation was not normal: three of the seven most powerful nations in the world had rejected the principle, had turned aggressively destructive. This led him to point to the dangers: "I weigh my words when I say I believe that our present Caucasian civilization is threatened by the greatest danger with which it has been confronted for four centuries."[38]

Two other aspects of the Stimson speech are worth noting. He pointed first to the fact of the shrinking world. This became a strong argument, particularly in the rhetoric of the internationalist since World War II; finally, he made an effort to refute, with his own prestige, the argument often advanced by the isolationists that a dictatorship would be created in the United States as too much power was going to the President. He said:

I am a Republican and the present administration is Democratic, but I have always tried to limit my partisanship in the zone of foreign affairs. I am a strong believer in the system of representative government, and from my observations I have come to the belief that in no sphere of government action is representative action so essential, so effective or so safe from abuse as in the conduct of foreign relations.

I am not impressed with the fear that in that zone Presidential discretion is likely to be abused. It is my observation that in no sphere of political action is the sobering effect of terrific responsibility upon one man so marked as in the sphere of our country's relations with the outside world.[39]

The beginnings of true internationalist thought had, thus, been made for America. An effort had begun after World War I, but it was defeated. In the chaotic period prior to World War II, the second attempt was advanced. As the world scene grew ever worse in the dark days before December 7, 1941, the public responded with some shift in its fundamentally isolationist mind. With the bombing of Pearl Harbor and the horrors of the war, America emerged not as it had after the first world struggle, but of a mind to participate actively in world affairs. It is this period to which we now turn.

The Apex of Internationalism

Clearly, at the end of World War II American attitudes and therefore the country's foreign policy had undergone what was almost a complete 180° rotation. By 1945 and 1946, the prevailing conception was one of international cooperation. Particularly in the years immediately following the war there was little if any effort made by any public figures which recommended the isolated American fortress.

As the result of the bombing of Pearl Harbor, an extremely destructive war started. It enveloped almost all the planet and news of it was broadcast over radio each night giving a real feeling of immediacy to the chaos, accented by the atomic bomb, towards the end. The oceans shrank and this country's dependence upon other nations to avoid the total execution of mankind became apparent. Harry Truman spoke at the final plenary session of the conference at which the United Nations charter was created and adopted, January 26, 1945. He said, "We have tested the principle of cooperation in this war [WWII] and have found that it works."[40]

37. Henry Stimson, "We Must Drop Our Isolation," *Vital Speeches*, 5 (April 15, 1939):399.
38. *Ibid.*
39. *Ibid.*, 400.
40. Harry Truman, "Speech at the Final Plenary Session," *Vital Speeches*, 11 (July 1, 1945):571.

So part of the argument in the Truman speech was that cooperation had been successful. But the case was not restricted to this rather limited observation. The primary position of President Truman at that time, and the internationalists since, rested on the impossibility of another war and the responsibility and duty of the United States, as well as that of all countries, to establish peace.

We all have to recognize—no matter how great our strength—that we must deny ourselves the license to do always as we please. No one nation, no regional group, can or should expect any special privilege which harms any other nation. If any nation would keep security for itself, it must be ready and willing to share security with all. That is the price which each nation will have to pay for world peace.[41]
Upon all of us, in all our countries, is now laid the duty of transforming into action these words which you have written [The United Nations Charter], upon our decisive action rests the hope of those who have fallen, those now living, those yet unborn—the hope for a world of free countries—with decent standards of living—which will work and cooperate in a friendly civilized community of nations.[42]

And, finally, the ultimate threat that prevents anyone who lives in the United States during the last half of the twentieth century from being an isolationist of the variety that spoke so loudly during the thirties:

Now in 1938 I stood on this platform right here and explained to you that our then isolationism would eventually lead to war. I made that speech after President Roosevelt made his speech at Chicago in 1937, in which he warned the United States that we were approaching another world war.
We can't stand another global war. We won't have another war unless it is total war, and that means the end of our civilization as we know it. We are not going to do that. We are going to accept that Golden Rule, and we are going forward to

meet our destiny, which I think Almighty God intended us to have—and we [the United States] are going to be the leader.[43]

Unlike 1919-20 when the League of Nations was defeated, the Senate accepted the United Nations by a vote of 82-2. The whole country was ready for America to participate in world problems cooperatively with other nations. Senators who had held strongly for an isolated United States in 1937, were now advocating support for cooperation. Arthur Vandenberg delivered a speech in the Senate on July 16, 1946, which concluded as follows:

Mr. President, in my view, peace hangs chiefly upon three factors which are inextricably interwoven:
One, the dependable and effective operation of the United Nations in behalf of justice courageously sustained by collective security.
Two, the successful outlawry of atomic bombs and kindred instruments of sudden, overwhelming mass destruction, under a tight system of total discipline which makes bad faith impossible.
Three, Mr. President, is my report to the Senate and the country regarding contemporary progress in the hard, perplexing task of doing in the name and cause of peace what our soldier sons did in the name and cause of war.
"Lord God of hosts, be with us yet, lest we forget, lest we forget."[44]

The first major crisis to test the newly instituted American internationalist foreign policy was the Korean struggle that began in 1950. For the next two or three years, there were a few of the respectable suggesting something of a return to isolationism.

---

41. *Ibid.*
42. *Ibid.*, 572.
43. Harry Truman, "Golden Rule for World Peace," *Vital Speeches*, 12 (October 15, 1945):3.
44. Arthur Vandenberg, "Peace with Justice the Supreme Necessity," *Vital Speeches*, 12 (August 1, 1946):620.

Their thinking will be analyzed in the next section of the chapter. The reversion toward this earlier point of view was minimal, however, and the United States continued its policy of collective security arguing as just previously described. On January 28, 1951, at a Founders' Day convocation at Northwestern University, the then Governor of Illinois, Adlai Stevenson, asked, "Are the universities to be stripped of students in order to defend our cultural heritage? The young of college age are the seed corn of a society and a nation. To survive must we eat our seed corn? And if we do, can we survive? We must and we will, I think, find at least a partial answer to that disturbing question. And we will find it in calm deliberation, not in frantic fright."[45]

The answer developed by Stevenson grew out of his analysis that the country was seriously threatened, and that all must learn that the response to the crisis must come from a collective sense of responsibility of all free nations:

Have we learned that our mission is the prevention, not just the survival of a major war? Have we discovered that there are no Gibraltars, no fortresses impregnable to death or ideas, anymore? . . . While the debate talks incessantly in terms of our national crisis and our national survival, it is not just our crisis, it is the crisis of the whole free world. . . . If we have not learned that having the most to lose we have the most to save, then, I say, let us pray.

But if we have, if the immensity of the responsibility and the stakes have dawned upon us, then the great debate has been a great blessing and we are on the way to thwart this latest greatest threat to all this University symbolizes.[46]

The answer to his opening then is affirmative; the country must stay in Korea and fight. And so with the other threats of Communism in the early fifties. The internationalist spirit was high in almost all of the country and its leaders, in or out of of-

fice. Truman described the actualities, to him, of the Communist threat on radio, December 15, 1950. After calling for major efforts in the face of the "grave danger," and issuing a national proclamation that a national emergency existed, he concluded his remarks with the theme:

No nation has ever had a greater responsibility than ours at the moment. We must remember that we are the leaders of the free world. We must understand that we cannot achieve peace by ourselves, but only by cooperating with other free nations and with the men and women who love freedom everywhere.

We must remember that our goal is not war but peace. Throughout the world our name stands for international justice and for a world based in the principles of law and order. We must keep it that way. We are willing to negotiate differences but we will not yield to aggression. Appeasement of evil is not the road to peace.[47]

With Dwight D. Eisenhower, yet to run and be elected to the presidency, on February 1, 1951, to the members of Congress, it was the same story.[48] Thomas Dewey, who was defeated by Truman in 1948, gave much the same speech as Truman's to the lawyers in New York City on December 14, 1950.[49] The times were threatening; internationalism was succeeding as the national response to the times.

The Democrats, Roosevelt and Truman, had launched the ship. The Republicans put their stamp of approval on it at the 1952 convention where Dwight Eisenhower defeated Robert Taft; and the coun-

---

45. Stevenson, "No Gibraltars," p. 285.
46. *Ibid.*, 287.
47. Harry Truman, "A National Emergency Exists," *Vital Speeches*, 17 (January 1, 1951):165.
48. Dwight Eisenhower, "The Defense of Western Europe," *Vital Speeches*, 17 (February 15, 1951):258-62.
49. Thomas Dewey, "National Mobilization," *Vital Speeches*, 17 (January 1, 1951):167-70.

try with the election of Eisenhower saw the firm and continuing development of the philosophy. The policy had served us in a time or two of crisis, but would it serve us as well as the chaos quieted under Eisenhower's administration?

During the Eisenhower years relative peace descended on the world. The Korean war was settled soon after Eisenhower took office, McCarthy was censured in late 1954, Stalin died and was condemned by Krushchev, Eisenhower produced the "spirit of Geneva" at the world's first summit meeting in 1955. The foreign policy that had been devised to solve world crises now had to modify—to address itself to keeping the peace. And it did. The policy no longer was addressed entirely to matters of security from war. It was extended to work toward solutions for poverty, oppression, injustice. Herbert Hoover, interestingly enough, while addressing a large audience at the opening of the Brussels Exposition on July 4, 1958, said "There is now some cooperation in organization of worldwide research. My country desires to see such cooperation expanded. Thus, the march of progress in the world would be faster."[50] Later in the speech, defending against the charge of United States imperialism, he stated, "Our people have *willingly* [italics mine] borne back-breaking taxes in these efforts [fighting foreign wars and the making of gifts to other nations] without any hope of returns. And they are today continuing this huge burden of taxation to aid in protecting the freedom of mankind and to relieve peoples from poverty."[51]

Hoover's son, acting Secretary of State, before the United Nations General Assembly on November 16, 1956, said:

Our goal must be a world in which nations and people can live side by side, whatever their internal political, economic, and social systems, without fear and with real hope of self-fulfillment. The United Nations can be an agency of inestimable value in helping to work toward this goal. We cannot ask if it will succeed in its job. We must make it succeed.

Nothing could be clearer than the fact that a more effective United Nations serves the interests of every nation. We must strive to develop institutions through which the rights of all nations can be respected and justice can be secured in peaceful ways. Let us join together here to build a bridge from the past to the future, across which we can walk together in a new spirit of confidence.[52]

This statement took the United States much further in its cooperation with other nations than arms and soldiers in immediate military struggles. This extended development of internationalism found formal recognition for the country in Dwight Eisenhower's second inaugural and reached an apex in John Kennedy's inaugural. Eisenhower said:

We must use our skills and knowledge and, at times, our substance, to help others rise from misery, however far the scene of suffering may be from our shores. For wherever in the world a people knows desperate want, there must appear at least the spark of hope, the hope of progress—or there will surely rise at last the flames of conflict.

We recognize and accept our own deep involvement in the destiny of men everywhere. We are accordingly pledged to honor, and to strive to fortify, the authority of the United Nations.[53]

The inaugural address of John Kennedy on January 20, 1961, was amazingly similar

---

50. Herbert Hoover, "The Invisible Forces Radiating from Nations," *Vital Speeches*, 24 (August 1, 1958):620.

51. *Ibid.*, 621.

52. Herbert Hoover, Jr., "The United Nations and the Present Crisis," *Vital Speeches*, 22 (December 1, 1956):100.

53. Dwight Eisenhower, "Our Destiny Lies with All Free Nations," *Vital Speeches*, 23 (February 1, 1957):248.

to that of Eisenhower in 1957. They are approximately the same length, relatively short. They both address themselves almost entirely to affairs of the world in general rather than laying particular stress on the domestic affairs of the United States. They both present the view of a united mankind struggling toward a better world of peace and security wherein problems of political conflict are solvable by men working together to eliminate want and to build human rights. The vision was broad and inspiring when Kennedy said:

Now the trumpet summons us again—not as a call to bear arms, though arms we need—not as a call to battle, though embattled we are—but a call to bear the burden of a long twilight struggle against the common enemies of man: tyranny, poverty, disease and war itself.

Can we forge against these enemies a grand and global alliance, north and south, east and west, that can assure a more fruitful life for all mankind? Will you join in that historic effort?

In the long history of the world, only a few generations have been granted the role of defending freedom in its hour of maximum danger. I do not shrink from this responsibility—I welcome it. I do not believe that any of us would exchange places with any other generation. The energy, the faith, the devotion which we bring to this endeavor will light our country and all who serve it—and the glow from that fire can truly light the world.[54]

Truly the apex of internationalist thought, thus far, had been reached. Isolationism was, for the moment, dead. The collective spirit of man raised in the common effort of aiding the world. But what of isolationism in the 1950s and 1960s. Did the cat have another life or two ahead of it?

Isolationism in Mid-Century America

Apparently the pressure of crisis is able to give some renewed life to one or another brand of isolationism. With the end of World War II, almost no one would call for an isolated America. While the United Nations was being established, the most that was offered by way of challenges to the concept of greater world participation for the United States were cautions. Virtually no denial of the concept of cooperation can be found. The objectors merely expressed hope, but with a degree of skepticism and warning. Herbert Hoover observed in the late part of 1945:

The preamble to the Charter [of the United Nations] contains a list of vital objectives. This preamble is an expression of hope. It is not a binding agreement. The test of the war-settlements and indeed of the Charter itself will be whether these ideals are applied to all people. If the nations fail in these particulars we shall have explosions which no Security Council can control. But if the ideas of this preamble be followed in the political and economic settlements of the war, the wounds of war can be healed, liberty restored in the world, the Charter strengthened and lasting peace can come to mankind.[55]

All went well for the internationalists until the pressure of the Korean crisis, and then isolationism reappeared, only slightly modified from that of the thirties. Extremism showed itself in the form of Joseph McCarthy and the Red witchhunts that lasted into 1954. The less radical, more soundly stated isolationism also reappeared in the persons of Herbert Hoover, Robert Taft, and Joseph P. Kennedy, whose remarks have been selected here as reflections of their thinking.

Herbert Hoover, in a general summary of the United States foreign policy on Decem-

---

54. John Kennedy, "For the Freedom of Man," *Vital Speeches*, 27 (February 1, 1961):227.
55. Herbert Hoover, "Progress Toward Enduring Peace," *Vital Speeches*, 11 (August 15, 1945):647.

ber 20, 1950, first reviewed world conditions for his radio audience. He concluded, "Alone [we, Americans] with sea and air power can so control the Atlantic and Pacific Oceans that there can be no possible invasion of the Western Hemisphere by Communist armies. They can no more reach Washington in force than we can reach Moscow."[56] Then he continued:

It is clear that the United Nations are defeated in Korea. It is also clear that other non-Communist nations did not or could not substantially respond to the U.N. call for arms to Korea. It is clear the U.N. cannot mobilize substantial military forces. It is clear Continental Europe has not in the three years of our aid developed that unity of purpose, and that will power necessary for its own defense. It is clear that our British friends are flirting with appeasement of Communist China. It is clear that the United Nations is in a fog of debate and indecision on whether to appease or not to appease.[57]

He proposed: "The Foundation of our national policies must be to preserve the world of this Western Hemisphere Gibraltar of Western Civilization." The United States should arm itself "to the teeth." There is the modification from an earlier policy of isolationism in his suggestion that we should continue to aid the hungry world so that they can be strong against the appeals of Communism. "We have a stern duty to work and sacrifice to do it." He pointed out that America is not blind to the need for the preservation of Europe, and the test is whether they have enough "spiritual Force."[58] The Europeans themselves must show it. The theme was the religiosity of old. Some updating of the old case was present, but the crucial tests are of old. The United States must avoid rash involvement of its military forces in hopeless campaigns. The policies suggested in the speech ". . . . do not relieve us of working to our utmost. They would preserve a stronghold

of Christian civilization in the world against any peradventure."[59]

It is clear that the isolationists had amended their position. But many of the old principles remained the same and were argued in the terms of an earlier America. Robert Taft, speaking in Tuxedo, New York, on May 21, 1951, said:

I believe the power of the United States is such that we can be safe if we use that power effectively, but there is one policy and only one policy which can destroy this Nation—the commitment to projects beyond our capacity to fulfill. Germany is in ruin because Hitler thought he could conquer the world when he could not do so. Italy was wrecked because Mussolini thought he could create an Italian empire. We cannot permit any emotional affection for other nations to divert us from the policy of American security.[60]

Joseph Kennedy, too, worried about the weakening of the United States with an overextension of our potential. Along with whatever the country might do in and for the world outside, it must remember that, primarily, its worry is itself:

As far back as March 18, 1946, I set forth in *Life* magazine what I considered should be the fundamentals of American policy. The first and foremost of these was that we should make and keep ourselves strong. Fundamental to any successful dealing with the world, was the maintenance here in the United States of a high standard of living. Whatever concrete action might be suggested, to bankrupt this nation in the pursuit of them would mean our self-destruction. I am not against generosity—generosity within our means. . . . A first step in the pursuit of this policy is to get out of

56. Herbert Hoover, "Our National Policies in This Crisis," *Vital Speeches*, 17 (January 1, 1951):165.
57. *Ibid.*, 166.
58. *Ibid.*
59. *Ibid.*, 167.
60. Robert Taft, "United States Relations with Western Europe," *Vital Speeches*, 17 (June 15, 1951):519.

Korea—indeed, to get out of any point in Asia which we do not plan realistically to hold in our own defense. . . . The next step in pursuit of this policy is to apply the same principle to Europe.[61]

The argument of the few isolationists of the early fifties, then, did recognize some responsibilities for the United States' participation with other nations. In that sense, the country did not return to the position of the thirties. Now, the struggle became one that said, "Some—as much as we can, but not more," and the "some" was limited. The position was advanced in the older terms, however. That is, the old understanding of the righteousness of America, the saving of the "Christian civilization" for the world was at the heart of the case. No longer were Washington and Jefferson used as the defense. Now, the "unsuccessful" World War II and the spiritual weakness of the rest of the world became the major premises. With these, the conclusion followed that the job of America was still the creation of fortress America.

With the relative peace of the late fifties and early sixties, the isolationist voice all but disappeared. The United States went on to reach the peak of international philosophy developed in the previous section of this chapter. All was calm in the great debate. But then two important new factors entered the scene which were to drive out a new clash in the last years of the sixties and continue with us into the seventies. The first of these was the military battle in Southeast Asia, particularly in South Vietnam. This might not, in itself, have been enough to start the debate again, but coupled with the second, a very new phenomenon in America, the debate assumed fresh life.

Large segments of the country began to find serious weaknesses in the "perfect" society. On all sides, important attacks were launched at fundamental American institutions. Inadequacies of the educational system appeared. The rights of certain minority groups proved to be far from ideal. The judicial system appeared weak. Crime in the streets reached epidemic proportions and won elections for opportunistic political candidates. Drugs became the frequent answer to youth, the hope of tomorrow, in facing the problems of the day while their parents remained calm with tranquilizers. Most of what the country had accepted to be the fulfillment of the dream of all mankind proved to many to be no more than a thin sugar coating on a rather unpleasant pill.

What would it take to face successfully each of these new factors? For Vietnam, if the war was right at all, and many in increasing numbers found it not to be, the need was for manpower, will power, and exceedingly large expenditures of funds. Such a demand takes tremendous energy from a society. For the domestic scene, the need was again manpower, will power, and exceedingly large expenditures of funds. In fact, the demands on the country have been so great during the last few years that the country is in a state of near exhaustion and frustration.

In the face of all the pressures there have emerged lines of thought which have many of the earmarks of an earlier isolationist stance though they are offered from a fundamentally different base. On December 3, 1970, Senator Frank Church set out elements of the new case. For the first section of his talk he described the obvious disunity in the country.

---

61. Joseph Kennedy, "Present Policy is Politically and Morally Bankrupt," *Vital Speeches,* 17 (January 1, 1951):170-71.

No longer do we face our problems together. Instead we divide into minority blocs and special interest groups; student militants, hard hats and Black Panthers, to name a few. Factionalizing is so much in fashion that those who claim no particular label are lumped together in a grouping of their own and touted as the "forgotten Americans."

As the balkanization of our society worsens, rational dialogue across the barriers all but ceases. "Non-negotiable demands" are leveled in language foul from faces flushed. <u>Power</u> is the ubiquitous symbol and catchword: white <u>power</u>, black <u>power</u>, red <u>power</u>, flower <u>power</u>.

Intolerant slogans depict the ugly mood:
"America, love it (my way) or leave it."
"Off the pigs."
"Tell it to Hanoi."
And on and on and on.

With Job, the time has come for America to implore: "How long will ye vex my soul and break me in pieces with words?"[62]

The causes he described as follows:

The dangerous generation gap, as I see it, has more to do with means than ends. Far too many bright sensitive college students are "turned off." Whatever word is used for describing their negative mood, whether it be alienated, disaffected, or disillusioned, the fact is that alarming numbers of young Americans are losing faith in the American political process. They believe the system is rigged for war, not peace; they suspect that representative government has lost its vitality, with only the pocketbook interests enjoying representation, not the people. Worst of all, they think that their entreaties, when voiced in the regular manner, go unheeded and unheard.[63]

He saw the symbol of all the problems to be Vietnam in particular and foreign policy in general:

Having witnessed the involvement of the United States in both great wars of the century, our contemporary leaders drew the conclusion that since we couldn't withdraw in isolation from the world, we must therefore take charge of it. . . . The United States, without much forethought, pledged itself to oversee the vast regions once occupied by the bankrupt European nations. Overnight, we became the policeman, banker and judge of most of the world.[64]

At this point of the speech we begin to see the Church solution, and though he disclaimed, quite justly, that he was an isolationist, the sounds of the proposal are not wholly unfamiliar:

The remedy—the only remedy—is to bring America home again, not to a neoisolationism of which I am sometimes accused; not to an abandonment of the United Nations or those alliances, such as NATO, which really contribute to our security; Not to a condition of military weakness which might tempt our enemies—but home again to the forgotten truth that the first mission of the federal government was never to decide which faction should govern some little country on the fringes of China, but to attend to the genuine needs of the American people!

For too long, our peoples' problems have gone unattended here at home. For too long, our presidents have been mesmerized by the quests of Caesar. For too long, our resources have been poured into distant lands, with which we have no former link or economic interest, no strategic stake or post-colonial responsibility.

The time has come to put right our priorities, before we exhaust ourselves in futile foreign adventures, as other great powers have done before us. At song fests we raise our voices to sing: "This land is our land." Well it cries out for more attention. American cities rot at their cores. The countryside empties of people, family farms disappear. Smog spreads it noxious mantle, water turns rancid, and the problems of waste disposal grow daily more severe. Race relations worsen, the streets are shamefully unsafe. Crime breeds on addictive drugs. And poverty persists amidst plenty.

This gathering crisis in our own land bears far more importantly on the future of the republic than anything we have now, or have ever had at stake, in Indo-China. Attention to these festering

---

62. Frank Church, "Foreign Policy: The Generation Gap," *Vital Speeches*, 37 (January 1, 1971):170.
63. *Ibid.*, 171.
64. *Ibid.*, 172.

problems on the homefront, reinforced by an iron-clad resolve to solve them, would do more than anything else to enlist the energies, quicken the interest, and restore the allegiance of the doubting young.[65]

Though obviously not from the isolationist mouth of Borah in the thirties, the speech has an element of similarity. Church observed that America has internal problems whose solution will go far to give America the sought after security and unity. This point was also developed by Borah in 1938.

But is the Church speech an isolationist speech? To answer this question we recall the history of internationalism and remember what it had become during the Eisenhower and Kennedy years.

First, we must be aware that the purpose of foreign policy is to foster a nation's security. Prior to Eisenhower and Kennedy, security was defined entirely in terms of military security. An isolationist was one who said we could be militarily secure, and therefore totally secure, on our own. The internationalist denied this premise saying that we had to have the help of others, militarily.

Eisenhower and Kennedy looked on security in military terms, to be sure, *and* in terms of the need to better the conditions of mankind, contending that the United States was only really secure as defenses were up and starvation and misery and oppression were down.

Church surely did not express the first kind of isolationism. He was very much aware that America needs to cooperate with its allies for military security. So in the old sense, Church is not an isolationist, but what of his denial of helping others in the world to achieve better living standards? What would he recommend? His speech is

not clear. To answer the question we would have to ask Senator Church and others today how they respond to this new brand of isolationist thought if in fact it does exist.

Closing Observations

The fight between the isolationists and the internationalists in the sense of the thirties is probably finished. With the H-bomb, intercontinental ballistic missiles, the prevalence of the revolutionary mind, none would hold that we can go it alone militarily.

The debate, if it appears with any strength at all in the seventies, will be centered not in the military aspects of the argument but in whether the United States should continue to help the less fortunate of the world. It appears that, if there is any life left in isolationism, the attacks will center there.

Certainly, however, we can be wise enough to avoid another improper dichotomy for ourselves. The argument must not be whether to help other peoples or just our own, but rather how much of each and in what ways. If we can, indeed, grant this direction for the debate, the cat may in fact be dead.

BIBLIOGRAPHY

Cantril, Hadley. *Public Opinion, 1935-1946.* Princeton: Princeton University Press, 1953. Anyone looking for the result of any of the public opinion surveys from their beginning in 1935 to 1946 should first check this volume. The survey sought will probably be present.

---

65. *Ibid.*

Lerche, Charles. *Foreign Policy of the American People.* Englewood Cliffs, N.J.: Prentice-Hall, 1967.
Shows major trends of American policy and then makes an effort to explain why the policies have been and are what they are.

Seabury, Paul. *Power, Freedom and Diplomacy.* New York: Vintage Books, 1963.
The Bancroft prize was awarded to this relatively short but excellent analysis and explanation for the relation of nation to nation.

20 America Confronts the Internal Communist Menace

Dale G. Leathers

For a period of nearly ten years following World War II, un-American was an epithet of almost unparalleled intimidation for the accused and of undisguised vituperation for the accuser. Seldom have Americans been so polarized, so fearful, and so preoccupied. They were preoccupied with the seemingly ineluctable conclusion that their lives would be gripped by one of two highly undesirable forces. Either they would lose many of their freedoms as an internal Communist conspiracy enveloped their country or they would lose many of their civil rights as the anti-Communists struggled to purge the country of subversives.

The establishment made the first move to rid the country of un-Americans in 1946. In that year Congress passed the Atomic Energy Act which forbade the disclosure of information regarding atomic weapons. President Harry Truman established the first federal loyalty program by executive order in 1947. Truman's security directive was followed in 1950 by the Internal Security Act, which provided for the deportation of Communists and other totalitarians as undesirables, and by the Imi- gration and Nationality Act of 1952 (Walter-McCarran Act) which drastically expanded the 1950 act by allowing the Attorney General to bar any alien if he believed him to be a security risk. In 1953, by executive order, President Eisenhower established his own security program which attempted to distinguish between disloyal employees and loyal security risks. Finally, the Foreign Agents' Registration Act, originally passed in 1938 and amended in 1953, required the agents of any "foreign principal" to register with the Department of Justice, to file statements about their activities and affairs, and to label any "political propaganda" they circulate.[1]

At the same time that the government was building an elaborate web of security legislation, a powerful and highly controversial instrument was emerging to examine the loyalty of an unprecedented number of Americans. This instrument was the legislative committee investigating un-American

---

1. Robert L. Cushman, *Civil Liberties in the United States: A Guide to Current Problems and Experiences* (Ithaca, N. Y.: Cornell University Press, 1956), pp. 166-74.

activities. Aggressive investigative commit-tees were soon to explore charges of Com-munism within virtually every major insti-tution in America.

As Telford Taylor writes in *The Grand Inquest: The Story of Congressional Invest-igations* (p. xiii):

Since 1946 three permanent Congressional com-mittees or subcommittees-the House Un-American Activities Committee, the Senate Internal Security Subcommittee, and Senate Permanent Investiga-ting Subcommittee—have been busily exploring and exposing the political activities, associations, and attitudes of American citizens. They have penetrated the most diverse surroundings and oc-cupations, among others the Hollywood motion picture industry, philanthropic foundations, pub-lic and private education at all levels, and industrial labor, with side glances into journalism, publish-ing, radio-television, and the clergy.

These powerful federal committees were joined at the statewide level in 1941 by the Fact-Finding Committee on Un-American Activities in California and in 1947 by the Joint Legislative Fact-Finding Committee on Un-American Activities in Washington as well as by innumerable ad hoc investiga-ting committees at various levels of govern-ment.[2]

All of the un-American investigating committees seemed to operate on the simi-lar assumption that an internal Communist conspiracy had penetrated to the heart of America's most vital institutions. The as-sumption was quickly put to the test.[3]

The un-American investigating commit-tees were, of course, the most visible and verbal manifestation of a deep concern, even fear, that gripped America in this pe-riod. Pollster Samuel Stouffer found that 71 percent of U.S. citizens felt that the American Communists represented a dan-ger to this country, and that 24 percent

viewed the American Communists as a great danger while 19 percent felt that they were a very great danger.[4]

This deepseated concern was no doubt reinforced by unofficial voices warning that "Communism is a phantom thing; it moves its cold ghostly fingers among us, it is eternally elusive; it is under the bed, in the closet, in the house, perhaps, of our next-door neighbor; it wields a subtle, mysterious weapon unlike a knife or a gun or even a hundred megaton bomb."[5] Others warned sinisterly that Communist fronts were manipulating newspapers, law-yers, and screen actors guilds, as well as the CIO Council, and culinary workers, musi-cians and employees unions.[6]

The official warnings were hardly less alarming. J. Edgar Hoover, alluding omi-nously to "spheres of activity" penetrated by the Communists in America, pointed to education, labor, civil rights, veterans groups, cultural organizations, minority groups, foreign born, youth peace move-

2. Vern Countryman, *Un-American Activities in the State of Washington* (Ithaca, N. Y.: Cornell University Press, 1951), p. 14.
3. See Index to the *Congressional Record*, 1950-1954. During the 1950-54 period alone for-mal hearings were held to investigate charges of Communist infiltration in the following American institutions: 1) Department of Defense; 2) Labor unions; 3) Voice of America; 4) State Department Information Program; 5) United States Army; 6) Printing Office; 7) Telegraph Industry; 8) Motion Picture Industry; 9) Radio-television industry; 10) Educational administration—secondary, high school, and college.
4. Samuel A. Stouffer, *Communism, Conformity and Civil Liberties: A Cross-Section of the Nation Speaks Its Mind* (Garden City, N.Y.: Doubleday, 1955), p. 171.
5. Roger Burlingame, *The Sixth Column* (Philadel-phia: Lippincott, 1962), p. 233.
6. David J. Saposs, *Communism in American Poli-tics* (Washington: Lippincott, 1962), p. 43.

ments, women, press-radio-television-motion pictures, and defense.[7]

Whether intentionally or not these cries of alarm served as a very serious indictment of the Truman administration and liberal Democrats. They had been the official keepers of the national security continuously since Franklin Roosevelt took office. Quickly, liberal Democrats developed a defensive public litany which was just as distinctive as that of the conservative McCarthyites. Leslie Fiedler writes that the liberal ritually repeated "Lattimore is pure, Hiss was framed; the Rosenbergs are a mirage; there never was a Klaus Fuchs; Harry Dexter White was maligned. . . *No harm has been done*, no harm has been done, no harm has been done!"[8] With equal determination and persistence the McCarthyite replied "Yalta and China, Hiss and Marzani and Harry Dexter White; treason and the coddling of treason; *guilty, guilty, guilty.*"[9]

The confrontation on the issue of internal Communism threw the United States into a paroxysm of soul-searching, accusations, denials, and recriminations. Accusation of un-American activities, rather than conviction, became sufficient to ruin reputations and careers. Such accusations proliferated very sharply in the early 1950s. In 1953 one legislative investigating committee alone, the House Committee on Un-American Activities, published the names of over 650 individuals who had been accused of Communist Party membership.[10]

Rarely, if ever, has there been a period in American history where the nature of public discourse had such a direct and immediate effect on the lives of so many Americans. For this reason above all others, the public discourse of this significant period requires careful analysis.

The purposes of this analysis are to 1) trace the genesis of domestic Communism as the dominant issue of the period; 2) reconstruct the bitter rhetorical confrontation on the issues of the period; 3) analyze the rhetorical legacy of the period.

Genesis of the Issues

Innumerable factors may have contributed to the explosive emergence of the Communist issue in the United States but six factors seem particularly important: 1) the symbolism of the intruder; 2) the rapid evolution of Soviet Russia from ally to enemy; 3) the loss of mainland China to Communism; 4) tangible evidence of Soviet espionage in high places; 5) fear of the atomic bomb; 6) public resentment of intellectuals in high places.

Communism may have become a major issue to many Americans because it represented what might be called the symbolism of the intruder. Talcott Parsons maintains that domestic Communism symbolized intrusion in two senses. First, many Americans felt that Communism represented a direct philosophical and economic threat to the free enterprise system. Secondly, the business community was particularly threatened by Communism because it represented the ultimate victory of a force

7. J. Edgar Hoover, *A Study of Communism* (New York: Holt, Rinehart, and Winston, 1962), p. 171.

8. Leslie A. Fiedler, *An End to Innocence: Essays on Culture and Politics* (Boston: Beacon Press, 1955), p. 76.

9. *Ibid.*

10. *Annual Report of the House Un-American Activities Committee*, 1953, pp. 64-75.

they violently opposed in theory but were forced to accept in practice—increased governmental control in return for governmental support.[11]

Public resentment and distrust of Soviet Russia was a second major force in the sudden emergence of the internal Communist issue. Nascent, private distrust of Russia as a wartime ally suddenly became virulent, public resentment of Russia as peacetime enemy. In the 1930s and during World War II Americans expressing philosophical sympathy with Communist goals were simply dismissed as indiscreet. By the end of the war they were publicly denounced as traitors.

Witnesses appearing before un-American activities committees recognized the sudden shift in public attitude and were quick to emphasize their dissociation with Communism, following World War II. Noted actor Larry Parks repeatedly emphasized this theme in an appearance before the House Committee on Un-American Activities in April, 1951. Parks noted emphatically that at present "I am not a Communist. I would like to point out that in my opinion there is a great difference between—and not a subtle difference between—being a Communist, a member of the Communist Party, say in 1941, 10 years ago, and being a Communist in 1951. To my mind this is a great difference and not a subtle one."[12]

Public resentment and fear of Communism was greatly exacerbated by the loss of mainland China to the Communists. Many Americans blamed the State Department. The loss of China simply represented another in a series of bungling, even treasonous, diplomatic efforts of a Democratic administration, to an increasing number of Americans, and public officials like Senator

Joseph McCarthy moved quickly to reinforce public resentment. On March 14, 1951, on the floor of the United States Senate, Senator McCarthy asked rhetorically "Whether we have heard one liberal voice raised in this Chamber or elsewhere in condemnation of Roosevelt's surrender to Russian imperialism at Yalta? This is the test, and by it we may measure the hypocrisy of the self-proclaimed liberal elements in this Chamber and in the country which have assisted in and applauded the surrender of all China to Russia without the firing of a single Russian shot."[13]

A fourth factor feeding the public fear of internal Communism was the real and apparent evidence of massive Soviet espionage in key governmental institutions. FBI director J. Edgar Hoover warned that "the relentless quest for information by Communist spies in the United States constitutes the most massive offensive of its type ever conducted by one nation against another in the history of international relations. The Soviet Union directs, controls, and coordinates Communist subversive and clandestine activities aimed at destroying the internal security of the United States."[14] Hoover not only warned of the Communists' objectives but of spy tech-

11. Talcott Parsons, "McCarthyism and American Social Tension: A Sociologist's View," *Yale Review* 44 (December, 1954):241.
12. U.S. Congress, House of Representatives, "Communist Infiltration of Hollywood Motion-Picture Industry—Part I," *Hearings Before the Committee on Un-American Activities*, March-April, 1951, p. 82.
13. Senator Joseph McCarthy, speech, February 20, 1950, "Communists in Government—Wheeling Speech," *Major Speeches and Debates of Senator McCarthy: 1950-1951* (Washington: U. S. Government Printing Office, 1953). Except when specified otherwise, McCarthy's speeches may be found in this volume.
14. Hoover, *A Study of Communism*, p. 147.

niques which would honor the memory of Ian Fleming. Russian spies, Hoover noted, could reduce a microfilmed page in size so that "it can be hidden in a period or other punctuation mark in what appears to be an innocent document."[15]

If Hoover's warnings were ominous, the terroristic rhetoric of ex-Communists like Louis Budenz and Elizabeth Bentley was positively incendiary. In *Men Without Faces* Budenz painted a frightening picture of the moral culpability of influential Americans and the effectiveness of the Soviet Fifth Column. As editor of the *Daily Worker*, Budenz "from the Eighth Floor (and frequently the Ninth) . . . watched, fascinated, as men and women of worldwide reputation were duped into carrying out plans laid for them by Stalin's secret police and special emmissaries. Wrap partyline bait in 'liberal' phrases and certain celebrities would bite over and over again."[16]

To make sure that the American public got his point, Budenz noted that "having thus lived for ten years in the company of Soviet spies and undercover agents, I find myself sometimes at a loss to understand the innocence and complacency of Americans concerning the extent of Communist infiltration and espionage."[17] Budenz's more detailed account of the activities of Soviet spies was reinforced by Elizabeth Bentley's chilling account of how the Soviet espionage network recruited the naive American intellectual.[18]

The fifth reason for the sudden public fear of internal Communism, development of the atomic bomb by the Soviet Union, seems sufficiently obvious not to require elaboration while the sixth factor, resentment of intellectuals in high places, is covered in the next section.

Confrontation on the Issues

The subject of Communism dominated public discourse in America in the period immediately following World War II. Even in the late 1940s the term Communism was sufficient to trigger the condemnatory, hyperbolic rhetoric which inflamed and divided Americans. Until 1950, however, the divisive rhetoric of anti-Communism did not coalesce around the two major issues of the period.

On February 9, 1950, Senator Joseph McCarthy "went to Wheeling to launch the public exposure of Communists in government."[19] The speech that McCarthy delivered in Wheeling, West Virginia, became bitterly controversial. McCarthy charged that the Department of State contained 205 known Communists, according to reporters on the scene. McCarthy denied the charge and claimed he simply identified 57 security risks.[20]

Whatever the exact nature of McCarthy's charge, the speech inflamed public sentiment and helped focus public opinion on the two dominant issues of the day: 1) Had the Communists actually mounted an internal conspiracy which extended to the heart of America's most vital institutions? 2) Were un-American activities committees protecting or destroying the safeguards of

---

15. *Ibid.*, p. 181.
16. Louis F. Budenz, *Men Without Faces: The Communist Conspiracy in the U.S.A.* (New York: Harper & Brother, 1950), p. 208.
17. *Ibid.*, p. 254.
18. Elizabeth Bentley, *Out of Bondage: The Story of Elizabeth Bentley* (New York: Devin-Adair, 1951), p. 140.
19. Joe McCarthy, *McCarthyism: The Fight for America* (New York: Devin-Adair, 1952), p. 9.
20. *Ibid.*

individual rights built into the United
States Constitution?

The Great Conspiracy—McCarthy and
his colleagues vigorously pressed the charge
that America was gripped by the insidious
effects of a great, internal Communist conspiracy. They charged, moreover, that liberal Democrats and the Truman administration were serving as important agents in
securing the aims of that conspiracy.

Senator McCarthy was the most visible
and verbal proponent of the conspiracy
theory. On March 14, 1951, McCarthy
enunciated the thesis of an internal conspiracy, a thesis which has served as the battle-
cry of anti-Communist forces until the
present time. He warned members of the
United States Senate that:

When the war ended and I got back to this country,
I was very forcibly impressed by the fact that this
foreign policy was being changed without the
knowledge, consent, or approval of the American
people, and was being changed without either of
the major political parties having ever advocated
the change which was taking place.[21]

Later McCarthy made his conspiracy
thesis more explicit by asking "who constitutes the highest circles of this conspiracy?
About that we cannot be sure . . . . I do not
believe that Mr. Truman is a conscious party to the great conspiracy, although it is
being conducted in his name."[22]

Finally, McCarthy warned Americans
about the sinister aims of the conspiracy
when he asked "what is the objective of the
great conspiracy? I think it clear from what
has occurred and is now occurring; to diminish the United States in world affairs, to
weaken us militarily, to confuse our spirit
with talk of surrender and to impair our
will to resist evil."[23] The United States
would ultimately be reduced to the de-

pressing fate of other nations gripped by a
conspiracy for there have "been many examples in history of rich and powerful
states which have been corrupted from
within, enfeebled and deceived until they
were unable to resist aggression.[24]

McCarthy was neither the first nor the
most persistent advocate of the internal
communist conspiracy theory, however.
Jack Tenney consistently expressed public
fear of the conspiracy during his long tenure as chairman of the California Fact-
Finding Committee on Un-American Activities. As far back as 1947, Tenney was
pressing his conspiracy theory upon Mrs.
Frederic March:

Chairman Tenney:	Do you have any sympathy for Communism Mrs. March?
Mrs. March:	I have stated in my state-ment, Senator, that I do not.
Chairman Tenney:	You have none whatso-ever? You do recognize Russia, I think, or you must if you read, has a dictator-ship, hasn't it?
Mrs. March:	Yes.
Chairman Tenney:	In which there are no free-doms?
Mrs. March:	I understand from what I read there are no freedoms.
Chairman Tenney:	That they have between fif-teen and twenty million Russian citizens in concen-tration camps and slave bat-talions?

---

21. McCarthy, speech, delivered to the United
States Senate, "American Foreign Policy," March
14, 1951.
22. McCarthy, speech, delivered to the United
States Senate, "Gen. Marshall and the Communist
Conspiracy," June 14, 1951.
23. *Ibid.*
24. *Ibid.*

Mrs. March:	I suppose so. I am told that.
Chairman Tenney:	You do recognize, I am sure, that they work conspiratorially; they take assumed names; they organize themselves into front groups with laudable purposes—the purposes are always good—and in that way they draw to themselves many Communists, and use them for their own purposes. You recognize that?[25]

Men like McCarthy, Tenney, Senator Jenner, and Congressman Velde moved quickly to give their internal conspiracy more specific direction in the early 1950s. They began by constantly repeating the charge that liberal Democrats were the tools of the Communists.

The charge against liberal Democrats is graphically captured in an exchange between Senator Lehman of Illinois and Senator McCarthy of Wisconsin:

Mr. Lehman:	Mr. President, Phillip Jessup is a great American who has served, and is serving his country with unsurpassed devotion, unselfishness, and loyalty. By character, by patriotism, by ability, and by useful services he belongs in the galaxy of those other outstanding American statesmen—Cordell Hull, Warren Austin, George C. Marshall, Henry L. Stimson, Averell Harriman, and John G. Winant.
Mr. McCarthy:	Mr. President, I am very sorry that the majority leader surrendered the floor before I could ask him any questions. This is a very serious matter. The majority leader has a very impor-

tant position. I am sure that he does not want to do what so many in his party have been doing—that is, labeling a once great party as a party which stands for the protection of Communists and crooks in Government.[26]

The charges of Democratic culpability became less guarded with the passage of time. McCarthy agonized publicly that "it makes me ill deep down inside when I hear cowardly politicians and self-proclaimed 'liberals,' too lazy to do their own thinking, parrot over and over this Communist Party line."[27]

At first, liberal Democrats were condemned as simply naive. Slowly a more damaging charge evolved. McCarthy and his followers intimated that Communists successfully sought liberal support because of a mutuality of goals. Communist, socialist, and Democrat became virtually interchangeable terms in the anti-Communist lexicon.

In the 1950s this charge became a preoccupation of the anti-Communists. It was not elaborated upon in detail until recently, however. Presently the charge has been given new life in a five hundred page

25. *Hearings before the California Fact-Finding Committee on Un-American Activities*, February, 1948. The complete set of transcripts of these committee hearings has never been made public and can only be pieced together. The most extensive and relevant reprints of these hearings can be found in Edward L. Barrett, *The Tenney Committee* (Ithaca, New York: Cornell University Press, 1951).
26. McCarthy, speech, delivered to the United States Senate, "Public Employees as Informants," August 9, 1951. Senator Lehman interrupted McCarthy's speech on this occasion.
27. McCarthy, *McCarthyism* p. 7.

polemic that has become the virtual hand-book of anti-Communist organizations in the 1960s. In *Fabian Freeway* Rose Martin writes:

The Socialist and Communist world movements are like the two faces of a coin—not identical, yet inseparable. Sometimes one side appears upper-most, sometimes the other; but at the core they are still one. Which side of this counterfeit coin might face up at a given time, probably depends upon the circumstances of the moment. It is, of course, to the interest of every man, woman and child in America, desiring personal liberty in a free and sov-ereign nation, that the fraudulent nature of this coin be recognized and exposed so that we may be forever spared the necessity of making such a spu-rious choice.[28]

The image of the liberal and Communist as ideological brothers was clearly icono-clastic on a personal level. Politically, it was not nearly so damaging as a companion charge. Once the liberals were charged with a commitment to Communist goals it seemed only logical for the anti-Commu-nists to charge that the Truman administra-tion was working conspiratorially to attain those same goals.

The Truman administration was consis-tently identified as "the administration that preaches a gospel of fear and . . . ex-pound[s] a foreign policy in the East based upon craven whimpering, appeasement."[29] Senator McCarthy had "yet to hear a single administration spokesman raise his voice against the policy of suppression, deceit, and false witness with which this admini-stration has protected the Soviet agents who have abstracted those secrets from us."[30]

The Communists planned and the Tru-man administration executed the goals of the great conspiracy according to the anti-Communists. Men like Tenney, Dies, and

Velde dolefully noted that all of America's major institutions were infiltrated by the Communists. Anti-Communists were parti-cularly concerned about the advanced states of infiltration in the defense industry as well as in the educational, communica-tion, and entertainment industries.[31]

President Truman did not escape blame for the conspiratorial machinations of his administration. In general, however, he was pictured as simply the vacillating, confused pawn of his scheming cabinet members. Dean Acheson and George Marshall were indicted by the anti-Communists as the chief conspirators.

Because of his imperious manner and close ties to the eastern intellectual estab-lishment, Secretary of State Dean Acheson proved to be a favorite target of anti-Com-munist rhetoric. Senator McCarthy was fond of referring to Acheson as the "perfid-ious Red Dean" and stated on the floor of the United States Senate that Acheson "is too far gone in mendacity and treason for his answer to carry any weight whatso-ever."[32]

McCarthy left little doubt that he be-lieved Acheson's sympathies and conspira-torial aims were identical with those of the Communists:

What does this whole sordid transaction teach us about the good faith of the advisers of Roosevelt and the assorted liberals, Communists, Communist

---

28. Rose L. Martin, *Fabian Freeway: Highway to Socialism in the USA* (Santa Monica, Cal.: Fi-delis, 1968) p. 16.

29. McCarthy, speech, "General Marshall and the Communist Conspiracy."

30. *Ibid.*

31. Barrett, *The Tenney Committee*, p. 335.

32. McCarthy, speech "General Marshall and the Communist Conspiracy."

sympathizers, and agents of the Kremlin—the Achesons, the Lattimores, the Phillips Jessups, and the Institute of Pacific Relations—the whole sorry crew who have for so long been insincerely befuddling the people with talk of imperialism and the people's rights in Asia?"[33]

The other "agent of the Kremlin" was Secretary of Defense George Marshall. In Marshall's important actions McCarthy found "a pattern which finds his decisions, maintained with great stubbornness and skill, always and invariably serving the world policy of the Kremlin."[34]

In perhaps his longest and most vitriolic speech on the floor of the United States Senate Joe McCarthy bitterly denounced George Marshall as the servant of the Kremlin. McCarthy made eighteen major charges against Marshall, that impugned his integrity and his patriotism. Among other things, McCarthy charged that:

It was Marshall who, at Tehran, made common cause with Stalin on the strategy of the war in Europe and marched side by side with him thereafter. It was Marshall, with Acheson and Vincent eagerly assisting, who created the China policy which, destroying China, robbed us of a great and friendly ally, a buffer against the Soviet imperialism with which we are now at war.
It was Marshall, who after long conferences with Acheson and Vincent, went to China to execute the criminal folly of the disastrous Marshall mission.[35]

The Un-American Activities Committee—Americans were alarmed by the charge of an internal Communist conspiracy. They were polarized by the charge of administration involvement in that conspiracy. Demands for a thorough investigation of the charges were immediate and widespread. Fortuitously or not the institutional vehicle for investigating such charges was already in existence and it was instantly pressed into service.

The vehicle was the legislative committee for investigating un-American activities. Ironically, the instrument used to explore the first great issue of the period—the great internal Communist conspiracy—quickly became a major issue itself. Almost immediately, the objectives and procedures of the un-American activities investigating committees became an issue of equal importance with that of the internal Communist conspiracy.

Public development of the two major issues differed drastically. The issue of the internal Communist conspiracy was developed primarily through the accusatory monologues of Senator McCarthy and his colleagues. In contrast the issue of un-American investigating committees was developed through the direct and bitter dialogue in the hearings of these same committees.

Specifically the issue was whether un-American activities committees represented an effective means for protecting the United States Constitution or an insidious means for destroying the individual rights so strongly identified with that constitution. That issue could be resolved only by debating three other integrally related issues: 1) The Fifth Amendment; 2) Guilt by Association; 3) Ex-Communist Informants.

The Fifth Amendment Question. The fifth amendment issue was bitterly contested. Few, if any, issues have ever had such a direct and dramatic impact on the lives of

---

33. *Ibid.*
34. *Ibid.*
35. *Ibid.*

Americans accused of wrongdoing. In theory a witness appearing before an un-American activities committee was guaranteed the right not to testify against himself. In practice the witness could exercise this right only at the risk of great personal peril.

In deciding whether to invoke the right of the fifth amendment the witness was faced with a very painful dilemma. If the witness did invoke the fifth amendment, he seemed to be conceding guilt of subversive activities to a large segment of a suspicious public. If the witness did not invoke the fifth amendment, he usually exposed himself to the hostile and insinuative interrogation of a committee which extended to him virtually none of the traditional safeguards of the American legal system.

Confrontations on this issue were intensified for a simple reason. The fifth amendment represented mutually irreconcilable things to committee members and witnesses. To the committee member, the fifth amendment represented a devious device for obfuscating the legitimate goal of investigating un-American activities. To the witness the fifth amendment represented a legal means of preventing illegitimate violations of their rights as American citizens.

Witnesses were acutely aware that subtle differences in their public stand on the fifth amendment question could have a major and permanent impact on their personal lives. The way a witness handled the fifth amendment issue was often the critical factor in determining whether his reputation was ruined or merely temporarily tainted by his mandatory appearance before a given committee.

Certainly the fifth amendment issue often resulted in personal anguish for the witness. This anguish is graphically illustrated in actor Larry Parks' statement to the House Committee on Un-American Activities:

> Don't present me with the choice of either being in contempt of this committee and going to jail or forcing me to really crawl through the mud to be an informer, for what purpose? I don't think this is a choice at all. I don't think it is really sportsmanlike. I don't think this is American. I don't think this is American justice. I think to do something like that is more akin to what happened under Hitler, and what is happening in Russia today. If you do this to me, I think it will impair the usefulness of this committee to a great extent, because it will make it almost impossible for a person to come to you, as I have done, and open himself to you and tell you the truth. So I beg of you not to force me to do this.[36]

Parks' obvious anguish suggests a singular irony that characterized confrontation on this issue. The fifth amendment is intended as protection for the individual's rights but during the era of the internal Communist menace it became a potential source of almost unlimited agony and punishment for the accused American.

As Parks' statement suggests, he took a rhetorically sophisticated position on the fifth amendment question. He refused to take the fifth amendment but at the same time he refused to answer committee questions about the allegedly subversive activi-

---

36. "Communist Infiltration of Hollywood Motion-Picture Industry—Part I," *Hearings before the Committee on Un-American Activities*, p. 107. The three major national committees investigating un-American activities were: 1) the House Committee on un-American Activities; 2) the Permanent Subcommittee on Investigations of the Committee on Government Operations; 3) the Subcommittee to Investigate the Administration of the Internal Security Act and other Internal Security Laws of the Committee on the Judiciary. The latter two were Senate committees and only the subcommittee designations will be used in future references.

ties of his close friends in the movie industry. To refuse testimony on grounds other than the fifth amendment was often impossible, however.

The witnesses' difficult rhetorical position is illustrated by an excerpt from the hearings of the Senate Subcommittee to Investigate the Administration of the Internal Security Act and Other Internal Security Laws:

Mr. Carpenter: Were you a member of the Communist Party and the Young Communist League at the time of your graduation from Dartmouth College?

Mr. Wilson: I decline to answer that question on two grounds: The first ground is that the first amendment to the Constitution fences off certain areas of association and belief from congressional legislation and therefore inquiry, and on that ground I am not required to answer the question. My second ground for refusing to answer the question is that I asserted my privilege under the fifth amendment not to be a witness against myself.

Senator Jenner: This committee will recognize your grounds not to answer that question under the fifth amendment, but this committee does not recognize your refusing to answer under the first amendment.[37]

Even if the witness took the fifth amendment, Senator McCarthy and other committee chairmen were quick to imply that this represented guilt. To illustrate, the following exchange took place between Senator McCarthy and the chairman of the mathematics department of Bronx High School:

Senator McCarthy: Have you ever attended any Communist Party meetings which were attended by any of your students?

Mr. Hlavaty: I must decline to answer that question.

Senator McCarthy: On the grounds that the answer might incriminate you?

Mr. Hlavaty: Yes, sir.

Senator McCarthy: Have you ever attempted to recruit any of your students into the Communist Party?

Mr. Hlavaty: I am afraid I must decline to answer all such questions.

Senator McCarthy: You can decline to answer that. You have a right to. If, as you say, you honestly think if you told us the truth, it would incriminate you, you have the right to decline to answer.

Mr. Hlavaty: That isn't the way I would say it, Senator.

Senator McCarthy: That is the only ground upon which you have the right. Otherwise we will not grant you that right. You are only entitled to the right to refuse to answer before this committee if you honestly think that if you told this committee the truth it would incriminate you. You understand that. It is only if you honestly

37. U.S. Congress, Senate, Judiciary Committee, "Interlocking Subversion in Government Departments" *Hearings Before the Subcommittee to Investigate the Administration of the Internal Security Act and Other Internal Security Laws,* United States Senate, July-August, 1954, p. 1490.

	feel that a truthful answer would incriminate you. Do you understand the question?
Mr. Hlavaty:	Yes, sir.
Senator McCarthy:	And your answer is that you decline to answer on the ground that your answer might incriminate you?
Mr. Hlavaty:	On the ground of the fifth amendment; yes, sir.[38]

McCarthy and his anti-Communist colleagues clearly used the fifth amendment as a weapon to attack committee witnesses. When one witness cited the fifth amendment before McCarthy's Permanent Subcommittee on Investigations, the senator's response was typical:

Is it not a fact that since the New York Board of Education passed a rule to the effect that it would not employ fifth amendment cases; that is, those who came before a committee and refused to answer whether or not they are Communists, since that time the Communist Parthy has given orders to all of the teachers in the New York area that they are to no longer attend Communist meetings, and to drop any outward evidence of membership in the Communist Party, so that they may continue to maintain their positions in the school system? Is that a correct statement of the order received from the Communist Party?[39]

Guilt by Association. Committee members and witnesses faced each other directly on the fifth amendment issue. A second major issue was more difficult to contest directly because it was seemingly so amorphous and so often developed by insinuation. Amorphous or not, no issue was more central to the rhetorical thrust of the anti-Communist era than guilt by association.

In an era of almost unprecedented distrust among Americans, guilt by association charges were particularly devastating. Aside from the hermit and the cloistered monk, virtually no American could be sure that his past associations were secure from

attack. No matter how indirect or how superficial one's contact with an alleged subversive, mere association was evidence of guilt to many in a nation which was seriously considering the plausibility of a conspiracy theory of history.

Charges of guilt by association took many forms. Contributions to Russia as wartime ally, legal defense of an accused subversive, solicitation by suspect humanitarian organizations, and even strong support of liberal causes was considered evidence of guilt by association.

Almost every transcript of the hearings of un-American activities committees featured guilt-by-association charges. This issue became a particular preoccupation with one chairman and one committee, however. Jack Tenney and his California Fact-Finding Committee on un-American Activities confronted almost every witness with guilt-by-association charges. Whether the target was the UCLA administraton, a famous actress, or a respected judge the charge was always the same.[40]

---

38. U.S. Congress, Senate, Government Operations Committee, "State Department Information Program—Voice of America," *Hearings Before the Permanent Subcommittee on Investigations*, United States Senate, March, 1953, p. 707.

39. U.S. Congress, Senate, Government Operations Committee, "Army Signal Corps—Subversion and Espionage," *Hearings Before the Permanent Subcommittee on Investigations*, United States Senate, December 14, 1953.

40. *Hearings before the California Fact-Finding Committee on Un-American Activities*, January, 1946. Chairman Tenney attacked UCLA provost Clarence A. Dykstra for allegedly allowing the University of California, Los Angeles, to become associated with subversive activities. Tenney warned Dykstra that such associations are "something you should watch, something you should take into consideration when you are being euchred into the position of loaning the University's name to these activities. I think if that is more carefully watched, we can avoid a lot of things."

The insinuative interrogation of Mrs. Frederic March was typical:

Question:	This particular statement Senator Tenney read to you concerned association with Communist groups.
Answer: (Mrs. March)	Yes, I think this followed the testimony of Mr. Leach. Now, Mr. Leach's testimony was the testimony that bore on things we had never done and most of which we had never heard of.
Question:	That was in 1940. Now, in 1945 when you joined the delegation with a known Communist, did it occur to you that you were putting yourself in a similar position as in 1940?
Answer:	I thought of it briefly, but you see I didn't believe that we could sit back in fear and never espouse any thing, for fear that some Communist might be on the Board. We can't afford to have them the only people in America who work for common decency.
Question:	Isn't it probable that could set a common pattern?
Answer:	I don't understand.
Question:	Isn't it possible by repeating the association with Communists that you would set a pattern of action?[41]

Tenney's treatment of distinguished judge Leon R. Yankwich seems to be the ultimate model of public pillory through guilt by association. Yankwich predictably was summoned before Tenney's committee for his allegedly subversive associations. Yankwich's single lecture before an educational organization resulted in the following confrontation with Tenney:

Tenney:	The Peoples Educational Center has been found to be a Communist front.
Yankwich:	That is right—
Tenney:	And their literature carried your name as either a lecturer or an instructor—I have forgotten which.
Yankwich:	No. I gave only one lecture.
Tenney:	They did carry your name on their literature.
Yankwich:	That is right—
Tenney:	Which, of course, is a Communist tactic of using a person in public life as "window dressing" for their organization. That was the gist of the action before the Committee...
Yankwich:	There was a man named Sam Jones who was a great prohibition advocate and one day he delivered a lecture and he asked for a contribution, and a man came up from the audience and put up a gold piece and threw it to the walk and he said, "I made this in the saloon business." He took the gold piece and threw it to the walk and he said, "Long enough you served the cause of the devil and now you serve the cause of God." Now, I don't know whether you understand it, but that is my attitude.
Tenney:	I think I know what you mean, but we don't want you to serve the cause of the devil either.[42]

41. *Hearings before the California Fact-Finding Committee on Un-American Activities*, February, 1948.
42. *Ibid.*

The day following Judge Yankwich's appearance Tenney felt compelled to have a statement read into the record of the committee hearing which attempted to establish in detail the allegedly subversive nature of Yankwich's associations.[43] Tenney did not stop there. The pursuit of Judge Yankwich on guilt by association charges culminated in the following official committee report on Judge Yankwich in 1948:

The committee finds that Judge Yankwich's conduct and attitude is a disgraceful reflection upon the federal bench. For anyone to fraternize with the enemies of the people of the United States, its Constitution and government, is bad enough in itself, but to dignify traitorous organizations, such as the Communist People's Educational Center, then no condemnation is strong enough to characterize such action. In these critical times, when the federal bench will be called upon to deal with cases involving the traitorous activities of Communist-Soviet agents, a man such as Yankwich is not qualified, because of his obvious bias and sympathy for pro-Communist, pro-Soviet causes, to sit on the federal bench.[44]

Ex-Communist Informants. The third issue which dominated debate in the public hearings of un-American activities committees was that of paid informants. Specifically the issue was the widespread and repeated use of a small group of ex-Communists as paid informers. To the anti-Communists these former conspirators were patriots of unquestioned probity. To many witnesses the ex-Communists were unprincipled, mercenary liars. In either case the ex-Communists did seem to function as unofficial judges in determining the guilt or innocence of countless Americans.

Clearly ex-Communists served as the main source for the identification and prosecution of alleged subversives. Senator McCarthy, in his own book, *McCarthyism: the Fight for America*, lists the names of fif-

teen individuals who had been named under oath as Communists or Soviet agents. Fourteen of the fifteen were identified by ex-Communists—Louis Budenz, Karl Wittfogel, Elizabeth Bentley, Gen. Alexander Barmine, Hede Messing, and Prof. William Canning.[45] The same reliance on the testimony of ex-Communists is exhibited in the Annual Report of the Committee on Un-American Activities for 1953 where hundreds of individuals are listed as "persons . . . identified as members of the Communist Party during the course of hearings held in San Francisco, California."[46] Identification was mainly by ex-Communists.

Senator McCarthy confirmed the nearly exclusive reliance on the testimony of a small group of ex-Communists. He wrote of Louis Budenz that "since he has renounced Communism, he has been used by the government as one of its principal witnesses in practically every criminal action or deportation proceeding against Communists."[47]

The ex-Communist as informant represented a great paradox of the period as Burlingame points out in *The Sixth Column*. While the anti-Communist committees were the implacable foes of the Communists, they relied almost entirely on the testimony of ex-Communists to prosecute the case against domestic Communists and alleged Communists. Men like McCarthy were publicly condemning Communists as liars and traitors at the same time they were

---

43. *Ibid.*
44. *Annual Report of the California Fact-Finding Committee on Un-American Activities*, 1948, pp. 348-50.
45. McCarthy, *McCarthyism*, pp. 55-56.
46. *Annual Report of the House Un-American Activities Committee*, p. 110.
47. McCarthy, *McCarthyism*, p. 3.

putting implicit faith in the critical testimony of ex-Communists. By public repentance the ex-Communists had seemingly become uncorruptible American patriots.

The bitter confrontation on this issue is perhaps best illustrated by the case of Edward Lamb. Lamb was a millionaire, a liberal attorney, a noted defender of humanitarian causes, and owner of numerous commercial television stations. As a close friend of Senator Estes Kefauver, Lamb had powerful connections within the government and, consequently, was able to mount an effective case against charges of subversive associations and actions.

Lamb was called before a hearing of the Federal Communications Commission for his allegedly subversive activities. At this hearing, the case against him was based solely on the testimony of ex-Communist informants. Ultimately, the use of the ex-Communists became the central issue of the hearings.

Nowhere is the confrontation on this issue more eloquently illustrated than in Lamb's autobiography, *No Lamb for Slaughter.* According to Lamb, "our nation had developed a new breed of scoundrel—the hatchet man for pay, the professional turncoat. Louis Budenz, who had been an editor of the Communist *Daily Worker*, became one of the better-paid informers; Whittaker Chambers and Elizabeth Bentley and other former Communists played a similar role of furnishing testimony for pay for many years."[48]

The testimony of ex-Communists has already been cited in this essay and it should be compared directly with Lamb's testimony. In the FCC hearing Lamb testified that:

I first heard that I was a member of the National Committee of the International Labor Defense from your own professional witness, Louis Budenz. . . . But I have heard more about it since you people have tried to hang these disgraceful Communist charges on me than I ever did before. You were the ones who hired the liars to repeat your manufactured slanders, and now we have the spectacle of your same people in the FCC passing judgment on the truth or falsity of your own manufactured evidence.[49]

Lamb expressed incredulity when he learned of the nature of evidence offered by ex-Communists—testimony that was willingly accepted by un-American activities committees. Budenz testified that the names of four hundred Communists had been given to him by a high Communist official named Jack Stachel and that these names were etched solely and secretly in his mind. Budenz claimed further "that after he had memorized the list, he and Stachel had torn it up. He said that this mythical list was a superconfidential catalogue of hidden Communist-party members in the United States."[50]

Lamb, like many other witnesses before him, objected violently to such diaphanous and mysterious evidence. Budenz's superconfidential list had of course been used many times to question the loyalty of countless Americans and to prove their disloyalty to the satisfaction of un-American activities committees and large segments of the public.

Even though acquitted of the charges against him, Lamb remained preoccupied with the issue of ex-Communist informants. Revealing a bitterness so characteristic of witnesses who had been prosecuted through such testimony, Lamb asked if

48. Edward Lamb, *No Lamb for Slaughter* (New York: Harcourt, Brace, and World, 1963), p. 135.
49. *Ibid.*, p. 176.
50. *Ibid.*, p. 142.

there was "any need to identify your political or business enemy? See Budenz—get the telephone number from your local FBI Office! You may say that all this is unbelievable. But many Americans went to jail because they appeared on this list of supposed subversives, a list existing only in an evil, profit-motivated informer's mind."[51]

The Rhetorical Legacy of the anti-Communist Era

Rarely have issues been so bitterly, even viciously, contested. The serious student of this period must be moved to ask whether the acrimonious confrontations on the issues left any lasting impact on American society. What is the legacy of this period in American history?

Historically, we still probably do not have sufficient perspective to analyze the long range effects of such confrontations. We can do no more than emphasize dominant historical features of the period. Those analysts who have looked back on this anti-Communist era agree on two things. First, the anti-Communists managed to create a public climate of almost unprecedented exploitation, repression, and fear. Second, the period was characterized by almost unlimited abuse of civil liberties.

Telford Taylor recaptures the intellectual tone of the period in *The Grand Inquest: The Story of Congressional Investigations*. He indicts the un-American activities committees as partisan political tools which were used to exploit public fears and punish personal misfortunes (p. xii):

Martin Dies, Jack Tenney, J. Parnell Thomas, Patrick McCarran, Eugene Cox, William Jenner, Joseph R. McCarthy, Harold Velde, Carroll Reece—whatever one's personal estimate of these men,

one thing is clear; they are not a representative group of American legislators. They are clustered at the extreme right end of the political color spectrum, where purple deepens into black. Largely for this reason, the Congressional loyalty investigations have been like a baseball game in which only one team ever comes to bat.

Barrett confirms Taylor's conclusion that these were dangerous and destructive men with the somewhat more qualified conclusion that "prosecution rather than investigation was the theme" in un-American activities investigations.[52]

The repressive climate of this anti-Communist period was perhaps manifested most dramatically in the persistent and flagrant abuses of civil liberties. Many of these abuses have been eloquently illustrated in the rhetorical confrontations reconstructed in these pages. Many others occurred even if they were not as immediately evident in public discourse.

Professor Robert Cushman demonstrates convincingly in his scholarly book that innumerable important civil liberties were violated by the anti-Communists. Above everything else, the anti-Communists managed to convolute and reverse assumptions which are most basic to the American system of justice. The accused subversive was presumed guilty until proven innocent and denied such elementary safeguards of due process as the right to face his accuser.[53]

While it is still too early to determine the ultimate historical legacy of the anti-Communist era, the rhetorical legacy is already identifiable. The anti-Communists developed a rhetorical posture and a set of techni-

---

51. *Ibid.*
52. Barrett, *The Tenney Committee*, p. 44.
53. Cushman, *Civil Liberties in the United States*, p. 179.

ques which have been adopted almost completely by the new Radical Right. Indeed the adopted rhetorical posture seems to account in large part for the unprecedented growth and affluence of the new Radical Right. [54]

A comparison of the dominant rhetorical features of the anti-Communists (1946-1954) and the new Radical Right (1960-to the present) confirms that revolutionary reactionaries like Robert Welch, Carl McIntire, and Billy James Hargis are the direct rhetorical descendants of Joe McCarthy, Pat McCarran, Jack Tenney and the other anti-Communists. [55] The features which dominated the rhetoric of the anti-Communists and the revolutionary reactionaries are very similar because the rhetoric was built on a common base.

Both the anti-Communists and the revolutionary reactionaries developed (1) a conspiracy theory of history which they made salable by the exploitation of a distrustful and disaffected public, (2) a rhetorical strategy which detached their message from the constraints of empirical verification, (3) a set of values which reinforced men's distrust of each other, their institutions, and democratic government.

From a rhetorical standpoint, few periods in American history were more hospitable to the credible development of a conspiracy theory of history than the post World War II period. To be truly effective, advocates of a conspiracy theory of history must be able to direct their message to an audience experiencing real and deep-seated fear. As suggested earlier, six historical forces combined, during the McCarthy era, to create an almost unparalleled climate of fear among Americans.

Once again in the mid-and late 1960s a set of historical factors coalesced which made the public particularly susceptible to a conspiracy theory. Administration officials consistently gave misleading reports on the state of the Viet Nam war and this seemingly intentional distortion of facts was made even more onerous by a compulsive secretiveness which appeared to envelope the Johnson administration.

In this environment of public suspicion and resentment of the government the revolutionary reactionaries moved quickly and vigorously to assert that the United States was once again in the insidious grips of an internal Communist conspiracy. [56] Like their anti-Communist predecessors, the men of the new Radical Right recognized the rhetorical axiom that a conspiracy theory of history receives a particularly receptive reading from a disillusioned and disaffected public.

To give their conspiracy theory credibility both the anti-Communists and the revolutionary reactionaries developed a

---

54. For a detailed description and analysis of the rise of the new Radical Right in the 1960s see Dale G. Leathers, "The Thrust of the Radical Right," *Preaching in American History*, ed. DeWitte Holland (New York: Abingdon Press, 1969), pp. 310-32, and Dale G. Leathers, "The Thrust of the Radical Right," *Sermons in American History*, ed. DeWitte Holland (Nashville, Tenn.: Abingdon Press, 1971), 413-50. For ease of identification McCarthy and his colleagues are referred to as the anti-Communists while the terms revolutionary reactionary and new Radical Right are used interchangeably to identify men like Robert Welch, Carl McIntire, and Billy James Hargis.

55. Interview with Dr. Billy James Hargis, founder-director of the Christian Crusade, at Crusade Headquarters, Tulsa, Oklahoma, March 11, 1965. In this interview Hargis emphasized that Senator Joseph McCarthy was his idol and that McCarthy had helped his Christian Crusade gain national prominence by praising Hargis's organization over the national media.

56. Dale G. Leathers, "Fundamentalism of the Radical Right," *Southern Speech Journal 33* (Summer, 1968), 251-55.

rhetorical strategy which detached their persuasive appeals from the burden of empirical verification.

To implement this rhetorical strategy, McCarthy and his colleagues used the fifth amendment, guilt by association, and ex-Communist informants to put their opponents in an untenable rhetorical position. If the accused un-American took the fifth amendment before un-American investigating committees, he was conceding guilt to many fearful Americans. If he waived fifth amendment protection, he found himself in an advocacy situation where the committee chairman held virtually all the procedural and persuasive prerogatives. The witness was almost defenseless.

In the same manner the American accused of guilt by association could hardly muster a factual refutation. The charges against him were rarely spelled out specifically and when they were spelled out they could not be empirically verified or disproven. They could not be subjected to empirical test because they allegedly involved the machinations of the internal Communist conspiracy, a conspiracy dedicated to the suppression of factual information.

Finally, the anti-Communists relied almost exclusively on the uncorroborated testimony of ex-Communists to support their charges and invariably the ex-Communists offered nothing more than the infallibility of their own memory to give credibility to their charges.

Through use of the fifth amendment, guilt-by-association charges, and the testimony of ex-Communists the anti-Communists stripped their opponents of any empirical means for refuting charges made against them. They further complicated their opponent's rhetorical position by denying the reliability of seemingly factual evidence on the grounds that the Communists controlled the major sources of information in America.

While the anti-Communists of the McCarthy era used the fifth amendment, guilt by association, and the testimony of ex-Communists to detach their persuasive message from the burden of empirical verification, the new Radical Right uses a somewhat more elaborate rhetorical strategy to attain the same objective.

The new Radical Right starts with the same basic assumption as their anti-Communist predecessors but extends the assumption much further—the Radical Right claims not only that appearances are deceiving, because of the internal Communist conspiracy, but that appearances are the exact opposite of what they seem to be. With this startling assumption as the touchstone of their rhetorical strategy, the revolutionary reactionaries can make the most implausible assertion appear to be plausible.

At present, the Radical Right builds its public rhetoric around this idea that appearances are the exact opposite of what they appear to be. Robert Welch labels this idea the Principle of Reversal and he first gained national prominence with the publication of a book based almost solely on this seemingly bizarre idea. In that book, *The Politician*, Welch argued that Dwight Eisenhower was undoubtedly a conscious agent of the Communist conspiracy because he was one of the last Americans anyone would suspect of Communist activities.

Strange as the Principle of Reversal may seem to many Americans, it has proven to be extremely useful for the Radical Right. Through the repeated and persistent use of the "principle" in their public rhetoric, the Radical Right has turned a highly disadvantageous historical situation to their advantage. While the polls show that the Radical Right has very little public support, Welch, McIntire, and Hargis, among others, quickly counter with the claim that appearances cannot be trusted. In fact they assert that the best evidence of the popularity of the Radical Right is the apparent unpopularity which is reflected in public opinion polls. After all, they ask, in a nation infiltrated by Communists who controls the public opinion polls?

The anti-empirical assumption, that appearances are the opposite of what they seem to be, is useful for two other reasons. Through consistent use of this principle the Radical Right is able to detach its message from the constraints of societal judgment and the constraints of history.

The reactionary message is detached from the pressures of societal judgment and evaluation because the reactionary is unconcerned about the judgment of a society which he believes to be thoroughly diseased and perverted by Communist infiltration. Furthermore, the reactionary message is detached from the judgment of history because the reactionary believes recorded history to be a sham and a delusion controlled by the internal Communist conspirators.[57]

The final part of the legacy passed on by the earlier anti-Communists to the reactionaries is a set of values which emphasize a basic distrust of man, his institutions, and above everything else a distrust of democratic government.[58] Distrust of their fellow man, and the institutions he has developed, was manifested over and over in the hearings of un-American activities committees and the same distrust is more blatantly exhibited in the present persuasion of the Radical Right.

Perhaps the most disturbing part of the legacy is the undeniable distrust, indeed fear, of democratic government. When Robert Welch attacks democratic government and stresses the motto of the John Birch Society, this is a republic—not a democracy, he is echoing the words of a very recent period in American history. Ironically, the anti-democratic legacy of the anti-Communists was never more evident than in un-American activities hearings which were pledged to defend that same democratic form of government.

In 1947 before the California Fact-Finding committee on un-American Activities, Jack Tenney captured the true legacy of anti-Communism:

Tenney: I might call your attention, Mrs. March, to this. Do you believe you are living in a democracy?

Mrs. March: Yes, I do.

Tenney: Did it ever occur to you that the word democracy does not appear in the Constitution of the United States?

Mrs. March: I am sorry, as a long time Jeffersonian Democrat, this would be very hard for me to adjust my thinking to.

Tenney: When I tell you it does not, I think you can depend on it. Ours is a republic. Under a democratic society the major party can vote the minority party out of

---

57. Dale G. Leathers, "Belief-Disbelief Systems: The Communicative Vacuum of the Radical Right," *Explorations in Rhetorical Criticism*, eds. Charles J. Stewart, *et al.*, (University Park, Penn.: The Pennsylvania State University Press, 1973), pp. 124-37.

58. Leathers, "Fundamentalism of the Radical Right," 247-51.

power. They can put them into slavery or take them out and shoot them, so our founding fathers felt it would be better to have a republic so that all would be protected. I think the word should be clarified so that we can understand what it means.[59]

BIBLIOGRAPHY

Anderson, Jack, and May, Ronald W. *McCarthy: the Man, the Senator, the Ism.* Boston: Beacon Press, 1952.
The authors analyze McCarthy's controversial Senate hearings on un-American activities.

Carr, Robert K. *The House Committee on Un-American Activities, 1945-1950.* Ithaca, New York: Cornell University Press, 1952.
As one in a series of impressively researched books on the anti-Communist era published by the Cornell University Press, Carr's is a particularly important publication. In his detailed study of un-American activities hearings Carr provides much additional information which helps highlight the rhetorical confrontations which are reconstructed in this chapter.

Commager, Henry Steele. *Civil Liberties Under Attack.* Philadelphia: University of Pennsylvania Press, 1951.
In a series of lectures Commager weighs the impact of anti-Communist activities on civil liberties.

Donner, Frank J. *The Un-Americans.* New York: Ballantine, 1961.
The House Un-American Activities Committee provides the focus for a lengthy and uncomplimentary study of the anti-Communists.

Ford, Sherman. *The McCarthy Menace: An Evaluation of the Facts and an Interpretation of the Evidence.* New York: William Frederick Press, 1954.
The author bitterly attacks McCarthy as a sinister threat to those very freedoms which he was ostensibly committed to defending.

Hook, Sydney, *Political Power and Personal Freedom: Critical Studies in Democracy, Communism and Civil Rights.* New York: Criterion, 1959.

Hook contrasts the ideological differences between communism and democracy with particular attention to such problems as fellow travelers and the Soviet espionage network.

McWilliams, Carey. *Witch Hunt: The Revival of Heresy.* Boston: Little, Brown, and Company. 1950.
In a decidedly polemical style, McWilliams indicts anti-Communism as a vehicle for personal persecution. He identifies the major cause of anti-Communism as economic and political insecurity.

---

59. *California Fact-Finding Committee on un-American Activities,* February, 1948.

21 The Black Revolution, 1954-1973

Arthur L. Smith

In the years between 1954 and 1964 there was a flowering of American idealism. This was especially true for blacks who saw their cause gain momentum. Young and old, white and black, people marched, sang, heard speeches, and above all, dreamed of a new way of life. The revolution sprang from a relatively innocuous beginning, a Supreme Court decision in 1954 entitled *Brown vs. Board of Education.* The significance of the decision was personalized by Rosa Parks, the woman in Montgomery, Alabama, who was "too tired" to relinquish her seat on the bus to a white man. And so began the 1955-56 Montgomery bus boycott.

Words alone cannot capture the spirit of people who were willing to endure fire hoses, cattle goads, and police dogs for the cause—equal justice and equal opportunity for all. These dreams of the "New Jerusalem" were shattered with the bullets which snatched away the lives of John Kennedy, Martin Luther King and then Robert Kennedy. This incredible succession of bloodshed, and the riots of 1965 marked the demise of one approach taken by blacks and

the beginnings of the development of other methods. The gains, while not satisfactory, were significant. In many places, attitudes had not changed, but some of the most blatant symbols such as signs reading "colored" and "white" no longer hung above the drinking fountains. While the separate, now unlabeled fountains remained, blacks knowingly drank from either. More than this, by relentless attacks upon the basic institutions of the United States, the black power movement has greatly changed the nation. Each attempt at change has met with opposition. In some cases, the opposition has been physical, while in other instances, it has been verbal. Both types reflect how deeply the attitudes of some are entrenched. Inasmuch as the institutions had made legitimate or legal the subordinate roles of blacks, they became the targets of legal, educational and confrontational protest. Thus, the society saw the awakening of its largest minority population in a monumental drive to alter the prevailing social conditions. Professor Pauli Murray has observed, "All Negro protest in a sense, has been directed against an inferior legal status either as defined by law or as applied in practice."[1] And so, the persistent campaigns against entrenched and traditional laws, customs and practices have made public speeches a capsule history of the black revolution.

The Frame of Protest

What were the fundamental assumptions about American society, the black man's status and the future of transracial relationships, held by black spokesmen from 1954 to 1968? To what extent were their rhetorical choices indicative of adjustments to the realities? Answering these questions will provide us with a frame for black revolutionary rhetoric.

The complexity of the social issues involved in black-white relations in the context of change gives rise to several rhetorical manifestations by the black spokesmen. However, only two ends are clearly identified in the protest movement: *integration* and *separation*. Every speaker who addresses himself to the solution of the racial conundrum chooses, either by design or chance, one or the other of these goals. Although there are several rhetorical manifestations, identified by themes and messages, there are only two explicit alternatives. The rhetorical manifestations of *integration* are equal opportunity or interdependence; of *separation*, separate states or back to Africa.

Equal opportunity has always been the most significant goal of black protest. In fact, it can be argued that black Americans generally have accepted the American Dream of equal opportunity to participate in prosperity and liberty with occasional deviation. Urged on by the developing black elite, protest leaders impelled American race relations into a more equalitarian

direction.[2] Most of the major civil rights organizations worked for integration as manifested in themes and messages devoted to equal opportunity. Thus NAACP, CORE and Urban League were, in a sense, equality organizations believing essentially that the black man's best hope consisted in the sharing of American society. Because these three organizations have represented the majority of active black protesters, they have wielded considerable influence in the protest campaign.

Interdependence as a theme in the rhetoric of blacks has always represented integration with a special quality: the subordinate position of the black man. This course, following Booker T. Washington, encourages blacks to seek integration without political or social rights. Economic development becomes the main component of a system of interdependence with blacks subservient to whites. Such a rhetorical venture, were it to be mounted by a contemporary black spokesman, would have almost no chance of succeeding. The social sensitivity and political sophistication of the masses of blacks have introduced a strikingly candid quality in black political thought. In the face of dignity, self-respect and pride, subservience and subordination as tactics of gaining acceptance within the society are anathema. This acceptance of one's self, one's heritage and one's color is a denial of any sociopolitical position that seeks a society with blacks in less than equal roles. Clearly, integration with whites and blacks unequal in terms of politics, society and economics is integration with a

---

1. Pauli Murray, "Protest Against the Legal Status of the Negro," *The Annals* 357 (January, 1965):56.
2. Arnold Rose, "The Negro Problem in the Context of Social Change," *The Annals*, 357 (January, 1965):4.

special qualification; integration in name only.

As thematic perspectives for the rhetoric of black revolution, both equal opportunity and interdependence have suggested one dimension of the protest. The speaker who approached the speech situation armed with historical data knew, although he may not have thoroughly understood, the essential problems of the society. While integration as a sociological concept has had currency among large portions of whites within recent years, it has always been a major theme of black leaders. Because black spokesmen were distracted by the concerns of whites that integration meant intermarriage, miscegenation and mongrelization, they often argued that integration did not mean what whites thought it meant. In fact, such a defensive rhetorical stance failed to stress the desirability of interethnic understanding and acceptance. Because integration was an emotional term, speakers were often careful not to exacerbate fears and anxieties.

Separation as a rhetorical theme has been manifested in two principal ways: speakers have argued for separate states within the United States and for a return to Africa. Always less than the received doctrine, promulgated by the major opinion-makers of both races, separation, for the most part, seldom occupied center stage in black history. The striking exception, of course, is Marcus Garvey's back-to-Africa movement of the 1920's. But since Garvey, black separatists have not been able to develop massive support for their schemes. Nevertheless, the black revolution of the 1960s was stimulated, perhaps put into second gear, by the manhood speeches of Malcolm X, the most powerful speaker of the Nation of Islam, and later, as El Hajj Malik Shabazz, the leader of his own socio-political group. But Malcolm X's political flirtation with separation was not longlasting; disenchanted with the Black Muslims, he began his own organization, and in the process divested himself of the notion of separation. What Malik Shabazz saw was the impracticability of separation as a political solution to the black man's problems. While it may have been rhetorically defensible, arguing from the position that years of protest had accomplished little, separation was not, in the long run, politically sound. Because Malik could see this, he was wary of contending the indefensible. And the mark of the brilliant orator is his ability to perceive what is and what is not defensible.

Back to Africa—Africa, as the ancestral home, has been the one abiding theme of the separatists. When arguments become vacuous and organizations cease to function, Africa has always been present. Thus, for people who feel betrayed and oppressed in a strange land, back-to-Africa draws considerable emotional blood. But the impracticality of that solution has tended to keep the contemporary movement small. There has been no effective back-to-Africa rhetoric since the 1920s. With the demise of Garvey's Universal Negro Improvement Association went massive black interest in African immigration as a solution to the American dilemma.

Separate States—Another solution employing separation as the principal basis has been called for by various organizations seeking to establish "black territories" within the United States. Speakers who have argued for this view have insisted that blacks and whites would be better off were they separated. But these orators have stopped short of calling for a return to Africa. Supporters of the separate state doctrine contend that blacks have as much claim to American land as whites. Thus, the Republic of New Africa and the Black Muslim organizations mobilized their followers to dream and even work toward acquiring land.

As thematic expressions in the speeches of the black revolution these four positions exercised black leaders during the 1960s. Integration or separation were the choices clearly delineated before the masses. Acceptance of one position meant the rejection of the other. The spokesmen for integration often assumed that the separation spokesmen were obstructing the black movement and the separatists thought the same of the integrationists. Most of the inventing black speakers utilized the conventions governing persuasive speeches as they argued their special beliefs. Thus, an integrationist's propositions were fashioned out of a certain perspective and from a particular interpretation of facts; so were the propositions of the separatists. In a real sense, this was primarily a question of resources, materials, and conditions that could be used by the speaker to create the necessary messages. But there are other fundamental questions that must be considered. Who will assent to the message? How will the audience be created and what use will be made of the message by the audience?

In assessing the integrationist's position, it is necessary to understand that more than anyone else in recent times Martin Luther King established the ground rules and principles of argument. As the most articulate spokesman for integration when it was most widely acclaimed, King stimulated the black audiences that had been prepared by World War II, A. Philip Randolph's labor agitation, and the buoyant expectation that Chief Justice Earl Warren would bring

a new era of justice. King gave new meaning to old arguments, recasting them in the language of Jesus and Gandhi. In so doing he created energetic audiences that listened to his rhetoric with the attentiveness of church-goers and then marched onto the streets. The position staked out by King became the battle line for numerous minor prophets who held tenaciously to his nonviolent line.

What King was to the integrationist position, Malcolm X was to the separatist view. He argued in the "Ballot or the Bullet" that he was for freedom, but he believed that separation was the best way to achieve it. Malcolm X scoffed at the idea that he was for separation and King was for integration. Simply put, the issue was not of substance but of method. Nevertheless, the outspoken leader of the Nation of Islam and later the Muslim Mosque Inc., became a symbol of black rage and alienation in the 1960s. Establishing the manner and the message of black militancy Malcolm X indelibly engraved his views on the black movement. As King had his followers, so little Malcolms soon poured forth the fiery words that had first been spoken by the mentor.

Accounting for the crescendo of black protest that developed and was sustained in the 1950s and 1960s takes the efforts of numerous scholars. The general agreement is that there were several causes for black protest: industrialization,[3] unemployment,[4] psychological pressures,[5] and social injustices. All of these problems were exacerbated in the 1950s and 1960s. Given

---

3. *Ibid.*, p. 2.
4. Herbert Hill, "Racial Inequality in Employment," *The Annals* 357 (January, 1965):31.
5. For an in-depth discussion of psychological pressures, see Price M. Cobbs and William H. Grier, *Black Rage,* (New York: Basic Books, 1968).

this set of circumstances the issues and audiences were easily created. Black spokesmen expressed the most profound aspirations of their constituents regarding the social condition. The rhetorical constellation from which they operated was encased in systems of reference influenced by American white society. In fact, what scholars have been studying consciously or unconsciously, when they study black protest, is the ideological attempt of blacks to escape the imposed systems of reference.

Thus, the frame of black protest is determined by the manifest sociopolitical situations inherent within an unequal society. Rhetoric functions in just such cases as an organizing instrument creating the possibilities and combinations that make life bearable for an oppressed people. Clearly integration and separation provided the black spokesmen of revolution (in the sense of drastic reformation) with the most feasible alternatives. Choosing one or the other the speaker often adapted his arguments from historical precedents. Martin Luther King, Jr. and Malcolm X were the principal figures in the rhetoric of the black revolution for over a decade; they established the contemporary norms, the topics, and the precise verbalizations that gave vision to their numerous followers. But their faith and manner of arguing had been employed by such men as William Whipple, Marcus Garvey, Reverdy Ransom, J.C. Price, to name a few. And the procession of men forced by sociopolitical pressures beyond their control to concentrate on integration or separation remains unbroken.

The Media of Protest

The emergence of black political socialization has been one of the major developments in recent black protest speeches, dis-cussion, and debates. Such a development had been coming for a long time. As early as 1943 Hortense Powdermaker had hypothesized that blacks of her day felt guilty about their conscious or unconscious feelings of hostility toward whites because of the Christian doctrine that it is sinful to hate.[6]

Fishman and Solomon speak of the emergence of a new social character.[7] Marvick writes of political socialization in terms of psychological transformation;[8] and Crawford and Naditch have referred to a psychology of Social Protest.[9] What are the contributing factors in the media to black political behavior since *Brown vs. Board of Education, Topeka?* In succeeding pages the argument shall be advanced that the mass media contributed to black political socialization and set the stage for substantial social and political debate by lifting speeches out of parochial contexts into national and often international contexts.

Television discovered the incipient King-led civil rights movement in the late 1950s. Mass meetings, demonstrations, escorted black students and epithet-shouting whites, and, eventually, freedom rides provided the most dramatic spectacle ever caught by television cameras. In the end the cameras

6. Hortense Powdermaker, "The Channeling of Negro Aggression by the Cultural Process," *American Journal of Sociology* 48 (May, 1943):753.
7. Jacob Fishman and Frederic Solomon, "Youth and Social Action: Perspectives on the Student Sit-In Movement," *American Journal of Orthopsychiatry* 33 (October, 1963):872-82.
8. Dwaine Marvick, "The Political Socialization of the American Negro," *The Annals* 361 (September, 1965):112-27.
9. Thomas Crawford and Murray Naditch, "Relative Deprivation, Powerlessness and Militancy: The Psychology of Protest," *Psychiatry* 33 (May, 1970):208-23.

would catch the urban protest confrontations of the 1960s. Stokely Carmichael, H. Rap Brown, and Malcolm X were given prime time along with Martin Luther King, Roy Wilkins, and Bayard Rustin. Watts exploded, and a hundred major revolts followed, and television was there. The Warren Commission seeking a cause of the disruptions, complained that the mass media acted irresponsibly in overplaying the role of violent spokesmen and actions. Clearly, the course of protest, nourished by the beaming sunshine of the cameras and lights in the 1950s, was clarified in the minds of blacks in the urban ghettos of the '60s. The lines of debate were drawn in full public view; and the results of what Boskin calls a "consensus of attitude" toward the black community and the larger society emerged in the abrupt expression of violence which was captured by television.[10]

Inasmuch as the American society of the 1960s increasingly became a village, the lines of separating blacks and whites were drawn even more sharply because ghetto blacks who had never seen white society "up close" were now exposed to it through television. In addition, Southern blacks who had experienced many kinds of deprivations were brought into a closer brotherhood with blacks in the North through television. This latter situation directly bears upon the rhetoric of black revolution as an indication of the generative expanding geographics of televised black protest. For blacks, one minute of King, Carmichael, or Cleaver on television was worth more than one hundred books on the common experience. In fact, the orator, whoever he might have been, often became the symbolic voice of the black community. This was true whether the black community completely sanctioned him or not; at that mo-

ment and before those cameras he was the only voice to the masses.

What blacks saw on television screens significantly affected the evolution of black protest. The creation of a McLuhanesque tribal village occurred on the one hand; but at the same time there was a much smaller compound being developed within the tribe that comprised blacks. While the televised speech of a political or social leader had a cohering effect on the audiences if based on no more than the fact that people were centering in on the event-message, it simultaneously encouraged polarization by making clear to blacks and whites the special separateness of the two groups as seen through the rhetoric of white racists and black revolutionaries. Thus television operated as an information source on two levels: the total community was focused upon an event-message, and black Americans experienced the utter frustration of thousands of other blacks across the nation. What happened in Birmingham or Watts was community-wide as blacks shared in the protest. "Black Power" by Carmichael illustrated how rapidly television could popularize a slogan. Although the slogan possessed innate potency because of the unique situational and temporal contexts, it could never have circulated so swiftly without television. What started as a local chant during a particularly tense demonstration became by virtue of the generative expanding geographics of televised protest a national call to confrontation. Television fashioned a national black coalition from the intellectual and social bases that were already present. The results of television

---

10. Joseph Boskin, "The Revolt of the Urban Ghettos: 1964-1967," *The Annals* 381 (March, 1969):1.

upon black protest are characteristically seen in the similarity of black rhetoric everywhere. There were hardly any better answers to be given to white liberals who demanded that blacks go slow than those given by King, or hardly any better reasons for self-defense than the ones given by Malcolm X. A national brotherhood had been erected from the materials of agony, frustration, and relative deprivation[11] experienced by black protesters.

Audiences, susceptible to the strategies of mythication and legitimation,[12] appeared in every community where blacks lived. Disturbances with political significance were the most outward signs of adherence to the rhetorical discourses suggesting body confrontation and "up against the wall" negotiations. Television as the town crier par excellence hailed blacks in Newark to see what Watts had done and demonstrated to blacks in Detroit how the brothers in Newark dealt with their situations. Thus, the rhetoric of revolution rode on the waves of television in a dramatic display of generative expanding geographies. The massive spontaneous rebellions had still another effect; black leaders hastened to crystallize the violent outbursts into some organized ideological channel and more often than not, the channel was Black Power. That the audiences had been prepared for this ideological direction is seen in the fact that traditional "civil rights" organizations began to lose membership rapidly and to face almost impossible odds at winning the young. Kopkind was wise to suggest that during this time the authentic political voice of the ghetto was that of the urban guerilla while the NAACP, Urban League, and to a lesser extent CORE became observers on the sidelines despite the insistence of their press releases.[13] Black Power, became for a moment in the revolution, the most provocative feature of an expanding movement. The Black Panthers, Revolutionary Action Committee, and FIGHT seized the momentum of revolution in much different language than had the NAACP, Urban League, and SCLC.

While there is some truth in the position that Black Power has roots in the black consciousness of the Harlem Renaissance of the 1920s, the strident rhetoric of the 1960s had more of the biting edge of cynicism than the previous movement. And television acted as transmitter of the "new mood" among blacks, thus bringing to the entire black community the engaging rhetoric of Black Power. With the aid of media Black Power became far more popular among blacks than W.E.B. Dubois' Pan Africanism or Marcus Garvey's Back to Africa had ever been. Clearly the electronic transmission of images, concepts, personalities and ideas influenced the transformation of the black masses. Public speaking became, during the black revolution, one means of getting on television. If a spokesman had something important or dramatic to say he could call a news conference or invite the press to the public speech. In fact, few leaders of the black revolution intended that their speeches remain local, they were national personalities addressing the nation even as they addressed black audiences on questions of significance. In some circles

---

11. For an in-depth analysis of relative deprivation as a reason for social protest, see Crawford and Naditch, "Relative Deprivation."
12. See Arthur L. Smith, *Rhetoric of Black Revolution* (Boston: Allyn and Bacon, 1969), chap. 3 for a discussion of these strategies.
13. See Andrew Kopkind, "Soul Power," *New York Review of Books*, August 24, 1967, pp. 3-6.

Stokely Carmichael was referred to as "T.V. Starmichael" because of the stagy character of many of his speeches. Television as a media of performance tended to focus on those qualities of drama which make for good camera shots.

The Kerner Commission gave ample space to analyzing the role of mass media in civil disturbances.[14] What the Commission discovered after careful investigation was that several generally-held conclusions concerning the mass media's role in racial disturbances were incorrect. Noting an initial belief that the media had sensationalized the disturbances by consistently overplaying violence and giving disproportionate amounts of time to emotional events and "militant" leaders, the Commission discovered that moderate black leaders were shown more frequently than militant leaders on television news broadcasts.[15] However, because of the nature of the medium and indeed ideologies, one minute of H. Rap Brown or Stokely Carmichael was more emotionally charged than five minutes of Roy Wilkins or Whitney Young. The significance of this is not to be found in arguing who was rational because the black revolution like most revolutions was born out of fire. Furthermore, in city after city the rhetoric of revolution transmitted by television awakened desires for involvement, excitement, and in some cases violence or outrage and hatred were kindled. Although the Commission refused to make a blanket indictment of television, it also failed to exonerate it. Suggesting that newsmen attempt a new level of sophistication, the Commission appeared to be saying that civil disorders are not just another story but something which can shake the pillars of the society. What was called for was an internal correction of deficiencies and con-

scientious attention to balance and sophistication in reporting. And too, because the most frequent "actor" appearances on television during the disturbances were black adult males and white public officials and law enforcement officers, the civil disorders were screened as black-white confrontation. The Commission recommended that the media should concentrate on the underlying cause of conflict.

But the Commission's recognition of television's power was the first official statement regarding mass media and the black revolution. It seemed clear to the commissioners, as it had to many viewers, that the television screens transmitted a kind of contagious hysteria that resulted in violence. While this reasoning always stood in the wings, the Commission played the theme of more responsibility from the cameramen and reporters. But like most Americans they were victims of a pervasive attitude, starstruck by "We Shall Overcome," and "Black Power" so that when "Burn, Baby Burn" appeared they could only respond as they previously had, with eager eyes and cameras to play up the most fluent rebels. The rebellions, of course, were not organized mass meetings protected by the sanctity of the church, but rather explosions caused by the youth who had sat at Malcolm X's feet while their parents and country relatives were inspired by Martin Luther King. So what the cameras caught, and what was transmitted, bore little resemblance to passionate orations by inspired preachers; the speakers were now

---

14. *Report of the National Advisory Commission on Civil Disorders*, (New York: Bantam Books, 1968), pp. 362-89.
15. *Ibid.*, p. 364.

cynical and their bold rhetoric inflammatory.[16]

The Language of Protest

The rhetoric of black revolution in the 1960s was most dramatic in the transformation of conventional language behavior as manifest in the public speeches of such figures as Malcolm X, Maulana Karenga, and Eldridge Cleaver. And indeed, the audiences were transformed by the overpowering images and concepts emerging from a new political consciousness and often expressed as a surrealistic collage.

When the "language of the street brothers" moved to the podium a new era had dawned in black rhetoric. This novel experience took several different forms, all of which had as their basis the soul and spirit of Malcolm X. One form drew directly from Malcolm X in its rhetorical directness as indicated in short and tense introductory statements. In the "Ballot or the Bullet" Malcolm X said, "Mr. Moderator, Brother Lomax, brothers and sisters, friends and enemies: I just can't believe everyone in here is a friend and I don't want to leave anybody out."[17] This style was followed by several speakers. Eldridge Cleaver, for instance, would often begin his speeches, "Hello, y'all out there in Babylon," and Maulana Karenga would say something like "Beautiful people, here we are." These speakers avoided the involved introductory comments of more traditional speakers who often saw art in setting the audience at ease. And as Malcolm X warned his audiences that his remarks were not meant to please or set them at ease, so the sons of Malcolm followed in step with terse introductions usually meant to establish a sense of distance by shocking the audience. Distance was usually easy to come by when a speaker made no attempt to find common ground with his audiences. But directness also demonstrated, or was meant to demonstrate, conviction. Inasmuch as the speaker appeared to disregard the traditional civilities of language he deliberately chose conviction over acceptance through audience adaptation.

More significant, perhaps was that for the first time black speakers en masse expressed their innermost thoughts and ideas about white people and white society.[18] Having started with the caustic attacks by the Nation of Islam's preachers, of whom Malcolm X was once chief, against "the blue-eyed devil" the diatribes against whites grew more vehement each day. In a sense black speakers had discovered, and the language reflected, that the whites were susceptible to black anger and hatred. This awareness was liberating for scores of angry blacks who had once been captive of a dehumanizing fear.

Such awareness was political as well as rhetorical, yet it was in the making of speeches that the surge of social consciousness was first recognized. Blacks began to talk about the right to define concepts applicable to blacks, the need to determine the destiny of black communities and the propagation of a black world view that would liberate the minds of the

---

16. "If we can't have freedom, no one will have freedom."
17. "The Ballot or the Bullet," in *Malcolm X Speaks* (New York: Grove Press, 1968) pp. 23-44, speech by Malcolm X in Cleveland, Ohio, April 1964.
18. To recognize this is to understand the public discourses of John Langston, Booker T. Washington, and even Marcus Garvey. With Malcolm X the whites became the objects of anger.

black masses. This talk was very expensive. For many blacks it meant a totally different orientation to life within these United States; it demanded a commitment to a perspective not yet clearly delineated. But theorists and propagandists were already in the making and they tried their various, sometimes novel ideas on the black community. The popular among them prevailed and the language of the public platform was that of the community; thus their community identity was firmly established. In fact, the speeches of the tacticians of protest rivaled the expressionism apparent in the behavior of the conscious blacks. Apart from the fact that the decision to wear the "natural look" was more significant than the Watts rebellion, the confident manner of the blacks signaled an acceptance of reality as well as rhetoric.

The language of protest, such as is used by black revolutionaries, extends the rhetorical sphere of both creators and audiences. While the black revolutionary speaker exhibits a strong appreciation for words, he is not overwhelmed by them but rather seeks to overwhelm his audiences by his word magic. Thus, the speaker assigns his word power over reality as he molds, alters, and transforms experiences. But this transformation is rhetorical; that is, it is persuasive or meant to be persuasive above all else, and therefore essentially directed toward the unbelievers and psychologically unaware.

In what demonstrations of language is the extension of reality supported? There is first of all the redefinition of individual terms. Several speakers emphasized the need for an overhauling of language which denigrates anything black; thus words like "blackmail" and "black lie" came to mean the opposite of their conventional defini-

tions. Instead of "black lie" or "blackmail" these speakers chose to speak of "white lie" and "whitemail." To them this shift of perspective clarified the symbolic predicament of the American society which had been unable to recognize the aspirations of black Americans even in the conception and structure of language. However, attempts at redefinition fall short of an overhaul of the American language because the best that can be accomplished is the deliberate alteration of the conventional meaning of a few words or terms. And too, this remains the province of the skilled speaker more than the mass public, unless, of course, there is an accompanying campaign for the dissemination of current alterations. Needless to say, nothing of the sort existed for the creative speakers of the 1960s except the occasional television excerpts of a speaker trying to "endarken" his audiences on a certain topic. There was something fad-like about these incursions into the vocabulary, although they were religiously made "out of conviction, not of convenience"[19] according to the speakers.

In yet another sense the extension of reality is demonstrated by the language of black revolution. Images discovered in the common experiences of black Americans are taken and used as instruments against their humiliating existence. Such use, however, extends the sphere of reality of the white audiences as it does that of the black audiences. This is so because the images conspired by the speakers of black revolution stand in precise contexts. When the speaker calls for the power of history, politics or religion, he seeks to establish precise meanings. The history of black Americans,

---

19. Speech by Maulana Karenga given at Purdue University, December 9, 1968.

with its pathos and victory, is often used in strange but exact contexts. The *spirituals* could become, in place of a quote by Camus or Frost, the particular poetic or philosophical expression needed by the black speaker for his black audiences, and the speaker was aware that politics had to be expressed in real terms; thus the revolutionary did not traffic in abstractions or dreams but on a two dimensional level—*either* and *or*. For the white audiences, acceptance of this perspective conceivably could be difficult if they insisted on retaining white superiority. What the black speakers did with their reversals of established order was to challenge accepted reality. Thus, they spoke of "black people," "blackness of sunshine," "the purity of blackness," and "my best day is a black day." No longer were the speakers guilty of condemning themselves; their language had reversed the traditional order. Inasmuch as several generations of blacks had grown accustomed to saying "white as snow" to signify purity, or some similar expression, the overthrow of this hierarchy was a singular achievement on the part of the black revolution. In this respect a transformation took place which had never before been imagined. What to most whites was absurd was precise to blacks and therein lies one of the conundrums of pluralism in American society.

To a lesser extent than the redefinition of single words and terms and the reversal of images, the extension of reality has been demonstrated by the use of profanity on the public platform. Where it would be difficult to imagine Frederick Douglass or Martin Luther King using obscenities in a public discourse, Eldrige Cleaver, in revolutionary tones, employed the language of the streets. In the view of Cleaver and others language was not obscene, actions were, and they pointed to rat infested apartments, poverty, and the Vietnam War as profane and immoral. Furthermore, the speakers often argued that they were using the language that could best be understood by the brothers in the community. But while there was an attempt to justify the unbridled use of obscene language, the speakers succeeded in producing mixed emotions in their audiences. And the extensive use of obscene language served to signal another stage in the dialectics of black protest.

What has been the cumulative impact of this language behavior on whites and blacks? How has the condition for this language behavior been created? When blacks utilized speech patterns and expressions which were nontraditional to whites, the reactions of whites took several forms depending upon their familiarity with black language. One reaction has been to reject the speaker and his speech as obscene or unethical. Such a response to a speech, meant to contain legitimate grievances, although employing profanity, was seen by the black speaker as an attempt to establish a white ethical hegemony, and this despite the fact that whites had abdicated their right to judge the morality of black language by their imprisonment of black life. Thus, outright rejection by white audiences failed to diminish the intensity of black revolutionary rhetoric. In fact, rejection signaled the black speaker that he was perfectly on target with his verbal punches. If whites rejected the statement of grievances, it was assumed that their rejection was based on an unwillingness to concede the legitimacy of grievances or black demands for restitution. However, the rejection, as whites frequently argued, was based on the language used rather than on the content conveyed. While this distinction has plagued black speakers and their white audiences, it has solidified many black audiences. White rejection of a speaker or speech provoked blacks to embrace the rejected object. Of course, these were irrational instances because blacks were responding to white reaction rather than reviewing the circumstances and responding to their evaluations.

Another response of white audiences to the rhetoric of blacks has been the acceptance of black language. Acceptance, of course, of the language does not commit a person to the speech content. Therefore, some whites who considered themselves as "hip" as the blacks approved of the language but rejected the politics. Hardly any whites accepted the politics without accepting the language.

When blacks, fired by Malcolm X's spirit, cast off the mantle of obsequiousness, they demanded a new accounting of reality. This accounting would dismantle the superimposed standards and values of whites. Thus, the use of profanity, while a part of some black communities, was an outgrowth of a new philosophical position which deemed white things contradictory to blacks, and the platform graces of traditional white society became one of those contradictory things. To accept white standards of ethics meant the loss of black integrity. If a speaker presumed to speak for black people, he had better be sure he was black (not a black-skinned man with white values) or else the wrath of the militants would be heaped upon his head. Let us now turn to the ideological struggle that has been a dominant characteristic of protest during the black revolution.

The Dialectics of Protest

When the decade of the 1960s opened black Americans were beginning to explore the social and philosophical grounds of legitimate protest against real abuses. By the end of the decade the exploration had almost exhausted itself in ever ascending rhetoric and continuous actions to outmaneuver the forces of repression and resistance. Thus, in ten dramatic years the leaders of black protest had run the gamut of possible methods of seeking redress. There had been boycotts, petitions, mass demonstrations, sit-ins, lie-ins, talk of guerrilla war, some violence, and many dead and wounded; the rhetoric and philosophy had frequently outpaced the masses. Furthermore, the response of white America was pathetically small compared to the sufferings and sacrifices of blacks. Peter Goldman summed up the decade by saying: "all the buffets of a decade—the false starts, the mixed counsel, the hopes raised and cheated—have left Negro Americans as a race sadder, a bit wiser, several shades blacker, and more impatient now than they have ever been."[20] But the process of getting blacker and madder was the result of a dialectics of protest begun in the early days of the decade.

Martin Luther King was the pivotal figure for most of the decade, and it was from his thought and rhetoric that new modes of confrontation and redress were derived and put into action. Soon he was no longer in the militant vanguard. Several spokesmen, who took their cue from him or who found counsel in the heroes of the past, outdistanced him in the virulence of rhetoric, though they never approached his wholeness of thought. The net effect, however, of this ideological movement, was the bypassing of King and the increased aggressiveness of the language.

---

20. Peter Goldman, *Report from Black America* (New York: Simon and Schuster, 1970), p. 18.

To put the dialectics in perspective it is necessary to mention King's vision.[21] His driving faith was that white Americans had consciences which would cause them to repudiate injustice if they observed the demonstration of those injustices against the oppressed. Hence, nonviolence was tactically wise, and for him, morally right as well. In his program of protest he organized marches, jail-ins, sit-ins, pray-ins, and boycotts to demonstrate the pervading nature of racism in the society. When his marchers, black and white, young and old, were attacked he counseled that they must not strike back because they could not allow the evil actions of the oppressor to dictate their actions. And too, there was the conviction, frequently expressed by him, that there was something redemptive in unjust suffering. It was this vision which was debated, discussed, and often abandoned in the turbulent 1960s.

An array of speakers with a babel of doctrines marched into black communities and onto television screens during the decade. And in the face of their inflamed rhetoric the black establishment leaders, Roy Wilkins, Whitney Young, and Bayard Rustin, retreated and took refuge in their past victories. King, as the most universally acclaimed spokesman of the decade, tried to field the rhetoric and counterattack for the traditional spokesmen, but the spiraling process had begun. Leading the attack was Malcolm X, a modern Jeremiah demanding black manhood, who looked upon King's philosophy as cowardice and upon King's acceptance of whites attacking black women as disgraceful for any race. To Malcolm X, there could be nothing redemptive in black men watching white men attack black women and children. Nonviolence was not an inherent good when it came to a man's rights; he must be willing to wage a struggle for his God-given prerogatives, according to Malcolm X. He argued that, "Black people are fed up with the dilly-dallying, pussyfooting, compromising approach that we've been using toward getting our freedom. We want freedom now, but we're not going to get it saying—'We shall overcome.' We've got to fight until we overcome."[22] Without mentioning King by name he had labeled King's movement as a pussyfooting approach, and he knew that most blacks, even if they did not see the means, would viscerally respond to a no-compromising position on freedom. Malcolm X systematically attacked the assumptions upon which King's movement was based. In his mind there had been no progress in the black man's predicament from the beginning of King's movement until 1964. "We're not even as far up as we were in 1954. We're behind where we were in 1954. There's more segregation now than there was in 1954. There's more racial animosity, more racial hatred, more racial violence today in 1964, than there was in 1954. Where is the progress?"[23] For those whose faith had been stirred by the romanticism of King's vision, this was a hard question to take. Even prejudiced southerners who had viewed King as a trouble-maker now looked at him with more favor. Clearly the public utterances of Malcolm X were rancorous compared to King's; and the acceptance of King's rhetoric was made easier because Malcolm X stood on the stage. So the first step of the dialectics of black pro-

---

21. Martin Luther King, *Strength to Love* (New York: Harper & Row, 1964); *Why We Can't Wait* (New York: Harper & Row, 1964); *Stride Toward Freedom* (New York: Harper & Brothers, 1958).
22. Malcolm X, "Ballot or Bullet," *Malcolm X Speaks*, p. 38. The entire black nationalism period of Malcolm X was filled with similar emphasis. Refer to other speeches in this book.
23. *Ibid.*, p. 31.

test was completed when Malcolm X became more news than King and when he was perceived as more of a threat than King.

And where King had tried to persuade a whole generation of southern blacks that freedom could be attained by peaceful marchers, Malcolm X spoke the words of violence and scared whites and blacks. Black nationalism he said meant, "Give it to us now. Don't wait for next year. Give it to us yesterday, and that's not fast enough."[24] And he was convinced that, "There is a new strategy coming in. It'll be molotov cocktails this month, hand grenades next month, and something else next month. It'll be ballots, or it'll be bullets. It'll be liberty, or it will be death. The only difference about this kind of death—it'll be reciprocal."[25] What this aggressive type of rhetoric produced was an exceedingly polarized public. Having created his own audiences Malcolm X had now become the object of venomous attacks equal to those he made upon others. Speaking militantly became the style of rhetoric employed by his votaries; speaking against Malcolm X became the style of many blacks and whites. His strident vilifications and caustic objectifications were so naked of congenial rhetorical embellishment that he shocked as well as antagonized much of the public with his audacity. He was the embodiment of "All the bad Niggers" who had ever lived. Speaking for blacks, Ossie Davis would intone at his funeral "He was our Manhood."[26] But the pronouncements of the prophet, the audaciousness of his faith, were not buried with him.

The sons of the prophet were numerous, mostly young black men who had worked in King's movement and had been inspired by Malcolm X's life; they took the banner of black nationalism to a new level as multitudes of college age blacks became politicized. The man so abused in life was now revered in death. Henry Austan of the Deacons for Defense and Justice said, "Malcolm X was my idol. Malcolm had not yet reached his peak, but I believe he was on the right road. The road I'm on is the one I think he was on. I think he believed that the black man in America had to unite and to stand up. I think this is what he was trying to do—unite the Negroes. He once said, 'Freedom by any means necessary'—which I made my motto."[27] Open for varied interpretations the words and speeches of Malcolm X became the Koran of his followers. But it was left for Stokely Carmichael, more a student of Martin Luther King than Malcolm X in the initial stages of his political development, to initiate the next step in the dialectics of protest. A little over a year after Malcolm X's death, Carmichael coined his now famous slogan "Black Power." Coming so soon after Malcolm X's plea for black nationalism, a concept which included political, economic, and social development, Black Power appeared to be a call to arms. Never in the history of Afro-American rhetoric had a slogan contained so much rhetorical electricity; and the shock waves are still reverberating. Over one hundred journal and magazine articles were written on Black Power within two years of Carmichael's chant. Books poured forth and debates ensued over the proper interpretation of this new concept.

24. *Ibid.*, p. 33.
25. *Ibid.*, p. 32.
26. Malcolm X, *The Autobiography of Malcolm X* (New York: Merit Press, 1967), p. 151.
27. George Breitman, *The Last Year of Malcolm X* (New York: Merit Press, 1967), p. 151.

As a national figure in his own right, Carmichael commanded the attention of the nation's young blacks who had participated in the Student Nonviolent Coordinating Committee voting rights drives in the South. He became the symbol of blacks frustrated with the slow pace of social change. In the mind of Carmichael, virtue had escaped white America and the nation stood guilty of all manner of injustice. "This country is a nation of thieves. It stole everything it has, beginning with Black people."[28] Indictment became the strategy of a militant blackness, and nothing was immune from the aggressive attacks of Black Power advocates. The institutions of American society, political, economic, and cultural, were targets for the fiery darts of the protest speakers. Led by Carmichael, the Black Power advocates believed that, "this country cannot justify any longer its existence."[29] Furthermore, "we have taken all the myths of this country and we have found them to be nothing but downright lies. This country told us that if we worked hard we would succeed, and if that were true we would own this country lock, stock, and barrel."[30] This is the rhetoric that shook the established order and emerged for three brief years as the moving force behind the black revolution. It was not a rhetoric that called for violence, but it demanded radical departures of thought. No longer would institutions be allowed to continue as if things were the same. Quite frankly, the indictments made by Carmichael changed institutional thinking as never before. Corporations and churches, schools and social agencies responded to the demands of the time with critical evaluations of their status. Thus, Carmichael had become the leading personality in the black revolution. Martin Luther King, first up-

staged by Malcolm X was still struggling with the Negro revolution. Carmichael, on the other hand, greatly inspired by Malcolm X during his last year, seized the time and heightened the contradictions.

H. Rap Brown took over the reins of SNCC from Stokely Carmichael and served as chairman from 1967 to 1968. However, in October, 1967, he was confined to New York City under house arrest, pending trial in Maryland on charges of inciting to riot. In June, 1968, he was convicted of a gun-carrying charge and sentenced to five years in prison and the maximum fine of two thousand dollars. In 1973, after a lengthy evasion of police, Brown was convicted of robbery and possession of dangerous weapons.

Brown's rhetoric complemented the momentum created by Carmichael, but it signaled another level of intensity in the black revolution. Clearly in Brown's terms Black Power meant political and, if necessary, violent force to counteract institutional racism. With H. Rap Brown it became fashionable to threaten the imminent destruction of America. He counseled blacks, "We have to decide if we will be killers; when we decide, we have to decide who we are going to kill, and when."[31] What Brown sought was the complete disregard of white society, "If white folks say it's more cultured to whisper, you talk loud. If white folks say gray

28. Speech by Stokely Carmichael given at Berkeley Black Power Conference of November 1966, Berkeley, California. Text of the speech is tape recorded and reproduced by permission of the Student Nonviolent Coordinating Committee, Atlanta, Georgia. For the text, see Charles W. Lomas, *The Agitator in American Society* (Englewood Cliffs, N.J.: Prentice-Hall, 1968), p. 144.
29. *Ibid.*
30. *Ibid.*, p. 145.
31. H. Rap Brown, *Die Nigger Die* (New York: Dial, 1968), p. 136.

suits are fashionable, you go buy a pink one. If they say America is great, you say America ain't shit."[32] However, redefinition in itself is not enough to be considered a heightening of the revolutionary fervor; there must be a more direct call for confrontation. So alongside the Carmichael type indictments and the Malcolm X type black pride themes, Brown introduced another dimension. "There is no redress of grievances for blacks in this country. When the government becomes the lawbreaker, people must become law enforcers."[33] On a similar note, Brown stated, "As the chairman says, 'Power comes from the barrel of a gun.' Freedom is not for sale. Freedom can only be bought with revolution."[34] Still further he spoke of revolutionary culture in these terms, "Write me a novel about how to infiltrate the FBI and destroy it. Write me poems that say more than that you are black and beautiful. Perform dances with guns to legitimatize guns as a weapon of struggle. If you examine any country that has undergone successful revolution, you will find that the cultural revolution has never come before actual armed confrontation, never before a contest for power was waged."[35] Thus, Brown saw armed confrontation as a distinct possibility in the black man's search for liberation. This was a step beyond the rhetoric of Carmichael who, despite popular beliefs, seldom spoke of armed confrontation in direct terms.

And then, the Black Panthers led by a host of revolutionary orators including Minister of Defense Huey P. Newton, Minister of Information Eldridge Cleaver, and Chairman of the Party Bobby Seale, sprang full bloom onto the national scene from their Oakland headquarters. Theirs was an extension of Brown's "baddest Nigger"

rhetoric which included active conflict in order to radicalize the black community. Thus, the speeches of the Black Panthers are stark, lacking in the conventional manners of the platforms. There were few attempts to persuade the white establishment to the views of the party; the party spokesmen were in open struggle with that establishment. Even prisoners converted to the politics of the Black Panthers and began to speak in revolutionary terms. In a dispatch from San Quentin a prisoner wrote, "We wish nothing more than to reenter the Black Community and take up our rightful role as Black men and warriors, helping to establish freedom for our people."[36] So the Panthers talked to themselves and their white radical allies who understood the nature of their mission. While the rhetoric was revolutionary, the ideology was traditional Marxist-Leninist. Huey Newton declared that, "History has bestowed upon the Black Panther Party the obligation to take these steps and thereby advance Marxism-Leninism to an even higher level along the path to a socialist state. We have the historical obligation to take the concept of internationalism to its final conclusion—The Destruction of Statehood itself."[37] As the party's chief theoretician, Newton articulated positions and modes of operation for the Black Panthers that moved them into the revolutionary forefront.

The talk of blacks defending themselves came to fruition with the Black Panthers urging members to "Kill the Pigs before

---

32. *Ibid.*., p. 137.
33. *Ibid.*
34. *Ibid.*, p. 140.
35. *Ibid.*, p. 14.
36. *Black Panther*, August 29, 1970.
37. *Ibid.*

they kill you."[38]   Raids and attacks on Black Panther headquarters and members have contributed to a rationale for malice as indicated by the following statements: "Ernest Scales was clubbed viciously for being black. . . . All Power to the people, Off the pig"; and "Tucker's raiders shoot, beat and murder, Lawrence Harris, a mentally disturbed black man. . . . All Power to the People, death to the fascist pigs."[39] Such rhetoric has spurred the founding of Black Panther chapters in nearly every major city in the nation. Their language and actions are signals of political intensification, or as they prefer to say "putting the pressure on" the power structure.

Speaking before the San Francisco Barristers Club in 1968 as a presidential candidate for the Peace and Freedom Party, thirty-three-year-old Eldridge Cleaver put the language and manifesto of the Black Panthers in focus. "I could go into the White House poor and come out fat fucking rich, but I'm too young. So I have to say fuck the White House, fuck the electoral system, and fuck all the pigs, and fuck the power structure. You're all chasing dollars, and there are other people here who are chasing dollars to buy guns to kill judges and police and corporation lawyers. We need lawyers today who have a lawbook in one hand and a gun in the other . . . so that if he goes to court and that shit doesn't come out right, he can pull out his gun and start shooting. . . ." Obviously this is not the rhetoric of Martin Luther King, Malcolm X, Stokely Carmichael or H. Rap Brown; a new dimension has been reached in the rhetoric of black protest with the emergence of the Black Panthers.

Angela Davis represented yet another attempt by a black speaker to resolve rhetorically the dilemma of being black in American society. Even though her rhetoric was interpreted politically because of her Communist membership, it was no different in ultimate objectives from the rhetoric of other black militants. As a teenager, she participated in civil rights activities and experienced the attacks on blacks epitomized in the killing of four black girls in a Birmingham church. Angela Davis later drew upon her experiences in the South to speak out against the treatment of black prisoners in California jails. She had shown brilliance as a student in America and Europe, but it was only when she was appointed to the faculty of the University of California, Los Angeles, and it became known that she was a member of the Communist Party that she became an active public speaker criticizing the judicial and prison systems.[40] Her critiques of social evils and injustice were more descriptive than analytic but contained power because they were given by a militant black woman. Furthermore, because she had attained high honors in the academic community and came from a middleclass background her militancy was not dependent upon ghetto experiences. Her alienation occurred even though she had achieved excellence in high school and college. This knowledge of "the system" made it possible for those in the academic world to relate to her in a way they had not been able to do with other black speakers. Angela Davis, therefore, was symbolic of

38. This expression is frequently found in the *Black Panther*. See, for example, March 16, 1968; September 13, 1969; and August 29, 1970.
39. Headlines protesting attacks and raids appear in virtually every issue of the *Black Panther*.
40. For a biographical sketch of Angela Davis and a discussion of her gradual estrangement from American society, see "The Making of a Fugitive," *Life Magazine*, September 11, 1970.

the rhetoric of revolution inasmuch as her public discourses suggested a radical transformation in American society, and she expressed her anger as a black militant Communist.

The foregoing discussion has dealt with the major outlines of the dialectics of black revolution. Several minor, sometimes parallel developments have existed, but the significant departures in rhetoric have been King's movement, Malcolm X's crusade, Carmichael's Black Power rhetoric, H. Rap Brown's rhetoric of confrontation, and the militant political rhetoric of the Black Panthers. That the ideology of one has been more threatening to the present social and political order, and in that sense more revolutionary than another, is attributable to the responses and reactions of various audiences.

In some cases the degree of acceptance or rejection by white audiences determined the extent to which the black spokesman would be accepted or rejected by militant blacks. Thus, a leader's need for followers often pressured him into more radical positions than he intended. And at the same time, some black protest speakers urged the rejection of other speakers, charging that they had abandoned the masses. The net effect of this volatile situation was the ever spiraling rhetoric which eventually led to a dead-end marked revolutionary activism. Beyond the position spoken and taken by the revolutionists was the revolution itself. However, the confrontation predicted is not necessarily inevitable; indeed a more plausible interpretation of this dialectic may be that any further social and political rhetoric will begin from a higher plane than the previous rhetoric. Arguments put forth, situations discussed and means debated in the 1960s may have accomplished their

ends; and if so, the future rhetoric of protest will answer different questions and seek different answers.

Conclusion

To sum up, the rhetoric of black revolution was prescribed by limited rhetorical possibilities as manifest in the black sociopolitical frame of reference. And the instruments of mass dissemination of images and speeches became the channels through which spokesmen were christened leaders, and their messages were received by the audiences. Introducing the novelty of redefinition of concepts and words, black spokesmen consummated the coming of blackness with a black perspective on social and political values, and by so doing brought surrealism to the public platform. And finally the religious desire for total liberation and freedom within the American society demanded that blacks exhaust every rhetorical and political means for resolution of the American moral problem.

BIBLIOGRAPHY

Boulware, Marcus H. *The Oratory of Negro Leaders.* Westport, Connecticut: Negro Universities Press, 1969.
This first history of twentieth century black speakers is fairly subjective in approach.

Breitman, George, ed. *Malcolm X Speaks* New York: Grove Press, 1965.
Presents in Malcolm's own words the major ideas which he expounded. It is a valuable source of materials.

Carmichael, Stokeley, and Himilton, Charles V. *Black Power: The Politics of Liberation in America.* New York: Random House, 1967.
The authors present their own solution for the racial problems in the United States.

Franklin, John H. *From Slavery to Freedom: A History of Negro Americans.* 3d ed. New York: Knopf, 1967.

This latest edition of the classic work provides an in-depth study of blacks from their African beginnings to the present. It is one of the best histories of black Americans.

Grant, Joanne, ed. *Black Protest: History, Documents, and Analysis, From 1919 to the Present.* Greenwich, Connecticut: Fawcett Publications, 1968.
The editor includes essays and opinions from a wide variety of black leaders.

Grier, William H., and Cobb, Price M. *Black Rage.* New York: Basic Books, 1968.
Analysis of the psychological implications of racism.

King, Martin L. *Why We Can't Wait.* New York: Harper and Row, 1964.
Includes King's polemic from the Birmingham jail which provides one ideological base for agitation by blacks.

Lincoln, Eric C. *The Black Muslims in America.* Boston: Beacon Press, 1961.
Describes the origins, doctrine, and organization of this active segment of the black community.

Lomax, Louis E. *The Negro Revolt.* New York: Harper and Row, 1962.

The author explains differences which exist between present organizations such as NAACP, SCLC, and the Urban League.

Malcolm X. *The Autobiography of Malcolm X.* New York: Grove Press, 1964.
Powerfully written book that has become a bible for many blacks. It also has given whites insights into the black experience.

Scott, Robert, and Brockriede, Wayne. *Rhetoric of Black Power.* New York: Harper and Row, 1968.
An excellent analysis of several civil rights speeches given in the 1960s.

Smith, Arthur L. *Rhetoric of Black Revolution.* Boston: Allyn and Bacon, 1969.
One of the earliest definitional studies of black protest discourse. It has formed a basis for much of the present studies in the field.

Smith, Arthur L., and Robb, Stephen. *The Voice of Black Rhetoric.* Boston: Allyn and Bacon, 1971.
A selection of speeches and key speakers from black history, providing biographical headnotes and presenting the materials chronologically.

22 Freedom of Speech in the 1960s

Thomas L. Tedford

On August 28, 1963, 200,000 Americans participated in a "March on Washington for Jobs and Freedom." This orderly demonstration, which included whites and blacks, was the climax of the generally peaceful civil rights protests of the 1950s and early 1960s. A few months later, in response to the appeals of civil rights advocates, Congress passed the Civil Rights Act of 1964, described as "the most far-reaching civil rights legislation since the Reconstruction era."[1] Two weeks following the passage of this bill riots broke out in Harlem, spread to the Bedford-Stuyvesant area of Brooklyn, and soon reached Rochester, Jersey City, Elizabeth and Patterson, New Jersey, Philadelphia, and other American cities. Thus began several years of violence in the black ghettos of the nation. Robert M. Fogelson reports that "most whites were . . . bewildered because blacks were disavowing the principles and tactics of nonviolent protest applied so successfully in the South in the late 1950s and early 1960s."[2]

On September 16, 1964, the Dean of Students of the University of California at Berkeley announced that students could no longer use a small strip of University property at the Bancroft and Telegraph entrance for political activities and the distribution of advocative literature concerning off-campus political issues. Strong student reaction to this regulation led to the formation of the Free Speech Movement, and the "Berkeley Invention" as it is called in the Scranton Report soon spread to campuses across the nation. Opposition to the war in Vietnam added to the rebellion of college students, and soon sit-ins, lie-ins, the heckling of visiting speakers from the "establishment," and various forms of violence became common occurrences on the college campus. The Decade of Dissent over racism, "repression" on the campus, and the Vietnam War reached its terrible climax in the spring of 1970 with the killing of several students, four by the National Guard at Kent State University, and two by the police at Jackson State College.

---

1. *Revolution in Civil Rights,* 4th ed. (Washington, D.C.: Congressional Quarterly Service, 1968), p. 53.
2. Robert M. Fogelson, *Violence as Protest* (Garden City, N.Y.: Doubleday, 1971), p. 2.

Commissions were appointed to study the violence. Speeches were made and articles and books were written, some attempting to explain "what went wrong" with the nation's commitment to peaceful and orderly change through freedom of speech and assembly, and others attempting to persuade the disruptive militants to return to the orderly processes of persuasion. Justices of the U.S. Supreme Court joined the polemics. In 1968 Justice Abe Fortas wrote that "violence is never defensible," and urged blacks, students, and antiwar dissenters to work within the system of freedom of expression to effect change.[3] And Justice William O. Douglas, dissenting, penned the remarkable opinion: "We must realize that today's Establishment is the new George III. Whether it will continue to adhere to his tactics, we do not know. If it does, the redress, honored in tradition, is . . . rebellion."[4]

What had gone wrong? Whereas the majority of free speech issues in the decades preceding the 1960s had been peacefully resolved in the courts by aggrieved parties, such as Jehovah's Witnesses, Communists, and Negroes,[5] the aggrieved of the 1960s—primarily students, blacks, and opponents of the war—expressed contempt for the slow, nonviolent process of evolutionary change which, theoretically, is made possible by free and open debate guaranteed by the Constitution. Was it true, as charged by the New Left, that freedom of speech had become nothing more than a psychological "safety valve" for blowing off steam rather than a realistic means of effecting change through argument, reason, and democratic decision-making?

What effect did the dissent of the 1960s have upon legal precedents in the area of free speech? How well did the First Amendment serve society? Does the freedom of expression actually promote change? What do aggrieved citizens do when they lose faith in free expression and the type of persuasion which it permits? We shall look at these questions from the perspective of the courts to determine the degree of freedom of expression granted to dissenters in the United States; and from the perspective of the protesting minorities to determine how well the freedom of expression served the purpose of effecting change.

Freedom of Speech in the Courts During the 1960s

First Amendment freedoms were expanded significantly during the 1960s as a result of numerous judicial decisions. As mentioned earlier, the decisions of the U.S. Supreme Court are of particular value in making this judgment. In the long view, court decisions will have more influence on the practice of freedom of expression in the nation than will any number of examples of violent protest, civil disobedience, or even peaceful demonstration. Henry Steele Commager voices an awareness of this principle when he notes that the courts, not by their power to strike down laws, but by their ability to expound law have a great impact upon society. Commager states, "It is as an educational institution that the Court may have

3. Abe Fortas, *Concerning Dissent and Civil Disobedience* (New York: New American Library, 1968), p. 80.

4. William O. Douglas, *Points of Rebellion* (New York: Vintage Books, 1970), p. 95.

5. Harry Kalven, Jr., *The Negro and the First Amendment* (Columbus: Ohio State University Press, 1965), p. 136.

its greatest contribution to make to the understanding and preservation of liberty."[6]

The First Amendment and Black Protest—Arthur I. Waskow describes the Negro sit-in movement, which began in February, 1960, as "creative disorder," and in so doing observes:

To the degree that the politics of disorder is aimed at bringing about change, it is generally invented by people who are "outside" a particular system of political order, and want to bring change about so that they can enter. In doing so, they tend to use new techniques that make sense to themselves out of their own experience, but that look disorderly to people who are thinking and acting inside the system.[7]

A series of court tests of this "creative disorder" was quick in coming. In the 1961 case of Garner v. Louisiana the Supreme Court reversed the convictions of a group of blacks who had conducted a sit-in at a white lunch counter.[8] The Court ruled that this type of peaceful protest was within the range of Constitutional protection.

In the same year as *Garner*, black demonstrators in Columbia, S.C. marched to the grounds of the South Carolina State House "to submit a protest to the citizens of South Carolina" concerning "discriminatory actions against Negroes."[9] The marchers were convicted in the state courts of breach of the peace, but the Supreme Court, in the 1963 reversal of the convictions, stated that "South Carolina infringed the petitioners' constitutionally protected rights of free speech, free assembly, and freedom to petition for redress of grievances."[10] The Court added that the protest in this case represented the "exercise of . . . basic constitutional rights *in their most pristine and classic form.*"[11] (Italics added.) Also decided in 1963 was the case

of NAACP v. Button in which the Supreme Court reversed a holding of the Virginia courts that the NAACP was guilty of improper solicitation of legal business.[12] The Supreme Court decided that the "activities of the NAACP, its affiliates and legal staff shown on this record are modes of expression and association protected by the First and Fourteenth Amendments," then added:

In the context of NAACP objectives, litigation is not a technique of resolving private differences; it is a means for achieving the lawful objectives of equality of treatment by all government, federal, state and local, for the members of the Negro community in this country. It is thus a form of political expression. Groups which find themselves unable to achieve their objectives through the ballot frequently turn to the courts. . . . And under the conditions of modern government, litigation may well be the sole practicable avenue open to a minority for redress of grievances.[13]

Two years later, in two cases entitled Cox v. Louisiana, the Supreme Court further defined the privileges and limitations of using public places for the exercise of First Amendment rights.[14] Cox had led a march of two thousand black college students to a point near the courthouse in downtown Baton Rouge. The police al-

_____

6. Henry Steele Commager, *Freedom and Order* (Cleveland: World Publishing Co., 1968), p. 49.
7. Arthur I. Waskow, *From Race Riot to Sit-In* (Garden City, N.Y.: Doubleday, Anchor, 1967), p. 278.
8. Garner v. Louisiana, 368 U.S. 157 (1961).
9. Edwards v. South Carolina, 372 U.S. 229 (1963), 230.
10. 372 U.S. 235.
11. *Ibid.*
12. NAACP v. Button, 371 U.S. 415 (1963).
13. 371 U.S. 428-430.
14. Cox v. Louisiana, 379 U.S. 536, and 379 U.S. 559 (1965).

lowed the demonstration for a time, then when the students refused an order to disperse, used tear gas to break up the meeting. Cox was arrested, charged, and later convicted of disturbing the peace, obstructing public passages, and picketing near a courthouse. Although the U.S. Supreme Court reversed the convictions of Cox because of the circumstances of the cases, the justices of the Court felt compelled to issue a warning that there was a difference between "pure speech" and speech which is part of picketing or marching, the latter being "speech plus" and therefore not as fully protected as the former. The Court said:

We emphatically reject the notion urged by . . . [Cox] that the First and Fourteenth Amendments afford the same kind of freedom to those who would communicate ideas by conduct such as patrolling, marching, and picketing on streets and highways, as these amendments afford to those who communicate ideas by pure speech.[15]

In Brown v. Louisiana, decided in 1966, the Supreme Court reversed the convictions of blacks who had conducted a brief "stand-up" in a public library which was reserved for the use of whites only.[16] The Court emphasized that the rights of the First Amendment "are not confined to verbal expression," adding that these rights "embrace appropriate types of action which certainly include the right in a peaceable and orderly manner to protest by silent and reproachful presence, in a place where the protestant has every right to be, the unconstitutional segregation of public facilities."[17]

There are some places where protestants do not have the right to be, however, as clarified in the 1966 case of Adderley v. Florida.[18] Adderley and a group of stu-

dents conducted a demonstration on the grounds of the Leon County, Fla. jail. In a 5-4 decision the Supreme Court affirmed their conviction pointing out that "in *Edwards*, the demonstrators went to the South Carolina State Capitol grounds in protest. In [Adderley] . . . they went to the jail. Traditionally, state capitol grounds are open to the public. Jails, built for security purposes, are not."[19]

In 1969 the Supreme Court reversed the conviction of Shuttlesworth, a black civil rights leader, who had been convicted in the Alabama courts of parading without a permit.[20] The Court pointed out that in this case the city ordinance under which the conviction was obtained was too broad, conferring upon the City Commission "virtually unbridled and absolute power to prohibit any 'parade,' 'procession,' or 'demonstration' on the city's streets or public ways."[21] Confirming the trend of the decade concerning the use of the streets for the exercise of First Amendment rights, the Court emphatically asserted that the privilege of using public places "for communication of views on national questions . . . must not, in the guise of regulation, be abridged or denied."[22] The ordinance was administered so as "in the words of Chief Justice Hughes, 'to deny or unwarrantedly abridge the right of assembly and the opportunities for the communication of

15. 379 U.S. 555.
16. Brown v. Louisiana, 383 U.S. 131 (1966).
17. 383 U.S. 141-42.
18. 385 U.S. 39 (1966).
19. 385 U.S. 41.
20. Shuttlesworth v. Birmingham, 394 U.S. 147 (1969).
21. 394 U.S. 150.
22. 394 U.S. 152.

thought . . . immemorially associated with resort to public places.' "[23]

In summary, black protest during the 1960s helped to establish a number of First Amendment principles. These principles include: (1) sit-ins, marches, parades, demonstrations, and picketing activities can be expressions of ideas, and are protected by the First Amendment; (2) the use of streets, parks, and similar public places for assembly, petition, and speaking is a basic right; (3) however, these activities are "speech plus," and are not as fully protected as is "pure speech"; (4) states can, by narrowly drawn statutes, control the use of public places as to time and place, but cannot absolutely deny their use; (5) and litigation and the use of the courts can be within itself a type of forum by which a minority can win a hearing for its grievances.

The First Amendment and Seditious Libel: the *New York Times* Case—Harry Kalven, Jr., asserts that "the absence of seditious libel as a crime is the true pragmatic test of freedom of speech." In other words, he argues, "a free society is one in which you cannot defame the government."[24] The seriousness with which the U.S. Supreme Court views the doctrine of sedition as a threat to free speech is basic to the 1964 landmark decision in New York Times Co. v. Sullivan.[25]

On March 29, 1960, an advertisement entitled "Heed Their Rising Voices" which had been placed by a group of Alabama civil rights activists appeared in the *New York Times*. The text charged that southern Negro students engaged in nonviolent demonstrations "in positive affirmation of the right to live in human dignity" were being met by an "unprecedented wave of ter-ror by those who would deny and negate" the Constitution and the Bill of Rights.[26] Specific examples of "terror" were cited in the advertisement, and an appeal for funds was made.

Even though he was not named in the advertisement, L.B. Sullivan claimed civil libel on the grounds that the statement contained falsehoods which reflected upon him since he was Commissioner of Public Affairs for Montgomery, and his duties included supervision of the Police Department. A number of factual errors in the advertisement were proved, and an Alabama jury awarded Sullivan damages of $500,000. The Alabama Supreme Court affirmed.

In reversing the decision of the Alabama courts, the U.S. Supreme Court drew parallels between the historical issue of sedition and the case in point. After referring to the Sedition Act of 1798 and quoting freely from James Madison and from the Virginia Resolution of 1798, the Court said, "Thus we consider this case against the background of a profound national commitment to the principle that *debate on public issues should be uninhibited, robust, and wide-open*, and that it may well include vehement, caustic, and sometimes unpleasantly sharp attacks on government and public officials."[27] (Italics added.) Recognizing that the advertisement in question did include some false statements, the Court reasoned that "erroneous" state-

---

23. 394 U.S. 159.
24. Kalven, *The Negro and the First Amendment*, p. 16.
25. 376 U.S. 254 (1964).
26. 376 U.S. 256.
27. 376 U.S. 270.

ments are bound to occur in free debate, but that such statements must be protected if a clash of views is to have the "breathing space" essential for survival. Libel, said the Court, "can claim no talismanic immunity from constitutional limitations. It must be measured by standards that satisfy the First Amendment."[28] The Court then phrased its "landmark" test: "The constitutional guarantees require, we think, a federal rule that prohibits a public official from recovering damages for a defamatory falsehood relating to his official conduct unless he proves that the statement was made with 'actual malice'—that is, with knowledge that it was false or with reckless disregard of whether it was false or not."[29]

The Court's action in *New York Times* set the stage for a series of rulings in which the Justices debate the place of freedom of speech in our society. The first such case, Garrison v. Louisiana, reversed the criminal libel conviction of the District Attorney of Orleans Parish, Louisiana, on the grounds that his criticisms of a number of judges was speech protected by the *Times* principle.[30] The Court stated, "Where criticism of public officials is concerned, we see no merit in the argument that criminal libel statutes serve interests distinct from those secured by civil libel laws, and therefore should not be subject to the same limitations."[31] Even the private reputation of a public official is covered by the *Times* decision, the Court asserted, for private matters of "dishonesty, malfeasance, or improper motivation" are part of the public's interest in determining whether or not a man is fit for office. The Court then ruled the Louisiana Criminal Defamation Statute unconstitutional because it failed to provide the "actual malice" test of *Times.*

In Rosenblatt v. Baer, decided a few months after *Garrison*, the Supreme Court reversed the libel conviction of newspaper columnist Rosenblatt, and in the process addressed itself to the matter of how far down the "hierarchy" of public officials the *Times* rule applied.[32] Rosenblatt had been critical of the administration of the Belknap County, N.H., Recreation Area, a resort owned and operated by the county. Baer, who was not named by Rosenblatt but who was supervisor of the area during the period about which Rosenblatt raised questions, sued on the grounds of defamatory falsehood. In explaining its decision to reverse, the Supreme Court stated:

There is, first, a strong interest in debate on public issues, and, second, a strong interest in debate about those persons who are in a position significantly to influence the resolution of those issues. Criticism of government is at the very center of the constitutionally protected area of free discussion. Criticism of those responsible for government operations must be free, lest criticism of government itself be penalized. It is clear, therefore, that the "public official" designation applies at the very least to those among the hierarchy of government employees who have, or appear to the public to have, substantial responsibility for or control over the conduct of governmental affairs.[33]

The *New York Times* case and those which were based upon it are significant for at least four reasons.[34] First, they show a willingness of the Court to grapple with

---

28. 376 U.S. 269-272.

29. 376 U.S. 279-280.

30. Garrison v. Louisiana, 379 U.S. 64 (1964).

31. 379 U.S. 67.

32. Rosenblatt v. Baer, 383 U.S. 75 (1966).

33. 383 U.S. 85.

34. See Time, Inc. v. Hill, 385 U.S. 374 (1967), in which the Court applied the *Times* doctrine to the area of invasion of privacy by the Press; and Curtis Publishing Co. v. Butts and Associated Press v. Walker, 388 U.S. 130 (1967), both decided in one opinion, which helps to clarify the meaning of "public official."

perplexing First Amendment problems; second, they provide a vehicle for a vigorous statement of the nation's commitment to free and open debate; third, they clearly demolish the traditional wall between libel and First Amendment freedoms; and finally, they establish that insofar as libel laws operate as sedition laws by silencing criticism of public officials the laws are unconstitutional except when actual malice is proved.

The First Amendment and Antiwar Dissent—One has only to compare the prosecutions of antiwar expression during the 1960s with those of World War I to see how far the nation has progressed in its dedication to the First Amendment and in its tolerance of vigorous dissent. Zechariah Chafee, Jr., reports that two thousand prosecutions were conducted under the Espionage Act of World War I, with almost all of the convictions based upon "expressions of opinion about the merits and conduct of the war."[35] However, the general tolerance of antiwar rhetoric in the 1960s was not without its critics. Representative Edward Hebert of Louisiana became so intent on seeing that war critics were punished that he suggested that the nation simply "forget the First Amendment."[36] And David Lawrence, in response to the Supreme Court's decision in the *Tinker* case, fulminated that the school children who wore black armbands to protest the Vietnam War were giving aid and comfort to the enemy, and were, therefore, guilty of "symbolic" treason.[37]

The U.S. Supreme Court addressed itself to the matter of freedom of speech and opposition to the war in its 1966 decision in the case of Bond v. Floyd.[38] Julian Bond had been prevented from taking his seat in the Georgia House of Representatives because he had endorsed an antiwar statement issued by the Student Nonviolent Coordinating Committee of which he was Communications Director. The lower courts had upheld the action of the Georgia House which had by a vote of 184 to 12 decided not to seat Bond because his antiwar statements had given aid and comfort to the enemy. In reversing the decision of the lower courts the Supreme Court said "there can be no question but that the First Amendment protects expressions in opposition to national foreign policy in Vietnam and the Selective Service system."[39] Going further, the Court stated that Bond's opinions were not a matter of disloyalty, but were matters of a "legislators' capacity to discuss [his] views of local or national policy."[40]

The symbolic protest of burning one's draft card was not viewed with the same sympathy as was Bond's "pure speech." In the 1968 case of United States v. O'Brien the Supreme Court upheld the conviction of David Paul O'Brien who in 1966 had burned his Selective Service registration certificate on the steps of the South Boston Courthouse.[41] O'Brien had been convicted in Federal District Court, but the Court of Appeals had reversed on First Amendment grounds. The Supreme Court agreed with the District Court in finding the law under

---

35. Zechariah Chafee, Jr., *Free Speech in the United States* (Cambridge, Mass.: Harvard University Press, 1964), p. 51.

36. Jessica Mitford, "Guilty as Charged by the Judge," *Atlantic*, August, 1969, p. 52.

37. David Lawrence, "Is Treason Permissible as Merely 'Free Speech'?" *U.S. News and World Report*, March 10, 1969, p. 108.

38. 385 U.S. 116 (1966).

39. 385 U.S. 132.

40. 385 U.S. 135.

41. United States v. O'Brien, 391 U.S. 367 (1968).

which O'Brien was convicted to be constitutional. "A law prohibiting destruction of Selective Service certificates," ruled the Court, "no more abridges free speech on its face than a motor vehicle law prohibiting the destruction of drivers' licenses, or a tax law prohibiting the destruction of books and records."[42] The Court pointed out that when "speech" and "nonspeech" elements are combined in a case, "a sufficiently important governmental interest in regulating the nonspeech element can justify incidental limitations on First Amendment freedoms."[43] The draft card serves at least four useful purposes, according to the decision:

1. The registration certificate serves as proof that the individual described thereon has registered for the draft . . . .
2. The information supplied on the certificates facilitates communication between registrants and local boards . . . .
3. Both certificates carry continual reminders that the registrant must notify his local board of any change of address, and other specified changes in his status. . . .
4. The regulatory scheme involving Selective Service certificates includes clearly valid prohibitions against the alteration, forgery, or similar deceptive misuse of certificates. The destruction or mutilation . . . increases the difficulty of detecting and tracing abuses such as these. Further, a mutilated certificate might itself be used for deceptive purposes.[44]

During the time that O'Brien's draft card case was being adjudicated a related case made its way into the courts. Following the demonstrations of Stop the Draft Week in October, 1967, Selective Service Director Hershey addressed a letter to each draft board urging that antiwar demonstrators be declared delinquent under the provisions of the Selective Service regulations. Hershey wrote that "illegal activity which interferes with recruiting or causes refusal of duty in

the military or naval forces could not by any stretch of the imagination be construed as being in the National interest."[45]

The National Student Association challenged Hershey's directive in the courts, arguing that it had a "chilling effect" upon the freedom of speech of the demonstrators. In June, 1969, the Court of Appeals for the District of Columbia agreed with the students in principle, and ruled that Hershey's memorandum was "not authorized by Selective Service laws or delinquency regulations." The Court stated that the memorandum did infringe upon free speech, for it might deter not only "validly proscribed conduct," but also "any protest activity which a registrant could plausibly expect his draft board to think unprotected or illegal."[46]

Two additional trials provide a climax to the adjudication of antiwar protest in the 1960s. In 1968 Dr. Benjamin Spock and his codefendants were tried for conspiracy to interfere with the operation of the Selective Service system. And in the winter of 1969-70 the "Great Conspiracy Trial" of the Chicago Seven, all of whom were charged with violation of the antiriot provisions of the Civil Rights Act of 1968 for their activities at the Democratic Convention held that year in Chicago, was conducted in the courtroom of Judge Julius Hoffman. In both cases the government, by sidestepping many First Amendment issues in charging *conspiracy*, indirectly recognized the high degree of protection provided by the courts to dissident speech. The principle is ex-

---

42. 391 U.S. 375.
43. 391 U.S. 376.
44. 391 U.S. 378-80.
45. Mitford, "Guilty as Charged," p. 51.
46. 37 *Law Week.* 3689 (1969).

plained by Jason Epstein in reference to the Chicago trial as follows:

The indictment [of the Chicago Seven] had nothing to do with freedom of speech or assembly [according to the government] but with certain criminal intentions, of which the defendants' speeches and rallies were merely the outward signs. The punishable crime, under the antiriot statute, occurred within the minds of the defendants, and the Constitution says nothing about states of mind. To [the prosecution] . . . therefore, the First Amendment was beside the point. Thus they persisted in their objections whenever the defense attempted to raise questions of freedom of expression or assembly. . . . The defendants' expressions were not at issue. It was their unexpressed intentions for which they were on trial.[47]

Defendants in both trials were found guilty, but the Court of Appeals reversed the convictions of Spock and one codefendant, and remanded the other codefendants for a new trial. The Chicago jury found that the defendants were not guilty of conspiracy, but convicted five of the seven on the lesser charge of crossing a state line with the intention of inciting a riot. This conviction is on appeal.

The First Amendment and the Schools— The case of Tinker v. Des Moines Independent Community School District, decided in 1969, is important to this analysis, not only because it arose from the antiwar dissent of the decade but also because it has wide implications for the free speech of students regardless of the stimulus for the expression.[48] In this case three public school pupils had been suspended for wearing black armbands to protest the war in Vietnam. Since the students were not disruptive, and since their method of dissent was "closely akin to 'pure speech,' " the Supreme Court ruled that the suspensions were improper. Teachers and students have

First Amendment rights, for, said the Court, "it can hardly be argued that either students or teachers shed their constitutional rights to freedom of speech or expression at the schoolhouse gate."[49] And in strong words the Court added:

In our system, state-operated schools may not be enclaves of totalitarianism. School officials do not possess absolute authority over their students. Students in school as well as out of school are "persons" under our Constitution. They are possessed of fundamental rights which the State must respect, just as they themselves must respect their obligations to the State. In our system, students may not be regarded as closed-circuit recipients of only that which the State chooses to communicate. They may not be confined to the expression of those sentiments that are officially approved. In the absence of a specific showing of constitutionally valid reasons to regulate their speech, students are entitled to freedom of expression of their views. . . .[50]

In Keyishian v. Board of Regents the Supreme Court confirmed that in its view, the academic freedom of teachers is "a special concern of the First Amendment."[51] And in Pickering v. Board of Education the Supreme Court upheld the right of a public school teacher to criticize the Board of Education without concern that his criticism would result in dismissal. Such a threat, the Court said, is a "potent means of inhibiting speech."[52] Finally, during the 1960s the lower federal courts ruled that the North Carolina speaker ban law and the proposed

47. Jason Epstein, *The Great Conspiracy Trial* (New York: Random House, 1970), p. 173.
48. Tinker v. Des Moines Independent Community School District, 393 U.S. 503 (1969).
49. 393 U.S. 506.
50. 393 U.S. 511.
51. Keyishian v. Board of Regents, 385 U.S. 589 (1967) at 603.
52. Pickering v. Board of Education, 391 U.S. 563 (1968), at 574.

speaker ban regulations of the Mississippi Board of Higher Education were unconstitutional, thus eliminating a threat to freedom of speech on the college campus and setting a precedent which will no doubt deter others who wish to censor speech in academe.[53]

The First Amendment and Broadcasting: The *Red Lion* Case—The significance of the case of Red Lion Broadcasting Co., v. Federal Communications Commission will become more apparent as one considers the question of access to the media raised by numerous dissenters during the 1960s and discussed later in this chapter.[54] In this case the Supreme Court upheld the "fairness doctrine" principle which requires broadcasters to provide fair coverage of each side of public issues. The Court ruled that the Red Lion Broadcasting Company did have to abide by a ruling of the FCC requiring free time for Fred J. Cook to reply to an attack made on him by Rev. Billy James Hargis in a "Christian Crusade" radio program.

Soon after the litigation in the *Red Lion* case began, the FCC adopted a new rule to make the "fairness doctrine" more precise. The new regulation went further than the "fairness doctrine," under which the broadcaster could himself present the view of the attacked party or select a third party to do so, by requiring "that the individual attacked himself be offered an opportunity to respond."[55] In addition, the new regulation specified that "where one candidate is endorsed in a political editorial, the other candidates must themselves be offered reply time to use personally or through a spokesman."[56] The Court, in rejecting the argument of the Radio Television News Directors Association and upholding the FCC, stated that "the right of free speech

of a broadcaster, the user of a sound truck, or any other individual does not embrace a right to snuff out the free speech of others."[57]

Freedom of Speech and the Dissenters of the 1960s.

The preceding discussion of court action in the area of freedom of speech demonstrates that the legal right to speak out on matters of race, war, education, governmental policy and other issues was expanded during the 1960s. Why, then, in the light of unprecedented freedom to speak did many individuals and groups choose violence? What, in effect, do the 1960s tell us about the strengths and weaknesses of free speech as an instrument for change in a complex, technical era? What follows is an attempt to suggest some of the answers to these questions by examining (1) typical successes of the dissenters, (2) the criticisms of freedom of speech voiced by many dissenters because of the difficulties in achieving some successes, and (3) significant proposals for correcting a major deficiency in First Amendment theory and practice as revealed by the dissenters of the period.

The mixture of legal and illegal protest employed during the decade enabled

---

53. For a discussion of the North Carolina speaker ban decision see *Free Speech*, the newsletter of the Committee on Freedom of Speech of the Speech Communication Association, March, 1968; the Mississippi case is summarized in 38 *Law Wk.* 2333 (1969).

54. Red Lion Broadcasting Co., Inc. v. Federal Communications Commission, and United States v. Radio Television New Directors Association, both decided in one opinion, 395 U.S. 367 (1969).

55. 395 U.S. 378.

56. *Ibid.*

57. 395 U.S. 387.

blacks, students, and opponents of the war to register notable successes in changing the minds and actions of others. Blacks were effective throughout the decade in securing their legal rights, primarily by constitutional means. This fact is supported by the cases reviewed earlier in this chapter, and by the legislative record which includes the Civil Rights Acts of 1960, 1964, 1965, 1967, and 1968.

Students registered many successes during the 1960s in their efforts to persuade faculties, administrators, and trustees to heed their grievances and to make changes in academia. In spite of many well-publicized examples of violence on the campus, most expressions of discontent were nonviolent, and the result has been and still is a serious reevaluation of higher education in America. In a 1971 address delivered to Rio Grande College, Alan Reitman, Associate Director of the American Civil Liberties Union, lists the following areas of discontent which have been resolved on numerous campuses as a result of student protest: (1) free and open discussion in the classroom; (2) a privileged relationship between student and teacher, including the confidentiality of student records; (3) student involvement in formulating academic policy; (4) full freedom in organizing clubs and societies, including the nondisclosure of membership lists and use of campus facilities; (5) freedom of selection of controversial speakers for student—sponsored forums; (6) freedom of expression in student newspapers and radio stations; (7) off-campus participation in political causes of the student's choice; (8) dress and grooming codes which support personal expression and taste; (9) full due process in disciplinary proceedings; and (10) only "single penalties" for committing off-campus offenses, without the institution invoking additional sanctions.[58]

Those who opposed the war in Vietnam enjoyed unprecedented freedom of expression to persuade the American public to accept their view—so successful, in fact, that deescalation of the conflict, troop withdrawal, and a peace agreement have become national policy. In general, the nation has been tolerant of the antiwar dissent and the courts have upheld the principle of constitutional protection for peaceful opposition to the war.

While it is generally true that the dissenters of the 1960s met with significant success in reaching and securing a hearing from their audiences, they also experienced frustrations and failures. The New Left has been particularly critical of free speech as a method of achieving change, arguing that it is too slow, that it really does not allow radical expression, and that the mass media which reflect and defend the status quo are not open to minority views. Thomas I. Emerson observes that these criticisms "are not without some factual foundation."[59]

Several schools of thought emerge from the debate over the relevance of the First Amendment to contemporary society. One school of thought argues that *violence* is the only effective means of protest open to today's minorities. Fogelson reports that the ghetto rioters of the 1960s felt "accomplishment," not because of the destruction, and not because they were revolutionaries,

58. Alan Reitman, "On Changing Value Patterns of Youth—and the Campus of the 70's," speech delivered at Rio Grande College, Ohio, February 9, 1971. (Typewritten.) Author has a copy.
59. Thomas I. Emerson, *The System of Freedom of Expression* (New York: Random House, 1970), pp. 726-27.

but because the riots were a "singularly successful attempt at communication."[60] Once the riots were underway, he adds, white society paid attention. Reporters, television crews, public officials, sociologists, and scholars rushed to the ghettos. Commissions were appointed. The President, governors, and mayors promised reform. And the militants of the ghettos "boasted that they had accomplished in a few days what older moderates had failed to do in a few decades."[61]

A second school of thought opposes violence but, lacking faith in the traditional procedure of debating the issues in the marketplace of ideas, urges the acceptance of nonviolent *civil disobedience* as a means of reaching the audience. Carl Cohen reports that a group of dissenters in Ann Arbor, Michigan, argued that even though they had practiced civil disobedience by deliberately violating a state law, their protest should be protected by the Constitution because it was "clearly a form of political speech."[62] Lawrence R. Velvel relates the issue of civil disobedience to freedom of speech in a different manner. He states:

To a certain extent, people engage in civil disobedience for the same reasons that people engage in free speech. Like speech, civil disobedience is an attempt to call attention to problems and to publicize views about how they should be solved. It is an attempt, in other words, to have certain ideas enter into the market place of ideas. Then, too, also like free speech, by calling attention to people's grievances and views, civil disobedience helps to make government and the public more aware of these grievances and views and more responsive to them. Finally, like free speech, it has a cathartic effect: it enables people to vent deep-seated feelings in a relatively peaceful way and thereby helps to keep the American cauldron from boiling over into even greater violence than we already have.[63]

A third school of thought, arguing that neither violence nor civil disobedience is necessary to compensate for the failures of free speech, presents a case of "status quo with repairs" by proposing the adoption by the government of imaginative *affirmative programs* for the promotion of First Amendment principles. The turmoil of the 1960s has provided significant momentum to this third school of thought, and it is this development—not the theorizing of Marcuse or the urgings of those who believe in violence or civil disobedience—which emerges as one of the most important developments of the Decade of Dissent.[64]

Charles A. Reich, examining the efforts of the blacks in the 1950s and early 1960s to be heard "in the impersonal din of the modern world," describes America's blacks as great innovators for their techniques of freedom rides, mass demonstrations, passive resistance, stand-ins, sit-ins, lie-ins, the March on Washington, and "an unprecedented recourse to law and the courts."[65]

60. Fogelson, *Violence as Protest*, p. 85.

61. *Ibid.*, p. 86.

62. Carl Cohen, "Law, Speech, and Disobedience," in *Civil Disobedience: Theory and Practice*, ed. Hugo A. Bedau (New York: Pegasus, 1969), p. 166.

63. Lawrence R. Velvel, *Undeclared War and Civil Disobedience: the American System in Crisis* (New York: Dunellen Publishing Co., 1970), p. 189.

64. Thomas I. Emerson seems to agree with this view when he states, "The most challenging problems in First Amendment theory today lie in the prospect of using law affirmatively to promote more effective functioning of the system of freedom of expression." Emerson, *The System*, p. 627. Note: The idea that free speech should be affirmatively promoted through law is not new. See Zechariah Chafee, Jr., *Government and Mass Communications: a Report from the Commission on Freedom of the Press* (Chicago: University of Chicago Press, 1947). What is new is the seriousness with which the idea is being considered as a result of the violence of the 1960s.

65. Charles A. Reich, "Making Free Speech Audible," *The Nation*, February 8, 1965, p. 138.

Affirmative steps are needed, he argues, to assist black Americans and other minorities in their recourse to persuasion through peaceful means. Among his recommendations are the following:

Government might make more public halls and auditoriums available free of charge for holding meetings, as is sometimes done with local school auditoriums. This helps free speech in general, and minorities in particular. Government might increase mailing subsidies for publications. The FCC could allocate more of the television spectrum for educational or public affairs, noncommercial broadcasting. And government might aid the arts, which are an important outlet for the expression of new ideas.[66]

Reich concludes by pointing out that without the affirmative support of law, freedom of expression—which he describes as an "18th-century privateer in an age of massed power"—is in danger of being significantly weakened. The effort to preserve our freedoms "is the great challenge for law and government, today and tomorrow."[67]

The subject was given a generous boost in 1967 with the publication of Jerome A. Barron's essay, "Access to the Press—A New First Amendment Right," in the *Harvard Law Review*.[68] Barron begins his article with this paragraph:

There is an anomaly in our constitutional law. While we protect expression once it has come to the fore, our law is indifferent to creating opportunities for expression. Our constitutional theory is in the grip of a romantic conception of free expression, a belief that the "marketplace of ideas" is freely accessible. But if ever there were a self-operating marketplace of ideas, it has long ceased to exist. The mass media's development of an antipathy to ideas requires legal intervention if novel and unpopular ideas are to be assured a forum—unorthodox points of view which have no claim on broadcast time and newspaper space as a matter of right are in poor position to compete with those aired as a matter of grace.[69]

Barron expresses agreement with the observation of W.H. Ferry that demonstrations have become the "free press of the movement to win justice for Negroes,"[70] adding that this indicates "the inadequacy of old media as instruments to afford full and effective hearing for all points of view."[71] He reaches the heart of his argument when he states:

What is required is an interpretation of the first amendment which focuses on the idea that restraining the hand of government is quite useless in assuring free speech if a restraint on access is effectively secured by private groups. A constitutional prohibition against governmental restrictions on expression is effective only if the Constitution ensures an adequate opportunity for discussion. Since this opportunity exists only in the mass media, the interests of those who control the means of communication must be accomodated with the interests of those who seek a forum in which to express their point of view.[72]

Barron suggests that access to the press could be accomplished in two ways, by judicial enforcement and by legislation, with the latter being the preferred solution. By way of illustration, Emerson in his analysis of Barron's thesis suggests four types of materials which the press might be compelled by law to publish:

66. *Ibid.*, p. 141.

67. *Ibid.*

68. Jerome A. Barron, "Access to the Press—A New First Amendment Right," *Harvard Law Review* 80 (1967):1641-78.

69. *Ibid.*, p. 1641.

70. W. H. Ferry, "Masscomm as Educator," *American Scholar* 35 (Spring, 1966):300. Ferry also states that demonstrations have become the free press for students who are attempting "to banish impersonality from the university and the corporation, and to spread the word that peace, not violence, is the only possible destiny for a nuclear-knowing world."

71. Barron, "Access to the Press," p. 1647.

72. *Ibid.*, p. 1656.

First, the newspaper might be required to accept paid noncommercial advertisements, in which controversial issues could be discussed or minority views expressed. Secondly, the newspaper might be compelled to grant roughly equal space in its columns to any person who has been libeled or personally attacked in order that he may make a reply. Thirdly, the newspaper might be made to open its letters-to-the-editor columns or make other space available for statements by individuals or groups on issues not reported or on viewpoints not represented by the paper. Finally, a kind of "fairness doctrine," similar to that employed in radio and television, could be imposed on newspapers, requiring them to provide on their own motion for coverage of all "newsworthy" subject matter and expression of all "responsible" viewpoints.[73]

In 1968 Barron was asked to present his views on the First Amendment to the Biennial National Conference of the American Civil Liberties Union. Following discussions on Barron's idea, the Conference made a number of recommendations in support of access to the media, including: (1) lawsuits to challenge the "discriminatory refusal" of advertisements and notices by publications; (2) a study of suits to challenge patterns of "lerogatory treatment" by publications of individuals and organizations where no opportunity for reply is allowed; (3) the distribution by "government instrumentalities" of pamphlets in which space is made available to all political candidates to state their platforms; (4) that a permanent citizens advisory commission be established for the purpose of evaluating "whether the mass media are improperly denying the right of access to competing views"; (5) a study of a recommendation that daily newspapers voluntarily institute a policy of providing editorial space to unedited news and opinion contributions from the public; (6) support for a program of government subsidy of public broadcasting.[74]

Even though the National Board of the ACLU decided not to implement the recommendations of the Conference on access to the media, extensive discussion of and continuing interest in the ideas advanced resulted. The 1970 annual meeting of the American Society of Newspaper Editors heard from its Freedom of Information Committee a report concerned with the subject of access to the media. Gilbert Cranberg, in reporting the development, observes that the attention given by the ASNE to the idea of "right of access" is unprecedented, and "is a measure of its impact during the three years since it was proposed by Professor . . . Barron."[75] He concludes wryly by noting that some officials of the newspaper industry are so disturbed over the proposals for access that they "wish Mr. Barron had never studied law."[76]

The most thorough consideration of the subject to date is presented by Thomas I. Emerson who believes that "government must affirmatively make available the opportunity for expression as well as protect it from encroachment."[77] His 1970 publication, *The System of Freedom of Expression*, includes a lengthy chapter on the problem, and provides an analysis of such matters as (1) furnishing facilities for the expression of ideas, (2) the regulation of radio and television, (3) the regulation of the

---

73. Emerson, *The System*, p. 670. Note: For an important court decision on the "fairness" principle, see the discussion of the *Red Lion* case earlier in this chapter.

74. "Report of 1968 Biennial Conference of the American Civil Liberties Union," New York, 1968, pp. 55-56, (Mimeographed.) Author has a copy.

75. Gilbert Cranberg, "Is 'Right of Access' Coming?" *Saturday Review*, August 8, 1970, p. 48.

76. *Ibid.*, p. 57.

77. Emerson, *The System*, p. 629.

press, and (4) the supplying of the "raw materials" of information, ideas, and alternative solutions, and improving the skills of understanding and appraisal necessary for the system of free speech to function properly. He concludes that the government "can probably do more to vitalize the system by supplying raw materials and improving the skills with which they are employed than by any other form of promotion."[78]

Conclusion

Despite many efforts at the "grassroots" of society to suppress freedom of speech during the 1960s, the right to protest, demonstrate, and express one's opinion both directly and indirectly was greatly expanded by the courts. This expansion proved inadequate, however, for many dissidents who discovered that the media were not open to them for the expression of opinions and for reaching the appropriate audience. One result was that violence and civil disobedience were adopted by many as alternatives to lawful dissent. These extra-legal activities, in conjunction with lawful means of expression, proved effective in reaching audiences and changing opinions and policies.

Out of the decade has emerged a constructive concern for providing access to the media so that, in the future, violence and civil disobedience will prove unnecessary as means of securing attention and communicating with the citizens of the nation. This development of support for affirmative promotion by the government of First Amendment rights is the quiet revolution in freedom of speech of the 1960s, and it deserves the most thoughtful consideration of those who believe that speech should continue to be a tool of democracy

useful for helping to resolve the issues of a contemporary society.

Bibliography

Chafee, Zechariah, Jr. *Free Speech in the United States.* Cambridge, Mass.: Harvard University Press, 1941.
Standard authority for the study of free speech from the time of the Alien and Sedition Acts to the 1940s. Includes Chafee's theory of the First Amendment. Useful for comparing contemporary First Amendment freedoms with those of the past.

Clark, David G., and Hutchison, Earl R., eds. *Mass Media and the Law: Freedom and Restraint.* New York: Wiley and Sons, 1970.
Excellent collection of viewpoints about the effect of the mass media upon freedom of speech and the democratic process. Subjects included cover prior restraint, right of access, and invasion of privacy.

Emerson, Thomas I. *The System of Freedom of Expression.* New York: Random House, 1970.
Surveys the development of First Amendment principles according to major problem areas, such as freedom of belief, external and internal security, obscenity, libel and privacy, and academic freedom. Develops Emerson's expression-action theory of freedom of speech, and includes a discussion of affirmative promotion of free speech by the government. A valuable reference work, lucid in style and comprehensive in scope.

Epstein, Jason. *The Great Conspiracy Trial.* New York: Random House, 1970.
An analysis of the trial of the Chicago Seven accused of conspiracy to provoke violence at the Democratic Convention in 1968. Presents an analysis of how the charge of conspiracy overwhelms traditional First Amendment freedoms.

Fogelson, Robert M. *Violence as Protest: A Study of Riots and Ghettos.* Garden City, N.Y.: Doubleday, 1971.
A study of the ghetto violence of the 1960s, developing the thesis that when minorities are denied access to lines of communication

---

78. *Ibid.*, pp. 627-73.

then riots become a means of speaking to the public about grievances.

Kalven, Harry, Jr. *The Negro and the First Amendment.* Columbus: Ohio State University Press, 1965.
Four lectures delivered by Professor Kalven in 1964 concerning how the civil rights movement has effected the "reworking of First Amendment doctrine" in the United States.

Mitford, Jessica. *The Trial of Dr. Spock.* New York: Alfred A. Knopf, 1969.
An account of the conspiracy trial of Dr. Benjamin Spock and his codefendants. Like Epstein, Mitford is concerned with the charge of conspiracy and how it infringes upon First Amendment freedoms.

Rucker, Bryce W. *The First Freedom.* Carbondale, Ill.: Southern Illinois University Press, 1968.
A study of how newspaper chains and monopolies and the centralizing of control in the wire services and in broadcasting interfere with the communication of minority viewpoints and thus inhibit freedom of speech. An updating of Morris L. Ernst's 1946 study which bears the same title.

Velvel, Lawrence R. *Undeclared War and Civil Disobedience: The American System in Crisis.* New York: The Dunellen Co., 1970.
A study of the principle of civil disobedience as practiced at various times in American history. Special application of the subject to war protest, together with interesting comments concerning the relationship of civil disobedience to freedom of speech.

Zinn, Howard. *Disobedience and Democracy: Nine Fallacies on Law and Order.* New York: Random House, Vintage, 1968.
An interesting point-by-point rebuttal to the arguments concerning civil disobedience advanced by Abe Fortas in *Concerning Dissent and Civil Disobedience*, Signet, 1968. Should be read in conjunction with the Fortas work.

23 Youth Rebels: A Decade of Protest

Gladys Ritchie

The Issues

According to a June, 1970, Gallup Poll, campus unrest was thought to be the nation's *main* problem. No doubt the recent deaths of five students during demonstrations and counter-demonstrations at Kent State and Jackson State Universities had weighed heavily in the voting of the citizens polled by Gallup. Yet Americans had been worrying their way through a decade of student protest that had begun quietly enough with passive sit-ins but had erupted into verbal confrontation, destruction of property, physical violence and death.

Establishment response to student protest, especially during the second half of the decade, focused largely on student tactics. When New York Senator Jacob Javits spoke to the Women's National Republican Club in May of 1968, he tried to call attention to the issues in the Columbia strike. "What the kids are fighting for at Columbia is a piece of the action. They want to be consulted, to have a vote, an opportunity to campaign for what they think is right. What's wrong with that?"

The ladies in the audience could not hold back their response. "No! No! Not *that* way!" they shouted.

The chairman of the club declared, "There is such a thing as law and order!"

To calm the ladies and to retain their support, Senator Javits had to speak a second time and qualify his early plea for attention to the issues of the students. "What I meant to say is that there is a need to learn what college youths are asking to obtain. I'm against sit-ins and anarchy and vandalism. . . . But this shouldn't divert us from the fact that there is a role for students to play in university life."[1]

Richard M. Nixon, campaigning in 1968 for the presidential nomination, felt no need to inquire into what college youths were asking to obtain; he was certain of their goal. He declared the Columbia uprising to be "the first major skirmish in a revolutionary struggle to seize the universities of this country and transform them into sanctuaries for radicals and . . . for revolutionary, political and social goals." Angered at student tactics, he warned his audience, "Rid the campus now of any groups that participated in or supported the recent disruptions that closed the school."[2]

1. *New York Times*, May 28, 1968, p. 31.
2. *New York Times*, May 10, 1968, p. 1.

In general, the American public was diverted from consideration of the issues behind student protest by the rage with which it responded to protest actions. Since rage is blind and fury deaf, many middle-aged Americans neither read nor listened to the student spokesmen who tried to present the issues.

One spokesman was Thomas Hayden, a young man who played many roles in the student "revolution" of the 1960s—beginning as founding president of Students for a Democratic Society, being present and accounted for at major student uprisings throughout the period, and ending the decade as a defendant in the infamous Chicago Seven Trial.

In 1961, Hayden, then editor of the daily University of Michigan newspaper, was writing about student disenchantment with the American way of life. In an open letter to the New Student Left, he accused America of failing "to deal with the hard facts of poverty" and placed the blame for that failure on "the drift of decision-making powers away from the directly representative legislative institutions into corporative and military hands." He charged that in America there persists "a racism that mocks our principles and corrupts everyday life." He condemned the "exploitation of our natural resources" and denounced "the ugliness and ill-planned nature of our cities."[3]

In a speech at the University of Michigan in 1962, Tom Hayden again indicted America, this time calling it a society that "basically values money and power, conformity and success, established habits and the status quo," a society that tolerates the "endless machines that grind up men's jobs, the few hundred corporations that exercise greater power over the economy and the country than in feudal societies. . . ."[4]

Protesting students envisioned the university as leader in the struggle of society to wrest control from endless machines, from the corporations, from the military. So they despised the university when it allowed itself to be used by that hierarchy of power. The university, they declared, should itself be the instrument to make men free.

During the Berkeley upheaval in 1964, the rhetoric of student leader Mario Savio echoed Hayden's indictment of the university and society. "There is a time," Savio shouted, "when the operation of the machine becomes so odious, makes you so sick at heart, that you can't take part; you can't even tacitly take part...."[5]

The early thrust of the student movement of the 1960s was toward the reform of society rather than of the university as such. Even the on-campus issues showed that tendency. Such early campus issues as the *in loco parentis* policy, the removal of university restraints on political expression and activity, the bans on controversial speakers—all seemed to activist students to be analogous to the larger social problems beyond the ivy walls.

In their writings, in their speeches, and in their organizational creeds, American student activists of the 1960s proclaimed their abhorrence of American hypocrisy. They would force America to strip itself of the self-delusion which corrodes ideals and can-

---

3. Thomas Hayden, "A Letter to the New (Young) Student Left," in *The New Student Left*, ed. Mitchell Cohen, and Dennis Hale (Boston: Beacon Press, 1967):2-3.

4. Thomas Hayden, "Student Social Action," pp. 284-85.

5. Mario Savio, quoted in Christopher G. Katope and Paul G. Zolbrod, eds., *Beyond Berkeley* (New York: World Publishing, 1966), pp. 88-89.

cels values. Out of despair over what they saw as the loss of the American dream, students asked that the empty promises of national mottoes, anthems and pledges be filled.

The Action

On February 1, 1960, four black students from North Carolina Agricultural and Technical College entered a store in Greensboro, sat at a segregated lunch counter, and asked for coffee. They were denied service, but they sat at the counter until the store closed. The first student sit-in of the decade had taken place.

In the next few months, white students joined the black in spontaneous sit-ins in the South, and northern students supported them with boycotts of the northern branches of the offending stores. Encouraged by the rapid growth and the early success of the sit-ins in the South, students formed the Student Non-Violent Coordinating Committee, dedicated to building a nonviolent protest movement among students.

While some students worked nonviolently to desegregate facilities in the South, others became involved with different issues. At Berkeley a student political party called SLATE urged students to take direct action to protest any restrictions of the freedoms guaranteed by the Constitution. By late 1961, students had begun to use nonviolent, direct-action techniques as a means to protest American foreign policy. Students marched on Washington, held peace vigils, and picketed the White House. SDS, then pushing for reform within the System, became the most widely publicized of the student political groups formed early in the decade.

Between 1960 and 1964, students protesting on campus did so through the normal channels of student government, still believing that once an issue could be brought to the attention of authorities, it would be only a matter of time before some response to it would come. Realization of the naiveté of that supposition began descending upon students in the middle of the decade. By summer of 1964, SNCC had begun to realize the futility of its venture into the Deep South. Eventually it gave up its passive confrontative efforts there, after the federal government proved it was in no hurry to end segregation, after the killers of civil rights workers Goodman, Chaney and Swerner were never brought to trial, and after white liberals failed to support the Mississippi challenge at the Democratic Party National Convention in Atlantic City.

After classes started in the fall of 1964, the Berkeley campus experienced a series of massive protest demonstrations, leading in December to a sit-in at the administration building, mass arrests and a strike. The Free Speech Movement had begun. For the first time in the decade, the concept of the "multiversity" and its indifference to the rights of students to personhood became a major issue. The Berkeley protest in 1964 also demonstrated that it was possible to involve large numbers of students in direct action against the administration. With the sudden and complete attention of the media given to the troubles at Berkeley, Americans became aware that the university campus could be a front line in a revolution against authority.

In December of 1964, SDS called for an April, 1965, march on Washington to protest the Vietnam War. By February of 1965, the bombing of North Vietnam had begun, and the administration was refusing to negotiate an end to the war. Twenty thousand students turned out for the April march. Afterward, hundreds of campuses staged "teach-ins" about the Vietnam War; it was now the central issue with activist students. With the fall of 1965 came waves of student demonstrations originated by local SDS chapters. According to Richard Peterson of the Educational Testing Service, SDS had organizations on 25% of the campuses at that time.[6]

In 1965, protest activity still was nonviolent, frequently taking the form of discussion and debate. Some draft cards were burned; but generally, civil disobedience was the rule. Gradually, however, students became disillusioned with failure to get results from their protest tactics. More students participated in each march, yet each major march was followed by some new escalation of the war. Students watching the news on television became horrified by what was happening to Vietnam citizens and disgusted with the corruption of the South Vietnam regime.

In 1966, General Hershey announced that some students would be drafted, designating those receiving the lowest grades to be the ones taken. Campus reaction was instant and heated. There were seizures of buildings and sit-ins at the University of Chicago, the City College of New York, Oberlin and other institutions. University of Chicago students experienced the exhilaration of success when they were able to close the university's administration building and directly confront the administration. Support of student activists from nonparticipating students was growing. Immediate and complete coverage from the news media brought the campus struggles into Everyman's life.

By June of 1966, SDS had begun a new phase. Its leadership changed, and ties to the original founders and their philosophies were severed. "Student Power" became the rebel cry on campus. Students wanted a voice in planning curricula and a seat on important administrative committees. They were no longer willing to submit to the dicta of authority. It was, as Senator Javits said, time for them to get a piece of the action. They were asking to play the role which, as citizens of the university community, they felt justifiably to be theirs.

Thus the student movement took a different turn after 1965. As the report submitted by Jerome H. Skolnick to the National Commission on the Causes and Prevention of Violence states, "Before 1965, the student movement embodied concern, dissent and protest about various social issues, but it generally accepted the legitimacy of the political community in general and especially the university." After 1965, Skolnick hypothesizes, "a considerable number of young people, particularly the activist core, experienced a progressive deterioration in their acceptance of national and university authority."[7] That progressive deterioration in student acceptance of national and university authority was the outstanding characteristic of the rebellion on campuses during the last half of the decade.

Evidence drawn from research findings of the American Council of Education, especially from Alan E. Bayer and Alex W. Astin's, "Violence and Disruption on the

6. Richard E. Peterson, *The Scope of Organized Student Protest in 1967-1968* (Princeton, N. J.: Educational Testing Service, 1968).

7. Jerome H. Skolnick, *The Politics of Protest* (New York: Ballantine Books, 1969), pp. 99-100.

U. S. Campus, 1968-69," published in the *Educational Record*, Fall, 1969, shows that one in three of the private universities in America experienced violent protest while one in eight public universities experienced incidents of comparative severity. Bayer and Astin define "violent protest" as any campus incident which involved (a) burning of buildings; (b) damage to buildings or furnishings; (c) destruction of files; (d) campus march or picketing or rally with physical violence; (e) injury or death to any person. Their studies show that approximately 70 percent of the private and 43 percent of the public universities experienced protest that was violent and disruptive during 1968-69.

Change and reform in American institutions were the goals behind the drive of the students who staged disruptions during the 1960s. History shows that violence and disruption have sometimes been effective goads to institutional change. Yet colleges and universities are the traditional bastions of rationality and civility. They do not readily explode into violence. Something deep and disturbing to the national equilibrium was at work. With the shootings of students on the Jackson State and Kent State campuses in 1970, the tide of violence and disruption on the nation's campuses during the decade of protest had crested.

The Rhetoric

The rhetorical strategy chosen by the four students at Greensboro was the sit-in: a rhetoric of nonviolent human action. Nonviolence as a rhetorical method seeks to persuade the opponent that he is wrong. It does not seek to defeat or humiliate or alienate the opponent; it wants to win his friendship and understanding.[8] A brief

look at some of the events which followed the first sit-in in Greensboro should show the functioning of the nonviolent sit-in as a rhetorical strategy in the South of the early 1960s.

By February 5, 1960, the integrated group at the S. H. Kress store in Greensboro was large enough to draw a crowd. They were surrounded by white high school toughs dressed in black leather jackets and carrying Confederate flags. The students sitting at the counter were very well dressed, many in suits and ties, and several carried Bibles. While the young whites taunted, snarled and jeered, the students remained silent, poised, determined.[9]

Twelve days after Greensboro one of the forty students sitting-in at a Nashville Woolworth store reported, "Young kids threw French fried potatoes at us and gum and cigarette butts. I looked down the counter at Barbara Crosby in a straight pink skirt and a white blouse and at Stephen in a dark suit with a calculus book."[10]

There was violence in Nashville later that day:

A white sit-inner, on a stool beside a Negro girl, became the object of attention. Someone kept calling him "nigger lover"! When he did not respond, he was pulled off the stool, thrown to the floor and kicked. A white man kept blowing cigar smoke into the face of a Negro student named LePrad. When he made no move, this infuriated the white taunter and he pulled LePrad off the stool and hit him. He got back on the stool again. He was pulled

8. Staughton Lynd, *Non-Violence in America: A Documentary History* (Indianapolis: Bobbs-Merrill, 1966), p. 391.
9. Jack Newfield, *A Prophetic Minority* (New York: New American Library, 1966), p. 35.
10. Candie Anderson, quoted in Howard Zinn, *SNCC: The New Abolitionists*, (Boston: Beacon Press, 1965), p. 21.

off the stool again and hit. The police came and arrested LePrad and the 17 students sitting in with him.[11]

Jane Stembridge, a student who was part of a jail-no-bail group in Atlanta in 1961 reminisced about the sit-in experience:

The most honest moment—the one in which I saw the guts-type truth stripped of anything but total fear and total courage—was when . . . Lana Taylor from Spellman was sitting next to me. The manager walked up behind her, said something obscene, and grabbed her by the shoulders. "Get the hell outta here, nigger." Lana was not going. I do not know whether she should have collapsed in a non-violent manner. She probably didn't know. She put her hands under the counter and held. He was rough and strong. She just held, and I looked down at that minute at her hands . . . brown, strained . . . every muscle holding. All of a sudden he let go and left. I thought he knew he could not move that girl, ever."[12]

Much of what these scenes show about the rhetoric of the sit-in is clear. The dress of the young students was a rhetorical act which spoke of order, dignity and nonviolence. Its contrast to the black jackets, long a symbol of violence and disregard for civil and moral law in this country, spoke of what those young people stood for. The Bibles they carried were symbols of brotherhood and love, were silent rhetorical challenges to the Confederate flag, a symbol of division and hate.

There was rhetoric in the calculus book, the volume of Goethe, and the biology texts, which demonstrated, by contrast the animal ignorance and behavior of the taunters and spectators. Paul LePrad, climbing back onto that stool, and Lana Taylor, holding with every muscle to the lunch counter, spoke to all who watched saying that the black students were determined to have their rights as citizens and their dignity as human beings.

Southern whites responded in yet another way to the rhetoric of the sit-in—they crowded their jails with students. And the students took their rhetoric of passive resistance to jail with them.

Words could not have achieved the student victory which was won over Sheriff Tyson in the Parchman Penitentiary in 1961. Stokeley Carmichael talked of that time in Parchman:

I'll never forget this Sheriff Tyson—he used to wear those big boots. He'd say, "You goddam smart nigger, why you always trying to be so uppity for? I'm going to see to it that you never get out of this place." They decided to take our mattresses because we were singing. . . . So they dragged Hank Thomas out and he hung onto his mattress and they took it and him and dropped it with a loud klunk on his back. . . . And then they put the wristbreakers on Freddy Leonard, which makes you twist around in a snake-like motion, and Tyson said, "Oh you want to hit me, don't you?" and Freddy just looked up at him meekly and said, "No, I just want you to break my arm." And Sheriff Tyson was shaken visibly, and he told the trusty, "Put him back." I hung onto the mattress and said, "I think we have a right to them and I think you are unjust," and he said, "I don't want to hear all that shit, nigger" and started to put on the wristbreakers. I wouldn't move and I started to sing, "I'm Gonna Tell God How You Treat Me," and everybody started to sing it and by this time Tyson was really to pieces. He called to the trustees, "Get him in there!" and he went out the door and slammed it, and left everybody else with their mattresses.[13]

When Stokeley *spoke* to Tyson about the injustice of what was being done to the students, he received, in return, verbal abuse. But the *act* of singing so flustered Tyson that he was forced to leave the room and drop the issue. Captain Maloney, at the Rock Hill jail, had responded

11. Zinn, *SNCC*, p. 21.
12. *Ibid.*, p. 39.
13. *Ibid.*, p. 57.

to the hymn singing of the jailed students by putting them into solitary, demonstrating that the message contained in the act of singing was more threatening to him than the cursing and disturbances made by other prisoners and ignored by Captain Maloney.

It is impossible, of course, to be certain of the impact of the rhetoric of those first sit-ins. Perhaps, as Jack Newfield puts it, the Greensboro sit-in was merely the catalyst that needed to be added to the existing chemicals of the 1954 school desegregation decision, the Montgomery bus boycott and the emerging nations of Africa, "in order to liberate the dammed up rivers of idealism, energy and courage that cascaded through the South those first weeks of 1960."[14]

The sit-in succeeded as a rhetorical strategy with a sensitive, intelligent, committed minority of American college students. It inspired them to pick up the cause of human dignity and go to work. In the beginning it was a handful of those students that left school to work for the civil rights movement. By 1963 hundreds of young people began to leave college for a summer, a semester, a year, to work in the South.[15] The nonviolent sit-in movement which became SNCC caused an upheaval in American colleges and universities that rocked America's complacency and alerted universities and the nation to the need for self-examination.

For some white American students, the civil rights movement of the early 1960s was a direct challenge to the official version of American life. It was a starting point from which the new student left moved in a number of directions. The history of the new left is one of the application, with varying degrees of success, of the lessons learned in

the civil rights movement to a number of different problems.[16]

Even though comparatively few students were involved in any form of direct action, and although student activity was, in 1960-62, restricted to relatively few campuses, some of the protesting students felt a need for organization. The *New York Times* of May 14, 1962, reported the formation of nine new student organizations on the Berkeley campus. In a survey of campuses across the nation, the *Times* found that although the political activity on American campuses involved only a small fraction of the student body (1 to 10 percent at most), "it was a fragment that was vocal, militant, organized, growing and full of determination."[17]

Looking for the spark which ignited the growth of student activity, the *Times* hypothesized that it came from the first sit-in at Greensboro in 1960. It was influenced, too, the *Times* asserted, by the election of John F. Kennedy as president, and by the emergence of a new student attitude toward college. Student activists were not looking at college as four years of fun before going to work. One student told the *Times*, "I think the grown-ups had better learn about these student groups. They dismiss us as beatniks. The beats don't engage in politics. They reject the real world. We're dying to jump in with both feet."[18]

It was during the period 1961-63 that SDS students, in seeking restoration of traditional American values, resorted to reasoned discourse through platform rhetoric

14. Newfield, *Prophetic Minority*, p. 39.
15. Zinn, *SNCC*, pp. 231-32.
16. Cohen and Hale, *New Student Left*, p. 24.
17. *New York Times*, May 14, 1962, p. 1.
18. *Ibid.*

and the writing of pamphlets and SDS publications. SDS rhetoric was a part of the ferment of the times. Their speeches and their
writings attempted to persuade America of
the salience of the issues of peace, civil liberties and unity. When SDS spoke, it was
usually to university audiences. Occasions
when SDS members were *invited* to speak
directly to the Establishment were unique.
Yet even when their immediate audience
(readers of school and SDS papers, groups
attending SDS meetings, participants in
student forums) was composed largely of
students, SDS rhetoric directed itself to a
larger, more elusive audience—the Establishment.

The tone of the writing, the tenor of the
speeches were not emotional, not anarchic.
Always reaching for the mind of the audience, the young idealists wrote and spoke
reasonably about their disappointment in
the state of affairs in America.

At this point, the student activists were
still looking for ways to work within the established system in order to bring about
needed change. SDS was still able, as was
SNCC, to accept the need for slow and ex-
hausting work, expecting it to take a life-
time. When Tom Hayden spoke, it was to
make a reasoned request. Student rhetoric
had not yet taken the form of ultimatum:

Thus far we have been quick to know what we oppose: racism, militarism, nationalism, oppression
of mind and spirit, unrestrained capitalism, provincialism of various kinds, and the bombs. It has
been almost an instinctive opposition. We have
been hurt by what exists, and we have responded
in outrage and compassion. We must move ahead
concertedly with our goal—the changing of society, not the assuaging of continuous ills. That
means politics as well as sentimentality. That
means writers and theoreticians as well as organizers and pickets. That means drawing on what remains of the adult labor, academic and political
communities, not just revolting in despair against

them and the world they have designed for us. . . .
Our gains will be modest, not sensational. It will be
slow and exhaustingly complex, lasting for at least
our lifetimes. For many of us it will not and cannot
be a college fling, a costless, painless tugging at our
liberal sentimentality. It will be longer, and the
cost great.[19]

The activist students moved ahead, as
Hayden suggested, provisionally and
strongly in the midst of their doubts. They
became a direct action group dedicated to
the restoration of the American dream,
speaking for that dream from the platform
at universities, at rallies—anywhere they
could be heard. They sought the social
order permeated by love to which SNCC
had pledged itself. But where SNCC trusted
in love to transcend hate, faith to reconcile
doubt, and mutual regard to cancel emnity,
SDS was considerably less hopeful, less
trusting. "I am beset by doubt at this point;
so, perhaps, are we all," said Tom Hayden
in 1961.[20]

The rhetoric of SDS was a strategic response to a situation of division. Students
like Tom Hayden sought an end to the division between generations by identifying
concepts of the young with those of their
elders: "the potential for self-cultivation,
self-direction, self-understanding and crea-
tivity." It was this potential that the young
SDS regarded as crucial and to which they
appealed, "not to the human potential for
violence, unreason, and submission to authority."[21]

In the spring of 1962, Tom Hayden, then
president of SDS, gave a speech at the University of Michigan. That speech, tran-

19. "A Letter to the New (Young) Left," reprinted in *New Student Left*, Cohen and Hale, p. 8.
20. Cohen and Hale, *New Student Left*, p. 9.
21. From *The Port Huron Statement*, reprinted in
Cohen and Hale, *New Student Left*, p. 12.

scribed on tape and printed in full in Cohen and Hale's *New Student Left*, was titled, "Student Social Action: From Liberation to Community." It was delivered in response to the expulsion from Southern University at Baton Rouge of a number of students who had participated in demonstrations against segregational practices in the community. The president of the university had called forth a university rule which reserved the right of the University to sever a student's connection with it for general inability to adjust himself to the pattern of the institution.

The first half of the speech is an indictment of the policy *in loco parentis*. It demonstrates the manner in which the student left used campus issues to point up bigger social problems. Hayden saw the student as essentially an outsider, "someone who takes what he gets or else," just as helpless as man in a technological society, a concept abhorrent to protesting students. His description of the university is Orwellian—in shades of *1984*, he shows the university forbidding the student certain associations, regulating academic life habits without explanation, and expelling the student at any moment he is found to be unable to adjust to the pattern of the university.

Hayden's own philosophy of education follows, and it states succinctly the cry echoed by student activists for the rest of the decade:

I believe education in a democracy should be threatening and renewing—threatening in that it should critically examine the deepest understandings of life, confronting taboo, habit, ritual, and personal ethics with a withering "why," unearthing the values that society buries for security's sake, and exposing these to the sunlight of the enquiring mind. . . .[22]

Hayden closed with a plea for "the con-

tinuous opening for the human potential," for restoration of values which would "unravel the heavy cape of impotence," for a sense of purpose which would "restore the dominance of human functional responsibilities and bring to men once more the will and the ability to exert real influence over events as citizens." From SDS thus came the call for participatory democracy, "resting on the independence of the ordinary people."

In referring to society as a struggle to wrest control somehow from the endless machines that grind up men's jobs, Hayden projected an image of society that Mario Savio would reiterate at Berkeley. In Hayden's speech we find a precise statement of the thinking that lay behind the student rebellion, a denunciation of the world they were about to inherit. As the SDS concept of the orientation of America spread to other campuses, it drove increasing numbers of students to take direct action against the university and society before the decade had passed.

Hayden's horror at the values of a technological, product-oriented society was echoed in student rhetoric across the country. His indictment of the university as victim and pawn of corporative and military power was the concept partly responsible for the holocaust at Kent State. His despair over the decomposition of democracy in America became the black gloom that left the activist students joyless during the late 1960s. His charge that the weaknesses and errors in university education and administration were symptomatic of ills that plague the whole of American society was flung again and again until the uni-

---

22. Quoted in Cohen and Hale, *New Student Left*, p. 282.

versities were forced to listen and to respond.

We hear in Hayden's speech a tone that
while it largely sounds like reasoned exhortation begins to take on the sound of demand. It would, as it despaired of winning
with logic, lead easily into a rhetoric of ultimatum. It promised that students must and
would be heard.

A study of student rhetoric, both oral
and written, of the period 1960-64 confirms that hypothesis that Hayden's speech
is typical of the kind of rhetorical strategy
chosen in the early sixties by students
across the country. During the first third of
the decade, Tom Hayden was perhaps the
most prolific writer and active student
speaker in the new student left. Yet other
students were about the business of persuasion: Charles McDew, with a speech
given at Antioch College in 1960, "Spiritual and Moral Aspects of the Student Nonviolent Struggle in the South"; Thomas
Kahn, speaking at the University of North
Carolina in 1962, "The Political Significance of the Freedom Rides"; Paul Potter,
writing an SDS working paper in 1964,
"The Intellectual and Social Change";
Robert A. Haber, writing for *Venture*, an
SDS publication, in 1960, "From Protest to
Radicalism: An Appraisal of the Student
Movement, 1960"; Todd Gitlin, writing an
SDS working paper in 1964, "The Battle-
field and the War"; and Carl Ogelsby,
speaking at the March on Washington to
End the War in Vietnam, 1965, "Let Us
Shape the Future."[23]

The general American public responded
to the early SDS pleas for change with indifference and silence. The printed media
are one reliable gauge of what America was
talking and writing about during those
three years when SDS was attempting to

reason with it from the platform and the
printed page. A study of the periodicals of
the period, both popular and educational,
reveals almost total ignorance or avoidance
of the wave of student protest rising from
SDS. Readers of the popular magazines
were being fed the image of American college students of which they had grown so
fond during the 1950s. Of the fifty title en-
tries under "College Students" in the *Reader's Guide to Periodical Literature of
1961-1963*, only three spoke of the protest
movement taking place on American campuses. Typical of the other titles were:
"Money, Books and Going Steady," "Suds,
Sex and Sand Promotion," and "College
Freshmen Are Better Than Ever."

Nor were those teachers and administrators who wrote for the education journals
of the period 1961-63 giving time or space
to responding to SDS or SNCC appeals.
Professionals in education were writing of
"Variety and Meaning of Premarital Het-
erosexual Experience for the College Student" as Tom Hayden was analogizing the
university to a corporation or new form of
business enterprise which produces "college graduates." Educators read in their
journals about the "Problems of Concentration among College Students" while
Tom Hayden accused the university of failure to challenge and truly educate a huge
bloc of students. A "Study of the Vocabulary Needs of a Class of Juniors and Sen-
iors at Alabama State" was a matter of
scholarly concern when Robert Haber decried the deep alienation of the students
from the decision-making institutions of
society.

In the first three years of the decade, the

---

23. For transcript of these speeches and essays, see
Cohen and Hale, *New Student Left*.

new student left was speaking harsh truths to a people who seemed to rest confortably in their preoccupation with the accumulation of goods. No matter that those young voices rose in anger, doubt and fear.

A small section of the student body at Berkeley had been involved in the civil rights movement in the South at various times during the period 1960-64. Increasing numbers of Berkeley students linked themselves with a series of issues, especially with the growing civil rights movement. Small units organized for direct action in the civil rights movement appeared on campus.

During the summer of 1964, when the Republican National Convention met in San Francisco, there were complaints from supporters of Barry Goldwater, a presidential nominee, that the university grounds were being used to organize disorderly forays on behalf of another nominee. In September the university administration undertook to enforce the existing regulations concerning the university's political neutrality. For months it had allowed such groups as SNCC and CORE to place their tables across the street side of Sproul Plaza and to solicit funds and volunteers for sit-ins. Actually, university regulations forbade both the soliciting of funds on university grounds and the use of university grounds for organizing outside political drives.

On September 29th, after the decision of the university to enforce its ban on such activities, four organizations (SNCC, CORE, Young Socialist Alliance and SLATE) set up their tables in front of Sather Gate in contravention of the rules.

It was at this point, when students at Berkeley refused to comply with orders or accept authoritative commands or requests as legitimate, that a new rhetorical choice was made by protesting students. The refusal to conform to rules came to be called "confrontation."

Robert L. Scott and Donald K. Smith talk of confrontation as a rhetoric because "this action, as diverse as its manifestations may be, is inherently symbolic. The act carries a message. It dissolves the line between marches, sit-ins, demonstrations, acts of physical violence, and aggressive discourse. In this way it informs us of the essential nature of discourse itself as human action."[24]

After four years of being generally ignored when they used traditional rhetorical tactics to press for changes within the system, the students found that confrontation got attention. As Scott and Smith ask, "How can administrators ignore the insurgency of those committed to jamming the machine of whatever enterprise is supposed to be ongoing? Those who would confront have learned a brutal art, practiced sometimes awkwardly and sometimes skillfully, which demands response,"[25]

In response to the students' confrontational tactics, the Berkeley administration insisted that the students who were defying the rules identify themselves, while allowing the tables to remain at Sather Gate. It must have been clear to students that the authorities were reluctant to act.

The next day about four hundred students signed petitions to the dean, declaring that they, too, were guilty of having manned the political tables in conscious violation of the university's rules. A nonvio-

24. Robert L. Scott and Donald K. Smith, "The Rhetoric of Confrontation," in *The Rhetoric of Revolution*, ed. Christopher Katope and Paul Zolbrod (Canada: Macmillan and Co., 1970), p. 210.

25. *Ibid.*, p. 211.

lent sit-in began which lasted into the early morning of October 1st. That day the university finally suspended eight students. Meanwhile, a continuing demonstration was maintained on the steps of the administration building.

Then came the first clash with the police. A police car appeared to take away a defiant student who had set up a card table for soliciting civil rights workers. As student observers described the incident, ". . . to the politically active student . . . the car symbolized the action of unjust authority and the threat to their political rights. To the rest of the students the car was a source of excitement, curiosity and a degree of sympathy."[26] The political students organized a sit-in around the car to prevent the defiant one from being taken away.

One of the students, Mario Savio, who from this point on in the two years of rebellion at Berkeley would assume the role of its major leader and advocate, leaped to the roof of the police car and began to address the students. Said an observer, "Savio's action captured the imagination of the crowd; he began by talking to them and ended by talking *for* them because he gave form and voice to the symbols of their rebellion. The police car, the crowd itself, the administration building in the background—all the symbols of resented authority and group strength—found their way into his address."[27]

Mario shouted, "We are being denied our rights by 'them' [pointing to the deans assembled on the balcony of the administration building]. We will stand around this police car until they negotiate with us."[28]

Consider the rhetorical elements inherent in this incident. A second kind of con-

frontation was taking place. The first confrontative act had been the defiance of the rule against setting up tables. The confrontation with police was dual in nature; it coupled the rhetorical tactic of placing the body against what was interpreted as injustice with the tactic of deliberate interference with the operation of established American institutions—the university and the police.

The message communicated by the action of surrounding the police car was clear—if the police would cooperate in the deprivation of a student's right to political participation (which they interpreted as the barring of free speech), then the students would act to remove the rights of policemen to take a hostage and deprive them of their freedom to leave the campus. The rhetoric in the students' act of defiance seemed to argue that if one believes the law to be immoral, then one must disobey it at any cost.

The students' physical rhetoric of resistance received national attention because the surrounding of the police car made "news." The three-day student demonstration at Berkeley was reported by the *New York Times* although it was relegated to its inside pages. The *Times* kept an eye on Berkeley through the remainder of October, and November. Rhetorically, then, the act of surrounding the police car was successful if it was intended to bring attention to the student fight for freedoms at Berkeley. The Free Speech Movement at Berkeley grew out of the belief that dangers to

26. Joseph Paff, Bill Cavala, and Jerry Berman, "The Student Riots at Berkeley: Dissent in the Multiversity," in *The New Student Left*, ed. Cohen and Hale, p. 238.
27. *Ibid.*, p. 239.
28. *Ibid.*

free speech were "many and diffuse in American society."[29] As student activists described it, the action against the police was "a rebellion over free speech which is a protest against bureaucracy and its impersonal processing of the student."[30]

Mario Savio's choice of using the police car as his podium was a rhetorical act. Placing himself literally on top of the law, he reinforced the intention of the activist students to prove the superiority of moral law over blind adherence to civil law. The act was a bold announcement of new student strategy: students would defy civil law if that rhetorical act was necessary to being seen and heard.

The audience to whom Savio's "speech" was addressed was only in part the students who surrounded the police car. It was no doubt designed to excite them into persisting in their act of civil disobedience. The *function* of the speech for those students, however, was, according to one, "to capture the imagination of that crowd, to speak for it, to give form as well as voice to the symbols of their rebellion."[31] In his talk, Mario Savio pointed to the deans of the university and said, "We are being denied our rights by *them*." His use of the third person when referring to the deans clearly indicates that it was not to them that his words were being flung. That part of Savio's audience to whom the act of defiance was addressed was the world outside the academic community—that part of America whose value system the new left had been trying to change.

Savio's speech marked the emergence of a kind of student rhetoric which in the remaining years of the decade was directed only secondarily to the listeners gathered around the speaker. Its admonishments and accusations were meant for an absent but much larger, more powerful audience—the Establishment. Theirs was a rhetoric that refused to identify with any values, concepts, images or attitudes of the elder generation. It sought to underscore division. It was a rhetoric which declared an enemy.

Another characteristic of student oratory at Berkeley demonstrated the nature of student rhetoric to come. Savio's rhetoric and that of students who followed him was not speechmaking in the traditional sense. Their oratory was nonstructured and spontaneous. Not a rhetoric of the manuscript, it was more the seizing of an opportunity for a student to "have his say," to assert leadership or to recruit nonactivist students into the rebellion. Very inoccasionally in the years of student protest remaining in the decade were protest speeches as carefully prepared, as well organized, or as coherent as were Tom Hayden's in the early days of SDS. Most student "speeches" were, like Savio's, impromptu outbursts filling a pause in the action at a student demonstration.

One other aspect of the police car incident is important to any study of the rhetorical choices made by students in protest during the 1960s. Savio's words shaped the pattern for a new kind of student rhetoric—a rhetoric of ultimatum. The rhetoric of ultimatum was heavily laced with strong verbs like "demand," "insist," and "must." The phrase "the only alternative" appeared again and again, indicating a refusal to compromise. It often threatened to bring the university to a halt, as it did when Savio said, "We must indicate to the people who run the machine that unless you're free, the

29. *Ibid.*, p. 240.
30. *Ibid.*
31. *Ibid.*, p. 239.

machine will be prevented from running at all."[32]

In another speech, Savio hit hard on the ultimatum: "Strong [an administrator] *must* say no to other suspensions. He *must* agree to meet with the political organization. There *must* be no discipline used against anyone. . . . And I am *publicly serving notice* that we are going to continue direct action until the administration accedes."[33] Threat rhetoric scorned the traditional attempt to establish grounds for identification between the speaker and his audience. Rarely if ever did activist students use the pronoun "we" to unite the speaker with his Establishment listener of whom the demands were being made. Theirs was a "we-versus-you" kind of rhetoric.

In the two years that followed the 1964 uprising, many changes took place at Berkeley, according to Wolin and Schaar, observers of the scene. The apparent victory of 1964 "had been hollowed out and hope had gone sour." Of all the differences between 1964 and 1966, the most striking was the difference in mood. In 1964 there was "much idealism and hope: the FSM was good-natured, ironical and humorous." By 1966 the campus was "tired, humorless and disillusioned."[34] When a second student strike was called in 1966, student activists threatened to destroy the university "if they take direct action against us rather than accede to our just demands."[35] With that promise to destroy the university, the rhetoric of threat had reached the ultimate in ultimata. In 1968, American students would cause universities to close their doors. The threat to destroy the university echoed through student rhetoric until the end of the decade.

The Chancellor at Berkeley described the kind of rhetoric taking place on the Plaza, ". . . a style of speech that is often vicious in intent, dishonest, laced with slander and character assassination, indifferent to evidence and truth, contemptuous of disagreement, and often charged with hatred."[36] Lewis Feuer marks the use of obscenity by student activists as one event in a long series of incidents revealing a gradual deterioration in ethics. He claimed that by 1965 student activists were possessed by "deceit, contempt, and disregard for other people's rights."[37]

There were other academics who, though they had consistently expressed by word and action their support of student ideals and of the rhetorical tactics used early in the Berkeley uprising, were led later to denounce the strategies of the students. One former ally was Professor Albert Hobbs. Writing in the *Inter-Collegiate Review* he reflected general Establishment response to the situation at Berkeley, "Tempting as it was to believe that the protest of SDS was motivated by reasoned idealism, as time went on even highly sympathetic observers, myself among them, found it increasingly difficult to reconcile verbal idealism with behavior which ranged from lack of consideration for the rights of

---

32. Katope and Zolbrod, *The Rhetoric of Revolution*, pp. 88-89.
33. Quoted in *The Berkeley Student Revolt* (New York: Doubleday, 1965), p. 111.
34. Sheldon S. Wolin and John N. Schaar, *The Berkeley Rebellion and Beyond* (New York: Vintage Books, 1970), pp. 46-47.
35. Lewis S. Feuer, *The Conflict of Generations: The Character and Significance of Student Movements* (New York: Basic Books, 1969), p. 458.
36. Wolin and Schaar, *Berkeley Rebellion*, pp. 50-51.
37. Lewis Feuer, "Pornopolitics and the University," *New Leader*, April 12, 1965, p. 15.

others to downright hooliganism."[38] Hobbs reported that a considerable number of competent observers (Nathan Glazer, Sidney Hook, William Peterson, Seymour Lipset and S.S. Wolin) concluded that the Free Speech Movement at Berkeley was only an excuse for an attempt on the part of malcontents to seize power without any clear idea of what to do with it.[39]

Careful observation of the rhetorical strategies of the student revolt of the 1960s will show that although the movement may at times have deteriorated into the kind of "hooliganism which lacked consideration for the rights of others," it was not born of that tendency, nor did it, in its infancy breed it. In the summer and fall of 1964, student activists had waged a battle over the principle of freedom. Its leaders had given themselves to the civil rights struggle in the South. Their outrage at finding on the university campus a level of repression analagous to the tactics of the white south led to the formation of the Free Speech Movement.

But if Professor Hobbs' response was at all typical, the alienation which student rhetoric seemed to be pursuing was well under way. The backlash had started. It was at this point in the decade of revolt that students appeared to be pursuing rhetorical strategies that doomed the movement. By having declared an enemy, they made one. By having abandoned the search for commonality, they removed the possibility for acting together to bring about reforms. By failing to live up to their own professed ideals, they cancelled the impact of their accusation of hypocrisy.

The sad fact is that in 1966 many Americans were unaware that nonviolent, reasonable rhetorical tactics had ever been used by student activists, so focused were they on the then-existing student tactics of confrontation and ultimatum. In general, America tuned in on the youth revolt after it had been active four years, too late to know any phase of its protest rhetoric except one which had abandoned nonviolence and reason for whatever rhetorical tactics would bring attention to their protest.

While events at Berkeley in 1964 set the mood for revolt, the uprising at Columbia University in 1968 was the Boston Tea Party of the student revolution. In the sense that the Columbia uprising deepened the alienation between generations, and in the manner in which the rhetorical tactics used at Columbia finalized the divorce of student rhetoric from reasoned discourse, Columbia finished what Berkeley had started.

The fires of student unrest which were kindled at Berkeley were kept smoldering on a few university and college campuses between 1966-68. Occasionally they had flared up into serious revolt, as they had at the University of Michigan and the University of Wisconsin; but the events at Columbia in April and May of 1968 stoked the fires of unrest to such heat that they ranged out of control during the last academic year of the decade.

For several years Columbia students who had objected to the status quo had confined their dissent to legitimate political protest. Their activities had rarely disrupted the normal functioning of the university. However, these acceptable forms of

----

38. Albert H. Hobbs, "The SDS Trip," reprinted in Katope and Zolbrod, *Rhetoric of Revolution*, p. 299.

39. *Ibid.*, p. 300.

protest had not won any meaningful reform.[40] Mark Rudd, who was one of the more radical students in SDS, was convinced that the old SDS political style was not leading the movement anywhere. When he became chairman of the Columbia chapter in March of 1968, tactics began to change. For example, when the New York City director of the Selective Service System appeared on campus to discuss draft regulations with students, the old SDS leaders suggested that the best way to respond was to fire probing questions at him. The more aggressive members had a different tactic ready. As the director started fielding questions from the floor, a group of students created a diversion at the rear of the auditorium. As everyone turned around, an unidentified assailant walked up to the colonel and pushed a lemon meringue pie in his face.[41]

Mark Rudd's defense of the pie rhetoric was that this tactic served radical goals at least as effectively as leafletting or dormitory canvassing. Few of the members of SDS agreed; most charged that the action had been terroristic. But soon Rudd's style of rhetoric won over a large segment of the Columbia chapter.[42] This energetic and aggressive faction of SDS began to dominate it. Known as the "action faction," it advocated confrontation politics.

Mark Rudd wrote the "October Proposals for Demonstrations at Columbia" as a call for students to reject the elder generation and the university it controlled. Where "The Port Huron Statement" had called for "human ... interdependence ... human brotherhood... personal links between man and man" and had stressed a need and desire for acting together to better the world, the "October Proposals" emphasized division between the generations and

proposed "confrontation," "the striking of blows," "the militant fight to achieve goals."

Rudd's plans included enticement of the news media into close coverage of radical activities, the incitement of spontaneous demonstrations around campus, the harassment of recruiters and of ROTC, a sit-in at Low Library—all in the Berkeley style of confrontation. The intent stated in the "October Proposals" was university capitulation. In October, Rudd interpreted the scene at Columbia as warlike; in April he felt the same way. This conception of the campus as battleground explains the SDS decision to use guerilla tactics: the young activists barricaded buildings; they took hostages; they destroyed "enemy" property; they defiled the work and/or possessions of individual "enemies"; they used obscenity labels for the "enemy."

The guerilla tactics of the students were addressed to a particular audience. As rhetoric they declared an end to reason as a means of persuasion. The use of such tactics expressed the activist philosophy that the end justifies any means. Guerilla tactics spoke of the SDS decision that all rules demanding rational discourse had been suspended, that the channels of communication had been blocked off, and that the speaker had as his intent the subjugation of an enemy.

A senior at Columbia explained the militant tactical decisions of the protesting students as a last desperate choice, "I played the game of rational discourse and persua-

---

40. Jerry L. Avorn, ed., and Columbia *Daily Spectator* staff members, *Up Against the Ivy Wall: A History of the Columbia Crisis* (New York: Atheneum, 1969):29.
41. *Ibid.*, p. 32.
42. *Ibid.*

sion. Now there is a mood of reconstruction. All the log jams are broken. Violence pays. The tactics of obstruction weren't right, weren't justifiable, but look what happened!"[43]

Lewis Cole, a radical leader, argued that Columbia students had exhausted every legal channel of protest. "It is regrettable that people can't attend classes and continue the normal functions but I would say the ends would justify the means—they are the only means allowable to us. Our rights and needs have been consistently unsatisfied."[44]

In defense of his tactics, Mark Rudd told a press conference:

Most of the campus agree with our demands but some people disagree with our tactics. These people must come to realize that intellectual support without action is worth nothing. During the course of the years we acted through standard channels to get results on IDA and the gym and we were rebuffed at every turn, rudely and irresponsibly. Thus the actions we took were necessary and just and we will not accept judgment or punishment from . . . the administration.[45]

Establishment reaction to student guerilla tactics initially was surprise, then disbelief, horror, anger and finally the urge to punish. If fear was any part of the Establishment reaction to student tactics it was likely to be the concern over where such lawlessness would lead.

Contributing further to the alienation of the generations was the use of obscenities in students' public speech. The role of obscenities in the rhetoric of student protest at Columbia is fascinating yet nebulous. Obscenity first became an issue in student rhetoric at Berkeley in 1965. But obscenities were never used as extensively at Berkeley as they were at Columbia.

Some of the radical students at Columbia adopted a slogan that contained an obscenity which became the "devil word" of the student movement at Columbia. They were handed the slogan by Mark Rudd on April 22nd, the day before it all began at Columbia. On that day Rudd wrote an open letter to President Grayson Kirk and printed it in an SDS paper as a rallying call for the demonstration planned for the next day.

In a long paragraph, he listed society's ills. Then he accused Grayson of being unable to understand positive values. The letter was laced throughout with threat rhetoric. It furnished a warning of the guerilla tactics and the "war" that lay ahead:

. . . if we win, we will take control of your world, your corporations, your university and attempt to mold a world in which we and other people can live as human beings. Your power is directly threatened since we will have to destroy that power before we take over. We will have to destroy at times, even violently, in order to end your power and your system.[46]

The final paragraph of Rudd's letter contained the slogan for radical revolution at Columbia: "There is only one thing left to say. It may sound nihilistic to you, since it is the opening shot in a war of liberation. I'll use the words of LeRoi Jones, whom I'm sure you don't like a whole lot: 'Up against the wall, motherfucker, this is a stick-up!' " "Up against the wall, you motherfucker!" became the battle cry of Columbia revolutionaries.

There is no shortage of theories about

43. *New York Times*, June 10, 1968, p. 53.
44. *Ibid.*
45. Avorn, *Up Against the Ivy Wall*, p. 137.
46. The complete text of Mark Rudd's letter to President Kirk is printed in Avorn, *Up Against the Ivy Wall*, pp. 25-27.

the reason for the use of obscenities by students in protest. One administrator told the *New York Times* that it was the "Get Dad" and "naughtiness" syndrome—the wicked children shocking the parents and the outside world.[47] A moderate student conjectured that the language revealed an attitude of disrespect. "Mark Rudd was putting down Nobel Prize winners and distinguished leaders in words that were profane and spiteful. It makes everybody equal."[48]

Mark Rudd explained the use of the rallying cry he gave to Columbia rebels. He claimed that to shout "Up against the wall, you motherfucker!" helped to define the strike. He thought nothing upset the "enemies" more than this slogan. "To them it seemed to show the extent to which we had broken with their norms, how far we had sunk to brutality, hatred and obscenity. Great!"[49] Rudd contended that the truth behind the use of the slogan was that it "defined Grayson Kirk, David Truman, the Trustees, many of the faculty, the cops, as our enemies. . . . The essence of the matter is that we are out for social and political revolution, nothing less."[50] He believed that the slogan put the administration and the interests it represents on one side and the leftist students and their interest in humanity on the other. Those in the middle were then forced to choose sides. By Rudd's admission, then, it was a fringe benefit for the new left if the slogan upset the enemy with its implication of depravity; its real intent was to separate the two sides in the battle.

Rudd offered still another explanation of his use of obscenity in the public speech of student protest. "We co-opted the word . . . from the ghetto much as we adopted the struggle of blacks and other oppressed as our own. When young people start calling those in power 'motherfuckers'

you know the structure of authority is breaking down."[51]

Another landmark in the Columbia uprising was the "bullshit speech," a brief talk by Mark Rudd before the Columbia faculty. Rudd's infamous speech took place at a meeting to which he had been invited by faculty members who had supported the student strike. They had told Rudd that the vote on amnesty was near and conjectured that if he appealed to the faculty, he might be able to swing a victory for amnesty.

Rudd stood in the back of the room while one faculty member painted an optimistic picture of the talks with rebellious black students. "Dialogue is still open, and the students are taking the night to think about various proposals," reported one professor. Another faculty member rose to give an encouraging report on the negotiations. Then one of them signaled Rudd, and the SDS leader moved to the front of the room to speak.

The speech was short. "We had exploratory talks . . . very exploratory, more in the line of bullshit. . . . It's going to be impossible to discipline people on these crimes. . . . There is only one solution: recognize that these are political acts and the reasons behind them are political. . . . I ask that this group grant amnesty with the understanding that what we did was right."[52]

The word "bullshit," though spoken casually by Rudd, negated everything the faculty speaker had just said. Rudd's speech forced the faculty to realize that action,

---

47. Avorn, *Up Against the Ivy Wall*, pp. 25-27.
48. *Ibid.*
49. *Ibid.*, p. 291.
50. *Ibid.*
51. *Ibid.*
52. *Ibid.*

not words, was the only thing the students respected and absolutely the only faculty move to which they would respond. As highly publicized as it was by the news media, the "bullshit speech" widened the rift between generations. It must have looked to the rest of the world as if it were too late for the divided generations to work out a rational resolution to their differences.

Not all students active in the Columbia uprising employed expletives as part of their rhetoric. It was the more radical activists who kept obscenity active in protest speech. The news media—finding a good story in the use of obscenities by students—made certain that the Establishment was exposed to the turn that student rhetoric had taken.

Before Mark Rudd finished his explanation of why the obscene slogans were used by SDS, he admitted that the reaction to the style was stronger than reaction to the content. Thus the use of obscenity in the new left rhetoric repeated the error it had made in the decision to use guerilla tactics—the method called attention to itself while the matter behind it was ignored.

The occasion for any kind of student oratory at Columbia in 1968 was most frequently the SDS-sponsored rally. Rally oratory usually emerged as response to immediately recent developments in the revolution. Sometimes the speaker planned his strategy aloud with his audience, acting out the SDS ideal of participatory democracy. For instance, at the rally held at the sundial on April 23, 1968, Mark Rudd's speech plans were altered in the moment before he climbed onto the sundial. Just then he had been handed a sealed letter sent to him by Columbia Vice-President David Truman. The letter stated that Low Library had been locked but that the Vice-Presi-

dent was prepared to meet with the entire group in the largest auditorium on campus to discuss the issues.

The first words from Rudd to the crowd were, "The doors to Low Library have been locked. The administration building has been closed down by us. Whether they realize it or not they are locked in and we, the free men, are outside."[53] Rudd had turned a quick rhetorical trick. He could have chosen to anger the crowd with the image of their being locked out of a building they had every right to enter, or he could have claimed that the students were in control of locks and keys and had chosen freedom for themselves. His choice of the second alternative injected the crowd with a sense of being on the right side in the "war"; it reinforced their sense of power; and it did not raise the pitch of the crowd too soon.

Next Rudd read aloud the complete text of the letter from Truman. With that rhetorical decision he made of his audience intimates with whom he shared a private message to Rudd from the second man in power. After finishing the letter, Rudd shouted, "He gives us this alternative because he is a very *li-ber-al* man," filling the word "liberal" with undisguised contempt. "After we've gone to the son of a bitch a million times and he hasn't responded to us, now he asks to meet with us at McMillin," he quickly added.[54]

Then Rudd outlined alternative courses of action which the demonstration could take that day. "We could have a demonstration inside McMillin with chanting and picketing. We could have Truman talk with us about IDA and the rest." Numerous listeners began to respond with "Yes!" or

---

53. *Ibid.*, p. 42.
54. *Ibid.*, p. 43.

"No!" Rudd did not allow his audience to entertain for long the thought of more discussion with the administration. He quickly added, "But if we go to McMillin, we will just talk and go through a lot of bullshit." At this point he looked up toward Low Library and received a signal that the huge door to Low was indeed locked. "The doors *are* locked at Low," he yelled. "We won't get in the fucking office. Maybe—"[55]

The uncertainty prompted by Rudd's "maybe" prompted a revolutionary named Hurwitz to leap onto the sundial and shout, "Did we come here to talk or did we come here to go to Low?" Raising his right arm to the sky, the radical jumped from the sundial and led the crowd to Low Library. Rudd, abandoning oratory for action, linked arms with his fellow revolutionaries and pushed to the front of the crowd that was following Hurwitz. He had paid the price for allowing his rhetoric to ramble and ultimately to rest in uncertainty—his audience had left him standing there with his mouth open.

From such snippets as these it is possible to make a few generalizations about student rally oratory. The speeches were a kind of reactionary rhetoric in the sense that they voiced response to momentary situations. An unexpected letter, a suggestion from a fellow revolutionary, audience feedback, a sudden turn of events—reactions to these happenings shaped student speeches at rallies. It was a rhetoric created by exigencies of the moment. Born of confusion, it often died of incoherence. Perhaps the SDS belief in participatory democracy deadened any desire in students to listen to or deliver well planned speeches. For whatever reason, the student uprising at Columbia was not noted for leaders who practiced the art of persuasive oratory. The gains made by students might more easily be traced to the Columbia brand of physical, confrontative rhetoric.

The uprising at Columbia University was ended by the students' departure from campus for summer work and play. But before they left there were commencement exercises to attend. The more radical students refused to attend the university's commencement exercises and staged their own. Those who listened to Columbia Professor Richard Hofstadter address the audience at the regularly scheduled exercises heard him contrast a reasoned approach to societal reform with the student strategies which had recently been used on Columbia's campus, "The technique of forceable occupation for closure of a university's buildings with the intention of bringing its activities to a halt is no ordinary bargaining device. It is a thrust into the vitals of university life."[56]

Hofstadter closed his address with a response to the question in the minds of people all over America: How can Columbia go on after this terrible wound? His only answer, he said, was "How can it *not* go on?"

The tone of Hofstadter's speech was deep concern; yet it expressed the hope amid chaos that Americans needed to hear at the moment. He vocalized the predominant American reaction to the crisis on campus: the students might be right in their call for reform but their tactics were wrong. No mention was being made at this point of the larger societal reforms for which stu-

_____

55. *Ibid.*
56. The complete text of Richard Hofstadter's commencement address can be found in *American Scholar*, Autumn, 1968, pp. 583-89.

dents had pressed early in the decade. Student strategies at Columbia finally focused so completely on university reform and amnesty for students that the issues of racism, military-corporate control, Vietnam and the draft were no longer the dominant concern of the student activists at Columbia.

In December, 1969, Yale President Kingman Brewster described student impatience, "While destructiveness is limited to a very small number, and while romantic visions of the university as a misty community without form or authority are confined to a limited minority, impatience is pervasive. Right, left, dull, bright, active, apathetic—the shadow of impatience touches them all."[57]

It was the impatience which finally erupted into violence. Once the elder generation resorted to police control of its youth, there was little hope that the division between the two generations could be bridged. When, in the spring of 1970, the National Guard troops at Kent State University and the State Police at Jackson State University fired on protesting students, their shots stunned the world and silenced the majority of student protesters on American campuses. By September, memories of those killings had blackmailed the generations into living together quietly.

In 1971 it is still quiet on American college and university campuses.

Reflections

"The campus has been virtually free of conflict throughout the entire year. By mutual consent academic activity has been restored to a style and tempo befitting one of the great intellectual centers of the world. . . . We have been through a harsh period of reassessment together and for the moment at least we are managing quite well."[58] These words were spoken to Columbia University's 1971 graduating class by President William McGill. The acknowledgement of "mutual consent" by which President McGill finds the academic community restored to "a style and tempo befitting a great university" is far from a jubilant declaration that the generations are now united in vision and acting together to create a better world. We may have here no more than an agreement between the generations not to wage war; i.e., if the "kids" will quit destroying university property and acting violently, the "grown-ups" will stop calling the cops.

True, there is a change of mood on American campuses in 1971. In 1968, Columbia's President Kirk could not dare to speak to the graduates because of the tension on campus; and even his noncontroversial substitute, the late Professor Hofstadter, was boycotted by dissenters who staged the first major "counter commencement." But peace, however tenuous, seems to reign in 1971.

Though relieved and grateful that the shrill and rebellious tone of recent years has been replaced by calm, the citizenry searches for an explanation of the quiet on campus. Have the rebellious students gone underground to regroup for the right time to start another "revolution?" Or is the rebellion done with, worn out, exhausted? There is no shortage of speculation about whether peace on campus is temporary or permanent.

---

57. Kingman Brewster, Jr., "If Not Reason, What?" *Vital Speeches*, Vol. 36, March 15, 1970, p. 348.

58. *New York Times*, June 6, 1971, p. E11.

It is possible to assess the nature of the gains made by students in protest during the 1960's. Studies of the issues behind the decade of protest show that student power on campus was the least emphasized of student goals.[59] Yet in the final analysis of those changes made in America during the decade, changes which might be traced to student dissent, the chief gain was in the area of greater voice in the governance of universities. Although it was concern for racial, social and political issues that began the protest at Greensboro and sustained it on most campuses for two-thirds of the decade, students were unable to trigger the reform of American society which they had called for early in the sixties.

SNCC and the young SDS had tried to reason with the Establishment about the need for reform, but SNCC was persecuted and SDS ignored. Then students stopped looking for commonality with the generation in power; daily they reinforced the division between generations. Finally, at Columbia, with the use of coercion, the final steps were taken to alienate the generations.

University tradition abhors the abandonment of reason for coercion, having always stood for the preservation of man's nobility. Given no alternative but to employ the despised tactic themselves, the Establishment may have been driven to a kind of self-hate bred by a sellout of one's convictions. That self-hate could in part have been responsible for the backlash response of the elder generation to the youth who caused their moral discomfort.

Peace on campus appears to have resulted from a decision to cease doing battle. That there could be a lasting peace when the generations seem to have found no other way of acting together than to lay down arms seems doubtful.

BIBLIOGRAPHY

Three valuable sources for insight into the early student civil rights movement, particularly the founding of SNCC and SDS, from the point of view of those who were directly involved. Where Lynd, Newfield and Zinn were not actually on the scene of events, they had access to records of students who were there and who recorded their firsthand observations:

Lynd, Staughton, ed. *Nonviolence in America: A Documentary History.* Indianapolis: Bobbs-Merrill, 1966.

Newfield, Jack. *A Prophetic Minority.* New York: The New American Library, 1966.

Zinn, Howard. *SNCC: The New Abolitionists.* Boston: Beacon Press, 1965.

Valubale collection of essays and speeches by active participants in the New Left student movement on American campuses during the 1960s:

Cohen, Mitchell, and Hale, Dennis, eds. *The New Student Left.* Boston: Beacon Press, 1967.

Primary source records of events during the Free Speech Movement at Berkeley in 1964-65:

Feuer, Lewis S. *The Conflict of Generations: The Character and Significance of Student Movements.* New York: Basic Books, 1969.

Schaar, John H., and Sheldon S. Wolin. *The Berkeley Rebellion and Beyond.* New York: Vintage Books, 1970.

A detailed history of events during the uprising at Columbia University in the spring of 1968, compiled by the members of the staff of the daily student newspaper at Columbia. Their documentation is a record of firsthand observations of twenty-five editors, reporters and researchers of the *Daily Spectator* staff who covered the crisis at Columbia:

Avorn, Jerry L., with Andrew; Crane, Jaffee, Mark; Root, Oren, Jr.; Starr, Paul; Stern, Michael; Stulberg, Robert. *Up Against the Ivy Walls.* New York: Atheneum, 1969.

59. See *Campus Tensions: Analysis and Recommendation,* Report of the Special Committee on Campus Tensions, American Council on Education, 1970; *Student Protests, 1969: Summary,* Report by Urban Research Corporation, 1970; *Youth in Turmoil,* Adapted from a special issue of *Fortune Magazine,* 1969; *Crisis at Columbia,* Report of the Fact-Finding Commission on Columbia Disturbances, 1968.

24 The Peace Movement and the Vietnam War

Jess Yoder

"Then conquer we must; for the cause, it is just," declares the American National Anthem. War is an intense, emotional national experience. In wartime a soldier is asked to lay his own life on the line for the sake of his country. When America commits her sons to battle she must assure her people that the cause is just; that their sons are not "dying in vain." When America commits her young men to face death on the battle line she must also assure her people that the war is necessary; that vital national interests are directly involved. In May of 1967, Assistant Secretary of Defense John T. McNaughton recognized that many Americans had not been assured that the United States involvement in the Vietnam War was necessary. In a note to Secretary Robert McNamara, McNaughton wrote, "A feeling is widely and strongly held that the 'Establishment' is out of its mind." Commenting further he said, "Related to this feeling is the increased polarization that is taking place in the United States with the seeds of the worst split in our people in more than a century."[1]

This chapter is concerned with the deep division within America over the Vietnam War. On the one side of the divide were the administration's spokesmen and policy makers who defended the U.S. actions taken in Vietnam; on the other side was an array of people, groups, and organizations who regarded the American involvement in Vietnam as a tragic mistake. Each side took its case to the people of America who in turn were asked to take a position on the war.

To a large extent the peace movement was shaped by events outside its own control. "The chief sustaining element in the Vietnam protest movement has been the war in Vietnam," the Skolnick Report reminds us.[2] Periods of escalation, such as the bombing of North Vietnam and the Cambodian invasion, became high points for the peace movement as it responded with spokesmen, demonstrations, protests, and campaigns against the war. The national elections of 1968, the party conventions, and the campaigning leading up to

---

1. *The New York Times, The Pentagon Papers* (New York: Bantam Books, 1971), p. 20.

2. Jerome H. Skolnick, *The Politics of Protest* (New York: Ballantine Books, 1969), pp. 31-32. This report was presented to the National Commission on the Causes and Prevention of Violence.

the elections provided another set of events that strengthened the peace movement. In the heated controversy over the war politicians running for national office often were forced to wear the "hawk" or "dove" labels. The rank and file citizens also experienced the hawk-dove tension as they supported their candidates and voted on the war issues.

The administration naturally carried the prestige of the president's office; its supporters in Congress and statehouses enjoyed White House prestige and rewards. The lack of progress in the war, low troop morale, stalemated peace talks, corruption in Saigon's government, and charges of deception in the Johnson strategy served to destroy the credibility of the administration and build up the credibility of its critics in the peace movement. Participants in the peace movement included senators, congressmen, governors, presidential candidates, former presidential advisors, professors, doctors, lawyers, authors, artists, movie stars, reporters, clergymen, union leaders, industrialists, students, even war veterans, and apparently officials in the Pentagon itself. While the administration claimed that it was privy to top secret information the opposition was able to gain prestige from its access to hard news, experts, and inside information.

Since the peace movement protested U.S. policy in Vietnam it seems appropriate first, to survey the development of the U.S. position in Vietnam; second, to examine the legal and the moral issues arising from this position; third, to analyze the development, strategies, and accomplishments of the peace movement; and finally, to summarize the implications of the movement from a rhetorical standpoint.

The Development of the U.S. Position in Vietnam

Most of the countries in Southeast Asia had secured their independence from colonial powers after World War II. The notable exception was French Indo-China. In 1941 the French negotiated with the Japanese to obtain control of Indo-China. At that point the Vietnamese nationalistic movement was suppressed and driven underground. The most important channel open to the Vietnamese nationals who desired to wrest their country from French control was the Communist party under the leadership of Ho Chi Minh. At that time the American Office of Strategic Services supported the Vietnamese nationalist movement which was known as the Vietminh. In spite of the opposition to colonialism the French refused to give up their Indo-China territories as did the Americans, French, British, and Dutch.

Roosevelt, who opposed the French occupation of Vietnam, called for the territory to become a United Nations trusteeship. However, the Truman administration came to the support of the French and agreed to underwrite up to two-thirds of their military costs in Vietnam, In mid-1954 the French forces capitulated to the Vietminh and the Geneva Conference was set up to arrange a settlement. The French government in Vietnam under the leadership of Bao Dai controlled about one-fourth of the country; the rest was controlled by the Vietminh.

The Geneva Accords, which grew out of the armistice agreement, provided a provisional *military* demarcation line in order to separate the Vietminh forces from the forces of the French Union. Disarmament was to be supervised by an International Control Commission and the mechanism for national elections was to be established. Elections were to be held at the end of a two-year period when the country was to be reunited under the newly elected leader. The United States agreed to honor the Geneva Conference Agreements, but it did not sign them.[3] In less than a year the French withdrew from Vietnam without honoring the election obligation. Boa Dai, formerly the French High Commissioner for Vietnam, took over the reigns of South Vietnam's government. Boa Dai appointed Ngo Dinh Diem as Premier of Vietnam. In October of 1955 a referendum was held in South Vietnam and Diem won the election. Diem had received the support of the United States. The government was reorganized and named the "Republic of Vietnam." Diem cancelled the elections which were scheduled for 1956 by the Geneva Agreements, declaring that his newly formed government was not a party to the Agreements. Apparently, the real reason was that Ho Chi Minh would have won the election.[4] This turn of events set into motion a wave of anti-Saigon sentiment in South Vietnam.

President Eisenhower, aware of the inequities and exploitation in South Vietnam, gave President Diem support on condition that the much needed land reforms and political reforms would be put into effect. Later Eisenhower's letter of support was used as evidence of the United States' commitment to Vietnam.[5]

The massive economic support given to the Diem government by the United States failed to stem the unrest in South Vietnam. The promised land reforms never materialized and the Diem rule became more repressive and corrupt. In the latter part of the 1950s the National Liberation Front (NLF) was organized to oppose the Diem tyranny. In its early years the NLF was opposed by Hanoi but in 1960 it received Hanoi's endorsement. In spite of clear evidence to the contrary, the official position of the United States was that the NLF was Hanoi's creation.[6]

The Kennedy administration significantly increased the U.S. commitment in Vietnam hoping to strengthen the faltering Saigon government. The Geneva Agreements limited the size of the U.S. mission (which was mainly military) in South Vietnam to 685 men. Ignoring these Agreements, which the U.S. had pledged to honor, Kennedy had by October, 1963, raised the Military Assistance Advisor Group (MAAG) to 16,732 men. The Ken-

3. See Donald Lancaster, "Power Politics at the Geneva Conference (1954)," in *Vietnam History, Documents, and Opinions*, ed. Marvin E. Gettleman (New York: New American Library, 1970), pp. 146-63. Lancaster says that Secretary of State Dulles did not want to sign an armistice involving concessions to Asian Communists.
4. President Eisenhower said, "I have never talked or corresponded with a person knowledgeable in Indo Chinese affairs who did not agree that had the elections been held at the time of the fighting possibly 80 percent of the population would have voted for Communist Ho Chi Minh as their leader rather than Chief of State Bao Dai," In Dwight D. Eisenhower, *Mandate for Change: The White House Years, 1953-1956* (London: Heinemann, 1963), p. 372.
5. Letter is printed in Gettleman, *Vietnam*, pp. 236-37.
6. The U. S. position was published later in the White Paper of 1965: *Agreesion from the North: The Record of North Vietnam's Campaign to Conquer South Vietnam*, U. S. Department of State Publication 7839, Far Eastern Series 130 (Washington, D. C., February, 1965). Also printed in Gettleman, *Vietnam*, pp. 324-57.

nedy administration also initiated the Strategic Hamlet Program to protect the people in rural areas from counter guerilla attacks. According to the Pentagon analysts the Hamlet Program "failed dismally." In the summer of 1963 Diem used the South Vietnamese Special Forces to put down Buddhist rebellions and raid pagodas. Washington officials were angered at Diem's action, especially after they financed the Special Forces program of South Vietnam.[7] Then in November of 1963 Diem and his brother, Ngo Dinh Nhu, were assassinated and a military junta took charge. Later in the same month President Kennedy was assassinated and it became Lyndon Johnson's responsibility to carry the U.S. policy forward.

Shortly after Kennedy's death United Nations Secretary U Thant and Premiere Charles DeGaulle had made offers to work on peace proposals for Vietnam. President Johnson, upon the advice of Secretary of State Rusk and Secretary of Defense McNamara, chose not to accept their overtures. Before negotiating was to begin the United States and South Vietnam wished to strengthen their bargaining position.[8] The pressures for a neutralist government had been quite strong under the leadership of the Minh junta. President Johnson suggested that neutralization of South Vietnam would only be another name for a Communist take-over and his administration began to take a more active role in building up South Vietnam militarily. An elaborate program of covert military operations against North Vietnam carrying the code name, Operation Plan 34A began on February 1, 1964.[9] The Minh junta was overthrown by General Khanh who aligned himself squarely with U.S. policy.

After the controversial "attack" upon the U.S. destroyers, the *Maddox* and the *Turner Joy*, took place in August of 1964, the American involvement in the war could be made public. Retaliation bombing raids were ordered immediately. The next day an administration-drafted resolution was presented to Congress. The resolution, which was passed immediately with only two dissenting votes in the Senate, gave the President authority "to take all necessary measures to repel any armed attack against the forces of the United States and to prevent further aggression." Section 2 of the resolution says that consonant with the United States Constitution and the United Nations Charter the United States is prepared, "as the President determines, to take all necessary steps, including the use of armed force, to assist any member or protocol state of the Southeast Asia Collective Defense Treaty requesting assistance in defense of its freedom."[10]

The Johnson administration contended that the Tonkin Gulf Resolution gave the President authority to conduct sustained bombing and, if necessary, to launch a ground war in Vietnam. Neither of these measures was taken until after President Johnson was reelected on a pledge not to enlarge the war. By February, 1965, Operation Rolling Thunder—sustained air war—was ordered and in April ground troops

---

7. *The Pentagon Papers*, p. 166.

8. George McTurnan Kahin, and John W. Lewis, *The United States in Vietnam* (New York: Dial Press, 1967), p. 152.

9. Neil Sheehan, "The Covert War and Tonkin Gulf: February-August, 1964," *The Pentagon Papers*, pp. 234ff.

10. For full text of the SEATO Defense Treaty see the U. S. Senate Committee on Foreign Relations publication, *Background Information Relating to Southeast Asia and Vietnam*, 4th rev. ed. (Washington, D. C., March, 1968), pp. 101ff; text of the Tonkin Resolution is on page 141.

were commanded to take offensive actions. The troop strength was steadily increased until it reached 565,000 in 1968. Neither the intense bombing nor the increased ground operations brought the predicted results. However, the increased antiwar pressure at home and the pessimistic reports from Vietnam prompted President Johnson to work hard for initiating peace talks. In March, 1968, the President halted bombing in North Vietnam and dramatically declared that he would not run for re-election. In January, 1969, the United States, South Vietnam, North Vietnam, and the National Liberation Front met in Paris to begin peace negotiations.

When Richard Nixon became president he reaffirmed the goals of his predecessors. Nixon pledged to bring the war to an end, win a just peace, and bring Americans home from Vietnam. Nixon set forth a plan of Vietnamization which called for a systematic withdrawal of American military personnel who were to be replaced by South Vietnam's military personnel. He pledged to reduce the U.S. troop strength in Vietnam by 150,000 in one year. In April, 1970, Nixon told the American people that American air strikes were being made in Laos in order to interdict supply routes to South Vietnam. In May the President announced the invasion into Cambodia. The American protest reaction was immediate and shortly thereafter four students at Kent State University and two students at Jackson State University were killed. Nixon insisted his action was necessary to save American lives and speed up troop withdrawal. The Cambodian invasion was terminated on July 1. Feelings subsided but the antiwar sentiment remained strong. Nixon was put under pressure to set a date for the withdrawal of all U.S. troops but he refused to set such a date. The President contended that setting a date would strengthen the hand of the enemy and be a "kiss of death" to American prisoners in North Vietnam. The North Vietnamese countered saying that they would not negotiate or return the American prisoners until the United States withdrew her troops. The stalemate has not been broken and the peace talks remain deadlocked.[11]

By mid-1971 more than 54,000 Americans had died in the Vietnam War and the casualty list had mounted to over 300,000 Americans. Thus far the American support of the South Vietnam regime has gone beyond the $120 billion mark. An analysis of the peace movement from a rhetorical standpoint must be seen in the context of these developing events. The peace movement emerged at the outset of the war and it became active when the United States' position developed from a covert war to an open commitment of troops and supplies. Naturally, the administration needed to justify and support its actions with arguments acceptable to the American public. The issues around which such arguments were centered became the points of controversy between the administration and the peace movement. The spokesmen for the peace movement in confronting the administration on the issues raised were in the same process constructing their own positions and rationale.

Why Are We In Vietnam? Legal Issues and Arguments

While President Eisenhower's administration gave military aid to South Vietnam

_____

11. At the time of this writing, December, 1971.

and Kennedy's administration increased the U.S. commitment to provide military advisors, it was during the Johnson administration that ground troops were fighting in Vietnam. Heavy bombing and shelling was also initiated by the Johnson administration. On July 28, 1965, President Johnson opened a White House Press Conference by reading a portion of a letter he had received from a lady in the midwest. Her question has persistently been asked during the war. She wrote:

Dear Mr. President: In my humble way I am writing to you about the crisis in Vietnam. I have a son who is now in Vietnam. My husband served in World War II. Our country was at war, but now, this time, it is just something I don't understand. Why?

The President said, "Well, I have tried to answer that question dozens of times and more in practically every state in this Union." Apparently his answer was not convincing, but he responded again declaring:

We insist and always will insist that the people of South Vietnam shall have the right of choice, the right to shape their own destiny in free elections in the South, or throughout all Vietnam under international supervision, and they shall not have any government imposed upon them by force and terror so long as we can prevent it.[12]

Earlier in a speech at Johns Hopkins University President Johnson stated that "the first reality is that North Vietnam has attacked the independent nation of South Vietnam. Its object is total conquest." Later in the speech the President said, "Our objective is the independence of South Vietnam, and its freedom from attack. We want nothing for ourselves, only that the people of South Vietnam be allowed to guide their own country in their own way."

There is another reality, contended President Johnson, "The rulers in Hanoi are urged on by Peking" the nation which destroyed freedoms in Tibet, India, and Korea is supporting the violence in Vietnam for its own purposes.[13]

The argument set forth by President Johnson assumes that South Vietnam is a separate independent state and that North Vietnam is another separate independent state which is depriving the people of the South of the right to govern themselves. The Geneva Agreements never made such claims; however, they did recognize a temporary military demarcation line behind which both the North and the South were asked to regroup their forces. After the elections scheduled for 1956 were held, the nation was to be reunited. The interpretation which President Johnson gave was necessary to justify the U.S. action; otherwise, the United States would be illegally interfering in a civil war. But Vietnam was not only divided into North and South Vietnam; South Vietnam was further divided into Saigon forces and the Viet Cong (NLF). President Johnson admitted, "Of course, some of the people of South Vietnam are participating in this attack on their own government. But trained men and supplies, orders and arms, flow in a constant stream from North to South."[14]

When pushed for documentation on the "external force" argument, Secretary of

---

12. Lyndon B. Johnson, "We Will Stand in Viet-Nam," printed by the Department of State, Publication 7937. Washington, D. C., August 16, 1965. pp. 1, 8.

13. Address by President Johnson, "Pattern for Peace in Southeast Asia," delivered April 17, 1965 at John Hopkins University. Department of State Bulletin, Washington, D. C., 1965):606-10. Also in Gettleman, *Vietnam*, pp. 364-70.

14. *Ibid.*, p. 606 in Gettleman, *Vietnam*.

State Rusk, in an address to the American Society of International Law, contended that the U.S. White Papers and the report of the International Control Commission establish evidence "beyond reasonable doubt" of North Vietnamese intervention. He added, "There is no evidence that the Viet Cong has any significant following in South Vietnam."[15] Secretary Rusk and the State Department failed to mention that the report of the International Control Commission accused the United States of far more serious violations of the Geneva Agreements, namely, supplying South Vietnam with "immense amounts of U.S. arms, military personnel, and war materials." The Control Commission found no cooperation from South Vietnam in policing peace agreements. This was in sharp contrast to the cooperation given by the Vietminh in the North.[16] The U.S. White Paper was the other source used to establish evidence of North Vietnam's aggression. I.F. Stone made an analysis of the evidence used to back up the charges set forth in the White Paper. Using the Pentagon's own data, Stone discovered that only 2.5 percent of the weapons confiscated in South Vietnam had come from North Vietnam. "The White Paper claimed 'that as many as 75 percent of the more than 7,000 Viet Cong who are known to have entered the South in 1964 were natives of North Vietnam.' But a careful reading of the text and the appendices turns up the names of only six North Vietnamese infiltrees."[17] In an address to Yeshiva University Senator Mike Mansfield said, "When the sharp increase in the American military effort began in early 1965, it was estimated that only about 400 North Vietnamese soldiers were among the enemy forces in the South, which totaled 140,000 at that time."[18] Senator Vance

Hartke said that the claim of the White Paper was "pure fairy tale" when it asserted our problem to be with Hanoi rather than with dissident elements in South Vietnam. Secretary Rusk concurred. "The fact is," Hartke said, "that the administration did put American troops in, did escalate the war, precisely because of the success of the dissident element inside of South Vietnam."[19]

President Johnson charged that the North Vietnamese were guilty of breaking the Geneva Agreements. He said that throughout the Eisenhower and Kennedy administrations as well as his own, the American goal has been to observe the Geneva Agreements of 1954. Senators Hartke, Morse, Gruening and others pointed out that the elections scheduled by the Agreements were not held because the United States supported Diem's refusal to permit the elections.

In addition to claiming that North Vietnam violated the freedom of South Vietnam and failed to keep the Geneva Agreements, President Johnson and Secretary of State Rusk repeatedly cited the SEATO Treaty as a basis of the American

---

15. Speech was given April 23, 1965. *Department of State Bulletin* 52 (Washington, May 10, 1965):694-700; also in *Vietnam*, ed. Gettleman, pp. 370-76 (Quotation on p. 375).

16. Gettleman records a number of the Commission reports, pp. 194-221.

17. I. F. Stone, "A Reply to the White Paper," *In A Time of Torment*, (New York, Random House, 1967), p. 213.

18. Mike Mansfield, "Viet-Nam and China," address given at Yeshiva University, New York, June 16, 1966. Quoted by Vance Hartke, *The American Crisis in Vietnam*, (Indianapolis: Bobbs, 1968), p. 68. These figures were confirmed by the Defense Department according to the *Washington Daily News*, June 23, 1966.

19. Hartke, p. 70.

commitment. "Let us be clear about our commitment in Vietnam," said Secretary Rusk. "It began with the Southeast Asia Treaty." Senator Hartke responded by pointing to the SEATO Treaty, Article I and Sections 1 and 2 in Article IV which state that international disputes are to be submitted to the Security Council of the United Nations. He charged that the United States deliberately bypassed the United Nations. "By no possible stretch of the English language does the SEATO Treaty commit us to any unilateral action. By no possible stretch of the imagination can the SEATO Treaty be a basis for the current policy being followed in Vietnam."[20] Senator J. William Fulbright told Secretary Rusk that the failure of the SEATO powers to act in behalf of South Vietnam was due to their belief that it was a civil war and they did not consider their own security at stake.

Antiwar groups raised another legal question stemming from the fact that the United States is a signatory to the Charter of the United Nations, the provisions of which are made obligatory upon its members. The Charter prohibits members from making threats or using force "against the territorial integrity or political independence of any state or in any other manner inconsistent with the purposes of the United Nations." It also states that the Security Council shall determine "the existence of any threat to the peace, breach of the peace, or act of aggression, and shall make recommendations or shall decide what measures shall be taken." A nation is permitted to respond to armed attack for self-defense if the Security Council has not had time to respond; that self-defense may also be a collective action, according to Article 51 of the Charter. The United States claim-

ed that intervention in Vietnam is sanctioned under Article 51 on the ground that South Vietnam is an independent state, that it had been attacked by North Vietnam, and that it was engaging in "collective self-defense" at the request of South Vietnam. Here again the opposition pointed out that the Geneva Accords recognized all of Vietnam as a single state, that attacks were not made by North Vietnam but by dissident South Vietnamese (the Viet Cong), and that the request for American assistance came from a puppet government created by the United States. Further, the government of South Vietnam was not a member of the United Nations because it could not meet the tests of membership. The United States, to operate in the spirit of the United Nations Charter, should at least have been willing to present the matter to the Security Council for a ruling.

Finally, the question of the constitutionality of the United States engaging in the Vietnam War was also raised. The President contended that the Tonkin Gulf Resolution expressed the intent of Congress because it authorized him to take "all necessary steps, including the use of armed force" when requested by a SEATO member. Since the Constitution grants the President, as Commander-in-Chief of Armed Forces, the power to deploy U.S. military forces, the argument continued, an explicit declaration of war in Vietnam was not necessary. The State Department, in a position paper, held that to declare war would

---

20. Hartke, pp. 34-35. Rusk's arguments on SEATO obligations are given in his statement before the U. S. Senate Committee on Foreign Relations, February 18, 1966 (Washington, D. C., *Department of State Bulletin* 54 March 7, 1966):1-17.

add a new psychological element to the international situation, reduce flexibility options for the President, and effect no changes on the legality issue.[21] Senator Wayne Morse in a speech, "Legal Issues of U.S. Position in Vietnam," declared that the President's "participation ends at the threshold of the decision whether or not to declare war. Under Article I, Section 8, Clause 11 [of the Constitution], that power if confided exclusively to Congress."[22]

Both President Johnson and President Nixon insisted that there had been no shift in the United State's commitment to South Vietnam since the time of President Eisenhower. The Eisenhower commitment provided economic and military aid to be used by the government of South Vietnam. The Kennedy commitment went a step further and provided advisors to give military training and counsel to the South Vietnamese army. President Johnson in his public statements implied that conducting bombing missions and sending in ground troops was no change in commitment. *The Pentagon Papers* point out that Johnson's strategy was to stress no changes in policy as he went about making changes. *The Papers* point out, "The fact that this departure from a longheld policy had momentous implications was well recognized by the Administration leadership. . . Mr. Johnson was greatly concerned that the step be given as little prominence as possible."[23] Obviously the antiwar leadership found no difficulty in noting the changes of policy.

The Crisis of Conscience: Moral and Religious Issues

President Johnson in an address to the National Legislative Conference at San An-

tonio, Texas, on September 29, 1967, said that while we cherish freedom and self-determination for all people, "the key to all that we have done in Vietnam is really in our own security."[24] The administration viewed communism as an evil, barbarous, and ruthless force with worldwide goals. In Vietnam it made no distinction between the communism of the National Liberation Front and North Vietnam. The communism in Vietnam was marked with the same evils ascribed to the communism in Red China and Russia. The dissenters and critics of American policies in Vietnam were accused of being soft on communism, giving encouragement to the enemy, destroying the morale of the fighting men, lacking the courage and willingness to persevere and pay the price for freedom, being ready to abandon commitments and treaties, and being disloyal and un-American. On occasion these charges were made openly in public speech, but more often they were unstated assumptions implied in the arguments and contentions of proadministration spokesmen. These charges had strong intonations of unethical motivations attributed to critics of the Vietnam war. In political rhetoric the administration's position, patriotism, and morality are seldom delineated, especially on issues pertaining to war and national defense.

---

21. *Ibid.*, pp. 168-69.

22. Speech to the U.S. Senate, Friday, February 25, 1966. Congressional Record: Proceedings of the 89th Congress, Second Session, Vol. 113, Part 3, p. 4158.

23. *The Pentagon Papers*, p. 382.

24. Lyndon Johnson, Address to the National Legislative Conference at San Antonio, Texas, September 29, 1967. U.S. Department of State Publication 8305: U.S. Government Printing Office, Washington, 1968, p. 2.

The clergy were not about to be intimidated by the disloyalty claims.[25] "I oppose the war in Vietnam because I love America,"[26] said Martin Luther King. Bishop James Pike exclaimed, "My King is God, not LBJ."[27] The Rt. Rev. John Burt in declaring his total opposition to the Vietnam War argued, "I do not believe I am giving moral approval to those against whom our forces now contend-the Viet Cong and the armies of Ho Chi Minh. Nor am I disparaging in the slightest the courage and sacrifice of those in our armed forces who are fighting there."[28] The Rev. Lee Lewellen Kester said from his pulpit, "The notion of our idealism to make Vietnam a holy war is built upon a thin veneer of religiosity. It is this distortion of Christian purpose that disturbs me most in our pragmatic argument of waging war. It arises out of our Communist neurosis, and our deification of democracy and some nebulous statement of freedom which sounds godly. . . ." Kester charged that the Vietnam War did not meet the standards of Christian morality:

Some hawks say our Vietnam war is a just war. I submit, however, that we have shattered the code of a just war. It must be waged under the authority of the state; it must be fought in the spirit of love; it must spare noncombatants; and there must be justice on one side only. The conditions have all been violated. . . . This is not a just war.[29]

During World War I and World War II the large majority of ministers and denominations lent their full support to the war efforts. "Clergymen have been especially prominent in the peace movement in contrast to their relative silence during former wars, " says the *Skolnick Report.*[30] Not one major church denomination in the United States has sanctioned the Vietnam War; in fact, each has condemned it on moral and religious grounds. Statement af-

ter statement condemning the war had come each year from religious denominational conferences; these include the American Jewish Congress, the Church of the Brethren, the Episcopal Church, the National Baptist Convention, the Society of Friends, the United Methodist Church, the United Presbyterian Church, the Lutheran Church, the Mennonite Church, and many others. Religious organizations also have spoken out against the war. A few examples are the Fellowship of Reconciliation, Clergy and Laymen Opposed to the War in Vietnam, Southern Christian Leadership Conference, Catholic Peace Fellowship, B'nai B'rith, American Friends Service Committee, Brethren Service Committee, and the Mennonite Central Committee. In early 1967 the Clergy and Laymen Concerned about Vietnam in a position paper said, "Each day we find allegiance to our na-

25. For a fuller discussion on the clergy and the Vietnam War see Jess Yoder, "The Protest of the American Clergy in Opposition to the War in Vietnam, " *Today's Speech* 17 (September, 1969): 51-59. A number of the issues for this discussion are drawn from that article.

26. Martin Luther King, "The Casualties of the War in Vietnam," an address to the Nation Institute, Los Angeles, California, February 25, 1967, published in a pamphlet entitled, *Dr. Martin Luther King, Jr., Dr. John C. Bennett, Dr. Henry Steele Commager, and Rabbi Abraham Heschel Speak on the War in Vietnam* (New York: Clergy and Laymen Concerned About Vietnam, n.d.), p. 8.

27. A sermon at the First Congregational Church, reprinted in the *San Francisco Chronicle,* July 22, 1968, p. 3.

28. An address at Kent State University, November 16, 1967. Rev. Burt is Episcopal Bishop of the Diocese of Ohio. Copies available through Episcopal Diocese of Ohio, Cleveland, Ohio.

29. A sermon, "Peace," *The Pulpit Digest,* May, 1968, pp. 29-30. Rev. Kester is minister of the Reformed Church, Oradell, N. J.

30. Skolnick, *Politics of Protest,* p. 61.

tion's policy more difficult to reconcile with allegiance to our God."[31]

But it was not only the conscience of the clergy that was disturbed; many of the "silent majority" were deeply disturbed.[32] As the war progressed, more and more people experiencing agony of conscience concluded with the late Martin Luther King, "A time comes when silence is betrayal."[33] New York Times reporter Neil Sheehan in his article, "Not a Dove, But No Longer a Hawk," expressed his anguish in these words:

I simply cannot help worrying that in the process of waging this war, we are not corrupting ourselves. I wonder when I look at the bombed-out peasant hamlets, the orphans begging and stealing in the streets of Saigon, and the women and children with napalm burns lying on the hospital cots, whether the United States or any other nation has the right to inflict this suffering and degradation on another people for its own ends.[34]

David Schoenbrun, another reporter, said that Sheehan's commentary "is the cry of anguish of an honest man who has gone far toward the realization that his country is doing something very wrong."[35]

Here are the words from a soldier in Vietnam who wrote to his parents: "Today we went on a mission, and I'm not proud of myself, my friends, or my country. We burned every hut in sight." He continued describing the frantic cries of an old man who in tears begged them not to throw a grenade into his hut, but his buddy had already pulled the pin.

After the explosion we found the mother, two children, and an almost new born baby. That is what the old man was trying to tell us! . . . IT WAS HORRIBLE!! The children's fragile bodies were torn apart, literally mutilated. We looked at each other and burned the hut.

The young man related the anguish he ex-

perienced when he burned the next hut that belonged to an old man who "just kept bowing, begging me not to burn his hut. . . I wish I could have cried," the son wrote to his father, "but I just can't anymore." The editor of the Akron Beacon Journal printed the letter and told his readers that this boy from their community "is sickened and conscience stricken at the murderous devastation he is ordered to commit. Here is a father who is torn between loyalty to his country and frustrated anger that his son should be plunged into such a mess. . . This is the way the United States is 'protecting' the rest of the world? Read the letter—and weep."[36]

A rash of war crimes books have appeared on the market in the past five years. They tell of atrocities, chemical warfare,

---

31. Ibid.

32. In fact, Ray H. Abrams in his book, Preachers Present Arms rev. ed. (Scottdale, Pa: Herald Press, 1969), commenting on the clergy during World War I said: "At least, their speeches and conduct differed in no wise from the mass of the people whom they had undertaken to lead" (p. 124). My discussion of preaching during World War II also indicates that the clergy reflected the views of the majority. [See Jess Yoder, "Preaching on Issues of War and Peace: 1915-1965," in Preaching in American History, ed. Dewitte Holland (New York, Abingdon Press, 1969), pp. 239-57.

33. Address, "Beyond Vietnam," given at Riverside Church Meeting in New York City sponsored by Clergy and Laymen Concerned about Vietnam on April 4, 1967. Published in King, et. al. Speak on the War (New York: Clergy and Laymen Concerned About Vietnam, 1967), p. 10.

34. Sheehan's article appeared in the New York Times Magazine, October 9, 1966; reprinted in Information Service vol. 45, no. 21 (New York: National Council of Churches, December 31, 1966), pp. 1-7.

35. David Schoenbrun, "Vietnam: The Case for Extrication," Christianity and Crisis, February 6, 1967, p. 4.

36. Akron Beacon Journal, March 27, 1967, editorial page.

defoliation, air war, refugees, obliterated villages, and guilt ridden consciences. Some veterans became so disturbed that they returned their Congressional Medals; others refused to accept them initially. So it was by no means only the clergy who raised the moral and religious issues. The American people are troubled by "the anguish of an aching conscience," said Rev. Howard Schomer.[37] The Americans voted their conscience on the Vietnam question when they rejected the belligerent position of presidential candidate Barry Goldwater and elected Lyndon Johnson who cautioned against using force and "dropping bombs that are likely to involve American boys in war in Asia with 700 million Chinese."[38] But when the elections were over the President shifted priorities from domestic concerns to the war. Those who spoke out against him, he vilified as "nervous Nellies," being "strangely silent" on the terrorism of the Viet Cong, maintaining "moral double bookkeeping," and wanting the United States "to tuck tail and run."[39] Senator Hartke said, "The massive nature of suffering in Vietnam has called forth an equally massive outpouring of agony by those who care for America."[40] The Harris poll of November 13, 1967, showed 65 percent of the American people wanted the President's Vietnam policy changed and only 23 percent approved of his handling of the war.[41] The real issue then was: *"Should America be fighting a war that violates the conscience of her people?"* The political answer may have been "Yes," but the moral answer had to be "No." Johnsonian patriotism brought with it a guilty conscience that could not be silenced.

Another serious moral issue raised by the Vietnam War was: *"Does the American goal justify the affliction and death rained*

upon both the North and South Vietnamese?" Since the war in Vietnam was never popular with the American people, the policy was to keep the American loss of life at a minimum. This appeared to be a legitimate moral goal, even an obligation, but when the resulting strategy is examined its morality appears flimsy. The American plan was to use bombing, antipersonnel weapons, crop poisoning and defoliation, and heavy fire-powered sweeps that were designed to make a countryside uninhabitable. In a guerrilla war where the enemy is scattered among the innocent it meant killing more civilians than enemy soldiers. Here are some reports of the plan in operation.

NBC reporter Bernard Fall described a bombing raid on a village in the Ca Mau peninsula. First, he said, napalm bombs were dropped:

The napalm bombs were intended to force the people out of their huts, to send them running into the open for fear of heat and burning, and then the wingplane came in with its antipersonnel fragmen-

37. Howard Schomer, President of Chicago Theological Seminary, was a member of an interfaith team sent to Vietnam by the Fellowship of Reconciliation in 1966. The quotation is from an undated report on that mission: "Facing the Vietnam Impasse Today." Available: Chicago Theological Seminary Library.

38. Dorth Dunbar Bromley, *Washington and Vietnam* (Dobbs Ferry, N. Y.: Oceana Publications, 1966), p. 26. Quotes Johnson's campaign speech of September 28, 1964.

39. The quotations are all from President Johnson's speeches found in the following issues of *New York Times*: "nervous Nellies," May 18, 1966, p. 8; "strangely silent," July 25, 1966, p. 4; "moral double bookkeeping," March 16, 1967, p. 9; "to tuck tail and run," June 28, 1967, p. 24.

40. Hartke, p. 8.

41. *Washington Post*, November 13, 1967; also in Hartke, p. 2.

tation weapons to destroy anyone who could not be seen running about the compound. Then we came in a second time with our 20-millimeter machine guns going full blast, raking over the village with our cannon.

A spotter plane followed to tally up the score. "It becomes important for the press to say: 520 Viet Cong killed, 12 Americans killed; therefore we have won 520 to 12. The score is totalled almost daily." But then Fall asked the agonizing question, "How many of those who were scored as dead that day were armed Viet Cong, and how many were simple peaceful villagers?"[42]

One pilot returning from a raid said, "I killed 40 Viet Cong today. That's the number they told me were in the village, anyway, and I leveled it."[43] Secretary of the Navy Paul Nitze in defending the United States' policy of destroying the Vietnamese countryside said such action was necessary in areas where neither the United States nor South Vietnamese forces could maintain continuous occupancy.[44] In the words of the American officer at Ben Tre, "It became necessary to destroy the town to save it." An estimated 1,000 to 1,500 civilians, 400 Viet Cong, and 20 to 30 Americans were killed in that act of salvation.[45]

Sweeps such as Operation Cedar Falls, Operation Junction City, and Iron Triangle were designed to clear areas of people and resources. Those who were within the free fire zone were shot as Viet Cong. Even women and children who survived the bombing, such as those at My Lai, were often, in the words of Lt. Calley, "wasted." Firepower was not the only means used to flush out the rural areas of Vietnam. "Never until the War in Vietnam has any nation so deliberately, extensively, and systematically destroyed a people's food

supplies as we are doing there," said Senator Vance Hartke.[46] In 1965 and the first half of 1966 alone 640,000 acres were defoliated. The use of chemical crop poisoning "had little effect on mobile enemy soldiers, but the tactics of starvation worked effectively against small children, pregnant women, the aged, and the sick," according to Harvard nutrition expert Dr. Jean Mayer.[47]

The full results of the U.S. military strategy in Vietnam will never be known. One thing is certain—the body count scores will not tell the story; they probably tell us more about ourselves than about the winning of the war. The estimate on the number of civilians killed have varied greatly. Harrison Salisbury of the *New York Times* was visiting North Vietnam at the time the air war was being intensified in the North. The *Pentagon Papers* report that Washington officials were irritated by his press reports stressing the high number of civilian deaths resulting from the bombing. But soon the intelligence reports of government estimated civilian deaths higher than Salisbury had reported. The official estimates were that four out of every five deaths were inflicted upon civilians.[48] According to the Pentagon report, in 1966 both the cost of the bombing and the number of missions conducted in the North were almost tripled but they "accomplished little more than in

42. Quoted by Rabbi Lelyveld, "The Values We Stand For," *Congress* 35 (March 25, 1968):16.

43. *In the Name of America*, commissioned and published by Clergy and Laymen Concerned About Vietnam (New York, 1968), p. 106.

44. *New York Times*, August 15, 1965, p. 3.

45. *New York Times*, February 8, 1968, p. 14.

46. Hartke, p. 126.

47. Skolnick, *Politics of Protest*, p. 83.

48. *Pentagon Papers*, p. 523.

1965." By 1967 McNamara reported to President Johnson that the bombing failed to interdict supplies going to the South, but it did result in unifying North Vietnam. "The picture of the world's greatest superpower killing or seriously injuring 1000 noncombatants a week, while trying to pound a tiny backward nation into submission on an issue whose merits are hotly disputed, is not a pretty one," the Secretary told the President.[49]

In South Vietnam the civilian losses were far greater than in the North for it was bombed over a longer period of time and the American and South Vietnamese armies which the bombers supported were located in the South. In April, 1971, Neil Sheehan reported that a minimum of 150,000 Vietnamese civilians were killed and another 350,000 were wounded or permanently maimed. In addition, the war made 5,000,000 refugees, nearly one-third of South Vietnam's entire population.[50] More than 50,000 Americans have died and over 300,000 have been wounded thus far in the conduct of this war. The carnage inflicted upon Vietnam and America cannot be removed from the consciences of Americans. Eugene Carson Blake, General Secretary of the World Council of Churches, asked, "But when the swamps of the Mekong Delta are filled with dead Vietnamese and when the flower of our youth lies dead with them, what victory will be won?"[51]

The Vietnam War raised another moral issue that is present in any war, but has never received such a high level of national attention as now. The issue is: *What should a man do who has been called to perform military service in a war that violates his conscience?* Selective Service has permitted young men opposed to all warfare to be classified as conscientious objectors. As

Chaplain William Overhalt at Boston University pointed out, those who regard the Vietnam War as morally wrong are forced to violate the law or their conscience. What should Senator McCloskey do if he were drafted? On "Meet the Press" he compared our military leaders' activities with those of General Jodl, a Nazi General executed at Nuremberg, in these words:

From 1965 until at least 1970 American military forces did exactly the same thing in South Vietnam. We burned over half of the villages in one province, Quang Nom, perhaps half in the six northern provinces. We did that because those were the areas of partisan support, Viet Cong support. We wanted to deny support and comfort that those villages provided. . . In my judgment we have performed over a five-year period precisely the same course of military conduct that we stated at Nuremberg was a war crime.[52]

What does a young man do who does not oppose all war as a matter of conscience but does oppose the Vietnam War for the reasons Senator McCloskey presented? What is a young man to do when he adheres to the doctrine of the "just war" and believes with Rev. Kester that "this is not a just war?" Is this doctrine of war, espoused by the majority of Catholics and Protestants, to be denied? Is the state to deny religious freedom on this issue and tell the church when a war is just?

Additionally there are many who have rejected the war in Vietnam, not for religious reasons but for humanitarian or phil-

---

49. *Ibid.*, p. 580.

50. Cleveland *Plain Dealer*, April 20, 1971, p. 16-A.

51. *New York Times*, April 27, 1967, p. 1.

52. Meet the Press TV broadcast by NBC on July 18, 1971. Printed in *Meet the Press* vol. 15, no. 28 (Washington, D. C.: Merkle Press, 1971), p. 8.

osophical reasons. These too have been denied the conscientious objector position. Bishop Pike charged, "An American soldier who is not convinced the United States is acting morally in the Vietnam War is guilty of 'individual murder.' "[53] One of the Boston Five stated his position in these words:

If there is such a thing as a just war, then there is such a thing as an unjust war; and whether just or unjust is finally a matter of individual conscience, for no man can properly surrender his conscience to the State. Our Puritan fathers came to these shores because they were committed to this principle. At the Nuremberg trials we faulted an entire nation for not accepting it.[54]

Because freedom of conscience has not been granted to the American youth who opposed the Vietnam War and who are not pacifists, hundreds of them have fled the country; some have gone to jail, many have never been called up, and others have fought with a guilty conscience. Some have disobeyed orders after being enlisted and have faced military prison sentences.

Though the United States Armed Forces have a number of volunteers the Selective Service System has been the main source of manpower for the war. The Selective Service System has operated upon the premise that a citizen has a moral obligation to serve his country, even if he cannot do so conscientiously. Many have feared that if the draft resister's conscience could overrule the call to military service the Selective Service system would collapse. The *Skolnick Report* says, "Nothing has aroused greater anxiety and outrage among people outside the movement than the burning of draft cards and the willingness of eminent citizens to stand beside resisters and applaud their patriotism."[55] National attention was focused on the Boston trial of Dr. Benjamin Spock, the Reverend William So-

loane Coffin, Jr., Marcus Raskin, Mitchell Goodman, and Michael Feber for their acts of "conspiracy" in aiding draft resisters. The Selective Service officials and other proadministration groups have attempted to charge draft resisters and deserters as disloyal, and un-American, and to associate them with left-wing conspiracy groups; however, they have never been able to reconcile the implications of the Nuremberg doctrine and the compulsory draft.

The fourth moral issue raised by the Vietnam War is concerned with the allocation of resources: *Is it morally right to curtail pressing domestic needs in order to prosecute the costly war in Vietnam?* Senator Charles Percy in his report of July, 1971, says that we have spent more than $120 billion to support the regime in South Vietnam. The Republican Blue Book, in May, 1967, stated that $300,000 was spent for each alleged dead enemy soldier.[56] Early in 1966 Senator Fulbright cautioned that the brave talk about having both "guns and butter" was deceptive. Speaking to the Bureau of Advertising of the American Newspaper Publishers Association, Fulbright said:

In concrete terms, the President simply cannot think about implementing the Great Society at home while he is supervising bombing missions over North Vietnam; nor is the Congress much inclined to debate—much less finance—expanded education programs when it is involved in debating— and paying for—an expanding war; nor can the American people be expected to think very hard or

---

53. Seattle Pacific College *Falcon*, September 22, 1967, p. 6.

54. Quoted from the *Yale Alumni Magazine*, March, 1967, by Skolnick, *Politics of Protest*, p. 74.

55. Skolnick, *Politics of Protest*, p. 73.

56. *Ibid.* p. 45.

do very much about improving their schools and communities when they are worried about casualty lists and the danger of a wider war.[57]

Similar sentiments were expressed by Martin Luther King when he declared that "the promises of the Great Society have been shot down on the battlefield of Vietnam."[58] Civil Rights leaders cautioned King on losing his effectiveness in the civil rights struggle by becoming involved in the antiwar movement. King responded that he could not be true to his conscience and be silent. "There is," he said, "at the outset a very obvious and almost facile connection between the war in Vietnam and the struggle I, and others, have been waging in America." He spoke of the hope for the poor— both black and white—through the Poverty Program.

Then came the build-up in Vietnam and I watched the program broken and enviscerated as if it were some idle political plaything of a society gone mad on war, and I knew that America would never invest the necessary funds or energies in rehabilitation of its poor so long as adventures like Vietnam continued to draw men and skills and money like some demonical destructive suction tube. So I was increasingly compelled to see the war as an enemy to the poor.[59]

As the war escalated the cut-backs in urban renewal, inner city programs, and welfare reforms revealed not only national economic priorities but also the moral principles used to determine those priorities.

Development, Strategies, and Accomplishments of the Peace Movement

America was born in a bloody revolution. The founding of Colonial America was possible because the revolutionary patriots were victorious on the battlefield.

Throughout the schools of America children have been taught that the Revolutionary War was instrumental in providing the liberties, freedoms, and inalienable rights set forth in the Constitution. The Civil War was instrumental in eradicating slavery and providing citizenship to former slaves. Americans fought in World War I to establish democracy abroad and free Europe from the tyranny of the Kaiser. Again in World War II Americans fought and died to wrest the world from ruthless fascist dictatorships. As the National Anthem declares—to see "the flag still there" by the light of the "rockets' red glare" is to see the cause of liberty, freedom, and justice triumph. Like a western movie on a grand scale, guns, bayonets, bombs, missiles, and military technology have been the precious means used to establish law, order, righteousness, and peace throughout America's history. Patriotism and righteousness consequently have been unquestionably identified and war has been recognized as the time-honored method used to destroy the evil and promote the good.

In the period following World War II Americans were so convinced about the rightness of war powers that they kept the draft, increased military testing and research, elected their top general and war hero to be president, and for the cause of peace stockpiled enough nuclear bombs to destroy all of mankind. To be certain that the ways of the "bad guys" were not confused with the ways of the "good guys" (both sides used similar means) after World

---

57. An address, "The Vietnam Fallout," given on April 28, 1966 in New York City. Available through Mennonite Central Committee, Peace Section, Akron, Pa.

58. King, "Casualties of the War," p. 6.

59. King, "Beyond Vietnam," p. 11.

War II public trials were convened at Nuremberg. Here fascist leaders were condemned for their demonic exercise of power, better known as war crimes, and the victors in their triumph were the heralds of righteousness. The Pentagon culture and ethic had permeated the American life style during the prosperous aftermath of World War II. The industrial military complex flourished during the booming years of cold war peace in the 1950s and early 1960s. Government sponsored military research contracts practically supported the prestigious universities and those industries concerned with the development of aerospace, electronics, and communication. The establishment contended that salvation was dependent on being ahead of the communists in the arms race.

The new generation of youth growing up in the 1960s did not find meaning for life in the prescription formulated by their fathers. They were not excited about dedicating their lives to keep ahead of the communists and perpetuating the cold war values of the industrial military complex. However, the call for a change of priorities in the 1960s did inspire them. Civil rights in schools, housing, and jobs were at long last to be extended to all citizens. Poverty was to be eradicated as America would become transformed into The Great Society. A mood of optimism calling for social change was "catching on."

As America moved into the decade of the 1960s the Freedom Movement was gaining momentum rapidly. Following the Montgomery Boycott of 1955, Dr. Martin Luther King emerged as the leader of the Civil Rights movement. Black Americans found new hope in the use of nonviolence and the Southern Christian Leadership Conference was organized to guide the movement. In February of 1960 four black freshmen sat down at a "whites only" lunch counter in Greensboro, North Carolina. They were refused service. The next day they returned, supported by seventy other students—white and black. Within a year the sit-in movement had spread to a hundred southern communities and more than fifty thousand people were participating. The sit-ins, using the means of nonviolence, were highly successful in bringing about more changes. The black minority became aware of new power but it also realized that token concessions were not adequate; voting power was needed to speed up change and to make it more universal. Groups such as SNCC (Student Nonviolent Coordinating Committee) were organized to implement voter registration. Marches, walks, boycotts, sit-ins, and demonstrations were recognized as effective methods of getting attention and communicating. The rhetoric of the streets was accompanied with position statements, news releases, speeches, interviews, signs, and often special television documentaries. The disenfranchised people of America had discovered that they had power to change the system and they set out to do it.

A number of pacifist religious groups such as the Fellowship of Reconciliation and The Society of Friends were heartened with the successes of the massive nonviolent actions employed in civil rights. For years they had advocated nonviolent actions with little tangible results. During the 1950s they had set up pickets at missile sites, held vigils at chemical and biological warfare centers, and sailed into nuclear testing areas. Other nonreligious pacifist groups were also actively supporting anti-war measures. These include the War Resister's League, the Committee for Non-

Violent Action, and the Society for Social Responsibility in Science. Historically religious and nonreligious pacifist groups viewed warfare and racial hatred as different expressions of the same problem—man's inhumanity to his fellow man. With cold war attitudes softening and disarmament talks started, it appeared that the virtues of nonviolence were finally recognized as a viable alternative to violence and war. Such optimism was short lived at home and abroad.

During the early 1960s some important shifts took place within both the civil rights movement and the peace movement. In civil rights Medgar Evers, three civil rights workers in Neshoba County, Mississippi, and four little girls in a Birmingham, Alabama, church were among the dead as a result of violent responses to nonviolent activities. In addition, the federal government failed to protect the workers within the movement. Blacks soon learned that their cause was not really being advanced by the white leadership. In 1966 SNCC excluded white leadership because of "the inability of whites to relate to the cultural aspects of Black society...."[60] White leaders were advised to work on their own race, which was where the civil rights problem really existed. While the war for civil rights and the war on poverty were being waged at home, American involvement in Vietnam was rapidly escalated during the mid-1960s. Many of the disenfranchized white civil rights leaders found in the antiwar movement a cause to demand all their energies. For example, Students for a Democratic Society which earlier stressed community organization among the blacks and poor whites focused more on the Vietnam War, the draft, and student power after 1965. The civil rights activity, nonetheless, pro-

vided models and training experiences which were important to the development of the peace movement.

The first significant dissent against the Vietnam War came in the spring of 1965 after President Johnson ordered "nonretaliatory" air attacks against North Vietnam, increased the number of ground troops, and publicly acknowledged the increased involvement in the war. Prior to this time the policy had been to conduct a covert war, hold no news conferences, and keep Congress and the public uninformed. The President then enjoyed high credibility and overwhelming popular endorsement. There were a few voices of skepticism and dissent. Only two senators, Morse and Gruening, considered the Gulf of Tonkin Resolution suspect and spoke against it. Before long reporters learned that they could not depend on the administration for hard news on the war. They began to observe field movements, study new activities in the Pentagon, look for leaks from within the administration, and listen to the reports of the Viet Cong and Hanoi. As the war progressed the independent reports of the press played an important function for the antiwar movement. When seasoned reporters as Neal Sheehan, Bernard Fall, Morley Saefer, Harrison Salisbury and others supplied evidence supporting the contentions of the peace advocates and refuting the contentions of the administration, American public opinion and support for the war diminished. Before the fact finding of American reporters, the International War Crimes Tribunal staged by Bertrand Russell and the writings of communist journalist Wilfred

---

60. SNCC, "A Position Paper on Race" in *Black Protest*, ed. Joanne Grant (Greenwich, Conn.: Fawcett Primer, 1968), p. 453.

Burchett carried little credibility with the American public. But after the fact finding of those American reporters, whom the people trusted, exposed false military reports and after the predicted progress in the war did not materialize the public withdrew much of its support for the war.[61]

The first organized opposition against the Vietnam War surfaced in the academic community. This opposition to the war began during the early period of escalation when most activities were covertly conducted. The academic community began by asking for explanations of little publicized reports. They called for public debates on the issues at "teach-in" sessions. Spokesmen for the administration soon charged that the university "teach-ins" were one-sided and not concerned with providing fair presentations. The Internal Security Subcommittee of the Senate, which investigated the teach-in movement, charged that it was more dedicated to protesting the war than holding open discussions and debate.[62] Between March 24, 1965, the date of the first teach-in, and May 15, 1965, the date of the National Teach-In in Washington, D.C., approximately fifty teach-ins were held at colleges and universities in every part of the country.

The National Teach-In at Washington gave the movement prestige and national attention. McGeorge Bundy, Special Assistant to President Johnson for national security affairs and one of the principal architects of American foreign policy, was scheduled to debate Professor George Kahin of Cornell University. The evening before the debate was to take place the White House withdrew Mr. Bundy from the debate. Nonetheless, the teach-in was held at the Sheraton-Park Hotel before an audience of about 5000. The debate was carried live by more than 130 radio stations and more than 100 campuses arranged special radio hookups. The total audience listening to the debate was estimated to exceed 100,000 persons.[63] *The New York Times* commented:

The 15½-hour teach-in yesterday was said to have cost between $20,000 and $30,000, not covering the costs of travel to Washington. All the speakers were to have donated their services. Most of the cost was said to have been already collected in small contributions, only a few more than $100 and only one of $1,000.

The investment brought an unusual amount of public press, radio, television interest in the discussions.[64]

Following the teach-ins of 1965, which provided opportunity for thinking through alternatives to the administration's policies, new positions concerning the Vietnam War began to take shape. The peace groups attempted to mobilize their forces and plan strategies to communicate their ideas. Because they came from varied backgrounds and differing philosophical orientations they never were able to become a political party, yet political power was needed to bring about the changes in policy. They were able to agree on one theme which was

---

61. Numerous examples which illustrate this credibility gap have been cited in the above section on "Legal Issues and Arguments."

62. Staff study, "The Anti-Vietnam Agitation and the Teach-In Movement," prepared for the Subcommittee to Investigate the Administration of the Internal Security Act and other Internal Security Laws to the Committee on the Judiciary (Washington, U. S. Government Printing Office; 1965), doc. no. 72.

63. *Ibid.*, p. 152, taken from *The New York Times*, May 16, 1965.

64. *Ibid.*, p. 149, taken from *The New York Times*, May 17, 1965.

"end the war and bring American troops home." There was disagreement about the uses of violent means to bring about these changes and the degree of cooperation that should be given to the existing structures. As it turned out many groups using different methods and operating at different levels attempted to bring the war to an end. Groups in the radical left portion of the movement asked Americans to support Hanoi and the Viet Cong. They supported such activities as destroying draft records and selective bombing of military research laboratories. Some were willing to destroy property but refused to participate in activities that would endanger lives. Others refused to endanger lives and destroy property but were willing to create confusion, inconvenience and the like by demonstrations and acts of noncooperation. Still others would support only methods such as lobbying, letter writing, advertising, and working for peace candidates.

Despite the apparent shortcomings resulting from the disunity and loose organization of the peace groups a number of factors were to their advantage as the movement developed: (1) American commanders who predicted an early end to the war and later claimed success from the military moves they had taken proved to be wrong on both counts. (2) The escalation of the war which cost thousands of American lives and billions of dollars was difficult to justify after the progress was evaluated. (3) Peace groups were able to demonstrate a surprising amount of support from the American public by the large attendance at their rallies. On several occasions they drew crowds ranging from 300,000 to 500,000 persons. (4) The peace groups were able to attract national leadership into their ranks. They received support from senators

Morse, Gruening, Fulbright, Mansfield, McCarthy, McGovern, Kennedy, Cooper, Church, Hatfield, Percy, Javits, McCloskey, Tunney, Hughes, Hartke, and Young. Nationally known church leaders such as the Rev. Martin Luther King, Bishop Pike, Rabbi Herschel, Bishop Sheen, Cardinal Cushing, the Rev. Blake and many others spoke out against the war. Actors such as Dick Gregory, Joan Baez, Dick and Tommy Smothers, Peter Boyle, Arlo Guthrie, Pete Seeger are only a small sampling of those who actively opposed the war. (5) The national elections provided a natural forum for the war to be discussed in the presidential campaigns of Robert Kennedy and Eugene McCarthy and in the senatorial and congressional races throughout the nation. The war was the major issue at the 1968 Democratic and Republican conventions. (6) The position of those opposing the war had a high moral appeal. Consequently much of the time the administration had to spend its time in face-saving and defending actions taken.

By the end of 1971 the leadership of both the Republican and Democratic parties viewed the Vietnam War as a tragic mistake. A Harris poll of April 16, 1971, indicated that 58 percent of Americans considered it to be morally wrong for the United States to be fighting in Vietnam.[65] How much of this change in attitude is to be credited to the peace movement is a matter of speculation. Was President Johnson's decision not to run for another term a result of the peace movement? The answers differ. Surely Nixon's decision to invade Cambodia brought forth a clear indication that Americans were unwilling to support the possi-

---

65. *Facts on File*, (New York: Facts on File, 1971), p. 291.

bility of further escalation. The weight of the war upon America's conscience made the draft unpopular and gave new impetus to the volunteer army. Clearly the war in Vietnam cannot be called a victory for South Vietnam or the United States. Perhaps as the war is being phased out by the Nixon administration one can also say that there has been no clear cut victory in the fight between the hawks and the doves. Both sides have attempted to claim success. There is no doubt that as a result of the Vietnam War American attitudes toward war as to the solution to international problems have undergone some radical changes.

BIBLIOGRAPHY

Falk, Richard A., ed. *The Vietnam War and International Law.* Princeton, N.J.: Princeton University Press, 1968-69.

Two-volume collection of papers giving an excellent analysis of legal questions and issues pertaining to the Vietnam War.

Gettleman, Marvin E., ed. *Vietnam: History, Documents, and Opinions On A Major World Crisis.* New York: New American Library, 1970.

Excellent compendium of documents including the writings, speeches of key political leaders, national statements of policy, international agreements, and special reports on the Vietnam War. It also provides articles that give the views of prominent writers and analysts. The reader has opportunity to examine the documents and study interpretations others have made in order to draw his own conclusions.

Halberstam, David. *The Making of a Quagmire.* New York: Random House, 1964.

American journalist's Pulitzer Prize winning account of the political and military events in South Vietnam from 1961 to 1964.

Kahin, George McT., and Lewis, John W. *The United States in Vietnam.* New York: Delta Books, 1967.

One of the most complete and best critiques of the U.S. position from its beginnings in Vietnam until 1967.

Melman, Seymour, ed. *In the Name of America.* New York: Clergy and Laymen Concerned about Vietnam, 1968.

Contains documents on laws on the conduct of war found in the International Conventions and United States laws. Infractions of these policies are classified with a listing of numerous cases of the violations of laws, agreements, and understandings.

Salisbury, Harrison. *Behind the Lines—Hanoi: December 23-January 7.* New York: Harper and Row, 1967.

The accounts of a *New York Times* reporter and editor who visited North Vietnam and reported on the United States bombings of civilians in that country.

Schoenbrun, David. *Vietnam: How We Got In, How To Get Out.* New York: Atheneum, 1968.

Well known journalist, broadcaster and critic of the United States policy in Vietnam gives a keen and spirited analysis of the issues.

Sheehen, Neil, *et al*, eds. *The Pentagon Papers.* New York: The *New York Times*, 1971.

The writing of the original *Pentagon Papers* commissioned by Secretary of Defense Robert S. McNamara, was a 47-volume work covering the American involvement in Indo-China from World War II to May, 1968. This published *New York Times* edition attempts to present the history in the form of a documentary narrative. It is a valuable source in that it presents the Pentagon's own interpretation of the Vietnam War.

Index